COMPUTATIONAL MODELS OF ARGUMENT

Frontiers in Artificial Intelligence and Applications

FAIA covers all aspects of theoretical and applied artificial intelligence research in the form of monographs, doctoral dissertations, textbooks, handbooks and proceedings volumes. The FAIA series contains several sub-series, including "Information Modelling and Knowledge Bases" and "Knowledge-Based Intelligent Engineering Systems". It also includes the biennial ECAI, the European Conference on Artificial Intelligence, proceedings volumes, and other ECCAI – the European Coordinating Committee on Artificial Intelligence – sponsored publications. An editorial panel of internationally well-known scholars is appointed to provide a high quality selection.

Series Editors:
J. Breuker, N. Guarino, J.N. Kok, J. Liu, R. López de Mántaras,
R. Mizoguchi, M. Musen, S.K. Pal and N. Zhong

Volume 216

Recently published in this series

ISSN 0922-6389 (print)
ISSN 1879-8314 (online)

Computational Models of Argument

Proceedings of COMMA 2010

Edited by

Pietro Baroni

Department of Information Engineering, University of Brescia, Italy

Federico Cerutti

Department of Information Engineering, University of Brescia, Italy

Massimiliano Giacomin

Department of Information Engineering, University of Brescia, Italy

and

Guillermo R. Simari

*Department of Computer Science & Engineering,
Universidad Nacional del Sur, Argentina*

IOS
Press

Amsterdam • Berlin • Tokyo • Washington, DC

ISBN 978-1-60750-618-8 (print)
ISBN 978-1-60750-619-5 (online)
Library of Congress Control Number: 2010933665

Publisher
IOS Press BV
Nieuwe Hemweg 6B
1013 BG Amsterdam
Netherlands
fax: +31 20 687 0019
e-mail: order@iospress.nl

Distributor in the USA and Canada
IOS Press, Inc.
4502 Rachael Manor Drive
Fairfax, VA 22032
USA
fax: +1 703 323 3668
e-mail: iosbooks@iospress.com

Computational Models of Argument
P. Baroni et al. (Eds.)
IOS Press, 2010

Preface

Argumentation as a field of inquiry has been attracting an increasing number of researchers from different areas. One of the main shared goals among these researchers is the pursuit of solutions to the many research problems found in the Knowledge Representation and Reasoning area of Artificial Intelligence using strategies akin to the commonsense approach displayed by humans. Practical applications of the basic research results have been gaining attention in several areas including in particular the Autonomous Agents and Multiagent Systems community. By the beginning of this decade, the need for a forum where these advances could be discussed in a specialized manner was recognized by the members of the argumentation community, leading to the decision of establishing a biennial conference with focus on the computational aspects of argumentation.

In September 2006, the First Conference on Computational Models of Argument was hosted, with resounding success, by the University of Liverpool; a similar response followed in May 2008 when the Second Conference on Computational Models of Argument was held in France, hosted by the Institut de Recherche en Informatique de Toulouse (IRIT).

This volume contains the papers forming the program of the Third Conference on Computational Models of Argument held in Desenzano del Garda, Italy, from Sept. 8th to 10th, 2010. This time the responsibility of hosting the conference was assumed by the University of Brescia. The papers in the volume address topics ranging from formal models of argumentation and the relevant theoretical questions, through algorithms and computational complexity issues, to the use of argumentation in several application domains, thus providing an up-to-date view of this vital research field.

The success of a conference depends on the contributions of many people. The organizers wish to thank the Steering Committee of COMMA for all the help received. We are deeply grateful to the members of the Program Committee, and additional reviewers, for the hard work of evaluating the submitted papers. Their reports and discussions greatly facilitated the final decisions that led to the content of this book, which includes two invited papers by prof. Gerhard Brewka and prof. Douglas Walton, 35 full papers and 5 short papers selected from 67 submissions.

We would like to thank Giovanni Perbellini for his contribution to the work of the Local Organizing Committee, Laura Folli for designing the conference logo and Diego Beda, Loretta Bettari, Luca Mori for their help concerning the venue of the conference. Finally, we gratefully acknowledge financial support from the Municipality of Desenzano del Garda and Taylor & Francis Group.

July, 2010

Pietro Baroni (General Conference Chair)
Federico Cerutti (Local Organization Co-chair)
Massimiliano Giacomin (Local Organization Chair)
Guillermo R. Simari (Programme Chair)

Programme Committee

Leila Amgoud (IRIT)

Kevin Ashley (University of Pittsburgh)

Katie Atkinson (University of Liverpool)

Trevor Bench-Capon (University of Liverpool)

Philippe Besnard (IRIT)

Guido Boella (University of Torino)

Ivan Bratko (University of Ljubljana)

Gerhard Brewka (University of Leipzig)

Simon Buckingham Shum (Open University)

Martin Caminada (University of Luxembourg)

Claudette Cayrol (IRIT)

Carlos Chesnevar (Universidad Nacional del Sur)

Sylvie Coste (Université d'Artois)

Jurgen Dix (Technical University of Clausthal)

Sylvie Doutre (IRIT)

Phan Minh Dung (Asian Institute of Technologies)

Paul E. Dunne (University of Liverpool)

John Fox (University of Oxford)

Dov M. Gabbay (King's College London – Bar-Ilan University – University of Luxembourg)

Alejandro Garcia (Universidad Nacional del Sur)

Lluis Godo (IIIA-CSIC)

Tom Gordon (Fraunhofer FOKUS)

Floriana Grasso (University of Liverpool)

Anthony Hunter (University College London)

Antonis Kakas (University of Cyprus)

Gabriele Kern-Isberner (University of Dortmund)

Paul Krause (University of Surrey)

Paolo Mancarella (University of Pisa)

Nicolas Maudet (University of Paris-Dauphine)

Peter McBurney (University of Liverpool)

Jerome Mengin (IRIT)

Sanjay Modgil (King's College London)

Tim Norman (University of Aberdeen)

Fabio Paglieri (ISTC-CNR)

Simon Parsons (City University of New York)

Henri Prade (IRIT)

Henry Prakken (University of Utrecht – University of Groningen)

Iyad Rahwan (Masdar Institute of Science & Technology)

Chris Reed (University of Dundee)

Giovanni Sartor (European University Institute)

Carles Sierra (IIIA-CSIC)

Francesca Toni (Imperial College)

Paolo Torroni (University of Bologna)

Leon van der Torre (University of Luxembourg)

Bart Verheij (University of Groningen)

Gerard Vreeswijk (University of Utrecht)

Doug Walton (University of Windsor)

Michael Wooldridge (University of Liverpool)

Additional Reviewers

Teresa Alsinet (IIIA-CSIC)
Manuel Atencia (IIIA-CSIC)
Davide Bacciu (University of Pisa)
Elizabeth Black (University of Utrecht)
Nils Bulling (Clausthal University of Technology)
Ana Casali (IIIA-CSIC)
Souhila Kaci (CRIL, CLLE-LTC)
Eric Kok (University of Utrecht)
Maxime Morge (University of Pisa)
Martin Mozina (University of Ljubljana)
Matt South (University of Oxford)
Tom van der Weide (University of Utrecht)
Wietske Visser (Delft University of Technology)

Contents

Part I

Invited Talks

Computational Models of Argument
P. Baroni et al. (Eds.)
IOS Press, 2010
© 2010 The authors and IOS Press. All rights reserved.
doi:10.3233/978-1-60750-619-5-3

Carneades and Abstract Dialectical Frameworks: A Reconstruction

Gerhard Brewka [a] and Thomas F. Gordon [b]

[a] *Universität Leipzig, Augustusplatz 10-11, 04109 Leipzig, Germany*
brewka@informatik.uni-leipzig.de
[b] *Fraunhofer FOKUS, Kaiserin-Augusta-Allee 31, 10589 Berlin, Germany*
thomas.gordon@fokus.fraunhofer.de

Abstract. Carneades is a rather general framework for argumentation. Unlike many other approaches, Carneades captures a number of aspects, like proof burdens, proof standards etc., which are of central importance, in particular in legal argumentation.

In this paper we show how Carneades argument evaluation structures can be reconstructed as abstract dialectical frameworks (ADFs), a recently proposed generalization of Dung argumentation frameworks (AFs). This not only provides at least an indirect link between Carneades and AFs, it also allows us to handle arbitrary argument cycles, thus lifting a restriction of Carneades. At the same time it provides strong evidence for the usefulness of ADFs as analytical/semantical tools in argumentation.

1. Introduction

The Carneades model of argumentation, introduced by Gordon, Prakken and Walton in [8] and developed further in a series of subsequent papers, e.g. [9], some of them appearing in this volume [2,10], is an advanced general framework for argumentation.[1] It captures both static aspects, related to the evaluation of arguments in a particular context based on proof standards for statements and on weights arguments are given by an audience, and dynamic aspects, covering for instance the shift of proof burdens in different stages of the argumentation process.

Unlike many other approaches, Carneades does not rely on Dung's argumentation frameworks (AFs) [5] for the definition of its semantics, more specifically its notion of acceptable arguments. One goal of this paper is to provide a link, albeit an indirect one, between Carneades and AFs. As we will see, both are instances of a more general framework. Moreover, in spite of this generality, Carneades suffers from a restriction: it is assumed that the graphs formed by arguments are acyclic. This is not as bad as it may first sound, as the use of pro and con arguments allows some conflicts to be represented which require cyclic representations in other frameworks, e.g. in Dung argumentation frameworks [5]. Still, cycles in argumentation appear so common that forbidding them

---

[1] As of June 2010, [8] is among the 10 most cited papers which appeared in the Artificial Intelligence Journal over the last 5 years.

right from the start is certainly somewhat problematic. And indeed, the authors in [8] write (page 882):

> "We ... leave an extension to graphs that allow for cycles through exceptions for future work."

Finishing this open task, that is, overcoming the mentioned limitation, is another main goal of this paper. We achieve this by translating Carneades argument evaluation structures to a framework which is able to handle cycles, and which offers a selection of adequate semantics. The target framework we will be using here are abstract dialectical frameworks (ADFs), and our second main goal is to provide evidence that these frameworks are indeed useful tools in argumentation.

ADFs are a powerful generalization of Dung-style argumentation frameworks [5] recently proposed by Brewka and Woltran in [4]. Dung argumentation frameworks have an implicit, fixed criterion for the acceptance of a node in the argument graph: a node is accepted iff all its parents are defeated. This acceptance criterion can be viewed as an implicit boolean function assigning a status to an argument based on the status of its parents. The basic idea underlying ADFs is to make this boolean function explicit, and then to allow arbitrary acceptance conditions for nodes to be specified.

As shown in [4], the standard semantics for Dung frameworks - grounded, preferred and stable - can be generalized to ADFs, the latter two to a slightly restricted class of ADFs called bipolar, where each link in the graph either supports or attacks its target node. Since all ADFs we are dealing with in this paper are bipolar, we will simply speak of ADFs and omit the adjective "bipolar" whenever there is no risk of confusion. Brewka and Woltran also discuss how acceptance conditions can conveniently be specified using weights of the links in an ADF. This also makes it possible to capture proof standards in a straightforward way. All this will come in handy for our reconstruction.

There are some issues that need to be addressed before we start our reconstruction. First of all, Carneades is a moving target: the framework has developed over time, and still is developing. We thus need to fix the particular version we are dealing with. We decided to choose the version presented in the book chapter [9], partly because we assume this chapter will have many readers, partly because this version is quite well-suited for our purposes, as we will see later.

Secondly, the dynamic features of Carneades have no counterpart in ADFs. ADFs were invented to capture the static evaluation of arguments, or more generally statements, given flexible forms of dependencies among them. We will restrict our discussion in this paper to the static part of Carneades. This is entirely sufficient for the purposes of this paper, and it allows us to slightly simplify the definitions from [9], stripping off dynamic aspects irrelevant to our goals. In particular, we do not discuss different argumentation stages. What we are interested in is the evaluation of stage specific Carneades argument structures.

The paper is organized as follows. We will first present Carneades, using simplified versions of the definitions in [9] which capture the relevant stage specific notions. We then present ADFs together with their semantics. The subsequent chapter contains the main results of the paper: it shows how to translate Carneades argument structures to ADFs, proves that the translation yields the desired results for acyclic Carneades structures, and discusses how this allows us to handle arbitrary cycles in argument structures.

2. Carneades

We start with the definition of arguments in Carneades [9]:

Definition 1 (argument). Let $\mathcal{L}$ be a propositional language. An **argument** is a tuple $\langle P, E, c \rangle$ where $P \subset \mathcal{L}$ are its **premises**, $E \subset \mathcal{L}$ with $P \cap E = \varnothing$ are its **exceptions** and $c \in \mathcal{L}$ is its **conclusion**. For simplicity, c and all members of P and E must be literals, i.e. either an atomic proposition or a negated atomic proposition. Let p be a literal. If p is c, then the argument is an argument **pro** p. If p is the complement of c, then the argument is an argument **con** p.

An argument evaluation structure was defined in [9] as a triple consisting of a stage, an audience, and a function assigning a proof standard to propositions. Since, as mentioned in the introduction, we are only interested here in stage specific argument evaluation, we skip the status part of the definition of stages (see [9]), keeping only the set of arguments. Furthermore, an audience is a pair consisting of a set of assumptions and a weight function. For simplicity we will represent these two parts explicitly, turning the triple into a quadruple:

Definition 2 (argument evaluation structure). A **(stage specific) Carneades argument evaluation structure** (CAES) is a tuple $\langle arguments, assumptions, weights, standard \rangle$, where

1. *arguments* is an acyclic[2] set of arguments,
2. *assumptions* is a consistent set of literals, those assumed by the current audience,
3. *weights* is a function assigning a real number n, $0 \leq n \leq 1$, to each argument, and
4. *standard* is a total function mapping propositions in $\mathcal{L}$ to a proof standard (to be defined below).

The acceptability of a proposition p in a CAES depends on its proof standard. Carneades distinguishes 5 such standards, each one based on a particular way of aggregating applicable pro and con arguments. The notion of applicability may in turn depend on the acceptability of (other) propositions:

Definition 3 (applicability). Let $\mathcal{S} = \langle arguments, assumptions, weights, standard \rangle$ be a CAES. An argument $\langle P, E, c \rangle \in arguments$ is **applicable** in $\mathcal{S}$ if and only if

- $p \in P$ implies $p \in assumptions$ or $[\overline{p} \notin assumptions$ and p is acceptable in $\mathcal{S}]$, and
- $p \in E$ implies $p \notin assumptions$ and $[\overline{p} \in assumptions$ or p is not acceptable in $\mathcal{S}]$.

What remains to be defined are the proof standards *scintilla of evidence*, *preponderance of evidence*, *clear and convincing evidence*, *beyond reasonable doubt* and *dialectical validity*, which we will abbreviate as se, pe, ce, bd and dv, respectively. We directly define acceptability under a particular proof standard.

Definition 4 (acceptability). Let $\mathcal{S} = \langle arguments, assumptions, weights, standard \rangle$ be a CAES. A proposition $p \in \mathcal{L}$ is **acceptable** in $\mathcal{S}$ if and only if one of the following conditions holds:

---

[2]A set of arguments is acyclic if its dependency graph is. The dependency graph has a node for each propositional atom appearing in some argument. Furthermore, there is a link from q to p whenever p depends on q, that is, whenever there is an argument pro or con p with q or $\neg q$ in its set of premises or exceptions.

- *standard*(p) = *se* and there is at least one applicable argument for p,
- *standard*(p) = *pe*, p satisfies *se*, and the maximum weight assigned to an applicable argument pro p is greater than the maximum weight of an applicable argument con p,
- *standard*(p) = *ce*, p satisfies *pe*, and the maximum weight of applicable pro arguments exceeds some threshold α, and the difference between the maximum weight of the applicable pro arguments and the maximum weight of the applicable con arguments exceeds some threshold β,
- *standard*(p) = *bd*, p satisfies *ce*, and the maximum weight of the applicable con arguments is less than some threshold γ,
- *standard*(p) = *dv*, and there is at least one applicable argument pro p and no applicable argument con p.

Note that, although acceptability is defined in terms of applicability, and applicability in terms of acceptability, the definitions are well-founded. This is due to the fact that the set of arguments is not allowed to contain cycles. However, this interdependency makes it quite difficult to generalize the definitions directly to the cyclic case. We will see how ADFs can be used to overcome this limitation.

3. Abstract Dialectical Frameworks

An ADF [4] is a directed graph whose nodes represent arguments or statements which can be accepted or not. The links represent dependencies: the status of a node s only depends on the status of its parents (denoted $par(s)$), that is, the nodes with a direct link to s. In addition, each node s has an associated acceptance condition C_s specifying the conditions under which s is accepted. This is where ADFs go beyond Dung argumentation frameworks. C_s is a boolean function yielding for each assignment of values to $par(s)$ one of the values *in*, *out* for s. As usual, we will identify value assignments with the sets of nodes which are *in*. Thus, if for some $R \subseteq par(s)$ we have $C_s(R) = in$, then s will be accepted provided the nodes in R are accepted and those in $par(s) \setminus R$ are not accepted.

Definition 5. An *abstract dialectical framework* is a tuple $D = (S, L, C)$ where

- S is a set of statements,
- $L \subseteq S \times S$ is a set of links,
- $C = \{C_s\}_{s \in S}$ is a set of total functions $C_s : 2^{par(s)} \rightarrow \{in, out\}$, one for each statement s. C_s is called acceptance condition of s.

S and L obviously form a graph, and we sometimes refer to elements of S as nodes. For the purposes of this paper we will only deal with a subset of ADFs, called bipolar in [4]. In such ADFs each link is either attacking or supporting:

Definition 6. Let $D = (S, L, C)$ be an ADF. A link $(r, s) \in L$ is

1. *supporting* iff, for no $R \subseteq par(s)$, $C_s(R) = in$ and $C_s(R \cup \{r\}) = out$,
2. *attacking* iff, for no $R \subseteq par(s)$, $C_s(R) = out$ and $C_s(R \cup \{r\}) = in$.

For simplicity we will only speak of ADFs here, keeping in mind that all ADFs in this paper are indeed bipolar.

It turns out that Dung's standard semantics - grounded, stable, preferred - can be generalized adequately to ADFs. We first introduce the notion of a model. Intuitively, in a model all acceptance conditions are satisfied.

Definition 7. Let $D = (S, L, C)$ be an ADF. $M \subseteq S$ is a *model* of D if for all $s \in S$ we have $s \in M$ iff $C_s(M \cap par(s)) = in$.

We first define the generalization of grounded semantics:

Definition 8. Let $D = (S, L, C)$ be an ADF. Consider the operator

$$\Gamma_D(A, R) = (acc(A, R), reb(A, R))$$

where

$$acc(A, R) = \{r \in S \mid A \subseteq S' \subseteq (S \smallsetminus R) \Rightarrow C_r(S' \cap par(r)) = in\}, \text{ and}$$
$$reb(A, R) = \{r \in S \mid A \subseteq S' \subseteq (S \smallsetminus R) \Rightarrow C_r(S' \cap par(r)) = out\}.$$

Γ_D is monotonic in both arguments and thus has a least fixpoint. E is the *well-founded model* of D iff for some $E' \subseteq S$, (E, E') is the least fixpoint of Γ_D.

For stable models we apply a construction similar to the Gelfond/Lifschitz reduct for logic programs. The purpose of the reduction is to eliminate models in which nodes are *in* just because of self supporting cycles:

Definition 9. Let $D = (S, L, C)$ be an ADF. A model M of D is a *stable model* if M is the least model of the reduced ADF D^M obtained from D by

1. eliminating all nodes not contained in M together with all links in which any of these nodes appear,
2. eliminating all attacking links,
3. restricting the acceptance conditions C_s for each remaining node s to the remaining parents of s.

Preferred extensions in Dung's approach are maximal admissible sets, where an admissible set is conflict-free and defends itself against attackers. This can be rephrased as follows: E is *admissible* in a Dung argumentation framework $A = (AR, att)$ iff for some $R \subseteq AR$

* R does not attack E, and
* E is a stable extension of $(AR\text{-}R, att \cap (AR\text{-}R \times AR\text{-}R))$.

This leads to the following generalization:

Definition 10. Let $D = (S, L, C)$, $R \subseteq S$. $D\text{-}R$ is the ADF obtained from D by

1. deleting all nodes in R together with their acceptance conditions and links they are contained in.
2. restricting acceptance conditions of the remaining nodes to the remaining parents.

Definition 11. Let $D = (S, L, C)$ be an ADF. $M \subseteq S$ is *admissible* in D iff there is $R \subseteq S$ such that

1. no element in R attacks an element in M, and
2. M is a stable model of D-R.

M is a *preferred* model of D iff M is (subset) maximal among the sets admissible in D.

Brewka and Woltran also introduced weighted ADFs where an additional weight function w assigns qualitative or numerical weights to the links in the graph. This allows acceptance conditions to be defined in a domain independent way, based on the weights of links rather than on the involved positions. They also showed how the proof standards proposed by Farley and Freeman [7] can be formalized based on this idea.

Since the - rather straightforward - treatment of weights in ADFs will be illustrated in our translation, we do not give further details here and refer the reader to [4].

4. The Translation

We now show how to translate a CAES $S = \langle arguments, assumptions, weights, standard \rangle$ into a dialectical framework $ADF(S)$ (more precisely: a weighted dialectical framework) such that the semantics of S, in other words the outcome of the evaluation, is preserved.

The translation has to take into account that, when scintilla of evidence is used as proof standard, both a proposition p and its complement $\bar{p}$ may be acceptable. For this reason we have to use two nodes for each literal appearing in one of the arguments, one representing the proposition, the other its complement.

We start with the translation of arguments. Let $a = \langle P, E, c \rangle$ be an argument with $P = \{p_1, \ldots, p_k\}$ and $E = \{e_1, \ldots, e_r\}$. The translation of a is the graph (V, R) with

$$V = \{p_1, \ldots, p_k, e_1, \ldots, e_r, c, \bar{c}, a\}$$
$$R = \{(p_i, a) \mid p_i \in P\} \cup \{(e_i, a) \mid e_i \in E\} \cup \{(a, c), (a, \bar{c})\}.$$

Note that it is not sufficient to have nodes representing the literals in the argument. We also need the node a representing the argument itself.[3] We will call the latter type of nodes argument nodes, the other nodes statement nodes.

The translation of all arguments in *arguments* gives us the graph underlying the ADF. We next define the weights associated with the links in the ADF.

Let argument a be as above. The weight function w is defined as follows:

$$
\begin{aligned}
w(x, a) &= + & &\text{for } x \in P \\
w(x, a) &= - & &\text{for } x \in E \\
w(a, c) &= (+, n) & &\text{where } n = weights(a) \\
w(a, \bar{c}) &= (-, n) & &\text{where } n = weights(a)
\end{aligned}
$$

Thus, the weights of arguments in Carneades are attached to the links connecting the corresponding argument node with the conclusion and its negation. In addition, pro argument links are marked with a +, con argument links with a −.

---

[3] One of the reasons for this is that otherwise the resulting ADFs might not be bipolar.

Example 1. Consider the argument

$$a = \langle \{bird\}, \{peng, ostr\}, flies \rangle$$

and assume $weights(a) = 0.8$. The ADF graph generated by this argument is shown in Fig. 1 (we mark links with their weights).

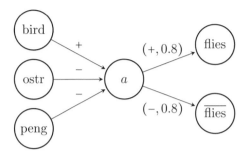

Figure 1. ADF representation of a Carneades argument

The effects of assumptions are represented via the acceptance conditions of argument nodes as follows. Let n be an argument node in the graph obtained from translating a set of arguments as described above. The acceptance condition C_n is defined as:

$C_n(R) = in$ iff
 (1) for all p_i with $w(p_i, a) = +$, $p_i \in assumptions$ or $\bar{p}_i \notin assumptions$ and $p_i \in R$, and
 (2) for all e_i with $w(e_i, a) = -$, $p_i \notin assumptions$ and $p_i \notin R$ or $\bar{p}_i \in assumptions$.

The acceptance conditions of statement nodes are directly derived from the proof standards for the propositions as specified by the function *standard*. Let m be a statement node, s the proof standard associated to the corresponding proposition via *standard*. We have to distinguish the 5 different cases (we let $max\emptyset = 0$; to avoid repetitions, we attach numbers in brackets to the conditions and use those instead of the conditions):

$s = se$: $C_m(R) = in$ iff [1] for some $r \in R$, $w(r, m) = (+, n)$.
$s = pe$: $C_m(R) = in$ iff [1] and
       [2] $max\{n \mid t \in R, w(t, m) = (+, n)\} > max\{n \mid t \in R, w(t, m) = (-, n)\}$.
$s = ce$: $C_m(R) = in$ iff [1] and [2] and
       [3] $max\{n \mid t \in R, w(t, m) = (+, n)\} > \alpha$ and
       [4] $max\{n \mid t \in R, w(t, m) = (+, n)\} - max\{n \mid t \in R, w(t, m) = (-, n)\} > \beta$.
$s = bd$: $C_m(R) = in$ iff [1] and [2] and [3] and [4] and
       [5] $max\{n \mid t \in R, w(t, m) = (-, n)\} < \gamma$
$s = dv$: $C_m(R) = in$ iff [1] and [6] for no $t \in R$, $w(t, m) = (-, n)$.

This concludes our translation. One may observe that, since cycles are not allowed in Carneades, the resulting ADF is acyclic. For such ADFs the semantics we presented earlier coincide:

Proposition 1. *Let the ADF $D = (S, L, C)$ be acyclic. Then D has a single preferred model which coincides with the single stable model and with the well-founded model.*

Proof (sketch): Since D is acyclic, we can show by induction on the number of elements in S that the well-founded model of D, $WF(D)$, is complete in the sense that, for each $s \in S$, $s \notin WF(D)$ implies $s \in E'$, where $(WF(D), E')$ is the least fixpoint of Γ_D. $WF(D)$ is thus the single (two-valued) model of D. Since D has no cycles, there can be no self-supporting links and the least model of the reduct $D^{WF(D)}$ coincides with $WF(D)$. $WF(D)$ is thus a stable model. Since stable models are preferred models, the set of preferred models cannot be empty. We can show, by induction on the number of iterations of the fixpoint operator Γ_D, that the well-founded model is a subset of each preferred model. A similar proof shows that, if $(WF(D), E')$ is the least fixpoint of Γ_D, then no element in E' can be contained in any preferred model of D. Thus, $WF(D)$ is also the single preferred model of D.   □

The following result shows that the translation actually preserves the meaning of a CAES.

Proposition 2. *Let* S = ⟨*arguments, assumptions, weights, standard*⟩ *be a CAES,* $ADF(S) = (S, L, C)$ *the dialectical framework resulting from translating* S *as defined above. The following holds:*

1. *An argument* $a \in$ *arguments is applicable in* S *iff the corresponding argument node* $a \in S$ *is contained in the well-founded (and thus the single preferred and the single stable) model of* $ADF(S)$.
2. *A proposition* p *is acceptable in* S *iff the corresponding statement node* $p \in S$ *is is contained in the well-founded (and thus the single preferred and the single stable) model of* $ADF(S)$.

Proof (sketch): We prove the proposition by induction on the number n of arguments in S. For $n = 0$ the result is obvious: there is neither an applicable argument nor an acceptable proposition in S, and since $ADF(S)$ is empty, we neither have an argument nor a statement node in the well-founded model of $ADF(S)$, denoted $WF(ADF(S))$.

Now assume the result holds for n arguments and consider a system with $n + 1$ arguments. Since arguments are acyclic, there must be an argument $a = \langle P, E, c \rangle$ such that c does not appear in the premises or exceptions of any other argument in S. If we disregard this argument we obtain a CAES S' for which, by induction hypothesis, the proposition holds. For a CAES S^*, let $App(S^*)$ denote the set of applicable arguments in S^*, $Acc(S^*)$ the set of acceptable nodes. Since neither applicability of arguments nor acceptability of propositions in S' depends on c there are only two cases: either $App(S) = App(S') \cup \{a\}$, or $App(S) = App(S')$. Furthermore, since the acceptability conditions of nodes in $ADF(S')$ do not depend on c, $WF(ADF(S'))$ is contained in $WF(ADF(S'))$. Now, since premises and exceptions of a are in $Acc(S')$ iff they are in the well-founded model of $WF(ADF(S'))$, and since the acceptance condition for a exactly mirrors the definition of applicability, we have $a \in WF(ADF(S))$ iff $a \in App(S)$. A similar argument shows that $c \in Acc(S)$ iff $c \in WF(ADF(S))$.   □

So far we have shown that a reconstruction of an acyclic CAES S as an ADF $ADF(S)$ is indeed possible. Our results also explain why the different Dung semantics do not show up in Carneades: the differences simply do not matter. However, the real advantage of our translation is that we can now lift the restriction of acyclicity, and then, of course, the different semantics do matter. Nothing in our translation hinges on the fact that the set of Carneades arguments is acyclic. Indeed, cycles in the set of arguments of

$\mathcal{S}$ will lead to cycles in $ADF(\mathcal{S})$, yet these cycles are handled - in different ways - by the available semantics of ADFs.

By a *generalized argument evaluation stucture* (GAES) we mean a CAES without the acyclicity restriction for the set of arguments. We define the semantics of GAES as follows:

Definition 12. Let $\mathcal{S}$ = $\langle arguments, assumptions, weights, standard \rangle$ be a GAES, $ADF(\mathcal{S})$ = (S, L, C) the dialectical framework resulting from translating $\mathcal{S}$ as defined above.

1. An argument $a \in arguments$ is applicable in $\mathcal{S}$ under grounded (credulous preferred, skeptical preferred, credulous stable, skeptical stable) semantics iff $a \in S$ is contained in the well-founded (all preferred, some preferred, all stable, some stable) model(s) of $ADF(\mathcal{S})$.
2. A proposition p is acceptable in $\mathcal{S}$ under grounded (credulous preferred, skeptical preferred, credulous stable, skeptical stable) semantics iff $p \in S$ is contained in the well-founded (all preferred, some preferred, all stable, some stable) model(s) of $ADF(\mathcal{S})$.

Example 2. Here is a simple example involving a cycle. Assume you are planning your vacation. You plan to go to Greece or to Italy, but cannot afford to visit both countries. Your arguments may thus be:

$$a_1 = \langle \varnothing, \{It\}, Gr \rangle, a_2 = \langle \varnothing, \{Gr\}, It \rangle.$$

These arguments obviously contain a cycle and thus cannot be handled by Carneades. Let n_1 be the weight of a_1, n_2 that of a_2. The translation yields the ADF shown in Fig. 2.

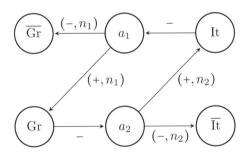

Figure 2. Greece vs. Italy

If we assume that both n_1 and n_2 are greater than α and β, and that further $\gamma > 0$, then the outcome is actually independent of the proof standard chosen for the statement nodes. We get 2 stable models, namely M_1 = $\{a_1, Gr\}$ and M_2 = $\{a_2, It\}$. These models are also the only preferred models. Thus both a_1 and a_2 are applicable under credulous stable and preferred semantics, but neither under skeptical stable nor under skeptical preferred semantics. Similarly, both Gr and It are acceptable under credulous stable and preferred semantics, but neither under skeptical stable nor under skeptical preferred semantics. The well-founded model is empty.

The approach presented here differs significantly from attempts to model proof standards using different Dung semantics, such as [1]. Although the various Dung semantics exhibit different degrees of cautiousness, we have doubts about using these different semantics as a basis for modeling proof standards. First of all, unless modularized variants of argumentation frameworks are used, as in [6] or [3], a chosen semantics is global and doesn't allow different proof standards to be applied to different issues within a single argumentation framework. More importantly, we doubt the various Dung semantics capture the intuitive meanings of legal proof standards. (For a detailed discussion see [9]). Our approach uses proof standards and Dung semantics for different purposes: proof standards are used to aggregate and accrue pro and con arguments about an issue; Dung semantics provide different ways to resolve cyclic arguments.

5. Conclusions

In this paper we have shown that Carneades argument evaluation structures can be reconstructed as abstract dialectical frameworks. This has several benefits, both from the point of view of ADFs and from the point of view of Carneades.

1. It shows that ADFs not only generalize Dung argumentation frameworks - which have been the starting point for their development. They also generalize Carneades argument evaluation structures. This provides evidence that the ADF framework is indeed a useful tool in the theory of argumentation.
2. It clarifies the relationship between Carneades and Dung AFs, showing that both are instances of ADFs. It thus helps to put Carneades on an equally solid formal foundation.
3. Finally, as we have seen, it allows us to lift the restriction of Carneades to acyclic argument structures.

References

[1]   Katie Atkinson and Trevor J. M. Bench-Capon. Argumentation and standards of proof. In *Proc. ICAIL*, pages 107–116, 2007.
[2]   Stefan Ballnat and Thomas Gordon. Goal selection in argumentation processes. In *Proc. COMMA* (this volume), 2010.
[3]   Gerhard Brewka and Thomas Eiter. Argumentation context systems: A framework for abstract group argumentation. In *LPNMR*, pages 44–57, 2009.
[4]   Gerhard Brewka and Stefan Woltran. Abstract dialectical frameworks. In *Proc. Principles of Knowledge Representation and Reasoning*, pages 102–111, 2010.
[5]   Phan Minh Dung. On the acceptability of arguments and its fundamental role in nonmonotonic reasoning, logic programming and n-person games. *Artif. Intell.*, 77(2):321–358, 1995.
[6]   Phan Minh Dung, Phan Minh Thang, and Nguyen 'Duy Hung. Modular argumentation for modelling legal doctrines of performance relief. In *ICAIL '09: Proceedings of the 12th International Conference on Artificial Intelligence and Law*, pages 128–136, New York, NY, USA, 2009. ACM.
[7]   Arthur M. Farley and Kathleen Freeman. Burden of proof in legal argumentation. In *Proc. ICAIL'95*, pages 156–164, 1995.
[8]   Thomas F. Gordon, Henry Prakken, and Douglas Walton. The Carneades model of argument and burden of proof. *Artif. Intell.*, 171(10-15):875–896, 2007.
[9]   Thomas F. Gordon and Douglas Walton. Proof burdens and standards. In Iyad Rahwan and Guillermo Simari, editors, *Argumentation in Artificial Intelligence*, pages 239–258. 2009.
[10] Matthias Grabmair, Thomas Gordon, and Douglas Walton. Probabilistic semantics for the Carneades argument model using Bayesian belief networks. In *Proc. COMMA* (this volume), 2010.

Computational Models of Argument
P. Baroni et al. (Eds.)
IOS Press, 2010
doi:10.3233/978-1-60750-619-5-13

Types of Dialogue and Burdens of Proof

Douglas Walton

University of Windsor, Windsor ON N9B 3Y1, Canada

Abstract

Burden of proof has recently come to be a topic of interest in argumentation systems for artificial intelligence (Prakken and Sartor, 2006, 2007, 2009; Gordon and Walton, 2007, 2009), but so far the main work on the subject seems to be in that type of dialogue which has most intensively been investigated generally, namely persuasion dialogue. The most significant exception is probably deliberation dialogue, where some recent work has begun to tentatively investigate burden of proof in that setting. In this paper, I survey work on burden of proof in the artificial intelligence literature on argumentation, and offer some thoughts on how this work might be extended to the other types of dialogue recognized by Walton and Krabbe (1995) that so far do not appear to have been much investigated in this regard.

1. Types of Dialogue and Dialectical Shifts

In this paper it is argued that the way forward toward a clearer, more precise and more useful grasp of burden of proof as a fundamental concept of argumentation is to recognize that there are different types of dialogue that function as normative frameworks of rational argumentation and that burden of proof is different in each type of dialogue. It is shown how burden of proof is determined in a dialogue by setting standards of proof, and by framing the dialogue in such a way that each party in the dialogue is obliged to meet the appropriate standard, and follow the procedural rules of the dialogue, in order to produce an argument that successful to achieve its goal of proof in that type of dialogue. According to the argument of the paper, requirements for burden proof need to set in each type of dialogue at different stages.

The six basic types of dialogue previously recognized in the argumentation literature (Walton and Krabbe, 1995) are inquiry, negotiation dialogue, information-seeking dialogue, deliberation, and eristic dialogue. Discovery dialogue (McBurney and Parsons, 2001) has been added in new list of the properties of the basic types of dialogue in Table 1. These dialogues are technical artifacts called normative models, meaning that they do not necessarily correspond exactly to real instances of persuasion or negotiation, and so forth, that may occur in a real conversational exchange. Each model of dialogue is defined by its initial situation, the participants' individual goals, and the aim of the dialogue as a whole.

Table 1. Seven Basic Types of Dialogue

Type of Dialogue	Initial Situation	Participant's Goal	Goal Of Dialogue
Persuasion	Conflict of Opinions	Persuade Other Party	Resolve or Clarify Issue
Inquiry	Need to Have Proof	Find and Verify Evidence	Prove (Disprove) Hypothesis
Discovery	Need to Find an Explanation of Facts	Find and Defend a Suitable Hypothesis	Choose Best Hypothesis for Testing
Negotiation	Conflict of Interests	Get What You Most Want	Reasonable Settlement Both Can Live With
Information-Seeking	Need Information	Acquire or Give Information	Exchange Information
Deliberation	Dilemma or Practical Choice	Co-ordinate Goals and Actions	Decide Best Available Course of Action
Eristic	Personal Conflict	Verbally Hit Out at Opponent	Reveal Deeper Basis of Conflict

A dialogue is formally defined as an ordered 3-tuple $\langle O, A, C \rangle$ where O is the opening stage, A is the argumentation stage, and C is the closing stage (Gordon and Walton, 2009, 5). Dialogue rules (protocols) define what types of moves are allowed by the parties during the argumentation stage (Walton and Krabbe, 1995). At the opening stage, the participants agree to take part in some type of dialogue that has a collective goal. Each party has an individual goal and the dialogue itself has a collective goal. The initial situation is framed at the opening stage, and the dialogue moves through the opening stage toward the closing stage. The type of dialogue, the goal of the dialogue, the initial situation, the participants, and the participant's goals are all set at the opening stage. In some instances, a burden of proof, called a global burden of proof, is set at the opening stage, applies through the whole argumentation stage, and determines which side was successful or not at the closing stage. In some instances, another kind of burden of proof, called a local burden of proof, applies to some speech acts made in moves during the argumentation stage (Walton, 1988).

Persuasion dialogue is adversarial in that the goal of each party is to win over the other side by finding arguments that defeat its thesis or casts it into doubt. Each party has a commitment set (Hamblin, 1971), and to win, a party must present a chain of argumentation that proves its thesis using only premises that are commitments of the other party. One very well known type of dialogue that can be classified as a type of persuasion dialogue is the critical discussion (van Eemeren and Grootendorst, 1992). The goal of a critical discussion is to resolve a conflict of opinions by rational argumentation. The critical discussion has procedural rules, but is not a formal model. However, the term 'persuasion dialogue' has now become a technical term of argumentation technology in artificial intelligence and there are formal models representing species of persuasion dialogue (Prakken, 2006).

Inquiry is quite different from persuasion dialogue because it is cooperative in nature, as opposed to persuasion dialogue which is highly adversarial. The goal of the inquiry, in its paradigm form, is to prove that a statement designated at the opening stage as the probandum is true or false, or if neither of these findings can be proved, to prove that there is insufficient evidence to prove that the probandum is true or false (Walton, 1998, chapter 3). The aim of this type of inquiry is to draw conclusions only from premises that can be firmly accepted as true or false, to prevent the need in the future to have to go back and reopen the inquiry once it has been closed. The most important characteristic of this paradigm of the inquiry as a type of dialogue is the property of cumulativeness (Walton, 1998, 70). To say a dialogue is cumulative means that once a statement has been accepted as true at any point in the argumentation stage of the inquiry, that statement must remain true at every point in the inquiry through the argumentation stage until the closing stage is reached. However, this paradigm of inquiry represents only one end of a spectrum where a high standard of proof is appropriate. In other inquiry settings, where there are conflicts of opinion and greater uncertainty, cumulativeness fails, but cooperativeness is a characteristic of inquiry. The model of inquiry dialogue built by Black and Hunter (2009) is meant to represent the cooperative setting of medical domains. Black and Hunter (2009, 174) model two subtypes of inquiry dialogue called in argument inquiry dialogues and warrant inquiry dialogues. The former allow to agents to share knowledge to jointly construct arguments, whereas the latter allow agents to share knowledge to construct dialectical trees that have an argument at each node in which a child node is a counterargument to its parent.

Inquiry dialogue can be classified as a truth-directed type of dialogue, as opposed to deliberation dialogue, which is not aimed at finding the truth that matter being discussed, but at arriving at a decision on what to do, where there is a need to take action. While persuasion dialogue is highly adversarial, deliberation is a collaborative type of dialogue in which parties collectively steer actions towards a common goal by agreeing on a proposal that can solve a problem affecting all of the parties concerned, taking all their interests into account. To determine in a particular case whether an argument in a text of discourse can better be seen as part of a persuasion dialog or a deliberation type of dialogue, one has to arrive at a determination of what the goals of the dialog and the goals of the participants are supposed to be. Argumentation in deliberation is primarily a matter of identifying proposals and arguments supporting them and finding critiques of other proposals (Walton et al., 2009). Deliberation dialogue is different from negotiation dialogue, because the negotiation deals with competing interests, whereas deliberation requires a sacrifice of one's interests.

Deliberation is a collaborative type of dialogue in which parties collectively steer group actions towards a common goal by agreeing on a proposal that can solve a problem affecting all of the parties concerned while taking their interests into account. A key property of deliberation dialogue is that proposal that is optimal for the group may not be optimal for any individual participant (McBurney et al. 2007, 98). Another property is that a participant in deliberation must be willing to share both her preferences and information with the other participants. This property does not hold in persuasion dialogue, where a participant presents only information that is useful to prove her thesis or to disprove the thesis of the opponent. In the formal model of deliberation of McBurney et al. (2007, 100), a deliberation dialogue consists of eight stages: open, inform, propose, consider, revise, recommend, confirm and close. Proposals for action that indicate possible action-options relevant to the governing question are put forward during the propose stage. Commenting on the proposals from various perspectives takes place during the consider stage. At the recommend stage a proposal for action can be recommended for acceptance or non-acceptance by each participant (Walton et al., 2010).

A dialectical shift is said to occur in cases where, during a sequence of argumentation, the participants begin to engage in a different type of dialogue from the one they were initially engaged in (Walton and Krabbe, 1995). In the following classic case (Parsons and Jennings, 1997, 267) often cited as an example, two agents are engaged in deliberation dialogue on how to hang a picture. Engaging in practical reasoning they come to the conclusion they need a hammer, and a nail, because they have figured out that the best way to hang the picture is on a nail, and the best way to put a nail in the wall is by means of a hammer. One knows where a hammer can be found, and the other has a pretty good idea of where to get a nail. At that point, the two begin to negotiate on who will get the hammer and who will go in search of a nail. In this kind of case, we say that the one dialogue is said to be embedded in the other (Walton and Krabbe, 1995), meaning that the second dialogue fits into the first and helps it along toward achieving its collective goal. In this instance, the shift to the negotiation dialogue is helpful in moving the deliberation dialogue along towards its goal of deciding the best way to hang the picture. For after all, if somebody has to get the hammer and nail, and they can't find anyone who is willing to do these things, they will have to rethink their deliberation on how best to hang the picture. Maybe they will need to phone a handyman, for example. This would mean another shift to an information-seeking dialogue, and involvement of a third party as a source of the information. This example of an embedding contrasts with an example of an illicit dialectical shift when the advent of the second type of dialogue interferes with the progress of the first. For example, let's consider a case in which a union-management negotiation deteriorates into an eristic dialogue in which each side bitterly attacks the other in an antagonistic manner. This kind of shift is not an embedding, because quarreling is not only unhelpful to the conduct of the negotiation, but is antithetical to it, and may very well even block it altogether, by leading to a strike for example.

2. Burden of Proof in Persuasion Dialogue

In all three versions of their set of rules for the critical discussion van Eemeren and Grootendorst set down a particular rule that governs burden of proof. In the 1992 version (van Eemeren and Grootendorst, 1992, 208), the rule governing burden of proof is simple. It only requires that "a party that advances the standpoint is obliged to defend it if the other party asks him to do so". For example, rule 8a of the formal dialogue system PPD (Walton and Krabbe, 1995, 136) says, "If one party challenges some assertion of the other party, the second party is to present, in the next move, at least one argument for that assertion". Hahn and Oaksford (2007, 47) have questioned whether van Eemeren and Grootendorst need to have rule 3 requiring burden of proof in a critical discussion. They think it makes sense to have a burden of proof for a participant's ultimate thesis set forth at the opening stage of the critical discussion, but they question why it is useful for each individual claim in the argumentative exchange to have an associated burden of proof. They concede that although there is a risk of non-persuasion in not responding to a challenge by putting forward an argument to defend one's claim, this risk is a relatively small factor in the outcome of the dialogue and "is entirely external to the dialogue and not a burden of proof in any conventional sense" (Hahn and Oaksford, 2007, 47). They have a point. It is worth asking what function the requirement of burden of proof has in a persuasion dialogue.

The addition of a third party audience to the persuasion dialogue affects brings out the utility of this function. If a party in a persuasion dialogue puts forward an argument, and then fails to defend it when challenged to do so, this failure will make his side appear weak to the audience who is evaluating the argumentation on both sides. They will ask why he put forward this particular claim if he can't defend it, and he may easily lose by default. This can come about because the audience has the role of being a neutral third party in the dialogue, and is not merely one of the contestants who is trying to get the best of the opposed party. It helps the audience to judge which side had the better argument if each side responds to challenges by putting forward arguments to support its claims. Law is an area where there is such a third party trier (a judge or jury) in addition to the opposed advocates on each side.

In legal argumentation of the kind found in a common law trial setting (a species of persuasion dialogue), there is a burden of persuasion set at the opening stage of a dialogue, and a burden of production of evidence is set during the argumentation stage. But there is also a tactical burden of proof that plays an important role in the formal system for modeling burden of proof of Prakken and Sartor (2009, 228). On their account, the burden of persuasion specifies which party has to prove some proposition that represents the ultimate probandum in the case, and also specifies to what proof standard has to be met. The judge is supposed to instruct the jury on what proof standard has to be met and which side estimated at the beginning of the trial process. Whether this burden has been met or not is determined at the end of the trial. The burden of persuasion remains the same throughout the trial, once it has been set. It never shifts from the one side to the other during the whole proceedings. The burden of production specifies which party has to offer evidence on some specific issue that arises during a particular point during the argumentation in the trial itself as it proceeds. The burden of production may in many instances only have to meet a low proof standard. If the evidence offered does not meet the standard, the issue can be decided as a matter of law against the burden party, or decided in the final stage by the trier. Both the burden of persuasion and the burden of production are assigned by law. The tactical burden of proof, on the other hand is decided by the party putting forward an argument at some stage during the proceedings. The arguer must judge the risk of ultimately losing on the particular issue being discussed at that point if he fails to put forward further evidence concerning that issue. The tactical burden is not ruled on or moderated by the judge. It pertains only to the two parties contesting on each side, enabling them to plan their argumentation strategies.

3. Burden of Proof in the Inquiry

The type of dialogue where use of the expression 'burden of proof' is most clearly appropriate is the inquiry. The aim of the inquiry is to collect sufficient evidence to either definitively prove the proposition at issue, or to show that it can be proved, despite the exhaustive effort was made to collect all the evidence that was available. The central aim of the inquiry is proof, where this term is taken to imply that a high standard of proof has been met. The negative aim of the inquiry is to avoid later retraction of the proposition that has been proved. And so the very highest standard of proof is appropriate. The inquiry is therefore the model of dialogue in which the expression 'burden of proof' has a paradigm status.

The inquiry as a type of dialogue is somewhat similar to the type of reasoning that Aristotle called a demonstration. On his account (1984, *Posterior Analytics*, 71b26), the premises of a demonstration are themselves indemonstrable, as the grounds of the conclusion, and must be better known than the conclusion and prior to it. He added that (1984, Posterior Analytics, 72b25) that circular argumentation is excluded from a demonstration. He argued that since demonstration must be based on premises prior to and better known than the conclusion to be proved, and since the same things cannot simultaneously be both prior and posterior to one another, circular demonstration is not possible (at least in the unqualified sense of the term 'demonstration'.

In contrast, persuasion dialogues, as well as deliberation dialogues and discovery dialogues, have to allow for retractions. It is part of the rationality of argumentation in a persuasion dialogue that if one party proves that the other party has accepted a statement that is demonstrably false, the other party has to immediately retract commitment to that statement. It does not follow that persuasion dialogue has to allow for retractions in all circumstances but, the default position is that it is presumed that retraction should generally be allowed, except in certain situations. In contrast, in the inquiry, the default position is to eliminate the possibility of retraction of commitments, except in certain situations.

Cumulativeness appears to be such a strict model of argumentation that many equate it with the Enlightenment ideal of foundationalism of the kind attacked by Toulmin (1959). To represent any real instance of an inquiry, it is useful to explore inquiry dialogue systems that are not fully cumulative. Black and Hunter (2007) have built a system of argument inquiry dialogues meant to be used in the medical domain to deal with the typical kind of situation in medical knowledge consisting of a database that is incomplete, inconsistent and operates under conditions of uncertainty. This kind of the inquiry dialogue they model represented by a situation in which many different health care professionals rule involved in the care of the patient and who must cooperate by sharing their specialized knowledge in order to provide the best care for the patient. To provide a standard for soundness and completeness of this type of dialogue, Black and Hunter (2007, 2) compare the outcome of one of their actual dialogues with the outcome that would be arrived at by a single agent that has as its beliefs that the union of the beliefs sets of both the agents participating in the dialogue. Their model assumes a form of cumulativeness in which an agent's belief set does not change during a dialogue, but they add that they would like to further explore inquiry dialogues to model the situation in which an agent has a reason for removing a belief from its beliefs at it had asserted earlier in the dialogue (Black and Hunter (2007, 6). To model real instances of argumentation inquiry dialogue, it would seem that ways of relaxing the strict requirement of cumulativeness need to be considered.

One difference between burden of proof in inquiry and persuasion dialogues is that the standard of proof generally needs to be set much higher in the inquiry type of dialogue. A similarity between the two types of dialogue is that the burden of proof, including the standard of proof, is set at the opening stage.

4. Discovery Dialogue

Discovery dialogue was first recognized as a distinct type of dialogue different from the any of the six basic types of dialogue by McBurney and Parsons (2001). On their account (McBurney and Parsons, 2001, 4), discovery dialogue and inquiry dialogue are distinctively different in a fundamental way. In an inquiry dialogue, the proposition that is to be proved true is designated prior to the course of the argumentation in the dialogue, whereas in a discovery dialogue the question was truth is to be determined only emerges during the course of the dialogue itself. According to their model of discovery dialogue, participants began by discussing the purpose of the dialogue, and then during the later stages they use data items, inference mechanisms, and consequences to present arguments to each other. Two other tools they use are called criteria and tests. Criteria, like novelty, importance, cost, benefits, and so forth, are used to compare one data item or consequence with another. The test is a procedure to ascertain the truth or falsity of some proposition, generally undertaken outside the discovery dialog.

The discovery dialogue moves through ten stages (McBurney and Parsons, 2001, 5) called open dialogue, discuss purpose, share knowledge, discuss mechanisms, infer consequences, discuss criteria, assess consequences, discuss tests, propose conclusions, and close dialogue. The names for these stages give the reader some idea of what happens at each stage as the dialogue proceeds by having the participants open the discussion, discuss the purpose of the dialogue, share knowledge by presenting data items to each other, discuss the mechanisms to be used, like the rules of inference, build arguments by inferring consequences from data items, discuss criteria for assessment of consequences presented, assess the consequences in light of the criteria previously presented, discuss the need for undertaking tests of proposed consequences, pose one or more conclusions for possible acceptance, close the dialogue. The stages of the discovery dialogue may be undertaken in any order and may be repeated, according to (2001, 6). They add that agreement is not necessary in a discovery dialogue, unless the participants want to have it.

McBurney and Parsons also present of formal system for discovery dialogue in which its basic components are defined. A wide range of speech acts (permitted locutions) that constitute moves in a discovery dialogue include the following: propose, assert, query, show argument, assess, recommend, accept, and retract. There is a commitment store that exists for each participant in the dialogue containing only the propositions which the participant has publicly accepted. All commitments of any participant can be viewed by all participants. They intend their model to be applicable to the problem of identifying risks and opportunities in a situation where knowledge is not shared by multiple agents.

To be able to identify when a dialectical shift from a discovery dialogue to an inquiry dialogue has occurred in a particular case, we first of all have to investigate how the one type of dialogue is different from the other. Most importantly, there are basic differences in how burden of proof, including the standard of proof, operates. In an inquiry dialogue the global burden of proof, that is operative during the whole argumentation stage, is set at the opening stage. In a discovery dialogue no global burden of proof is set at the opening stage that operates over both subsequent stages of the dialog. McBurney and Parsons (2001, 418) express this difference by writing that in inquiry dialogue, the participants "collaborate to ascertain the truth of some question", while in discovery dialog, we want to discover something not previously known, and "the question whose truth is to be ascertained may only emerge in the course of the dialog itself". This difference is highly significant, as it affects how each of the two types of dialogue is fundamentally structured.

In an inquiry dialogue, the global burden of proof is set at the opening stage and is then applied at the closing stage to determine whether the inquiry has been successful or not. This feature is comparable to a persuasion dialogue, where the burden of persuasion is set at the opening stage (Prakken and Sartor, 2007). At the opening stage of the inquiry dialogue, a particular statement has to be specified, so that the object of the inquiry as a whole is to prove or disprove this statement. In a persuasion dialogue, this burden of proof can be imposed on one side, or imposed equally on both sides (Prakken and Sartor, 2006). However, in an inquiry dialogue there can be no asymmetry between the sides. All participants collaborate together to bring forward evidence that can be amassed together to prove or disprove the statement at issue. Discovery dialogue is quite different in this respect. There is no statement set at the beginning in such a manner that the goal of the whole dialogue is to prove or disprove this statement. The basic reason has been made clear by McBurney and Parsons. What is to be discovered is not known at the opening stage of the discovery dialog. The aim of the discovery dialog is to try to find something, and until that thing is found, it is not known what is, and hence it cannot be set as something to be proved or disproved at the opening stage as the goal of the dialogue.

5. Burden of Proof in Deliberation Dialogue

Burden of proof is not the only type of burden one can have in the dialogue. Most of the types of dialogue that have been studied so far in the argumentation literature, like persuasion dialogue, concern claims that are put forward in the form of a proposition that is held to be true or false. The central aim of the argumentation is to prove that such a proposition is true or false. But other types of dialogue, like deliberation and negotiation, do not have the central aim of proving that a particular proposition is true or false. Still other dialogues are not mainly about argumentation. Some are about the giving and receiving of explanations, for example. In this kind of dialogue, there is no burden of proof, because the central aim is not to prove something but to explain something that the questioner claims to fail to understand. However, in this type of dialogue when a questioner asks for an explanation, there is an obligation on the part of the other party to provide one, assuming he is in a position to do that. So generally, in all types of dialogue of the kind that provide normative structures for rational communication, there are obligations to respond in a certain way to a request made in a prior move by the other party. These obligations are quite general, but the notion of burden of proof is more restricted, and only applies where a response to an expression of doubt by one party as to whether some proposition is true or not needs to be made by offering an attempt to prove that the proposition is true or false. For obvious reasons, this type of dialogue exchange is centrally important in science and philosophy, but the problem is that the vocabulary used to describe its operation has a tendency to be carried over into other types of dialogue where the central purpose is not to prove or disprove something.

There is no global burden of proof in a deliberation dialogue, because no thesis to be proved or disproved is set into place for each side at the opening stage (Walton, 2010). Deliberation is not an adversarial type of dialogue, and that the opening stage all options are left open concerning proposals that might be brought forward to answer the governing question. At the opening stage, the governing question cites a problem that needs to be solved cooperatively by the group were party to the deliberations, a problem that concerns choice of actions by the group. The goal of the dialogue is not to prove or disprove anything, but to arrive at a decision on which is the best course of action to take. Hence the expression 'burden of proof' is not generally appropriate for this type of dialogue.

During a later stage, proposals for action are put forward, and what takes place during the argumentation stage is a discussion that examines the arguments both for and against each proposal, in order to arrive at decision on which proposal is best. Something like the standard of proof called the preponderance of the evidence in law is operative during this stage. The outcome in a deliberation dialogue should be to select the best proposal, even if that proposal is only marginally better than others that have been offered. A party who offers a proposal is generally advocating it is the best course of action to take, even though in some instances a proposal may merely be put forward hypothetically is something to consider but not necessarily something to adopt is the best course of action. In such instances is reasonable to allow one party to deliberation dialogue to ask another party to justify the proposal that the second party has put forward, so that the reasons behind it can be examined and possibly criticized. Hence there is a place in deliberation dialogue for something comparable to burden of proof. It could be called a burden of defending or justifying a proposal. What needs to be observed is that this burden only comes into play during the argumentation stage where proposals are being put forward, question and defended. In contrast with the situation in persuasion dialogue, and of these proposals is formulated and set into place at the opening stage is something that has to be proved or cast into doubt by one of the designated parties in the dialogue. In this regard, persuasion dialogue and deliberation are different in their structures. Since persuasion dialogue (the critical discussion type of dialogue) has been most discussed in the argumentation literature, it seems natural to think that there must be something comparable to burden of proof that is also operative in deliberation dialogue. But this expectation is misleading.

In deliberation dialogue, there is no burden of persuasion set the opening stage, because the proposals will only be formulated as recommendations for particular courses of actions at the later argumentation stage. A deliberation dialogue arises from the need for action, as expressed in a governing question formulated at the opening stage, like 'Where shall we go for dinner tonight?', and proposals for action arise only at a later stage in the dialogue (McBurney et al, 2007, 99). There is no burden of proof set for any of the parties in a deliberation at the opening stage. However, at the later argumentation stage, once a proposal has been put forward by a particular party, it will be reasonably assumed by the other participants that this party will be prepared to defend his proposal by using arguments, for example like the argument that his proposal does not have negative consequences, or the argument that his proposal will fulfill some goal that is taken to be important for the group. How burden of proof figures during the argumentation stage can be seen by examining some of the permissible locutions (speech acts allowed as moves). One of these is the ask-justify locution (McBurney et al., 2007, 103), quoted below.

The locution **ask_justify** (*Pj*, *Pi*, *type*, *t*) is a request by participant *Pj* of participant *Pi*, seeking justification from *Pi* for the assertion that sentence *t* is a valid instance of type *type*. Following this, *Pi* must either retract the sentence *t* or shift into an embedded persuasion dialogue in which *Pi* seeks to persuade *Pj* that sentence *t* is such a valid instance.

What we see here is that one participant in a deliberation dialogue can ask another participant to justify a proposition that the second party has become committed to through some previous move of a type like an assertion or proposal. As long as the proposition is in the second party's commitment set, the first party has a right to ask him to justify it or retract it. But notice that when the second party offers such a justification attempt, the dialogue shifts into an embedded persuasion dialogue in which the second party tries to persuade the first party to become committed to this proposition by using a valid argument. So what we see here is the burden of proof is involved during specific groups of moves at the argumentation stage, but when the attempt is made by the respondent to fulfill the request for justification, there is a shift of persuasion dialogue. By this means the notion of burden of proof appropriate for the persuasion dialogue can be used to evaluate the argument offered.

A key factor that is vitally important for persuasion dialogue is that the participants agree on the issue to be discussed at the opening stage. Each party must have a thesis to be proved. This setting of the issue is vitally important for preventing the discussion from wandering off and never concluding, or by shifting the burden of proof back and forth and never concluding. In deliberation dialogue however, the proposals are not formulated until a later stage. It makes no sense to attempt to fix the proposals at the opening stage, because they need to arise out of the brainstorming discussions that take place after the opening stage. Burden of proof only arises during the argumentation stage in relation to specific kinds of moves made during that stage, and when it does arrive there is a shift of persuasion dialogue which allows the appropriate notion of burden of proof to be brought in from the persuasion dialogue. Hence we see that burden of proof please only a very small role in deliberation dialogue itself. The role performs is best described not as a burden of proof but as a burden of justification.

6. Information-seeking dialogue, Negotiation and Eristic Dialogue

There seems to be little to say about burden of proof in information-seeking dialogues at first sight, but there are at least two ways in which burden of proof might enter into this type of dialogue. Information dialogue is not exclusively taken up with the putting forward of ask and tell questions, or with the kind of searching for information one might do when using Google. One reason is that there is a concern not only with obtaining raw information, but with determining the quality of this information by judging its reliability. Judgments of reliability of collected information would seem to involve standards of proof, and therefore also may involve burdens of proof. Another reason is that in many instances of information seeking dialogue, the requesting agent needed to provide the responding agent with an argument in order to obtain access to the information requested. As noted in (Doutre et al., 2006), such dialogues may be viewed as consisting only of ask and tell locutions if this argument component of them is not considered. But if this argument component is considered as part of the information-seeking dialogue, then burden of proof is involved.

There also seems to be little to say, or that has been said, about burden of proof either negotiation dialogue or eristic dialogue, at least that I am aware of, but the reason may be that burden of proof is not an appropriate requirement in either of these types of dialogue. Anyone who adopts the approach to proving something to the other party by means of evidence that fulfills a burden of proof would be likely to perform very badly in either of these types of dialogue. For proving something by using evidence to support your claims is, or should not be the central goal in either of these types of dialogue. However, in both types of dialogue there are typically intervals where there is a shift from one of them to another type of dialogue where burden of proof is important. For example a contractor in homeowner may be negotiating a price for installing a new basement in the house, and at some point in the dialog may become important for the contractor to try to convince homeowner that the building code for walls in basements in that area specifies certain requirements that have to be met, for example discerning the thickness of the walls. In such a case, the notion of burden of proof may not play any direct role in the negotiation argumentation itself, but when there is a shift from it to a persuasion dialogue where they contractor tries to convince homeowner the walls of a certain minimum thickness are mandatory, burden of proof may be an important factor in evaluating his arguments. It may be, as well, that agents argue about receiving permission to get information during an information-seeking dialogue, there has been a shift to some other type of dialogue like a persuasion dialogue.

7. Conclusions

Global burden of proof in a dialogue is defined as a 3-tuple $\langle P, T, S \rangle$ where P is a set of participants, T is an ultimate *probandum*, a proposition to be proved or cast into doubt by a designated participant and S is the standard of proof required to make a proof successful. If there is no thesis to be proved or cast into doubt in a dialogue, there is no burden of proof in that dialogue, except where it may enter by a dialectical shift. The local burden of proof defines what requirement of proof has to be fulfilled for a speech act, or move like making a claim, during the argumentation stage. The global burden of proof is set at the opening stage, but during the argumentation stage, as particular arguments are put forward and replied to, there is a local burden of proof for each argument that can change. This local burden of proof can shift from one side to the other during the argumentation stage as arguments are put forward and critically questioned. Once the argumentation has reached the closing stage, the outcome is determined by judging whether one side or the other has met its global burden of proof, according the requirements set at the opening stage.

It seems fair to conclude that although the bulk of the literature on burden of proof so far is on persuasion dialogue, it should also be important to investigate burden of proof in inquiry dialogue where it is a central concept. Burden of proof is only significant in deliberation dialogue when there has been a shift to a persuasion dialogue. Burden of proof is important in information seeking dialogue when arguments need to be brought forward to get permission to receive the information, or when the reliability of the information is a concern. Burden of proof is especially important in the study of scientific argumentation because of the characteristic shift in scientific research from the discovery stage to the inquiry stage.

References

[1] Aristotle (1984). Posterior Analytics, The Complete Works of Aristotle, vol. 1. ed. J. Barnes, Princeton: Princeton University Press.
[2] Black, E. and Hunter, A. (2007). A Generative Inquiry Dialogue System. Sixth International Joint Conference on Autonomous Agents and Multi-agent Systems, 1010-1017.
[3] Black, E. and Hunter, A. (2009). An Inquiry Dialogue System, Autonomous Agent and Multi-Agent Systems 19, 173–209.
[4] Doutre, S., McBurney, P., Wooldridge, M. and Barden, W. (2006). Information-seeking Agent Dialogs with Permissions and Arguments, Fifth International Joint Conference on Autonomous Agents and Multiagent Systems. Technical Report: www.csc.liv.ac.uk/research/techreports/tr2005/ulcs-05-010.pdf
[5] Gordon, T. F. Prakken, H. and Walton, D. (2007). The Carneades Model of Argument and Burden of Proof, Artificial Intelligence, 171, 875-896.

[6] Gordon, T. F. and Walton, D. (2009). Proof Burdens and Standards, *Argumentation and Artificial Intelligence*, ed. I. Rahwan and G. Simari, Dordrecht: Springer, 2009.

[7] McBurney, P. and Parsons, S. (2001). Chance Discovery Using Dialectical Argumentation. New Frontiers in Artificial Intelligence, ed. T. Terano, T. Nishida, A. Namatame, S. Tsumoto, Y. Ohsawa and T. Washio (Lecture Notes in Artificial Intelligence, vol. 2253), Berlin, Springer Verlag, 414-424.

[8] McBurney, P. Hitchcock, D. and Parsons, S. (2007). The Eightfold Way of Deliberation Dialogue, *International Journal of Intelligent Systems*, 22, 95-132.

[9] Parsons, S. and Jennings N. (1997). Negotiation through Argumentation: A Preliminary Report. Proceedings of the Second International Conferecne on Multi-Agent Systems, ed. Mario Tokoro. Menlo Park, California: AAAI Press, 267-274.

[10] Prakken, H. (2006). Formal Systems for Persuasion Dialogue. *The Knowledge Engineering Review*, 21, 163-188.

[11] Prakken, H. and Sartor, G. (2006). Presumptions and Burdens of Proof, *Legal Knowledge and Information Systems: JURIX 2006: The Nineteenth Annual Conference*, ed. T. M. van Engers, Amsterdam: IOS Press, 21-30.

[12] Prakken, H. and Sartor, G. (2007). Formalising Arguments about the Burden of Persuasion. Proceedings of the Eleventh International Conference on Artificial Intelligence and Law. New York: ACM Press, 97-106.

[13] Prakken, H. and Sartor, G. (2009). A Logical Analysis of Burdens of Proof. Legal Evidence and Burden of proof, ed. Hendrik Kaptein, Henry Prakken and Bart Verhiej. Farnham: Ashgate, 223- 253.

[14] Walton, D. (1988). Burden of Proof, Argumentation, 2, 233-254.

[15] Walton, D. (1998). The New Dialectic: Conversational Contexts of Argument. Toronto: University of Toronto Press.

[16] Walton, D. (2010). Burden of Proof in Deliberation Dialogs, Proceedings of ArgMAS 2009, ed. P. McBurney et al, Lecture Notes in Computer Science 6057, Heidelberg, Springer, 2010, 1-22.

[17] Walton, D. Atkinson, K. Bench-Capon, T. J. M. Wyner, A. and Cartwright, D. (2010). Argumentation in the Framework of Deliberation Dialogue, Arguing Global Governance, ed. Bjola, C. and Kornprobst, M. London: Routledge, 210-230.

[18] Walton, D. and Krabbe, E. C. W (1995). Commitment in Dialogue. Albany: SUNY Press.

Part II

Regular Papers

Computational Models of Argument
P. Baroni et al. (Eds.)
IOS Press, 2010
doi:10.3233/978-1-60750-619-5-27

A characterization of collective conflict for defeasible argumentation

Teresa ALSINET [a,1], Ramón BÉJAR [a] and Lluís GODO [b]

[a] *Department of Computer Science. University of Lleida,* SPAIN
[b] *Artificial Intelligence Research Institute (IIIA-CSIC), Bellaterra,* SPAIN

Abstract.

In this paper we define a recursive semantics for warrant in a general defeasible argumentation framework by formalizing a notion of collective (non-binary) conflict among arguments. This allows us to ensure direct and indirect consistency (in the sense of Caminada and Amgoud) without distinguishing between direct and indirect conflicts. Then, the general defeasible argumentation framework is extended by allowing to attach levels of preference to defeasible knowledge items and by providing a level-wise definition of warranted and blocked conclusions. Finally, we formalize the warrant recursive semantics for the particular framework of Possibilistic Defeasible Logic Programming, characterize the unique output program property and design an efficient algorithm for computing warranted conclusions in polynomial space.

Keywords. Defeasible argumentation, collective conflict, recursive warrant semantics.

1. Introduction and motivation

Possibilistic Defeasible Logic Programming (P-DeLP) [3] is a rule-based argumentation framework which is an extension of Defeasible Logic Programming (DeLP) [10] in which defeasible rules are attached with weights (belonging to the real unit interval $[0, 1]$) expressing their belief or preference strength and formalized as necessity degrees. As many other argumentation frameworks [8,14], P-DeLP can be used as a vehicle for facilitating rationally justifiable decision making when handling incomplete and potentially inconsistent information. Actually, given a P-DeLP program, justifiable decisions correspond to warranted conclusions (with a maximum necessity degree), that is, those which remain undefeated after an exhaustive dialectical analysis of all possible arguments for and against.

In [6] Caminada and Amgoud propose three *rationality postulates* which every rule-based argumentation system should satisfy. One of such postulates (called *Indirect Consistency*) claims that the closure of warranted conclusions with respect to the set of strict rules must be consistent. A number of rule-based argumentation systems are identified in which such postulate does not hold (including DeLP [10] and Prakken & Sartor's [13], among others). As a way to solve this problem, the use of *transposed rules* is proposed in [6] to extend the representation of strict rules.

Since the dialectical analysis based semantics of P-DeLP does not satisfy indirect consistency, in [2,1] a level-wise approach to compute warranted conclusions, called

---

[1]Correspondence to: T. Alsinet. Department of Computer Science, University of Lleida. C/Jaume II, 69. Lleida, Spain. Tel.: +34 973702734; Fax: +34 973702702; E-mail: tracy@diei.udl.cat

level-based P-DeLP, was defined ensuring the indirect consistency postulate without extending the representation of strict rules with transposed rules. In contrast with DeLP and other argument-based approaches [8,14,5,15], the level-based P-DeLP framework does not require the use of dialectical trees as underlying structures for characterizing the semantics for warranted conclusions. The level-based P-DeLP framework distinguishes two types of conflicts between arguments, direct and indirect. Direct conflicts occur when there exists an inconsistency emerging from arguments supporting contradictory literals. Indirect conflicts occur in a given program when there exists an inconsistency emerging from the set of strict rules of the program and a set of non-defeated (due to a direct conflict) arguments. The level-based P-DeLP framework therefore establishes an implicit evaluation order between conflicts, in the sense that if a conclusion is involved in both a direct and indirect conflict, the direct conflict invalidates the indirect one. On the other hand, although the level-based P-DeLP semantics for warranted conclusions is skeptical, in [1] it was shown that some circular definitions of conflict between arguments can arise and they can lead to different extensions of warranted conclusions.

Recently Pollock defined [12] a recursive semantics for defeasible argumentation (without levels of preference) where circular definitions of defeat between arguments were characterized by means of *inference-graphs*, representing (binary) support and defeat relations between the conclusions of arguments. Following this approach, our aim in this paper is to formally characterize circular definitions of conflict among arguments that cause different extensions of warranted conclusions in the level-based P-DeLP framework. However, because of the above mentioned implicit evaluation order between conflicts and its undesired side-effect, we are in need for a new and general notion of conflict among arguments which, besides of ensuring the Caminda and Amgoud's rationality postulates, allows us to safely reason about circular definitions of conflict between arguments.

To this end, in this paper we first define a recursive semantics for warranted conclusions in a quite general framework (without levels of strength) by formalizing a new collective (non-binary) notion of conflict between arguments ensuring indirect consistency without distinguishing between direct and indirect conflicts. Second we extend the recursive semantics to an argumentation framework with levels of preference by providing a level-wise definition of warranted and blocked conclusions. A warranted conclusion is a justified conclusion which is only based on warranted information and which does not generate a conflict, while a blocked conclusion is a conclusion which, like warranted conclusions, is only based on warranted information, but it does generate a conflict. Third, we specialize the warrant recursive semantics for the particular framework of P-DeLP, we refer to this formalism as RP-DeLP, characterize the condition under which a program has a unique output based on what we call *warrant dependency graph*, and design an efficient algorithm for computing warranted conclusions in polynomial space.

2. General defeasible argumentation framework

We will start by considering a rather general framework for defeasible argumentation based on a propositional logic $(\mathcal{L}, \vdash)$ with a special symbol $\perp$ for contradiction[2]. For any set of formulas A, if $A \vdash \perp$ we will say that A is contradictory, while if $A \not\vdash \perp$ we

---

[2]If not stated otherwise, in this and in the next section $(\mathcal{L}, \vdash)$ may be taken as classical propositional logic.

will say that A is consistent. A knowledge base (KB) is a triplet $\mathcal{P} = (\Pi, \Delta, \Sigma)$, where $\Pi, \Delta, \Sigma \subseteq \mathcal{L}$, and $\Pi \not\vdash \bot$. Π is a finite set of formulas representing strict knowledge (formulas we take for granted they hold to be true), Δ is another finite set of formulas representing the defeasible knowledge (formulas for which we have reasons to believe they are true) and Σ denotes the set of formulas over which arguments can be built. In many argumentation systems, Σ is taken to be a set of literals.

The notion of *argument* is the usual one. Given a KB $\mathcal{P}$, an argument for a formula $\varphi \in \Sigma$ is a pair $\mathcal{A} = \langle A, \varphi \rangle$, with $A \subseteq \Delta$ such that:

1. $\Pi \cup A \not\vdash \bot$, and
2. A is minimal (w.r.t. set inclusion) such that $\Pi \cup A \vdash \varphi$.

If $A = \emptyset$, then we will call $\mathcal{A}$ a s-argument (s for strict), otherwise it will be a d-argument (d for defeasible). The notion of *subargument* is referred to d-arguments and expresses an incremental prove relationship between arguments which is formalized as follows.

Definition 1 (Subargument) *Let $\langle B, \psi \rangle$ and $\langle A, \varphi \rangle$ be two d-arguments such that the minimal sets (w.r.t. set inclusion) $\Pi_\psi \subseteq \Pi$ and $\Pi_\varphi \subseteq \Pi$ such that $\Pi_\psi \cup B \vdash \psi$ and $\Pi_\varphi \cup A \vdash \varphi$ verify that $\Pi_\psi \subseteq \Pi_\varphi$. Then, $\langle B, \psi \rangle$ is a subargument of $\langle A, \varphi \rangle$, written $\langle B, \psi \rangle \sqsubset \langle A, \varphi \rangle$, when either $B \subset A$ (strict inclusion for defeasible knowledge), or $B = A$ and $\Pi_\psi \subset \Pi_\varphi$ (strict inclusion for strict knowledge), or $B = A$ and $\Pi_\psi = \Pi_\varphi$ and $\psi \vdash \varphi$ and $\varphi \not\vdash \psi$* [3].

A formula $\varphi \in \Sigma$ will be called *justifiable* w.r.t. $\mathcal{P}$ if there exists an argument for φ, i.e. there exists $A \subseteq \Delta$ such that $\langle A, \varphi \rangle$ is an argument.

The usual notion of attack or defeat relation in an argumentation system is binary. However in certain situations, the conflict relation among arguments is hardly representable as a binary relation. For instance, consider the following KB $\mathcal{P}_1 = (\Pi, \Delta, \Sigma)$ with

$$\Pi = \{a \wedge b \to \neg p\}, \Delta = \{a, b, p\} \text{ and } \Sigma = \{a, b, p, \neg p\}.$$

Clearly, $\mathcal{A}_1 = \langle \{p\}, p \rangle, \mathcal{A}_2 = \langle \{b\}, b \rangle, \mathcal{A}_3 = \langle \{a\}, a \rangle$ are arguments that justify p, b and a respectively, and which do not pair-wisely generate a conflict. Indeed, $\Pi \cup \{a, b\} \not\vdash \bot$, $\Pi \cup \{a, p\} \not\vdash \bot$ and $\Pi \cup \{b, p\} \not\vdash \bot$. However the three arguments are collectively conflicting since $\Pi \cup \{a, b, p\} \vdash \bot$, hence in this $\mathcal{P}_1$ there is a non-binary conflict relation among several arguments. In the following we will formalize this notion of collective, or non-binary, conflict among in principle valid arguments and which arises when we compare them with the strict part of the knowledge base.

The following notion of acceptable argument with respect to a set (possibly empty) of justifiable conclusions W will play a key role. If we think of W as a consistent set of already warranted conclusions, an acceptable argument captures the idea of an argument which is based on subarguments already warranted.

Definition 2 (Acceptable argument) *Let W be a set of justifiable conclusions which is consistent w.r.t. Π, i.e. $\Pi \cup W \not\vdash \bot$. A d-argument $\mathcal{A} = \langle A, \varphi \rangle$ is an acceptable argument for φ w.r.t. W iff:*

---

[3]Notice that if $(\Pi, \Delta, \Sigma) = (\{r\}, \{r \to p \wedge q\}, \{p, q, p \wedge q\})$ and $A = \{r \to p \wedge q\}$ then $\mathcal{A}_1 = \langle A, p \rangle$, $\mathcal{A}_2 = \langle A, q \rangle$ and $\mathcal{A}_3 = \langle A, p \wedge q \rangle$ are arguments for different formulas with a same support and thus, in our framework, $\mathcal{A}_3 \sqsubset \mathcal{A}_1$ and $\mathcal{A}_3 \sqsubset \mathcal{A}_2$ are the subargument relations between arguments $\mathcal{A}_1$, $\mathcal{A}_2$ and $\mathcal{A}_3$ since $p \wedge q \vdash p$, $p \wedge q \vdash q$, $p \not\vdash p \wedge q$ and $q \not\vdash p \wedge q$.

1. if $\langle B, \psi \rangle$ is a subargument of $\langle A, \varphi \rangle$ then $\psi \in W$
2. $\Pi \cup W \cup \{\varphi\} \nvdash \bot$

In the above example, arguments $\mathcal{A}_1$, $\mathcal{A}_2$ and $\mathcal{A}_3$ are acceptable w.r.t. Π and the empty set of conclusions $W = \emptyset$. However $\mathcal{A}_4 = \langle \{a, b\}, \neg p \rangle$ is an argument for $\neg p$, but $\mathcal{A}_4$ is not acceptable w.r.t. $W = \emptyset$ since $\mathcal{A}_2$ and $\mathcal{A}_3$ are subarguments of $\mathcal{A}_4$ but obviously $a, b \notin W$.

Now we are ready to introduce the notion of collective conflict relative to a consistent set of justifiable conclusions. The idea of defining a warrant semantics on the basis of conflicting sets of arguments was proposed in [16] and [11]. The difference between these approaches and our notion of collective conflict is that in [16] the notion of conflict is not relative to a set of already warranted conclusions and [11] defines a generalization of Dung's abstract framework with sets of attacking arguments not relative to the strict part of the knowledge base.

Definition 3 (Conflict among arguments) *Let* $\mathcal{P} = (\Pi, \Delta, \Sigma)$ *be a KB, let W be a consistent set of justifiable conclusions w.r.t.* Π *and let* $\mathcal{A}_1 = \langle A_1, \varphi_1 \rangle, \ldots, \mathcal{A}_k = \langle A_k, \varphi_k \rangle$ *be acceptable arguments w.r.t. W. We say that the set of arguments* $\{\mathcal{A}_1, \ldots, \mathcal{A}_k\}$ *generates a conflict w.r.t. W iff the two following conditions hold:*

(C) *The set of argument conclusions* $\{\varphi_1, \ldots, \varphi_k\}$ *is contradictory w.r.t.* $\Pi \cup W$, *i.e.* $\Pi \cup W \cup \{\varphi_1, \ldots, \varphi_k\} \vdash \bot$.

(M) *The set* $\{\mathcal{A}_1, \ldots, \mathcal{A}_k\}$ *is minimal w.r.t. set inclusion satisfying (C), i.e. if* $S \subset \{\varphi_1, \ldots, \varphi_k\}$, *then* $\Pi \cup W \cup S \nvdash \bot$.

Consider the previous KB $\mathcal{P}_1$. According to Definition 3, it is clear that the set of acceptable arguments $\{\mathcal{A}_1, \mathcal{A}_2, \mathcal{A}_3\}$ for p, b and a respectively generates a (collective) conflict (w.r.t. $W = \emptyset$). The intuition is that this collective conflict should block the conclusions a, b and p to be warranted. Now, this general notion of conflict is used to define a recursive semantics for warranted conclusions of a knowledge base. Actually we define below an output of a KB $\mathcal{P} = (\Pi, \Delta, \Sigma)$ as a pair $(Warr, Block)$ of subsets of Σ of warranted and blocked conclusions respectively, all of them based on warranted information but, while warranted conclusions do not generate any conflict, blocked conclusions do.

Definition 4 (Output for a KB) *An output for a KB* $\mathcal{P} = (\Pi, \Delta, \Sigma)$ *is any pair* $(Warr, Block)$, *where* $Warr = s\text{-}Warr \cup d\text{-}Warr$ *with* $s\text{-}Warr = \{\varphi \mid \Pi \vdash \varphi\} \cap \Sigma$, *and* $d\text{-}Warr$ *and Block are required to satisfy the following recursive constraints:*

1. *A d-argument* $\langle A, \varphi \rangle$ *is called* valid *(or not rejected) if it satisfies the following two conditions:*

   (i) for every $\langle B, \psi \rangle \sqsubset \langle A, \varphi \rangle$, $\psi \in d\text{-}Warr$,
   (ii) $\langle A, \varphi \rangle$ *is acceptable w.r.t. the set* $W = \{\psi \mid \langle B, \psi \rangle \sqsubset \langle A, \varphi \rangle\}$.

2. *For every valid argument* $\langle A, \varphi \rangle$ *we have that*
   - $\varphi \in d\text{-}Warr$ *whenever there does not exist a set of valid arguments G such that*

     (i) $\langle A, \varphi \rangle \not\sqsubset \langle C, \chi \rangle$ *for all* $\langle C, \chi \rangle \in G$
     (ii) $G \cup \{\langle A, \varphi \rangle\}$ *generates a conflict w.r.t.* $W = \{\psi \mid$ *there exists* $\langle B, \psi \rangle \sqsubset \langle D, \gamma \rangle$ *for some* $\langle D, \gamma \rangle \in G \cup \{\langle A, \varphi \rangle\}\}$

- *otherwise,* $\varphi \in Block.$

The intuition underlying this definition is as follows: an argument $\langle A, \varphi \rangle$ is either warranted or blocked whenever for each subargument $\langle B, \psi \rangle$ of $\langle A, \varphi \rangle$, ψ is warranted; then, it is eventually warranted if φ is not involved in any conflict, otherwise it is blocked.

Example 5 *Consider the KB* $\mathcal{P}_2 = (\Pi, \Delta, \Sigma)$, *with*

$$\Pi = \{a \rightarrow y, b \wedge c \rightarrow \neg y\}, \, \Delta = \{a, b, c, \neg c\} \text{ and } \Sigma = \{a, b, c, \neg c, y, \neg y\}.$$

According to Definition 4, s-Warr $= \emptyset$ *and the arguments* $\langle \{a\}, a \rangle$, $\langle \{b\}, b \rangle$, $\langle \{c\}, c \rangle$ *and* $\langle \{\neg c\}, \neg c \rangle$ *are valid. Now, for every such valid argument there exists a set of valid arguments which generates a conflict w.r.t.* $W = \emptyset$: *indeed both sets of valid arguments* $\{\langle \{a\}, a \rangle, \langle \{b\}, b \rangle, \langle \{c\}, c \rangle\}$ *and* $\{\langle \{c\}, c \rangle, \langle \{\neg c\}, \neg c \rangle\}$ *generate a conflict (since* $\Pi \cup \{a, b, c\} \vdash \perp$ *and* $\Pi \cup \{c, \neg c\} \vdash \perp$). *Therefore a, b, c and* $\neg c$ *are blocked conclusions. On the other hand, the arguments* $\langle \{a, b\}, \neg c \rangle$, $\langle \{a\}, y \rangle$ *and* $\langle \{b, c\}, \neg y \rangle$ *are not valid since they are based on conclusions which are not warranted. Hence y and* $\neg y$ *are considered as rejected conclusions. Thus, the (unique) output for* $\mathcal{P}$ *is the pair* $(Warr, Block) = (\emptyset, \Delta)$. *Intuitively this output for* $\mathcal{P}$ *expresses that all conclusions in Block are valid, however all together are contradictory w.r.t.* Π.

The KB $\mathcal{P}_2$ was also considered in [2], where direct conflicts were evaluated before indirect conflicts, and thus, every blocked literal invalidated all rules in which that literal occurred. Hence, in [2], c and $\neg c$ were considered as blocked conclusions but a, b and y were warranted conclusions.

Next we prove that if $(Warr, Block)$ is an output for a KB the set *Warr* of warranted conclusions satisfies indirect consistency and the closure postulate (in the sense of Caminada and Amgoud) with respect to the strict knowledge.

Proposition 6 (Indirect consistency) *Let* $\mathcal{P} = (\Pi, \Delta, \Sigma)$ *be a KB and let* $(Warr, Block)$ *be an output for* $\mathcal{P}$. *Then,* $\Pi \cup Warr \not\vdash \perp$.

Proof: Suppose that $\Pi \cup Warr \vdash \perp$. Obviously, it should be that $\Pi \cup W \vdash \perp$ for some $W \subseteq d\text{-}Warr$. However, by Definition 4, for every $\varphi \in d\text{-}Warr$ there does not exist a set $W' \subseteq d\text{-}Warr$ such that $\Pi \cup W' \cup \{\varphi\} \vdash \perp$, and therefore, $\Pi \cup W \not\vdash \perp$ for all $W \subseteq d\text{-}Warr$. □

Proposition 7 (Closure) *Let* $\mathcal{P} = (\Pi, \Delta, \Sigma)$ *be a KB and let* $(Warr, Block)$ *be an output for* $\mathcal{P}$. *If* $\Pi \cup Warr \vdash \varphi$ *with* $\varphi \in \Sigma$, *then* $\varphi \in Warr$ *whenever there exits an acceptable argument for* φ *w.r.t. Warr.*

Proof: Suppose that for some $W \subseteq Warr$, $\Pi \cup W \vdash \varphi$ and $\varphi \notin Warr$, for some formula $\varphi \in \Sigma$ such that there exists an argument $\langle A, \varphi \rangle$ satisfying that if $\langle B, \psi \rangle$ is a subargument of $\langle A, \varphi \rangle$ then $\psi \in W$. On the one hand, if $A = \emptyset$, it must be that $\Pi \vdash \varphi$. Then, as $\varphi \in \Sigma$, $\varphi \in Warr$. On the other hand, as $\Pi \cup Warr \not\vdash \perp$ and $\Pi \cup W \vdash \varphi$, $\Pi \cup W \cup \{\varphi\} \not\vdash \perp$, and thus, $\langle A, \varphi \rangle$ is a valid argument for φ. Then, if $\varphi \notin Warr$, there exits a set of valid arguments G such that (i) $\langle A, \varphi \rangle \not\sqsubset \langle C, \chi \rangle$ for all $\langle C, \chi \rangle \in G$, and (ii) $G \cup \{\langle A, \varphi \rangle\}$ generates a conflict w.r.t. $W' = \{\psi \mid$ there exists $\langle B, \psi \rangle \sqsubset \langle D, \gamma \rangle$ for some $\langle D, \gamma \rangle \in G \cup \{\langle A, \varphi \rangle\}\}$. According to Definition 3, if $G \cup \{\langle A, \varphi \rangle\}$ generates a conflict w.r.t. W', then $\Pi \cup W' \cup \{\varphi\} \cup \{\psi \mid \langle B, \psi \rangle \in G\} \vdash \bot$ (condition (C)), and $\Pi \cup W' \cup S \nvdash \bot$, for all set $S \subset \{\varphi\} \cup \{\psi \mid \langle B, \psi \rangle \in G\}$ (condition (M)). Now, as $W \subseteq W'$ and $\Pi \cup W \vdash \varphi$, if $\Pi \cup W' \cup \{\varphi\} \cup \{\psi \mid \langle B, \psi \rangle \in G\} \vdash \bot$, then $\Pi \cup W' \cup \{\psi \mid \langle B, \psi \rangle \in G\} \vdash \bot$, and thus, $\varphi \in Warr$.   □

We remark that, as it will be discussed in Section 4, a KB may have multiple outputs. For instance, consider the KB $\mathcal{P}_3 = (\Pi, \Delta, \Sigma)$ with $\Pi = \emptyset$, $\Delta = \{p, q, \neg p \vee \neg q\}$ and $\Sigma = \{p, q, \neg p, \neg q\}$. Then, one can check that there are two outputs, $Warr_1 = \{p\}, Block_1 = \{q, \neg q\}$, and $Warr_2 = \{q\}, Block_2 = \{p, \neg p\}$.

3. Extending the framework with a preference ordering on arguments

In the previous section, we have considered knowledge bases containing formulas describing knowledge at two epistemic levels, strict and defeasible. A natural extension is to introduce several levels of defeasibility or preference among different pieces of defeasible knowledge.

A *stratified knowledge base* (sKB) is a tuple $\mathcal{P} = (\Pi, \Delta, \preceq, \Sigma)$, such that (Π, Δ, Σ) is a KB (in the sense of the previous section) and $\preceq$ is a *suitable* total pre-order on the set of defeasible formulas Δ. Suitable means for us that this pre-order is representable by a necessity measure defined on the set of formulas of $\mathcal{L}$, namely $\varphi \preceq \psi$ iff $N(\varphi) \leq N(\psi)$ for each $\varphi, \psi \in \Delta \cup \Pi$, where N is a mapping $N : \mathcal{L} \to [0, 1]$ such that

1. $N(\top) = 1, N(\bot) = 0$,
2. $N(\varphi \wedge \psi) = \min(N(\varphi), N(\psi))$, and further
3. $N(\varphi) = 1$ iff $\Pi \vdash \varphi$

Then we define the *strength of an argument* $\langle A, \varphi \rangle$, written $s(\langle A, \varphi \rangle)$, as follows[4]:

$$s(\langle A, \varphi \rangle) = 1 \text{ if } A = \emptyset, \text{ and } s(\langle A, \varphi \rangle) = \min\{N(\psi) \mid \psi \in A\}, \text{ otherwise.}$$

Since we are considering several levels of strength among arguments, the intended construction of the sets of conclusions $Warr$ and $Block$ is done level-wise, starting from the highest level and iteratively going down from one level to next level below. If $1 > \alpha_1 > \ldots > \alpha_p \geq 0$ are the strengths of d-arguments that can be built within a sKB $\mathcal{P} = (\Pi, \Delta, \preceq, \Sigma)$, we define $d\text{-}Warr = \{d\text{-}Warr(\alpha_1), \ldots, d\text{-}Warr(\alpha_p)\}$ and $Block = \{Block(\alpha_1), \ldots, Block(\alpha_p)\}$, where $d\text{-}Warr(\alpha_i)$ and $Block(\alpha_i)$ are respectively the sets of warranted and blocked justifiable conclusions with strength α_i. Then, we safely write $d\text{-}Warrr(> \alpha_i)$ to denote $\cup_{\beta > \alpha_i} d\text{-}Warr(\beta)$, and analogously for $Block(> \alpha_i)$, defininig $d\text{-}Warr(> \alpha_1) = s\text{-}Warr$ and $Block(> \alpha_1) = \emptyset$.

Definition 8 (Output for a sKB) *An output for a sKB* $\mathcal{P} = (\Pi, \Delta, \preceq, \Sigma)$ *is any pair* $(Warr, Block)$, *where* $Warr = s\text{-}Warr \cup d\text{-}Warr$ *with* $s\text{-}Warr = \{\varphi \mid \Pi \vdash \varphi\} \cap \Sigma$, *and* $d\text{-}Warr$ *and* $Block$ *are required to satisfy the following recursive constraints:*

1. *A d-argument* $\langle A, \varphi \rangle$ *of strength* α_i *is called* valid *(or not rejected) if it satisfies the follov ing three conditions[5]:*

---

[4]Actually, several N's may lead to a same pre-order $\preceq$, but we can take any of them to define the degree of strength since only the relative ordering is what matters.

[5]Notice that if $\langle A, \varphi \rangle$ is an acceptable argument w.r.t. $d\text{-}Warr(> \alpha_i)$, then $\langle A, \varphi \rangle$ is valid whenever condition (iii) holds.

(i) for every subargument $\langle B, \psi \rangle \sqsubset \langle A, \varphi \rangle$ of strength α_i, $\psi \in$ d-Warr(α_i);

(ii) $\langle A, \varphi \rangle$ is acceptable w.r.t.
$$W = d\text{-}Warr(> \alpha_i) \cup \{\psi \mid \langle B, \psi \rangle \sqsubset \langle A, \varphi \rangle \text{ and } s(\langle B, \psi \rangle) = \alpha_i\};$$

(iii) $\varphi \notin$ d-Warr$(> \alpha_i) \cup$ Block$(> \alpha_i)$ and $\{\varphi, \psi\} \nvdash \bot$ for all $\psi \in$ Block$(> \alpha_i)$.

2. *For every valid argument $\langle A, \varphi \rangle$ of strength α_i we have that*

- $\varphi \in$ d-Warr(α_i) *whenever there does not exist a set G of valid arguments of strength α_i such that*

   (i) $\langle A, \varphi \rangle \not\sqsubset \langle C, \chi \rangle$ for all $\langle C, \chi \rangle \in G$

   (ii) $G \cup \{\langle A, \varphi \rangle\}$ generates a conflict w.r.t. $W = d\text{-}Warr(> \alpha_i) \cup \{\psi \mid$ there exists $\langle B, \psi \rangle \sqsubset \langle D, \gamma \rangle$ for some $\langle D, \gamma \rangle \in G \cup \{\langle A, \varphi \rangle\}\}$

- *otherwise, $\varphi \in$ Block(α_i).*

There are two main remarks when considering several levels of strength among arguments. On the one hand a d-argument $\langle A, \varphi \rangle$ of strength α_i is valid whenever there does not exist a different valid argument for φ of strength greater than α_i and φ is consistent with each valid argument of strength greater than α_i. On the other hand, a valid argument $\langle A, \varphi \rangle$ of strength α_i becomes blocked as soon as it leads to some conflict among arguments of strength α_i.

Example 9 *Consider the KB $\mathcal{P}_1$ in the previous section*
$$\Pi = \{a \wedge b \rightarrow \neg p\}, \Delta = \{a, b, p\} \text{ and } \Sigma = \{a, b, p, \neg p\}.$$
extended with levels of defeasibility as follows: $\{a, b\} \prec p$. Assume α_1 is the level of p and α_2 the level of a and b, obviously with $1 > \alpha_1 > \alpha_2$. According to Definition 8, s-Warr $= \emptyset$ and the argument for $\langle\{p\}, p\rangle$ is the only valid argument with strength α_1. Then, at level α_1, we get d-Warr$(\alpha_1) = \{p\}$ and Block$(\alpha_1) = \emptyset$. At level α_2, we have that $\langle\{a\}, a\rangle$ and $\langle\{b\}, b\rangle$ are valid arguments for conclusions a and b respectively. However, since $\Pi \cup$ d-Warr$(\alpha_1) \cup \{a, b\} \vdash \bot$, the conclusions a and b are blocked, and thus, d-Warr$(\alpha_2) = \emptyset$ and Block$(\alpha_2) = \{a, b\}$. Notice that the argument $\langle\{a, b\}, \neg p\rangle$ for $\neg p$ is not acceptable since it is based on a and b and $a, b \notin$ d-Warr(α_2).

Example 10 *Consider the KB $\mathcal{P}_2$ of Example 5:*
$$\Pi = \{a \rightarrow y, b \wedge c \rightarrow \neg y\}, \Delta = \{a, b, c, \neg c\}, \text{ and } \Sigma = \{a, b, c, \neg c, y, \neg y\},$$
extended with three levels of defeasibility as follows: $\neg c \prec c \prec \{a, b\}$. Assume α_1 is the level of a and b, α_2 is the level of c, and α_3 is the level of $\neg c$, with $1 > \alpha_1 > \alpha_2 > \alpha_3$. Then, s-Warr $= \emptyset$ and, at level α_1, we have not only the conclusions a, b and y with valid arguments not generating conflict, but also $\langle\{a, b\}, \neg c\rangle$ is a valid argument for $\neg c$ which does not generate conflict. Therefore, d-Warr$(\alpha_1) = \{a, b, y, \neg c\}$ and Block$(\alpha_1) = \emptyset$. At level α_2, we have arguments for c and $\neg y$. Since $\Pi \cup$d-Warr$(\alpha_1) \cup \{c\} \vdash \bot$, the argument $\langle\{c\}, c\rangle$ is not acceptable w.r.t. d-Warr(α_1), and thus, c is a rejected conclusion. Then, as the argument $\langle\{b, c\}, \neg y\rangle$ for $\neg y$ is based on c, $\neg y$ is also a rejected conclusion, and therefore d-Warr$(\alpha_2) =$ Block$(\alpha_2) = \emptyset$. Finally, at level α_3 we have the argument $\langle\{\neg c\}, \neg c\rangle$, but since $\neg c$ is already in d-Warr(α_1), we also have d-Warr$(\alpha_3) =$ Block$(\alpha_3) = \emptyset$.

4. A particular case: recursive P-DeLP

In this section we particularize the framework and recursive warrant semantics for stratified knowledge bases defined in the previous section to the case of the P-DeLP programs. As mentioned in Section 1, P-DeLP is a rule-based argumentation system extending the well-known DeLP system in which weights are attached to defeasible rules expressing their belief or preference strength and formalized as necessity degrees. For a detailed description of the P-DeLP argumentation system based on dialectical trees the reader is referred to [3].

Although the original syntax and inference of P-DeLP are a bit different (e.g. the weights are explicit in the formulas and arguments), here we will present them in a way so to adapt them to the framework introduced in the previous sections. We will refer to this particular framework as RP-DeLP. Hence we define the logic $(\mathcal{L}_R, \vdash_R)$ underlying RP-DeLP as follows. The language of RP-DeLP is inherited from the language of logic programming, including the notions of atom, literal, rule and fact. Formulas are built over a finite set of propositional variables $p, q, \ldots$ which is extended with a new (negated) atom "$\sim p$" for each original atom p. Atoms of the form p or $\sim p$ will be referred as literals, and if P is a literal, we will use $\sim P$ to denote $\sim p$ if P is an atom p, and will denote p if P is a negated atom $\sim p$. Formulas of $\mathcal{L}_R$ consist of rules of the form $Q \leftarrow P_1 \wedge \ldots \wedge P_k$, where $Q, P_1, \ldots, P_k$ are literals. A fact will be a rule with no premises. We will also use the name *clause* to denote a rule or a fact. The inference operator $\vdash_R$ is defined by instances of the modus ponens rule of the form: $\{Q \leftarrow P_1 \wedge \ldots \wedge P_k, P_1, \ldots, P_k\} \vdash_R Q$. A set of clauses Γ is *contradictory*, denoted $\Gamma \vdash \bot$, if , for some atom q, $\Gamma \vdash_R q$ and $\Gamma \vdash_R \sim q$.

A RP-DeLP program $\mathcal{P}$ is just a stratified knowledge base $(\Pi, \Delta, \preceq, \Sigma)$ over the logic $(\mathcal{L}_R, \vdash_R)$, where Σ consists of the set of all literals of $\mathcal{L}_R$. We will assume that $\preceq$ is representable by a necessity measure N, so we will often refer to numerical weights for defeasible clauses and arguments rather than to the pre-ordering $\preceq$. Also, for the sake of a simpler notation we will get rid of Σ from a program specification.

As we have mentioned in the previous section, in some cases the output (*Warr, Block*) for a stratified knowledge base in general, and for a RP-DeLP program in particular, is not unique, due to circular definitions of warranty that emerge when considering conflicts among arguments. Such circular definitions of warranty are characterized next by means of what we call *warrant dependency graph* of a RP-DeLP program. In [12] a similar graph structure, called inference-graph, was defined to represent inference (support) and defeat relations among arguments allowing to detect circular defeat relations when considering recursive semantics for defeasible reasoning. The main difference between both approaches is that in our case we handle collective conflicts among arguments in order to preserve direct consistency among warranted conclusions and indirect consistency with respect to the strict knowledge .

In the following, given a RP-DeLP program $\mathcal{P} = (\Pi, \Delta)$ with preference levels $1 > \alpha_1 > \ldots > \alpha_m > 0$, if W denotes a set of justifiable literals, we will denote by $W(\alpha)$ the subset of literals Q from W for which there exist an argument $\langle A, Q \rangle$ with maximum strength α, $W(\geq \alpha) = \cup_{\beta \geq \alpha} W(\beta)$, and $W(> \alpha) = \cup_{\beta > \alpha} W(\beta)$ with $W(> \alpha_1) = W(1)$.

Definition 11 (Warrant dependency graph) *Let* $\mathcal{P} = (\Pi, \Delta)$ *be a RP-DeLP program and let* W *be a set of justifiable conclusions consistent with* Π. *Let* $\mathcal{A}_1 =$

$\langle A_1, Q_1 \rangle, \ldots, A_k = \langle A_k, Q_k \rangle$ *be acceptable arguments of a same strength* α *w.r.t.* W *such that for all* i, $Q_i \notin W(\geq \alpha)$. *Moreover, let* $\mathcal{B}_1 = \langle B_1, P_1 \rangle, \ldots, \mathcal{B}_n = \langle B_n, P_n \rangle$ *be arguments of the same strength* α *such that for all* j, $P_j \notin W(\geq \alpha)$, $P_j \notin \{Q_1, \ldots, Q_k\}$, *and there exists an argument* $\mathcal{S} \in \{A_1, \ldots, A_k\}$ *with* $\mathcal{S} \sqsubset \mathcal{B}_j$. *Then, the warrant dependency graph* (V, E) *for* $\{A_1, \ldots, A_k\}$ *w.r.t.* W *and* $\{\mathcal{B}_1, \ldots, \mathcal{B}_n\}$ *is defined as follows:*

1. *For every literal* $L \in \{Q_1, \ldots, Q_k\} \cup \{P_1, \ldots, P_n\}$, *the set of vertices* V *includes one vertex* v_L.
2. *For every pair of literals* $\{L_1, L_2\}$ *such that* $L_1 = \sim L_2$ *with* $L_1 \in \{P_1, \ldots, P_n\}$ *and* $L_2 \in \{Q_1, \ldots, Q_k\}$, *the set of directed edges* E *includes one edge* (v_{L_1}, v_{L_2})[6].
3. *For every pair of literals* $\{L_1, L_2\}$ *such that* $L_1 \in \{Q_1, \ldots, Q_k\}$, $L_2 \in \{P_1, \ldots, P_n\}$ *and the argument of* L_1 *is a subargument of the argument of* L_2, *the set of directed edges* E *includes one edge* (v_{L_1}, v_{L_2})[7].
4. *For every strict rule* $L \leftarrow L_1 \wedge \ldots \wedge L_m$ *of* Π *such that*

   - *either* $\sim L \in W(\geq \alpha)$ *or* $\sim L \in \{Q_1, \ldots, Q_k\}$, *and*
   - *for every* L_i ($i = 1, \ldots, m$), *either* $L_i \in W(\geq \alpha)$ *or* $L_i \in \{Q_1, \ldots, Q_k\} \cup \{P_1, \ldots, P_n\}$,

   the set of directed edges E *includes one edge* (v_{L_i}, v_{L_j})[8] *for every pair of literals* $\{L_i, L_j\} \subseteq \{L_1, \ldots, L_m\}$ *with* $L_i \in \{P_1, \ldots, P_n\}$ *and* $L_j \in \{Q_1, \ldots, Q_k\}$ *whenever the argument of* L_j *is not a subargument of the argument of* L_i.
5. *Elements of* V *and* E *are only obtained by applying the above construction rules.*

Intuitively, the warrant dependency graph for a set of arguments represents conflict and support dependences among arguments in $\{A_1, \ldots, A_k\}$ and arguments in $\{\mathcal{B}_1, \ldots, \mathcal{B}_n\}$ w.r.t. a set of justified conclusions W.

Example 12 *Consider a RP-DeLP program defined from the KB* $\mathcal{P}_3$ *of Section 2; i.e. a RP-DeLP program with an empty set of strict clauses and the following set of defeasible clauses with just one defeasibility level:*
$$\Delta = \{p, q, \sim p \leftarrow q, \sim q \leftarrow p\}.$$
Now, consider the empty set of conclusions $W = W(1) = \emptyset$ *and arguments for conclusions* p *and* q; *i.e.* $A_1 = \langle \{p\}, p \rangle$ *and* $A_2 = \langle \{q\}, q \rangle$. *Finally, consider the arguments for conclusions* $\sim p$ *and* $\sim q$; *i.e.* $\mathcal{B}_1 = \langle \{q, \sim p \leftarrow q\}, \sim p \rangle$ *and* $\mathcal{B}_2 = \langle \{p, \sim q \leftarrow p\}, \sim q \rangle$.
  Figure 1 (a) shows the warrant dependency graph for A_1 *and* A_2 *w.r.t.* $W = \emptyset$, $\mathcal{B}_1$, *and* $\mathcal{B}_2$. *Conflict and support dependences between literals are represented as dashed and solid arrows, respectively. The cycle of the graph expresses that (1) the warranty of* p *depends on a (possible) conflict with* $\sim p$; *(2) the support of* $\sim p$ *depends on* q *(i.e. the validity of* $\sim p$ *depends on the warranty of* q); *(3) the warranty of* q *depends on a (possible) conflict with* $\sim q$; *and (4) the support of* $\sim q$ *depends on* p *(i.e. the validity of* $\sim q$ *depends on the warranty of* p).
  Consider now the RP-DeLP program $\mathcal{P}_4 = (\Pi, \Delta)$, *with*
$$\Pi = \{y, \sim y \leftarrow p \wedge r, \sim y \leftarrow q \wedge s\} \text{ and } \Delta = \{p, q, r \leftarrow q, s \leftarrow p\}$$
with just one defeasibility level. Moreover consider the set of justified conclusions $W =$

---

[6]The directed edge (v_{L_1}, v_{L_2}) represents a conflict dependence of L_2 w.r.t. L_1.
[7]The directed edge (v_{L_1}, v_{L_2}) represents a support dependence of L_2 w.r.t. L_1.
[8]The directed edge (v_{L_i}, v_{L_j}) represents a conflict dependence of L_j w.r.t. L_i.

$W(1) = \{y\}$ and arguments for conclusions p and q; i.e.
$$\mathcal{A}_1 = \langle\{p\}, p\rangle \text{ and } \mathcal{A}_2 = \langle\{q\}, q\rangle.$$
Finally, consider arguments for conclusions r and s; i.e.
$$\mathcal{B}_1 = \langle\{q, r \leftarrow q\}, r\rangle \text{ and } \mathcal{B}_2 = \langle\{p, s \leftarrow p\}, s\rangle.$$
Figure 1 (b) shows the warrant dependency graph for $\mathcal{A}_1$ and $\mathcal{A}_2$ w.r.t. W, $\mathcal{B}_1$, and $\mathcal{B}_2$. The cycle of the graph expresses that (1) the warranty of p depends on a (possible) conflict with r; (2) the support of r depends on q (i.e. the validity of r depends on the warranty of q); (3) the warranty of q depends on a (possible) conflict with s; and (4) the support of s depends on p (i.e. the validity of s depends on the warranty of p).

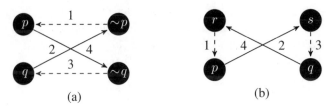

Figure 1. Warrant dependency graphs: (a) for $\mathcal{P}_3$, (b) for $\mathcal{P}_4$.

The characterization of the *unique output property* for a program $\mathcal{P} = (\Pi, \Delta)$ is done level-wise, starting from the highest level and iteratively going down from one level to next level below. For every level it consists in checking whether for some literal L, the warranty of L recursively depends on itself based on the topology of a warrant dependency graph defined as follows.

Definition 13 (Graph for a literal) *Let* $\mathcal{P} = (\Pi, \Delta)$ *be a RP-DeLP program, let* *(Warr, Block) be an output for* $\mathcal{P}$ *and let* L *be a literal such that* $L \in \text{Warr}(\alpha)$, *for some level* α. *The graph for* L *w.r.t. Warr is the warrant dependency graph* (V, E) *for arguments* $\{\mathcal{A}_1, \dots, \mathcal{A}_k\}$ *w.r.t.* W *and* $\{\mathcal{B}_1, \dots, \mathcal{B}_n\}$ *where*

- $W = \text{Warr}(\geq \alpha) \backslash \{L\}$,
- $\mathcal{A}_1 = \langle A_1, Q_1\rangle, \dots, \mathcal{A}_k = \langle A_k, Q_k\rangle$ *are all arguments with strength* α^9 *that are acceptable w.r.t.* W *(according to Definition 2) and such that* $Q_j \notin \text{Warr}(> \alpha)$ *and* $Q_j, \sim Q_j \notin \text{Block}(> \alpha)$, *and*
- $\mathcal{B}_1 = \langle B_1, P_1\rangle, \dots, \mathcal{B}_n = \langle B_n, P_n\rangle$ *are all arguments with strength* α *that satisfy the following conditions* [10]:

  (i) $P_j \notin \text{Warr}(> \alpha)$ *and* $P_j \notin \{Q_1, \dots, Q_k\}$,
  (ii) $P_j, \sim P_j \notin \text{Block}(> \alpha)$,
  (iii) *for all* $\langle C, R\rangle \sqsubset \mathcal{B}_j$ *with strength* $\beta > \alpha$, $R \in \text{Warr}(\beta)$ *and for all* $\langle C, R\rangle \sqsubset$ $\mathcal{B}_j$ *with strength* α, $R \in \{Q_1, \dots, Q_k\} \cup \{P_1, \dots, P_n\}$,
  (iv) $\Pi \cup \text{Warr}(> \alpha) \cup \{\langle C, R\rangle \sqsubset \mathcal{B}_j\} \cup \{P_j\} \nvdash \bot$,
  (v) *there exists an argument* $\mathcal{S} \in \{\mathcal{A}_1, \dots, \mathcal{A}_k\}$ *such that* $\mathcal{S} \sqsubset \mathcal{B}_j$, *and*

---

[9]Remark that for all argument $\mathcal{A}_j \in \{\mathcal{A}_1, \dots, \mathcal{A}_k\}$ with $Q_j \neq L$, $\mathcal{A}_j$ does not depend on L and either $Q_j \in \text{Warr}(\alpha)$ or $Q_j \in \text{Block}(\alpha)$.

[10]Remark that for all argument $\mathcal{B}_j \in \{\mathcal{B}_1, \dots, \mathcal{B}_k\}$, either $\mathcal{B}_j$ depends on L and $(P_j, \alpha) \in \text{Warr}(\alpha) \cup \text{Block}(\alpha)$ or $\mathcal{B}_j$ depends on some $Q_j \in \text{Block}(\alpha)$.

(vi) for every argument $\mathcal{S} \in \{\mathcal{A}_1, \ldots, \mathcal{A}_k\}$ such that $\mathcal{S} \sqsubset \mathcal{B}_j$, there does not exist a set of arguments $G \subseteq \{\mathcal{A}_1, \ldots, \mathcal{A}_k\} \backslash \{\mathcal{S}\}$ such that $G \cup \{\mathcal{S}\}$ generates a conflict w.r.t. W.

Proposition 14 (RP-DeLP program with unique output) *Let $\mathcal{P} = (\Pi, \Delta)$ be a RP-DeLP program and let $(Warr, Block)$ be an output for $\mathcal{P}$. $(Warr, Block)$ is the unique output for $\mathcal{P}$ iff for all literal $L \in Warr$ there is no cycle in the graph for L w.r.t. Warr.*

Intuitively, given a literal L such that $L \in Warr(\alpha)$, for some program preference level α, Definition 13 builds the warrant dependency graph for L and all acceptable arguments $\{\mathcal{A}_1, \ldots, \mathcal{A}_k\}$ of strength α that do not depend on L w.r.t. arguments $\{\mathcal{B}_1, \ldots, \mathcal{B}_n\}$ of strength α whose supports depend on L or on some argument in $\{\mathcal{A}_1, \ldots, \mathcal{A}_k\}$. Then, according to Definition 11, the existence of a cycle expresses that the warranty of the argument for L depends on the validity of some $\mathcal{B} \in \{\mathcal{B}_1, \ldots, \mathcal{B}_n\}$, which depends on the warranty of some $L' \in \{\mathcal{A}_1, \ldots, \mathcal{A}_k\}$ with $L \neq L'$, which in turn depends on the validity of some $\mathcal{B}' \in \{\mathcal{B}_1, \ldots, \mathcal{B}_n\}$ with $\mathcal{B}' \neq \mathcal{B}$, which in turn depends on the warranty of L. Thus, for arguments of L and L' there does not exist a (unique) conflict evaluation order. Obviously, for RP-DeLP programs with unique output the set of warranted conclusions for every level α can be (computed) defined by an unique conflict evaluation order between arguments. Next we show that programs of Example 12 have multiple outputs.

Example 15 *According to Definition 8, $Output_1 = (Warr_1, Block_1)$ with $Warr_1 = \{p\}$ and $Block_1 = \{q, \sim q\}$, is an output for program $\mathcal{P}_3$ of Example 12. Then, according to Definition 13, Figure 1 shows the graph for p w.r.t. $Warr_1$; i.e. the warrant dependency graph for arguments $\{\mathcal{A}_1, \mathcal{A}_2\}$ w.r.t. W and $\{\mathcal{B}_1, \mathcal{B}_2\}$ with*

$$\mathcal{A}_1 = \langle \{p\}, p \rangle, \mathcal{A}_2 = \langle \{q\}, q \rangle, W = \emptyset,$$
$$\mathcal{B}_1 = \langle \{q, \sim p \leftarrow q\}, \sim p \rangle \text{ and } \mathcal{B}_2 = \langle \{p, \sim q \leftarrow p\}, \sim q \rangle.$$

Therefore, according to Proposition 14, $Output_1$ is not the unique output for $\mathcal{P}_3$ since there is a cycle in the graph for p w.r.t. $Warr_1$. Notice that $Output_2 = (Warr_2, Block_2)$ with $Warr_2 = \{q\}$ and $Block_2 = \{p, \sim p\}$, is also an output for program $\mathcal{P}_3$ and the graph for q w.r.t. $Warr_2$ also contains a cycle.

Consider now the RP-DeLP program $\mathcal{P}_4$ of Example 12. According to Definition 8, $Output_1 = (Warr_1, Block_1)$ with $Warr_1 = \{y, p\}$ and $Block_1 = \{q, s\}$, is an output for $\mathcal{P}_4$. Then, according to Definition 13, Figure 1 shows the graph for p w.r.t. $W = Warr_1(1) = \{y\}$ proving that the output for $\mathcal{P}_4$ is not unique. Indeed, notice that $Output_2 = (Warr_2, Block_2)$ with $Warr_2 = \{y, q\}$ and $Block_2 = \{p, r\}$, is also an output for program $\mathcal{P}_4$ and the graph for q w.r.t. $Warr_2$ also contains a cycle.

One of the main advantages of the warrant recursive semantics for RP-DeLP is from the implementation point of view. Actually, warrant semantics based on dialectical trees and, in general, rule-based argumentation frameworks like DeLP [7,9], might consider an exponential number of arguments with respect to the number of rules of a given program. In contrast, in our framework, at least for the particular case of RP-DeLP programs with unique output, it is not necessary to explicitly compute all the possible arguments for a given literal to check whether it is warranted, as we can implement an algorithm[11] (not shown here due to space limitations) with a worst-case complexity in P^{NP}.

---

[11]Details can be found in the extended version at *http://ia.udl.cat/ramon/comma2010full.pdf*

5. Conclusions and future work

In this paper we have introduced a new recursive semantics for determining the warranty status of arguments in defeasible argumentation. The distinctive features of this semantics, e.g. with respect to Pollock's critical link semantics, are: (i) it is based on a non-binary notion of conflict in order to preserve consistency with the strict knowledge and (ii) besides the set of warranted and rejected conclusions, we introduce the set of blocked conclusions, which are those conclusions which are based on warranted information but they generate a conflict with other already warranted conclusions of the same strength.

As future work we plan to formalize the maximal ideal output for RP-DeLP programs which will allow us to characterize the relationship between this unique output based on the recursive warrant semantics and the output of DeLP [10] and other general argumentation frameworks [5,4] based on the use of dialectical trees as underlying structures for characterizing the semantics of warranted conclusions.

Acknowledgments Authors are thankful to the anonymous reviewers for their helpful comments. Research partially funded by the Spanish MICINN projects MULOG2 (TIN2007-68005-C04-01/02) and ARINF (TIN2009-14704-C03-01/03), CONSOLIDER (CSD2007-0022), and ESF Eurocores-LogICCC/MICINN (FFI2008-03126-E/FILO), and the grant JC2009-00272 from the Ministerio de Educación.

References

[1]   T. Alsinet, C.I. Chesñevar, and L Godo. Enforcing indirect consistency in possibilistic defeasible logic programming: a level-based approach. In *IPMU'08*, pages 497–504, 2008.
[2]   T. Alsinet, C.I. Chesñevar, and L Godo. A level-based approach to computing warranted arguments in possibilistic defeasible logic programming. In *COMMA'08*, pages 1–12, 2008.
[3]   T. Alsinet, C.I. Chesñevar, L. Godo, and G. Simari. A logic programming framework for possibilistic argumentation: Formalization and logical properties. *Fuzzy Sets and Systems*, 159 (10): 1208–1228, 2008.
[4]   L. Amgoud and C. Cayrol. On the Acceptability of Arguments in Preference-based Argumentation. In UAI'08, pages 1–7, 1998.
[5]   P. Besnard and A. Hunter. *Elements of Argumentation*. The MIT Press, 2008.
[6]   M. Caminada and L. Amgoud. On the evaluation of argumentation formalisms. *Artificial Intelligence*, 171 (5-6): 286–310, 2007.
[7]   L. Cecchi, P. Fillottrani, and G. Simari. On the complexity of DeLP through game semantics. In NMR Workshop, pages 386–394, 2006.
[8]   C. Chesñevar, A. Maguitman, and R. Loui. Logical Models of Argument. *ACM Computing Surveys*, 32 (4): 337–383, 2000.
[9]   C.I. Chesñevar, G. Simari, and L. Godo. Computing dialectical trees efficiently in possibilistic defeasible logic programming. In *LPNMR'05*, pages 158–171, 2005.
[10] A. García and G. Simari. Defeasible Logic Programming: An Argumentative Approach. *Theory and Practice of Logic Programming*, 4 (1): 95–138, 2004.
[11] S.H. Nielsen and S. Parsons. A Generalization of Dung's Abstract Framework for Argumentation: Arguing with Sets of Attacking Arguments. In *ArgMAS'06*, pages 54–73, 2006.
[12] J.L. Pollock. A recursive semantics for defeasible reasoning. In Iyad Rahwan and Guillermo R. Simari, editors, *Argumentation in Artificial Intelligence*, chapter 9, pages 173–198. Springer, 2009.
[13] H. Prakken and G. Sartor. Argument-based extended logic programming with defeasible priorities. *Journal of Applied Non-classical Logics*, 7: 25–75, 1997.
[14] H. Prakken and G. Vreeswijk. Logical Systems for Defeasible Argumentation. In D. Gabbay and F. Guenther, editors, *Handbook of Phil. Logic*, pages 219–318. Kluwer, 2002.
[15] I. Rahwan and G. Simari, editors. *Argumentation in Artificial Intelligence*. Springer, 2009.
[16] G. Vreeswijk. Abstract Argumentation Systems. *Artificial Intelligence*, 90(1-2): 225–279,1997.

Computational Models of Argument
P. Baroni et al. (Eds.)
IOS Press, 2010
doi:10.3233/978-1-60750-619-5-39

Generalizing stable semantics by preferences

Leila AMGOUD [a,1] and Srdjan VESIC [a]

[a] *Institut de Recherche en Informatique de Toulouse*

Abstract.

Different proposals have been made in the literature for refining Dung's argumentation framework by preferences between arguments. The idea is to ignore an attack if the attacked argument is stronger than its attacker. Acceptability semantics are then applied on the remaining attacks. Unfortunately, these proposals may return some unintended results, in particular, when the attack relation is asymmetric.

In this paper, we propose a new approach in which preferences are taken into account at the semantics level. In case preferences are not available or do not conflict with the attacks, the extensions of the new semantics coincide with those of the basic ones. Besides, in our approach, the extensions (under a given semantics) are the maximal elements of a *dominance relation* on the powerset of the set of arguments. Throughout the paper, we focus on stable semantics. We provide a full characterization of its dominance relations; and we refine it with preferences.

1. Introduction

Argumentation is a reasoning model based on the construction and the evaluation of arguments. An argument gives a reason to believe a statement, to perform an action, etc.

The most abstract argumentation framework in the literature has been proposed in [8]. It consists of a set of *arguments* and a binary relation that captures *attacks* among them. Different *acceptability semantics* have been proposed in the same paper. A semantics amounts to define sets of acceptable arguments, called *extensions*. In this framework, arguments are assumed to have all the same strength. Besides, in [5,7,11], it has been argued that some arguments may be stronger than others. In [2], a first *abstract* preference-based argumentation framework (PAF) has been proposed. It takes as input a set of arguments, an attack relation, and a preference relation between arguments which is abstract and can thus be instantiated in different ways. This proposal has been generalized in [10] in order to reason even about preferences. Thus, arguments may support preferences about arguments. The last extension has been proposed in [4]. It assumes that each argument promotes a value, and a preference between two arguments comes from the importance of the respective values that are promoted by the two arguments. Whatever the source of the preference relation is, the idea is to ignore an attack if the attacked argument is stronger than its attacker. Dung's semantics are then applied on the remaining attacks. Unfortunately, these proposals may return some unintended results, in

---

[1]Corresponding Author: amgoud@irit.fr.

particular, when the attack relation is not symmetric. Besides, in [1], it has been shown that the attack relation should not be symmetric because otherwise the corresponding argumentation framework violates the postulate on consistency [6].

Example 1 *Let* $\Sigma = \{x, \neg y, x \rightarrow y\}$ *be a propositional knowledge base s.t.* x *is more certain than the two other formulas. The following arguments[2] are built from this base:*

$a_1 :< \{x\}, x >$	$a_2 :< \{\neg y\}, \neg y >$
$a_3 :< \{x \rightarrow y\}, x \rightarrow y >$	$a_4 :< \{x, \neg y\}, x \wedge \neg y >$
$a_5 :< \{\neg y, x \rightarrow y\}, \neg x >$	$a_6 :< \{x, x \rightarrow y\}, y >$

The figure below depicts the attacks wrt "assumption attack"[3] [9].

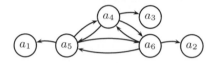

Finally, assume that arguments are compared using the weakest link principle[4] *[5]. According to this relation, the argument* a_1 *is strictly preferred to the others, which are themselves equally preferred. The classical approaches of PAFs remove the attack from* a_5 *to* a_1 *and get* $\{a_1, a_2, a_3, a_5\}$ *as a stable extension. Note that this extension, which intends to support a* coherent *point of view, is conflicting since it contains both* a_1 *and* a_5 *and supports thus* x *and* $\neg x$.

In this paper, we propose a new approach for PAFs in which preferences are taken into account at the semantics level. The idea is that, instead of modifying the inputs of Dung's framework, we extend the semantics with preferences. In case these preferences are not available or do not conflict with the attacks, the extensions of the new semantics coincide with those of the basic ones. Besides, in our approach, the extensions (under a given semantics) are the maximal elements of a *dominance relation* on the powerset of the set of arguments. A dominance relation encodes thus an acceptability semantics in our case. Contrarily to existing semantics which partition the powerset of arguments into two subsets: the extensions and the non-extensions, our approach provides more information since it compares all susbsets of arguments. Another novelty of our approach is that it defines a semantics through a set of postulates. The postulates describe the desirable properties of a dominance relation. In this paper, we focus only on stable semantics. We provide a full characterization of its dominance relations; and we refine it with preferences. A representation theorem is given; it describes the extensions of the new semantics, called *pref-stable*.

The paper is organized as follows: The next section recalls Dung's framework. Then, we propose our new approach for PAFs. Next, we characterize the dominance relations that encode stable semantics. Then, we show how to refine stable semantics with preferences. The last section is devoted to some concluding remarks and future work.

---

[2]An *argument* is a pair $< H, h >$ where H is its *support* and h its *conclusion*. H is a minimal subset of Σ that is consistent and infers classically h.

[3]An argument a *attacks* b iff the conclusion of a is the contrary of a formula in the support of b.

[4]An argument a is *preferred* to an argument b if the least certain formula in the support of a is more certain than the least certain formula in the support of b.

2. Basic argumentation framework

In the seminal paper [8], an *argumentation framework* (AF) is a pair $\mathcal{F} = (\mathcal{A}, \mathcal{R})$ where $\mathcal{A}$ is a set of *arguments* and $\mathcal{R}$ is an *attack relation* between arguments ($\mathcal{R} \subseteq \mathcal{A} \times \mathcal{A}$). The notation $(a, b) \in \mathcal{R}$ or $a\mathcal{R}b$ means that the argument a attacks the argument b. Different *acceptability semantics* for evaluating arguments have been proposed in the same paper. Each semantics amounts to define sets of acceptable arguments, called *extensions*. For the purpose of our paper, we only need to recall *stable* semantics.

Definition 1 (Conflict-free, Stable semantics) *Let $\mathcal{F} = (\mathcal{A}, \mathcal{R})$ be an AF and $\mathcal{B} \subseteq \mathcal{A}$.*

- $\mathcal{B}$ is conflict-free iff $\nexists$ a, $b \in \mathcal{B}$ s.t. $a\mathcal{R}b$.
- $\mathcal{B}$ is a stable extension iff it is conflict-free and attacks any argument in $\mathcal{A} \setminus \mathcal{B}$.

$\mathsf{Ext}(\mathcal{F})$ *denotes the set of stable extensions of $\mathcal{F}$.*

Note that some argumentation frameworks may not have stable extensions.

3. A new approach for PAFs

A *preference-based argumentation framework* (PAF) takes as input three elements: a set $\mathcal{A}$ of arguments, a binary relation $\mathcal{R}$ capturing attacks between arguments, and a (partial or total) preorder[5] $\geq$ on the set $\mathcal{A}$. This latter encodes differences in strengths of arguments. The expression $(a, b) \in \geq$ or $a \geq b$ means that the argument a is at least as strong as b. The symbol $>$ denotes the strict relation associated with $\geq$. Indeed, $a > b$ iff $a \geq b$ and not $(b \geq a)$.

Definition 2 (PAF) *A PAF is a tuple $\mathcal{T} = (\mathcal{A}, \mathcal{R}, \geq)$, where $\mathcal{A}$ is a set of arguments, $\mathcal{R}$ is an attack relation on $\mathcal{A}$, and $\geq$ is a (partial or total) preorder on $\mathcal{A}$.*

The new approach amounts to define *new acceptability semantics* that take into account the preference relation between arguments. A semantics is defined by a *dominance relation*, denoted by $\succeq$, on the powerset $\mathcal{P}(\mathcal{A})$ of the set of arguments. We say also that a dominance relation $\succeq$ *encodes* a semantics. For $\mathcal{E}, \mathcal{E}' \in \mathcal{P}(\mathcal{A})$, writing $(\mathcal{E}, \mathcal{E}') \in \succeq$ (or equivalently $\mathcal{E} \succeq \mathcal{E}'$) means that the set $\mathcal{E}$ is at least as good as the set $\mathcal{E}'$. The relation $\succ$ is the strict version of $\succeq$, that is for $\mathcal{E}, \mathcal{E}' \in \mathcal{P}(\mathcal{A})$, $\mathcal{E} \succ \mathcal{E}'$ iff $\mathcal{E} \succeq \mathcal{E}'$ and not $(\mathcal{E}' \succeq \mathcal{E})$.

Like the basic semantics of Dung, the new semantics computes extensions of arguments. These latter are the maximal elements of the dominance relation $\succeq$ that encodes the semantics. The notion of maximality is defined as follows.

Definition 3 (Maximal elements) *Let $\mathcal{E} \in \mathcal{P}(\mathcal{A})$ and $\succeq \subseteq \mathcal{P}(\mathcal{A}) \times \mathcal{P}(\mathcal{A})$. $\mathcal{E}$ is maximal wrt $\succeq$ iff $\forall \mathcal{E}' \in \mathcal{P}(\mathcal{A})$, $\mathcal{E} \succeq \mathcal{E}'$.*

As we will see in the next sections, not any relation $\succeq$ can be used for evaluating arguments in a PAF. An appropriate relation should, for instance, ensure the conflict-freeness of its maximal elements. Recall that this property is at the heart of all Dung's semantics, as it avoids inconsistent conclusions.

---

[5] A binary relation is a *preorder* iff it is *reflexive* and *transitive*.

Definition 4 (Extensions of a PAF) *Let $T = (\mathcal{A}, \mathcal{R}, \geq)$ be a PAF, and $\mathcal{E} \in \mathcal{P}(\mathcal{A})$. The set $\mathcal{E}$ is an* extension *of T under the dominance relation $\succeq \; \subseteq \mathcal{P}(\mathcal{A}) \times \mathcal{P}(\mathcal{A})$ iff $\mathcal{E}$ is a maximal element of $\succeq$.*
Let $\text{Ext}_{\succeq}(T)$ denote the set of extensions of T wrt $\succeq$.

Notation: Let $T = (\mathcal{A}, \mathcal{R}, \geq)$ be a PAF. $\mathcal{CF}(T)$ denotes the conflict-free (wrt $\mathcal{R}$) sets of arguments. At some places, we abuse notation and use $\mathcal{CF}(\mathcal{F})$ to denote the conflict-free sets of arguments of a basic framework $\mathcal{F} = (\mathcal{A}, \mathcal{R})$.

Assumptions: Let $T = (\mathcal{A}, \mathcal{R}, \geq)$ be a PAF. Throughout the paper, we assume that:

1. The set $\mathcal{A}$ is finite.
2. T does not contain self-attacking arguments.

In the remainder of the paper, we will propose a new acceptability semantics, called *Pref-stable*. This semantics generalizes stable semantics with preferences between arguments. In case preferences are not available or are not conflicting with the attacks, the extensions of the two semantics coincide.

4. Stable semantics as a dominance relation

In the previous section, we have shown that our new semantics are defined as dominance relations on the power set of the set of arguments. The new semantics should recover the basic semantics of Dung in some cases. Before showing how to extend stable semantics with preferences, it is important to encode this semantics in the new setting, i.e. to define it as a dominance relation on the power set of the set of arguments. The following theorem characterizes the dominance relations that encode stable semantics.

Theorem 1 *Let $\mathcal{F} = (\mathcal{A}, \mathcal{R})$ be an AF and $\succeq \; \subseteq \mathcal{P}(\mathcal{A}) \times \mathcal{P}(\mathcal{A})$. Then, $\forall \mathcal{E} \in \mathcal{P}(\mathcal{A})$, $(\mathcal{E} \in \text{Ext}(\mathcal{F}) \Leftrightarrow \mathcal{E}$ is maximal wrt $\succeq)$ iff:*

1. *$\forall \mathcal{E} \in \mathcal{P}(\mathcal{A})$, if $\mathcal{E} \notin \mathcal{CF}(\mathcal{F})$ then $\exists \mathcal{E}' \in \mathcal{P}(\mathcal{A})$ s.t. $\neg(\mathcal{E} \succeq \mathcal{E}')$*
2. *if $\mathcal{E} \in \mathcal{CF}(\mathcal{F})$ and $\forall a' \notin \mathcal{E}$, $\exists a \in \mathcal{E}$ s.t. $a\mathcal{R}a'$, then $\forall \mathcal{E}' \in \mathcal{P}(\mathcal{A})$ it holds that $\mathcal{E} \succeq \mathcal{E}'$*
3. *if $\mathcal{E} \in \mathcal{CF}(\mathcal{F})$ and $\exists a' \in \mathcal{A} \setminus \mathcal{E}$ s.t. $\nexists a \in \mathcal{E}$ and $a\mathcal{R}a'$, then $\exists \mathcal{E}' \in \mathcal{P}(\mathcal{A})$ s.t. $\neg(\mathcal{E} \succeq \mathcal{E}')$.*

In other words, a relation $\succeq$ encodes stable semantics if and only if it verifies the three conditions given in this theorem.

It is worth mentioning that there are several relations $\succeq$ that encode stable semantics. All these relations return the same maximal elements (i.e. the same extensions). However, they compare in different ways the remaining sets of arguments. An example of a relation that encodes stable semantics is the following:

Relation 1. Let $\mathcal{F} = (\mathcal{A}, \mathcal{R})$ be an AF and $\mathcal{E}, \mathcal{E}' \in \mathcal{P}(\mathcal{A})$. $\mathcal{E} \succeq_1 \mathcal{E}'$ iff

- $\mathcal{E} \in \mathcal{CF}(\mathcal{F})$ and $\mathcal{E}' \notin \mathcal{CF}(\mathcal{F})$, or
- $\mathcal{E}, \mathcal{E}' \in \mathcal{CF}(\mathcal{F})$ and $\forall a' \in \mathcal{E}' \setminus \mathcal{E}$, $\exists a \in \mathcal{E} \setminus \mathcal{E}'$ s.t. $a\mathcal{R}a'$.

Let us illustrate this relation on the following simple example.

Example 2 *Consider the AF* $\mathcal{F} = (\mathcal{A}, \mathcal{R})$ *where* $\mathcal{A} = \{a, b\}$ *and* $\mathcal{R} = \{(a, b), (b, a)\}$. *It is clear that:* $\{a\}, \{b\} \succeq_1 \{\} \succeq_1 \{a, b\}$. *The two sets* $\{a\}$ *and* $\{b\}$ *are equally preferred. The maximal elements of* $\succeq_1$ *(its stable extensions) are* $\{a\}$ *and* $\{b\}$.

Note that Dung's approach returns only two classes of subsets of arguments: the extensions and the non-extensions. In Example 2, the two sets $\{a\}$ and $\{b\}$ are stable extensions while it does not say anything about the sets $\{a, b\}$ and $\{\}$. Our approach compares even the non-extensions. Indeed, according to $\succeq_1$, the set $\{\}$ is preferred to $\{a, b\}$. The fact of comparing non-extensions makes it possible to have more than one relation for stable semantics.

5. Pref-stable semantics

This section defines a new semantics, called *pref-stable*, that extends the stable one by preferences. Recall that there are two basic requirements behind stable semantics: i) conflict-freeness, and ii) external attack. The first property ensures that the extensions of a framework are conflict-free, while the second ensures that any argument outside an extension is attacked by an argument of the extension. These requirements are considered in the definition of the extensions themselves. In our approach, the requirements of pref-stable semantics are given as *postulates* that a dominance relation $\succeq$ should satisfy.

Like stable semantics, the new semantics requires that the extensions of a PAF are conflict-free wrt the attack relation. This is important since an extension represents a coherent point of view. In our approach, since all subsets of arguments are compared, we assume that a conflict-free set of arguments is preferred to any conflicting one.

Postulate 1 *Let* $\mathcal{T} = (\mathcal{A}, \mathcal{R}, \geq)$ *and* $\mathcal{E}, \mathcal{E}' \subseteq \mathcal{A}$. *Then,*

$$\frac{\mathcal{E} \in \mathcal{CF}(\mathcal{T}) \quad \mathcal{E}' \notin \mathcal{CF}(\mathcal{T})}{\mathcal{E} \succ \mathcal{E}'} 6$$

It is easy to show that if a relation satisfies this postulate, then its maximal elements are conflict-free.

Property 1 *Let* $\mathcal{T} = (\mathcal{A}, \mathcal{R}, \geq)$ *be a PAF and* $\succeq \subseteq \mathcal{P}(\mathcal{A}) \times \mathcal{P}(\mathcal{A})$ *satisfies Postulate 1. For all* $\mathcal{E} \in \mathtt{Ext}_\succeq(\mathcal{T})$, *it holds that* $\mathcal{E} \in \mathcal{CF}(\mathcal{T})$.

The following requirement ensures that a dominance relation is entirely based on the distinct elements of any two subsets of arguments.

Postulate 2 *Let* $\mathcal{T} = (\mathcal{A}, \mathcal{R}, \geq)$ *be a PAF, and* $\mathcal{E}, \mathcal{E}' \in \mathcal{CF}(\mathcal{T})$. *Then,*

$$\frac{\mathcal{E} \succeq \mathcal{E}'}{\mathcal{E} \backslash \mathcal{E}' \succeq \mathcal{E}' \backslash \mathcal{E}} \qquad \frac{\mathcal{E} \backslash \mathcal{E}' \succeq \mathcal{E}' \backslash \mathcal{E}}{\mathcal{E} \succeq \mathcal{E}'}$$

The two following postulates show how preferences between arguments are taken into account in a semantics that generalize stable semantics. As already explained, the basic idea is that if an argument a attacks another argument b and $b > a$, then the set

---
[6]The notation $\frac{X \quad Y}{Z}$ means that if X and Y hold, then Z holds as well.

$\{b\}$ is privileged. Thus, $\{b\}$ should be strictly preferred to $\{a\}$. However, if the two arguments are equally preferred or incomparable or even $a > b$, then the set $\{a\}$ should be strictly preferred to $\{b\}$.

The next postulate describes when a set should not be preferred to another. The idea is that: if an argument of a set $\mathcal{E}$ cannot be compared with arguments in another set $\mathcal{E}'$ (since it is neither attacked nor less preferred to any argument of the other set), then the set $\mathcal{E}$ cannot be less preferred to $\mathcal{E}'$.

Postulate 3 *Let* $\mathcal{T} = (\mathcal{A}, \mathcal{R}, \geq)$ *be a PAF, and* $\mathcal{E}, \mathcal{E}' \in \mathcal{CF}(\mathcal{T})$ *s.t.* $\mathcal{E} \cap \mathcal{E}' = \emptyset$. *Then,*

$$\frac{(\exists x' \in \mathcal{E}')(\forall x \in \mathcal{E}) \ \neg(x\mathcal{R}x' \wedge \neg(\ x'>x)) \wedge \neg(x>x')}{\neg(\mathcal{E} \succeq \mathcal{E}')}$$

The last postulate describes when a set is preferred to another when preferences between arguments are taken into account. The idea is that if for any argument of a set, there is at least one argument in another set which 'wins the conflict' with it, then the latter should be preferred to the former. There are two situations in which an argument x wins a conflict against x': either x attacks x' and x' does not defend itself since it is not stronger than x wrt $\geq$, or x' attacks x but x is strictly preferred to x'.

Postulate 4 *Let* $\mathcal{T} = (\mathcal{A}, \mathcal{R}, \geq)$ *be a PAF and* $\mathcal{E}, \mathcal{E}' \in \mathcal{CF}(\mathcal{T})$ *s.t.* $\mathcal{E} \cap \mathcal{E}' = \emptyset$. *Then,*

$$\frac{(\forall x' \in \mathcal{E}')(\exists x \in \mathcal{E}) \ s.t. \ (x\mathcal{R}x' \wedge \ \neg(x'>x)) \ or \ (x'\mathcal{R}x \wedge x>x')}{\mathcal{E} \succeq \mathcal{E}'}$$

Now that the four postulates are introduced, we are ready to define the pref-stable semantics.

Definition 5 (Pref-stable semantics) *Let* $\mathcal{T} = (\mathcal{A}, \mathcal{R}, \geq)$ *be a PAF. A relation* $\succeq \subseteq \mathcal{P}(\mathcal{A}) \times \mathcal{P}(\mathcal{A})$ *encodes pref-stable semantics iff* $\succeq$ *satisfies Postulates 1, 2, 3 and 4.*

Throughout the paper, a relation that encodes pref-stable semantics will be called *pref-stable relation*, and its maximal elements are called *pref-stable extensions*.

It can be checked that a pref-stable relation strictly prefers a conflict-free set to all its strict subsets.

Property 2 *Let* $\mathcal{T} = (\mathcal{A}, \mathcal{R}, \geq)$ *be a given PAF,* $\mathcal{E}, \mathcal{E}' \in \mathcal{CF}(\mathcal{T})$. *If* $\succeq$ *is a pref-stable relation, then* $\mathcal{E}' \succ \mathcal{E}$ *whenever* $\mathcal{E} \subsetneq \mathcal{E}'$.

Like stable semantics, there are several relations that encode pref-stable semantics. However, the differences between them are not significant, and we can show that they all return the same pref-stable extensions.

Theorem 2 *Let* $\mathcal{T} = (\mathcal{A}, \mathcal{R}, \geq)$ *be a PAF. If* $\succeq, \succeq' \subseteq \mathcal{P}(\mathcal{A}) \times \mathcal{P}(\mathcal{A})$ *are pref-stable relations, then* $\text{Ext}_{\succeq}(\mathcal{T}) = \text{Ext}_{\succeq'}(\mathcal{T})$.

Finally, we can show that a pref-stable semantics generalizes stable semantics. This means that when preferences are not available or do not conflict with attacks in a given PAF, then pref-stable relations are a subset of those encoding stable semantics (i.e. they satisfy the three conditions of Theorem 1.

Theorem 3 *Let* $\mathcal{T} = (\mathcal{A}, \mathcal{R}, \geq)$ *be a PAF and* $\mathcal{F} = (\mathcal{A}, \mathcal{R})$ *its basic version. If* $\succeq$ *is a pref-stable relation and* $\nexists a, b \in \mathcal{A}$ *such that* $a\mathcal{R}b$ *and* $b > a$, *then:*

- $\text{Ext}(\mathcal{F}) = \text{Ext}_{\succeq}(\mathcal{T})$
- $\succeq$ *satisfies the three conditions of Theorem 1*

Let us now consider an example of a pref-stable relation. This relation extends $\succeq_1$ which encodes stable semantics.

Relation 2 (Relation 1 extended). Let $\mathcal{T} = (\mathcal{A}, \mathcal{R}, \geq)$ be a PAF and $\mathcal{E}, \mathcal{E}' \in \mathcal{P}(\mathcal{A})$. $\mathcal{E} \succeq_2 \mathcal{E}'$ iff at least one of the following conditions holds:

- $\mathcal{E} \in \mathcal{CF}(\mathcal{T})$ and $\mathcal{E}' \notin \mathcal{CF}(\mathcal{T})$
- $\mathcal{E}, \mathcal{E}' \in \mathcal{CF}(\mathcal{T})$ and $(\forall a' \in \mathcal{E}' \setminus \mathcal{E})(\exists a \in \mathcal{E} \setminus \mathcal{E}')$ s.t. $(a\mathcal{R}a' \wedge a' \not> a) \vee (a > a')$.

Property 3 $\succeq_2$ *is a pref-stable relation.*

Let us illustrate this relation on the following simple example.

Example 3 *Let* $\mathcal{A} = \{a, b\}$, $\mathcal{R} = \{(a, b)\}$ *and* $b \geq a$. *It can be checked that the set* $\{b\}$ *is the only maximal element of relation* $\succeq_2$. *Figure 1 shows the preferences among elements of* $\mathcal{P}(\mathcal{A})$ *wrt* $\succeq_2$.

Figure 1. $\succeq_2 \subseteq \mathcal{P}(\mathcal{A}) \times \mathcal{P}(\mathcal{A})$

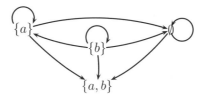

Let us now reconsider the example presented in the introduction.

Example 1 (Cont): It can be checked that every pref-stable relation returns exactly two pref-extensions: $\{a_1, a_2, a_4\}$ (whose base is $\{x, \neg y\}$) and $\{a_1, a_3, a_6\}$ (whose base is $\{x, x \rightarrow y\}$). Thus, the bases corresponding to both extensions are consistent.

5.1. General and specific pref-stable relations

As already said, there are several relations that encode pref-stable semantics. The aim of this section is to define the upper and lower bounds of these relations.

The following relation, denoted by $\succeq_g$, is the most general pref-stable relation. It returns $\mathcal{E} \succeq_g \mathcal{E}'$ if and only if it can be proved from the four postulates that $\mathcal{E}$ must be preferred to $\mathcal{E}'$.

Definition 6 (General pref-stable relation) *Let* $\mathcal{T} = (\mathcal{A}, \mathcal{R}, \geq)$ *be a PAF and* $\mathcal{E}, \mathcal{E}' \in \mathcal{P}(\mathcal{A})$. $\mathcal{E} \succeq_g \mathcal{E}'$ *iff:*

- $\mathcal{E} \in \mathcal{CF}(\mathcal{T})$ *and* $\mathcal{E}' \notin \mathcal{CF}(\mathcal{T})$, *or*
- $\mathcal{E}, \mathcal{E}' \in \mathcal{CF}(\mathcal{T})$ *and* $(\forall a' \in \mathcal{E}' \backslash \mathcal{E})(\exists a \in \mathcal{E} \backslash \mathcal{E}')$ *s.t.* $(a\mathcal{R}a' \wedge a' \not> a) \vee (a'\mathcal{R}a \wedge a > a')$.

Property 4 $\succeq_g$ *is a pref-stable relation.*

The next relation, denoted by $\succeq_s$, is the most specific pref-stable relation. It returns $\mathcal{E} \succeq_s \mathcal{E}'$ if and only if from the four postulates it cannot be proved that $\neg(\mathcal{E} \succeq_s \mathcal{E}')$.

Definition 7 (Specific pref-stable relation) *Let* $\mathcal{T} = (\mathcal{A}, \mathcal{R}, \geq)$ *be a PAF and* $\mathcal{E}, \mathcal{E}' \in \mathcal{P}(\mathcal{A})$. $\mathcal{E} \succeq_s \mathcal{E}'$ *iff:*

- $\mathcal{E}' \notin \mathcal{CF}(\mathcal{T})$, *or*
- $\mathcal{E}, \mathcal{E}' \in \mathcal{CF}(\mathcal{T})$ *and* $(\forall a' \in \mathcal{E}' \backslash \mathcal{E})(\exists a \in \mathcal{E} \backslash \mathcal{E}')$ *s.t.* $(a\mathcal{R}a' \wedge a' \not> a) \vee (a > a')$.

Property 5 $\succeq_s$ *is a pref-stable relation.*

Let us illustrate the differences between the three relations $\succeq_2$, $\succeq_s$ and $\succeq_g$ on the following example.

Example 4 *Let* $\mathcal{A} = \{a, b, c\}$, $\mathcal{R} = \{(a, b)\}$ *and* $a \geq c$. *For example, it holds that* $\{a\} \succeq_2 \{c\}$, $\{a\} \succeq_s \{c\}$ *and* $\neg(\{a\} \succeq_g \{c\})$. *That is, for relations* $\succeq_2$ *and* $\succeq_s$ *the strict preference between* a *and* c *is enough to prefer* $\{a\}$ *to* $\{c\}$. *For relation* $\succeq_g$, *since* c *is not attacked by* a, *there is no preference between the sets* $\{a\}$ *and* $\{c\}$. *The fact that* a *is stronger is not important, because there is no conflict between those arguments.*

Another difference is that for the relation $\succeq_s$, *all conflicting sets are equally preferred. For example,* $\{a, b, c\} \succeq_s \{a, b\}$ *and* $\{a, b\} \succeq_s \{a, b, c\}$. *Besides, relations* $\succeq_2$ *and* $\succeq_g$ *encode the idea that a contradictory point of view cannot be accepted as a standpoint. Thus, it is not even possible to compare two contradictory sets of arguments. For example* $\neg(\{a, b, c\} \succeq_2 \{a, b\})$.

The next result shows that any pref-stable relation is "between" the general and the specific relations.

Theorem 4 *Let* $\mathcal{T} = (\mathcal{A}, \mathcal{R}, \geq)$ *be a PAF and* $\mathcal{E}, \mathcal{E}' \in \mathcal{P}(\mathcal{A})$. *Let* $\succeq$ *be a pref-stable relation.*

- *If* $\mathcal{E} \succeq_g \mathcal{E}'$ *then* $\mathcal{E} \succeq \mathcal{E}'$.
- *If* $\mathcal{E} \succeq \mathcal{E}'$ *then* $\mathcal{E} \succeq_s \mathcal{E}'$.

A simple consequence of the previous result is that, if $\mathcal{E} \succeq_g \mathcal{E}'$ and $\mathcal{E} \succeq_s \mathcal{E}'$, then $\mathcal{E} \succeq \mathcal{E}'$ for any pref-stable relation.

5.2. Corresponding Semantics

This section characterizes pref-stable extensions without referring to pref-stable relations. Indeed, the next theorem proves that it is not necessary to compare all sets of arguments in order to know whether a given subset of arguments is a pref-stable extension of a PAF.

Theorem 5 *Let* $\mathcal{T} = (\mathcal{A}, \mathcal{R}, \geq)$ *be a PAF and* $\succeq$ *a pref-stable relation.* $\mathcal{E} \in \mathtt{Ext}_{\succeq}(\mathcal{T})$ *iff:*

- $\mathcal{E} \in \mathcal{CF}(\mathcal{T})$, *and*
- $(\forall a' \in \mathcal{A} \setminus \mathcal{E}) \, (\exists a \in \mathcal{E})$ *s.t.* $(a\mathcal{R}a' \wedge a' \not> a) \vee (a'\mathcal{R}a \wedge a > a')$.

This result is of great importance since it shows how to compute directly the pref-stable extensions of a PAF without bothering about pref-stable relations. This is particularly the case when we do not want to compare all the elements of $\mathcal{P}(\mathcal{A})$.

Another way to compute the pref-stable extensions of a PAF is to "invert" the direction of attacks when they are not in accordance with the preferences between arguments. We apply then stable semantics on the basic framework that is obtained. More precisely, we start with a PAF $\mathcal{T} = (\mathcal{A}, \mathcal{R}, \geq)$. We compute an AF $\mathcal{F} = (\mathcal{A}, \mathcal{R}')$ where $\mathcal{R}'$ is defined as follows:

$$\begin{cases} \text{If } (a, b) \in \mathcal{R} \text{ and } b \not> a \text{ then } (a, b) \in \mathcal{R}' \\ \text{If } (a, b) \in \mathcal{R} \text{ and } b > a \text{ then } (b, a) \in \mathcal{R}' \end{cases}$$

then we apply stable semantics on the new framework $(\mathcal{A}, \mathcal{R}')$. This result is proved in the following theorem.

Theorem 6 *Let* $\mathcal{T} = (\mathcal{A}, \mathcal{R}, \geq)$ *be a PAF and* $\succeq$ *be a pref-stable relation. Let* $\mathcal{R}' = \{(a, b) \mid (a\mathcal{R}b \wedge b \not> a) \vee (b\mathcal{R}a \wedge a > b)\}$. *It holds that* $\mathtt{Ext}_{\succeq}(\mathcal{T}) = \mathtt{Ext}((\mathcal{A}, \mathcal{R}'))$.

Let us illustrate this result through a simple example.

Example 5 *Let us consider the PAF represented in Figure 2. It can be checked that any pref-stable relation will return exactly one pref-stable extension:* $\mathtt{Ext}_{\succeq}(\mathcal{T}) = \{\{b, d, e\}\}$. *The argumentation framework that is obtained after inverting arrows is de-*

Figure 2. PAF $\mathcal{T} = (\mathcal{A}, \mathcal{R}, \geq)$ (Example 5)

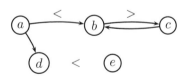

picted in Figure 3. It is easy to see that the only stable extension of this framework is the set $\{b, d, e\}$.

Figure 3. Framework $(\mathcal{A}, \mathcal{R}')$

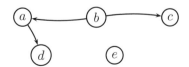

6. Conclusion

Several proposals have been made in the literature on how to integrate preferences in an argumentation system. In this paper, we have shown that those proposals may return undesirable results when the attack relation is asymmetric. We have then proposed a novel approach to compute the extensions of a PAF. The idea is to define new acceptability semantics that take into account both attacks and preferences between arguments.

In our approach, a semantics is defined by a dominance relation on the powerset of the set of arguments. The extensions of a PAF are the maximal elements of this relation. This approach offers great advantages. First, it shows clearly the impact of preferences on the result of a PAF. Second, it allows to compare all the elements of the powerset of arguments. Thus, it offers more information.

In this paper, we have mainly focused on generalizing Dung's semantics [8], in particular stable one. We have defined a new semantics, called pref-stable, that recovers stable semantics in case preferences between arguments are not available or do not conflict with the attacks. We have proposed a full characterization of pref-stable semantics both in terms of dominance relations that encode it and also in a declarative way.

To the best of our knowledge, the only related work is that proposed in [3]. In that paper, three "particular" relations that extend respectively stable, preferred and grounded semantics are provided. As shown in our paper, those relations are unfortunately not unique. We have provided a full picture on the way of extending stable semantics into pref-stable using postulates.

References

[1]   L. Amgoud and P. Besnard. Bridging the gap between abstract argumentation systems and logic. In *International Conference on Scalable Uncertainty Management (SUM'09)*, pages 12–27, 2009.

[2]   L. Amgoud and C. Cayrol. A reasoning model based on the production of acceptable arguments. *Annals of Mathematics and Artificial Int.*, 34:197–216, 2002.

[3]   L. Amgoud and S. Vesic. Repairing preference-based argumentation systems. In *Proceedings of IJCAI'09*, pages 665–670. AAAI Press, 2009.

[4]   T. J. M. Bench-Capon. Persuasion in practical argument using value-based argumentation frameworks. *J. of Logic and Computation*, 13(3):429–448, 2003.

[5]   S. Benferhat, D. Dubois, and H. Prade. Argumentative inference in uncertain and inconsistent knowledge bases. In *Proceedings of UAI'93*, pages 411–419, 1993.

[6]   M. Caminada and L. Amgoud. On the evaluation of argumentation formalisms. *AIJ*, 171 (5-6):286–310, 2007.

[7]   C. Cayrol, V. Royer, and C. Saurel. Management of preferences in assumption-based reasoning. *Lecture Notes in Computer Science*, 682:13–22, 1993.

[8]   P. Dung. On the acceptability of arguments and its fundamental role in nonmonotonic reasoning, logic programming and n-person games. *AIJ*, 77:321–357, 1995.

[9]   M. Elvang-Gøransson, J. Fox, and P. Krause. Acceptability of arguments as 'logical uncertainty'. In *Proceedings of ECSQARU'93*, number 747, pages 85–90. 1993.

[10] S. Modgil. Reasoning about preferences in argumentation frameworks. *AIJ*, 173(9-10):901–934, 2009.

[11] G. Simari and R. Loui. A mathematical treatment of defeasible reasoning and its implementation. *AIJ*, 53:125–157, 1992.

Appendix

Proof of Property 1 Let us assume that $\mathcal{E} \in \text{Ext}_{\succeq}(\mathcal{T})$. Thus, $\mathcal{E} \succeq \emptyset$. Since $\emptyset \in \mathcal{CF}(\mathcal{T})$, then from Postulate 1, $\mathcal{E} \in \mathcal{CF}(\mathcal{T})$.

Proof of Property 2 From Postulate 2, it follows that $\mathcal{E} \succeq \mathcal{E}'$ iff $\emptyset \succeq \mathcal{E}' \setminus \mathcal{E}$. From Postulate 3, $\neg(\emptyset \succeq \mathcal{E}' \setminus \mathcal{E})$. Consequently $\neg(\mathcal{E} \succeq \mathcal{E}')$. Postulate 4 implies that $\mathcal{E}' \setminus \mathcal{E} \succeq \emptyset$. From Postulate 2, $\mathcal{E}' \succeq \mathcal{E}$. This fact, together with $\neg(\mathcal{E} \succeq \mathcal{E}')$, leads to conclusion $\mathcal{E}' \succ \mathcal{E}$.

Proof of Property 3 To show that $\succeq_2$ is a pref-stable relation, we show that it satisfies all postulates. Postulate 1 is satisfied since from the first item of the definition of $\succeq_2$, any conflict-free set is preferred to any conflicting set. Postulate 2 is satisfied since from the second item of the same definition, when comparing two sets $\mathcal{E}$ and $\mathcal{E}'$, common elements are not taken into account. The second condition of the definition of $\succeq_2$ is exactly the negation of the condition of Postulate 3. Since Postulate 4 implies the second item of this definition, then it is verified.

Proof of Property 4 Postulates 1 and 2 are verified for the same reasons as for $\succeq_2$. Postulate 3 implies that the second item of Definition 6 is not satisfied. Postulate 4 is trivially verified.

Proof of Property 5 We see from the first item of Definition 7 that all (conflict-free and non conflict-free) sets are better than non conflict-free sets. A non conflict-free set, however, cannot be better than conflict-free set. Thus, Postulate 1 is satisfied. Postulates 2, 3 and 4 are verified for same reasons as in the case of relation $\succeq_g$.

Proof of Theorem 1. $\Rightarrow$ Assume that $((\forall \mathcal{E} \subseteq \mathcal{A})$ we have $\mathcal{E} \in \text{Ext}(\mathcal{F}) \Leftrightarrow \mathcal{E}$ is a maximal element of $\succeq)$. We will prove that the three above conditions are satisfied.

1. Assume that $\mathcal{E} \subseteq \mathcal{A}$ and $\mathcal{E} \notin \mathcal{CF}(\mathcal{F})$. So, $\mathcal{E}$ is not a stable extension of $(\mathcal{A}, \mathcal{R})$. From what we supposed, $\mathcal{E}$ is not a maximal element of $\succeq$. In other words, $\exists \mathcal{E}' \subseteq \mathcal{A}$ s.t. $\neg(\mathcal{E} \succeq \mathcal{E}')$.
2. Assume that $\mathcal{E} \in \mathcal{CF}(\mathcal{F})$ and that $\forall a' \notin \mathcal{E}$, $\exists a \in \mathcal{E}$ s.t. $(a, a') \in \mathcal{R}$. Thus, $\mathcal{E}$ is a Dung's stable extension of $(\mathcal{A}, \mathcal{R})$. From what we supposed, it must be that $\mathcal{E}$ is a maximal element of $\succeq$. Consequently, $(\forall \mathcal{E}' \subseteq \mathcal{A}) \mathcal{E} \succeq \mathcal{E}'$.
3. Assume that $\mathcal{E} \in \mathcal{CF}(\mathcal{F})$ and $\exists a' \in \mathcal{A} \setminus \mathcal{E}$ s.t. $\nexists a \in \mathcal{E}$ and $(a, a') \in \mathcal{R}$. It is obvious that $\mathcal{E}$ is not a Dung's stable extension of $(\mathcal{A}, \mathcal{R})$. From $(\mathcal{E} \in \text{Ext}(\mathcal{F}) \Leftrightarrow \mathcal{E}$ is a maximal element of $\succeq)$ we conclude that $\mathcal{E}$ is not a maximal element of $\succeq$. Thus, $(\exists \mathcal{E}' \subseteq \mathcal{A}) \neg(\mathcal{E} \succeq \mathcal{E}')$.

$\Leftarrow$ Let $\succeq$ satisfy the three conditions.

- Let $\mathcal{E}$ be a stable extension of $(\mathcal{A}, \mathcal{R})$ and let $\mathcal{E}' \subseteq \mathcal{A}$. From the second condition, $\mathcal{E} \succeq \mathcal{E}'$. Thus, $\mathcal{E}$ must be a maximal element wrt $\succeq$.
- If $\mathcal{E}$ is not a stable extension of $(\mathcal{A}, \mathcal{R})$ but $\mathcal{E} \in \mathcal{CF}(\mathcal{F})$, from the third condition we have that $\mathcal{E}$ is not a maximal element wrt $\succeq$.
- If $\mathcal{E}$ is not a stable extension of $(\mathcal{A}, \mathcal{R})$ and $\mathcal{E} \notin \mathcal{CF}(\mathcal{F})$ then, from the first condition, $\mathcal{E}$ is not a maximal element wrt $\succeq$.

Proof of Theorem 2 $\Rightarrow$ Let $\mathcal{E} \in \text{Ext}_{\succeq}(\mathcal{T})$. We will prove that $\mathcal{E} \in \text{Ext}_{\succeq'}(\mathcal{T})$. From Postulate 1, $\mathcal{E} \in \mathcal{CF}(\mathcal{T})$. Let $\mathcal{E}' \subseteq \mathcal{A}$. If $\mathcal{E}'$ is not conflict-free then, from Postulate 1, $\mathcal{E} \succeq' \mathcal{E}'$. Else, from Postulate 2, $\mathcal{E} \succeq' \mathcal{E}'$ iff $\mathcal{E} \setminus \mathcal{E}' \succeq' \mathcal{E}' \setminus \mathcal{E}$. Let $\mathcal{E}_1 = \mathcal{E} \setminus \mathcal{E}'$ and $\mathcal{E}_2 = \mathcal{E}' \setminus \mathcal{E}$. $\mathcal{E}_1$ and $\mathcal{E}_2$ are disjoint conflict-free sets. If condition of Postulate 4 is satisfied for $\mathcal{E}_1$ and $\mathcal{E}_2$, then $\mathcal{E}_1 \succeq' \mathcal{E}_2$. Let us study the case when this condition is not satisfied. Condition of Postulate 3 is not satisfied since $\mathcal{E} \in \text{Ext}_{\succeq}(\mathcal{T})$. Thus, it must be that $(\exists x' \in \mathcal{E}_2)$ s.t. $(\nexists x \in \mathcal{E}_1)((x, x') \in \mathcal{R} \wedge (x', x) \not\gg) \vee ((x', x) \in \mathcal{R} \wedge (x, x') \gg)$ and $(\exists x \in \mathcal{E}_1)(x, x') \gg$. Let $X = \{x \in \mathcal{E}_1 | (x, x') \gg\}$. X is conflict-free. From Postulate 3, $\neg(\mathcal{E}_1 \setminus X \succeq \{x'\})$. Postulate 2 implies that $\neg(\mathcal{E}_1 \setminus X \cup (X \cup (\mathcal{E} \cap \mathcal{E}')) \succeq \{x'\} \cup (X \cup (\mathcal{E} \cap \mathcal{E}')))$, i.e. $\neg(\mathcal{E} \succeq \{x'\} \cup (X \cup (\mathcal{E} \cap \mathcal{E}')))$. Contradiction with $\mathcal{E} \in \text{Ext}_{\succeq}(\mathcal{T})$. Thus, condition of Postulate 4 is satisfied for $\mathcal{E}_1$ and $\mathcal{E}_2$, and $\mathcal{E}_1 \succeq' \mathcal{E}_2$. Consequently, $\mathcal{E} \succeq' \mathcal{E}'$. This means that $\mathcal{E} \in \text{Ext}_{\succeq'}(\mathcal{T})$.

$\Leftarrow$ In the first part of proof, we showed that for all pref-stable relations $\succeq_1, \succeq_2$, it holds that if $\mathcal{E} \in \text{Ext}_{\succeq_1}(\mathcal{T})$ then $\mathcal{E} \in \text{Ext}_{\succeq_2}(\mathcal{T})$. Contraposition of this rule gives if $\mathcal{E} \notin \text{Ext}_{\succeq_2}(\mathcal{T})$ then $\mathcal{E} \notin \text{Ext}_{\succeq_1}(\mathcal{T})$. Since this was proved for arbitrary relations which satisfy all postulates, we conclude: if $\mathcal{E} \notin \text{Ext}_{\succeq}(\mathcal{T})$ then $\mathcal{E} \notin \text{Ext}_{\succeq'}(\mathcal{T})$.

Proof of Theorem 3

- Let $\mathcal{T}$ be a preference-based argumentation system s.t. $(\nexists a, b \in \mathcal{A})(a, b) \in \mathcal{R} \wedge (b, a) \in >$.
  $\Rightarrow$ Let $\mathcal{E} \in \text{Ext}(\mathcal{F})$. We prove that $\mathcal{E} \in \text{Ext}_{\succeq}(\mathcal{T})$. Let $\mathcal{E}' \in \mathcal{P}(\mathcal{A})$. If $\mathcal{E}' \notin \mathcal{CF}(\mathcal{T})$ then, from Postulate 1, $\mathcal{E} \succeq \mathcal{E}'$. Let $\mathcal{E}' \in \mathcal{CF}(\mathcal{T})$. Since $\mathcal{E} \in \text{Ext}(\mathcal{F})$ then $(\forall x' \in \mathcal{E}' \backslash \mathcal{E})(\exists x \in \mathcal{E} \backslash \mathcal{E}')(x, x') \in \mathcal{R}$. We supposed $(\nexists a, b \in \mathcal{A})(a, b) \in \mathcal{R} \wedge (b, a) \in >$. Thus, from Postulate 4, $\mathcal{E} \backslash \mathcal{E}' \succeq \mathcal{E}' \backslash \mathcal{E}$. Now, Postulate 2 implies $\mathcal{E} \succeq \mathcal{E}'$. Since $\mathcal{E}'$ was arbitrary, then $\mathcal{E} \in \text{Ext}_{\succeq}(\mathcal{T})$.
  $\Leftarrow$ Let $\mathcal{E} \in \text{Ext}_{\succeq}(\mathcal{T})$. We will show that $\mathcal{E} \in \text{Ext}_{\succeq}(\mathcal{F})$. From Postulate 1, $\mathcal{E} \in \mathcal{CF}(\mathcal{T})$. Let $x' \notin \mathcal{E}$. Since $\mathcal{E} \in \text{Ext}_{\succeq}(\mathcal{T})$ then it must be $\mathcal{E} \succeq \{x'\}$. From Postulate 3, $(\exists x \in \mathcal{E})(x, x') \in \mathcal{R} \vee (x, x') \in >$. If $(\exists x \in \mathcal{E})(x, x') \in \mathcal{R}$, the proof is over. Let us suppose the contrary. Then $(\nexists x \in \mathcal{E})(x, x') \in \mathcal{R}$. Let $X = \{x \in \mathcal{E} | x > x'\}$. From Postulate 3, $\neg(\mathcal{E} \setminus X \succeq \{x'\})$. This fact and Postulate 2 imply $\neg(\mathcal{E} \succeq (X \cup \{x'\}))$. Contradiction with $\mathcal{E} \in \text{Ext}_{\succeq}(\mathcal{T})$. Thus, $\mathcal{E} \in \text{Ext}(\mathcal{F})$.
- In the first part of the proof, we have shown that for every PAF $\mathcal{T} = (\mathcal{A}, \mathcal{R}, \geq)$ s.t. $(\nexists a, b \in \mathcal{A})a\mathcal{R}b \wedge b > a$ and for every pref-relation $\succeq$, it holds that maximal elements wrt $\succeq$ are exactly stable extensions of argumentation framework $\mathcal{F} = (\mathcal{A}, \mathcal{R})$. Informally speaking, $\succeq$ generalizes stable semantics. Formally, from the fact that for any $\mathcal{E} \subseteq \mathcal{A}$ is holds that ($\mathcal{E}$ is a maximal element wrt $\succeq$ iff $\mathcal{E} \in \text{Ext}(\mathcal{F})$), Theorem 1 implies that three items of that theorem must be verified by $\succeq$.

Proof of Theorem 4

- Let $\mathcal{E} \succeq_g \mathcal{E}'$. This means that $\mathcal{E} \in \mathcal{CF}(\mathcal{T})$. If $\mathcal{E}' \notin \mathcal{CF}(\mathcal{T})$, then from Postulate 1, $\mathcal{E} \succeq \mathcal{E}'$. We study the case when $\mathcal{E}' \in \mathcal{CF}(\mathcal{T})$. From Postulate 2, we have $\mathcal{E} \succeq \mathcal{E}'$ iff $\mathcal{E} \setminus \mathcal{E}' \succeq \mathcal{E}' \setminus \mathcal{E}$. From Definition 6 and Postulate 4, $\mathcal{E} \setminus \mathcal{E}' \succeq \mathcal{E}' \setminus \mathcal{E}$. Thus, $\mathcal{E} \succeq \mathcal{E}'$.
- If $\mathcal{E}, \mathcal{E}' \notin \mathcal{CF}(\mathcal{T})$ then, Definition 7 implies $\mathcal{E} \succeq_s \mathcal{E}'$. Case $\mathcal{E} \notin \mathcal{CF}(\mathcal{T})$, $\mathcal{E}' \in \mathcal{CF}(\mathcal{T})$ is not possible because of Postulate 1. If $\mathcal{E} \in \mathcal{CF}(\mathcal{T})$, $\mathcal{E}' \notin \mathcal{CF}(\mathcal{T})$, then from Definition 7, $\mathcal{E} \succeq_s \mathcal{E}'$. In the non-trivial case, when $\mathcal{E}, \mathcal{E}' \in \mathcal{CF}(\mathcal{T})$, from Postulate 2, $\mathcal{E} \setminus \mathcal{E}' \succeq \mathcal{E}' \setminus \mathcal{E}$. Suppose that $\neg(\mathcal{E} \setminus \mathcal{E}' \succeq_s \mathcal{E}' \setminus \mathcal{E})$. Now, Definition 7 implies $(\exists x' \in \mathcal{E}' \setminus \mathcal{E})(\nexists x \in \mathcal{E} \setminus \mathcal{E}')$ s.t. $((x, x') \in >) \vee ((x, x') \in \mathcal{R} \wedge (x', x) \notin >)$. From this fact and Postulate 3, it holds that $\neg(\mathcal{E} \setminus \mathcal{E}' \succeq \mathcal{E}' \setminus \mathcal{E})$. Contradiction.

Proof of Theorem 5 Since both relations $\succeq$ and $\succeq_g$ verify Postulates 1, 2, 3 and 4, then from Theorem 2, $\text{Ext}_{\succeq}(\mathcal{T}) = \text{Ext}_{\succeq_g}(\mathcal{T})$. This means that it is sufficient to prove that $\mathcal{E} \in \text{Ext}_{\succeq_g}(\mathcal{T})$ iff the two conditions of theorem are satisfied.

$\Rightarrow$ Let $\mathcal{E} \in \text{Ext}_{\succeq_g}(\mathcal{T})$. Since $\mathcal{E}$ is a pref-extension, according to Property 1, $\mathcal{E} \in \mathcal{CF}(\mathcal{T})$. Let $x' \in \mathcal{A} \setminus \mathcal{E}$. We supposed that $(\nexists a \in \mathcal{A})$ s.t. $(a, a) \in \mathcal{R}$, so it must be that $\{x'\}$ is conflict-free. Since $\mathcal{E} \in \text{Ext}_{\succeq_g}(\mathcal{T})$, it holds that $\mathcal{E} \succeq_g \{x'\}$. Since $\mathcal{E}$ and $\{x'\}$ are conflict-free, Definition 6 implies $(\exists x \in \mathcal{E})$ s.t. $(((x, x') \in \mathcal{R} \wedge (x', x) \notin >) \vee ((x', x) \in \mathcal{R} \wedge (x, x') \in >))$.

$\Leftarrow$ Let $\mathcal{E}$ be conflict-free set and let $(\forall x' \in \mathcal{A} \setminus \mathcal{E}) \ (\exists x \in \mathcal{E})$ s.t. $(((x, x') \in \mathcal{R} \wedge (x', x) \notin >) \vee ((x', x) \in \mathcal{R} \wedge (x, x') \in >))$. Let us prove that $\mathcal{E} \in \text{Ext}_{\succeq_g}(\mathcal{T})$.

- Since $\mathcal{E} \in \mathcal{CF}(\mathcal{T})$ then for every non conflict-free set $\mathcal{E}'$ it holds that $\mathcal{E} \succeq_g \mathcal{E}'$.
- Let $\mathcal{E}' \subseteq \mathcal{A}$ be an arbitrary conflict-free set of arguments. If $\mathcal{E}' \subseteq \mathcal{E}$, the second condition of theorem is trivially satisfied. Else, let $x' \in \mathcal{E}' \setminus \mathcal{E}$. From what we supposed, we have that $(\exists x \in \mathcal{E} \setminus \mathcal{E}')$ s.t. $((x, x') \in \mathcal{R} \wedge (x', x) \notin >)$ or $((x', x) \in \mathcal{R} \wedge (x, x') \in >)$. Thus, $\mathcal{E} \succeq_g \mathcal{E}'$.

From those two items, we have that $\mathcal{E} \in \text{Ext}_{\succeq_g}(\mathcal{T})$.

Proof of Theorem 6 Since both relations $\succeq$ and $\succeq_g$ verify Postulates 1, 2, 3 and 4, then from Theorem 2, $\text{Ext}_{\succeq}(\mathcal{T}) = \text{Ext}_{\succeq_g}(\mathcal{T})$. This means that it is sufficient to prove that $\mathcal{E} \in \text{Ext}_{\succeq_g}(\mathcal{T})$ iff $\mathcal{E} \in \text{Ext}((\mathcal{A}, \mathcal{R}'))$. Note also that $\mathcal{E} \in \mathcal{CF}(\mathcal{T})$ iff $\mathcal{E}$ is conflict-free in $(\mathcal{A}, \mathcal{R}')$. Thus, we will simply use the notation $\mathcal{E} \in \mathcal{CF}$ to refer to both of those cases since they coincide.

$\Rightarrow$ Let $\mathcal{E} \in \text{Ext}_{\succeq_g}(\mathcal{T})$. From Theorem 5, $\mathcal{E} \in \mathcal{CF}$ and $(\forall x' \in \mathcal{A} \setminus \mathcal{E}) \ (\exists x \in \mathcal{E})$ s.t. $(((x, x') \in \mathcal{R} \wedge (x', x) \notin >) \vee ((x', x) \in \mathcal{R} \wedge (x, x') \in >))$. This means that $(\forall x' \in \mathcal{A} \setminus \mathcal{E}) \ (\exists x \in \mathcal{E})$ s.t. $(x, x') \in \mathcal{R}'$. In other words, $\mathcal{E} \in \text{Ext}((\mathcal{A}, \mathcal{R}'))$.

$\Leftarrow$ Let $\mathcal{E} \in \text{Ext}((\mathcal{A}, \mathcal{R}'))$. Trivially, $\mathcal{E} \in \mathcal{CF}$. Let $\mathcal{E}' \subseteq \mathcal{A}$. If $\mathcal{E}' \notin \mathcal{CF}$, then $\mathcal{E} \succeq \mathcal{E}'$. Else, let $\mathcal{E}' \in \mathcal{CF}$. Since $\mathcal{E} \in \text{Ext}((\mathcal{A}, \mathcal{R}'))$, then $(\forall x' \in \mathcal{A} \setminus \mathcal{E})(\exists x \in \mathcal{E})(x, x') \in \mathcal{R}'$. This is equivalent to $(\forall x' \in \mathcal{A} \setminus \mathcal{E})$ $(\exists x \in \mathcal{E})$ s.t. $(((x, x') \in \mathcal{R} \wedge (x', x) \notin >) \vee ((x', x) \in \mathcal{R} \wedge (x, x') \in >))$. Trivially, $(\forall x' \in \mathcal{E}' \setminus \mathcal{E})$ $(\exists x \in \mathcal{E} \setminus \mathcal{E}')$ s.t. $(((x, x') \in \mathcal{R} \wedge (x', x) \notin >) \vee ((x', x) \in \mathcal{R} \wedge (x, x') \in >))$. That means that $\mathcal{E} \in \text{Ext}_{\succeq}(\mathcal{T})$.

Computational Models of Argument
P. Baroni et al. (Eds.)
IOS Press, 2010
doi:10.3233/978-1-60750-619-5-51

Goal Selection
in Argumentation Processes

A Formal Model of Abduction in Argument Evaluation Structures

Stefan BALLNAT [1] and Thomas F. GORDON [2]

Fraunhofer FOKUS, Berlin

Abstract. When argumentation is conceived as a kind of *process*, typically a dialogue, for reasoning rationally with limited resources under conditions of incomplete and inconsistent information, arguers need heuristics for controlling the search for arguments to put foward, so as to move from stage to stage in the process in an efficient, goal-directed way. For this purpose, we have developed a formal model of abduction in argument evelution structures. An argument evaluation structure consists of the arguments of a stage, assumptions about audience and an assignment of proof standards to issues. A derivability relation is defined over argument evaluation structures for the literals 'in' a stage. Literals which are not derivable in a stage are 'out'. Abduction is defined as a relation between an argument evaluation structure and sets of literals, called 'positions', which, when the assumptions are revised to include the literals of the position, would make a goal literal in or out, depending of the standpoint of the agent. Soundness, minimiality, consistency and completeness properties of the abduction relation are proven. A heuristic cost function estimating how difficult it is to find or construct arguments pro a literal in the domain can be used to order positions and literals within positions. We compare our work to abduction in propositional logic, in particular the Assumption-Based Truth Maintenance System (ATMS).

Keywords. Abduction, Argumentation, Argument Evaluation, Dialogues, Heuristics, Process Models, Proof Standards, Relevance

1. Introduction

We view argumentation as a kind of process for reasoning rationally about problems which are not well-formed or semi-decidable with incomplete or inconsistent information and limited computational resources [1,2]. Persuasion dialogues [3] between a proponent and respondent about some claim or thesis are the prototypical type of argumentation process, but argumentation processes in our conception are not restricted to dialogues, in their usual sense as conversations between two or more persons.[3]

---

[1] stefan.ballnat@fokus.fraunhofer.de

[2] thomas.gordon@fokus.fraunhofer.de

[3] Dialogues in philosophy and AI are often generalized to cover as well the reasoning processes of single agents, switching between pro and con roles. Presumably most if not all argumentation processes can be viewed as dialogues in this generalized sense.

Figure 1 shows a simple argumentation process, where an *agent* is preparing his case, to be presented later to the audience, by constructing arguments from information found using some *information service*.

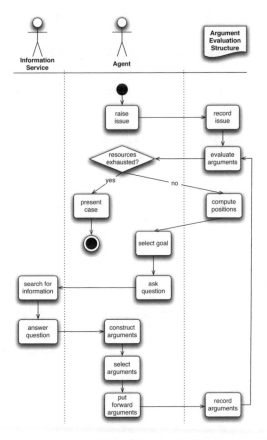

Figure 1. A Simple Argumentation Process

Arguments are put forward, recorded and evaluated in an *argument evaluation structure*, taking into consideration applicable *proof standards* [4,5,6] and assumptions about the *audience*. The agent needs to formulate some kind of impression of his audience, in order to avoid expending resources trying to prove propositions which the audience would accept without proof and also to select arguments which are likely to be persuasive.

Each time through the loop, if resources remain, the agent will use the argument evaluation structure to abduce alternative *positions*, where, similar to [7], a position is a set of propositions which, if added to the assumptions, would make the main issue provable (in) or not provable (out), depending of the standpoint of the agent. From these alternative positions, a subgoal is then selected to work on next, taking into consideration the estimated cost of proving each proposition of a position.

Our focus here is on the task of selecting the next goal to work on. This is an essential, central task of all argumentation processes. An agent cannot argue well without some means of efficiently choosing subgoals which are likely to lead to arguments which are effective for helping to resolve the main issue in a favorable way, given the agent's standpoint.

For the purpose of supporting goal selection, this paper presents a formal model of abduction in argument evaluation structures. Abduction has several meanings in logic. It can mean a method for inferring explanations of observations, but we are using the term by analogy to a more formal meaning, where abduction is one of three kinds of inference relations, together with deduction and induction.

The rest of the paper is organized as follows. The next section presents the formal model. This is followed with a section presenting an example illustrating the model. The paper closes with a discussion of related and possible future work.

2. The Formal Model

The model of goal selection builds on our prior work on argument evaluation structures [5,6]. To make this paper self-contained, we begin by summarizing this prior work.

We begin with the concept of an argument. Informally, an argument is a structure linking a set of premises to a conclusion. Some of the critical questions of the argumentation scheme used to construct the argument are modeled as exceptions of the argument.

Definition 1 (argument) *Let $\mathcal{L}$ be a propositional language. An **argument** is a tuple $\langle P, E, c \rangle$ where $P \subset \mathcal{L}$ are its **premises**, $E \subset \mathcal{L}$ are its **exceptions** and $c \in \mathcal{L}$ is its **conclusion**. For simplicity, c and all members of P and E must be literals, i.e. either an atomic proposition or a negated atomic proposition. Let p be a literal. If p is c, then the argument is an argument **pro** p. If p is the complement of c, then the argument is an argument **con** p.*

Arguments do not need to be deductively valid. For example, premises needed to make the argument deductively valid can be left implicit. (Such arguments are called 'enthymemes'.) An argument is dialectically valid only if it furthers the goals of the argumentation process [3]. One way to assess the dialectically validity of an argument is to check whether it is an instance of an argumentation scheme which is accepted by the procedural rules (protocol) of the particular argumentation process in the problem domain.

Argumentation is viewed as a process. To fully model different kinds of proof burdens, it is useful to divide the process into three phases, an open, argumentation and closing phase and to distinguish between claimed and questioned propositions. But for our purposes here these details are not necessary.

Definition 2 (argumentation process) *An **argumentation process** is a sequence of **stages** where each stage is a set of arguments. In every chain of arguments, $a_1, \ldots a_n$, constructable from the arguments in a stage by linking the conclusion of an argument to a premise or exception of another argument, a conclusion of an argument a_i may not be a premise or exception of an argument a_j, if $j < i$. A set of arguments which violates this condition is said to contain a* cycle *and a set of arguments which complies with this condition is called* cycle-free.

Notice that arguments both pro and con some proposition can be included in the arguments of a stage without causing a cycle.

Next we need a structure for evaluating arguments, to assess the acceptability of propositions at issue. As in value-based argumentation frameworks [8,9] arguments are evaluated with respect to assumptions about an *audience*.

Definition 3 (audience) *An* audience *is a structure* $\langle \Phi, f \rangle$, *where* $\Phi \subset \mathcal{L}$ *is a consistent set of literals assumed to be acceptable by the audience and f is a partial function mapping arguments to real numbers in the range* $0.0 \ldots 1.0$, *representing the relative weights assumed to be assigned by the audience to the arguments.*

An argument evaluation structure associates an audience with a stage of process and assigns proof standards to issues, providing a basis for evaluating the acceptability of propositions to this audience.

Definition 4 (argument evaluation structure) *An* **argument evaluation structure** *is a tuple* $\langle \Gamma, \mathcal{A}, g \rangle$, *where* Γ *is a stage in a argumentation process,* $\mathcal{A}$ *is an audience and g is a total function mapping propositions in* $\mathcal{L}$ *to their applicable proof standards in the process. A* **proof standard** *is a function mapping tuples of the form* $\langle p, \Gamma, \mathcal{A} \rangle$ *to the Boolean values true and false, where p is a literal in* $\mathcal{L}$.

Given an argument evaluation structure, the acceptability of a proposition is defined by its proof standard.

Definition 5 (acceptability) *Let* $\mathcal{S} = \langle \Gamma, \mathcal{A}, g \rangle$ *be an argument evaluation structure, where* $\mathcal{A} = \langle \Phi, f \rangle$. *A literal p is* **acceptable** *in* $\mathcal{S}$ *if and only if* $g(p)(p, \Gamma, \mathcal{A})$ *is true.*

Derivability in an argument evaluation structure can then be defined as a kind of nonmonotonic inference relation as follows:

Definition 6 (derivability) *Let* $\mathcal{S} = \langle \Gamma, \mathcal{A}, g \rangle$ *be an argument evaluation structure, where* $\mathcal{A} = \langle \Phi, f \rangle$. *A literal p is* **in** *S, denoted* $(\Gamma, \Phi) \vdash_{f,g} p$, *if and only if*

- $p \in \Phi$ *or*
- $(\neg p \notin \Phi$ *and p is acceptable in* $S)$

Otherwise p is **out**, *denoted* $(\Gamma, \Phi) \nvdash_{f,g} p$.

Obviously much of the work of argument evaluation has been delegated to the proof standards. All the proof standards we have defined make use of the concept of argument applicability, so let us define this concept first.

Definition 7 (argument applicability) *Let* $\mathcal{S} = \langle \Gamma, \mathcal{A}, g \rangle$ *be an argument evaluation structure. An argument* $\langle P, E, c \rangle$ *is* **applicable** *in this argument evaluation structure if and only if*

- *the argument is a member of* Γ, *the arguments of the stage*
- *every proposition* $p \in P$ *is in*
- *every proposition* $p \in E$ *is out*

In [6] we defined five proof standards, most of them modeling legal proof standards: 1) scintilla of the evidence, 2) preponderance of the evidence, 3) clear and convincing evidence, 4) beyond a reasonable doubt and 5) dialectical validty. To illustrate proof standards we present here the definition of two of these standards, dialectical validity and preponderance.

Definition 8 (dialectical validity) *Let* $\langle \Gamma, \mathcal{A}, g \rangle$ *be an argument evaluation structure and let p be a literal in $\mathcal{L}$. $dv(p, \Gamma, \mathcal{A}) = true$ if and only if there is at least one applicable argument pro p in Γ and no applicable argument con p in Γ.*

Definition 9 (preponderance of the evidence) *Let* $\langle \Gamma, \mathcal{A}, g \rangle$ *be an argument evaluation structure and let p be a literal in $\mathcal{L}$. $pe(p, \Gamma, \mathcal{A}) = true$ if and only if*

- *there is at least one applicable argument pro p in Γ and*
- *the maximum weight assigned by the audience $\mathcal{A}$ to the applicable arguments pro p is greater than the maximum weight of the applicable arguments con p.*

Given these preliminaries we can now turn to our primary task, of defining abduction and computing goals. We begin by the defining the *labels* of literals and arguments in an argument evaluation structure, where each label is a propositional formula. Each literal has two labels. The labels express conditions which, if accepted by the audience, would make the literal in or, respectively, out. Similarly, arguments also have two labels, expressing conditions which, if accepted by the audience, would make the argument applicable or, respectively, not applicable.

The base case in the definition of the labels of literals covers the case where the literal is assumed to have been accepted or rejected by the audience. If however the literal has not been assumed to have been accepted or rejected by the audience, then the label is a function of the proof standard assigned to the literal.

Definition 10 (literal labels) *Let $\mathcal{S} = \langle \Gamma, \mathcal{A}, g \rangle$ an argument evaluation structure with $\mathcal{A} = \langle \Phi, f \rangle$. The* in *and* out *labels of a literal p are defined as:*

- $in\text{-}label(p, \mathcal{S}) := \begin{cases} \top & if\ p \in \Phi \\ p & if\ \neg p \in \Phi \\ ps\text{-}in\text{-}label(p, \mathcal{S}) & otherwise \end{cases}$

- $out\text{-}label(p, \mathcal{S}) := \begin{cases} \neg p & if\ p \in \Phi \\ \top & if\ \neg p \in \Phi \\ ps\text{-}out\text{-}label(p, \mathcal{S}) & otherwise \end{cases}$

where the helping functions ps-in-label and ps-out-label are defined as follows:

- $ps\text{-}in\text{-}label(p, \mathcal{S}) := \begin{cases} dv\text{-}in\text{-}label(p, \mathcal{S}) & if\ g(p) = dv \\ ba\text{-}in\text{-}label(p, \mathcal{S}) & if\ g(p) = pe \end{cases}$

- $ps\text{-}out\text{-}label(p, \mathcal{S}) := \begin{cases} dv\text{-}out\text{-}label(p, \mathcal{S}) & if\ g(p) = dv \\ ba\text{-}out\text{-}label(p, \mathcal{S}) & if\ g(p) = pe \end{cases}$

To save space, the definitions of ps-in-label and ps-out-label handle only the two proof standards defined above, preponderance of evidence and dialectical validity, but they can be extended in a straightforward manner to handle other proof standards.

Before defining the labeling functions for these two specific proof standards we first define argument labels. Using the definition of argument applicability, the in-label of arguments is the conjunction of all in-labels of its premises and of all the out-labels of its exceptions. The out-label of an argument is simply the negation of its in-label, where the negation of a literal's in-label is the literal's out-label and vice versa, not the negation of the literal represented by the in-label.

Definition 11 (argument labels) *Let $S = \langle \Gamma, \mathcal{A}, g \rangle$ be an argument evaluation structure and $a = \langle P, E, c \rangle \in \Gamma$ be an argument. We define the **argument labels** for a as follows:*

- $in\text{-}label(a, S) := \bigwedge_{p \in P} in\text{-}label(p, S) \wedge \bigwedge_{e \in E} out\text{-}label(e, S)$
- $out\text{-}label(a, S) := \bigvee_{p \in P} out\text{-}label(p, S) \vee \bigvee_{e \in E} in\text{-}label(e, S)$

Next, we present the labeling functions for the two proof standards, using the argument labels, beginning with dialectical validity. The in-label for a literal assigned the dialectical validity standard is defined as the conjunction of the out-labels of all its con-arguments and the disjunction of the in-labels of all its pro-arguments. We also add the literal itself as a disjunct to the label in order to later enable goals to be derived for all literal nodes in an argument graph and not just leaves. Notice that the dialectical validity out-label is almost the negation of its in-label.

Definition 12 (dialectical validity label) *Let $S = \langle \Gamma, \mathcal{A}, g \rangle$ be an argument evaluation structure and $p \in \mathcal{L}$ a literal. The **dialectical validity label** for p in S is defined as follows:*

- $dv\text{-}in\text{-}label(p, S) := (\bigvee_{a \in Pro} in\text{-}label(a, S) \wedge \bigwedge_{a \in Con} out\text{-}label(a, S)) \vee p$
- $dv\text{-}out\text{-}label(p, S) := \bigwedge_{a \in Pro} out\text{-}label(a, S) \vee \bigvee_{a \in Con} in\text{-}label(a, S) \vee \neg p$

where Pro and Con denote the sets of pro- and con-arguments for p in Γ.

Coming to the second proof standard, preponderance of the evidence, we must consider the weights of the arguments. The label of a literal assigned this standard is the disjunction of the in-labels of all its pro-arguments (assuring the existence of an applicable pro-argument) combined with the conjunction of the out-labels of all its con-arguments with greater or equal weight (assuring all applicable con-arguments have less weight). We again add the literal itself to the label. For the out-label we again turn the tables and require that either every pro-argument be not applicable or that there exist an applicable con-argument of greater or equal weight.

Definition 13 (preponderance label) *Let $S = \langle \Gamma, \mathcal{A}, g \rangle$ be an argument evaluation structure and $p \in \mathcal{L}$ a literal. The **preponderance label** for p in S is defined as follows:*

- $ba\text{-}in\text{-}label(p, S) := (\bigvee_{a \in Pro} [in\text{-}label(a, S) \wedge \bigwedge_{\substack{b \in Con, \\ f(a) \leq f(b)}} out\text{-}label(b, S)]) \vee p$

- $ba\text{-}out\text{-}label(p, \mathcal{S}) := (\bigwedge_{a \in Pro} [out\text{-}label(a, \mathcal{S}) \vee \bigvee_{\substack{b \in Con, \\ f(a) \leq f(b)}} in\text{-}label(b, \mathcal{S})]) \vee \neg p$

where Pro and Con denote the sets of pro and con arguments for p in Γ.

It is easy to see that the out-label of a literal is in general not the same as the in-label of the literal's complement. To make this clear, consider a small example of an argument evaluation structure $\mathcal{S}$ with just one literal q, no arguments and no assumptions for the audience. No matter what proof standard is assigned to q we obtain out-label$(q, \mathcal{S}) = \top \vee \neg q$ for the out-label whereas the in-label for the complement of q is in-label$(\neg q, \mathcal{S}) = \neg q$.

Labels for further proof standards can be defined similarly.

A label of a statement is transformed into a set of positions by first reducing the label to minimal disjunctive normal form and then interpreting the clauses of the formula as alternative positions consisting of the corresponding literals.

Definition 14 (position sets) *Let l be a label of a literal p in an argument evaluation structure $\mathcal{S}$. Let $\lambda_l = C_1 \vee \ldots \vee C_n$ be a formula equivalent to l in minimal disjunctive normal form. We define the **position set** of the label, denoted $ps(l)$, as follows: $ps(l) = \{gl_{C_i} \mid 1 \leq i \leq n\}$ where $gl_{C_i} = \{L_{ij} \mid 1 \leq j \leq m\}$ for $C_i = L_{i1} \wedge \ldots \wedge L_{im}$*

Abduction is defined as a relation between an argument evaluation structure and a position, which holds if adding the literals of the position to the assumptions about the audience would make a goal literal in or out, depending of the standpoint of the agent.

Definition 15 (abduction) *Let $\mathcal{S}$ be an argument evaluation structure and let $p \in \mathcal{L}$ be a literal. We define two abductive inference relations, $\Vdash_{in}$ and $\Vdash_{out}$ as follows.*

- $(p, \mathcal{S}) \Vdash_{in} \Delta$ *if and only if* $\Delta \in ps(in\text{-}label(p, \mathcal{S}))$
- $(p, \mathcal{S}) \Vdash_{out} \Delta$ *if and only if* $\Delta \in ps(out\text{-}label(p, \mathcal{S}))$

We have proved that these abduction relations are sound, minimal, consistent and complete with respect to the underlying derivability inference relation. There is space only to present sketches of the proofs of these properties here. The full proofs are available in a technical report [10].

First we need to take care of a technical issue, namely aggregating two positions in such a way that the literals of one position replace the complementary literals of the other position. We need this operator to revise the assumptions the agent makes about literals accepted by the audience after persuading the audience to accept a position.

Definition 16 (assumption revision) *Let Φ be the set of literals assumed to be accepted by the audience and let Δ be a position which the agent wants to persuade the audience to accept. The **revised assumptions** about the audience are $\Phi \uplus \Delta = \{L \mid L \in \Delta \vee (L \in \Phi \wedge \neg L \notin \Delta)\}$*

By soundness, we mean that revising the assumptions about the audience to include the literals of a position makes the issue in or out in the resulting argument evaluation structure, depending on whether the agent is interested in proving or disproving the literal at issue. This is the most important property, because it assures the agent that persuading the audience to accept the literals of a position should be effective in persuading the audience to accept the agent's standpoint with respect to the literal at issue.

Theorem 1 (soundness) *Let* $\mathcal{S} = \langle \Gamma, \mathcal{A}, g \rangle$ *be an argument evaluation structure with an audience* $\mathcal{A} = \langle \Phi, f \rangle$. *Let* $p \in \mathcal{L}$ *be a literal and* Δ *be a position. The following statements hold:*

- $(p, \mathcal{S}) \Vdash_{in} \Delta \Rightarrow (\Gamma, \Phi \uplus \Delta) \vdash_{f,g} p$
- $(p, \mathcal{S}) \Vdash_{out} \Delta \Rightarrow (\Gamma, \Phi \uplus \Delta) \nvdash_{f,g} p$

The proof is straight-forward because we defined the statement and argument labels on the basis of the acceptability and applicability definitions. Assumption revision preserves the consistency of the assumptions of the audience.

Theorem 2 (minimality) *Let* $\mathcal{S} = \langle \Gamma, \mathcal{A}, g \rangle$ *be an argument evaluation structure and* $p \in \mathcal{L}$ *be a literal. For all* Δ_1 *and* Δ_2, *if* $(p, \mathcal{S}) \Vdash_{in} \Delta_1$ *and* $(p, \mathcal{S}) \Vdash_{in} \Delta_2$ *or if* $(p, \mathcal{S}) \Vdash_{out} \Delta_1$ *and* $(p, \mathcal{S}) \Vdash_{out} \Delta_2$, *then* $\Delta_1 \not\subset \Delta_2$.

Minimality follows from the use of minimal disjunctive normal form to transform labels into position sets.

Theorem 3 (consistency) *Let* $\mathcal{S} = \langle \Gamma, \mathcal{A}, g \rangle$ *be an argument evaluation structure,* $p \in \mathcal{L}$ *a literal and* Δ *a position. If* $(p, \mathcal{S}) \Vdash_{in} \Delta$ *or* $(p, \mathcal{S}) \Vdash_{out} \Delta$ *then* Δ *is a consistent set of literals in classical propositional logic.*

Consistency follows from the use of minimal disjunctive normal form to transform the label of an issue into a position set, since the literal of the issue is added as a disjunct of the formula.

Finally, completeness guarantees that all possible positions enabling the agent to prove or disprove the literal at issue are abduced.

Theorem 4 (completeness) *Let* $\mathcal{S} = \langle \Gamma, \mathcal{A}, g \rangle$ *be an argument evaluation structure with an audience* $\mathcal{A} = \langle \Phi, f \rangle$. *Let* $p \in \mathcal{L}$ *be a literal and* Δ *a position. The following statements hold:*

- $(\Gamma, \Phi \uplus \Delta) \vdash_{f,g} p \Rightarrow \exists \Delta' \subseteq \Delta.(p, \mathcal{S}) \Vdash_{in} \Delta'$
- $(\Gamma, \Phi \uplus \Delta) \nvdash_{f,g} p \Rightarrow \exists \Delta' \subseteq \Delta.(p, \mathcal{S}) \Vdash_{out} \Delta'$

The proof of completeness concentrates on the definition of literal labels, in particular its use of specific labels for each proof standard, to show that all sets of assumptions that make a literal acceptable (or not acceptable) are covered by its labels.

Having defined positions, we can heuristically select a subset of the positions, as part of a reasoning strategy, using a total order on positions. Such an order could be defined, e.g., using an estimate of the cost of proving each literal. This would enable the agent to select one of the cheapest positions to work on next.

Definition 17 (preferred positions) *Let* S *be an argument evaluation structure,* $p \in \mathcal{L}$ *a literal at issue, and* $\leq$ *a total order on positions. A position* Δ *for proving* p, *where* $(p, \mathcal{S}) \Vdash_{in} \Delta$, *is a **preferred position** if and only if* $\forall \Delta'.(p, \mathcal{S}) \Vdash_{in} \Delta' \Rightarrow \Delta \leq \Delta'$.

Similarly, if Δ *is a position for disproving* p, *where* $(p, \mathcal{S}) \Vdash_{out} \Delta$, *then* Δ *is a preferred position if and only if* $\forall \Delta'.(p, \mathcal{S}) \Vdash_{out} \Delta' \Rightarrow \Delta \leq \Delta'$.

Finally, we define two relevance properties of arguments. Intuitively, an argument is relevant for a proving a goal literal, if its conclusion is a member of a position for this literal. The stronger relevance property requires in addition that the conclusion of the argument be a member of a preferred position.

Definition 18 (relevance) *Let* $a = \langle P, E, c \rangle$ *an argument and* $\mathcal{S}$ *be an argument evaluation structure and* $p \in \mathcal{L}$ *be an issue.*

- *The argument* a *is **weakly relevant** in* $\mathcal{S}$ *if and only if* $\exists \Delta.[(p, \mathcal{S}) \Vdash_{in} \Delta \vee (p, \mathcal{S}) \Vdash_{out} \Delta] \wedge c \in \Delta$
- *The argument* a *is **strongly relevant** in* $\mathcal{S}$ *if and only if* c *is a member of a preferred position for* p *in* $\mathcal{S}$.

This notion of relevance is analogous to Sperber and Wilson's [11], who define relevance by two conditions. Weak relevance is similar to the first condition, requiring "large effects" on the "context". The context is here the argument evaluation structure; the large effect of proving a weakly relevant statement is to bring the agent "one step closer" to proving or disproving the main issue. Strongly relevance is analogous to the second condition of "small effort" because we take the total order on the positions into account to select the "cheapest" position.

3. Example

Figure 2 shows a small argument graph for which it is already hard to see what goal to choose next. In the argument evaluation structure $\mathcal{S} = \langle \Gamma, \mathcal{A}, g \rangle$ we have the stage $\Gamma = \{a_1, a_2, a_3, a_4, a_5\}$ and the audience $\mathcal{A} = \langle \Phi, f \rangle$, where $\Phi = \{\neg q, s, \neg t, \neg v, w\}$ and the weights assigned by f are as shown in the figure. The proof standard assigned by g is preponderance of the evidence for all literals. The issue is p.

In the figure, literals are shown in boxes and arguments in circles. The weights assigned by the audience to arguments are shown above the circles. Pro arguments are displayed with filled arrowheads; con arguments with open arrowheads. Premises are visualized by a solid line linking a proposition to an argument; Exceptions are visualized with dashed lines. By convention, only positive literals are displayed in boxes. Negative conclusions are visualized using con arguments. Negated premises are shown with a cross mark on the link between the premise and the argument, but there is no example in this figure. Literals assumed to have been accepted by the audience are shown with a check mark in the lower left corner of the box for the literal; literals assumed to have been rejected by the audience are shown with an X mark. (Acceptance of a literal P implies rejection of $\neg P$ and vice versa.)

Computing the labels for p and its complement we obtain:

- in-label$(p, \mathcal{S}) = (\top \wedge q \wedge (\top \vee v \vee t \vee \neg r)) \vee p \equiv q \vee p$
- out-label$(p, \mathcal{S}) = \neg s \vee \top \vee (u \wedge \top \wedge \top) \vee r \vee \neg p \equiv \top$
- in-label$(\neg p, \mathcal{S}) = (u \wedge \top \wedge \top) \vee r \vee \neg p \equiv u \vee r \vee \neg p$
- out-label$(\neg p, \mathcal{S}) = \top \vee v \vee t \vee \neg r \vee p \equiv \top$

The four corresponding sets of positions are:

- $\{q\}$ and $\{p\}$ if the agent wants to prove p

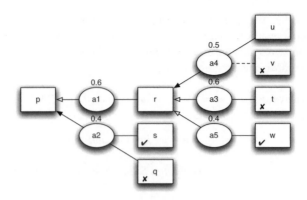

Figure 2. An example argument graph

- {} if the agent wants to disprove p.
- $\{u\}$, $\{r\}$ and $\{\neg p\}$ if the agent wants to prove $\neg p$.
- {} if the agent wants to disprove $\neg p$.

So, if the agent is interested in disproving p or $\neg p$ no further arguments should be needed to persuade the audience, since neither literal currently satisfies its proof standard. If however the agent wants to prove p, he can either try to construct another argument pro p or arguments sufficient to make q acceptable to the audience. The agent need not be concerned yet about rebutting the argument con p because it is not currently applicable.

4. Discussion

We have presented a model of abduction in an argument evaluation structure which enables a principled method for selecting goals to work on in argumentation processes, to help agents to construct arguments in an efficient, goal-directed way.

Again, we are using the term abduction by analogy to its formal meaning, as one of three kinds of inference relations, together with deduction and induction, not as a method for inferring causes of observations. The role of deduction is played by the derivability relation in our system, which infers literals which 'in' an argument evaluation structure. Induction in our system would be the inference of further arguments which would make a goal statement in if the arguments are added to the stage of the argument evaluation structure. Finally, abduction in this framework is the inference of literals which, if added to the set of literals assumed to be accepted by the audience, would make a goal literal derivable (in) in the argument evaluation structure.

This work was inspired by de Kleer's Assumption-Based Truth Maintenance System (ATMS) [12,13] and its application to controlling problem-solvers [14]. Whereas the ATMS performs abduction in a subset of classical propositional logic, our system performs abduction in an argumentation evaluation structure, which is a kind of non-monotonic inference relation. Junker showed how to use the ATMS for nonmonotonic reasoning [15], but the semantics of his inference relation does not meet the requirements we have identified for evaluating arguments, such as support for proof standards. Rather than trying to develop a new argument evaluation structure which meets our requirements on top of the ATMS, we have opted to develop a model of abduction sufficient for the purpose of goal selection on top of our existing Carneades argument evaluation structure.

The definition of relevance presented here continues our prior work on modeling issues [16,17,18], where issues are understood as relevant, contested statements. The details of these models vary considerably, as a consequence of their very different underlying formal models of argument. This line of work is not related to relevance logic, which aims to weaken classical logic to avoid claimed paradoxes of material and strict implication.

Assumption revision in our system is much simpler than general belief revision [19], since all of the formulas in a set of assumptions have been restricted to literals.

In [20], decision theory was used to select arguments to put forward in a formal argument game, making use of the expected utility of an argument, the probability of an argument being successful and the costs of the argument. Although this work is quite different from ours, since our aim is to help agents to select goals to work on, by searching for information which can be used to construct arguments about the goal, not to select from amoung a fixed set of arguments, both have in common the goal of helping agents with strategic issues when making moves in argumentation processes and both use cost functions for this purpose. An issue for further research is whether expected utilities, as well as costs, could be useful in our context.

Computational complexity issues may be interesting to investigate. The problem of computing positions is presumably intractable, since it depends on the reduction of formulas to their minimal disjunctive normal form, which is itself in general an intractable problem. However it may be possible to reformulate our problem to make it less complex, by using the structure of argument graphs to incrementally construct labels in minimal disjunctive normal form, rather than reducing them to this normal form after they have been constructed.

The model of abduction presented here has been implemented in the latest version of our Carneades[4] argumentation software. Our next steps include the development of pilot applications, as part of an effort to validate the model.

References

[1]   Horst W.J. Rittel and Melvin M. Webber. Dilemmas in a general theory of planning. *Policy Science*, 4:155–169, 1973.

[2]   Ronald P. Loui. Process and policy: resource-bounded non-demonstrative reasoning. *Computational Intelligence*, 14:1–38, 1998.

[3]   Douglas Walton. *The New Dialectic: Conversational Contexts of Argument*. University of Toronto Press, Toronto; Buffalo, 1998. 24 cm.

[4]   Kathleen Freeman and Arthur M. Farley. A model of argumentation and its application to legal reasoning. *Artificial Intelligence and Law*, 4(3-4):163–197, 1996.

[5]   Thomas F. Gordon, Henry Prakken, and Douglas Walton. The Carneades model of argument and burden of proof. *Artificial Intelligence*, 171(10-11):875–896, 2007.

[6]   Thomas F. Gordon and Douglas Walton. Proof burdens and standards. In Iyad Rahwan and Guillermo Simari, editors, *Argumentation in Artificial Intelligence*, pages 239–260. Springer-Verlag, Berlin, Germany, 2009.

[7]   Adam Wyner, Tom van Engers, and Anthony Hunter. Working on the argument pipeline: Through flow issues between natural language argument, instantiated arguments, and argumentation frameworks. In

---

[4]http://carneades.berlios.de

Proceedings of the Workshop on Computational Models of Natural Argument, Lisbon, Portugal, August 2010. to appear.

[8]   Trevor Bench-Capon. Persuasion in practical argument using value-based argumentation frameworks. *Journal of Logic and Computation*, 13(3):429–448, 2003.

[9]   Trevor J.M. Bench-Capon, Sylvie Doutre, and Paul E. Dunne. Audiences in argumentation frameworks. *Artificial Intelligence*, 171(42-71), 2007.

[10]   Stefan Ballnat and Thomas F. Gordon. Goal selection in argumentation processes – a formal model of abduction in argument evaluation structures. Technical report, Fraunhofer FOKUS, Berlin, Germany, 2010.

[11]   Dan Sperber and Deirde Wilson. *Relevance: Communication and cognition*. Blackwell Publishers, 1995.

[12]   Johan de Kleer. An assumption-based TMS. *Artificial Intelligence*, 28(2):127–162, 1986.

[13]   J. De Kleer. A general labeling algorithm for assumption-based truth maintenance. In *Proceedings of the 7th national conference on artificial intelligence*, pages 188–192, San Francisco, California, USA, 1988. Morgan Kaufmanns Publishers.

[14]   Johann De Kleer. Problem solving with the ATMS. *Artificial Intelligence*, 28(2):197–224, 1986.

[15]   Ulrich Junker. A correct non-monotonic ATMS. In *Proceedings of the 11th International Joint Conference on Artificial Intelligence*, pages 1049–1054. Morgan Kaufmann Publishers, Detroit, Michigan, 1989.

[16]   Thomas F. Gordon. Issue spotting in a system for searching interpretation spaces. In *Proceedings of the Second International Conference on Artificial Intelligence and Law*, pages 157–164. Association for Computing Machinery (ACM), New York, 1989.

[17]   Thomas F. Gordon. An abductive theory of legal issues. *International Journal of Man-Machine Studies*, 35:95–118, 1991.

[18]   Thomas F. Gordon. *The Pleadings Game; An Artificial Intelligence Model of Procedural Justice*. Springer, New York, 1995. Book version of 1993 Ph.D. Thesis; University of Darmstadt.

[19]   Carlos E. Alchourron, Peter Gärdenfors, and David Makinson. On the logic of theory change: Partial meet contraction and revision functions. *The Journal of Symbolic Logic*, 50(2):510–530, June 1985.

[20]   Régis Riverert, Henry Prakken, Antonio Rotolo, and Giovanni Sartor. Heuristics in argumentation: A game-theoretical investigation. In Philippe Besnard, Sylvie Doutre, and Anthony Hunter, editors, *Compuational Models of Argument, Proceedings of COMMA 2008*, pages 324–335, 2008.

Computational Models of Argument
P. Baroni et al. (Eds.)
IOS Press, 2010
doi:10.3233/978-1-60750-619-5-63

On Extension Counting Problems in Argumentation Frameworks

Pietro BARONI [a] Paul E. DUNNE [b] Massimiliano GIACOMIN [a]

[a] *Dip. Ingegneria dell'Informazione, University of Brescia, Italy.*
[b] *Department of Computer Science, The University of Liverpool, U.K.*

Abstract. We consider the problem of *counting* (without explicitly enumerating) extensions prescribed by multiple-status semantics in abstract argumentation. Referring to Dung's traditional stable and preferred semantics and to the recently introduced resolution-based grounded semantics (GR^*), we show that in general extension counting is computationally hard (actually #P–complete). We then identify non-trivial topological classes of argumentation frameworks where extension counting is tractable. In particular we show, by providing and analyzing the relevant algorithms, that in symmetric argumentation frameworks counting GR^* extensions is tractable (but is still hard for stable and preferred estensions), while counting is tractable for all the considered semantics in tree-like argumentation frameworks.

Keywords. Computational properties of argumentation; Argumentation Frameworks; Extension-based semantics; Counting.

1. Introduction

The abstract model of argumentation by Dung [12] is now established as a basis for much research on computational aspects of argumentation, see, e.g. the survey of Bench-Capon and Dunne [7]. In Dung's approach the basic abstraction is an *argumentation framework* (AF) comprising a pair $\langle \mathcal{A}, \mathcal{R} \rangle$ wherein $\mathcal{A}$ represents a set of abstract atomic *arguments* and $\mathcal{R} \subseteq \mathcal{A} \times \mathcal{A}$ defines the so-called *attack relation*. This relation describes a view of two arguments being "incompatible" in the sense that if $\langle x, y \rangle \in \mathcal{R}$ then the argument x *attacks* the argument y. A major emphasis of subsequent study has been in defining diverse formalisms describing intuitive ideas of "collection of acceptable arguments". Typically such proposals are formulated in terms of some predicate $\sigma : 2^{\mathcal{A}} \to \langle \top, \bot \rangle$ so that acceptable collections are those $S \subseteq \mathcal{A}$ for which $\sigma(S)$ holds. In addition to the canonical forms presented in [12] – grounded, admissible, preferred and stable sets – a number of alternatives have been put forward: a detailed review of such argumentation semantics may be found in the survey of Baroni and Giacomin [4].

The *resolution-based* family of semantics presented by Baroni and Giacomin [3] differs from such proposals in being *parametric*. That is, given any semantics σ, the *resolution–based* σ semantics is well-defined. In particular the resolution-based *grounded* semantics is known to have a number of important properties not only in terms of its semantic characteristics, as shown in [3], but also with respect to its computational tractability [1]. Given the likely intractability of key decision problems in all but the grounded semantics of [12] – a review of computational complexity results in this field is presented in Dunne and Wooldridge [14] – the fact that a number of standard questions may be efficiently decided within resolution-based grounded semantics provides a powerful supporting case for its adoption.

Our principal interest in this paper concerns a natural problem which has been largely neglected in the study of multiple status semantics, i.e. those σ for which $|\{\, S \subseteq \mathcal{A} \, : \, \sigma(S)\}|$ may be greater than 1: that of *counting* the number of distinct subsets that meet the criteria of a given semantics. Although a number of *enumeration* techiques have been studied e.g. [10,9] so that the counting problem is solved as a side-effect of enumerating all extensions of a particular type, little direct study of counting *without* explicit enumeration has been undertaken. Direct counting techniques may be useful to get a rough assessment of the uncertainty inherent to an argumentation framework w.r.t. a given semantics, to assess the proportion of acceptance of an argument with respect to the total number of extensions, or to be exploited as a bound for an enumeration algorithm.

The present work aims at filling the above mentioned gap by analyzing basic computational properties and providing algorithms for the extension counting problem. The paper is organised as follows. In Section 2 we provide background concepts concerning abstract argumentation frameworks and their semantics. In particular we introduce preferred ($\mathcal{PR}$), stable ($\mathcal{ST}$), and resolution-based grounded (GR^*) semantics and recall several useful properties and technical results available in the literature. Our main results are presented in Section 3: specifically we prove that the problem of counting the number of extensions in the general case is computationally hard in the sense of being #P–complete for $\mathcal{PR}$, $\mathcal{ST}$ and GR^*. In contrast to this negative result, however, we present polynomial time[1] methods for two classes of AFs. For *symmetric* AFs counting turns out to be tractable for GR^* (but still intractable for $\mathcal{PR}$ and $\mathcal{ST}$) while for "tree-like" AFs counting is tractable for all $\mathcal{PR}$, $\mathcal{ST}$ and GR^*. Conclusions and directions for further work are outlined in Section 5.

2. Basic concepts

The following concepts were introduced in Dung [12].

Definition 1 *An* argumentation framework *(AF) is a pair* $\mathcal{G} = \langle \mathcal{A}, \mathcal{R} \rangle$ *(also denoted as* $\mathcal{G}(\mathcal{A}, \mathcal{R})$*), in which* $\mathcal{A}$ *is a finite set of* arguments *and* $\mathcal{R} \subseteq \mathcal{A} \times \mathcal{A}$ *is the* attack *relationship for* $\mathcal{G}$*. A pair* $\langle x, y \rangle \in \mathcal{R}$ *is referred to as 'y is attacked by x' or 'x attacks y'. For S, T subsets of arguments in the* AF $\mathcal{G}(\mathcal{A}, \mathcal{R})$*, we say that* $t \in T$ *is attacked by S – written* $attacks(S, t)$ *– if there is some* $s \in S$ *such that* $\langle s, t \rangle \in \mathcal{R}$*. An argument* x *is* self-attacking *if* $\langle x, x \rangle \in \mathcal{R}$*. We denote by* S^+ *the set of all arguments* $t \in \mathcal{A}$ *for which* $attacks(S, t)$ *and by* S^- *the set of those arguments* t *such that* $attacks(t, S)$*. For* $x \in \mathcal{A}$*, every argument* y *in* $\{x\}^- \cap \{x\}^+$ *is involved in a* mutual attack *with* x*, i.e.* $\{\langle x, y \rangle, \langle y, x \rangle\} \subseteq \mathcal{R}$*. The restriction of* $\mathcal{G}(\mathcal{A}, \mathcal{R})$ *to a set of arguments* $S \subseteq \mathcal{A}$*, denoted as* $\mathcal{G} \downarrow_S$*, is defined as* $\mathcal{G} \downarrow_S = \langle S, \mathcal{R} \cap (S \times S) \rangle$*.*

An argumen $x \in \mathcal{A}$ is acceptable *with respect to a set* $S \subseteq \mathcal{A}$ *if* $\forall y \in \{x\}^-$ $\exists z \in S \cap \{y\}^-$*. The function* $\mathcal{F}_\mathcal{G} : 2^\mathcal{A} \to 2^\mathcal{A}$ *which, given a set* $S \subseteq \mathcal{A}$*, returns the set*

---

[1]We recall that in the case of *function* problems, such as counting structures, "polynomial" means in the number of bits needed to encode *both* input instances and results.

of the acceptable arguments with respect to S, is called the characteristic function *of $\mathcal{G}$.*
We will also use the notation $\mathcal{F}_{\mathcal{G}}^{0}(S) \triangleq \mathcal{F}_{\mathcal{G}}(S)$ *and for* $i > 0$, $\mathcal{F}_{\mathcal{G}}^{i}(S) = \mathcal{F}_{\mathcal{G}}(\mathcal{F}_{\mathcal{G}}^{i-1}(S))$.

It is proved in [12], that in every finite AF $\mathcal{G}(\mathcal{A}, \mathcal{R})$, $\mathcal{F}_{\mathcal{G}}^{j}(\emptyset)$ has a least-fixed point, i.e. there is a finite value, i for which $\mathcal{F}_{\mathcal{G}}^{i}(\emptyset) = \mathcal{F}_{\mathcal{G}}^{i+k}(\emptyset)$ for all $k \geq 0$. The *grounded extension* of $\mathcal{G}$ is the (unique) subset of $\mathcal{A}$ given by $\min_{i \geq 0 \,:\, \mathcal{F}_{\mathcal{G}}^{i}(\emptyset) = \mathcal{F}_{\mathcal{G}}^{i+1}(\emptyset)} \mathcal{F}_{\mathcal{G}}^{i}(\emptyset)$. We use $\mathcal{E}_{GR}(\mathcal{G})$ to denote the set whose (sole) element is the subset of $\mathcal{A}$ forming the *grounded extension* of $\mathcal{G}$. For $\mathcal{G}(\mathcal{A}, \mathcal{R})$ with $\mathcal{E}_{GR}(\mathcal{G}) = \{S\}$, we will denote as $\text{CUT}(\mathcal{G})$ the AF with arguments $\mathcal{A}_S = \mathcal{A} \setminus (S \cup S^+)$ and attack relation $\mathcal{R}_S = \mathcal{R} \cap \mathcal{A}_S \times \mathcal{A}_S$.

More generally, given a predicate $\sigma : 2^{\mathcal{A}} \to \langle \top, \bot \rangle$ defining an argumentation semantics via subsets of arguments, we use $\mathcal{E}_{\sigma}(\langle \mathcal{A}, \mathcal{R} \rangle)$ to denote those $S \subseteq \mathcal{A}$ for which $\sigma(S)$ holds in $\langle \mathcal{A}, \mathcal{R} \rangle$, these sets being usually called *extensions* of the relevant argumentation semantics.

We recall first the definitions of traditional Dung's *stable* ($\mathcal{ST}$) and *preferred* ($\mathcal{PR}$) semantics.

Definition 2 *Let $\mathcal{G} = \langle \mathcal{A}, \mathcal{R} \rangle$ be an* argumentation framework. *A set $S \subseteq \mathcal{A}$ is* conflict-free *iff $\not\exists x, y \in S$ such that $\langle x, y \rangle \in \mathcal{R}$. A set $S \subseteq \mathcal{A}$ is* admissible *iff S is conflict-free and $S \subseteq \mathcal{F}_{\mathcal{G}}(S)$. A set $S \subseteq \mathcal{A}$ is a* preferred extension *iff S is a maximal (wrt. $\subseteq$) admissible set. A set $S \subseteq \mathcal{A}$ is a* stable extension *iff S is conflict-free and $S^+ = \mathcal{A} \setminus S$.*

We will denote as $\mathcal{MCF}(\mathcal{G}(\mathcal{A}, \mathcal{R})) \subseteq 2^{\mathcal{A}}$ the set of maximal (w.r.t. inclusion) conflict-free sets of $\mathcal{G}$.

The more recent notion of *resolution-based extension semantics* was introduced by Baroni and Giacomin [3]. Given $\mathcal{G}(\mathcal{A}, \mathcal{R})$, let $M_{\mathcal{G}} \subseteq \mathcal{R}$ be the set of mutual attacks in $\mathcal{G}$ (note that self-attacking arguments are *not* considered to define mutual attacks), i.e. for which (with $x \neq y$) $\langle x, y \rangle \in M_{\mathcal{G}}$ if and only if $\langle y, x \rangle \in M_{\mathcal{G}}$. A (partial) resolution of $\mathcal{G}$ is defined by any subset $\beta \subseteq M_{\mathcal{G}}$ for which *at most one element* of each of the pairs $\langle x, y \rangle$, $\langle y, x \rangle$ is in β. The AF $\mathcal{G}_{\beta}$ arising from the partial resolution β is $\langle \mathcal{A}, \mathcal{R} \setminus \beta \rangle$. A *full resolution* is any partial resolution in which *exactly* one element of each mutual attack occurs, hence the AF $\mathcal{G}_{\gamma}$ arising from any full resolution γ of $\mathcal{G}$ contains no mutually attacking arguments. On this basis, we can now give the definition of *resolution-based grounded semantics* (GR^*).

Definition 3 *Given an* AF $\mathcal{G} = \langle \mathcal{A}, \mathcal{R} \rangle$ *the set of extensions of* resolution-based grounded semantics *is defined as:* $\mathcal{E}_{GR^*}(\mathcal{G}) = \min\{ S \subseteq \mathcal{A} : \mathcal{E}_{GR}(\mathcal{G}_{\beta}) = \{S\}$ *for some full resolution β of $\mathcal{G}\}$ (where* min *is with respect to $\subseteq$).*

We will also use the graph theoretical notion of strongly-connected component (SCC). Given an AF $\mathcal{G}(\mathcal{A}, \mathcal{R})$ the set of its SCCs (denoted as $\text{SCC}(\mathcal{G})$) consists of the equivalence classes induced by the relation $\rho(x, y)$ defined over $\mathcal{A} \times \mathcal{A}$ so that $\rho(x, y)$ holds if and only if $(x = y)$ *or* there are directed paths from x to y *and* from y to x in $\mathcal{G}(\mathcal{A}, \mathcal{R})$.

Let $\{\mathcal{A}_1, \ldots, \mathcal{A}_k\}$ be the SCCs of $\mathcal{G}(\mathcal{A}, \mathcal{R})$ and, for $i = 1 \ldots k$, $\mathcal{C}_i = \mathcal{G} \downarrow_{\mathcal{A}_i}$. The partial order $\prec$ over $\mathcal{C} = \{\mathcal{C}_1, \ldots, \mathcal{C}_k\}$ is defined as $(\mathcal{C}_i \prec \mathcal{C}_j)$ if and only if $(i \neq j)$ and $\exists x \in \mathcal{A}_i$, $y \in \mathcal{A}_j$ for which there is a directed path from x to y. With a little abuse of terminology we will refer to the pair $(\mathcal{C}, \preceq)$ as SCC *decomposition*.

A specific class of SCCs will play an important role in the paper.

Definition 4 *Let* $\mathcal{G}(\mathcal{A}, \mathcal{R})$ *be an* AF *with* SCC *decomposition* $(\mathcal{C}, \preceq)$. *We define the* minimal relevant components *of* $\mathcal{G}$, *denoted* $\mathcal{MR}(\mathcal{G})$, *to be those* $\mathcal{C}_i$ *such that* $\neg(\mathcal{C}_j \prec \mathcal{C}_i)$ *for all* $j \neq i$ *and* $\mathcal{C}_i$ *contains no directed cycle of three or more arguments* nor any *self-attacking argument.*

Notice that if $\mathcal{C}_i \in \mathcal{MR}(\mathcal{G})$ then its cycles can only be formed by *mutually attacking arguments*.

As a matter of fact, mutual attacks will play a significant role in this paper, hence a specific terminology is needed. An AF $\mathcal{G}(\mathcal{A}, \mathcal{R})$ is *symmetric* iff $\langle x, y \rangle \in \mathcal{R} \Leftrightarrow \langle y, x \rangle \in \mathcal{R}$. An AF $\mathcal{G}(\mathcal{A}, \mathcal{R})$ is *SCC-symmetric* iff for any $\mathcal{A}_i \in \mathrm{SCC}(\mathcal{G})$ $\mathcal{G}{\downarrow}_{\mathcal{A}_i}$ is symmetric.

Different semantics have been shown to be in agreement, i.e. to prescribe exactly the same extensions, on symmetric [11] and SCC-symmetric [2] argumentation frameworks[2].

Proposition 1 *Let* $\mathcal{G}(\mathcal{A}, \mathcal{R})$ *be an* AF. *If* $\mathcal{G}$ *is symmetric then* $\mathcal{E}_{ST}(\mathcal{G}) = \mathcal{E}_{PR}(\mathcal{G}) = \mathcal{MCF}(\mathcal{G})$. *If* $\mathcal{G}$ *is SCC-symmetric then* $\mathcal{E}_{ST}(\mathcal{G}) = \mathcal{E}_{PR}(\mathcal{G})$.

3. Intractability results for counting in multiple–status semantics

To begin we show that, in general, counting extensions for GR^*, $\mathcal{PR}$, $\mathcal{ST}$ is computationally hard, i.e. #P–complete[3]. We denote by $Count_\sigma(\mathcal{G})$ the *function* (as opposed to decision) problem of determining $|\mathcal{E}_\sigma(\mathcal{G})|$.

Theorem 1 $Count_{GR^*}$ *is #P–complete.*

Proof: That $Count_{GR^*} \in$ #P is immediate from [1, Thm. 3] which shows that deciding $S \in \mathcal{E}_{GR^*}(\mathcal{G})$ can be done in polynomial time. To establish #P–hardness we use a reduction from the problem of counting satisfying assignments of a given CNF formula, $\varphi(Z_n)$ over the variables $\{z_1, \ldots, z_n\}$. Given an instance $\varphi(Z_n)$ with clauses $\{C_1, C_2, \ldots, C_m\}$ form the instance $\langle \mathcal{A}_\varphi, \mathcal{R}_\varphi \rangle$ having[4]

$$\mathcal{A}_\varphi = \{\varphi, \psi\} \cup \{C_j : 1 \leq j \leq m\} \cup \{z_i, \neg z_i : 1 \leq i \leq n\}$$

$$\mathcal{R}_\varphi = \{\langle C_j, \varphi \rangle : 1 \leq j \leq m\} \cup$$
$$\{\langle z_i, C_j \rangle : z_i \text{ occurs in } C_j\} \cup$$
$$\{\langle \neg z_i, C_j \rangle : \neg z_i \text{ occurs in } C_j\} \cup$$
$$\{\langle z_i, \neg z_i \rangle, \langle \neg z_i, z_i \rangle : 1 \leq i \leq n\} \cup$$
$$\{\langle \varphi, \psi \rangle, \langle \psi, \varphi \rangle\}$$

The #P–hardness of $Count_{GR^*}$ follows from the fact that

$$Count_{GR^*}(\langle \mathcal{A}_\varphi, \mathcal{R}_\varphi \rangle) = 2^n + |\{\alpha \in \langle \top, \bot \rangle^n : \varphi(\alpha)\}|$$

which in turn allows the number of satisfying assignment of $\varphi(Z_n)$ to be calculated given $Count_{GR^*}(\langle \mathcal{A}_\varphi, \mathcal{R}_\varphi \rangle)$.

---

[2]In [12] an AF where stable and preferred extensions coincide is called *coherent*.

[3]This class of function problems was introduced by Valiant [17]. We refer the reader to Papadimitriou [16, Chap. 18] for background.

[4]Modulo the additional argument ψ and its mutual attack on φ this is identical to the reduction of [1, Thm. 4].

To prove this, notice that each satisfying assignment, α, yields two distinct $S_\alpha \in \mathcal{E}_{GR^*}(\langle \mathcal{A}_\varphi, \mathcal{R}_\varphi \rangle)$ via

$$S_\alpha^1 = \{\varphi\} \cup \{ z_i \; : \; z_i = \top \text{ under } \alpha \} \cup \{\neg z_i \; : \; z_i = \bot \text{ under } \alpha\}$$
$$S_\alpha^2 = \{\psi\} \cup \{ z_i \; : \; z_i = \top \text{ under } \alpha \} \cup \{\neg z_i \; : \; z_i = \bot \text{ under } \alpha\}$$

On the other hand, every unsatisfying assignment, β, yields only

$$S_\beta = \{\psi\} \cup \{ z_i \; : \; z_i = \top \text{ under } \alpha \} \cup \{\neg z_i \; : \; z_i = \bot \text{ under } \alpha\} \cup$$
$$\cup \{C_j \; : \; C_j \text{is false under } \beta\}$$

Taking into account that the total number of (either satisfying or not satisfying) assignments to Z_n is 2^n, it is easy to see that the desired result holds. □

Theorem 2 $Count_{ST}$ *and* $Count_{\mathcal{PR}}$ *are* #P–*complete.*

Proof: Given the relatively simple structure of the argumentation framework used in Thm. 1, it is easy to see that all extensions S_α^1, S_α^2, S_β are stable (they attack all elements not included in them) and that no other stable extensions exist in this case. It follows that stable extensions coincide with GR^* extensions and $Count_{ST}$ is #P–complete. It is also easy to see that this argumentation framework is SCC-symmetric, hence by Proposition 1 preferred extensions coincide with stable extensions and $Count_{\mathcal{PR}}$ is #P–complete. □

4. Tractability of counting in restricted frameworks

In this section we examine cases for which $|\mathcal{E}_\sigma(\mathcal{G})|$ can be computed efficiently (for selected extension semantics σ).

4.1. Counting in symmetric frameworks

The fact that $Count_\sigma$ is computationally hard, i.e. #P–complete, for the class of *symmetric* AFs with $\sigma \in \{ST, \mathcal{PR}\}$ follows immediately from Valiant [18] and Proposition 1.[5] In the case of GR^*, however, we have

Theorem 3 *If $\mathcal{G}$ is a symmetric framework then* $Count_{GR^*}(\mathcal{G})$ *can be computed in polynomial time.*

Before presenting the proof of this result, we recall some standard terminology and properties of trees.

Definition 5 *Let $T(V, E)$ be a tree with vertex set $V = \{v_1, \ldots, v_n\}$. The* orientation *of T with root $v \in V$, assigns a direction $d(\{x, y\}) \in \{\langle x, y \rangle, \langle y, x \rangle\}$ to every $\{x, y\} \in E$ according to the following scheme:*

    a. $W \; := V \setminus \{v\}$ *and* $U := \{v\}$

---

[5] Valiant's result is phrased in terms of counting "maximal cliques" (in undirected graphs), however these are exactly the same as maximal conflict-free sets in the dual graph, i.e. that formed by including $\{\langle x, y \rangle, \langle y, x \rangle\}$ if and only if $\{x, y\}$ is not an edge.

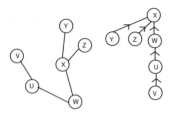

Figure 1. An orientation of T with root x

b. **while** $W \neq \emptyset$ **do**

   b1. *Choose any $w \in W$ for which $\exists u \in U$ having $\{w, u\} \in E$.*
   b2. $d(\{w, u\}) := \langle w, u \rangle$
   b3. $W := W \setminus \{w\}; U := U \cup \{w\}$

Note that an orientation is actually an argumentation framework. The orientation of T with root v is denoted as $T_v = (V, E(T_v))$ where $E(T_v) = \{d(\{x, y\}) \mid x, y \in V \wedge x \neq y\}$. For an orientation T_x the notation $n(T_x)$ refers to the set of its nodes.

Given an orientation T_x of $T(V, E)$ and a node $y \in V$, the vertices $w \in V$ such that $\langle w, y \rangle \in E(T_v)$ are called children *of y in the orientation T_x and are denoted as $child(T_x, y) \subseteq V$. In a similar manner, the* grandchildren *of y, denoted $grchild(T_x, y)$ are $\cup_{z \in child(T_x, y)} child(T_x, z)$. For any $y \in V$, the orientation corresponding to the subtree of T_x with root y is denoted as T_x^y. The set of vertices in T_x which have no children are called the* leaf vertices *(w.r.t. T_x) and denoted as $Leaf(T_x)$.*

An example orientation is given in Fig. 1.
The following functions will play a key role in our construction:

$$\mu(T_x^y) = |\{ S \subseteq n(T_x^y) : S \in \mathcal{MCF}(T_x^y)\}|$$
$$\nu(T_x^y) = |\{ S \subseteq n(T_x^y) \setminus \{y\} : S \in \mathcal{MCF}(T_x^y)\}|$$

An important relation between $\mu()$ and $\nu()$ is demonstrated by Wilf in [19].

Fact 1 *Given an orientation T_x of $T(V, E)$, for all $y \in V$ it holds that*

$$\mu(T_x^y) = \begin{cases} 1 \text{ if } child(T_x, y) = \emptyset \\ 2 \text{ if } child(T_x, y) \neq \emptyset \text{ and } grchild(T_x, y) = \emptyset \\ \nu(T_x^y) + \prod_{z \in grchild(T_x, y)} \mu(T_x^z) \text{ otherwise} \end{cases}$$

$$\nu(T_x^y) = \begin{cases} 0 \text{ if } child(T_x, y) = \emptyset \\ 1 \text{ if } child(T_x, y) \neq \emptyset \text{ and } grchild(T_x, y) = \emptyset \\ \prod_{z \in child(T_x, y)} \mu(T_x^z) - \prod_{z \in child(T_x, y)} \nu(T_x^z) \text{ otherwise} \end{cases}$$

Note that from the relationships in Fact 1 we have a straightforward dynamic programming algorithm for counting maximal conflict-free sets in trees which completes in polynomial (in fact linear) time in $|\mathcal{A}|$.

We also recall some properties of the set $\mathcal{E}_{GR^*}(\mathcal{G})$ demonstrated in [1].

Fact 2

   a. *For any $\mathcal{G}(\mathcal{A}, \mathcal{R})$, $\mathcal{E}_{GR}(\mathcal{G}) = \mathcal{E}_{GR^*}(\mathcal{G})$ if and only if $\mathcal{MR}(\text{CUT}(\mathcal{G})) = \emptyset$.*

b. *For any* $\mathcal{G}(\mathcal{A},\mathcal{R})$ $|\mathcal{E}_{GR^*}(\mathcal{G})| = |\mathcal{E}_{GR^*}(\text{CUT}(\mathcal{G}))|$.

c. *For any* $\mathcal{G}(\mathcal{A},\mathcal{R})$ *consisting of a unique* SCC*:*

- $\mathcal{E}_{GR^*}(\mathcal{G}) = \mathcal{MCF}(\mathcal{G})$ *if* $\mathcal{G}$ *satisfies the conditions for minimal relevant components stated in Definition 4;*
- $\mathcal{E}_{GR^*}(\mathcal{G}) = \{\emptyset\}$ *otherwise.*

Using Facts 1 and 2 we obtain the proof of Thm. 3.

Proof: (of Thm. 3) First note that from the fact that $\mathcal{G}$ (and hence also $\text{CUT}(\mathcal{G})$) is symmetric it follows that $\mathcal{G}$ (and analogously $\text{CUT}(\mathcal{G})$) consists only of SCCs which are minimal with respect to $\prec$ (i.e. there can not be attacks between arguments belonging to distinct SCCs).

Now from Fact 2(a) $Count_{GR^*}(\mathcal{G}) = 1$ if $\mathcal{MR}(\text{CUT}(\mathcal{G})) = \emptyset$ which can be checked in polynomial time, as shown in [1, Cor. 3]. Otherwise, if $\mathcal{MR}(\text{CUT}(\mathcal{G})) \neq \emptyset$, let $(\mathcal{C},\preceq)$ be the SCC decomposition of $\text{CUT}(\mathcal{G})$. We show that $Count_{GR^*}(\mathcal{G}) = Count_{GR^*}(\text{CUT}(\mathcal{G})) = \prod_{\mathcal{C}_i \in \mathcal{C}} Count_{GR^*}(\mathcal{C}_i) = \prod_{M \in \mathcal{MR}(\text{CUT}(\mathcal{G}))} Count_{GR^*}(M) = \prod_{M \in \mathcal{MR}(\text{CUT}(\mathcal{G}))} |\mathcal{MCF}(M)|$. The first equality follows from Fact 2(b). For the second one observe that, as noted above, the SCCs of $\text{CUT}(\mathcal{G})$ are not connected each other. It is then easy to see, through Definition 3, that any set resulting from the union of one GR^* extension taken from each $\mathcal{C}_i$ is a GR^* extension of $\mathcal{G}$ and viceversa (formally this derives from the property of *directionality* of GR^* [3]). From Fact 2(c) it follows that for each $\mathcal{C}$ in the SCC decomposition of $\text{CUT}(\mathcal{G})$ $Count_{GR^*}(\mathcal{C}) \neq 1$ only for elements of $\mathcal{MR}(\text{CUT}(\mathcal{G}))$ (hence the third equality) and that their GR^* extensions coincide with their maximal conflict-free sets (hence the fourth equality). Finally, observe that since each component M contains neither cycles with more than two arguments nor self-attacks then the *undirected* graph defined from M is a tree. Hence counting maximal conflict-free sets of each element M of $\mathcal{MR}(\text{CUT}(\mathcal{G}))$ can be done in polynomial time using Wilf's algorithm.   □

4.2. Counting in tree-like frameworks

In this subsection we focus on a specific class of frameworks called "tree-like" and show that, in this context, counting extensions is tractable for GR^*, $\mathcal{PR}$ and $\mathcal{ST}$.

Definition 6 *An argumentation framework,* $\mathcal{G}(\mathcal{A},\mathcal{R})$ *is tree-like iff it satisfies both of the following conditions:*

a. *the* undirected *graph* $G(V,E)$ *with* $V = \mathcal{A}$ *and* $E = \{\{p,q\} \ : \ \langle p,q \rangle \in \mathcal{R}$ *or* $\langle q,p \rangle \in \mathcal{R}\}$ *is acyclic.*

b. *The* SCC *decomposition* $(\mathcal{C},\prec)$ *of* $\mathcal{G}$ *with* $\mathcal{C} = \{\mathcal{C}_1,\ldots,\mathcal{C}_k\}$, *has exactly one maximal element w.r.t.* $\prec$, *i.e. element* $\mathcal{C}_i$ *for which* $\forall \, \mathcal{C}_j \ (j \neq i) \, \mathcal{C}_j \prec \mathcal{C}_i$.

It turns out that any tree-like framework is SCC-symmetric.

Proposition 2 *If an argumentation framework* $\mathcal{G}(\mathcal{A},\mathcal{R})$ *is tree-like then it is SCC-symmetric.*

Proof: For any arguments x, y belonging to the same SCC of $\mathcal{G}$ and such that $\langle x,y \rangle \in \mathcal{R}$ we want to show that $\langle y,x \rangle \in \mathcal{R}$. Note first that since $\mathcal{G}$ is tree-like, $x \neq y$. Suppose by contradiction that $\langle y, x \rangle \notin \mathcal{R}$: since x and y belong to the same SCC there must be a path from y to x involving at least another element z, but then there is a cycle of at least three elements in $\mathcal{G}$ contradicting the fact that $\mathcal{G}$ is tree-like. □

The following property of tree-like frameworks is important in our approach to computing $Count_{GR^*}(\mathcal{G})$.

Proposition 3 *Let $\mathcal{G}(\mathcal{A}, \mathcal{R})$ be tree-like with SCC decomposition $(\{\mathcal{C}_1, \ldots, \mathcal{C}_k\}, \prec)$ and $\mathcal{C}_{\max}$ be the (unique) maximal element w.r.t. $\prec$. For all $\mathcal{C}_i \in \{\mathcal{C}_1, \ldots, \mathcal{C}_k\} \setminus \{\mathcal{C}_{\max}\}$, $\mathcal{C}_i$ has* exactly *one immediate successor w.r.t $\prec$, i.e. there is a unique element $\mathcal{C}_{succ(i)}$ for which*

$$\mathcal{C}_i \prec \mathcal{C}_{succ(i)} \quad and \quad \forall\, j \neq succ(i) \ (\mathcal{C}_i \prec \mathcal{C}_j \Rightarrow \mathcal{C}_{succ(i)} \prec \mathcal{C}_j)$$

Proof: Suppose by contradiction that $\mathcal{G}$ is tree-like and that some component $\mathcal{C}_i$ has at least two immediate successors, $\mathcal{C}_{i_1}$ and $\mathcal{C}_{i_2}$ say (where $i_i \neq i_2$). Let $\mathcal{C}_{\max}$ be the unique maximal component. Then

$$\mathcal{C}_i \prec \mathcal{C}_{i_1} \prec \mathcal{C}_{\max} \quad and \quad \mathcal{C}_i \prec \mathcal{C}_{i_2} \prec \mathcal{C}_{\max}$$

It is easy to see that according to these conditions, the undirected graph $G(V, E)$ contains a cycle (containing a vertex from each of $\{\mathcal{C}_i, \mathcal{C}_{i_1}, \mathcal{C}_{i_2}, \mathcal{C}_{\max}\}$), contradicting the hypothesis that $\mathcal{G}$ is tree-like. □

The three multiple-status semantics considered in this paper are in agreement in tree-like argumentation frameworks.

Proposition 4 *For any tree-like argumentation framework $\mathcal{G}(\mathcal{A}, \mathcal{R})$, $\mathcal{E}_{\mathcal{PR}}(\mathcal{G}) = \mathcal{E}_{\mathcal{ST}}(\mathcal{G}) = \mathcal{E}_{GR^*}(\mathcal{G})$.*

Proof: $\mathcal{E}_{\mathcal{PR}}(\mathcal{G}) = \mathcal{E}_{\mathcal{ST}}(\mathcal{G})$ follows from $\mathcal{G}$ being SCC-symmetric (Prop. 2) and then from Prop. 1. Let us now show that $\mathcal{E}_{\mathcal{ST}}(\mathcal{G}) = \mathcal{E}_{GR^*}(\mathcal{G})$. First note that since $\mathcal{G}$ is tree-like, the AF $\mathcal{G}_\beta$ arising from any full resolution β of $\mathcal{G}$ is acyclic. It is known [12] that the grounded extension S of any acyclic AF is stable (i.e. attacks all arguments outside it) and clearly this property holds for S also in $\mathcal{G}$, since the attacks in $\mathcal{G}_\beta$ are a subset of those in $\mathcal{G}$. It follows that $\{\ S \subseteq \mathcal{A} \ : \ \mathcal{E}_{GR}(\mathcal{G}_\beta) = \{S\}$ for some full resolution β of $\mathcal{G}\} \subseteq \mathcal{E}_{\mathcal{ST}}(\mathcal{G})$. Since no stable extension can be a proper subset of another one it follows $\{\ S \subseteq \mathcal{A} \ : \ \mathcal{E}_{GR}(\mathcal{G}_\beta) = \{S\}$ for some full resolution β of $\mathcal{G}\} = \min\{\ S \subseteq \mathcal{A} \ : \ \mathcal{E}_{GR}(\mathcal{G}_\beta) = \{S\}$ for some full resolution β of $\mathcal{G}\} = \mathcal{E}_{GR^*}(\mathcal{G})$ and hence $\mathcal{E}_{GR^*}(\mathcal{G}) \subseteq \mathcal{E}_{\mathcal{ST}}(\mathcal{G})$.

To show now that $\mathcal{E}_{\mathcal{ST}}(\mathcal{G}) \subseteq \mathcal{E}_{GR^*}(\mathcal{G})$ note first that for any stable extension E of $\mathcal{G}$ it is easy to identify a full resolution β of $\mathcal{G}$ such that E is a stable extension of $\mathcal{G}_\beta$ (it suffices to resolve any mutual attack involving an element x of E "in favour" of x). Since $\mathcal{G}_\beta$ is acyclic, again E is also the grounded extension of $\mathcal{G}_\beta$, hence $E \in \{\ S \subseteq \mathcal{A} \ : \ \mathcal{E}_{GR}(\mathcal{G}_\beta) = \{S\}$ for some full resolution β of $\mathcal{G}\}$. To show that E is also minimal in this set (and hence $E \in \mathcal{E}_{GR^*}(\mathcal{G})$) suppose by contradiction that it is not, namely that exists $E' \in \mathcal{E}_{GR^*}(\mathcal{G})$ such that $E' \subsetneq E$. From the first part of the proof we know that E' is a stable extension of $\mathcal{G}$ but this is impossible since it is known that no stable extension can be a proper subset of another one. □

To show tractability of $Count_\sigma(\mathcal{G})$ for all $\sigma \in \{GR^*, \mathcal{PR}, \mathcal{ST}\}$ we refer to Algorithm 1 where the following notation is used: as usual $(\mathcal{C}, \prec)$ denotes the SCC decompo-

---

Algorithm 1 $Count_\sigma$ for tree-like $\mathcal{G}(\langle \mathcal{A}, \mathcal{R} \rangle)$ and $\sigma \in \{GR^*, \mathcal{PR}, \mathcal{ST}\}$

1: Compute $\langle \mathcal{C}, \prec \rangle$.
2: **for** Each $\mathcal{C}_i \in \mathcal{C}$ **do**
3:      Mark $\mathcal{C}_i$ as **uncounted**.
4: **end for**
5: **while** $\mathcal{C}_{max}$ is marked **uncounted do**
6:      Choose any $\mathcal{C}_i$ which is uncounted *and* such that every *immediate* predecessor of $\mathcal{C}_i$ under $\prec$ is marked *counted*
7:      **if** $to(i) \neq \emptyset$ **then**
8:          **for** each $x \in to(i)$ **do**
9:              Add to $\mathcal{C}_i$ a child $z(x)$ of x and label $z(x)$ with $\mu(z(x)) = \prod_{y \in \{x\}^- \setminus \mathcal{C}_i} \mu(y)$ and $\nu(z(x)) = \prod_{y \in \{x\}^- \setminus \mathcal{C}_i} \nu(y)$.
10:              Add to $\mathcal{C}_i$ a child $z'(x)$ of $z(x)$ and label $z'(x)$ with $\mu(z'(x)) = \nu(z(x))$ and $\nu(z'(x)) = 0$.
11:              Delete all attackers (and relevant attacks to x) in $\{x\}^- \setminus (\mathcal{C}_i \cup \{z(x)\})$.
12:          **end for**
13:      **end if**
14:      **if** $fr(i) \neq \emptyset$ **then**
15:          $T_p :=$ orientation of $\mathcal{C}_i$ with root the only element p of $fr(i)$.
16:      **else**
17:          $T_p :=$ arbitrary orientation.
18:      **end if**
19:      Label each $v \in T_p$ with $\langle \mu(T_p^v), \nu(T_p^v) \rangle$ using Wilf's algorithm.
20:      Mark $\mathcal{C}_i$ as **counted**.
21:      **if** $\mathcal{C}_i = \mathcal{C}_{max}$ **then**
22:          **return** $\mu(T_p^p)$.
23:      **end if**
24: **end while**

---

sition of $\mathcal{G}$, $\mathcal{C}_i, \mathcal{C}_j$ denote generic elements of $\mathcal{C}$, $\mathcal{C}_{max}$ denotes the element of $\mathcal{C}$ which is maximal with respect to $\prec$ and, given an element x of $\mathcal{A}$, a child of x is an element y which attacks x. Moreover for $\mathcal{C}_i = \langle \mathcal{A}_i, \mathcal{R}_i \rangle$ we denote by $fr(i)$ and $to(i)$ the following sets[6]:

$$fr(i) = \{p \in \mathcal{A}_i \ : \ \exists \, \mathcal{C}_j \ (i \neq j) \text{ and } q \in \mathcal{A}_j \text{ s.t. } \langle p, q \rangle \in \mathcal{R}\}$$
$$to(i) = \{p \in \mathcal{A}_i \ : \ \exists \, \mathcal{C}_j \ (i \neq j) \text{ and } q \in \mathcal{A}_j \text{ s.t. } \langle q, p \rangle \in \mathcal{R}\}.$$

Note that, since $\mathcal{G}$ is tree-like, any $\mathcal{C}_i$ is symmetric and the undirected graph defined from it is a tree: an orientation of $\mathcal{C}_i$ (see lines 15 and 17) is an orientation of such a tree plus the nodes and the edges added in lines 9 and 10 of the algorithm.

Theorem 4 $Count_\sigma(\mathcal{G})$ *is polynomial time computable whenever $\mathcal{G}$ is a tree-like framework and $\sigma \in \{GR^*, \mathcal{PR}, \mathcal{ST}\}$.*

Proof: It is easy to see that Algorithm 1 terminates in polynomial time wrt. $|\mathcal{A}|$. First, the fact that computing the SCC decomposition can be done in linear time is a well-known

---

[6]Note that since $\mathcal{G}$ is tree-like, for any $\mathcal{C}_i$ $fr(i)$ is either empty or a singleton.

result in graph theory. Then, since $\prec$ induces a partial order on SCCs and $\mathcal{G}$ is tree-like, the main while loop and the non-deterministic choice it includes are well-founded: $\mathcal{C}_{max}$ will be necessarily chosen after all other SCCs have been marked. Hence the algorithm terminates after a number of iterations equal to the number of SCCs, in turn bounded by $|\mathcal{A}|$. It is also easy to see that each iteration involves only operations (including runs of Wilf's algorithm) whose execution time is polynomial with respect to $|\mathcal{A}|$.

To show that Algorithm 1 correctly computes $Count_\sigma(\mathcal{G})$ for $\sigma \in \{GR^*, \mathcal{PR}, \mathcal{ST}\}$ we proceed by induction along the SCCs in $\mathcal{C}$, always referring in the following to the original SCCs, i.e. not modified by steps 9 and 10 of the algorithm. Given a set of nodes S contained in a SCC $\mathcal{C}_i$, we will denote as $\mathrm{sccanc}(S)$ the set including S and the nodes of all SCCs $\mathcal{C}_j$, with $j \neq i$, such that there is a directed path from an element of $\mathcal{C}_j$ to an element of S.

As to the basis step, considering an SCC $\mathcal{C}_i$ which is minimal with respect to $\prec$ it is easy to see that Algorithm 1 reduces to an invocation of Wilf's algorithm on a particular orientation of $\mathcal{C}_i$: since the undirected graph defined by $\mathcal{C}_i$ is a tree, by reasoning as in the proof of Theorem 3 it can be seen that the correct $(\mu(), \nu())$ labelling of the chosen root p is obtained, corresponding to $|\mathcal{E}_{GR^*}(\mathcal{G}{\downarrow}_{\mathcal{C}_i})|$ and $|E \in \mathcal{E}_{GR^*}(\mathcal{G}{\downarrow}_{\mathcal{C}_i}) : p \notin E|$, respectively (and the same result holds for preferred and stable extensions by Prop. 4).

As to the inductive step, referring to stable extensions (since this simplifies the proof) suppose that for all the elements $\mathcal{C}_j$ preceding an element $\mathcal{C}_i$ the chosen root for $\mathcal{C}_j$, i.e. $fr(j)$, has been labelled with $\mu(fr(j)) = |\mathcal{E}_{ST}(\mathcal{G}{\downarrow}_{\mathrm{sccanc}(\mathcal{C}_j)})|$ (i.e. the total number of extensions of the sub-tree of SCCs rooted in $\mathcal{C}_j$) and $\nu(fr(j)) = |\{E \in \mathcal{E}_{ST}(\mathcal{G}{\downarrow}_{\mathrm{sccanc}(\mathcal{C}_j)}) : fr(j) \notin E\}|$ (i.e. the number of those extensions not including $fr(j)$). We have then to show that Algorithm 1 produces a correct $(\mu(), \nu())$ labelling of the chosen root p for $\mathcal{C}_i$, i.e. $\mu(p) = |\mathcal{E}_{ST}(\mathcal{G}{\downarrow}_{\mathrm{sccanc}(\mathcal{C}_i)})|$ and $\nu(p) = |\{E \in \mathcal{E}_{ST}(\mathcal{G}{\downarrow}_{\mathrm{sccanc}(\mathcal{C}_i)}) \mid p \notin E\}|$ (in particular this implies that the algorithm returns the correct value when $\mathcal{C}_i = \mathcal{C}_{max}$).

To this purpose we proceed in turn by induction along the arguments of T'_p, i.e. the chosen orientation T_p excluding the arguments added by the algorithm at steps 9 and 10 (notice that T'_p is an orientation such that $n(T'_p) = \mathcal{C}_i$): we prove that the algorithm assigns to each element x of T'_p the label $\mu(x) = |\mathcal{E}_{ST}(\mathcal{G}{\downarrow}_{\mathrm{sccanc}(n(T'^x_p))})|$ and $\nu(x) = |\{E \in \mathcal{E}_{ST}(\mathcal{G}{\downarrow}_{\mathrm{sccanc}(n(T'^x_p))}) \mid x \notin E\}|$ (entailing the desired conclusion for $x = p$). As to the basis step, consider $x \in Leaf(T'_p)$ (in this case $n(T'^x_p) = \{x\}$). If $x \notin to(i)$ then the application of Wilf's algorithm at line 19 correctly returns $\mu(x) = 1$ and $\nu(x) = 0$. In the other case, let $\mathcal{DP}(x)$ denote the set of components $\mathcal{C}_j$ (with $j \neq i$) such that $fr(j)$ attacks x: it can be observed that the total number of stable extensions of $\mathcal{G}{\downarrow}_{\mathrm{sccanc}(\{x\})}$ coincides with the product of the numbers of stable extensions of $\mathcal{G}{\downarrow}_{\mathrm{sccanc}(\mathcal{C}_j)}$ for any $\mathcal{C}_j \in \mathcal{DP}(x)$. In fact, given the tree-like structure of $\mathcal{G}$ the union of any stable extension of $\mathcal{G}{\downarrow}_{\mathrm{sccanc}(\mathcal{C}_j)}$ for any $\mathcal{C}_j \in \mathcal{DP}(x)$ with any other stable extension of $\mathcal{G}{\downarrow}_{\mathrm{sccanc}(\mathcal{C}_j)}$ for any other $\mathcal{C}_j \in \mathcal{DP}(x)$ preserves the properties of being conflict-free and of attacking all elements not included in it. Moreover x can only be added to or attacked by an extension obtained in this way, hence no additional stable extensions arise. In summary, the correct $\mu(x)$ is equal to $\prod_{\mathcal{C}_j \in \mathcal{DP}(x)} \mu(fr(j))$. Moreover, since x is attacked by any $fr(j)$, x is outside all these stable extensions, except those where each of the arguments $fr(j)$ is not present. It follows that the correct $\nu(x)$ is equal to $\prod_{\mathcal{C}_j \in \mathcal{DP}(x)} \mu(fr(j)) - \prod_{\mathcal{C}_j \in \mathcal{DP}(x)} \nu(fr(j))$. Consider now what Algorithm 1 does. It adds to x a child $z(x)$ such that $\mu(z(x)) = \prod_{\mathcal{C}_j \in \mathcal{DP}(x)} \mu(fr(j))$ and $\nu(z(x)) =$

$\prod_{C_j \in \mathcal{DP}(x)} \nu(fr(j))$ and a grandchild $z'(x)$ (child of $z(x)$) such that $\mu(z'(x)) = \nu(z(x))$ and $\nu(z'(x)) = 0$. All attacks to x are then deleted and Wilf's algorithm is applied, in a situation where x has a single child $z(x)$ and a single grandchild $z'(x)$. It follows $\nu(x) = \mu(z(x)) - \nu(z(x)) = \prod_{C_j \in \mathcal{DP}(x)} \mu(fr(j)) - \prod_{C_j \in \mathcal{DP}(x)} \nu(fr(j))$ and $\mu(x) = \nu(x) + \mu(z'(x)) = \prod_{C_j \in \mathcal{DP}(x)} \mu(fr(j)) - \prod_{C_j \in \mathcal{DP}(x)} \nu(fr(j)) + \prod_{C_j \in \mathcal{DP}(x)} \nu(fr(j)) = \prod_{C_j \in \mathcal{DP}(x)} \mu(fr(j))$. Hence the labelling produced by Algorithm 1 is correct.

Consider now an argument $x \in C_i$ such that $child(T'_p, x) \neq \emptyset$, and suppose inductively that for any $v \in child(T'_p, x)$ $\mu(v) = |\mathcal{E}_{ST}(\mathcal{G}{\downarrow}\text{sccanc}(n(T'^v_p)))|$ and $\nu(v) = |\{E \in \mathcal{E}_{ST}(\mathcal{G}{\downarrow}\text{sccanc}(n(T'^v_p))) \mid v \notin E\}|$. If $x \notin to(i)$ then the result follows from the application of Wilf's algorithm, therefore in the following we consider the more interesting case that x receives attacks from other SCCs. With a similar reasoning as above, we can determine first the total number of stable extensions of the subtrees external to C_i directly linked to x, namely the cardinality of set $\mathcal{S} = \{S \in \mathcal{E}_{ST}(\mathcal{G}{\downarrow}\text{sccanc}(\{x\}) \setminus \{x\}))\}$. It can be seen that $|\mathcal{S}| = \mu'(x) = \prod_{y \in \{x\}^- \setminus C_i} \mu(y)$. Similarly one can determine the number $\Gamma(x)$ of these stable extensions which do not attack x, namely the cardinality of set $\mathcal{T} = \{S \in \mathcal{S} \mid \neg attacks(S, x)\}$. It holds that $|\mathcal{T}| = \Gamma(x) = \prod_{y \in \{x\}^- \setminus C_i} \nu(y)$. Now consider each child $v \in child(T'_p, x)$ and the correct value $\nu(x) = |\{E \in \mathcal{E}_{ST}(\mathcal{G}{\downarrow}\text{sccanc}(n(T'^x_p))) \mid x \notin E\}|$, i.e. the number of of stable extensions of the tree rooted in x and such that they do not include x. It holds that $\nu(x) = (\prod_{v \in child(T'_p, x)} \mu(v)) * \mu'(x) - (\prod_{v \in child(T'_p, x)} \nu(v)) * \Gamma(x)$. In fact, every stable extension involving a subtree rooted in any child of x in T'_p can be combined with any stable extension involving a subtree rooted in another child of x in T'_p and with a stable extension of the subtree linked to x with elements outside C_i (this corresponds to the term $(\prod_{v \in child(T'_p, x)} \mu(v)) * \mu'(x)$), preserving the properties of being conflict-free and of attacking all arguments outside it (including x), with the exception of those combinations where no element attacking x is included (this corresponds to the term $(\prod_{v \in child(T'_p, x)} \nu(v)) * \Gamma(x)$). The correct value for $\mu(x)$, i.e. the total number of stable extensions of the tree rooted in x, is then given by $\nu(x)$ plus a term concerning the number of the stable extensions where x is included. As far as the nodes included in C_i are concerned, it can be seen that adding x to any combination of stable extensions taken from each subtree rooted in a grandchild of x yields a conflict-free set attacking all elements in $n(T_x^x)$ not included in it (the number of these sets is $\prod_{v \in grchild(T'_p, x) \cap C_i} \mu(v)$). Moreover each of these sets can be combined with any of the stable extensions of the subtree linked to x and not included in C_i (namely the set $\mathcal{T}$), provided that this stable extension does not attack x (the number of these sets is $\Gamma(x)$). Combining these considerations it turns out that the additional term is given by $(\prod_{v \in grchild(T'_p, x) \cap C_i} \mu(v)) * \Gamma(x)$ and that then $\mu(x) = \nu(x) + (\prod_{v \in grchild(T'_p, x) \cap C_i} \mu(v)) * \Gamma(x)$.

Referring now to Algorithm 1 it can be seen that, in virtue of the replacement carried out in lines 9 and 10, the $\mu(), \nu()$ labelling produced for any node x coincides with the values stated above and therefore is correct. This completes the proof. $\qquad\Box$

5. Conclusions and Further work

In Dung's framework, we have considered the problem of counting extensions prescribed by the main traditional multiple status semantics and a more recent proposal. Although counting is #P–complete for general AFs, we have presented polynomial time solution methods for GR^* in symmetric and for all semantics in "tree-like" AFs. These results provide the basis for a number of directions for future work. One immediate challenge concerns investigating other classes of AFs where counting is tractable for the semantics considered in this paper. Furthermore the analysis of the counting problem might be developed for other multiple status semantics notions such as complete [12], semi-stable [8] or CF2 [5] semantics, and might be extended as well to semantics notions defined for formalisms derived from augmentations of the Dung's framework such as [6,15,13].

References

[1] P. Baroni, P. E. Dunne, and M. Giacomin. Computational properties of resolution-based grounded semantics. In *Proc. 21st IJCAI*, pages 683–689, 2009.
[2] P. Baroni and M. Giacomin. Characterizing defeat graphs where argumentation semantics agree. In *Proc. of ArgNMR, Workshop on Argumentation and Non-Monotonic Reasoning*, pages 33–48, 2007.
[3] P. Baroni and M. Giacomin. Resolution-based argumentation semantics. In *Proc. 2nd Int. Conf. on Computational Models of Argument (COMMA 2008)*, volume 172, pages 25–36, Toulouse, F, 2008.
[4] P. Baroni and M. Giacomin. Semantics of abstract argument systems. In I. Rahwan and G. Simari, editors, *Argumentation in AI*, chapter 2, pages 25–44. Springer-Verlag, 2009.
[5] P. Baroni, M. Giacomin, and G. Guida. SCC-recursiveness: a general schema for argumentation semantics. *Artificial Intelligence*, 168(1-2):165–210, 2005.
[6] T. J. M. Bench-Capon. Persuasion in Practical Argument Using Value-based Argumentation Frameworks. *Journal of Logic and Computation*, 13(3):429–448, 2003.
[7] T. J. M. Bench-Capon and P. E. Dunne. Argumentation in artificial intelligence. *Artificial Intelligence*, 171:619–641, 2007.
[8] M. Caminada. Semi-stable semantics. In P. E. Dunne and T. J. M. Bench-Capon, editors, *Proc. 1st Int. Conf. on Computational Models of Argument*, volume 144 of *FAIA*, pages 121–130. IOS Press, 2006.
[9] M. Caminada. An algorithm for computing semi-stable semantics. In *Proc. of ECSQARU 2007, 9th European Conference on Symbolic and Quantitative Approaches to Reasoning with Uncertainty*, pages 222–234, Hammamet, Tunisia, 2007.
[10] C. Cayrol, S. Doutre, and J. Mengin. On Decision Problems related to the preferred semantics for argumentation frameworks. *Journal of Logic and Computation*, 13(3):377–403, 2003.
[11] S. Coste-Marquis, C. Devred, and P. Marquis. Symmetric argumentation frameworks. In L. Godo, editor, *Proc. 8th European Conf. on Symbolic and Quantitative Approaches to Reasoning With Uncertainty (ECSQARU)*, volume 3571 of *LNAI*, pages 317–328. Springer-Verlag, 2005.
[12] P. M. Dung. On the acceptability of arguments and its fundamental role in nonmonotonic reasoning, logic programming, and N-person games. *Artificial Intelligence*, 77:321–357, 1995.
[13] P. E. Dunne, A. Hunter, P. McBurney, S. Parsons, and M. Wooldridge. Inconsistency tolerance in weighted argument systems. In *Proc. 8th AAMAS*, pages 851–858, 2009.
[14] P. E. Dunne and M. Wooldridge. Complexity of abstract argumentation. In I. Rahwan and G. Simari, editors, *Argumentation in AI*, chapter 5, pages 85–104. Springer-Verlag, 2009.
[15] S. Modgil. Reasoning about preferences in argumentation frameworks. *Artificial Intelligence*, 173(9–10):901–934, 2009.
[16] C. H. Papadimitriou. *Computational Complexity*. Addison-Wesley, 1994.
[17] L. G. Valiant. The complexity of computing the permanent. *Theor. Comp. Sci.*, 8:189–201, 1979.
[18] L. G. Valiant. The complexity of enumeration and reliability problems. *SIAM J. Comput.*, 8:410–421, 1979.
[19] H. S. Wilf. The number of maximal independent sets in a tree. *SIAM J. Alg. Disc. Meth.*, 7:125–130, 1986.

Computational Models of Argument
P. Baroni et al. (Eds.)
IOS Press, 2010
doi:10.3233/978-1-60750-619-5-75

Expanding Argumentation Frameworks: Enforcing and Monotonicity Results

Ringo Baumann and Gerhard Brewka

Universität Leipzig, Augustusplatz 10-11, 04109 Leipzig, Germany
{baumann, brewka}@informatik.uni-leipzig.de

Abstract. This paper addresses the problem of revising a Dung-style argumentation framework by adding finitely many *new* arguments which may interact with *old* ones. We study the behavior of the extensions of the augmented argumentation frameworks, taking also into account possible changes of the underlying semantics (which may be interpreted as corresponding changes of proof standards). We show both possibility and impossibility results related to the problem of enforcing a desired set of arguments. Furthermore, we prove some monotonicity results for a special class of expansions with respect to the cardinality of the set of extensions and the justification state.

Keywords. argumentation theory, belief revision, dynamics of argumentation

1. Introduction

Argumentation theory has become a popular research area in Artificial Intelligence (a very good overview is given in [1]). Argumentation frameworks (AFs), as introduced in Dung's seminal paper [2], are set-theoretically just directed graphs whose nodes are arguments and whose edges represent conflicts between them. There is a rich variety of semantics, which define the acceptable sets of arguments, so-called *extensions*. The motivations of these semantics range from the desired treatment of specific examples to fulfilling a number of abstract principles. A number of papers are engaged with the investigation of the properties and interrelations between the different semantics. Baroni and Giacomin [3] introduced several general criteria for comparing and evaluating semantics.

Dung's argumentation frameworks are static: they specify sets of acceptable arguments given a fixed set of arguments and attacks among them. Since argumentation is a dynamic process, it is natural to investigate the dynamic behavior of AFs. More precisely, we are interested in how extensions of an AF change when new arguments and/or attack relations are added. This task can be subsumed under the term *argument revision*[1]. Since arguments in the end support propositions, it can also be viewed as a particular form of belief revision. In particular, we want to investigate whether, and if so how, it is possible to modify a given AF in such a way that a desired set of arguments becomes an extension. This question is certainly of great interest in a multi-agent scenario where an agent wants another agent to accept a particular set of arguments.

---

[1]Boella et. al. [4] called this task *argument-attack refinement*.

The modifications we allow include expansions of the AF which add arguments and possibly new attack relations, but we also allow changing the semantics. In this respect our approach is more general than existing work (see Conclusion). Changes in the semantics are of interest as they correspond to changes in the degree of cautiousness which have been correlated with different proof standards [5]. Including also deletions of arguments and attacks would not be overly interesting as this trivializes the problem (one could then just delete everything and add the wanted arguments without any attacks).[2]

Our contributions to this topic are:

- impossibility results w.r.t. enforcing[3] a desired set of arguments
- possibility results for enforcing desired sets for specific semantics
- monotonicity results for weak expansions[4] concerning the number of extensions and the justification state of arguments

The paper is organized as follows: Section 2 reviews the necessary definitions at work in argumentation systems. The third section introduces new definitions, namely several kinds of expansions and enforcments. Section 4, the main part of this paper, contains the (im)possibility and monotonicity results. The last section discusses related results and conclusions.

2. Background

2.1. Argumentation Frameworks

Definition 1. An *argumentation framework* $\mathcal{A}$ is a pair (A, R), where A is a non-empty finite set whose elements are called *arguments* and $R \subseteq A \times A$ is a binary relation, called *attack relation*.

If $(a, b) \in R$ holds we say that a attacks b, or b is attacked by a. In the following we consider a fixed countably infinite set $\mathcal{U}$ of arguments, called *universe*. Quantified formulae refer to this universe and all denoted sets are finite subsets of $\mathcal{U}$ or $\mathcal{U} \times \mathcal{U}$, respectively. We introduce some useful abbreviations.

Definition 2. Let $\mathcal{A} = (A, R)$ be an AF, B and B' subsets of A and $a \in A$. Then

1. $(B, B') \bar{\in} R \Leftrightarrow_{def} \exists b \exists b' : b \in B \wedge b' \in B' \wedge (b, b') \in R$,
2. B is unattacked in $\mathcal{A} \Leftrightarrow_{def} (A \backslash B, B) \bar{\notin} R$,
3. a is defended by B in $\mathcal{A} \Leftrightarrow_{def} \forall a' : a' \in A \wedge (a', a) \in R \rightarrow (B, \{a'\}) \bar{\in} R$,
4. B is conflict-free in $\mathcal{A} \Leftrightarrow_{def} (B, B) \bar{\notin} R$,
5. $\mathcal{A}_{\downarrow B}$ is the restriction of $\mathcal{A}$ to $B \Leftrightarrow_{def} \mathcal{A}_{\downarrow B} = (B, R \cap (B \times B))$.

---

[2]Since we assume an infinite universe of arguments just enumerating all supersets of the arguments and checking whether they produce the intended set of arguments is not a viable option.

[3]Enforcing means modifying an AF and/or changing the semantics with the result that a desired set becomes an extension (see Definition 6).

[4]A weak expansion adds further arguments which do not attack previous arguments (see Definition 5).

2.2. Extension-Based Semantics

Semantics of argumentation frameworks specify certain conditions for selecting subsets of a given AF $\mathcal{A}$. The selected subsets are called *extensions*. The set of all extensions of $\mathcal{A}$ under semantics $\mathcal{S}$ is denoted by $\mathcal{E}_{\mathcal{S}}(\mathcal{A})$. We consider the classical (stable, preferred, complete, grounded [2]) and the ideal semantics [6].

Definition 3. Let $\mathcal{A} = (A, R)$ be an AF and $E \subseteq A$. E is a

1. *stable extension* ($E \in \mathcal{E}_{st}(\mathcal{A})$) iff
   $(E, E) \notin R$ and for every $a \in A \backslash E$ holds: $(E, \{a\}) \bar{\in} R$;
2. *admissible extension*[5] ($E \in \mathcal{E}_{ad}(\mathcal{A})$) iff
   $(E, E) \notin R$ and each $a \in E$ is defended by E in $\mathcal{A}$,
3. *preferred extension* ($E \in \mathcal{E}_{pr}(\mathcal{A})$) iff
   $E \in \mathcal{E}_{ad}(\mathcal{A})$ and for each $E' \in \mathcal{E}_{ad}(\mathcal{A})$ holds: $E \not\subset E'$,
4. *complete extension* ($E \in \mathcal{E}_{co}(\mathcal{A})$) iff
   $E \in \mathcal{E}_{ad}(\mathcal{A})$ and for each $a \in A$ defended by E in $\mathcal{A}$ holds: $a \in E$,
5. *grounded extension* ($E \in \mathcal{E}_{gr}(\mathcal{A})$) iff
   $E \in \mathcal{E}_{co}(\mathcal{A})$ and for each $E' \in \mathcal{E}_{co}(\mathcal{A})$ holds: $E' \not\subset E$,
6. *ideal extension* of $\mathcal{A}$ ($E \in \mathcal{E}_{id}(\mathcal{A})$) iff
   $E \in \mathcal{E}_{ad}(\mathcal{A})$, $E \subseteq \bigcap_{P \in \mathcal{E}_{pr}(\mathcal{A})} P$ and for each $A \in \mathcal{E}_{ad}(\mathcal{A})$ w.t.p. $A \subseteq \bigcap_{P \in \mathcal{E}_{pr}(\mathcal{A})} P$ holds $E \not\subset A$

The defined semantics are only a subset of all existing semantics. There are several inter-relations between them. Two important ones are $\mathcal{E}_{st}(\mathcal{A}) \subseteq \mathcal{E}_{pr}(\mathcal{A}) \subseteq \mathcal{E}_{co}(\mathcal{A}) \subseteq \mathcal{E}_{ad}(\mathcal{A})$ and $|\mathcal{E}_{gr}(\mathcal{A})| = |\mathcal{E}_{id}(\mathcal{A})| = 1$, i.e grounded and ideal semantics follow the unique-status approach [7]. The definitions of the semantics are guided by general principles [3]. Some of them will be introduced in the following. The set of all AFs $\mathcal{A}$ with at least one extension under semantics $\mathcal{S}$ and the set of all unattacked subsets in $\mathcal{A}$ are denoted as $\mathcal{D}_{\mathcal{S}}$ or $\mathcal{US}(\mathcal{A})$, respectively.

Definition 4. (abstract principles) A semantics $\mathcal{S}$ satisfies

1. *admissibility*,
2. *reinstatement*,
3. *conflict-freeness*,
4. *the directionality principle*

if and only if for any argumentation framework $\mathcal{A} \in \mathcal{D}_{\mathcal{S}}$, any extension $E \in \mathcal{E}_{\mathcal{S}}(\mathcal{A})$ and any unattacked set $U \in \mathcal{US}(\mathcal{A})$ it holds that:

1. $\forall a \; (a \in E \rightarrow \forall b \; (b \in A \wedge (b, a) \in R \rightarrow (E, \{b\}) \bar{\in} R))$,
2. $\forall a \; (\forall b \; (b \in A \wedge (b, a) \in R \rightarrow (E, \{b\}) \bar{\in} R) \rightarrow a \in E)$,
3. $(E, E) \notin R$,
4. $\mathcal{E}_{\mathcal{S}}(\mathcal{A}_{\downarrow U}) = \{(E \cap U) | E \in \mathcal{E}_{\mathcal{S}}(\mathcal{A})\}$.

Stable semantics does not fulfill directionality and the admissible semantics does not satisfy the reinstatement principle. Apart from that all considered semantics satisfy all mentioned principles. A good overview about these results is given in [8].

---

[5]Note that it is more common to speak about admissible sets instead of the admissible semantics. For reasons of unified notation we used the uncommon version.

3. Expansions and Enforcements

Argumentation is a dynamic process. We focus in this paper on expansions $\mathcal{A}^*$ of an AF $\mathcal{A} = (A, R)$ where new arguments and attacks may be added but the attacks among the old arguments remain unchanged. We thus assume that - before adding new arguments - the attack relationships among arguments put forward earlier have been fully clarified and there is no further dispute concerning these relations. The following definition takes this idea into account.

Definition 5. An AF $\mathcal{A}^*$ is an *expansion* of AF $\mathcal{A} = (A, R)$ iff $\mathcal{A}^* = (A \cup A^*, R \cup R^*)$ for some nonempty A^* disjoint from A. An expansion is

1. *normal* $(\mathcal{A} <^N \mathcal{A}^*)$ iff $\forall ab \ ((a,b) \in R^* \rightarrow a \in A^* \vee b \in A^*)$,
2. *strong* $(\mathcal{A} <^N_S \mathcal{A}^*)$ iff $\mathcal{A} <^N \mathcal{A}^*$ and $\forall ab \ ((a,b) \in R^* \rightarrow \neg(a \in A \wedge b \in A^*))$,
3. *weak* $(\mathcal{A} <^N_W \mathcal{A}^*)$ iff $\mathcal{A} <^N \mathcal{A}^*$ and $\forall ab \ ((a,b) \in R^* \rightarrow \neg(a \in A^* \wedge b \in A))$.

Normal expansions contain new arguments and possibly new attack relations. The latter have to involve at least one new argument. Strong and weak expansions[6] restrict the possible attacks between A and A^* to a single direction. The following figure illustrates a normal expansion. The dashed arrows are those that can be added.

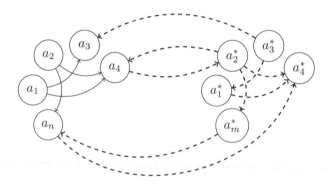

Figure 1. Normal Expansion of $\mathcal{A}$

Enforcing an extension E^* means modifying an argumentation framework in such a way that E^* becomes one of its extensions[7]. The modifications we are interested in here are (a) normal expansions and (b) changes in the semantics. The former correspond to additional arguments that are brought into play together with the attack relations among them and older arguments. The latter can be viewed as a switch in the applied proof standard, for instance a switch from stable semantics to the more cautious grounded semantics.

---

[6]The terms are inspired by the fact that added arguments never receive attacks from previous arguments (*strong* arguments) or attack previous arguments (*weak* arguments), respectively.

[7]Note that there is a range of possibilities to define an enforcement, e.g. E^* is a subset of an extension, or all elements of E^* are credulously (sceptically) justified, or E^* is the only extension and so on. We provide a very basic and extendable definition for enforcing.

Definition 6. Let $\mathcal{A} = (A, R)$ be an AF, S a semantics. Furthermore, let E^* be a *desired* set which is not an extension, i.e. $E^* \notin \mathcal{E}_S(\mathcal{A})$. An $(\mathcal{A}, S)$-*enforcement* of E^* is a pair $\mathcal{F} = (\mathcal{A}^*, S^*)$ such that (1) $\mathcal{A}^* = \mathcal{A}$ or $\mathcal{A} <^N \mathcal{A}^*$, and (2) $E^* \in \mathcal{E}_{S^*}(\mathcal{A}^*)$. $\mathcal{F}$ is called

1. *conservative if $S = S^*$,*
2. *conservative strong if $\mathcal{A} <^N_S \mathcal{A}^*$ and $S = S^*$,*
3. *conservative weak if $\mathcal{A} <^N_W \mathcal{A}^*$ and $S = S^*$,*
4. *liberal if $S \neq S^*$,*
5. *liberal strong if $\mathcal{A} <^N_S \mathcal{A}^*$ and $S \neq S^*$,*
6. *liberal weak if $\mathcal{A} <^N_W \mathcal{A}^*$ and $S \neq S^*$.*

Whenever $\mathcal{A}$ and S are clear from context we simply speak of enforcements of E^*. We call the first three types *conservative* because the considered semantics remains constant. Almost all existing papers dealing with belief revision consider a fixed semantics. Liberal enforcements change the semantics. As mentioned earlier, this may be interpreted as a change of proof standard or paradigm shift. Imagine a judicial proceeding. It is vitally important whether you are accused on the base of criminal or civil law. The required evidence is different and hence the acceptable sets of arguments differ.

Note that more general modifications like leaving out previous attack relations or adding further attacks between previous arguments are excluded by our definition. If these types of manipulation are allowed the problem becomes trivial because one may add or delete arguments and attack relations at will.

To familiarize the reader with enforcements we give two examples.

Example 1. Let $\mathcal{A}$ be the following AF:

Let S be stable semantics and $E^* = \{a_1, a_3\}$ the *desired* set of arguments. Obviously we have $E^* \notin \mathcal{E}_S(\mathcal{A})$. How to enforce E^*? Define a liberal enforcement with $\mathcal{A} = \mathcal{A}^*$ and $S^* = pr$. One can check that E^* is indeed a preferred extension of $\mathcal{A}^*$.

Example 2. Let $\mathcal{A} = (A, R) = (\{a_1, a_2, a_3\}, \{(a_1, a_2), (a_2, a_1), (a_2, a_3)\})$ be an AF:

Let S be grounded semantics and $E^* = \{a_1^*, a_2\}$ the *desired* set of arguments. Obviously $E^* \notin \mathcal{E}_S(\mathcal{A})$ since $a_1^* \notin A$. How to enforce E^*? Define a conservative enforcement with $\mathcal{A}^* = (A \cup \{a_1^*\}, R \cup \{(a_1^*, a_1)\})$. E^* is the grounded extension of $\mathcal{A}^*$.

4. Manipulating Argumentation Scenarios

The examples above illustrate the possibility to enforce extensions. This is not the case in general, i.e. not all *desired* sets are enforceable[8]. In the next two subsections we want to study necessary and sufficient conditions for the enforcement problem.

4.1. Impossibility Results (Enforcing of Extensions)

We now show some useful interrelations between subsets of an AF, its normal expansions and abstract principles of semantics. The following properties are pretty obvious and hardly need any proof. Being aware of this fact, we still present them in the form of a proposition to be able to refer to them later on.

Proposition 1. *(simple properties) Let $\mathcal{A} = (A, R)$ be an AF and $\mathcal{S}$ a semantics.*

1. *If $\mathcal{S}$ satisfies admissibility and $A' \subseteq A$ does not defend all its elements in $\mathcal{A}$, then there is no conservative enforcement of A'.*
2. *If $\mathcal{S}$ satisfies reinstatement and $A' \subseteq A$ does not contain all defended elements in $\mathcal{A}$, then there is no conservative weak enforcement of A'.*
3. *If $\mathcal{S}$ satisfies conflict-freeness and $A' \subseteq A$ is conflicting, i.e. $(A', A') \not\in R$, then there is no conservative enforcement of A'', if $A' \subseteq A''$ holds.*
4. *If $A' \subseteq A$ is unattacked in $\mathcal{A}$, i.e. $A' \in \mathcal{US}(\mathcal{A})$, then A' is unattacked in each weak expansion $\mathcal{A}^*$ of $\mathcal{A}$.*

Proof: Remember that normal expansions never delete previous arguments and never add or delete attacks between them. The equality-case ($\mathcal{A} = \mathcal{A}^*$) is obvious for all propositions.

1. given that A' does not defend all its elements we conclude $\exists ab\,(a \in A' \wedge b \in A \wedge (b, a) \in R \wedge (A', \{b\}) \not\in R)$; using $A' \subseteq A, b \in A$ and $\mathcal{A} <^N \mathcal{A}^*$, i.e. further attack relations have to involve at least one new argument, we conclude $(A', \{b\}) \not\in R \cup R^*$, hence $A' \not\in \mathcal{E}_\mathcal{S}(\mathcal{A}^*)$;
2. given that A' does not contain all defended arguments in $\mathcal{A}$ we conclude $\exists a \in A \backslash A'$: $\forall b\,(b \in A \wedge (b, a) \in R \rightarrow (A', \{b\}) \in R)$; considering that $\mathcal{A} <^N_W \mathcal{A}^*$ it follows that all possible attackers of a are already elements of A, hence A' does not contain all defended arguments in $\mathcal{A}^*$, i.e. $A' \not\in \mathcal{E}_\mathcal{S}(\mathcal{A}^*)$;
3. obvious, supersets of conflicting sets are conflicting;
4. obvious, unattacked previous arguments stay unattacked if all additional attacks go to *new* elements.   □

It is important to emphasize that these results are strict in the following sense: The conclusions of proposition 1.1, 1.2 and 1.4 are not necessarily true (or false) for supersets and subsets of A'. The same holds for subsets of conflicting sets. The following example illustrates the subset-case for proposition 1.1:

Example 3. Consider the following normal expansion $\mathcal{A}^*$ of $\mathcal{A} = (\{a_1, a_2\}, \{(a_1, a_2)\})$:

---

[8]Note that we consider conservative and liberal enforcements (Def. 7). With arbitrary modifications (elimination of arguments, new attack relations between *old* arguments) arbitrary extensions can be generated.

The set $A' = \{a_1, a_2\}$ does not defend a_2 in $\mathcal{A}$. Consider now the normal expansion $\mathcal{A}^* = (A \cup \{a_1^*\}, R \cup \{(a_1, a_1^*)\})$ of $\mathcal{A}$. On the one hand the set $\{a_1\} \subseteq A'$ is a stable[9] extension of $\mathcal{A}^*$, i.e. $\{a_1\} \in \mathcal{E}_{st}(\mathcal{A}^*)$ (existence of a conservative enforcement) and on the other hand the set $\{a_2\} \subseteq A'$ is itself a set, which does not defend all its elements in $\mathcal{A}$ (i.e., prop. 1.1 is applicable), hence there is no conservative enforcement of $\{a_2\}$.

Propositions 1.1, 1.2 and 1.3 present obvious necessary conditions for the enforcement problem[10]. The following impossibility theorems are more sophisticated than the mentioned proposition. The first one shows limitations for exchanging believed with unattacking arguments.

Theorem 2. *(conservative (liberal) enforcing [exchanging arguments]) Given an AF $\mathcal{A} = (A, R)$ and*

1. *a semantics $\mathcal{S}$ satisfying reinstatement,*
2. *a semantics $\mathcal{S}^*$, satisfying admissibility and conflict-freeness,*
3. *a set E such that $E \in \mathcal{E}_{\mathcal{S}}(\mathcal{A})$ and*
4. *two sets E', C such that $E' \subseteq E$, $C \subseteq A\backslash E$, $C \neq \emptyset$, $(C, A\backslash\{E' \cup C\}) \not\subseteq R$ and $E^* := E' \cup C \notin \mathcal{E}_{\mathcal{S}}(\mathcal{A})$*

For all normal expansions $\mathcal{A}^*$ of $\mathcal{A}$ we have $E^* \notin \mathcal{E}_{\mathcal{S}^*}(\mathcal{A}^*)$.

Proof (reduction to the absurd) given $\mathcal{A}^* = (A \cup A^*, R \cup R^*)$ such that $\mathcal{A} \prec^N \mathcal{A}^*$ and $E^* \in \mathcal{E}_{\mathcal{S}^*}(\mathcal{A}^*)$; C is a nonempty subset of $A\backslash E$, hence $\exists c : c \in C \wedge c \notin E$; using the reinstatement property of $\mathcal{S}$ and $E \in \mathcal{E}_{\mathcal{S}}(\mathcal{A})$ we deduce $\exists b : b \in A \wedge (b, c) \in R \wedge (E, \{b\}) \not\subseteq R$ (*); it obviously holds that $b \in A \cup A^* \wedge (b, c) \in R \cup R^*$, taking admissibility of $\mathcal{S}^*$ and $E^* \in \mathcal{E}_{\mathcal{S}^*}(\mathcal{A}^*)$ into account we conclude $(E^*, \{b\}) \bar{\in} R \cup R^*$; this formula is fulfilled if $(E^*, \{b\}) \bar{\in} R \vee (E^*, \{b\}) \bar{\in} R^*$ holds; the latter disjunct is false because new attack relations have to involve at least one new argument; the former disjunct is equivalent to $(E', \{b\}) \bar{\in} R \vee (C, \{b\}) \bar{\in} R$; $(E', \{b\}) \bar{\in} R$ contradicts $(E, \{b\}) \not\subseteq R$ (compare (*)) because $E' \subseteq E$ holds; we deduce $b \notin E^*$ because $\mathcal{S}^*$ satisfies conflict-freeness and the assumption $E^* \in \mathcal{E}_{\mathcal{S}^*}(\mathcal{A}^*)$; hence $b \in A\backslash\{E' \cup C\}$, i.e. $(C, \{b\}) \not\subseteq R$ because of the fourth premise $(C, A\backslash\{E' \cup C\}) \not\subseteq R$. $\square$

Intuitively, the theorem says the following: if the involved semantics satisfy the specified properties, then it is impossible to find a normal expansion which possesses an extension E^* composed of a subset of an old extension E and some formerly unaccepted arguments C, given no element of C attacks some element which is not in the new extension.

The second impossibility theorem demonstrates limitations for eliminating arguments of existing extensions.

Theorem 3. *(conservative (liberal) weak enforcing [eliminating arguments]) Given an AF $\mathcal{A} = (A, R)$ and*

1. *a semantics $\mathcal{S}$, satisfying admissibility and conflict-freeness,*
2. *a semantics $\mathcal{S}^*$, satisfying reinstatement,*
3. *a set E such that $E \in \mathcal{E}_{\mathcal{S}}(\mathcal{A})$ and*

---

[9]Stable semantics satisfies the admissibility principle.

[10]Proposition 1.4 is not a conclusion about the set of extensions. It is essential to prove the monotonicity result (compare Theorem 4).

4. *a set C such that $C \nsubseteq E$, $(C, A\backslash E) \not\equiv R$ and $E^* := E\backslash C \notin \mathcal{E}_S(\mathcal{A})$*

For all weak expansions $\mathcal{A}^*$ of $\mathcal{A}$ we have $E^* \notin \mathcal{E}_{S^*}(\mathcal{A}^*)$.

Proof (reduction to the absurd) Given $\mathcal{A}^* = (A \cup A^*, R \cup R^*)$ such that $\mathcal{A} <_W^N \mathcal{A}^*$ and $E^* \in \mathcal{E}_{S^*}(\mathcal{A}^*)$; C is not empty because $E \in \mathcal{E}_S(\mathcal{A})$ and $E^* \notin \mathcal{E}_S(\mathcal{A})$ hold, hence we conclude $\exists c : c \in C \wedge c \notin E^*$; using the reinstatement property of S^* and $E^* \in \mathcal{E}_{S^*}(\mathcal{A}^*)$ we deduce $\exists b : b \in A \cup A^* \wedge (b, c) \in R \cup R^* \wedge (E^*, \{b\}) \not\equiv R \cup R^*$; it obviously holds $(E^*, \{b\}) \not\equiv R$ (*) and due to the fact that $\mathcal{A}^*$ is a weak expansion we have $(b, c) \in R \wedge b \in A$; $c \in E$, admissibility of S and $E \in \mathcal{E}_S(\mathcal{A})$ yield $(E, \{b\}) \equiv R$, hence $b \in A\backslash E$ (**) because of the conflict-freeness of S; $(E, \{b\}) \equiv R$ is equivalent to $(E^*, \{b\}) \equiv R \vee (C, \{b\}) \equiv R$; $(E^*, \{b\}) \equiv R$ contradicts (*) and $(C, \{b\}) \equiv R$ contradicts (**), given the fourth premise $(C, A\backslash E) \not\equiv R$.   □

Intuitively, the theorem says the following: if the involved semantics satisfy the specified properties, then it is impossible to find a weak expansion possessing an extension which is a proper subset of an old extension and not already an extension of the original AF, unless one of the arguments left out in the new extension attacks an element which was not in the old extension.

Due to the use of abstract principles, these theorems establish a connection between the set of extensions of the AF $\mathcal{A}$ under the semantics S and the set of extensions of the normal or weak expansion $\mathcal{A}^*$ under the semantics S^*. They represent sufficient conditions for the impossibility to enforce a desired set.

4.2. Possibility Result (Enforcing of Extensions)

Consider the following simple AF $\mathcal{A}$:

Proposition 1 (as well as Theorem 2) implies that $\{a_2\}$ never can be an extension of a normal expansion $\mathcal{A}^*$ of $\mathcal{A}$ under a semantics S satisfying admissibility. What about the following weaker claim: Is there a normal expansion $\mathcal{A}^*$ of $\mathcal{A}$ with an extension E^* such that a_2 is an element of E^*? In this subsection we want to prove the positive answer for all defined semantics. Furthermore we will prove the uniqueness or superset-property of this extension.

Theorem 4. *(conservative strong enforcing [$\sigma \in \{st, ad, pr, co, gr, id\}$]) Let $\mathcal{A} = (A, R)$ be an AF and $C \subseteq A$ a conflict-free set such that $C \notin \mathcal{E}_\sigma(\mathcal{A})$. There is a strong expansion $\mathcal{A}^*$ of $\mathcal{A}$ such that $C \subset E^*$ for some $E^* \in \mathcal{E}_\sigma(\mathcal{A}^*)$. Moreover, it is possible to construct $\mathcal{A}^*$ in such a way that (1) $|E^*\backslash C| = 1$ and (2) E^* is the unique extension of $\mathcal{A}^*$ (for $\sigma \in \{st, pr, co, gr, id\}$) or the set-inclusion maximal extension of $\mathcal{A}^*$ (for $\sigma = ad$).*

Proof: Without loss of generality we assume $A = \{a_1, ..., a_n\}$ and $C = \{a_1, ..., a_i\}$. Consider the strong expansion $\mathcal{A}^* = (A \cup \{a_1^*\}, R \cup \{(a_1^*, a_{i+1}), ..., (a_1^*, a_n)\})$ of $\mathcal{A}$ and let $E^* = C \cup \{a_1^*\}$. We show $E^* \in \mathcal{E}_\sigma(\mathcal{A}^*)$.
Given $C \notin \mathcal{E}_\sigma(\mathcal{A})$ we conclude $i < n$ (for all σ); furthermore $C \cup \{a_1^*\}$ is conflict-free in $\mathcal{A}^*$ by construction.

1. ($\sigma = st$) for every $a_j \in \{A \cup \{a_1^*\}\} \setminus \{C \cup \{a_1^*\}\}$ holds $(a_1^*, a_j) \in R^*$; (uniqueness) given $E^{**} \in \mathcal{E}_{st}(\mathcal{A}^*)$, therefore $a_1^* \in E^{**}$ holds because it is unattacked; hence for all $a_j \in \{a_{i+1}, ..., a_n\}$ holds $a_j \notin E^{**}$ (conflict); furthermore C has to be a subset of E^{**} because no element is attacked by a_1^* and they are pairwise conflict-free, i.e. $E^{**} = E^*$.

2. ($\sigma = ad$) each $a_j \in E^*$ is defended by E^* in $\mathcal{A}^*$ because every possible attacker in the complement $\{A \cup \{a_1^*\}\} \setminus \{C \cup \{a_1^*\}\}$ is counterattacked by a_1^*; (super-set-property) given an extension $E^{**} \in \mathcal{E}_{ad}(\mathcal{A}^*)$; for every $a_j \in \{a_{i+1}, ..., a_n\}$ we have $a_j \notin E^{**}$ because there is no counterattack to a_1^*, hence $E^{**} \subseteq E^*$.

3. ($\sigma = pr$) admissibility is clear (compare 2.); maximality follows by the super-set-property of E^*; (uniqueness) given $E^{**} \in \mathcal{E}_{pr}(\mathcal{A}^*)$, hence $E^{**} \in \mathcal{E}_{ad}(\mathcal{A}^*)$; we conclude $E^{**} \subseteq E^*$ (super-set-property) and finally $E^{**} = E^*$ because it has to be maximal.

4. ($\sigma = co$) admissibility is clear (compare 2.); furthermore, for all $a_j \in \{a_{i+1}, ..., a_n\}$ (i.e. $a_j \notin E^*$) holds: a_j is not defended by $C \cup \{a_1^*\}$ in $\mathcal{A}^*$ because a_1^* is unattacked; (uniqueness) given $E^{**} \in \mathcal{E}_{pr}(\mathcal{A}^*)$, hence $E^{**} \in \mathcal{E}_{ad}(\mathcal{A}^*)$; we conclude $E^{**} \subseteq E^*$, assuming that $E^{**} \neq E^*$ yields a contradiction because a_1^* has to be in E^{**} (unattacked, thus defended by E^{**}) and all elements in C are defended by a_1^*, consequently by supersets of a_1^* (like E^{**}) too.

5. ($\sigma = gr$) $E^* \in \mathcal{E}_{co}(\mathcal{A}^*)$ follows by the first part and minimality by the second part (uniqueness) in 4.; (uniqueness) obvious, because it is a unique-status approach.

6. ($\sigma = id$) admissibility is clear (compare 2.); furthermore, $E^* = \mathcal{E}_{pr}(\mathcal{A}^*)$ (compare 3.), hence $E^* \subseteq \bigcap_{P \in \mathcal{E}_{pr}(\mathcal{A}^*)} P$ holds; in addition E^* is the maximal admissible set (super-set-property compare 2.), hence for each $A \in \mathcal{E}_{ad}(\mathcal{A}^*)$ such that $A \subseteq \bigcap_{P \in \mathcal{E}_{pr}(\mathcal{A}^*)} P$ holds $E^* \not\subset A$; (uniqueness) obvious, because it is a unique-status approach. □

The theorem shows that whenever a set C is conflict-free we may add one additional argument a and certain attacks so that the union of C and a is the unique extension of the constructed AF. It is important to emphasize that in special cases the enforcement of the desired set may be reached with less additional attack relations. Our construction shows the potential possibility only. To exemplify the standard construction consider the following AF.

Example 4. Let $\mathcal{A}^* = (A \cup \{a_1^*\}, R \cup \{(a_1^*, a_1), (a_1^*, a_3), (a_1^*, a_5)\})$ be the following strong expansion of $\mathcal{A} = (A, R)$:

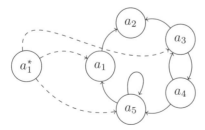

$C = \{a_2, a_4\}$ is the desired set of arguments. C is conflict-free and $C \notin \mathcal{E}_\sigma(\mathcal{A})$ holds for all $\sigma \in \{st, ad, pr, co, gr, id\}$, i.e. Theorem 3 is applicable. Hence, the standard-construction has the property that the set $E^* = \{a_2, a_4, a_1^*\}$ is the only extension of $\mathcal{A}^*$ **for all** semantics $\sigma \in \{st, pr, co, gr, id\}$[11].

---

[11] For $\sigma = ad$ the super-set-property holds (compare 2.).

4.3. Monotonic Relations Between Sets of Extensions

Adding new arguments and their associated interactions obviously may change the outcome of an AF in a nonmonotonic way: arguments accepted earlier may become unaccepted, others become accepted; the number of extensions may shrink - or increase, depending on the new arguments. In this section we will identify special cases where arguments accepted earlier survive, and where the number of extensions can only increase. We will show that this holds for the class of weak expansions of an AF $\mathcal{A}$ and a semantics $\mathcal{S}$ satisfying the directionality principle. Here, every old belief set is contained in a new one and furthermore every new belief set is the union of an old one and a (possibly empty) set of new arguments.

Theorem 5. *(monotonicity) Given an AF* $\mathcal{A} = (A, R)$ *and a semantics* $\mathcal{S}$ *satisfying directionality, then for all weak expansions* $\mathcal{A}^*$ *of* $\mathcal{A}$ *the following holds:*

1. $|\mathcal{E}_{\mathcal{S}}(\mathcal{A})| \leq |\mathcal{E}_{\mathcal{S}}(\mathcal{A}^*)|$,
2. $\forall E \in \mathcal{E}_{\mathcal{S}}(\mathcal{A}) \; \exists E^* \in \mathcal{E}_{\mathcal{S}}(\mathcal{A}^*) : E \subseteq E^*$ *and*
3. $\forall E^* \in \mathcal{E}_{\mathcal{S}}(\mathcal{A}^*) \; \exists E_i \in \mathcal{E}_{\mathcal{S}}(\mathcal{A}) \; \exists A_i^* \subseteq A^* : E^* = E_i \cup A_i^*$

Proof: Given $\mathcal{A}^* = (A \cup A^*, R \cup R^*)$ such that $\mathcal{A} <_W^N \mathcal{A}^*$ and a semantics $\mathcal{S}$ satisfying the directionality principle; obviously we have $A \in \mathcal{US}(\mathcal{A}^*)$[12], hence the directionality principle yields $\mathcal{E}_{\mathcal{S}}(\mathcal{A}^*_{\downarrow A}) = \{(E^* \cap A) | E^* \in \mathcal{E}_{\mathcal{S}}(\mathcal{A}^*)\}$ (*); using that $\forall ab \in R^* : a \in A^* \vee b \in A^*$ holds, we conclude $\mathcal{A}^*_{\downarrow A} = \mathcal{A}$, hence $\mathcal{E}_{\mathcal{S}}(\mathcal{A}^*_{\downarrow A}) = \mathcal{E}_{\mathcal{S}}(\mathcal{A})$; (this is used for the following proofs)
1. (reduction to the absurd) Let $n, m \in \mathbf{N}$ and assume that $m = |\mathcal{E}_{\mathcal{S}}(\mathcal{A})| > |\mathcal{E}_{\mathcal{S}}(\mathcal{A}^*)| = n$ holds, consequently $|\mathcal{E}_{\mathcal{S}}(\mathcal{A}^*_{\downarrow A})| = m$; on the other hand with $|\mathcal{E}_{\mathcal{S}}(\mathcal{A}^*)| = n$ we get $|\{(E^* \cap A) | E^* \in \mathcal{E}_{\mathcal{S}}(\mathcal{A}^*)\}| \leq n$, i.e. $|\mathcal{E}_{\mathcal{S}}(\mathcal{A}^*_{\downarrow A})| \neq |\{(E^* \cap A) | E^* \in \mathcal{E}_{\mathcal{S}}(\mathcal{A}^*)\}|$, hence $\mathcal{E}_{\mathcal{S}}(\mathcal{A}^*_{\downarrow A}) \neq \{(E^* \cap A) | E^* \in \mathcal{E}_{\mathcal{S}}(\mathcal{A}^*)\}$ (contradicts (*)).
2. (reduction to the absurd) Assume that $\exists E \in \mathcal{E}_{\mathcal{S}}(\mathcal{A}) \; \forall E^* \in \mathcal{E}_{\mathcal{S}}(\mathcal{A}^*) : E \nsubseteq E^*$; i.e. $E \in \mathcal{E}_{\mathcal{S}}(\mathcal{A}^*_{\downarrow A})$; we infer $E \nsubseteq E^* \cap A$ for all $E^* \in \mathcal{E}_{\mathcal{S}}(\mathcal{A}^*)$ from $E \nsubseteq E^*$, i.e. $E \neq E^* \cap A \; \forall E^* \in \mathcal{E}_{\mathcal{S}}(\mathcal{A}^*)$; hence $E \notin \{(E^* \cap A) | E^* \in \mathcal{E}_{\mathcal{S}}(\mathcal{A}^*)\}$ and consequently $\mathcal{E}_{\mathcal{S}}(\mathcal{A}^*_{\downarrow A}) \neq \{(E^* \cap A) | E^* \in \mathcal{E}_{\mathcal{S}}(\mathcal{A}^*)\}$ (contradicts (*)).
3. (reduction to the absurd) $\exists E^* \in \mathcal{E}_{\mathcal{S}}(\mathcal{A}^*) \; \forall E_i \in \mathcal{E}_{\mathcal{S}}(\mathcal{A}) \; \forall A_i^* \subseteq A^* : E^* \neq E_i \cup A_i^*$; we deduce $E^* \cap A \neq E_i$ for all $E_i \in \mathcal{E}_{\mathcal{S}}(\mathcal{A})$ because assuming the existence of an E_i such that $E^* \cap A = E_i$ we may find an $A_i^* \subseteq A^*$ (set $A_i^* = E^* \backslash A$), so that $E^* = E_i \cup A_i^*$; hence $E^* \cap A \notin \mathcal{E}_{\mathcal{S}}(\mathcal{A})$ and consequently $\mathcal{E}_{\mathcal{S}}(\mathcal{A}^*_{\downarrow A}) \neq \{(E^* \cap A) | E^* \in \mathcal{E}_{\mathcal{S}}(\mathcal{A}^*)\}$ (contradicts (*)). □

The second and the third parts of Theorem 5 imply nice properties with respect to the justification state[13] of an argument a.

Corollary 6. *Given the same assumptions as in Theorem 5, then*

1. $\displaystyle \bigcup_{E \in \mathcal{E}_{\mathcal{S}}(\mathcal{A})} E \subseteq \bigcup_{E^* \in \mathcal{E}_{\mathcal{S}}(\mathcal{A}^*)} E^*$ *(credulously justified args persist),*

---

[12]The general interrelation between unattacked sets of $\mathcal{A}$ and a weak expansion $\mathcal{A}^*$ of $\mathcal{A}$ is the following: $\forall U \; (U \in \mathcal{US}(\mathcal{A}) \rightarrow U \in \mathcal{US}(\mathcal{A}^*))$. Compare proposition 1.4.
[13]A very good overview about justification states is given in [1] (chapter 2.4).

2. $\displaystyle\bigcap_{E \in \mathcal{E}_S(\mathcal{A})} E \subseteq \bigcap_{E^* \in \mathcal{E}_S(\mathcal{A}^*)} E^*$ *(skeptically justified args persist)*.

That means, a skeptically (credulously) justified argument in $\mathcal{A}$ is skeptically (credulously) justified in $\mathcal{A}^*$. Remember that the grounded, complete, preferred and ideal semantics as well as CF2 [9] and the prudent version of the grounded semantics [10] satisfy the directionality principle. A weak expansion of an AF considered under any of these semantics behaves in a monotonic fashion with respect to the cardinality of the set of extensions as well as the mentioned subset-properties. Note that we cannot strengthen the cardinality statement in the sense of excluding equality.

Example 5. Consider the following two weak expansions $\mathcal{A}_1^*$, $\mathcal{A}_2^*$ of $\mathcal{A} = (\{a_1\}, \varnothing)$:

Let S be preferred semantics, hence $\mathcal{E}_S(\mathcal{A}) = \{\{a_1\}\}$, i.e. $|\mathcal{E}_S(\mathcal{A})| = 1$. The set of extensions of the first weak expansion stays equal ($\mathcal{E}_S(\mathcal{A}_1^*) = \{\{a_1\}\}$) in contrast to the second weak expansion ($\mathcal{E}_S(\mathcal{A}^*) = \{\{a_1, a_2^*\}, \{a_1, a_3^*\}\}$).

The monotonicity result is of interest as it provides a simplified method for checking whether an argument a is in some, respectively all extensions of an AF $\mathcal{A}$. First we introduce a new concept.

Definition 7. Let $C = \langle \mathcal{A}_0, ..., \mathcal{A}_n \rangle$ be a sequence of AFs, $\mathcal{A}$ an AF. C is called *expansion chain of $\mathcal{A}$* iff

1. $\mathcal{A} = \mathcal{A}_n$ and
2. $\mathcal{A}_i <^N \mathcal{A}_{i+1}$ ($\mathcal{A}_{i+1}$ is a normal expansion of $\mathcal{A}_i$) for all i: $0 \leq i \leq n - 1$.

C is called *weak* (resp. *strong*) if all expansions in the chain are weak (resp. strong).

Corollary 7. *Let $C = \langle \mathcal{A}_0, ..., \mathcal{A}_n \rangle$ be a weak expansion chain of $\mathcal{A}$, and let i be the smallest integer such that $\mathcal{A}$ covers a.[14] Given the same assumptions as in Theorem 5, we get: a is in some/all extensions of $\mathcal{A}$ iff a is in some/all extensions of $\mathcal{A}_i$.*

The corollary shows that it is sufficient to check the acceptability of an argument a in the chain-member $\mathcal{A}_i$ which is the first AF in which a appears. The following example illustrates this method.

Example 6. Acceptability of a_5 in the shaded AF decides its acceptability in the whole AF.

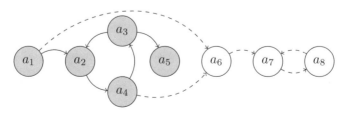

---

[14] $\mathcal{A} = (A, R)$ covers a whenever $a \in A$.

5. Related Work and Conclusions

We investigated a particular type of dynamics in Dung-style AFs. We provided theoretical insights about the impact of further arguments and attack relations. In particular, we investigated conditions for the (im)possibility to enforce a *desired* set of arguments. Moreover, we showed that the class of weak expansions behaves monotonically w.r.t. the cardinality of extensions and justification state of arguments if the considered semantics satisfies directionality. The use of abstract principles makes our results general enough to cover semantics which may be defined in the future.

There are several papers dealing with adding new information in argumentation. The closest to ours is [11]. Cayrol et al. proposed a typology of revisions (one new argument, one new interaction). Furthermore they proved sufficient conditions for being of a certain revision type. Other papers like [12] as well as [13] include additional knowledge from which arguments and attack relations can be justified. A further work worth mentioning in this context is [14]. Rotstein et al. define a warrant-prioritized revision operation which adds one additional argument that must be accepted afterwards. None of these papers establishes relationships between abstract properties of semantics and the (im)possibility of enforcements, as we do.

Future work may involve further abstract principles like I-maximality or several kinds of scepticism-adequacy [3]. Another direction is the investigation of similar properties for AFs with integrated preferences.

References

[1]   I. Rahwan and G. Simari (editors), "Argumentation in Artificial Intelligence" Springer 2009, Berlin, Germany

[2]   P.M.Dung, "On the acceptability of arguments and its fundamental role in nonmonotonic reasoning, logic programming and n-person games", Artificial Intelligence 77 (1995), p. 321-357

[3]   Baroni, P. and Giacomin, M. 2006. "Evaluation and comparison criteria for extension-based argumentation semantics", Proceedings of COMMA 2006 P. E. Dunne and T. J. Bench-Capon, Eds. Frontiers in Artificial Intelligence and Applications, vol. 144. IOS Press, Amsterdam, The Netherlands, p. 157-168

[4]   Boella, G., Kaci, S. and van der Torre, L. 2009b. "Dynamics in argumentation with single extensions: attack refinement and the grounded extension" In Proc. AAMAS 2009, p. 1213-1214

[5]   K. Atkinson, T. Bench-Capon , "Argumentation and Standards of Proof" Proceedings of 11th international conference on Artificial intelligence and law 2007, Stanford, California

[6]   P.M. Dung, P. Mancarella, F. Toni, "A dialectic procedure for sceptical, assumption-based argumentation" in: P.E. Dunne, T. Bench-Capon (Eds.), Proceedings of the 1st COMMA 2006, IOS Press, Liverpool, UK, 2006, pp. 145-156

[7]   H. Prakken, G.A.W. Vreeswijk, "Logics for defeasible argumentation" in: D.M. Gabbay, F. Guenthner (Eds.), Handbook of Philosophical Logic, second ed., Kluwer Academic Publishers, Dordrecht, 2001

[8]   Baroni, P. and Giacomin, M. 2007, "On principle-based evaluation of extension-based argumentation semantics", Artif. Intell. 171, 10-15 (Jul. 2007), p. 675-700

[9]   P. Baroni, M. Giacomin, "Solving semantic problems with odd-length cycles in argumentation" in: EC-SQARU 2003, LNAI 2711, Springer-Verlag, Aalborg, Denmark, 2003, p. 440-451

[10] S. Coste-Marquis, C. Devred, P. Marquis, "Prudent semantics for argumentation frameworks, in: Proceedings of the 17th ICTAI 2005, IEEE Computer Society, Hong Kong, China, 2005, p. 568-572

[11] Cayrol, C., Dupin de Saint-Cyr, F. and Lagasquie-Schiex, M.- C. 2008. "Revision of an argumentation system", In Proc. KR 2008, p. 124-134

[12] Wassermann, R. 1999, "Full acceptance through argumentation - a preliminary report", in Proc. of IJCAI Workshop Practical Reasoning and Rationality

[13] Falappa, M., Garcia, A. and Simari, G. 2004, "Belief dynamics and defeasible argumentation in rational agents", in Proc. of NMR, p. 164-170

[14] Rotstein, N. D., Moguillansky, M. O., Falappa, M. A., Garcia, A. J. and Simari, G. R. 2008a, "Argument theory change: Revision upon warrant", in Proc. COMMA 2008, p. 336-347

Computational Models of Argument
P. Baroni et al. (Eds.)
IOS Press, 2010
doi:10.3233/978-1-60750-619-5-87

Using Defeasible Logic Programming for Argumentation-Based Decision Support in Private Law

C. BEIERLE [a], B. FREUND [a], G. KERN-ISBERNER [b], M. THIMM [b]

[a] *FernUniversität in Hagen, Germany*
[b] *Technische Universität Dortmund, Germany*

Abstract. Legal reasoning is one of the most obvious application areas for computational models of argumentation as the exchange of arguments and counterarguments is the established means for making decisions in law. In this paper we employ Defeasible Logic Programming (DeLP) for representing legal cases and for giving decision-support, exemplary for private law. We give a formalization of legal provisions that can be used easily by judges for supporting their decision process and present a working system that resembles the decision-making in legal reasoning, in particular, with respect to the *burden of proof*.

1. Introduction

Although AI and Law is a long-established discipline (see [3] for an overview of past developments and present problems), the number of expert systems in actual use by judges—if any—is very low. Instead, legal professionals use computers for writing, communication, and as databases substituting their traditional libraries. There are only few tools to support the decision-making itself. This is especially remarkable since legal reasoning is essentially rule-based, and therefore seems to invite automation. The low motivation of judges for using expert systems can partly be explained by a certain conservatism that characterizes the legal system. But the reluctance to embrace counsel based on computation runs deeper than tradition and nostalgia. To rely on an expert system, a judge—more than any other kind of expert—needs to have not only a basic, but a profound understanding of the formal model and inference mechanism the system is based on. Although new forms of logic and models of argumentation have been studied in legal theory as well (e. g. [14,15,8,19,3]), they never really affected the curriculum. Classical legal theory, based on aristotelian-scholastic reasoning, is still all the logical training judges routinely get. It forms the core of most textbooks on legal method and lies at the heart of legal reasoning as it is taught at law schools both in common law [2] (US) and civil law countries [11] (China), [4] (Germany), [13] (Switzerland). It is therefore the natural key to the comprehension and acceptance of expert systems by judges.

In this paper, we will focus on these general principles that govern judicial legal reasoning, and elaborate on its argumentative inference structures, in particular with respect to the *burden of proof*. We will show that defeasible logic programming (DeLP) [5] suits the judicial way of reasoning especially well, and present an argumentative system for decision support in private law that has been implemented based on DeLP. The expert system introduced here, LiZ, focuses on this perspective of a judge, and thus is to be taken with a grain of salt when compared to the more sophisticated models recently used in AI and law which have been mentioned above. In contrast to these, it does not strive to model externally the way legal experts actually think (or argue), but it takes the internal position of a judge. Moreover, by using DeLP to implement the model, it becomes possible to add defeasible reasoning at the level of subsuming (or classifying) cases while at the same time respecting the classical structure of the law. The system is not confined to material law rules, but takes into account the procedural aspects of the law paramount for the work of a judge, particularly, the burden of proof, necessary indications to the parties, intermediary decisions to manage the process and so on. However, we abstract as far as possible from idiosyncratic aspects of specific jurisdictions. In line with current research in comparative law [20] we focus on a common core of legal procedure, ensuring broader applicability of the formal model. In general, various kinds of burden of proof can be distinguished; for a recent and thorough analysis and survey see [7].

In Sec. 2 we give a brief introduction to legal reasoning in private law and afterwards extract and compare its essential aspects with methods for defeasible argumentation. In Sec. 3 we establish a model of legal reasoning by exemplifying some legal concepts, and further refine our model by formalizing knowledge representation in Sec. 4. Section 5 recalls the relevant technical aspects of DeLP, and Sec. 6 presents our approach of an argumentation-based decision-support system using DeLP. In Sec. 7 we conclude.

2. Legal reasoning and defeasible argumentation

Legal reasoning is rule-based. This holds true for all legal systems and all areas of law. Moreover, the structure of the rules, whether contained in judgements, statutes, legal literature or even in practitioners' minds, is more ore less universal. A simple private law case, as it might appear in a student textbook, shall help to illustrate this structure.

Example 1. Consider the following scenario: *Bobby Buyer (B) has contracted with Sally Seller (S), the local car dealer, for the delivery of a brand new car. However, at the agreed date, S does not deliver. Can B demand delivery of the car from S?*

To begin with, we need a rule to decide the case. Let's assume B and S live in land where the *UNIDROIT Principles* [9] apply. Then our case would be governed by the following article (Art. 7.2.2 of the UNIDROIT Principles):

> "*Where a party who owes an obligation other than one to pay money does not perform, the other party* **may require performance**, *unless*
>
> (a) *performance is impossible in law or in fact;*
> (b) *performance or, where relevant, enforcement is unreasonably burdensome or expensive;*
> (c) *the party entitled to performance may reasonably obtain performance from another source;*
> (d) *performance is of an exclusively personal character; or*
> (e) *the party entitled to performance does not require performance within a reasonably time after it has, or ought to have, become aware of the non-performance.*"

Thanks to the clear-cut way in which this provision is designed, it is rather simple to extract the rule incorporated in it, or, more precisely, the conditions and the consequence of the rule. In a semi-formal notation, one might put it like this:

[*obligation*(X,Y,O) **and**	// meaning "X owes O to Y"
not_money(O) **and**	// true if O isn't a sum of money
no_performance(X,Y,O) **and**	// X hasn't delivered O to Y
not (*performance_impossible*(X,O) **or**	// X cannot deliver O
performance_too_burdensome(X,O) **or**	
alternative_source_available(O) **or**	
personal_obligation(X,Y,O) **or**	
time_limit_exceeded(X,Y,O))]	// Y didn't bring his claim in time
⤳ *right_to_performance*(Y,X,O)	// Y can demand performance (i. e., delivery)

To answer the question of the case, one would aim at gathering information about all atoms mentioned in the body of the rule and then derive formally whether the formula specified in the head holds.

However, it should be emphasized that classical logic is not an appropriate framework for processing rules as the one given in Ex. 1, for two reasons: First, legal rules have usually been amended, over time, by exceptions and counter-exceptions. Therefore, legal rules are not strict, but *defeasible*, as we can rarely rely on them not having exceptions (indicated by *unless* in Art. 7.2.2.) [17,6]. Second, there is the nature of the situation in which legal cases typically arise. Usually there are two or more parties involved, one bringing a claim and the other one defending against it. Since both of them have their stakes in it, they can hardly be expected to be objective in their description of the situation. Yet they are often the only ones with first-hand knowledge about the relevant facts, and thus are the natural starting point when collecting these facts. This raises the question of how to reconcile the two conflicting views presented by the parties to the judge. Since a judge *must* ultimately find a decision, the conflict has to be solved. A way of dealing with contradictory and missing information has to be found, as it is not possible to send the plaintiff home with a mere "*sorry, I don't know*". So, legal reasoning cannot be *logical* (or else would trivialize, or run into blazing contradictions), but it has to be *rational*, and, what is particularly important in this domain, *justifiable*. The question is what consequences may correctly be inferred from a set of defeasible, possibly contradicting legal rules. Legal theory provides some guidance, as it has developed requirements of formal or procedural justice. These requirements will be mimicked by restrictions for inference mechanisms applicable to our model of law. All inference mechanisms that observe these restrictions—and the results that can be inferred by applying them—will be called *justifiable*. The goal is not to completely determine the inference, but to set out a frame within which several inference mechanisms can exist. We assume the following restrictions to form the basic requirements for justifiability:

Strictness Strict legal rules—like e. g. the first article of the basic law in Germany: "The dignity of a human being is inviolable."—are to be treated as in classical logic (accordingly, a knowledge base containing contradicting *strict* rules is corrupt).

Specificity Exceptions to a rule have a higher priority than the rule itself, as the idea is that an exception, if its conditions are met, defeats the rule.

Equality Equal cases are to be treated equally.

The last requirement, "Equality", means that the inference mechanism is not randomized, so that using the same knowledge base and entering the same facts repeatedly yields the same result. This, of course, is only one of the implications of "Equality". The concept goes further in theory, but insofar cannot be properly formalized here. The reason is that the expert system cannot decide whether two real-life situations are "alike". It only asks for the relevant facts, which are then to be entered by the user. In other words the inference mechanism guarantees formal equality (same input, same output), while the user has to guarantee material equality (similar situations, same input).

Beyond justifiability, there are some standard conflict rules [21]. The following three, given in their original latin form, date back to medieval times, when the *ius commune* governed continental Europe, and still serve as important guidelines for the administration of justice:

1. Lex specialis derogat legi generali. (*The special rule defeats the general rule.*)
2. Lex superior derogat legi inferiori. (*The superior rule defeats the inferior rule.*)
3. Lex posterior derogat legi priori. (*The younger rule defeats the older rule.*)

The idea of the first conflict rule is that a rule having additional conditions is based on more information and therefore preferable to one based on less information. This is meant by a "special" rule, which applies only to a part of the situations where the "general" rule applies, because it has additional preconditions. The second conflict rule makes use of a hierarchy of laws, where e. g. the Constitution is at the top. The rationale behind the third conflict rule is similar to that of the first one: a legal rule that has been created at a later stage, for example by an act of parliament, is based on more information because the lawgiver of the future knows more than the lawgiver of the past.

There are many more formal (and, of course, material) criteria for justice proposed in legal theory, but none of them have received universal acceptance. Taking the aspects described above as a specification of minimal requirements for a justifiable inference mechanism, defeasible argumentation appears to be an optimal framework for a system that is able to support judicial decisions. The standard version of DeLP [5], which we used for the LiZ system, is an adequate inference engine for defeasible argumentation. It turns out that the additional assumptions made in DeLP to add plausibility to the results inferred (like "Generalized Specificity" as a comparision criterion for arguments and the "concordance" of argumentation lines) are remarkably similar to the standard conflict rules used in legal theory. We will come back to this issue later, but first we go on with a general formalization of the legal concepts of "burden of proof" and "legal trees".

3. Legal trees and the burden of proof

Gathering information on a legal case is not always simple. Considering again the rule formalized in Ex. 1, already the first condition *obligation*(X,Y,O) is problematic. Though it seems clear that S has promised to B to deliver the car and is thereby obliged to do so, so that *obligation*(S,B,CAR) should be true, an obligation per definition belongs to the *legal sphere*. It is not tangible or measurable as a real-life object, there is no physical detector for it. Instead, we need another legal rule to tell us when an obligation arises. In fact, we find such a rule in the UNIDROIT Principles [9, Art. 1.3], a specialized version of which would contain the following rules (again in semi-formal notation):

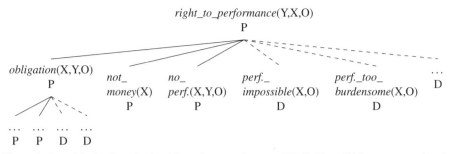

Figure 1. Part of the *legal tree* for the claim *right_to_performance*(Y,X,O). The solid lines correspond to *if*, a dashed line to *unless*. The labels P (plaintiff) and D (defendant) indicate the *burden of proof*.

(1) *sales_contract*(X,Y,PRICE,O) ⤳ *obligation*(X,Y,money)   // the buyer's obligation
(2) *sales_contract*(X,Y,PRICE,O) ⤳ *obligation*(Y,X,O)   // the seller's obligation

In applying Art. 7.2.2 to the example, we would take recourse to the second one of the above rules to determine whether a non-monetary obligation between B and S exists. We will call rules which are invoked in this way (i. e., to explain, define or otherwise determine the conditions of another rule) *secondary rules*, as opposed to the *primary rules* that directly raise a legal claim as their consequence (in this case: "Can B demand delivery of the car?", which is answered by Art. 7.2.2).

The secondary rule tells us that if the condition *sales_contract*(B,S,PRICE,O) is met, we can derive *obligation*(S,B,O). The question whether such a contract exists is almost a matter of fact, since we would expect that the sales contract exists as a real-life object. Therefore, in breaking down our initial question "*Can B demand delivery?*", we have reached a rather basic level were the legal question is turned into tiny factual bits of information we can provide easily. Of course, this is only the ideal (see [12] for an account of the age-old criticism of this method and [10] for a recent investigation of the relationship between legal argumentation and language). Often questions remain which are not answered so easily (like "*is the enforcement unreasonably burdensome?*", see Art. 7.2.2 lit. b), and would provide even greater difficulty if they should be answered by artificial intelligence. Yet the method just described has proven workable and is practiced by judges and lawyers around the globe. Due to the complexity of the law itself, this method carries far enough potential for computer-assistance even without the possibility to automatically find the basic factual information finally needed to decide the case.

Breaking down a rule by using secondary rules leads to a tree structure, as Fig. 1 illustrates. The conditions of the primary rule are "explained" by secondary rules, the conditions of which may in turn be explained by further secondary rules, and so on. This goes on until there are no more rules available for any of the conditions that have not already been explained. It should then be possible to determine these conditions—represented by the leafs of the tree—with relative ease by collecting appropriate "real-life" evidence. These conditions pose the decisive questions of the case. Answering them means to collect the "relevant facts", which then allows deciding on the secondary rules step by step—moving from the leafs to the root of the tree—and finally deciding whether the primary rule applies to the given case or not.

Collecting "relevant facts" imposes the next issue that has to be dealt with in order to integrate all information for a given case. As discussed before, usually, there are multiple parties involved in legal reasoning and the question at hand is, what to do when these parties provide contradictory or incomplete information? Or more general, which of the parties is responsible in bringing forward essential information needed to solve a given case in an adequate manner? Courts all over the world have developed more or less the same solution to this problem. The approach is rather simple. First, a kind of *assumption* is created for every single one of the relevant facts. If the parties cannot help to clarify the fact in question, the fact is either assumed to be given or absent. This provides a way of dealing with incomplete information. Second, if the parties do say something but contradict each other, evidence is collected from both sides. If the evidence suffices to establish the fact (or its absence), this result becomes part of the basis for the decision. If however the evidence remains inconclusive, again recourse is taken to the assumption created earlier to circumvent the contradiction presented by the parties.

The legal term associated with the creation of the assumption is *burden of proof* (see [16], [18], or [7] for an AI and Law perspective on this subject, and e. g. [1] for an analysis from within legal theory). Saying that a party has the burden to prove fact "A" means that the assumption for this fact is "NOT A". Saying a party has the burden to prove "NOT A" means that the assumption is "A". Logically it is not important which of the parties carries the burden, but which content the burden has (to prove "A" or to prove "NOT A"). However, legal experts are not used to talking about the content at all. They don't have to. For a human being, the content of the burden can easily be derived from the knowledge of who carries it. A party would only try to either prove a fact or to prove the absence of it, depending on what suits the party best. When the plaintiff likes to prove "A", the defendant will always like to prove "NOT A", and both will be clear from the context. Therefore, knowing who carries the burden of proof regarding a certain fact is equivalent to knowing the content of the burden, and thus the corresponding assumption. In anglo-american terminology, this relationship is depicted very clearly: when one party has the burden of proof, the other one is said to have the *benefit of assumption* (i. e., it benefits if the assumption is resorted to).

Naturally, jurists have developed rules to determine the burden of proof. The general rule is that a party carries the burden of proof for those facts that, if given, would favor the party, i. e. facts that would either (a) support the party's claim or (b) support its defense against the other party's claim. However, this general rule is sometimes tricky to apply. The question it raises is whether a certain fact is the negative condition of a claim or rather the positive condition of a defense to it (or vice versa), which may be hard to say since the wording of the law can be ambivalent. From the perspective of classical logic, presupposing an omniscient observer, it wouldn't make a difference. Yet, in a court scenario with the possibilities of contradictory and incomplete information, it makes a difference in determining the assumptions and therefore in deciding most real cases. To illustrate this, we will use the concept of an exception to a rule. An exception to a rule can be derived from the rule by adding further conditions and negating the consequence. For example, if [A **and** B **and** C] $\rightsquigarrow$ Z is a rule, then [A **and** B **and** C **and** D] $\rightsquigarrow$ NOT Z is an exception.

Back to the problem of the burden of proof we find that exceptions usually constitute the basis for a defense against a claim, whereas exceptions to exceptions in turn support the claim, and so on; this kind of proof burden corresponds to the *burden of production* in [7]. That means, when the plaintiff claims Z under the rule above, he has the burden of proof for A, B, and C. In turn, the burden of proof for D lies with the defendant, as it only occurs as part of the exception which naturally only the defendant would like to support. The assumptions would be "NOT A", "NOT B", "NOT C" and "NOT D". If, however, we dropped the exception and modified the strict rule by adding the additional literal from the exception in negated form as a condition, we would get the single (strict) rule: [A **and** B **and** C **and** (**not** D)] $\leadsto$ Z.

In this scenario, the plaintiff claiming Z would have to prove A, B, C and also "NOT D", as all these are conditions for the rule supporting his claim. The resulting assumptions would be "NOT A", "NOT B", "NOT C" and "D", so in contrast to the first scenario, "D" would be assumed. If the plaintiff can show A, B, and C, but the parties disagree on D, and neither of them can provide sufficient evidence, then in the latter scenario the plaintiff loses the case (for failing to establish the conditions of the rule supporting the claim), while winning in the first scenario (where the defendant fails to establish the conditions of the exception). Generally, the absence of a fact is often hard to show, which is why negated conditions are kept to a minimum in legal rules (although they do exist). Instead they are put into exceptions, where they occur in positive form.

Until now, we have only applied the concept of burden of proof to primary rules, but it can be elegantly extended to the whole *legal tree* introduced in Fig. 1. To do so, we start at the root of the tree and mark the root and the conditions of the primary rule with a "P" for plaintiff, and the conditions of exceptions to the primary rule with a "D" for defendant. Then we work our way down the tree: In the illustration given in Fig. 1, this means that the burden of proof is inherited from the parent node along solid lines, but inverted along dashed lines. Thus, not only the relevant facts needed to solve a given case but also the respective burden of proof for each of the facts (and, therefore, the assumptions that follow) can easily and automatically be calculated. The only knowledge necessary is the rules (and their exceptions).

4. Legal Knowledge Modelling and Reasoning

We will now further extend and formalize our model. As a general starting point we will allow rules to be either strict or defeasible, while the latter will be the standard.

Legal provisions In order to represent legal rules in a concise fashion, we will represent exceptions within their corresponding rule. The concept of rules and exceptions correctly reflects the theoretical structure of the law, but at a somewhat low level. For example, a single article from any given statute usually contains more than one rule (and can contain multiple exceptions, cf. Art. 7.2.2). Therefore, a meta-structure comprising all those rules seems convenient. In our model, rules with the same consequence are incorporated in a *legal provision* (cf. Def. 1 below). Grouping rules with the same consequence in this way also helps to deal with alternatives. In accordance to the way legal experts conceive and apply legal rules, alternative conditions, corresponding to a logical disjunction, are removed by introducing extra rules for every alternative. Therefore, in our legal model, the conditions of a rule will always be *cumulative*, i. e. a conjunction of literals.

Subsumption When applying a legal rule, after breaking it down as far as possible to its constituents (i. e. the conditions of the lowest secondary rules in the "legal tree"), there inevitably comes the task of *subsuming* the given case under these constituents. Although there are no more legal rules available to decide whether these conditions are fulfilled, one will usually find further lexical rules to do so. Taking a trivial example, to decide whether an obligation is "non-monetary" (see Art. 7.2.2), "money" could be looked up in a dictionary, which would probably enumerate the forms in which money comes along or its characteristics. Such definitions are nothing else than further rules. Our model therefore allows for *subsumption rules* to be added to the database. They have the same form as legal rules and are treated likewise in the inference process. They are only named differently to make clear that they do not share the same authority due to their non-legal origin.

Open concepts and antagonistic rules As mentioned, legal rules in the knowledge base are usually meant to be *defeasible*, i. e. open to exceptions and refutation. Although modelling law by using defeasible rules is probably against the intuition of many legal experts, it is suitable for the reasons given above. Moreover, defeasible rules can also be used for modelling the arguments that are used in law in dealing with open concepts like "burdensome" (cf. Art. 7.2.2), "reliable", "adequate" etc. For instance, as adequacy is a very broad and fuzzy concept, indicators have been developed for the adequacy and inadequacy of damages to make the handling of the law easier and more foreseeable. Such arguments can be seen as *antagonistic* rules, where the consequence of one rule is the negation of the consequence of the other.

In the knowledge base, not only rules with the same consequence, but also their antagonistic counterparts become part of one single *legal provision*:

Definition 1 (legal provision). A *legal provision* is a triple $P = (c, \mathcal{B}, \overline{\mathcal{B}})$ with $\mathcal{B} = \{B_1, \ldots, B_k\}$ and $\overline{\mathcal{B}} = \{B_{k+1}, \ldots, B_{k+l}\}$ where $k \geq 1$ is the number of legal rules having c as their consequence, and $l \geq 0$ is the number of corresponding antagonistic rules. Each B_i is of the form $B_i = ((b_1, \ldots, b_n), E_1, \ldots, E_m)$ where the b_j are the *conditions* and E_j sequences of *exceptions* for the i-th rule with $n \geq 1$, and $m \geq 0$.

For instance, in an attribute-value pair notation for legal provisions (in LiZ, an XML representation is used), Art. 7.2.2 is given by the following knowledge base entry:

Art. 7.2.2 = (consequence = *right_to_performance*(Y,X,O),
              rules = ((conditions = (*obligation*(X,Y,O), *not_money*(X),
                                       no_performance(X,Y,O)),
                        exception = (*performance_impossible*(X,O)),
                        exception = (*performance_too_burdensome*(X,O)),...)))

A *legal knowledge base* is a set $KB = \{P_1, \ldots, P_n\}$ of legal provisions. For each claim c, such a knowledge base uniquely determines a legal tree $ltree(c, KB)$ with root c and whose further nodes and arrows are constructed from KB. For the general case, we extended the legal tree construction as illustrated in Fig. 1 accordingly:

- Multiple rules with the same consequence: Outgoing arrows of a node are grouped together if they belong to the same rule.
- Conjunctions of exceptions: The respective arrows are grouped accordingly.
- Antagonistic rules: Introduce *not-if* and *not-unless* arrows.

Note that the computation of the burden of proof within the legal tree carries over smoothly to antagonistic rules: The burden of proof is inverted along *not-if* arrows, but inherited along *not-unless* arrows.

We continue with a brief excursus to some technical details of DeLP that will be used to represent and to reason with the model formalized above.

5. Defeasible Logic Programming

The basic elements of *Defeasible Logic Programming* (DeLP) are facts and rules. A single atom h or a negated atom $\sim h$ (in DeLP negation is denoted by $\sim$) is called a literal or *fact*. Rules are divided into strict rules of the form $h \leftarrow B$ and defeasible rules of the form $h \prec B$ where h is a literal and B is a set of literals. A literal h is *derivable* from a set of facts, strict rules, and defeasible rules X, denoted by $X \mathrel{\mid\!\sim} h$, iff it is derivable in the classical rule-based sense treating strict and defeasible rules equally. A set X is *contradictory*, denoted $X \mathrel{\mid\!\sim} \bot$, iff both $X \mathrel{\mid\!\sim} h$ and $X \mathrel{\mid\!\sim} \sim h$ holds for some h. A *defeasible logic program* (*de.l.p.*) P is a tuple $P = (\Pi, \Delta)$ with a non-contradictory set of strict rules and facts Π and a set of defeasible rules Δ. Using rules and facts arguments can be constructed as follows.

Definition 2 (Argument, Subargument). Let $h \in \mathcal{L}$ be a literal and let $P = (\Pi, \Delta)$ be a *de.l.p.*. Then $\langle \mathcal{A}, h \rangle$ with $\mathcal{A} \subseteq \Delta$ is an *argument* for h, iff $\Pi \cup \mathcal{A} \mathrel{\mid\!\sim} h$, $\Pi \cup \mathcal{A} \mathrel{\mid\!\not\sim} \bot$, and $\mathcal{A}$ is minimal with respect to set inclusion. An argument $\langle \mathcal{B}, q \rangle$ is a *subargument* of an argument $\langle \mathcal{A}, h \rangle$, iff $\mathcal{B} \subseteq \mathcal{A}$.

Two literals h and h_1 *disagree* regarding a *de.l.p.* $P = (\Pi, \Delta)$, iff the set $\Pi \cup \{h, h_1\}$ is contradictory. An argument $\langle \mathcal{A}_1, h_1 \rangle$ is a *counterargument* to an argument $\langle \mathcal{A}_2, h_2 \rangle$ at a literal h, iff there is a subargument $\langle \mathcal{A}, h \rangle$ of $\langle \mathcal{A}_2, h_2 \rangle$ such that h and h_1 disagree.

In order to deal with counterarguments, a central aspect of defeasible logic programming is a formal comparison criterion among arguments. Bearing in mind the context of legal reasoning *Generalized Specificity* [5] seems to be the most appropriate choice. According to this criterion an argument is preferred to another argument, iff the former one is more *specific* than the latter, i. e., (informally) iff the former one uses more facts or less rules. For example, $\langle \{c \prec a, b\}, c \rangle$ is more specific than $\langle \{\sim c \prec a\}, \sim c \rangle$, denoted by $\langle \{c \prec a, b\}, c \rangle \succ \langle \{\sim c \prec a\}, \sim c \rangle$, cf. [5]. Then an argument $\langle \mathcal{A}_1, h_1 \rangle$ is a *defeater* of an argument $\langle \mathcal{A}_2, h_2 \rangle$, iff there is a subargument $\langle \mathcal{A}, h \rangle$ of $\langle \mathcal{A}_2, h_2 \rangle$ such that $\langle \mathcal{A}_1, h_1 \rangle$ is a counterargument of $\langle \mathcal{A}_2, h_2 \rangle$ at literal h and either $\langle \mathcal{A}_1, h_1 \rangle \succ \langle \mathcal{A}, h \rangle$ (*proper defeat*) or $\langle \mathcal{A}_1, h_1 \rangle \not\succ \langle \mathcal{A}, h \rangle$ and $\langle \mathcal{A}, h \rangle \not\succ \langle \mathcal{A}_1, h_1 \rangle$ (*blocking defeat*).

When considering sequences of arguments, the definition of defeat is not sufficient to describe a conclusive argumentation line since it disregards the dialectical structure of argumentation, cf. [5].

Definition 3 (Acceptable Argumentation Line). Let $P = (\Pi, \Delta)$ be a *de.l.p.*. Let $\Lambda = [\langle \mathcal{A}_1, h_1 \rangle, \ldots, \langle \mathcal{A}_m, h_m \rangle]$ be a sequence of some arguments. Λ is called an *acceptable argumentation line*, iff 1.) Λ is a finite sequence, 2.) every argument $\langle \mathcal{A}_i, h_i \rangle$ with $i > 1$ is a defeater of its predecessor $\langle \mathcal{A}_{i-1}, h_{i-1} \rangle$ and if $\langle \mathcal{A}_i, h_i \rangle$ is a blocking defeater of $\langle \mathcal{A}_{i-1}, h_{i-1} \rangle$ and $\langle \mathcal{A}_{i+1}, h_{i+1} \rangle$ exists, then $\langle \mathcal{A}_{i+1}, h_{i+1} \rangle$ is a proper defeater of $\langle \mathcal{A}_i, h_i \rangle$, 3.) $\Pi \cup \mathcal{A}_1 \cup \mathcal{A}_3 \cup \ldots$ is non-contradictory (*concordance of supporting arguments*), 4.) $\Pi \cup \mathcal{A}_2 \cup \mathcal{A}_4 \cup \ldots$ is non-contradictory (*concordance of interfering arguments*), and 5.) no argument $\langle \mathcal{A}_k, h_k \rangle$ is a subargument of an argument $\langle \mathcal{A}_i, h_i \rangle$ with $i < k$.

In DeLP a literal h is *warranted*, if there is an argument $\langle \mathcal{A}, h \rangle$ which is non-defeated in the end. To decide whether $\langle \mathcal{A}, h \rangle$ is defeated or not, every acceptable argumentation line starting with $\langle \mathcal{A}, h \rangle$ has to be considered.

Definition 4 (Dialectical Tree). Let $P = (\Pi, \Delta)$ be a *de.l.p.* and let $\langle \mathcal{A}_0, h_0 \rangle$ be an argument. A *dialectical tree* for $\langle \mathcal{A}_0, h_0 \rangle$, denoted $\mathcal{T}_{\langle \mathcal{A}_0, h_0 \rangle}$, is defined as follows:

1. The root of $\mathcal{T}$ is $\langle \mathcal{A}_0, h_0 \rangle$.
2. Let $\langle \mathcal{A}_n, h_n \rangle$ be a node in $\mathcal{T}$ and let $\Lambda = [\langle \mathcal{A}_0, h_0 \rangle, \ldots, \langle \mathcal{A}_n, h_n \rangle]$ be the sequence of nodes from the root to $\langle \mathcal{A}_n, h_n \rangle$. Let $\langle \mathcal{B}_1, q_1 \rangle, \ldots, \langle \mathcal{B}_k, q_k \rangle$ be the defeaters of $\langle \mathcal{A}_n, h_n \rangle$. For every defeater $\langle \mathcal{B}_i, q_i \rangle$ with $1 \leq i \leq k$ such that the argumentation line $\Lambda' = [\langle \mathcal{A}_0, h_0 \rangle, \ldots, \langle \mathcal{A}_n, h_n \rangle, \langle \mathcal{B}_i, q_i \rangle]$ is acceptable, the node $\langle \mathcal{A}_n, h_n \rangle$ has a child $\langle \mathcal{B}_i, q_i \rangle$. If there is no such $\langle \mathcal{B}_i, q_i \rangle$, the node $\langle \mathcal{A}_n, h_n \rangle$ is a leaf.

In order to decide whether the argument at the root of a given dialectical tree is defeated or not, it is necessary to perform a *bottom-up*-analysis of the tree. Every leaf of the tree is marked "undefeated" and every inner node is marked "defeated", if it has at least one child node marked "undefeated". Otherwise it is marked "undefeated". Let $\mathcal{T}^*_{\langle \mathcal{A}, h \rangle}$ denote the marked dialectical tree of $\mathcal{T}_{\langle \mathcal{A}, h \rangle}$. We call a literal h *warranted*, iff there is an argument $\langle \mathcal{A}, h \rangle$ for h such that the root of the marked dialectical tree $\mathcal{T}^*_{\langle \mathcal{A}, h \rangle}$ is marked "undefeated". Then $\langle \mathcal{A}, h \rangle$ is a *warrant* for h.

6. Using DeLP for Legal Reasoning

One advantage of the representation for legal knowledge described in Sec. 4 is the similarity to a *de.l.p.*. The legal knowledge can be transformed into DeLP rules straightforwardly. The relevant facts of the case can then be added as DeLP facts.

For example, Art. 7.2.2 in DeLP rules becomes:

R1: *right_to_performance*(Y,X,O) $\prec$ *obligation*(X,Y,O), *not_money*(X), *no_performance*(X,Y,O).
R2: ~*right_to_performance*(Y,X,O) $\prec$ *obligation*(X,Y,O), *not_money*(X),
    no_performance(X,Y,O), *performance_impossible*(X,O).
R3: ~*right_to_performance*(Y,X,O) $\prec$ *obligation*(X,Y,O), *not_money*(X),
    no_performance(X,Y,O), *performance_too_burdensome*(X,O).

Likewise, secondary and antagonistic rules are translated to DeLP, for instance:

R4: *performance_too_burdensome*(X,O) $\prec$ *performance_req_excessive_expense*(X,O).
R5: ~*performance_too_burdensome*(X,O) $\prec$ *obstacles_were_foreseeable*(X,O).
R6: *performance_req_excessive_expense*(X,O) $\prec$ *severe_short_of_goods*(O), *out_of_stock*(X,O).

For the general case, let $P = (c, \mathcal{B}, \overline{\mathcal{B}})$ be a legal provision as in Def. 1 and let $B = ((b_1, \ldots, b_n), E_1, \ldots, E_m)$ with $E_i = (e_{i,1}, \ldots, e_{i,r_i})$. If $B \in \mathcal{B}$, the following $m + 1$ DeLP rules are generated:

$$c \prec b_1, \ldots, b_n.$$
$$\sim c \prec b_1, \ldots, b_n, e_{1,1}, \ldots, e_{1,r_1}.$$
$$\ldots$$
$$\sim c \prec b_1, \ldots, b_n, e_{m,1}, \ldots, e_{m,r_m}.$$

For $B \in \overline{\mathcal{B}}$, the DeLP rules generated are obtained from the rules above by replacing c (resp. $\sim c$) in each rule head by $\sim c$ (resp. c).

When passi: g the rules {R1, ..., R6} together with the facts *obligation*(X,Y,O), *not_money*(O), n _performance*(X,Y,O), *severe_short_of_goods*(O), *out_of_stock*(X,O), *obstacles_were_foreseeable*(X,O) to the DeLP interpreter and asking for the status of the claim *right_to_performance*(Y,X,O), it generates the dialectical tree shown in Fig. 2. Since the root of this tree is undefeated, DeLP warrants its claim.

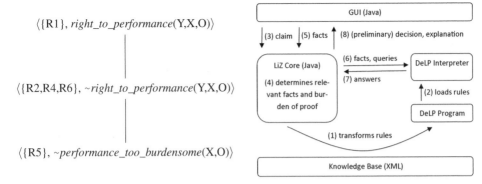

$\langle\{R1\}, right\_to\_performance(Y,X,O)\rangle$

$\langle\{R2,R4,R6\}, \sim right\_to\_performance(Y,X,O)\rangle$

$\langle\{R5\}, \sim performance\_too\_burdensome(X,O)\rangle$

Figure 2. Example of a dialectical tree generated by DeLP

Figure 3. Illustration of the LiZ system. The system is interactive, steps 5 to 8 are repeated during the legal procedure until no more relevant facts are submitted.

It is obvious that the inference mechanism of DeLP is *justifiable* according to our definition in Sec. 2. This is true regardless of the concrete comparison criterion used to decide between conflicting rules (DeLP allows for different criteria), as long as this criterion prefers exceptions over the corresponding rule. Above that, the standard criterion of "generalized specificity" is particularly suitable for modeling legal reasoning. The concept of "generalized specificity" is twofold. First, it prefers "more precise" rules, where rule A is more precise than rule B if the conditions of B are a true subset of the conditions of A. Secondly, it prefers more concise arguments, where an argument is more concise when it makes less use of rules than another. This concept corresponds remarkably well to the widely acclaimed standard rules of interpretation in legal theory that we recalled in Sec. 2. Indeed, generalized specificity incorporates the same idea as the *lex specialis*.

As an extension to this work, also the ideas of *lex superior* and *lex posterior* could be easily implemented on the basis of DeLP. For this, only the priority relation between arguments has to be changed, e. g., by combining generalized specificity with information about time and law hierarchies in a lexicographic way.

The structure of the LiZ system itself is illustrated in Fig. 3. It interactively follows the course of a civil action from the judge's point of view. First, the user enters general information about the case, especially the kind of claim. Then, LiZ searches the knowledge base for rules that might support such a claim, collects all the secondary rules needed to interpret them, and constructs and shows the legal tree(s). It also determines the burden of proof for the relevant facts. The user can then successively enter the relevant facts as presented by plaintiff and defendant through the GUI. Whenever a new fact is entered, LiZ updates the three fact sets (view of the plaintiff/defendant, view to be taken by the judge), transforms them to DeLP facts and passes them on to the DeLP interpreter, along with a query as to whether the claim would be supported under each of the fact sets. The results are transformed into plain text as used by judges, the user can base his or her intermediary decisions on them (e. g., ask the defendant to produce further evidence to avoid losing the case). Thus, the system shows the decision that would have to be made at any given time, which becomes the final decision once all facts have been entered. Currently, the LiZ database contains rules from the law of obligations of the German Civil Code, but the design of LiZ is in no way specifically tailored to the German jurisdiction.

7. Conclusions and Further Work

We presented an approach to an argumentation-based system that supports a judge in deciding private law cases. Starting from a focus on general principles governing judicial legal reasoning, we argued that the defeasibility inherent in laws and rules as well as the way rules are aggregated, compared, and preferred match the reasoning behavior of DeLP, together with the power of generalized specificity that is used as comparison criterion among arguments. The introduced knowledge representation model based on the notion of legal provisions has been implemented with an XML representation in the LiZ system. In particular, LiZ automatically determines the burden of proof that is essential for argumentation, exploits the defeasible reasoning facilities of the DeLP system, and provides interface functionalities as required from a private law judge point of view. As part of our future work, we plan to modify the priority relation among arguments in such a way as to take superiority of laws into account, or to favor more recent laws. Moreover, the modelling of further and more intricate cases will be necessary for a thorough usability and acceptance evaluation of the LiZ system.

References

[1]   A. Aarnio. *The Rational as Reasonable*. D. Reidel Publ. Co., Dordrecht, 1987.

[2]   R. J. Aldisert. *Logic for Lawyers*. National Institute for Trial Advocacy, 3rd edition, 1997.

[3]   T. Bench-Capon and H. Prakken. Introducing the logic and law corner. *J. of Logic and Computation*, 18(1):1–12, 2008.

[4]   E. Bund. *Juristische Logik und Argumentation*. Rombach & Co., Freiburg im Breisgau, 1983.

[5]   Alejandro J. García and Guillermo R. Simari. Defeasible logic programming: An argumentative approach. *Theory and Practice of Logic Programming*, 4(1):95–138, 2004.

[6]   D. M. Godden and D. Walton. Defeasibility in judicial opinion: Logical or procedural? *Informal Logic*, 28(1):6–19, 2008.

[7]   T. F. Gordon and D. Walton. Proof burdens and standards. In I. Rahwan and G. Simari, editors, *Argumentation in Artificial Intelligence*, pages 239–260–144. Springer, 2009.

[8]   J. Horovitz. *Law and Logic*. Springer, 1972.

[9]   International Institute for the Unification of Private Law. *UNIDROIT Principles of International Commercial Contracts*. UNIDROIT, Rome, 2nd edition, 2004.

[10]   M. Klatt. *Making the law explicit*. Hart Publishing, Oxford, 2008.

[11]   X. Minghui. On the inference rules in legal logic. *Social Sciences in China*, 30:58–74, 2009.

[12]   K. Olivecrona. *Law as Fact*. Steven and Sons, London, 1971.

[13]   E. Ott. *Die Methode der Rechtsanwendung*. Schulthess Polygraphischer Verlag AG, Zürich, 1979.

[14]   A. Peczenik. *On Law and Reason*. Springer Science + Business Media B.V., 2009.

[15]   A. Podlech, editor. *Rechnen und Entscheiden, Mathematische Modelle juristischer Argumentation*. Duncker & Humblot, Berlin, 1977.

[16]   H. Prakken. A formal model of adjudication dialogues. *AI and Law*, 16(3):333–359, 2008.

[17]   H. Prakken and G. Sartor. The role of logic in computational models of legal argument: A critical survey. In A. C. Kakas and F. Sadri, editors, *Computational Logic: Logic Programming and Beyond*, volume 2408 of *Lecture Notes in Computer Science*, pages 342–381. Springer, 2002.

[18]   G. Sartor. Defeasibility in legal reasoning. In Z. Bankowski, I. White, and U. Hahn, editors, *Informatics and the Foundations of Legal Reasoning*, pages 119–157. Kluwer, 1995.

[19]   M. J. Sergot, F. Sadri, R. A. Kowalski, F. Kriwaczek, P. Hammond, and H. T. Cory. The British nationality act as a logic program. *Commun. ACM*, 29(5):370–386, 1986.

[20]   V. Varano. Some reflections on procedure, comparative law, and the common core approach. *Global Jurist Topics*, 3(2):395–418, 2003.

[21]   E. Vranes. The definition of 'norm conflict' in international law and legal theory. *The European Journal of International Law*, 17(2):395–418, 2006.

Computational Models of Argument
P. Baroni et al. (Eds.)
IOS Press, 2010
doi:10.3233/978-1-60750-619-5-99

A formal analysis of the AIF in terms of the ASPIC framework

Floris BEX [a], Henry PRAKKEN [b] and Chris REED [a]

[a] *Argumentation Research Group, School of Computing, University of Dundee*
[b] *Department of Information and Computing Sciences, Utrecht University*
Faculty of Law, University of Groningen

Abstract In order to support the interchange of ideas and data between different projects and applications in the area of computational argumentation, a common ontology for computational argument, the Argument Interchange Format (AIF), has been devised. One of the criticisms levelled at the AIF has been that it does not take into account formal argumentation systems and their associated argumentation-theoretic semantics, which are part of the main focus of the field of computational argumentation. This paper aims to meet those criticisms by analysing the core AIF ontology in terms of the recently developed ASPIC argumentation framework.

Keywords. ontology, argument interchange, formal argumentation framework

1. Introduction

Argumentation is a rich research area, which uses insights from such diverse disciplines as artificial intelligence, linguistics, law and philosophy. In the past few decades, AI has developed its own sub-field devoted to computational argument, in which significant theoretical and practical advances are being made. This fecundity, unfortunately, has a negative consequence: with many researchers focusing on different aspects of argumentation, it is increasingly difficult to reintegrate results into a coherent whole. To tackle this problem, the community has initiated an effort aimed at building a common ontology for computational argument, which will support interchange between research projects and applications in the area: the Argument Interchange Format (AIF) (4; 12). The AIF's main practical goal is to facilitate the research and development of various tools for argument manipulation, argument visualization and multi-agent argumentation (4). In addition to this, the AIF also has a clear theoretical goal, namely to provide a general core ontology that encapsulates the common subject matter of the different (computational, linguistic, philosophical) approaches to argumentation.

Although the AIF takes its inspiration from different disciplines, its roots and goals are firmly in the field of computational argument. There therefore has to be a clear connection between the AIF core ontology and computational theories of argument. However, the AIF does as of yet not fully take into account such theories; while the work that has discussed the AIF to date (13; 14) deals with issues which are important for computational argument, such as argumentation schemes (17) and dialogues (16), the examples and the general flavour of this work clearly stem from philosophical argumentation theory. Most importantly, the relation between the AIF and the various logics for argumentation and their associated argumentation-theoretic semantics (such as (5)) has not yet been clarified.

In this paper, we aim to meet the above-mentioned criticisms of the AIF by interpreting the AIF core ontology in terms of a formal (logical) argumentation theory. More specifically, we explicitly show the connection between the elements of the AIF ontology and the recently developed ASPIC framework for argumentation (9). This framework is well-suited as a formal basis for the ontology because, like the AIF, it attempts to integrate ideas from different approaches in the literature (5; 8; 15; 10). Furthermore, because the ASPIC framework is explicitly linked to the argumentation-theoretic semantics of (5), giving arguments expressed using the AIF ontology meaning in terms of the ASPIC framework allows the arguments to be evaluated in these semantics.

The rest of this paper is organized as follows. In section 2 we discuss the core Argument Interchange Format and give a simple example which we will refer to in the rest of the paper. Section 3 discusses the relevant parts of the ASPIC framework as set out by (9). Section 4 formalizes the connection between the AIF and the ASPIC framework. First, we show how an AIF argumentation graph can be conceived of as an ASPIC argumentation theory (section 4.1) and then (section 4.2) we define how ASPIC arguments can be translated as an AIF argumentation graph. Section 5 concludes the paper and discusses some related and future research.

2. The Argument Interchange Format

The AIF is a communal project which aims to consolidate some of the defining work on (computational) argumentation (4). It works under the assumption that a common vision and consensus on the concepts and technologies in the field promotes the research and development of new argumentation tools and techniques. In addition to practical aspirations, such as developing a way of interchanging data between tools for argument manipulation and visualization, the AIF project also aims to develop a commonly agreed-upon core ontology that specifies the basic concepts used to express arguments and their mutual relations. The purpose of this ontology is not to replace other (formal) languages for expressing argument but rather to serve as an interlingua that acts as the centrepiece to multiple individual reifications.

The core AIF ontology (Figure 1) falls into two natural halves: the Upper Ontology and the Forms ontology (13; 12). In the ontology, arguments and the relations between them are conceived of as an *argument graph*. The Upper Ontology defines the language of nodes with which a graph can be built and the the Forms Ontology defines the various argumentative concepts or *forms* (e.g. argumentation schemes).

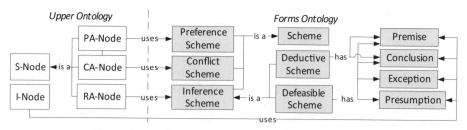

Figure 1. The Upper and Forms Ontologies of the AIF

The AIF ontology places at its core a distinction between *information*, such as propositions and sentences, and *schemes*, general patterns of reasoning such as inference or attack. Accordingly, the Upper Ontology defines two types of nodes: information nodes (I-nodes) and scheme nodes (S-nodes). Scheme nodes can be rule application nodes (RA-nodes), which denote applications of an inference rule or scheme, conflict application nodes (CA-nodes), which denote a specific conflict, and preference application nodes (PA-nodes), which denote specific preferences. Nodes are used to build an *AIF argument graph* (called argument networks by (13; 12)), which can be defined as follows:

Definition 2.1 An *AIF argument graph* G is a simple digraph (V, E) where

- $V = I \cup RA \cup CA \cup PA$ is the set of nodes in G, where I are the I-nodes, RA are the RA-nodes, CA are the CA-nodes and PA are the PA-nodes; and
- $E \subseteq V \times V \setminus I \times I$ is the set of the edges in G; and
- if $v \in N \setminus I$ then v has at least one direct predecessor and one direct successor.

We say that, given two nodes $v_1, v_2 \in V$ v_1 is a *direct predecessor* of v_2 and v_2 is a *direct successor* of v_1 if there is an edge $(v_1, v_2) \in E$.

For current purposes, we assume that a node consists of some content (i.e. the information or the name of the scheme that is being applied) and some identifier. I-nodes can only be connected to other I-nodes via S-nodes: there must be a scheme that expresses the rationale behind the relation between I-nodes. S-nodes, on the other hand, can be connected to other S-nodes directly (see Figure 2). The ontology does not type the edges in a graph; instead, semantics for edges can be inferred from the node types they connect.

In addition to the Upper Ontology, which defines the basic language for building argument graphs,[1] (13) introduced the Forms Ontology, which contains the abstract argumentative concepts. In the AIF ontology a pattern of reasoning can be an inference scheme, a conflict scheme or a preference scheme, which express a support relation (A therefore B), a conflict relation (A attacks B) and a preference relation (A is preferred to B), respectively. Scheme types can be further classified. For example, inference schemes can be deductive or defeasible and defeasible inference schemes can be subdivided into more specific argumentation schemes (e.g. Expert Opinion or Witness Testimony, see (17)). We will not explicitly define these schemes but simply assume the Forms Ontology is a set $\mathcal{F}$ which contains the relevant forms. The Forms Ontology is connected to the Upper Ontology, so that it is clear exactly what kind of form a particular node type uses (i.e. instantiates). For example, an application of an inference rule (RA node) uses an inference scheme from the Forms Ontology.

Figure 2 gives an example of an AIF argument graph, in which I-nodes are shown as rectangles and S-nodes as ellipses. The forms have been indicated above the nodes in italics. Here, the scheme for Witness Testimony (a defeasible scheme) is used to infer I_2 from I_1 and a deductive scheme is then used to subsequently infer I_3. Note that some nodes use multiple forms; I_2, for example, is the conclusion of the first inference step (that uses RA_1) but the premise of the second (that uses RA_2). RA_1 is attacked by its exception, I_4, through a Witness Bias conflict scheme. I_4 is itself attacked by I_5 and vice versa, and I_5 is preferred over I_4.

---

[1]It should be noted that, in a sense, the choice of the representational language is arbitrary. It would, for example, be perfectly acceptable to model arguments not as graphs but as sequences of sentences, as long as the information, schemes applications and the connection between them are somehow represented.

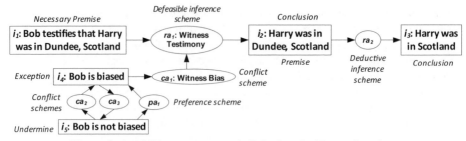

Figure 2. An AIF argument graph linked to the Forms Ontology

The abstract AIF ontology as presented here is purely intended as a language for expressing arguments. In order to do anything meaningful with such arguments (e.g. visualize, query, evaluate and so on), they must be expressed in a more concrete language so that they can be processed by additional tools and methods. For example, (13) reified the abstract ontology in RDF, a Semantic Web-based ontology language, which may then be used as input for a variety of Semantic Web argument annotation tools. In a similar vein, (11) have formalized the AIF in Description Logic, which allows for the automatic classification of schemes and arguments. In the current paper, one of the aims is to show how AIF argument graphs can be evaluated, that is, how a certain defeat status can be assigned to the elements of an argument graph using the argumentation-theoretic semantics of (5). To this end, the abstract ontology needs to be reified in a general framework for formal argumentation, in this case the ASPIC framework that will be explained in the next section.

3. The ASPIC framework

The framework of (9) further develops the attempts of (1; 3) to integrate within (5)'s abstract approach the work of (8; 15; 10) on rule-based argumentation. The framework instantiates Dung's abstract approach by assuming an unspecified logical language and by defining arguments as inference trees formed by applying deductive (or 'strict') and defeasible inference rules. The notion of an argument as an inference tree naturally leads to three ways of attacking an argument: attacking an inference, attacking a conclusion and attacking a premise. To resolve such conflicts, preferences may be used, which leads to three corresponding kinds of defeat: undercutting, rebutting and undermining defeat. To characterize them, some minimal assumptions on the logical object language must be made, namely that certain well-formed formulas are a contrary or contradictory of certain other well-formed formulas. Apart from this the framework is still abstract: it applies to any set of inference rules, as long as it is divided into strict and defeasible ones, and to any logical language with a contrary relation defined over it. The framework also abstracts from whether inference rules are domain-specific (as in e.g. default logic and logic programming) or whether they express general patterns of inference, such as the deductive inferences of classical logic or defeasible argumentation schemes. In the rest of this section, the framework will be defined; an extended example is given in section 4, where we translate the graph from Figure 2 to the ASPIC framework.

The basic notion of the framework is that of an argumentation system.

Definition 3.1 [Argumentation system] An *argumentation system* is a tuple $AS = (\mathcal{L}, {}^-, \mathcal{R}, \leq)$ where

- $\mathcal{L}$ is a logical language,
- ${}^-$ is a contrariness function from $\mathcal{L}$ to $2^{\mathcal{L}}$
- $\mathcal{R} = \mathcal{R}_s \cup \mathcal{R}_d$ is a set of strict ($\mathcal{R}_s$) and defeasible ($\mathcal{R}_d$) inference rules such that $\mathcal{R}_s \cap \mathcal{R}_d = \emptyset$,
- $\leq$ is a partial preorder on $\mathcal{R}_d$.

Definition 3.2 [Logical language] Let $\mathcal{L}$, a set, be a logical language. If $\varphi \in \overline{\psi}$ then if $\psi \notin \overline{\varphi}$ then φ is called a *contrary* of ψ, otherwise φ and ψ are called *contradictory*. The latter case is denoted by $\varphi = -\psi$ (i.e., $\varphi \in \overline{\psi}$ and $\psi \in \overline{\varphi}$).

Arguments are built by applying inference rules to one or more elements of $\mathcal{L}$. Strict rules are of the form $\varphi_1, \ldots, \varphi_n \to \varphi$, defeasible rules of the form $\varphi_1, \ldots, \varphi_n \Rightarrow \varphi$, interpreted as 'if the antecedents $\varphi_1, \ldots, \varphi_n$ hold, then *necessarily / presumably* the consequent φ holds', respectively. As is usual in logic, inference rules can be specified by schemes in which a rule's antecedents and consequent are metavariables ranging over $\mathcal{L}$.

Arguments are constructed from a knowledge base, which is assumed to contain three kinds of formulas.

Definition 3.3 [Knowledge bases] A *knowledge base* in an argumentation system $(\mathcal{L}, {}^-, \mathcal{R}, \leq)$ is a pair $(\mathcal{K}, \leq')$ where $\mathcal{K} \subseteq \mathcal{L}$ and $\leq'$ is a partial preorder on $\mathcal{K} \setminus \mathcal{K}_n$. Here $\mathcal{K} = \mathcal{K}_n \cup \mathcal{K}_p \cup \mathcal{K}_a$ where these subsets of $\mathcal{K}$ are disjoint and

- $\mathcal{K}_n$ is a set of (necessary) *axioms*. Intuitively, arguments cannot be attacked on their axiom premises.
- $\mathcal{K}_p$ is a set of *ordinary premises*. Intuitively, arguments can be attacked on their ordinary premises, and whether this results in defeat must be determined by comparing the attacker and the attacked premise (in a way specified below).
- $\mathcal{K}_a$ is a set of *assumptions*. Intuitively, arguments can be attacked on their ordinary assumptions, where these attacks always succeed.

The following definition of arguments is taken from (15), in which for any argument A, the function `Prem` returns all the formulas of $\mathcal{K}$ (called *premises*) used to build A, `Conc` returns A's conclusion, `Sub` returns all of A's sub-arguments, `Rules` returns all inference rules in A and `TopRule` returns the last inference rule used in A.

Definition 3.4 [Argument] An *argument* A on the basis of a knowledge base $(\mathcal{K}, \leq')$ in an argumentation system $(\mathcal{L}, {}^-, \mathcal{R}, \leq)$ is:

1. φ if $\varphi \in \mathcal{K}$ with: $\text{Prem}(A) = \{\varphi\}$; $\text{Conc}(A) = \varphi$; $\text{Sub}(A) = \{\varphi\}$; $\text{Rules}(A) = \emptyset$; $\text{TopRule}(A) = $ undefined.
2. $A_1, \ldots A_n \to/\Rightarrow \psi$ if $A_1, \ldots, A_n$ are arguments such that there exists a strict/defeasible rule $\text{Conc}(A_1), \ldots, \text{Conc}(A_n) \to/\Rightarrow \psi$ in $\mathcal{R}_s/\mathcal{R}_d$.
   $\text{Prem}(A) = \text{Prem}(A_1) \cup \ldots \cup \text{Prem}(A_n)$,
   $\text{Conc}(A) = \psi$,
   $\text{Sub}(A) = \text{Sub}(A_1) \cup \ldots \cup \text{Sub}(A_n) \cup \{A\}$.
   $\text{Rules}(A) = \text{Rules}(A_1) \cup \ldots \cup \text{Rules}(A_n) \cup \{\text{Conc}(A_1), \ldots, \text{Conc}(A_n) \to/\Rightarrow \psi\}$
   $\text{TopRule}(A) = \text{Conc}(A_1), \ldots \text{Conc}(A_n) \to/\Rightarrow \psi$

Furthermore, $\texttt{DefRules}(A) = \texttt{Rules}(A) \setminus \mathcal{R}_s$. Then A is: *strict* if $\texttt{DefRules}(A) = \emptyset$; *defeasible* if $\texttt{DefRules}(A) \neq \emptyset$; *firm* if $\texttt{Prem}(A) \subseteq \mathcal{K}_n$; *plausible* if $\texttt{Prem}(A) \not\subseteq \mathcal{K}_n$.

The framework assumes a partial preorder $\preceq$ on arguments, such that $A \preceq B$ means B is at least as 'good' as A. $A \prec B$ means that B is strictly preferred to A, where $\prec$ is the strict ordering associated with $\preceq$. The argument ordering is assumed to be 'admissible', i.e., to satisfy two further conditions: firm-and-strict arguments are strictly better than all other arguments and a strict inference cannot make an argument strictly better or worse than its weakest proper subargument. In this paper we assume that the argument ordering is somehow defined in terms of the orderings on $\mathcal{R}_d$ and $\mathcal{K}$ (definitions 3.1 and 3.3). Because of space limitations we refer to (9) for two example definitions. The notion of an argument ordering is used in the notion of an argument theory.

Definition 3.5 [Argumentation theories] An *argumentation theory* is a triple $AT = (AS, KB, \preceq)$ where AS is an argumentation system, KB is a knowledge base in AS and $\preceq$ is an admissible ordering of the set of all arguments that can be constructed from KB in AS (below called the set of arguments on the basis of AT).

If there is no danger for confusion the argumentation system will below be left implicit.

As indicated above, when arguments are inference trees, three syntactic forms of attack are possible: attacking a premise, a conclusion, or an inference. To model attacks on inferences, it is assumed that applications of inference rules can be expressed in the object language. The general framework of (9) leaves the nature of this naming convention implicit. In this paper we assume that this can be done in terms of a subset $\mathcal{L}_R$ of $\mathcal{L}$ containing formulas of the form r or r_i. For convenience we will also use elements of $\mathcal{L}_R$ at the metalevel, as names for inference rules, letting the context disambiguate.

Definition 3.6 [Attacks]
• Argument A *undercuts* argument B (on B') iff $\texttt{Conc}(A) \in \overline{r}$ for some $B' \in \texttt{Sub}(B)$ with a defeasible top rule r.
• Argument A *rebuts* argument B on (B') iff $\texttt{Conc}(A) \in \overline{\varphi}$ for some $B' \in \texttt{Sub}(B)$ of the form $B_1'', \ldots, B_n'' \Rightarrow \varphi$. In such a case A *contrary-rebuts* B iff $\texttt{Conc}(A)$ is a contrary of φ.
• Argument A *undermines* B (on φ) iff $\texttt{Conc}(A) \in \overline{\varphi}$ for some $\varphi \in \texttt{Prem}(B) \setminus \mathcal{K}_n$. In such a case A *contrary-undermines* B iff $\texttt{Conc}(A)$ is a contrary of φ or if $\varphi \in \mathcal{K}_a$.

Next these three notions of attack are combined with the argument ordering to yield three kinds of defeat. In fact, for undercutting attack no preferences will be needed to make it result in defeat, since otherwise a weaker undercutter and its stronger target might be in the same extension. The same holds for the other two ways of attack as far as they involve contraries (i.e., non-symmetric conflict relations between formulas).

Definition 3.7 [Successful rebuttal, undermining and defeat]
Argument A *successfully rebuts* argument B if A rebuts B on B' and either A contrary-rebuts B' or $A \not\prec B'$.
Argument A *successfully undermines* B if A undermines B on φ and either A contrary-undermines B or $A \not\prec \varphi$.
Argument A *defeats* argument B iff A undercuts or successfully rebuts or successfully

undermines B. Argument A *strictly defeats* argument B if A defeats B and B does not defeat A.

The definition of successful undermining exploits the fact that an argument premise is also a subargument. In (9), structured argumentation theories are then linked to Dung-style abstract argumentation theories:

Definition 3.8 [DF corresponding to an AT] An *abstract argumentation framework* DF_{AT} *corresponding to an argumentation theory* AT is a pair $\langle \mathcal{A}, Def \rangle$ such that $\mathcal{A}$ is the set of arguments on the basis of AT as defined by Definition 3.4, and Def is the relation on $\mathcal{A}$ given by Definition 3.7.

Thus, any semantics for abstract argumentation frameworks can be applied to arguments in an ASPIC framework. In (9) it is shown that for the four original semantics of (5), ASPIC frameworks as defined above satisfy (3)'s rationality postulates (if they satisfy some further basic assumptions).

4. Analysing AIF using the ASPIC argumentation framework

In this section the connection between the core AIF ontology (section 2) and the ASPIC argumentation framework (section 3) will be clarified. This explicit connection between the informal AIF ontology and the formal ASPIC framework tells us what the AIF notation means in terms of the formal framework. While there are, of course, other ways to give meaning to the elements of the ontology, an advantage of the current approach is that by formally grounding the AIF ontology in the ASPIC framework, specific boundaries for rational argumentation are set. There are not many constraints on an argument graph, as some flexibility is needed if one wants the AIF to be able to take into account natural arguments, which are put forth by people who will not always abide by strict formal rules that govern the structure of arguments. However, one of the aims of the AIF is to provide tools for structuring arguments so that, for example, inconsistencies among arguments may be discovered. By reifying AIF argument graphs in the ASPIC framework, the arguments are expressed in a more concrete language which allows such inconsistency checking and further evaluation of complex argument graphs.

A valid question is whether the boundaries set by the ASPIC framework are the right ones, that is, is the ASPIC framework a good argumentation logic for expressing and evaluating natural arguments? Fully answering this question is beyond the scope of this paper and we restrict ourselves to some remarks. To start with, ASPIC's tree structure of arguments fits well with many textbook accounts of argument structure and with may argument visualisation tools. Second, as argued by (9), its distinction between strict and defeasible inference rules allows a natural formalisation of argument schemes, which is an important concept from argumentation theory. Moreover, the ASPIC framework is embedded in the widely accepted semantic approach of (5) while, finally, under certain reasonable conditions it satisfies the rationality postulates of (3). On the other hand, not all features of the AIF can be translated into ASPIC, such as reasons for contrary relations and for preferences; the current boundaries to rational argumentation are thus limited to those forms of argumentation that can be expressed in the ASPIC framework. In this respect, the exercise of trying to translate the elements of the AIF ontology into the ASPIC framework tests the limits and flexibility of this formal logical framework.

4.1. From the AIF ontology to the ASPIC framework

If we want to show the connection between the AIF ontology and the ASPIC framework, we first need to show how an AIF argument graph can be interpreted in the ASPIC theory. Since in ASPIC the argumentation framework (Definition 3.8) is calculated from an argumentation theory (Definition 3.5), all that needs to be extracted from the AIF graph is the elements of such a theory. In particular, the AIF graph does not need to directly represent the notions of an argument, argument ordering, attack and defeat. This fits the philosophy behind the AIF: graphs are as basic as possible so that they are maximally interchangeable. Properties such as defeat are *calculated properties* of an AIF graph, properties which can be calculated by some specific tool or framework that processes the graph.

Definition 4.1 Given an AIF argument graph G and a set of forms $\mathcal{F}$, an ASPIC argumentation theory AT based on G is as follows:

1. $\mathcal{L} = I \cup RA$, where $\mathcal{L}_R = RA$;
2. $\mathcal{K} = \mathcal{K}_n \cup \mathcal{K}_p \cup \mathcal{K}_a$ where $\mathcal{K}_{n/p/a} = \{v \in I \mid v$ is an initial node and uses a form *axiom/premise/assumption*\}.
3. $\mathcal{R}_s/\mathcal{R}_d$ is the smallest set of inference rules $v_1, \ldots, v_n \;\rightarrow/\Rightarrow\; v$ (where $v_1, \ldots, v_n, v \in \mathcal{L}$) for which there is a node $v_k \in RA$ such that:

    (a) v_k uses a *deductive/defeasible scheme* $\in \mathcal{F}$; and
    (b) v_k's direct predecessors are $v_1, \ldots, v_n$ and v_k has a direct successor v.

4. $v_i \in \overline{v_j}$ iff there is a node $v_k \in CA$ such that ca has a direct predecessor v_i and a direct successor is v_j.
5. $\leq' = \{(v_i, v_j) \mid v_i, v_j \in \mathcal{K},$ there is a node $v_k \in PA$ such that pa has a direct predecessor v_i and direct successor $v_j\}$.
6. $\leq = \{(r_i, r_j) \mid r_i, r_j \in \mathcal{R}$ and $ra_i, ra_j \in RA,$ there is a node $v_k \in PA$ such that v_k has a direct predecessor ra_i and direct successor $ra_j\}$.

The above definition translates elements of an AIF graph into elements of an ASPIC argumentation theory. The language of the argumentation theory consists of all I- and RA-nodes in the graph. In the case of the example from Figure 2, this means that $\mathcal{L} = \{i_1, \ldots, i_5\} \cup \{r_1, r_2\}$ (I-nodes are referred to by their identifier). $\mathcal{K}$ contains all I-nodes which are themselves not derived from other I-nodes (in the example i_1, i_4, i_5), distributed among the different subsets of $\mathcal{K}$ according to the form they use. In the example, assume that $i_1 \in \mathcal{K}_n$ (that Bob testified can not be sensibly denied) and that i_4 and i_5 are ordinary premises in $\mathcal{K}_p$. Inference rules in the ASPIC framework are constructed from the combination of RA nodes and their predecessors and successors. The type of inference rule is determined by the form that the RA node uses (the translation of schemes in the Forms Ontology to rule schemes in the ASPIC framework is left implicit). The example graph translates to the sets of inference rules as follows: $\mathcal{R}_s = \{r_2 = i_2 \rightarrow i_3\}$ and $\mathcal{R}_d = \{r_1 = i_1 \Rightarrow i_2\}$, where r_1 and r_2 correspond to ra_1 and ra_2, respectively. Contrariness is determined by whether two nodes are connected through a CA-node; in the example, $i_4 \in \overline{r_1}$, $i_4 \in \overline{i_5}$ and $i_5 \in \overline{i_4}$ (i.e. i_4 and i_5 are each other's contradictories while i_4 is a contrary of r_1). Finally, a PA-node between two initial I-nodes or between two RA-nodes translates into preferences between either elements of $\mathcal{K}$ or inference rules, respectively. In the example there is one such explicit preference: $i_4 \leq' i_5$.

Now, given the elements of the example ASPIC theory as laid out above, the following arguments can be constructed: A_1: i_1, A_2: $A_1 \Rightarrow i_2$, A_3: $A_2 \rightarrow i_3$, A_4: i_4, A_5: i_5. According to definition 3.6, A_4 undercuts both A_2 and A_3 (it attacks the application of r_1), A_4 rebuts A_5 and A_5 rebuts A_4. In order to determine defeat relations, first a preference ordering on arguments must be set. In the example, this ordering can be safely assumed to be $A_4 \prec A_5$, because $i_4 \leq' i_5$ and i_4 and i_5 are A_4 and A_5's only components. Definition 3.7 then says that A_4 defeats A_2 and A_3 (because it undercuts them), and A_5 defeats A_4 (because it successfully rebuts it). Given these defeat relations, any of (5)'s semantics can be applied. In the example, it is clear that A_1, A_2, A_3 and A_5 are acceptable: A_1 is not attacked and A_5 successfully reinstates A_2 and A_3. Argument A_4 is not acceptable because, no matter which semantics are chosen, it is not in the extension.

Most elements of an AIF argument graph can be interpreted in the ASPIC framework. However, an AIF graph may contain elements or subgraps which are not properly expressible in ASPIC. This may be due to limitations of the AIF. For example, the preferences in the graph, which are translated into orderings by clauses (4) and (5) of Definition 4.1, may not satisfy the rational constraints imposed on them by ASPIC, since users of the AIF are free to ignore these constraints. In such cases the ASPIC framework sets the rational boundaries for argumentation. However, in some cases the inability to express a part of the graph may be due to limitations of the ASPIC framework. For example, in an AIF graph PA- or CA-nodes can be supported or attacked by an I-node through an RA- or CA-node. Thus reasons for and against preferences or contrariness may be given, which is perfectly acceptable (e.g. linguistic, legal or social reasons may be given for why "married" and "bachelor" are contradictory). In its current state, the ASPIC framework does not allow such reasons to be expressed.

4.2. From the ASPIC framework to the AIF ontology

We next define a translation from ASPIC to AIF. Since the AIF is meant for expressing arguments instead of (closures of) knowledge bases, we define the translation for a given set of arguments constructed in ASPIC on the basis of a given argumentation theory. As above, the translation does not concern the notions of attack and defeat, since these can be derived from the given elements of an argumentation theory. We also assume that $\mathcal{A}$ only contains undercutters for other arguments in $\mathcal{A}$. Finally, for any function f defined on arguments we overload the symbol f to let for any set $S = \{A_1, \ldots, A_n\}$ of arguments $f(S)$ stand for $f(A_1) \cup \ldots \cup f(A_n)$.

Definition 4.2 Given a set of arguments $\mathcal{A}_{AT}$ on the basis of an ASPIC argumentation theory AT, an AIF graph G and a set of forms $\mathcal{F}$ on the basis of $\mathcal{A}_{AT}$ is as follows:

1. I is the smallest set of consisting of distinct nodes v such that:
   (a) $v \in \text{Conc}(\text{Sub}(\mathcal{A})) \setminus \mathcal{L}_R$;
   (b) if $v \in \mathcal{K}_{n/p/a}$ then v uses a form *axiom/premise/assumption* $\in \mathcal{F}$.

2. RA is the smallest set consisting of distinct nodes v for each rule r in $\text{Rules}(\mathcal{A})$, where if $r \in \mathcal{R}_{s/d}$ then v uses a *deductive scheme/defeasible scheme* $\in \mathcal{F}$, respectively (we say that v corresponds to r).

3. CA is the smallest set consisting of distinct nodes v for each pair $\varphi, \psi \in \text{Conc}(\text{Sub}(\mathcal{A}))$ and $\varphi \in \overline{\psi}$ (we say that v corresponds to (φ, ψ));

4. PA is the smallest set consisting of distinct nodes v for each a pair (k, k') in $\leq'$ such that $k, k' \in \text{Prem}(\mathcal{A})$ and for each pair (r, r') in $\leq$ such that $r, r' \in \text{Rules}(\mathcal{A})$} (we say that v corresponds to (k, k') or to (r, r'));
5. E is the smallest set such that for all v, v' in G:

   (a) If $v \in I$ and $v' \in RA$ and v' corresponds to r, then:

       i. $(v, v') \in E$ if v is an antecedent of r;
       ii. $(v', v) \in E$ if v is the consequent of r;

   (b) If $v, v' \in RA$, v corresponds to r and v' corresponds to r', then $(v, v') \in E$ if r' (as a wff of $\mathcal{L}_R$) is the consequent of r;
   (c) If $v \in I \cup RA$ and $v' \in CA \cup PA$ and v' corresponds to (φ, ψ), then:

       i. $(v, v') \in E$ if $v = \varphi$;
       ii. $(v', v) \in E$ if $v = \psi$.

The above definition builds an AIF graph based on the elements of an ASPIC argumentation theory. The I-nodes consist of all the premises and conclusions of an argument in $\mathcal{A}$ (denoted by $\text{Conc}(\text{Sub}(\mathcal{A}))$). In the example (see AT as defined below definition 4.1 and Figure 2), there are five I-nodes based on the formulas $\{i_1, \ldots, i_5\}$. The set of RA-nodes consist of all inference rules applied in an argument in $\mathcal{A}$; the type of inference rule determines which form an RA-node uses. In the example, there are two inference rules, r_1 and r_2, which corresponding to the two RA-nodes ra_1 and ra_2 that use a defeasible and a deductive scheme, respectively. CA nodes correspond to conflicts between formulas occurring in arguments in $\mathcal{A}$ as determined by the contrariness relation. In Figure 2, the nodes ca_1, ca_2, ca_3 are based on the contrariness between i_4 and i_5 and i_4 and r_1. PA-nodes correspond to the preferences in AT between the rules used in arguments in $\mathcal{A}$ (i.e. a subset of $\leq$) or between the premises of arguments in $\mathcal{A}$ (a subset of $\leq'$). In the example AT there is only one such preference, namely $i_4 \leq' i_5$, which translates into pa_1 in Figure 2. Since the argument ordering $\preceq$ of AT is defined in terms of $\leq$ and $\leq'$, it is not part of the AIF graph.

The edges between the nodes are determined in terms of the relations between the corresponding elements in the AT. I-nodes representing an inference rule's antecedents and consequents are connected to the RA-node corresponding to the rule (viz., for example, the edges from i_1 to ra_1 to i_2 in Figure 2). Reasons for inference rules can be appropriately translated as links from RA-nodes to RA-nodes: condition 5b says that for any rule r in an argument with as its conclusion another rule $r' \in \mathcal{L}_R$, the RA-node corresponding to r is connected to the RA-node corresponding to r'. In this way, an argument that concludes that an inference rule should be applied (e.g. a reason for why there is no exception) can be expressed. Links from or to PA- and CA-nodes are connected to I- and RA-nodes according to the preference and contrariness relations in AT. For example, the edges from i_5 to pa_1 to i_4 are based on the fact that $i_4 \leq' i_5$. An undercutter is expressed as a link from the conclusion of the undercutter (an I-node, i_4 in the example) to a CA-node (ca_1) and a link from this CA-node to the RA-node denoting the undercut rule (ra_1). Definition 4.2 does not define the translation of edges between, for example, CA-nodes to CA-nodes, which are needed to express reasons against contrariness relations, as the ASPIC framework cannot express such reasons.

5. Conclusions and future research

In this paper we have shown how argument graphs as defined by the AIF can be formally grounded in the ASPIC argumentation framework. We have given the AIF ontology a sound formal basis and demonstrated how a formal framework can aid in tracing possible inconsistencies in a graph. Because of the formal scope of the ASPIC framework, we have also implicitly shown the connection between the AIF and other formal argumentation frameworks. In addition to the ASPIC framework's obvious relation to (5; 8; 15; 10), several other well-known argumentation systems (e.g. (2)) are shown by (9) to be special cases of the ASPIC framework. The connection between the AIF and ASPIC can therefore be extended to these systems. A topic for future research is to see what the relation is between the AIF and other formal frameworks that fall outside the scope of the ASPIC framework; this would also further clarify the relation between the ASPIC framework and these other frameworks. Thus, one of the main theoretical aims of the AIF project, namely, to integrate various results into a coherent whole, can be realized. This in turn lays a foundation for tackling the practical aims of the AIF work: to build a bridge between tools that support humans in the analysis, conduct and preparation of arguments, and the techniques and systems developed in formal computer science for reasoning with and reasoning about arguments. By building this bridge, we hope ultimately to be able to support improved human argumentation.

The paper shows that a relatively simple AIF argument graph contains enough information for a complex formal framework such as ASPIC to work with. Information that is not contained in the graph, such as defeat relations, can be calculated from the graph as desired. This conforms to the central aim of the AIF project: the AIF is intended as a language for expressing arguments rather than a language for, for example, evaluating or visualizing arguments. That said, the discussion on what should be explicitly represented in the graph and what should count as a calculated property is by no means settled. In this regard, it would be interesting to explore how and if the AIF can be directly connected to abstract argumentation frameworks, which have the notion of argument as one of its basic components. One possibility is to introduce new nodes – A-nodes perhaps – which link to all the components (I-nodes, RA-nodes, etc.) from which the argument is composed. An implementation of this idea has been trialled in a tool for computing acceptability semantics.[2] One problem, however, is how to characterize A-nodes precisely – they seem to have some of the character of an I-node, but on the other hand, could be interpreted just as sets of properties of other nodes. Given both these ontological problems and further challenges in implementation we currently leave A-nodes to future work.

Some properties of argumentation represented in an AIF graph cannot be expressed in the ASPIC framework, in particular reasons for contrariness relations and preferences. Some of these shortcomings are being addressed: (7) present an extension of the ASPIC system along the lines of (6), in which attacks on attacks can be modelled with arguments about preference relations between premises or defeasible inference rules. In an AIF graph, such arguments about preference statements are represented as PA-nodes supported by I-nodes through RA-nodes. In our future work we intend to fully develop these ideas so as to keep the translation functions between the AIF and ASPIC up-to-date with new versions of the ASPIC framework.

---

[2]The tool is called OVA-gen and is accessible online at *http://ova.computing.dundee.ac.uk/ova-gen/*

Finally, a necessary topic for future research and development is to further test the limits of the current ASPIC reification of the AIF ontology by considering less trivial examples of natural argument.

References

[1] L. Amgoud, L. Bodenstaff, M. Caminada, P. McBurney, S. Parsons, H. Prakken, J. van Veenen, and G.A.W. Vreeswijk. Final review and report on formal argumentation system. Deliverable D2.6, ASPIC IST-FP6-002307, 2006.

[2] A. Bondarenko, P.M. Dung, R.A. Kowalski, and F. Toni. An abstract, argumentation-theoretic approach to default reasoning. *Artificial Intelligence*, 93:63–101, 1997.

[3] M. Caminada and L. Amgoud. On the evaluation of argumentation formalisms. *Artificial Intelligence*, 171:286–310, 2007.

[4] C.I. Chesñevar, J. McGinnis, S. Modgil, I. Rahwan, C. Reed, G. Simari, M. South, G. Vreeswijk, and S. Willmott. Towards an argument interchange format. *The Knowledge Engineering Review*, 21:293–316, 2006.

[5] P.M. Dung. On the acceptability of arguments and its fundamental role in nonmonotonic reasoning, logic programming, and n–person games. *Artificial Intelligence*, 77:321–357, 1995.

[6] S. Modgil. Reasoning about preferences in argumentation frameworks. *Artificial Intelligence*, 173:901–934, 2009.

[7] S. Modgil and H. Prakken. Reasoning about preferences in structured argumentation frameworks. *These proceedings*.

[8] J.L. Pollock. Justification and defeat. *Artificial Intelligence*, 67:377–408, 1994.

[9] H. Prakken. An abstract framework for argumentation with structured arguments. *Argument and Computation*, 1, 2010. *To appear*.

[10] H. Prakken and G. Sartor. Argument-based extended logic programming with defeasible priorities. *Journal of Applied Non-classical Logics*, 7:25–75, 1997.

[11] I. Rahwan, I Banihashemi, C. Reed, Walton D., and S. Abdallah. Representing and classifying arguments on the semantic web. *Knowledge Engineering Review*, 2010. *To appear*.

[12] I. Rahwan and C. Reed. The argument interchange format. In I. Rahwan and G. Simari, editors, *Argumentation in Artificial Intelligence*. Springer, 2009.

[13] I. Rahwan, F. Zablith, and C. Reed. Laying the foundations for a world wide argument web. *Artificial Intelligence*, 171:897–921, 2007.

[14] C. Reed, S. Wells, J. Devereux, and G. Rowe. Aif+: Dialogue in the argument interchange format. In Ph. Besnard, S. Doutre, and A. Hunter, editors, *Proceedings of COMMA-2008*, pages 311–323. IOS Press, 2008.

[15] G.A.W. Vreeswijk. Abstract argumentation systems. *Artificial Intelligence*, 90:225–279, 1997.

[16] D.N. Walton. *Logical dialogue-games and fallacies*. University Press of America, Inc., Lanham, MD., 1984.

[17] D.N. Walton, C. Reed, and F. Macagno. *Argumentation Schemes*. Cambridge University Press, Cambridge, 2008.

Computational Models of Argument
P. Baroni et al. (Eds.)
IOS Press, 2010
doi:10.3233/978-1-60750-619-5-111

Support in Abstract Argumentation

G. BOELLA [a]   D. M. GABBAY [b,c]   L. VAN DER TORRE [c]   S. VILLATA [a]

[a] *University of Turin, Italy*
[b] *King's College London, United Kingdom*
[c] *University of Luxembourg, Luxembourg*

Abstract. In this paper, we consider two drawbacks of Cayrol and Lagasque-Schiex's meta-argumentation theory to model bipolar argumentation frameworks. We consider first the "lost of admissibility" in Dung's sense and second, the definition of notions of attack in the context of a support relation. We show how to prevent these drawbacks by introducing *support meta-arguments*. Like the model of Cayrol and Lagasque-Schiex, our formalization confirms the use of meta-argumentation to reuse Dung's properties. We do not take a stance towards the usefulness of a support relation among arguments, though we show that if one would like to introduce them, it can be done without extending Dung's theory. Finally, we show how to use meta-argumentation to instantiate an argumentation framework to represent *defeasible* support. In this model of support, the support relation itself can be attacked.

Keywords. Abstract argumentation theory, bipolar argumentation, meta argumentation, modelling

1. Introduction

Cayrol and Lagasque-Schiex [8] discuss the following drawback of their meta-argumentation theory for bipolar argumentation, which we aim to solve in this paper. The bipolar argumentation framework $BAF = \langle A, \rightarrow, \Rightarrow \rangle$ visualized in Figure 1.a has —using their semantics—the extension of acceptable arguments $\{d, e\}$, whereas $\{d, e\}$ is not an admissible extension of the argumentation framework $AF = \langle A, \rightarrow \rangle$, i.e. if we do not consider the support relation and we consider standard Dung semantics [9].

Figure 1. (a) $BAF = \langle A, \rightarrow, \Rightarrow \rangle$, with arguments $A = \{a, b, c, d, e\}$, attack relation $\{b \rightarrow d, e \rightarrow c\}$ and support relation $\{a \Rightarrow b, b \Rightarrow c\}$. (b) The BAF of Figure 1.a. in our meta-argumentation framework.

The extension $\{d, e\}$ would not be admissible in Dung's setting, because there is no argument in the extension $\{d, e\}$ attacking argument b, whereas b attacks argument d. However, a bipolar argumentation framework extends Dung's abstract argumentation framework with a second binary relation $\Rightarrow$ among arguments, representing support among arguments, and in the theory of Cayrol and Lagasque-Schiex [8], this makes the extension $\{d, e\}$ admissible. In this paper we address the following research question:

- How to analyze and prevent Cayrol and Lagasque-Schiex drawback where extensions can be inadmissible for the Dung's framework without support?

In this paper, we distinguish between deductive support, which means that argument a supports argument b if the acceptance of a implies the acceptance of b, and defeasible support, which means that the implication holds only by default and it can be attacked. Our research question therefore breaks down in the following sub-questions:

1. Why do they [8] run into the loss of Dung's admissibility drawback?
2. How can we solve this drawback if we consider deductive support only?
3. How can we extend deductive support to defeasible support?

Cayrol and Lagasque-Schiex [8], as explained in more detail in Section 2, run into this drawback, because they turn a bipolar argumentation framework into a "collective" meta-argumentation framework in which meta-arguments represent sets of arguments called coalitions. Their meta-argumentation framework is introduced to reuse Dung's principles, properties and algorithms, and to solve problems in their earlier approaches [7,1]. Moreover, their approach has an additional drawback. Suppose that Liverpool wins Premier League (lpl) if it wins the last match (wlm) or Manchester does not win its own one (mnw). We have two implications: "Liverpool wins last match" supports "Liverpool wins Premier League", ($wlm \Rightarrow lpl$), and "Manchester does not win last match" supports "Liverpool wins Premier League", ($mnw \Rightarrow lpl$). If an argument a attacks "Liverpool wins last match" ($a \rightarrow wlm$) then it attacks also "Liverpool wins Premier League". This is counterintuitive because lpl is supported also by argument mnw. This kind of attack has the form "if $a \Rightarrow b$ and $c \rightarrow a$ then $c \rightarrow b$" and it is called secondary attack [8].

Our approach also uses meta-argumentation and therefore also reuses Dung's principles, algorithms and properties [5,3]. However, we represent the deductive support of argument a to argument b by the attack of argument b to an auxiliary argument called $Z_{a,b}$, together with the attack of argument $Z_{a,b}$ to argument a. Instead of secondary attacks, we introduce mediated attacks representing the following constraint: if $a \Rightarrow b$ and $c \rightarrow b$ then a mediated attack $c \rightarrow a$ is added. As visualized in Figure 1.b the set of acceptable arguments $\{d, e\}$ is admissible because given that $b \rightarrow d$, e *defends* d against b with a mediated attack $e \dashrightarrow b$ and $\{d, e\}$ is stable because $a \notin \{d, e\}$ and argument $e \in \{d, e\}$ attacks a with the mediated attack $e \dashrightarrow a$, due to the mediated attack $e \dashrightarrow b$. So the set of acceptable arguments $\{d, e\}$ is admissible in Dung's sense in our model thanks to these mediated attack and the absence of "collective" meta-arguments.

Moreover, given a bipolar argumentation framework, we introduce second-order attacks to model defeasible support. These attacks can be of two kinds: attacks from an argument or an attack relation to another attack relation and attacks from an argument to a support relation. Attacks on support lead to an override of the constraints for deductive support described above.

The layout of this paper follows the three research questions and is as follows. Section 2 presents the existing bipolar argumentation frameworks [8]. In Section 3, we propose the representation of deductive support using meta-argumentation. Section 4 introduces defeasible support and second-order attacks. Conclusions end the paper.

2. Cayrol and Lagasquie-Schiex's bipolar argumentation framework

In this section we summarize the definitions of bipolar argumentation frameworks with the terminology used by Cayrol and Lagasquie-Schiex [8].

Definition 1 (Bipolar Argumentation Framework BAF [8]) *A bipolar argumentation framework* $\langle A, \rightarrow, \Rightarrow \rangle$ *consists of a finite set A called arguments and two binary relations on A called attack and support respectively.*

The purpose of Cayrol and Lagasquie-Schiex [8] is to define a meta-argumentation framework, consisting only of a set of meta-arguments and a conflict relation between these meta-arguments. Their idea is that a meta-argument makes sense if its members are somehow related by the support relation [8].

Definition 2 (Conflict free) *Given an argumentation framework $AF = \langle A, \rightarrow \rangle$, a set $C \subseteq A$ is conflict free, denoted as $cf(C)$, iff there do not exist $\alpha, \beta \in C$ such that $\alpha \rightarrow \beta$.*

Meta-arguments are called elementary coalitions in [8] and are defined as follows:

Definition 3 (Elementary coalitions [8]) *An elementary coalition of BAF is a subset $EC = \{a_1, \ldots, a_n\}$ of A such that*

1. *there exists a permutation $\{i_1, \ldots, i_n\}$ of $\{1, \ldots, n\}$ such that the sequence of support $a_{i_1} \Rightarrow a_{i_2}, \ldots, \Rightarrow a_{i_n}$ holds;*
2. *$cf(EC)$;*
3. *EC is maximal (with respect to $\subseteq$) among the subsets of A satisfying (1) and (2).*

EC denotes the set of elementary coalitions of BAF and $ECAF = \langle EC(A), c\text{-}attacks \rangle$ is the elementary coalition framework associated with BAF. Cayrol and Lagasquie-Schiex [8] define a conflict relation on $EC(A)$ as follows:

Definition 4 (c-attacks relation [8]) *Let EC_1 and EC_2 be two elementary coalitions of BAF. EC_1 c-attacks EC_2 if and only if there exists an argument a_1 in EC_1 and an argument a_2 in EC_2 such that $a_1 \rightarrow a_2$.*

Definition 5 (Acceptability semantics [8])

- *S is a ecp-extension of BAF if and only if there exists $\{EC_1, \ldots, EC_p\}$ a preferred extension of $ECAF$ such that $S = EC_1 \cup \ldots \cup EC_p$.*
- *S is a ecs-extension of BAF if and only if there exists $\{EC_1, \ldots, EC_p\}$ a stable extension of $ECAF$ such that $S = EC_1 \cup \ldots \cup EC_p$.*
- *S is a ecg-extension of BAF if and only if there exists $\{EC_1, \ldots, EC_p\}$ a grounded extension of $ECAF$ such that $S = EC_1 \cup \ldots \cup EC_p$.*

Definition 5 provides preferred, stable and grounded extensions, but it can be defined more generally for any semantics defined on Dung's argumentation framework. In general, there is a function g that defines extensions of extended argumentation frameworks in terms of extensions of meta-arguments. In Definition 5, the extensions of arguments are obtained by taking the union of the extensions of meta-arguments. So a $BAF = \langle A, \Rightarrow, \rightarrow \rangle$ is flattened to a framework $AF = \langle MA, \longmapsto \rangle$ where MA is the set called meta arguments and $\longmapsto$ is a binary relation on meta-arguments called meta-attack relation. In this way, Definition 5 becomes: $\mathcal{E}(BAF) = \{\mathcal{E}_{EC_1} \cup \ldots \cup \mathcal{E}_{EC_p} | \mathcal{E}_{EC_i} \in \mathcal{E}(AF)\}$ where $\mathcal{E}(AF) : 2^{\mathcal{U}} \times 2^{\mathcal{U} \times \mathcal{U}} \to 2^{2^{\mathcal{U}}}$ is Dung's acceptance function. For example, if $\mathcal{E}(AF) = \{\{\{a,b\},\{c\}\},\{\{d,e\}\}\}$ then $\mathcal{E}(BAF) = \{\{a,b,c\},\{d,e\}\}$. As we discuss in the following section, in our meta argumentation theory we do not take the union, but we filter away auxiliary arguments like the arguments $Z_{a,b}$ in Figure 1.b.

Given bipolar argumentation frameworks, Cayrol and Lagasquie-Schiex [8] define supported and secondary attacks based on attack and support as shown in Figure 2.a-b.

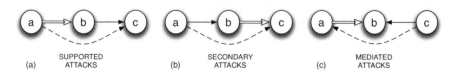

	SUPPORTED ATTACKS		SECONDARY ATTACKS		MEDIATED ATTACKS
(a)		(b)		(c)	

Figure 2. The three attack relations based on attack and support defined for bipolar argumentation frameworks.

This figure should be read as follows. If there is a support of argument a to argument b and there is an attack from argument b to argument c, then [8] claim that there is a supported attack from a to c. If there is an attack from a to b and b supports c, then Cayrol and Lagasquie-Schiex [8] claim that there is a secondary attack from a to c. Supported and secondary attacks are defined for a sequence of support relations and an attack relation, e.g., in Figure 2.a there may be $d \Rightarrow e$, $e \Rightarrow a$ in addition to $a \Rightarrow b$.

The drawback of the meta-argumentation proposed by [8] is, as they call it, the loss of admissibility in Dung's sense. The authors of [8] claim also that this loss of admissibility is neither surprising nor really problematic for them. They motivate this claim observing that admissibility is lost because it takes into account "individual" attack whereas, with their meta-argumentation, they want to consider "collective" attack. First we underline that the aim of using meta-argumentation is to preserve all Dung's properties and principles and second we do not agree that meta-arguments make sense if their members are somehow related by the support relation, as assumed by [8]. In this paper we prevent this drawback by using our meta-argumentation methodology and adding a new kind of attack called mediated attacks. Let us consider again the example of Figure 1. Given this BAF and the mediated attacks we add in our model, the extension $\{d, e\}$ becomes an admissible extension also for the corresponding Dung's argumentation framework where the support relation is not considered.

A further drawback of the approach presented in [8] is, as described by the football example in the introduction, that secondary attacks lead to inconsistencies, i.e., if the argument "Liverpool wins last match" is attacked then this does not mean that argument "Liverpool wins Premier League" is attacked too since it is supported also by another argument, "Manchester does not win last match". We avoid the introduction of this kind of attack called secondary attacks in [8]. For a further discussion about bipolar argumentation frameworks, see [7,1,8].

3. Modelling deductive support

In this section, we present how to model deductive support in meta-argumentation. How to model support in argumentation is a controversial issue. There is no a single notion of "support", as witnessed by Toulmin [12] where support is a relation between data and claims, but it may be expected that there are many, which can be used in different applications. However, in Dung's framework of abstract argumentation [9], support could also be represented by Dung's notion of defence [9], or by instantiating abstract arguments [11]. The aim of this paper is not to take a position in this debate but to provide a new way to model support in bipolar argumentation frameworks. We introduce notions as deductive support and defeasible support which are different from Cayrol et al. [7,1,8]. Moreover, we introduce a methodology which makes it possible to define various kinds of support in a relatively easy way without the need to introduce additional machinery.

We want deductive support to satisfy the following conditions on the acceptability of supported arguments: if argument a supports argument b, and a is acceptable, then b must be acceptable too, and if argument a supports argument b, and b is not acceptable, then a must be not acceptable either. Moreover, the extensions must be admissible, if the acceptance function of the basic argumentation framework is admissible too.

We illustrate the difference between the meta-argumentation used by Cayrol and Lagasquie-Schiex [8] and the one we introduce in this paper, using an example. Consider the bipolar argumentation framework in Figure 3.1, where argument d supports argument c, argument c attacks argument b, argument b attacks argument a, and argument e attacks argument c.

Figure 3. An example of bipolar argumentation framework.

According to Cayrol and Lagasquie-Schiex [8], the intuitive extension of this bipolar argumentation framework is the extension $\{b, e\}$. They obtain this extension in two steps. First, they define meta-arguments as sets of arguments, and define meta-attack relations as attacks between sets of arguments. As illustrated in Figure 3.2, this means that the meta-argument $\{d, c\}$ attacks argument b.

In our meta-argumentation methodology, we do not group arguments together in meta-arguments, but we add meta-arguments. As illustrated in Figure 3.3, we add meta-arguments $X_{x,y}$ and $Y_{x,y}$ for each attack of argument x to argument y. Meta-argument $X_{x,y}$ is read as "the attack from x to y is not active" and meta-argument $Y_{x,y}$ is read as "the attack from x to y is active". Moreover, we introduce a meta-argument $Z_{d,c}$ and if argument d supports argument c, then we add the attack relations from $acc(c)$ to $Z_{d,c}$, and from $Z_{d,c}$ to $acc(d)$. Meta-argument $Z_{d,c}$ is read as "argument d does not support argument c".

We [5,3] instantiate Dung's theory with meta-arguments, *such that we use Dung's theory to reason about itself*. Meta-argumentation is a particular way to define mappings from argumentation frameworks to extended argumentation frameworks: arguments are interpreted as meta-arguments, of which some are mapped to "argument a is accepted", $acc(a)$, where a is an abstract argument from the extended argumentation framework EAF. The meta-argumentation methodology is summarized in Figure 4.

We use a so-called acceptance function $\mathcal{E}$ mapping a bipolar argumentation framework $\langle A, \rightarrow, \Rightarrow \rangle$ to its set of extensions, i.e., to a set of sets of arguments, where the universe of arguments $\mathcal{U}$ is the set of all generated arguments.

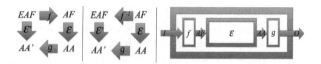

Figure 4. The meta-argumentation methodology.

Definition 6 *Let* $\mathcal{U}$ *be a set called the universe of arguments. An acceptance function* $\mathcal{E}_{BAF} : 2^{\mathcal{U}} \times 2^{\mathcal{U} \times \mathcal{U}} \times 2^{\mathcal{U} \times \mathcal{U}} \rightarrow 2^{2^{\mathcal{U}}}$ *is a partial function defined for each bipolar argumentation framework* $\langle A, \rightarrow, \Rightarrow \rangle$ *with finite* $A \subseteq \mathcal{U}$ *and* $\rightarrow \subseteq A \times A$ *and* $\Rightarrow \subseteq A \times A$, *and mapping a bipolar argumentation framework* $\langle A, \rightarrow, \Rightarrow \rangle$ *to sets of subsets of* A: $\mathcal{E}_{BAF}(\langle A, \rightarrow, \Rightarrow \rangle) \subseteq 2^{A}$.

The function f assigns to each argument a in the EAF, an argument "argument a is accepted" in the basic argumentation framework. We use Dung's acceptance function $\mathcal{E} : 2^{\mathcal{U}} \times 2^{\mathcal{U} \times \mathcal{U}} \rightarrow 2^{2^{\mathcal{U}}}$ to find functions $\mathcal{E}'$ between extended argumentation frameworks EAF and the acceptable arguments AA' they return. The accepted arguments of the argumentation framework are a function of the extended argumentation framework $AA = \mathcal{E}'(EAF)$. The transformation function consists of two parts: a function f^{-1} transforms an argumentation framework AF to an extended argumentation framework EAF, and a function g transforms the acceptable arguments of the basic AF into acceptable arguments of the EAF. Summarizing $\mathcal{E}' = \{(f^{-1}(a), g(b)) \mid (a, b) \in \mathcal{E}\}$ and $AA' = \mathcal{E}'(EAF) = g(AA) = g(\mathcal{E}(AF)) = g(\mathcal{E}(f(EAF)))$.

The first step of our approach is to define the set of extended argumentation frameworks. The second step consists in defining flattening algorithms as a function from this set of EAFs to the set of all basic argumentation frameworks: $f : EAF \rightarrow AF$.

As in [8], we generalize the key concept of attack between two arguments by combining a sequence of support relations and a direct attack relation. If there is a support of argument a to argument b and there is an attack from argument c to argument b, then we claim that there is a mediated attack from c to a. Mediated attacks are defined as follows:

Definition 7 (Mediated attacks) *Let* $a, b \in A$, *a mediated attack for* b *by* a *is a sequence* $a_1 R_1 \ldots R_{n-2} a_{n-1}$ *and* $a_n R_{n-1} a_{n-1}$, $n \geqslant 3$, *with* $a_1 = b, a_n = a$, *such that* $R_{n-1} = \rightarrow$ *and* $\forall i = 1 \ldots n\text{-}2, R_i = \Rightarrow$.

Mediated attacks are illustrated in Figure 2.

Example 1 *Let* BAF_1 *be defined by arguments* $A = \{a, b, c, d, e\}$, *support relation* $\{d \Rightarrow c\}$ *and attack relation* $\{b \rightarrow a, c \rightarrow b, e \rightarrow c\}$ *as shown in Figure 5.a.* BAF_1 *has one supported attack, because given* $d \Rightarrow c \rightarrow b$ *we add* $d \dashrightarrow b$ *and one mediated attack, because given* $d \Rightarrow c$ *and* $e \rightarrow c$ *we add* $e \dashrightarrow d$ *where* $\dashrightarrow$ *are supported and mediated attacks. The set of acceptable arguments is* $\{e, b\}$ *and this is the only preferred, grounded and stable extension.*

Example 2 *Let* BAF_2 *be defined by arguments* $A = \{a, b, c, d, e\}$, *support relation* $\{c \Rightarrow b, c \Rightarrow d\}$ *and attack relation* $\{a \rightarrow b, d \rightarrow e\}$ *as shown in Figure 5.b. We have two new attacks according to Definition 7:* $a \dashrightarrow c$ *is a mediated attack and* $c \dashrightarrow e$ *is a supported attack. So there is only one preferred extension which is also stable and*

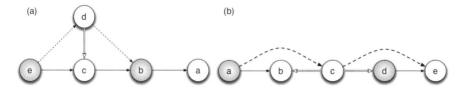

Figure 5. (a) BAF_1 and (b) BAF_2, with the supported and mediated attacks.

grounded $\{a, d\}$, as for the associate Dung's AF, while the preferred, grounded and stable extensions of [8] for BAF_2 is $\{a, e\}$. This is because, first, the mediated attack $a \dashrightarrow c$ is not considered, [8] claim there is no attack of an element of the set $\{a, e\}$ against c. Introducing explicitly mediated attacks allows us to preserve admissibility in Dung's sense. Second, in [8], b, c, d are considered as a meta-argument thus acceptable only as a whole.

Definition 8 presents the instantiation of a basic argumentation framework as a bipolar argumentation framework using meta-argumentation. This allows us to have not only that arguments can support other arguments but also that arguments can support attack relations and that attack relations can support other attack relations. In this way we do not restrict the support relation of being only between arguments but also between binary relations themselves.

The flattening of the support relations can be summarized in the following way. Given a support relation $a \Rightarrow b$, it holds that if argument b is not acceptable then argument a is not acceptable either and if argument a is acceptable then argument b is acceptable too. The universe of meta-arguments is $MU = \{acc(a) \mid a \in \mathcal{U}\} \cup \{X_{a,b}, Y_{a,b} \mid a, b \in \mathcal{U}\} \cup \{Z_{a,b} \mid a, b \in \mathcal{U}\}$, and the flattening function f is given by $f(EAF) = \langle MA, \longmapsto \rangle$ where MA is the set called meta-arguments and $\longmapsto$ is a binary relation called meta-attack. For a set of arguments $B \subseteq MU$, the unflattening function g is given by $g(B) = \{a \mid acc(a) \in B\}$, and for sets of arguments $AA \subseteq 2^{MU}$, it is given by $g(AA) = \{g(B) \mid B \in AA\}$.

Definition 8 *Given a bipolar argumentation framework $BAF = \langle A, \rightarrow, \Rightarrow \rangle$, the set of meta-arguments $MA \subseteq MU$ is $\{acc(a) \mid a \in A\} \cup \{X_{a,b}, Y_{a,b} \mid a, b \in A\} \cup \{Z_{a,b} \mid a, b \in A\}$ and $\longmapsto \subseteq MA \times MA$ is a binary relation on MA such that:*
$acc(a) \longmapsto X_{a,b}$ iff $a \rightarrow b \wedge X_{a,b} \longmapsto Y_{a,b}$ iff $a \rightarrow b \wedge Y_{a,b} \longmapsto acc(b)$ iff $a \rightarrow b$,
$acc(b) \longmapsto Z_{a,b}$ iff $a \Rightarrow b \wedge Z_{a,b} \longmapsto acc(a)$ iff $a \Rightarrow b$.

For a given flattening function f, the acceptance function of the extended argumentation theory $\mathcal{E}'$ is defined using the acceptance function of the basic abstract argumentation theory $\mathcal{E}$: an argument of an EAF is acceptable if and only if it is acceptable in the flattened basic AF.

The following propositions hold for our meta-argumentation with supported and mediated attacks.

Proposition 1 (Conflict free for supported and mediated attacks) *Given a bipolar argumentation framework BAF, if there is a supported or mediated attack from a to b, and a is acceptable, then b is not acceptable.*

Proof: *We prove the contrapositive. If there is a supported or mediated attack from a to b, and b is acceptable, then a is not acceptable. So assume that there is a supported or mediated attack from a to b, and $acc(b)$ is acceptable. Then meta-argument $Y_{a,b}$ is not acceptable and $X_{a,b}$ is acceptable. Consequently, $acc(a)$ is not acceptable.*

Proposition 2 (Semantics of support) *Given a bipolar argumentation framework BAF, if it holds that $a \Rightarrow b$ and argument a is acceptable, $a \in \mathcal{E}(BAF)$, then argument b is acceptable too.*

Proof: *We prove the contrapositive. If it holds that $a \Rightarrow b$ and argument b is not acceptable, then argument a is not acceptable. Assume that $a \Rightarrow b$ and meta-argument $acc(b)$ is not accepted, then meta-argument $Z_{a,b}$ is acceptable. Consequently, meta-argument $acc(a)$ is not acceptable.*

Proposition 3 *Given a bipolar argumentation framework BAF, if we add a supported attack such that $a \to c$ if $a \Rightarrow b$ and $b \to c$, then the extensions do not change, using our meta-argumentation and one of Dung's semantics.*

Proof: *We use reasoning by cases. Case 1: $acc(a)$ is acceptable, then also $acc(b)$ is acceptable following Proposition 2, and given $b \to c$, $a \to c$ can be deleted without changing the extension. Case 2: $acc(a)$ is not acceptable, then $a \to c$ can be deleted. Case 3: $acc(a)$ is undecided, then also $acc(b)$ is undecided and $acc(c)$ is undecided.*

It may be argued that our representation of deductive support is in contrast with other interpretations of support. Specifically, the fact that a supports b is modeled by the flattening function with a path from $acc(b)$ to $acc(a)$, i.e. $acc(a)$ is acceptable only if $acc(b)$ is acceptable. It does not correspond to the other view of support from a to b, i.e. the acceptance of b yield the acceptance of a and not vice versa.

Note that, given $a \Rightarrow b$, in meta-argumentation we condense all the attacks which are both on b and thus on a (both from b and thus from a) using only meta-argument $Z_{a,b}$, see Proposition 4. This means that the closure rules do not change the extensions of the meta-argumentation framework. In this way we simplify the representation of the meta-argumentation framework in which supported and mediated attacks occur.

Proposition 4 *Given a bipolar argumentation framework BAF in our meta-argumentation where $a \Rightarrow b$ and $c \to b$ and there is a mediated attack $c \to a$, if $Y_{c,a}$ is acceptable then $Z_{a,b}$ and $Y_{c,b}$ are acceptable too.*

Proof: *We prove the contrapositive. If it holds that $Z_{a,b}$ and $Y_{c,b}$ are not acceptable then $Y_{c,a}$ is not acceptable. Assume that $acc(c)$ is not acceptable, so $X_{c,b}$ and $X_{c,a}$ are acceptable and $Y_{c,b}$ and $Z_{a,b}$ are not acceptable. Consequently, $Y_{c,a}$ is not acceptable.*

Example 3 *Let BAF_3 be defined by $A = \{a, b, c\}$, $\{a \Rightarrow b\}$, $\{b \to c\}$ and BAF_4 be defined by $A = \{a, b, c\}$, $\{a \Rightarrow b\}$, $\{c \to b\}$. The instantiation of a classical argumentation framework as BAF_3 and BAF_4 is described in Figure 6.*
The sets of meta-arguments are $MA_3 = \{acc(a), acc(b), acc(c), X_{b,c}, Y_{b,c}, Z_{a,b}\}$ and $MA_4 = \{acc(a), acc(b), acc(c), X_{c,b}, Y_{c,b}, Z_{a,b}\}$. In BAF_3, we have that the set of meta-attack relations is composed by $acc(b) \longmapsto X_{b,c} \longmapsto Y_{b,c} \longmapsto acc(c)$

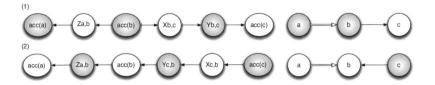

Figure 6. Turning BAF_3 and BAF_4 into meta-argumentation.

and by the support relation $acc(b) \longmapsto Z_{a,b} \longmapsto acc(a)$. The same happens for BAF_4 where we have $acc(c) \longmapsto X_{c,b} \longmapsto Y_{c,b} \longmapsto acc(b)$ and the support relation $acc(b) \longmapsto Z_{a,b} \longmapsto acc(a)$. The set of acceptable arguments for each BAF is represented by the grey arguments. We have that $\mathcal{E}'(BAF_3) = \{a, b\}$ and $\mathcal{E}'(BAF_4) = \{c\}$ are the acceptable arguments. The sets of acceptable arguments for the meta-argumentation frameworks are $\mathcal{E}(f(BAF_3)) = \{acc(a), acc(b), Y_{b,c}\}$ and $\mathcal{E}(f(BAF_4)) = \{acc(c), Z_{a,b}, Y_{c,b}\}$ and by filtering these sets we obtain the same acceptable arguments of the starting $BAFs$, $\mathcal{E}'(BAF_3) = g(\mathcal{E}(f(BAF_3))) = \{a, b\}$ and $\mathcal{E}'(BAF_4) = g(\mathcal{E}(f(BAF_4))) = \{c\}$. Meta-argument $Z_{a,b}$ represents in a compact way that every attack from b to an argument c leads to an attack from a to c (BAF_3) and that every attack to b from an argument c leads to an attack from c to a (BAF_4).

Example 4 Let BAF_5 be defined by $A = \{a, b, c, d\}$, $\{a \Rightarrow b, b \Rightarrow c, a \Rightarrow d\}$, $\{d \rightarrow c\}$ as in Figure 7. The set of acceptable arguments is $\{d\}$ as for the associated Dung's argumentation framework. In bipolar argumentation [8], the set of acceptable arguments is $\{a, b, d\}$, or $\{a, d\}$ if elementary coalitions are considered.

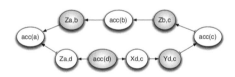

Figure 7. Turning BAF_5 into meta-argumentation.

Our approach allows us to reuse all the principles, algorithms and properties defined for standard Dung's argumentation framework without loosing admissibility in Dung's sense. Using our meta-argumentation admissibility is not lost because we take into account individual attacks and defence while Cayrol and Lagasquie-Schiex [8] consider "collective" attacks and defence for coalitions. A recent approach to represent support in argumentation has been proposed by Brewka and Woltran [6]. In this paper they introduce a generalization of Dung-style argumentation where each node comes with an associated acceptance condition.This allows to model different types of dependencies, e.g. support and attack, within a single framework. Given that $a \Rightarrow b$, they represent support as $acc(a) \longmapsto Z_{a,b} \longmapsto b$ without posing constraints as we do. We can extend our meta-argumentation to consider also this model of support but it is not evident how the approach of [6] can be extended in order to introduce our constraints and second-order attacks.

4. Modelling defeasible support

In this section, we define defeasible support. We highlight two possible kinds of second-order attacks and we present how to instantiate Dung's AF with an extended argumentation framework with support relations and second-order attack relations.

The two kinds of second-order attacks are, first, attacks from an argument or an attack relation to another attack relation and second, attacks from an argument to a support relation. The first kind of second-order attack has received a lot of attention in the last years and similar proposals using a meta approach have been proposed [10,4,2]. The difference is that we are able to treat also the case in which an attack relation attacks another attack relation. Concerning the second kind of second-order attacks, it has not been considered yet in the context of bipolar argumentation frameworks. Definition 9 presents the instantiation of a basic argumentation framework as a bipolar second-order argumentation framework using meta-argumentation. The flattening function f is as in Definition 8.

Definition 9 *Given an extended argumentation framework $EAF = \langle A, \to, \Rightarrow, \to^2 \rangle$ where $A \subseteq \mathcal{U}$ is a set of arguments, $\to \subseteq A \times A$, $\Rightarrow \subseteq A \times A$ and $\to^2$ is a binary relation on $(A \cup \to) \times (\to \cup \Rightarrow)$, the set of meta-arguments $MA \subseteq MU$ is $\{acc(a) \mid a \in A\} \cup \{X_{a,b}, Y_{a,b} \mid a, b \in A\} \cup \{Z_{a,b} \mid a, b \in A\} \cup \{X_{a,b \to c}, Y_{a,b \to c} \mid a, b, c \in A\}$ and $\longmapsto \subseteq MA \times MA$ is a binary relation on MA such that:*
$acc(a) \longmapsto X_{a,b}$ iff $a \to b \wedge X_{a,b} \longmapsto Y_{a,b}$ iff $a \to b \wedge Y_{a,b} \longmapsto acc(b)$ iff $a \to b$,
$acc(b) \longmapsto Z_{a,b}$ iff $a \Rightarrow b \wedge Z_{a,b} \longmapsto acc(a)$ iff $a \Rightarrow b$,
$acc(a) \longmapsto X_{a,b \to c}$ iff $a \to^2 (b \to c) \wedge X_{a,b \to c} \longmapsto Y_{a,b \to c}$ iff $a \to^2 (b \to c)$ $\wedge Y_{a,b \to c} \longmapsto Y_{b,c}$ iff $a \to^2 (b \to c)$,
$Y_{a,b} \longmapsto Y_{c,d}$ iff $(a \to b) \to^2 (c \to d)$,
$acc(c) \longmapsto X_{c,Z_{a,b}}$ iff $c \to^2 (a \Rightarrow b) \wedge X_{c,Z_{a,b}} \longmapsto Y_{c,Z_{a,b}}$ iff $c \to^2 (a \Rightarrow b)$ $\wedge Y_{c,Z_{a,b}} \longmapsto Z_{a,b}$ iff $c \to^2 (a \Rightarrow b)$.

Example 5 *Let BAF_3 be extended with the second-order attack relation $\{d \to (b \to c)\}$, as in Figure 8.1. The set of acceptable arguments is $\{a, b, c, d\}$ since the attack from b to c is made ineffective by argument d. Let BAF_4 be extended with the second-order attack relation $\{d \to (c \to b)\}$, as in Figure 8.2. The set of acceptable arguments is again $\{a, b, c, d\}$. Note that since b is no more attacked and can be accepted, also a can be accepted in this example.*

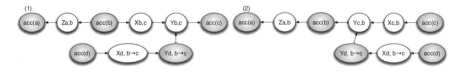

Figure 8. BAF_3 and BAF_4 with second-order attacks.

What does it mean that the support relation between two arguments does not hold anymore? It means that, given $a \Rightarrow b$, when b is not acceptable, a can be acceptable and converse when a is acceptable than b can be not acceptable.

Example 6 *Let BAF_3 be extended with the second-order attack relation $\{d \rightarrow (a \Rightarrow b))\}$, as in Figure 9.1. The set of acceptable arguments is $\{a, b, d\}$. Let BAF_4 be extended with the second-order attack relation $\{d \rightarrow (a \Rightarrow b))\}$, as in Figure 9.2. The set of acceptable arguments is $\{a, c, d\}$. Note that b is attacked by argument c and it is not acceptable but a is acceptable because the support relation has been made ineffective by the attack of d.*

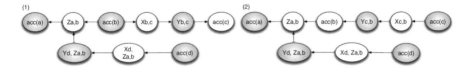

Figure 9. BAF_3 and BAF_4 with an attack on the support relation.

Our model of defeasible support allows us to represent both rebut and undercut in meta-argumentation. Rebut is modeled when $a \Rightarrow b$ and $c \rightarrow b$, as discussed in the previous section, while undercut is modeled when $c \rightarrow (a \Rightarrow b)$ so when the support relation itself is attacked. Let us consider the following example: the fact that Tweety is a bird (tb) provides support for its flying ability (tf). Then it turns out that Tweety is a pinguin (tp). Argument "Tweety flies" is attacked by "Tweety is a pinguin", $tp \rightarrow tf$. Following our constraints, does it mean that Tweety is not a bird? No, we have that argument tp attacks both the argument tf but also the fact that being a bird supports the flying ability of Tweety, $tp \rightarrow (tb \Rightarrow tf)$.

5. Conclusions and Future Work

Table 1 summarizes the comparison between Cayrol and Lagasquie-Schiex's [8] approach and our one.

Table 1. Comparison between Cayrol and Lagasquie-Schiex [8] and our approach

	Their meta-argumentation	Our meta-argumentation
Additional attacks	supported, secondary	supported, mediated
Meta-arguments	sets of arguments	additional meta-arguments
Function g	union of meta-arguments	filtering meta-arguments
Admissibility in Dung's sense	no	yes
Attacks on support relation	no	yes

We can prevent the drawbacks of [8] by considering deductive support where given $a \Rightarrow b$ it holds that: if a is acceptable then b is acceptable too and if b is not acceptable then a is not acceptable either. Moreover, we consider that if $a \Rightarrow b$ and $c \rightarrow b$ then the mediated attack $c \rightarrow a$ is added. These attacks substitute [8]'s secondary attacks. Secondary attacks lead to inconsistencies, i.e., when it is the case that an argument is supported by two different arguments. If one of the two supporter arguments is attacked then also the supported argument is attacked even if it is supported also by the another unattacked argument. Moreover, mediated attacks avoid the "loss of admissibility" as shown by the examples of Section 3.

We extend deductive support to defeasible support by allowing second-order attacks not only on attack relations but also on support relations. Given $a \Rightarrow b$ and a second-order attack on this support relation $c \rightarrow (a \Rightarrow b)$, we have that the semantics of deductive support does not hold anymore. In [8], no attacks to the support relations are introduced and it is not clear how it could be done with their "collective" meta-arguments.

Due to the modelling perspective, we have to observe that there is no a single notion of "support", but there are many, which can be used in different applications. We introduce notions which are different from [8] and [6]. Moreover, we introduce a methodology which makes it possible to define various kinds of support in a relatively easy way, without the need to introduce additional machinery. Since there are various kinds of support, it is better not to extend argumentation frameworks, but to instantiate them.

A topic for future research is how to model attacks and support with strengths. For example we may say that if there is an attack and a support with the same strength on argument a, then argument a is undecided. A way of representing strengths consists in having, instead of X and Y attack arguments, arguments X_1, Y_1, X_2, Y_2 and so on. Likewise we can have Z_1, Z_2, Z_3 and so on for support relations, and we have that Y_i attacks Z_j if $i > j$ and Z_i attacks Y_j if $i > j$. As observed above, there are various kinds of support, so it is better to instantiate argumentation frameworks. In that way, we can add new notions of support under the form of patters. The definition of the patterns for deductive support and defeasible support is left for further research.

References

[1] L. Amgoud, C. Cayrol, M.-C. Lagasquie-Schiex, and P. Livet. On bipolarity in argumentation frameworks. *Int. J. Intell. Syst.*, 23(10):1062–1093, 2008.

[2] P. Baroni, F. Cerutti, M. Giacomin, and G. Guida. Encompassing attacks to attacks in abstract argumentation frameworks. In C. Sossai and G. Chemello, editors, *ECSQARU*, volume 5590 of *Lecture Notes in Computer Science*, pages 83–94. Springer, 2009.

[3] G. Boella, D. M. Gabbay, L. van der Torre, and S. Villata. Meta-argumentation modelling i: Methodology and techniques. *Studia Logica*, 93(2-3):297–355, 2009.

[4] G. Boella, L. van der Torre, and S. Villata. Social viewpoints for arguing about coalitions. In T. D. Bui, T. V. Ho, and Q.-T. Ha, editors, *PRIMA*, volume 5357 of *Lecture Notes in Computer Science*, pages 66–77. Springer, 2008.

[5] G. Boella, L. van der Torre, and S. Villata. On the acceptability of meta-arguments. In *Proc. of the 2009 IEEE/WIC/ACM International Conference on Intelligent Agent Technology, IAT 2009*, pages 259–262. IEEE, 2009.

[6] G. Brewka and S. Woltran. Abstract dialectical frameworks. In *Proc. of the 20th International Conference on the Principles of Knowledge Representation and Reasoning (KR 2010)*, pages 102–111, 2010.

[7] C. Cayrol and M.-C. Lagasquie-Schiex. On the acceptability of arguments in bipolar argumentation frameworks. In L. Godo, editor, *ECSQARU*, volume 3571 of *Lecture Notes in Computer Science*, pages 378–389. Springer, 2005.

[8] C. Cayrol and M.-C. Lagasquie-Schiex. Coalitions of arguments: A tool for handling bipolar argumentation frameworks. *Int. J. Intell. Syst.*, 25(1):83–109, 2010.

[9] P. M. Dung. On the acceptability of arguments and its fundamental role in nonmonotonic reasoning, logic programming and n-person games. *Artif. Intell.*, 77(2):321–358, 1995.

[10] S. Modgil and T. J. M. Bench-Capon. Integrating object and meta-level value based argumentation. In P. Besnard, S. Doutre, and A. Hunter, editors, *COMMA*, volume 172 of *Frontiers in Artificial Intelligence and Applications*, pages 240–251. IOS Press, 2008.

[11] H. Prakken. A logical framework for modelling legal argument. In *Proc. of the 4th Int. Conf. on Artificial intelligence and Law, ICAIL, ACM*, pages 1–9, 1993.

[12] S. Toulmin. *The Uses of Argument*. Cambridge University Press, 1958.

Computational Models of Argument
P. Baroni et al. (Eds.)
IOS Press, 2010
doi:10.3233/978-1-60750-619-5-123

Software Agents in Support of Human Argument Mapping

Simon BUCKINGHAM SHUM[a], Maarten SIERHUIS[b,c,d],
Jack PARK[a], Matthew BROWN[e]
[a] *Knowledge Media Institute, The Open University, UK*
[b] *NASA Ames Research Center, USA*
[c] *Carnegie Mellon University, Silicon Valley, USA*
[d] *Man-Machine Interaction, Delft University of Technology, NL*
[e] *University of Utah, Salt Lake City, USA*

Abstract. This paper reports progress in realizing human-agent argumentation, which
we argue will be part of future Computer-Supported Collaborative Argumentation
(CSCA) tools. With a particular interest in argument mapping, we present two
investigations demonstrating how a particular agent-oriented language and architecture
can augment CSCA: (i) the use of the *IBIS* formalism enabling *Brahms* agents to
simulate argumentation, and (ii) the extension of the *Compendium* tool by integrating
it with Brahms agents tasked with detecting related discourse elsewhere.

Keywords. Argument Mapping, IBIS, Compendium, Brahms, Multi-Agent Systems

1. Introduction

Computer-Supported Collaborative Argumentation (CSCA) research seeks to augment
human dialogue, deliberation and argumentation with appropriate software support, with a
significant interest in how the visualization of these discourse structures can augment
personal and shared cognition [1,2,3]. As part of a long-term research programme, we
have been developing an open source and open architecture tool for CSCA mapping called
Compendium [4]. In tandem with experimenting with the technological possibilities (e.g.
through integration with video-conferencing, social media, or AI planning [4]), we are
studying its use in authentic contexts, in order to determine the work practices that make
such tools effective [5,6].

Argumentation in Multi-Agent Systems (MAS) research is investigating how
argumentation theory can provide software agents with greater capacity to reason and
negotiate, in order to resolve competing priorities or recommended courses of action.
Parallel to this, our long-term objective is the design of human-agent interaction (HAI), a
subset of which implicates human-agent argumentation. In this paper, we report on two
investigations into how Brahms, a particular agent-oriented language and architecture
developed at NASA [7] can augment CSCA. The efforts we report on cover (i) the use of
the Issue-Based Information System (IBIS) formalism [8] enabling software agents to
interact about competing options using argumentation, and (ii) the extension of the
Compendium CSCA tool by integrating it with agents tasked with detecting related
discourse elsewhere and enabling the ability to share discussion topics and argumentation

between different context. To convey the kind of use case that we are designing for, consider this scenario:

Susan is one of a team of analysts at a commodities trading firm. The team is seeking to understand how climate change may impact the markets they follow, and have assigned different staff to specific topics. Aware that this is a highly contested issue, Susan creates a new project in her argument mapping tool, and records the results of her research in a set of maps, tracking Questions, potential Answers, and relevant Arguments to help reflect on the trustworthiness of the information she is gathering. She skims a climatology book to identify major themes, before going online to examine government advice, business analyses, and climate change advocacy groups from the different sides. Her argument-mapping tool includes a supporting personal software agent that in the background has access to a network of other intelligent software agents that can check if there are related conversations/analyses on the net. She can view suggestions from her agent, and add the most relevant to her own analysis. Some of the suggestions come from agents monitoring her colleagues' maps; others are mining online discussions in interoperable platforms, while others are trained to perform their own research on specific online databases. Moreover, some agents are capable of working together to construct their own argument maps around a given issue, which are then proposed to the analyst as contributions.

In order to examine the modelling and implementation requirements raised by this, we start (§2) by introducing our previous work in CSCA, in particular our development of the Compendium software tool to support IBIS and other notations. We then introduce the Brahms agent language, and summarise progress to date on human-agent argument mapping from a series of NASA field trials (§3). This sets the context for a deeper level of integration, which serves as the core of this paper, namely the extension of Brahms agents to conduct IBIS-based analyses (§4), and the extension of Compendium with Brahms agents to identify potentially relevant IBIS content in remote databases (§5). We then draw conclusions and consider future work.

2. Our Previous Work in CSCA

In [9] we trace the work of design and policy planning theorist Horst Rittel, whose characterisation in the 1970's of "wicked problems" continues to resonate with today's societal challenges: "Wicked and incorrigible [problems]... defy efforts to delineate their boundaries and to identify their causes, and thus to expose their problematic nature" [10]. In such domains, the complexity of the arguments invites CSCA support, although as we discuss elsewhere [11], the evidence is that before deep dialogue has helped to build common ground and trust, clear argumentation on its own will never be sufficient. Rittel concluded that real world policy dilemmas are qualitatively different to those that could be solved by formal models or methodologies, classed as the 'first-generation' design methodologies. Instead, an *argumentative* approach to such problems was required: "First generation methods seem to start once all the truly difficult questions have been dealt with. ... [Argumentative design] means that the statements are systematically challenged in order to expose them to the viewpoints of the different sides, and the structure of the process becomes one of alternating steps on the micro-level; that means the generation of solution specifications towards end statements, and subjecting them to discussion of their pros and cons." [10]

Rittel's work has proven influential in CSCA research, through his proposal of the Issue-Based Information System (IBIS) as a method and notation for conducting "argumentative design". The gIBIS prototype [12] and the subsequent QuestMap product, rendered IBIS as a graphical-hypertext network. A root *Issue* provides the orientation to a map, establishing the problematic context for the discussion. The analyst then maps possible responses to these, and relevant arguments. An important strand of our work has sought to articulate the skillset that practitioners deploy when they use such tools to add value to Design Rationale capture, and other forms of knowledge-intensive work [6].

Several discourse-modelling methodologies have developed around the capabilities of Compendium. *Dialogue Mapping* is a set of skills developed by Conklin [13] for mapping IBIS structures in real time during a meeting in order to support the analysis of wicked problems, as defined by Rittel. *Issue Mapping* is conducted asynchronously, without the pressure of real time knowledge representation, permitting more reflection prior to crafting the map, which is more typical of argument diagramming tools. In Dialogue and Issue Mapping, nodes are usually unconstrained free-text expressions summarising an agenda item or a participant's contribution (Figure 1). "Arguments" are typically no more formally expressed than as shown in the examples below, because the demands of real time mapping do not permit greater analysis and formalization.

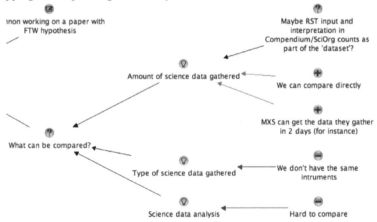

Figure 1: Example of an IBIS map constructed in an online meeting, shared live over the internet

The more disciplined *Conversational Modelling* technique [14,15] incorporates and extends Dialogue Mapping by using a modelling methodology as the driver for the particular kinds of Issues, Answers and Pros/Cons that are mapped. *Templates* are defined to seed particular genres of analysis, optionally constraining node labels to machine-readable strings, and using node typing and tags to assist automation. Conversational Modelling templates have particular relevance for argument modelling in general, and for this paper in particular. Firstly, we have reported how Walton's critical questions associated with different presumptive argumentation schemes, once published in XML by Reed and Walton, were then further transformed into IBIS Conversational Modelling templates in Compendium [11]. For instance, a *challenges* link, which is in fact making an *argument by analogy*, can be 'exploded' into a template map showing the implicit premises, and the associated critical questions that can be asked about them.

Secondly, in the context of two space exploration field trials, we have reported how templates enabled software agents both to read and write Compendium maps [16], enabling Compendium to play a multiplicity of roles:

- As a way to create formal information structures for understanding by software agents, from informal discussions by people.
- As a way to navigate richly linked data and metadata in maps written by software agents;
- As a real time discourse mapping environment for both co-located and online meetings;
- As an asynchronous medium for distributed team conversation;
- As an asynchronous medium for scientists to program software agents;
- Combining planned, formal modelling, with interpretive scientific and project management discourse which could move in unpredictable directions.

Compendium is implemented as an open source, cross-platform, Java application that can swap between either the MySQL or Apache Derby relational databases. SQL and XML export/import assists data interoperability between clients and servers, and a number of projects have used RDF for data interchange. Public Java application interface classes provide an interface for other systems to read and write to the database directly, so maps can be generated from another data source or interpreted for processing by another system. A shared MySQL database supports group working over a local area network or Internet. Maps can be published for web browsers to view as interactive image-maps, or as linear HTML outline documents. An active user and developer community are supported by the Compendium Institute, which has logged over 30,000 downloads of the tool to date [17].

Recent years have seen the emergence of other web platforms for structured deliberation, whose core ontology is IBIS. Debategraph [18], Deliberatorium [19], and Cohere [20] seek to exploit the benefits of a web user interface and Web 2.0 services. An ongoing project is designing and testing a common serialization format for these platforms [21]. Apart from the possibility for diverse platforms to exchange data, web services and agent architectures point to the possibility of federating IBIS dialogue/argumentation [22].

This represents the current state of our agent-augmented CSCA research, and computational platform, and serves as the point of departure for the new work. The purpose of the work presented here was to show the feasibility of our approach, in order to ultimately develop an agent system that enables an agent-supported discussion, enabling software agents to negotiate with each other and/or people. Our prototype systems presented in sections 4 and 5 are a step towards showing that software agents can both simulate and support a human discussion using the IBIS argumentation framework. The idea is that if software agents can use IBIS, then it will be possible to enable human-agent discussions in a specific domain. These presented examples are a first step towards proving this hypothesis and ultimately developing a MAS system that can do this.

3. An Agent Language for Supporting CSCA

Brahms [7] is an agent-oriented language and agent simulation and execution environment that has been under development for over a decade. It provides a way to model activity and communication practices of groups of people and multi-agent systems, and contrasts to other belief-desire-intention (BDI) agent languages, as discussed in [23].

Brahms is a mature agent architecture used at NASA's International Space Station Mission Control Center [24], and underpinning large scale e-science infrastructures such as the Mobile Agents Architecture (MAA), which provides a means for modelling, simulating, implementing and managing a computer-supported Mars/Earth-based science work system [25].

Brahms agents are belief-based and use situation-action rules to perform activities. One type of activity is communicating with other agents, whether other Brahms agents or agents implemented in the Java language. The Brahms language provides a communications library enabling the design of specific agent communication protocols, based on speech act theory [26], as defined by the FIPA agent communication standard [27]. Using a combination of belief-based Brahms agents and a standardized communications protocol for IBIS conversations between agents, we developed our Brahms framework for collaborative argumentation (CA). It is our belief that this CA framework can be extended to become a general framework for human-agent CA. Here we explain the Brahms communication library. In the next section we discuss the Brahms IBIS protocol.

The Brahms communication library defines the FIPA communication act as the Brahms object class *CommunicationAct*. An instance (called a *comact*) of this class has to be created by the agent that wants to communicate about a particular topic (called the *payload* of the comact). The other attribute of a comact is the comact's *envelope*, specifying the sender and receiver information. The Brahms *Communicator* group defines a number of activities for creating comacts and communicating (i.e. sending) comacts to other agents (a Brahms activity is a predefined action or plan taking an amount of time to complete). The payload content of a comact is not defined in the CommunicativeAct class, but is specified by FIPA and can be designed by the modeler.

4. Extending Brahms Agents to Conduct IBIS Conversations

Perhaps the biggest change in transitioning from human to agent IBIS argumentation is the role of the facilitator. For human IBIS argumentation, the facilitator is responsible for both translating specific comments made by the group into individual IBIS nodes as well as maintaining the overall structure of the IBIS conversation. With agent IBIS argumentation, there is no longer a need for the facilitator to parse suggestions and ideas from the participants into their proper IBIS notation. Instead, we can develop agents that are capable of expressing their beliefs directly through IBIS nodes. While the agent facilitator is no longer required to perform translation, the task of maintaining the structure of an IBIS conversation between agents is much more difficult than in the human case. It is easy enough for a human facilitator to identify if an idea being proposed has already been summarized in the IBIS conversation. Agents lack this innate ability and thus the agent facilitator must search through the IBIS conversation to ensure that an IBIS node is unique before adding it to the conversation. Without intervention, duplicate IBIS nodes would, at a minimum, increase the amount of computation without adding any semantic value, and in the worst case could result in infinite loops.

At an abstract level, the process of creating an agent capable of understanding and communicating in IBIS is straightforward. In order to understand IBIS, an agent has to be aware of the various types of IBIS nodes and the function that they serve. The type of IBIS node received, the beliefs encapsulated by the IBIS node, and the current beliefs of the agent determine how an agent responds to a given IBIS node.

4.1. Implementing IBIS-agents in Brahms

The IBIS framework is defined by two interfaces, IBISParticipantAgent and IBISFacilitatorAgent. These interfaces present the functions, which must be implemented with domain knowledge in order to conduct IBIS argumentation.

IBISParticipantAgent
- *preArgumentationActivity()*
  - ◦ defines the actions taken by an agent before the argumentation begins, this may include the sending of the initial IBIS nodes that start the argumentation
- *postArgumentationActivity()*
  - ◦ defines the actions taken by an agent after the argumentation has concluded, this may include deciding the outcome of the argumentation
- *processQuestionNode(IBISNode node), processIdeaNode(IBISNode node), processProNode(IBISNode node), processConNode(IBISNode node)*
  - ◦ defines the actions taken by an agent when processing the various types of IBIS nodes, this may include the creation of new beliefs and/or responding with an IBIS node

IBISFacilitatorAgent
- *checkForDuplicate(IBISNode node)*
  - ◦ defines the process by which IBIS nodes are determined to be unique or duplicate

Each IBISParticipantAgent starts its execution by calling *preArgumentationActivity()*. Then for a predefined amount of time the IBISParticipantAgents will periodically check with the IBISFacilitatorAgent for new IBIS nodes. Each IBISParticipantAgent will process new IBIS nodes by calling the appropriate function for that type of IBIS node to see if it matches any of the preconditions for generating a response. After time has expired, each IBISParticipantAgent calls *postArgumentationActivity()* and then quits. The IBISFacilitatorAgent waits to receive an IBIS node from an IBISParticipantAgent. When it does, it calls *checkForDuplicate()* on the incoming node to see if it has already received an identical node. If it hasn't, then the node is added to the IBIS conversation.

IBIS nodes and IBIS notation play an enhanced role in agent IBIS argumentation. In human IBIS argumentation, the IBIS notation is not the same as the discussion, but the IBIS notation is used as a captured summary of the real-life dialogue, serving to focus and improve the quality of the discussion and create shared understanding between the discussion participants. Contrast this with the agent IBIS argumentation case, where the actual "discussion"[1] between agents is taking place directly through the IBIS notation. Therefore, it is necessary to give the IBIS nodes for agent argumentation additional expressive power that is not present in human IBIS argumentation. IBIS nodes are represented in the framework as shown in Figure 2.

The most important aspect of an IBIS node is the *content* attribute. When an agent goes to process a new IBIS node, they can determine what beliefs are associated with this node by looking at the objects referenced in *content*. A problem arises when multiple IBIS nodes refer to a single object, as it is no longer possible to determine which beliefs should be associated with which node. This problem is circumvented by having each agent create a new copy of the object they want to talk about and reference the copy in *content*, which ensures that each IBIS node refers to unique objects.

---

[1] The word discussion is purposefully in between quotation marks, signifying the realization that agents are not having actual discussions, but are simply sending IBIS-like messages to each other, which are then interpreted in agent specific ways to partake in individual agent activity outside of the IBIS communication activity being held.

```
class IBISNode extends SerializableObject{
  attributes:
    int weight; //the weight of the IBIS node when deciding the outcome of the
                argumentation
    IBISParticipantAgent sender; //sender of the IBIS node
    IBISNode parentNode; //IBIS node that this IBIS node is responding to
    map content; //map that contains references to all objects that appear in
                 the beliefs associated with this node
    string label; //text description of IBIS node (display use only)
    boolean isDuplicate; //indicates if an identical IBIS node has been seen
                         before
  relations:
    IBISNode childNode; //IBIS nodes that respond to this IBIS node
}
```

Figure 2: Representing IBIS nodes in the Brahms framework

4.2. Brahms IBIS-agents: preliminary evaluation

Simulating the Federal Aviation Administration's (FAA) Collaborative Convective Forecast Product (CCFP) chat sessions tested our agent IBIS argumentation framework. This online, text-based chat consists of meteorologists representing a variety of organizations (Aviation Weather Center, regional Air Route Traffic Control Centers, airlines, etc.) collaborating to form a consensus weather forecast. The forecaster for the Aviation Weather Center (AWC) is responsible for leading the chat as well as producing the final forecast. A typical CCFP chat begins with the AWC forecaster presenting their initial forecast. They then open up the discussion to see if any participants have modifications to suggest. The final forecast is then used as the primary weather analysis for the FAA's strategic planning teleconference.

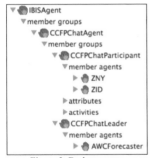

Figure 3. Brahms group membership for IBIS Framework

The text-based nature of the chat sessions appears to have a negative impact on the effectiveness of the collaboration. Problems include participants responding to questions out of order, failing to identify the question to which they are responding, and suggesting ideas without any kind of justification. As a result, the chat transcripts become convoluted, which diminishes their value as a record of the participants' decision-making process and serves to decrease the overall amount of participation. For these reasons, rather than simulating the CCFP chat sessions verbatim, we are suggesting the use of IBIS as a method for structuring the discussion.

The model we describe next is a first prototype of a scenario in which some of the knowledge held currently by human participants can be held and negotiated by agents. The model shows that the human collaboration during the CCFP chat can be formalized and modeled in an agent-based simulation, using the IBIS formalism.

Figure 3 shows that the *IBISAgent* interface is implemented by *CCFPChatAgent*. *CCFPChatAgent* is further extended by *CCFPChatLeader* and *CCFPChatParticipant*. The *AWC forecaster* agent is a member of the group *CCFPChatLeader*, where as all other participant agents are members of *CCFPChatParticipant*. The flexibility of the framework allows you to define multiple classes of agents that are capable of participating in IBIS argumentation. This could range from conducting IBIS argumentation with entirely homogeneous participants to having unique behaviors defined for each participant. Figure 4 specifies the beliefs held by the three IBIS agents in Figure 3.

```
agent AWCForecaster memberof CCFPChatLeader{
        initial_beliefs:
            (current updatedWeatherEvents unknown);
            (current.weatherReport = AWCForecasterWeatherReport);
            (AWCForecasterWeatherReport twoHourForecast WeatherEvent1);
            (WeatherEvent1.name = "weather_event_1");
            (WeatherEvent1.confidence = 1);
            (WeatherEvent1.growth = 1);
            (WeatherEvent1.tops = 1);
            (WeatherEvent1.coverage = 1);
            (WeatherEvent1.speed = 25);
            (WeatherEvent1.direction = 45);
}
agent ZID memberof CCFPChatParticipant{
        initial_beliefs:
            (current updatedWeatherEvents unknown);
            (current.weatherReport = ZIDWeatherReport);
            (ZIDWeatherReport twoHourForecast WeatherEvent1);
            (WeatherEvent1.name = "weather_event_1");
            (WeatherEvent1.confidence = 1);
            (WeatherEvent1.growth = 1);
            (WeatherEvent1.tops = 2);
            (WeatherEvent1.coverage = 2);
            (WeatherEvent1.speed = 25);
            (WeatherEvent1.direction = 45);
}
agent ZNY memberof CCFPChatParticipant{
        initial_beliefs:
            (current updatedWeatherEvents unknown);
            (current.weatherReport = ZNYWeatherReport);
            (ZNYWeatherReport twoHourForecast WeatherEvent1);
            (WeatherEvent1.name = "weather_event_1");
            (WeatherEvent1.confidence = 2);
            (WeatherEvent1.growth = 2);
            (WeatherEvent1.tops = 2);
            (WeatherEvent1.coverage = 1);
            (WeatherEvent1.speed = 25);
            (WeatherEvent1.direction = 45);
}
```

Figure 4: Three Brahms IBIS agents with beliefs derived from the CCFP use case

When we simulate the CCFP chat session conducted by running these agents in the Brahms environment, an IBIS conversation is produced: Figure 6 shows the Brahms simulation output, and Figure 7 shows the visualization of their IBIS argumentation, an initial result that gives us confidence that this approach has potential. However, Figure 5 shows the exponential rate at which simulation time increases with the number of IBIS nodes generated. Work needs to be done to bring this rate closer to linear before the framework will scale. The performance issues are due to the fact that an agent is required to create a copy of each object that it references in an IBIS node before communicating it to the facilitator. Finding a solution to this issue should help reduce the memory footprint of the framework, which in turn should increase the overall performance. Another issue facing the IBIS framework is the difference in complexity of the code for the framework, compared to that of the domain specific implementation. While the framework itself is simple and straightforward, the domain specific implementation is convoluted and repetitive. Making the framework more sophisticated should lead to a reduction in the amount of both code and effort necessary to apply it to new domains.

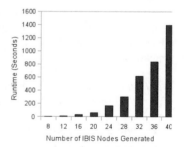

Figure 5: Runtimes for simulated CCFP IBIS conversations

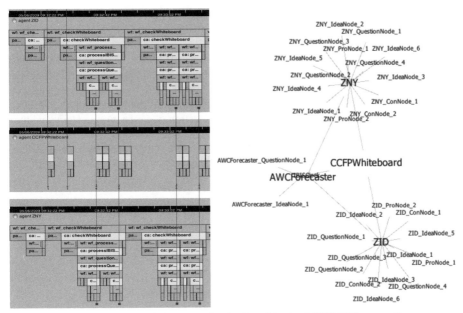

Figure 6. Brahms simulation output visualization of simulated CCFP IBIS conversation

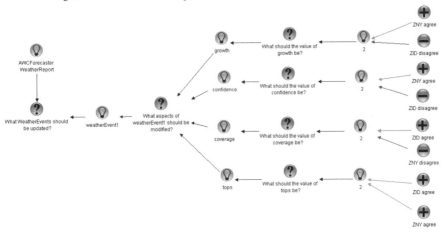

Figure 7: Compendium visualization of simulated CCFP IBIS conversation

5. Extending Compendium with Brahms Agents

We turn now to the second investigation into human-agent argument mapping: extending our CSCA mapping tool (Compendium) with agents (Brahms), in order to enable agent-based search of remote IBIS maps. Coupling Compendium to Brahms entails the creation of a Java class that serves, within Compendium, as a host for Brahms. Compendium's code was modified to accommodate these additional capabilities to support this framework: (i) core Compendium was modified to create the agent host class which, on

booting establishes an instance of a Brahms agent ready to communicate'
(ii) Compendium's user interface was extended (see below); (iii) an SQL query was added
responding to requests from other agents.

A Brahms agent was programmed to operate in the IBIS environment, and an adapter
framework was created that couples a Brahms instance to a Compendium. Brahms agents
communicate with each other, and with their Compendium hosts. To generalize this
picture, any compatible IBIS platform could be substituted for the Compendium platforms.
To define terms that will be used in the following section, we refer to one Compendium-
Agent pair as *local*, and other pairs as *remote*. In our user scenario, a local pair serves
"Susan" as her argument-mapping platform. One or more remote pairs behave as if they
are database servers capable of responding to simple queries.

Figure 8 illustrates the additional feature that provides a menu
item for requesting an agent to
search for nodes to satisfy a given
query. Figure 9 illustrates the
query being formed. Note that the
'%' character serves as a wildcard:
the query will match IBIS nodes
that offer 'climate' inside any
sentence. The query is broadcast
from the local Brahms agent to
available remote agents. Our first
iteration restricts that broadcast to
one remote agent coupled to a
second instance of Compendium,

Figure 8: Compendium 'Search Agents' menu selection

the database containing other IBIS conversations. Our prototype implements a simple SQL
query to the remote Compendium's database. Any node that has a statement that includes
the word "climate" will be returned, as illustrated in Figure 10.

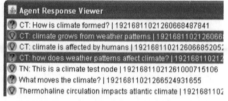

Figure 9: Composing a query   Figure 10: Search results returned from the agent
                                                    network

The user can select one or more responses from the Agent Response Viewer, which
leads to the addition of nodes to the original target node.

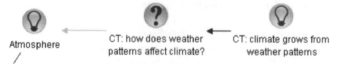

Figure 11: The local IBIS conversation expanded by query results

This serves as a proof of concept to demonstrate the feasibility of agent-mediated
search within Brahms, invoked from within the Compendium client user interface, with

results from a remote IBIS database being inserted, at the analyst's discretion, into her local IBIS map. We consider future developments next.

6. Conclusions and Future Work

Our research is designed towards realizing practical CSCA tools to help people cope with the complexity of knowledge intensive work in organizations, and with the challenges now facing society at large. Part of this future includes, we propose, software agents to help scaffold human reasoning: while agents can already be delegated simple tasks in order to release human effort for higher order reasoning, research in argumentation and MAS now points to the potential of human-agent argumentation.

In this paper we have motivated two investigations into how a particular agent-oriented language and architecture can augment CSCA: (i) the use of the IBIS formalism enabling Brahms agents to interact about competing options using argumentation, and (ii) the extension of the Compendium CSCA tool by integrating it with Brahms agents tasked with detecting related discourse elsewhere.

These results provide proof of the concept of human-agent argumentation. There is significant work left to develop this infrastructure to the point where we can begin to evaluate it in authentic contexts, such as the NASA field trials reviewed at the start. Brahms agents could be extended from the current simulation of Issue Mapping in IBIS, to identify when a particular kind of argument is being made, in order to deploy the IBIS argumentation schemes we have as Compendium templates [28].

Brahms already provides the low-level protocols for distributed internet-based MAS. IBIS-agents seeking to connect and federate IBIS conversations over the Internet will need to infer potential connectedness based on different (non-exclusive) strategies, currently under review [22]. One strategy seeks to exploit the contextual cues provided by IBIS structure, for instance, if two Issues in two different maps are similar, then arguably, they establish similar contexts for comparing the nodes connected to them. Another strategy would add more sophisticated language processing to parse node labels. A third strategy is to use topic mapping federation techniques.

Finally and most ambitiously, the Brahms language has been shown in a range of NASA mission contexts to be capable of modelling and implementing multi-agent systems to scaffold authentic work practices. This expands our vision for computational modelling of argumentation: it could be possible to move beyond modelling the micro-worlds of agent-agent and human-agent argumentation, to conceiving and modelling the broader work system in which this takes place, considering the actors and contexts that cause new issues to be raised, constraining the options and tradeoffs, and with an understanding of who or what may then make use of the results of argumentation.

Acknowledgements: We gratefully acknowledge the support of NASA Ames Research Center in conducting the IBIS Brahms agent research. Compendium is currently funded by the Hewlett Foundation (OpenLearn & OLnet Projects), and previously by the UK AHRC, EPSRC, ESRC and JISC.

7. References

1   Kirschner, P. Buckingham Shum, S. and Carr, C. (Eds.) *Visualizing Argumentation.* Springer: London.
2   Okada, A., Buckingham Shum, S. and Sherborne, T. (2008). *Knowledge Cartography.* Springer: London
3   Reed, C., Walton, D. & Macagno, F. (2007). Argument diagramming in logic, law and artificial intelligence. *Knowledge Engineering Review*, 22 (1), 87-109
4   Buckingham Shum, S., et al. (2006). Hypermedia Support for Argumentation-Based Rationale: 15 Years on from gIBIS and QOC. In: *Rationale Management in Software Engineering.* Dutoit, R. et al.. Springer: Berlin
5   de Moor, A. and Aakhus, M. (2006). Argumentation Support: From Technologies to Tools. *Communications of the ACM*, 49, (3), pp.93-98
6   Selvin, A., Buckingham Shum S.J. & Aakhus, M. (In Press). The Practice Level in Participatory Design Rationale: Studying Practitioner Moves and Choices. *Human Technology Journal*
7   Sierhuis, M., W. J. Clancey, et al. (2009). Brahms: An Agent-Oriented Language for Work Practice Simulation and Multi-Agent Systems Development. *Multi-Agent Programming*, Rafael, H. et al. Springer
8   Rittel, H.W.J., Second Generation Design Methods. *Interview in: Design Methods Group 5th Anniversary Report: DMG Occasional Paper*, 1972. 1: p. 5-10. Reprinted in: *Developments in Design Methodology*, N. Cross (Ed.), 1984, pp. 317-327, J. Wiley & Sons: Chichester
9   Buckingham Shum, S. and N. Hammond (1994). "Argumentation-Based Design Rationale: What Use at What Cost?" *International Journal of Human-Computer Studies,* 40(4): 603-652
10   Rittel, H.W.J., Second Generation Design Methods. *Interview in: Design Methods Group 5th Anniversary Report: DMG Occasional Paper*, 1972. 1: p. 5-10. Reprinted in: *Developments in Design Methodology*, N. Cross (Ed.), 1984, pp. 317-327, J. Wiley & Sons: Chichester
11   Buckingham Shum, S. and Okada, A. (2008). Knowledge Cartography for Controversies. In: *Knowledge Cartography,* (Eds.) Okada, A., Buckingham Shum, S. and Sherborne, T. Springer: London
12   Conklin, J. and M.L. Begeman (1988). gIBIS: A Hypertext Tool for Exploratory Policy Discussion. *ACM Transactions on Office Information Systems*, 4 (6): p. 303-331.
13   Conklin, J. (2006) *Dialogue Mapping.* Wiley & Sons: Chichester
14   Sierhuis, M. and Selvin, A. (1996). Towards a framework for collaborative modeling and simulation. *Workshop on Strategies for Collaborative Modeling and Simulation*, ACM CSCW '96, Boston, MA
15   Selvin A. (1999) Supporting Collaborative Analysis and Design with Hypertext Functionality. *Journal of Digital Information*, 1 (4): http://journals.tdl.org/jodi/article/view/jodi-17/15
16   Sierhuis, M. and Buckingham Shum, S. (2008). Human-Agent Knowledge Cartography for e-Science. In *Knowledge Cartography.* (Eds.) Okada, A., Buckingham Shum, S. and Sherborne, T. Springer: London
17   Compendium Institute: http://compendium.open.ac.uk/institute
18   Debategraph: www.debategraph.org
19   Klein, M. and Iandoli, L. (2008). Supporting Collaborative Deliberation Using a Large-Scale Argumentation System: The MIT Collaboratorium. *Conference on Online Deliberation.*
20   Buckingham Shum, S. (2008). Cohere: Towards Web 2.0 Argumentation. *2nd International Conference on Computational Models of Argument*, 28-30 May 2008, Toulouse. IOS Press: Amsterdam
21   IBIS Interchange Specification: http://projects.kmi.open.ac.uk/hyperdiscourse/docs/IBIS-0.1.pdf
22   Park, J. (2010). Boundary Infrastructures for IBIS Federation: Design Rationale, Implementation, and Evaluation. *Technical Report KMI-10-01*, Knowledge Media Institute, Open University, UK
23   Sierhuis, M. (2007). "It's not just goals all the way down" – "It's activities all the way down." *Engineering Societies in the Agents World VII*, 7th International, Workshop, ESAW 2006, Dublin, 2006, Revised Selected and Invited Papers. G. M. P. O'Hare, A. Ricci, M. J. O'Grady and O. Dikenelli. Dublin, Ireland, Springer. LNCS 4457/2007: 1-24
24   Sierhuis, M., Clancey, W.J. et al. (2009). NASA's OCA Mirroring System: An application of multiagent systems in Mission Control. *Autonomous Agents and Multi Agent Conference* (Industry Track). Budapest
25   Clancey, W.J., et al. (2005). Automating CapCom Using Mobile Agents and Robotic Assistants. *American Institute of Aeronautics and Astronautics 1st Space Exploration Conference*, Orlando, FL
26   Searle, J., R. (1975). A taxonomy of illocutionary acts. *Language, Mind, and Knowledge.* K. Gunderson. Minneapolis, University of Minnesota. 1-29: 344-369
27   FIPA. (2002). "FIPA Communicative Act Library Specification." Retrieved 12/10, 2004, from http://www.fipa.org/repository/aclspecs.html
28   Argumentation Schemes in IBIS: http://compendium.open.ac.uk/compendium-arg-schemes.html

Computational Models of Argument
P. Baroni et al. (Eds.)
IOS Press, 2010
doi:10.3233/978-1-60750-619-5-135

Argument Analysis: Components of Interpersonal Argumentation

Katarzyna BUDZYNSKA [a]

[a] *Institute of Philosophy, Cardinal Stefan Wyszynski University in Warsaw, Poland*

Abstract. The aim of the paper is to propose a robust model of interpersonal argumentation (IP). The IP-arguments directly address participants of communication, i.e. they refer to speech acts rather than to propositional contents. Argumentation theory recognizes several IP-arguments, e.g. argument from position to know or *ad hominem* arguments. The model proposed in the paper enables to describe references to different types of speech acts - not only assertives, but also commissives and directives. The IP-arguments are assumed to be warranted by the component of authorizing an agent to perform a given speech act. Consequently, the wider class of IP-communication can be expressed in the extended model, such as e.g. the structure of generic *ad hominem* can be explicitly represented as the undercutter.

Keywords. argumentation structure, argumentation schemes, speech acts

Introduction

The aim of the paper is to provide a model for a structure and schemes of argumentation, which directly addresses participants of communication. That is, it contains statements that refer to an agent's speech act such as e.g. "The expert asserts that global warming is a myth", "The witness testified that the suspect was guilty". Throughout the paper, I call it interpersonal argumentation (IP) using the framework proposed in [30,29]. Argumentation theory recognizes several arguments from the IP-level, e.g., appeal to expert opinion, appeal to witness testimony or *ad hominem* arguments. The class of IP-arguments is also known as source indicators reasoning (see e.g. [26]) or ethotic argumentation [6]. The representation of IP-arguments finds application in computational models of argument, which build upon and use the concepts of argumentation's structure and schemes such as e.g. ARGUMED [22], Araucaria [17], the AIF [7], ArgDF [15] or Avicenna [16].

The standard treatment of the IP-argumentation does not account for some of its aspects. First, it allows only to describe references to assertives (such as "i asserts A" in argument from position to know), while in natural contexts also other types of speech acts are objects of reference (such as a promise). For instance, a real-life argument may have the following form "John promised he would come back, so he'll come back". The representation of this type of arguments is troublesome, since it is not clear what could be a warrant for such an inference. In the case of assertives, the fact that i is in position to know A warrants the reasoner to conclude that A (presumably) holds. Furthermore, in the standard treatment only appealing to one type of authority is describable (the appeal to the cognitive authority, i.e. to expert opinion). As a result, there is no scheme for the appeal to an administrative authority (one who has right to exercise command or influence).

The next group of problems is related to *ad hominem* arguments. The standard representation of its basic type, i.e. GENERIC AH, does not reflect its counter-argumentative structure. That is, the attack present in GENERIC AH is not explicitly represented as a relation (denoted by an arrow in the diagram). And finally, the accusation such as "the witness i testimony is unreliable" can have an ambiguous representation, since it can be treated either as a premise of GENERIC AH, i.e. as a support for a conclusion "i's argument should not be accepted" (as assumed in [26]), or explicitly as an undercutter, i.e. as an attack against e.g. the relation between a reason and its conclusion (as assumed in DEFLOG [24]). The novelty of this paper is that I propose an extended model of interpersonal argumentation which allows to avoid those problems.

The paper is organized into two parts. The first part does not represent a contribution of this work. It describes concepts that I employ (Section 1) and the standard treatment of the IP-argumentation (Section 2). The second part of the paper introduces an extended model of interpersonal argumentation. Section 3 presents basic structure of IP-arguments and attacks on IP-components, Section 4 discusses an example of complex interactions at the IP-level, and, finally, Section 5 shows an example of applying the proposed model in the formal representation of arguments in DEFLOG.

1. Background

This section presents frameworks, which I employ to discuss and extend the model of the IP-argumentation: interpersonal level in argument analysis (Section 1.1), speech act theory (Section 1.2), and broad definition of argumentation (Section 1.3).

1.1. Interpersonal level

The first framework proposed by M. Załęska distinguishes three levels in the argument analysis: textual, ideational (related to content) and interpersonal [30,29]. Originally, this distinction was introduced by M. Halliday [10] for analyzing phenomena on the stage of an utterance. According to the hallidayan model, the interpersonal metafunction concerns the linguistic means through which the speaker participates at the communicative situation, establishing a relation with the hearer in order to influence him. Halliday includes into the interpersonal metafunction an expression of the speaker's commitments, attitudes and evaluations.

In the paper, I focus on how other's utterance is framed by a metatextual term signaling the reported speech. In particular, if an utterance refers to the performance of an agent's communicative act (e.g. his assertion, promise, etc.), then it is treated here as belonging to the interpersonal level. When such an utterance is performed in argumentation, we talk about the interpersonal argumentation. Arguments such as appeal to expert opinion, appeal to witness testimony, argument from position to know, argument from popular opinion or *ad hominem* arguments belong to the IP-level. On the contrary, arguments such as argument from sign or analogy are content-based arguments and operate within the ideational level. Observe that this concept of the IP-arguments differs from the concept of interpersonal reasoning introduced in [28]. Walton and Krabbe examined the reasoning in the context of dialogue and, as a result, proposed a taxonomy of different arguments (e.g. persuasion or negotiation dialogue). The relation between the IP-arguments and the types of dialogues remains outside the scope of this paper.

1.2. Speech acts

The second framework used in the paper is speech act theory introduced by J. Austin [2] and further developed by J. Searle [18,19] and J. Searle and D. Vanderveken [20]. I assume that a speech act $F(A)$ consists of an illocutionary force F and a propositional content A [20]. The same structure of speech acts $(claim(A), why(A), \text{etc.})$ is assumed in dialogue systems (see e.g. [14]). An illocutionary force is an intention of uttering a propositional content. For instance, John may utter A with an intention of asserting, asking, warning, promising and so on.

A speech act can be felicitous or infelicitous depending on whether or not it successfully performs a given action. For example, my act of promise that I met you yesterday is infelicitous. The rules that determine what constitutes a successful speech act are called the *constitutive rules*. In [18], Searle distinguishes four classes of those rules: (1) *propositional content rules*: some illocutions can only be achieved with an appropriate propositional content, e.g. a promise may refer only to what is in the future and under the control of a speaker, (2) *preparatory rules*: they determine what a speaker presupposes in performing a speech act, e.g. a speaker cannot marry a couple unless he is legally authorized to do so, (3) *sincerity rules*: they tell what psychological state is expressed (e.g. an assertion expresses belief, a promise expresses an intention to do something) and a speech act is sincere only if a speaker is actually in this state, (4) *essential rules*: they determine what a speech act consists in essentially, e.g. a promise commits a speaker to perform an act expressed in a propositional content. Thus, my promise that I met you yesterday was infelicitous, since I did not fulfil the propositional content condition (the propositional content does not refer to a future action).

The essential conditions are then used to build a taxonomy of speech acts. Both Austin [2] and Searle [19] proposed their taxonomies. However, throughout the paper I will use a slightly improved taxonomy by K. Bach and R. Harnish [3]. They distinguish four classes of speech acts: (1) *assertives* (constatives): they express a speaker's belief and his desire that a hearer forms a similar one, they also commit a speaker to the truth of the propositional content, e.g. claiming, conceding, testifying, deducing, arguing, denying, criticizing, rebutting, (2) *commissives*: they express the speaker's intention to do something and the belief that his utterance obliges him to do it, they also commit a speaker to do something, e.g. promising, threatening, offering, (3) *directives*: they express some attitude about a possible future act performed by a hearer and the intention that his utterance be taken as reason for the hearer's action, e.g. asking, commending, requesting, advising, (4) *acknowledgments*: they express feelings toward the hearer, e.g. apologizing, congratulating, thanking.

1.3. Broad notion of argumentation

The last concept that I adopt to represent the IP-argumentation is a broad notion of argument proposed by R. Pinto [12] and then formally specified by D. Hitchcock [11]. They claim that not only assertives may be a conclusion of argumentation. In fact, it can be any other speech act: (1) a commissive, e.g. "I know that you don't like to stay home alone for a long time, so I promise that I'll come back soon", (2) a directive, e.g. "John felt cold, so he asked me to close the window", or (3) an acknowledgment, e.g. "My conduct was inexcusable, so I apologize most sincerely".

2. Standard model of interpersonal argumentation

In this section, I present what I will call "standard model of interpersonal argumentation". Recall that argumentation theory distinguishes several IP-arguments. In this paper, I limit the considerations to argument from expert opinion, argument from position to know, and the basic type of *ad hominem* argument - GENERIC AH.[1] Section 2.1 presents Walton's account of IP-argumentation schemes. Section 2.2 shows how the IP-arguments are diagrammed and formalized in Verheij's ARGUMED and DEFLOG.

2.1. Walton's schemes of IP-argumentation

In D. Walton's model, position to know and expert opinion arguments are represented by the following schemes and critical questions (see e.g. [25,27]):

ARGUMENT FROM POSITION TO KNOW
i is in a position to know whether A is true or false.
i asserts that A is true (false).
Therefore, A may plausibly be taken to be true (false).

(CQ1) Is i in a position to know whether A is true (false)?
(CQ2) Is i an honest (trustworthy, reliable) source?
(CQ3) Did i assert that A is true (false)?

ARGUMENTATION SCHEME FOR APPEAL TO EXPERT OPINION
(Major premise) Source i is an expert in domain D containing proposition A.
(Minor premise) i asserts that proposition A (in domain D) is true (false).
Therefore, A may plausibly be taken to be true (false).

(CQ1) Expertise critical question: How credible is i as an expert source?
(CQ2) Field critical question: Is i an expert in the field that A is in?
(CQ3) Opinion critical question: What did i assert that implies A?
(CQ4) Trustworthiness critical question: Is i personally reliable as a source?
(CQ5) Consistency critical question: Is A consistent with what other experts assert?
(CQ6) Backup Evidence critical question: Is i's assertion based on evidence?

GENERIC AH is specified as follows ([26]: 249):

ARGUMENTATION SCHEME FOR GENERIC AH
i is a bad person.
Therefore, i's argument α should not be accepted.

(CQ1) Is the premise true (or well supported) that i is a bad person?
(CQ2) Is the allegation that i is a bad person relevant to judging i's argument α?

---

[1]For the specification of other IP-arguments the reader is referred e.g. to [27].

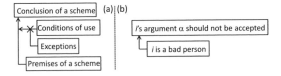

Figure 1. The argumentation schemes in ARGUMED: (a) a general form, (b) GENERIC AH.

(CQ3) Is the conclusion of the argument α should be (absolutely) rejected even if other evidence to support α has been presented, or is the conclusion merely (the relative claim) that α should be assigned a reduced weight of credibility, relative to the total body of evidence available?

2.2. Verheij's ARGUMED and DEFLOG

B. Verheij proposes the logical system DEFLOG, which allows to analyze prima facie justified assumptions [24]. These assumptions are not treated as definitely true, but are allowed to be defeated by some additional information. This corresponds to the idea of defeasible reasoning, what enables to link together Verheij's formalization and (defeasible) argumentation schemes [23]. The argumentation schemes are visually represented in the automated argument assistant ARGUMED based on DEFLOG [22]. This section gives a brief overview of Verheij's proposal.

In [23], Verheij introduces a method for formal analysis of argumentation schemes. The basic components of a scheme are its premises and conclusion. Additionally, each scheme has its *condition of use*, which corresponds to Toulmin's warrant [21], and Pollock-style [13] undercutting *exceptions of use*, which block the use of the scheme (Fig. 1a). Verheij also proposes how to diagram GENERIC AH (Fig. 1b).

DEFLOG's language has two connectives: dialectical negation $\times$, and primitive implication $\rightsquigarrow$. The dialectical negation $\times\varphi$ expresses that the statement φ is defeated. When the dialectical negation of a prima facie justified assumption is (actually) justified, the assumption is not actually justified, but defeated. The primitive implication $\varphi \rightsquigarrow \psi$ expresses elementary conditional relations, which can be a subject of attack or defeat. It only validates Modus Ponens. In DEFLOG, a warrant and an undercutter are treated as the support and, respectively, attack of the relation between a reason and its conclusion. Thus, a warrant corresponds to condition of scheme's use and is expressed by $\varphi \rightsquigarrow (\psi \rightsquigarrow \chi)$, while an undercutter corresponds to an exception of scheme's use and is expressed by $\varphi \rightsquigarrow \times (\psi \rightsquigarrow \chi)$.

Consider the example from [23]. Suppose that we have two prima facie assumptions:

```
testimony,
testimony ⤳ guilty,
```

where "testimony $\rightsquigarrow$ guilty" means that there is a witness testimony that implies the suspect's guilt. The application of Modus Ponens arrives at a conclusion that the suspect is guilty. Now, two additional prima facie assumptions are introduced:

```
unreliable,
unreliable ⤳ × (testimony ⤳ guilty),
```

Figure 2. The basic components of the IP-argumentation diagrammed according to: (a) Toulmin's model, (b) ARGUMED, and (c) Walton's model.

where "`unreliable`" means that the testimony is unreliable, and the second sentence expresses that if the witness testimony is unreliable, it is defeated that the testimony implies the suspect's guilt. Now, if the four assumptions are assumed to be prima facie justified, the prima facie assumption that the testimony implies guilt, is defeated, and it does not follow that the suspect is guilty.

The standard model of the IP-argumentation has some limitations. The next sections discuss those problems and propose an extension, which allows to avoid them.

3. Basic structure of IP-argumentation in the extended model

In this section, I propose the model for the basic components of IP-argumentation and for two types of interactions among them: support (Section 3.1) and attack (Section 3.2).

3.1. Relation of support

Following the specification of argument proposed by Pinto and Hitchcock (see Section 1.3), I assume that the argumentation may include different speech acts. However, I extend this approach by allowing not only a conclusion, but also a premise to be a speech act. Such an extension is implicitly assumed by, e.g., Walton's model of argument from position to know, where one of the premises is *assertive* "i asserts A", e.g. "John says that it is raining, so it is raining". I consider two further types of speech acts as premises: *commissives*, e.g. "John promised he would come back, so he'll come back", and *directives*, e.g. "John commanded me to close the window, so I should close the window". In this paper, I do not consider the acknowledgment class of speech acts.

A conclusion of the IP-argumentation will be true or accepted as true, if the intention of a speech act is satisfied. Following Bach and Harnish's taxonomy of speech acts (see Section 1.2), a conclusion for an assertive will be accepted by a hearer (I will accept that it is raining), when the hearer takes the speaker's commitment as reason to form a similar belief (I will treat John's commitment as a reason to believe that it is raining). A conclusion for a commissive will be accepted by (I will accept that John will come back), when the hearer takes the speaker's commitment to an action as reason to form a belief about that action (I will treat John's commitment to come back as a reason to believe that John will come back). A conclusion for a directive will be accepted by a hearer (I will accept that I should close the window), when the hearer takes the speaker's utterance as reason for his action (I will treat John's command as a reason to close the window).

Whether or not a hearer takes a speaker's utterance as reason for belief or action is determined by the *constitutive rules* for performing illocutionary acts (see Section 1.2). In other words, the hearer has to give the speaker an *authorization* to perform a given speech act. For example, I will accept that it is raining on the basis of John's assertion

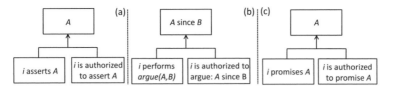

Figure 3. IP-arguments with: (a) a simple assertive, (b) a compound assertive $argue(A, B)$, and (c) a commissive $promise(A)$.

that it is raining, if I think he is authorized to make assertions with respect to the weather. In particular, I can give him an authorization on the ground of sincerity condition, since I think that he declares his actual belief. Similarly, I will accept that John will come back on the basis of his promise, if I think he is authorized to make promises with respect to his coming back. In particular, I may give him an authorization on the ground of propositional content conditions, since I think that this action is under his control.

The component of authorization can be viewed as a warrant of IP-arguments in Toulmin's sense [21] (see Fig. 2a). In Verheij's model, the warrant refers to the *condition of use* (see Fig. 2b).[2] Finally, it corresponds to the *major premise* in Walton-like argumentation scheme (see Fig. 2c).

The proposed IP-model is easily reducible to the traditional approach, where only assertions are allowed. To this end, I consider only one type of speech acts: $F(A)$, in which F belongs to assertives. The interesting question is what assertives should be allowed in such IP-argumentation. The narrow approach is to allow only $F(A)$, where F can have a form such as $assert, claim, affirm, state, assure, inform, report$, etc. (Fig. 3a). This type of IP-arguments corresponds to the argument from position to know. On the other hand, we could allow F to be an assertive $argue$, which according to Segmented Discourse Representation Theory (SDRT) [1] has relational characterization, i.e. F refers to a pair of propositional contents. Then, the speech act of arguing has a form: $argue(A, B)$ (Fig. 3b). This type of assertive can be also denoted as $argue(A)$, where A is composed of $prem(A)$, i.e. the set of premises of A, and $conc(A)$, i.e. a conclusion of A (see e.g. [14]). The rules, which determine whether a hearer gives a speaker authorization to perform $argue$, are explored by F. van Eemeren and R. Grootendorst as identity and correctness conditions [9]. Finally, since the extended model takes into account the speech acts, which belong to commissives or directives, IP-arguments can have also a form such as in Fig. 3c.

3.2. Attacks on IP-components

Attacks on the components of IP-arguments are expressed by different *ad hominem* arguments. In this section, I explore the limitations of the standard representation of AH and propose its modifications. I describe the proposal on the basic type of *ad hominem*, i.e. on GENERIC AH.

AH arguments attack a speaker's authorization to perform a given speech act or more generally they try to discredit an agent as a rightful participant of the social discourse.

---

[2]Observe that in Verheij's approach the selection of "condition of use" for a scheme is somehow arbitrary. It means that we could assume alternative condition of use: "If i perform $F(A)$ and i is authorized to perform $F(A)$, then A". In the paper, I focus on the simpler option.

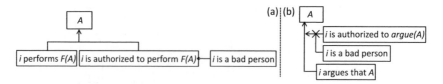

Figure 4. GENERIC AH in: (a) a Walton-like model, (b) ARGUMED.

The first limitation of the standard treatment is that it focuses on questioning an agent's right to perform a speech act *argue*, while in natural contexts any speech act may be questioned. Second, the standard model does not recognize AH as counter-arguments, at least not at their structural level. Attacks are commonly modeled by means of a relation on a set of arguments (denoted by arrows in the diagram), such as e.g. in Dung's [8] abstract framework. In Walton's model, the GENERIC AH attack is not explicitly represented, but only "reconstructible" from the content of its premise and conclusion: they describe that someone attacked other agent ("you are a bad person") questioning his argument ("your argument should not be accepted").

Let us start with the second limitation. It is not clear how to understand that i's argument should not be accepted. One reasonable interpretation is that i's conclusion is not rejected, but "undermined". Thus, the attack's effect may be viewed as similar to the effect that undercutters have, i.e. i's conclusion is not accepted since e.g. the inferential link between the premise and the conclusion is blocked.[3] If this is the case, then the GENERIC AH attack "i is a bad person" is directed at the component "i is authorized to perform $F(A)$" (Fig. 4a). Moreover, since in Verheij's model the component of authorization constitutes the condition of use, then GENERIC AH becomes an exception of use. That is, the attack "i is a bad person" is an exception to use i's authorization as a warrant for accepting i's argument A (Fig. 4b).

In order to avoid the first limitation of the standard treatment, we should allow GENERIC AH to attack authorization to perform any speech act. In particular, i's right can be diminished to perform the complex assertive: $argue(A)$. This case corresponds to Walton's account where the effect of *ad hominem* is to not accept i's argument. Moreover, GENERIC AH is allowed to attack also simple assertives such as: $claim(A)$, as well as commissives or directives. In the future work, I plan to consider the possibility of representing the IP-type of attacks in Dung's framework.

4. More complex IP-structures: appeal to expert opinion

The extended model enables to enrich the standard treatment of appeal to expert opinion in several manners. First, it allows to capture the distinction between two types of authorities to which arguments may appeal: *cognitive* (*de facto, epistemic*) *authority* and *administrative* (*de jure, deontic*) *authority*. Walton recognizes the ambiguity of "authority" as a problem, since it may disturb the analysis and evaluation of the acceptability of a given appeal to an authority ([25]: 76–79). Therefore, in such cases it is important to allow these types of authorities to be explicitly represented in the diagram. The *cognitive*

---

[3] At this point, we do not need to decide how to precisely specify a goal of undercutter: as an inferential link [13], a generalization [5], or a premise [4].

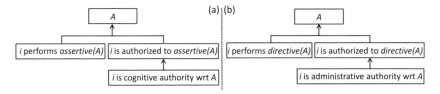

Figure 5. Two types of authority: (a) cognitive (expert), (b) administrative.

authority refers to a relationship between two agents where one (say i) is an expert in a field of knowledge and i's pronouncement in the field have a special weight (importance) for the other agent. This could be narrowly interpreted as appealing to i's simple assertive such as $claim(A)$. That option corresponds to Walton's argumentation scheme for appeal to expert opinion. The broader interpretation would allow to appeal to any i's assertive including the complex ones such as $argue(A)$ (see Fig. 5a). The *administrative authority* refers to a relationship between two agents where i has a right to exercise command or influence. Depending on applications, we can allow only some directives to be involved in this type of appeal, i.e. those that have a high degree of strength of the illocutionary point[4] (such as $command(A)$, $require(A)$, $forbid(A)$), or any i's directive including e.g. $ask(A)$ (in some applications in multi-agent systems, it may be assumed that only some agents have a right to query; then, those agents could be treated as possessing the administrative authority). The latter option is diagrammed in Fig. 5b.

Next, observe that some of critical questions in the argument from expert opinion seem to be very general, i.e. not specific for the case of expert (applying also to witness testimony etc.) such as trustworthiness critical question, while other critical questions are directly related to the properties of expertise such as field critical question. This intuition can be represented with the use of the extended model. In Fig. 6, the argument from expert opinion is diagrammed according to ARGUMED. Suppose that someone refers to Bob's assertion that A holds, and treats Bob as an expert with respect to A. How may his argument be critically questioned? The first class of questions (Fig. 6a and 6b) refers to the basic IP-argument (the grey elements in Fig. 6): if Bob asserts A, then (assuming that he is authorized to make this assertion) A holds. The other class of questions (Fig. 6c and 6d) refers to the "expertise" IP-subargument that support the component of authorization (the dashed-bordered elements in Fig. 6): if Bob is an expert with respect to A, then (assuming that experts on A are authorized on A) Bob is authorized to assert A.

The questions related to the components of the *basic IP-argument* can be of two kinds. One subclass refers to questioning the basic condition of use, i.e. the authorization to perform a speech act (Fig. 6a). Trustworthiness critical question (CQ4) and backup evidence question (CQ6) belong to this subclass. Such representation will have consequences on how an attack based on this type of question is formalized in DEFLOG (see the next section). Another subclass involves questions regarding truth of the basic premise, i.e. the precision of reporting the performance of a speech act (Fig. 6b). This includes questions such as opinion critical question (CQ3). There are also two types of critical questions specific for the *appeal to authority*. One subclass refers to questioning its condition of use, i.e. the expert's authorization (Fig. 6c). This question indicates an

---

[4]Two speech acts can achieve the same point (aim) with different degree of strength (see e.g. [20]). For instance, asking and commanding that a hearer do something both have the point of attempting to get him to do that thing. However, the latter is stronger than the former.

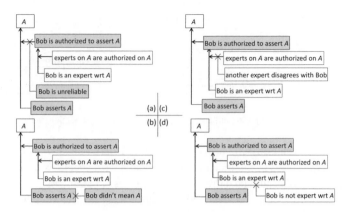

Figure 6. Classes of critical questions in argument from expert opinion, questioning: (a) the basic condition of use, (b) the basic premise, (c) the specific (expertise) condition of use, (b) the specific (expertise) premise.

exception when our trust to the expert's opinion should be suspended (or cancelled). That subclass includes consistency critical question (CQ5). The last subclass involves questions regarding truth of the premise, i.e. i's authority or expertise (Fig. 6d). This includes questions such as expertise critical question (CQ1) and field critical question (CQ2).

    Finally, the extended model enables to enrich IP-argumentation schemes and critical questions such that they could refer to the broader class of communicative activities, i.e. not only to assertives, but also commissives and directives. Especially interesting is a possibility to formulate the specification for appeal to administrative authority. However, its precise elaboration needs further investigations into the essential properties of this type of authority, what is outside the scope of this paper.

5. An example of application: DEFLOG

In argumentation theory, the accusation of someone's unreliability can be treated as (non-fallacious) GENERIC AH. Consequently, DEFLOG allows the utterance "the witness is unreliable" to be formalized in two different manners. In [23], the ARGUMED diagram represents GENERIC AH as "monologic" argumentation (at least at its structural level with no attack relation, see Fig. 1b). On the other hand, in the example discussed in [23] the accusation of witness's unreliability is represented as an undercutter (see Section 2.2). In this section, I briefly show how the extended model enables to unify the formalization.

    The exceptions of scheme's use correspond in DEFLOG to undercutters. Therefore, the specification of GENERIC AH proposed in the extended model allows to explicitly represent a statement "i is a bad person" as an *undercutting attack* in Verheij's sense (i.e. as an attack on the relation between a reason and its conclusion). Suppose that someone says: "Harry is a British subject, since John says so", and the other person reacts with GENERIC AH: "John is a liar". Let p be a statement that John says that Harry is a British subject, q - Harry is a British subject, and r - John is a liar. Initially, there are two prima facie assumptions:

p,

$p \rightsquigarrow q$.

At this point, it follows that q. However, the GENERIC AH attack "John is a liar" adds two other prima facie assumptions:

r,

$r \rightsquigarrow \times (p \rightsquigarrow q)$.

Now, if the four assumptions are assumed to be prima facie justified, the prima facie assumption $p \rightsquigarrow q$ is defeated, and it does not follow that q.

In DEFLOG, the *warrant* is interpreted as the support of the relation between a reason and its conclusion. Therefore, the *component of authorization* could be generally treated as φ in a formula $\varphi \rightsquigarrow (\psi \rightsquigarrow \chi)$. In the example, the warrant "John is authorized to assert that Harry is a British subject" (denoted by s) supports the relation between "John says that Harry is a British subject" and "Harry is a British subject", i.e.

$s \rightsquigarrow (p \rightsquigarrow q)$.

As a result, in the extended model GENERIC AH "behaves" in a similar manner as undercutting exceptions do. In particular, it is represented similarly to the exceptions which are determined by critical questions such as (CQ4) in argument from expert opinion. Thus, the formalization of such cases becomes unified.

Conclusions

The paper provides a model for analyzing various aspects of the interpersonal argumentation. I assume that the basic components of IP-structure are a speech act and an authorization to perform this speech act. The model allows to describe the properties of IP-arguments expressible in the standard treatment, e.g. the position to know argument from the standard model corresponds to the basic type of the IP-argumentation with speech acts limited to simple assertives.

Moreover, the model proposed in the paper enriches the standard treatment in several manners. First, it allows to infer a propositional content from any assertive, commissive or directive. For instance, the appeal to witness testimony can be treated as a subspecies of the basic type of IP-argument with an assertive of a type $testify$. The inference is warranted by the speaker's authorization to perform a speech act. The authorization is determined by the constitutive rules distinguished by Searle. Next, the attack in GENERIC AH is explicitly represented as an undercutter and *ad hominem* may attack not only the opponent's argument, but any of his speech act. Finally, the appeal to expert opinion may be represented as complex argumentation, where the "expert" subargument supports the basic IP-argument. Consequently, its critical questions divide into two classes depending on whether they refer to the basic IP-argument (such as trustworthiness critical question) or to the "expertise" IP-subargument (such as field critical question). It is also possible to express the appeal to an administrative authority.

The extended model finds an application wherever the concepts of argumentation structure and schemes are explored. In the paper, I show that it allows to treat the accusation of unreliability as GENERIC AH and, as a result, to unify the formalization in DEFLOG. Moreover, the extended model could enrich the argument analysis e.g. represented by the AIF or supported by Araucaria or ArgDF. It can be also applied in formal dialogue systems (such as e.g. [14]) to specify a new type of supports or attacks based on authorization of a participant of a dialogue to perform a move in the dialogue.

Acknowledgements

The author gratefully acknowledges the support from Polish Ministry of Science and Higher Education under grant N N101 009338.

References

[1]   N. Asher and A. Lascaride, *Logics of Conversation*, Cambridge University Press, 2003.
[2]   J. L. Austin, *How to Do Things with Words*, Oxford: Clarendon, 1962.
[3]   K. Bach and R. Harnish, *Linguistic Communication and Speech Acts*, M.I.T. Press, Cambridge, 1979.
[4]   P. Besnard and A. Hunter, *Elements of Argumentation*, MIT Press, 2008.
[5]   F. Bex, S. van den Braak, H. van Oostendorp, H. Prakken, B. Verheij and G. Vreeswijk, Sense-making software for crime investigation: how to combine stories and arguments?, *Law, Probability and Risk* **6** (2007), 145–168.
[6]   A. Brinton, Ethotic argument, *History of Philosophy Quarterly* **3** (1986), 245–257.
[7]   C. Chesnevar, J. McGinnis, S. Modgil, I. Rahwan, C. Reed, G. Simari, M. South, G. Vreeswijk, and S. Willmott, Towards an Argument Interchange Format, *The Knowledge Engineering Review* **21(4)** (2006), 293–316.
[8]   P.M. Dung, On the acceptability of arguments and its fundamental role in nonmonotonic reasoning, logic programming, and n-person games, *Artificial Intelligence* **77** (1995), 321–357.
[9]   F. H. van Eemeren and R. Grootendorst, *Argumentation, Communication, and Fallacies. A Pragma-Dialectical Perspective*, Lawrence Erlbaum Associates, Inc., 1992.
[10] M.A.K. Halliday, *An Introduction to Functional Grammar*, Arnold, London, 1985.
[11] D.Hitchcock, Informal logic and the concept of argument, *Handbook of the Philosophy of Science*, Elsevier **5** (2006), 101–129.
[12] R. Pinto, Generalizing the notion of argument, *Argument, Inference and Dialectic* (2001), 10–20.
[13] J.L. Pollock, *Cognitive Carpentry*, MIT Press, 1995.
[14] H. Prakken, Coherence and flexibility in dialogue games for argumentation, *Journal of Logic and Computation* **15** (2005), 1009–1040.
[15] I. Rahwan, F. Zablith, and C. Reed, Laying the Foundations for aWorldWide Argument Web, *Artificial Intelligence* **171(10-15)** (2007), 897–921.
[16] I. Rahwan, B. Banihashemi, C. Reed, D. Walton and S. Abdallah, Representing and Classifying Arguments on the Semantic Web, *The Knowledge Engineering Review* (2010), to appear.
[17] C. Reed and G. Rowe, Araucaria: Software for argument analysis, diagramming and representation, *International Journal of AI Tools* **14(3-4)** (2004), 961–980.
[18] J. Searle, *Speech Acts: An essay in the philosophy of language*, Cambridge University Press, 1969.
[19] J. Searle, A taxonomy of illocutionary acts, *Language. Mind and Knowledge, Minnesota Studies in the Philosophy of Science* **VII** (1975), 344–369.
[20] J. Searle and D. Vanderveken, *Foundations of Illocutionary Logic*, Cambridge University Press, 1985.
[21] S. Toulmin, *The Uses of Argument*, Cambridge University Press, 1958.
[22] B. Verheij, Automated argument assistance for lawyers, *Proc. of Conference on Artificial Intelligence and Law* (1999), 43–52.
[23] B. Verheij, Dialectical argumentation with argumentation schemes: an approach to legal logic, *Artificial Intelligence and Law* **11** (2003), 167–195.
[24] B. Verheij, DefLog: on the logical interpretation of prima facie justified assumptions, *Journal of Logic and Computation* **13(3)** (2003), 319–346.
[25] D. Walton, *Appeal to Expert Opinion: Arguments from Authority*, University Park, Pa., 1997.
[26] D. Walton, *Ad Hominem Arguments*, University of Alabama Press, Tuscaloosa, 1998.
[27] D. Walton, *Fundamentals of Critical Argumentation*, Cambridge University Press, 2006.
[28] D. Walton and E. Krabbe, *Commitment in Dialogue: Basic Concepts of Interpersonal Reasoning*, State University of N.Y. Press, 1995.
[29] M. Załęska, Dimensione interpersonale dell'argomentazione, (2010), in press.
[30] M. Załęska, Citing a name which counts. Quotation in the academic discourse from an interpersonal perspective, *Beiträge der Europäischen Slavistischen Linguistik (Polyslav)* (2005), 214–222.

Computational Models of Argument
P. Baroni et al. (Eds.)
IOS Press, 2010
doi:10.3233/978-1-60750-619-5-147

An Algorithm for Stage Semantics

Martin CAMINADA [a]

[a] *University of Luxembourg*

Abstract. In the current paper, we re-examine the concept of stage semantics, which is one of the oldest semantics for abstract argumentation. Using a formal treatment of its properties, we explain how the intuition behind stage semantics differs from the intuition behind the admissibility based semantics that most scholars in argumentation theory are familiar with. We then provide a labelling-based algorithm for computing all stage extensions, based on earlier algorithms for computing all preferred, stable and semi-stable extensions.

1. Introduction

The concept of stage semantics for abstract argumentation was first introduced by Verheij [15] and has subsequently been worked out in Verheij's DEFLOG system [16,17], which can be regarded as a generalization of the abstract argumentation theory of Dung [10]. Although stage semantics is one of the oldest semantics for abstract argumentation, it has so far remained relatively unknown, which might have to do with the fact that it was originally stated not in terms of the usual extensions approach, but in the form of pairs (J, D) where J is a set of justified arguments and D is a set of defeated arguments [15]. Nevertheless, there exist good reasons for treating stage semantics as one of the main-stream semantics for abstract argumentation, not only because it can be expressed using a relatively simple and elegant principle, but also because it implements a fundamentally different intuition than the traditional admissibility based semantics (such as complete, grounded and preferred [10], ideal [11] or semi-stable [15,5]).

Despite of the differences between stage semantics and the traditional admissibility-based semantics, it is still possible to provide an algorithm for computing all stage extensions, that is very close to previously stated algorithms for computing all preferred, stable and semi-stable extensions [6,14], as is demonstrated in the current paper.

2. Stage Semantics

In Verheij's original work [15] stage semantics was defined in terms of pairs of sets of arguments. In the current paper, however, we will describe stage semantics in terms of the more commonly applied extensions approach. We assume familiarity with basic argumentation concepts, such as that of an argumentation framework, conflict-free sets, admissible sets, complete extensions, preferred extensions, stable extensions and the grounded extension. Definitions of these can be found in [10]. In the current paper, we only consider finite argumentation frameworks.

If A is an argument then we write A^+ for the set of arguments attacked by A. Similarly, if $Args$ is a set of arguments then we write $Args^+$ to refer to the set of arguments attacked by at least one argument in $Args$.

Definition 1. *Let $AF = (Ar, att)$ be an argumentation framework. A stage extension is a conflict-free set $Args \subseteq Ar$ where $Args \cup Args^+$ is maximal (w.r.t. set inclusion) among all conflict-free sets.*

Stage semantics can to some extent be compared to semi-stable semantics, which is essentially an admissible set $Args$ where $Args \cup Args^+$ is maximal. In the remainder of this paper, we refer to $Args \cup Args^+$ as the *range* of $Args$, a term that was first introduced in [15]. Thus, where semi-stable extensions are admissible sets with maximal range, stage extensions are conflict-free sets with maximal range.

One could examine whether the same principle can also be applied to other semantics. That is, what if for instance one would look at complete, preferred or stable extensions with maximal range? It turns out that doing so does not yield any additional semantics. Complete extensions with maximal range, as well as preferred extensions with maximal range, are semi-stable extensions.[1] Stable extensions by definition have a maximal range, so selecting the stable extensions with maximal range simply means selecting all stable extensions. An overview of the effects of selecting sets and extensions with maximal range is provided in Table 1.

input extensions/sets	conflict-free sets	admissible sets	complete extensions	preferred extensions	stable extensions
result when selecting for maximal range	stage extensions	semi-stable extensions	semi-stable extensions	semi-stable extensions	stable extensions

Table 1. Selecting the extensions with a maximal range, given a semantics.

As an example of how stage semantics operates, consider the first argumentation framework on the left of Figure 1. Here, there exist five conflict-free sets: $\emptyset$, $\{A\}$, $\{B\}$, $\{C\}$ and $\{A, C\}$. Both $\{B\}$ and $\{A, C\}$ are maximal, but only $\{A, C\}$ has a maximal range, so only $\{A, C\}$ is a stage extension. This illustrates that selecting a maximal conflict-free set is different than selecting a conflict-free set with maximal range.[2]

Another example is the second argumentation framework of Figure 1. Here, there exist pricisely two stage extensions: $\{A, D\}$ and $\{B, D\}$ (both of which have a range of $\{A, B, C.D\}$). Hence, the results of stage semantics of this example are in line with the results of more established semantics like preferred, stable and semi-stable.

In the third argumentation framework of Figure 1, the two-cycle of the previous example has been replaced by a three-cycle. Here, there exist three stage extensions $\{A, E\}$, $\{B, E\}$ and $\{C, E\}$ (with corresponding ranges $\{A, B, D, E\}$, $\{B, C, D, E\}$ and $\{C, A, D, E\}$). This is in contrast with the admissibility based semantics (grounded, preferred, complete, ideal and semi-stable) which all yield $\emptyset$ as the only extension.

---

[1]The equivalence between admissible sets with maximal ranges and complete extensions with maximal ranges has been proved in [5], and the equivalence between complete extensions with maximal ranges and preferred extensions with maximal ranges can be proved in a similar way.

[2]Just like selecting a maximal admissible set (preferred) is different than selecting an admissible set with a maximal range (semi-stable).

Hence, one of the advantages of stage semantics is that odd and even loops are treated equally. The only other well-known semantics with this property is CF2 [3].[3]

The fourth argumentation framework of Figure 1 is where stage semantics yields a different result than obtained by the admissibility based semantics, as well as by CF2. The only stage extension here is $\{B\}$, where the admissibility based semantics all yield $\emptyset$ as the only extension.

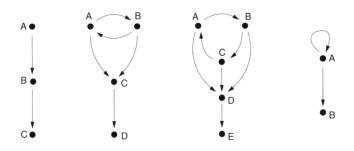

Figure 1. Four argumentation frameworks

It holds that every stable extension is a stage extension (just like every stable extension is a semi-stable extension [5]).

Theorem 1. *Let $\mathcal{A}rgs$ be a stable extension of argumentation framework (Ar, att). $\mathcal{A}rgs$ is also a stage extension of (Ar, att).*

Proof. Let $\mathcal{A}rgs$ be a stable extension of (Ar, att). Then $\mathcal{A}rgs$ is a conflict-free set that attacks every argument in $Ar \backslash \mathcal{A}rgs$. This means that $\mathcal{A}rgs \cup \mathcal{A}rgs^+ = Ar$. Therefore, $\mathcal{A}rgs \cup \mathcal{A}rgs^+$ is maximal (it cannot be a proper superset of Ar). Therefore, $\mathcal{A}rgs$ is a stage extension.   □

It also holds that if there exists at least one stable extension, then every stage extension is also a stable extension (just like if there exists at least one stable extension, then every semi-stable extension is also a stable extension [5]).

Theorem 2. *Let (Ar, att) be an argumentation framework that has at least one stable extension. It then holds that every stage extension is also a stable extension.*

Proof. Let $\mathcal{A}rgs$ be a stable extension of (Ar, att). It then holds that $\mathcal{A}rgs$ is a conflict-free set with $\mathcal{A}rgs \cup \mathcal{A}rgs^+ = Ar$. Therefore, every stage extension $\mathcal{A}rgs'$ will have to satisfy $\mathcal{A}rgs' \cup \mathcal{A}rgs'^+ = Ar$ in order to have a maximal range. This means that every stage extension will also be a stable extension.   □

Theorem 1 and 2 can be seen as special instances of the results obtained in DEFLOG [16,17]. Apart from the extensions approach, it is also possible to describe stage semantics in terms of argument labellings [4,8,7].

---

[3]CF2 semantics does have the advantage that the grounded extension is a subset of *every* CF2 extension, whereas for stage semantics one has the weaker property that the grounded extension is a subset of *at least one* stage extension. See [7] for more details.

Definition 2. *Let* (Ar, att) *be an argumentation framework. A labelling is a function* $\mathcal{L}ab : Ar \rightarrow \{\text{in}, \text{out}, \text{undec}\}$.

If $\mathcal{L}ab$ is a labelling then we write $\text{in}(\mathcal{L}ab)$ for $\{A \mid \mathcal{L}ab(A) = \text{in}\}$, $\text{out}(\mathcal{L}ab)$ for $\{A \mid \mathcal{L}ab(A) = \text{out}\}$ and $\text{undec}(\mathcal{L}ab)$ for $\{A \mid \mathcal{L}ab(A) = \text{undec}\}$. Since a labelling is a function, it can be represented as a set of pairs. In this paper we will sometimes use an alternative way to represent a labelling, as a partition $(\text{in}(\mathcal{L}ab), \text{out}(\mathcal{L}ab), \text{undec}(\mathcal{L}ab))$.

Definition 3. *Let* (Ar, att) *be an argumentation framework. A conflict-free labelling is a labelling such that for every* $A \in Ar$ *it holds that:*

1. *if* $\mathcal{L}ab(A) = \text{in}$ *then* $\forall B \in Ar : (B\,att\,A \supset \mathcal{L}ab(B) \neq \text{in})$
2. *if* $\mathcal{L}ab(A) = \text{out}$ *then* $\exists B \in Ar : (B\,att\,A \wedge \mathcal{L}ab(B) = \text{in})$

The definition of a conflict-free labelling is almost equal to that of an admissible labelling in [8]. The only difference is that for an admissible labelling, the first clause is "if $\mathcal{L}ab(A) = \text{in}$ then $\forall B \in Ar : (B\,att\,A \supset \mathcal{L}ab(B) = \text{out})$)", which is stronger than the first clause of Definition 3. It immediately follows that every admissible labelling is also a conflict-free labelling, just like every admissible set is also a conflict-free set.

Definition 4. *Let* (Ar, att) *be an argumentation framework.* $\mathcal{L}ab$ *is a stage labelling iff* $\mathcal{L}ab$ *is a conflict-free labelling where* undec *is minimal (w.r.t. set inclusion) among all conflict-free labellings.*

It can be verified that stage extensions and stage labellings stand in a one-to-one relationship to each other.

Proposition 1. *Let* $AF = (Ar, att)$ *be an argumentation framework.*

1. *If* $\mathcal{A}rgs$ *is a stage extension of* AF *then* $\text{Ext2Lab}(\mathcal{A}rgs)$ *is a stage labelling of* AF, *where* $\text{Ext2Lab}(\mathcal{A}rgs) = (\mathcal{A}rgs, \mathcal{A}rgs^+, Ar\backslash(\mathcal{A}rgs \cup \mathcal{A}rgs^+))$.
2. *If* $\mathcal{L}ab$ *is a stage labelling of* AF *then* $\text{Lab2Ext}(\mathcal{L}ab)$ *is a stage extension of* AF, *where* $\text{Lab2Ext}(\mathcal{L}ab) = \text{in}(\mathcal{L}ab)$.

Moreover, when restricted to stage extensions and stage labellings, the functions Ext2Lab *and* Lab2Ext *become bijective and each other's inverses.*

The proof of Proposition 1 is included in [7], where it is also proved that every stable labelling (in the sense of [4,8]) is also a stage labelling, and that if there exists at least one stable labelling, then every stage labelling is also a stable labelling.

3. An Algorithm

In the current section we provide an algorithm for computing all stage labellings of a given argumentation framework. Using the result of Proposition 1 we then also obtain the stage extensions of the argumentation framework, which are after all simply the sets of in-labelled arguments of the stage labellings.

The basic idea of the algorithm is to start with a labelling in which every argument is labelled in. This labelling will subsequently be referred to as the *all*-in labelling. Then, a sequence of *transition steps* is applied, where each step resolves a conflict between two in-labelled arguments where one attacks the other. The algorithm described in the current section is a slightly modified version of the earlier developed algorithm for computing all semi-stable labellings[4] [6]. The main difference is that where the semi-stable algorithm is based on the notion of an admissible labelling, the currently presented stage algorithm is based on the notion of a conflict-free labelling.

Definition 5. *Let $\mathcal{L}ab$ be a labelling of argumentation framework $AF = (Ar, att)$.*

1. *an* in-*labelled argument A is called* illegally in *iff* $\exists B \in Ar : (B \, att \, A \land \mathcal{L}ab(B) = \text{in}) \lor \exists B \in Ar : (A \, att \, B \land \mathcal{L}ab(B) = \text{in})$
2. *an* out-*labelled argument A is called* illegally out *iff* $\neg \exists B \in Ar : (B \, att \, A \land \mathcal{L}ab(B) = \text{in})$

In essence, an argument is illegally in iff it violates point 1 of Definition 3 and is illegally out iff it violates point 2 of Definition 3. It then follows that a labelling is conflict-free iff it does not have any argument that is illegally in or illegally out.

Definition 6. *Let $\mathcal{L}ab$ be a labelling of argumentation framework (Ar, att) and $A \in Ar$ and argument that is illegally* in *in $\mathcal{L}ab$. A transition step* on A in $\mathcal{L}ab$ *consists of the following:*

1. *the label of A is changed from* in *to* out
2. *for every $B \in \{A\} \cup A^+$, if B is illegally* out *then the label of B is changed from* out *to* undec

It can be observed that each transition step preserves the absence of arguments that are illegally out. That is, if a labelling does not have any argument that is illegally out before a transition step, then there will still be no argument that is illegally out after the transition step. Moreover, since each transition step reduces the number of illegally in-labelled arguments by at least one, subsequently applying transition steps starting from the all-in labelling ultimately yields a labelling without any illegally in-labelled arguments.

Definition 7. *A transition sequence is a list $[\mathcal{L}ab_0, A_1, \mathcal{L}ab_1, A_2, \mathcal{L}ab_2, \ldots, A_n, \mathcal{L}ab_n]$ ($n \geq 0$) where $\mathcal{L}ab_0$ is the all-in labelling, each A_i ($1 \leq i \leq n$) is an argument that is illegally* in *in $\mathcal{L}ab_{i-1}$, and every $\mathcal{L}ab_i$ ($1 \leq i \leq n$) is the result of doing a transition step on A_i in $\mathcal{L}ab_{i-1}$. A transition sequence is called* terminated *iff $\mathcal{L}ab_n$ does not have any argument that is illegally* in.

Since we only consider finite argumentation frameworks, it holds that every transition sequence can be extended to a terminated transition sequence, in which a finite number of transitions have been performed. We say that a transition sequence *yields $\mathcal{L}ab$* if its last labelling is $\mathcal{L}ab$.

As an example of a transition sequence, consider the third argumentation framework of Figure 1. Starting with the all-in labelling $\mathcal{L}ab_0 = (\{A, B, C, D\}, \emptyset, \emptyset)$, one could, for instance, select argument A to do a transition step on, resulting in the labelling $\mathcal{L}ab_1 = (\{B, C, D, E\}, \{A\}, \emptyset)$. Subsequently one could, for instance, select argument

---

[4]Other variations of the same algorithm exist for computing all preferred and all stable labellings [6].

C to do a transition step on. Once C is relabelled out, A becomes illegally out and is therefore relabelled undec in the same transition step. Hence the resulting labelling $\mathcal{L}ab_2$ is $(\{B, D, E\}, \{C\}, \{A\})$. Subsequently, one could select argument D to do a transition step on, resulting in the labelling $\mathcal{L}ab_3 = (\{B, E\}, \{C, D\}, \{A\})$. This labelling does not have any argument that is illegaly in, so the transition sequence is terminated. The overall transition sequence is $[\mathcal{L}ab_0, A, \mathcal{L}ab_1, C, \mathcal{L}ab_2, D, \mathcal{L}ab_3]$.

Lemma 1. *Let $[\mathcal{L}ab_0, A_1, \mathcal{L}ab_1, \ldots, A_n, \mathcal{L}ab_n]$ be a terminated transition sequence. It holds that $\mathcal{L}ab_n$ is a conflict-free labelling.*

Proof. Since the all-in labelling does not have any argument that is illegally out (it has no out-labelled argument at all) and each transition step preserves the absence of illegally out-labelled arguments, it follows that each terminated transition sequence yields a labelling without any illegally out-labelled arguments. Since a terminated transition sequence also yields a labelling without any illegally in-labelled arguments (otherwise the transition sequence would not be terminated), it follows that the result yielded by a terminated transition sequence is a conflict-free labelling. □

As an example, consider the argumentation framework on the left of Figure 1. An example of a (terminated) transition sequence is, starting from the all-in labelling, first to perform a transition step on B, resulting in a labelling $(\{A, C\}, \{B\}, \emptyset)$, which is conflict-free, thus terminating the transition sequence. Another possibility would be first to perform a transition step on A, resulting in a labelling $(\{B, C\}, \emptyset, \{A\})$, and subsequently performing transition steps on B or C, resulting in the conflict-free labellings $(\{C\}, \emptyset, \{A, B\})$ and $(\{B\}, \{C\}, \{A\})$, respectively. Other transition sequences also exist. Only the first obtained labelling is a stage labelling. All other labellings that are yielded by terminated transition sequences are conflict-free but not stage. Fortunately, it holds that, as a general rule, every stage labelling is included in the results yielded by the terminated transition sequences, as is expressed by the following theorem.

Theorem 3. *Let $\mathcal{L}ab_{stage}$ be a stage labelling of argumentation framework (Ar, att). There exists a terminated transition sequence which yields $\mathcal{L}ab_{stage}$.*

Proof. We prove the theorem by, given a stage labelling, constructing a terminated transition sequence that yields it. The idea is to construct this transition sequence in two phases, first by doing transition steps on the arguments that are labelled out by $\mathcal{L}ab$, then by doing transition steps on the arguments that are labelled undec by $\mathcal{L}ab$.

Let $\mathcal{L}ab_{stage}$ be a stage labelling. Let $[\mathcal{L}ab_0, A_1, \mathcal{L}ab_1, \ldots, A_m, \mathcal{L}ab_m]$ $(m \geq 0)$ be a (possibly unterminated) transition sequence where $A_1, \ldots, A_m$ are the arguments that are labelled out by $\mathcal{L}ab_{stage}$ (that is: $\{A_1, \ldots, A_m\} = \text{out}(\mathcal{L}ab_{stage})$). This is a correct transition sequence, because every A_i $(1 \leq i \leq m)$ will be illegally in until it is relabelled to out (this is because every A_i is legally out in $\mathcal{L}ab_{stage}$, so it has an attacker that is labelled in by $\mathcal{L}ab_{stage}$, and since we do not relabel this attacker in any of the transition steps, it will be labelled in by every $\mathcal{L}ab_i$ $(0 \leq i \leq m)$). Furthermore, none of the transition steps will relabel any out-labelled argument to undec because every out-labelled argument will stay legally out throughout the transition sequence. This implies that $\text{undec}(\mathcal{L}ab_m) = \emptyset$. Furthermore, since transition steps are done on every argument that is labelled out by $\mathcal{L}ab_{stage}$, it follows that $\text{out}(\mathcal{L}ab_m) = \text{out}(\mathcal{L}ab_{stage})$. Since no transition steps are done on arguments that are labelled in by $\mathcal{L}ab_{stage}$, it holds that

$\text{in}(\mathcal{L}ab_m) \supseteq \text{in}(\mathcal{L}ab_{stage})$.

We now continue the transition sequence, this time by doing transition steps not on arguments that are labeled out by $\mathcal{L}ab_{stage}$, but on arguments that are labelled undec by $\mathcal{L}ab_{stage}$. The idea is to keep doing this until there are no more arguments in $\text{undec}(\mathcal{L}ab_{stage})$ that are illegally in in the transition sequence. Thus, the extended transition sequence becomes $[\mathcal{L}ab_0, A_1, \mathcal{L}ab_1, \ldots, A_m, \mathcal{L}ab_m, A_{m+1}, \mathcal{L}ab_{m+1}, \ldots, A_{m+n}, \mathcal{L}ab_{m+n}]$ $(m, n \geq 0)$ where:

(1) $\{A_{m+1}, \ldots, A_{m+n}\} \subseteq \text{undec}(\mathcal{L}ab_{stage})$, and

(2) $\mathcal{L}ab_{m+n}$ does not have any illegally in-labelled argument that is an element of $\text{undec}(\mathcal{L}ab_{stage})$.

Not only does $\mathcal{L}ab_{m+n}$ not have any illegally in-labelled argument that is an element of $\text{undec}(\mathcal{L}ab_{stage})$, it also does not have any illegally in-labelled argument that is an element of $\text{out}(\mathcal{L}ab_{stage})$ (this is because these arguments have been relabelled to out in the first part of the transition sequence), and it also does not have any illegally in-labelled argument that is an element of $\text{in}(\mathcal{L}ab_{stage})$ (this is because if there exists such an argument (say A), then it must have a conflict with an in-labelled argument from $\text{undec}(\mathcal{L}ab_{stage})$ (say B), but then it follows that B is also illegally in in $\mathcal{L}ab_{m+n}$: contradiction). From the fact that $\mathcal{L}ab_{m+n}$ does not have any illegally in-labelled argument that is in $\text{undec}(\mathcal{L}ab_{stage})$, in $\text{out}(\mathcal{L}ab_{stage})$ or in $\text{in}(\mathcal{L}ab_{stage})$, it holds that $\mathcal{L}ab_{m+n}$ does not have any illegally in-labelled argument at all. This means that the transition sequence is terminated, and that therefore (Lemma 1) $\mathcal{L}ab_{m+n}$ is a conflict-free labelling. Since no transition steps on any arguments in $\text{in}(\mathcal{L}ab_{stage})$ were performed, it holds that $\text{in}(\mathcal{L}ab_{m+n}) \supseteq \text{in}(\mathcal{L}ab_{stage})$. Furthermore, since $\text{out}(\mathcal{L}ab_m) = \text{out}(\mathcal{L}ab_{stage})$, and none of the transition steps following $\mathcal{L}ab_m$ relabels any of these out-labelled arguments to undec (they will always stay legally out because they all have attackers in $\text{in}(\mathcal{L}ab_{stage})$ that are not selected for any transition steps) it also holds that $\text{out}(\mathcal{L}ab_{m+n}) \supseteq \text{out}(\mathcal{L}ab_{stage})$. From the fact that $\text{in}(\mathcal{L}ab_{m+n}) \supseteq \text{in}(\mathcal{L}ab_{stage})$ and $\text{out}(\mathcal{L}ab_{m+n}) \supseteq \text{out}(\mathcal{L}ab_{stage})$ it follows that $\text{undec}(\mathcal{L}ab_{m+n}) \subseteq \text{undec}(\mathcal{L}ab_{stage})$. However, since $\mathcal{L}ab_{stage}$ is a stage labelling and $\mathcal{L}ab_{m+n}$ is a conflict-free labelling, it follows that $\text{undec}(\mathcal{L}ab_{m+n})$ cannot be a strict subset of $\mathcal{L}ab_{stage}$. Therefore, it must hold that $\text{undec}(\mathcal{L}ab_{m+n}) = \text{undec}(\mathcal{L}ab_{stage})$. It then follows that $\text{in}(\mathcal{L}ab_{m+n}) = \text{in}(\mathcal{L}ab_{stage})$ and $\text{out}(\mathcal{L}ab_{m+n}) = \text{out}(\mathcal{L}ab_{stage})$. This means that $\mathcal{L}ab_{m+n} = \mathcal{L}ab_{stage}$. $\qquad\square$

Since each terminated transition sequence yields a labelling that is conflict-free, Theorem 3 allows for a simple way of obtaining all stage labellings: simply produce all terminated transition sequences and select the results with minimal undec. Fortunately, it is not necessary to compute *all* of the terminated transition sequences. This is because during the course of a transition sequence, the set of undec-labelled arguments either stays the same or increases, as is stated in the following proposition.

Proposition 2. *Let* $[\mathcal{L}ab_0, A_1, \mathcal{L}ab_1, \ldots, A_n, \mathcal{L}ab_n]$ *be a transition sequence. For any* $1 \leq i \leq n$ *it holds that* $\text{undec}(\mathcal{L}ab_{i-1}) \subseteq \text{undec}(\mathcal{L}ab_i)$.

Suppose we have already computed a terminated transition sequence yielding labelling $\mathcal{L}ab$, and we are currently computing a (not yet terminated) transition sequence whose last labelling is $\mathcal{L}ab_i$. If $\text{undec}(\mathcal{L}ab) \subsetneq \text{undec}(\mathcal{L}ab_i)$ then Proposition 2 tells us that the current transition sequence will never yield a stage extension once it is terminated, and that it would therefore be a good idea to backtrack to another possibility. This allows us to prune the search space, a possibility that was not available in Verheij's original treatment of the dynamics of stage semantics [16,17].

Overall, the algorithm for computing the stage labellings of a given argumentation framework can be described as follows.

```
potential_stage_labs := ∅;    find_stage_labs(all-in);
print potential_stage_labs;    end;

procedure find_stage_labs(Lab)
   # if we found something that is worse than found earlier
   # then prune the search tree and backtrack
   if ∃Lab' ∈ potential_stage_labs: undec(Lab') ⊊ undec(Lab) then return;
   # now see if our current transition sequence has terminated
   if Lab does not have an argument that is illegally in then
      for each Lab' ⊆ potential_stage_labs
         # if an old candidate is worse than the new candidate: remove
         if undec(Lab) ⊊ undec(Lab') then
            potential_stage_labs := potential_stage_labs - {Lab'};
         endif;
      endfor;
      # add our newly found labelling as a candidate
      # we already know that it is not worse than what we already have
      potential_stage_labs := potential_stage_labs ∪ {Lab};
      return; # we are done with this one; try next possibility
   else
      for each argument A that is illegally in in Lab
         find_stage_labs(transition_step(A, Lab));
      endfor;
   endif;
endproc;

procedure transition_step(A, Lab)
   Lab' := Lab;
   # relabel argument A from in to out
   Lab' := (Lab' − {(A, in)}) ∪ {(A, out)};
   # relabel any resulting illegal out to undec
   for each B in {A} ∪ A⁺
      if B is illegally out then Lab' := (Lab' − {(B, out)}) ∪ {(B, undec)};
   endfor;
   return Lab';
endproc;
```

A software implementation of the above algorithm is presented at the COMMA demo session. Apart from computing the stage labellings (extensions), the software is also able to compute the grounded, preferred, stable and semi-stable labellings (extensions) using the algorithms described in [6,14].

4. Stage Semantics and Maximal Consistency

There exists an alternative way to describe the concept of stage semantics. In essence, what stage semantics does is taking a maximal subgraph of the argumentation framework that has at least one stable extension. A stage extension is then a stable extension of such a maximal subgraph. Similar observations have been made in the context of DEFLOG [16,17]. In the current section, however, we treat these results in the context of abstract argumentation.

Definition 8. *Let* $AF = (Ar, att)$ *be an argumentation framework and* $Args \subseteq Ar$. *We define a* subframework $AF|_{Args}$ *of* AF *as* $(Args, att \cap (Args \times Args))$. *If* $AF|_{Args_1}$ *and* $AF|_{Args_2}$ *are subframeworks of* AF *then we say that* $AF|_{Args_2}$ *is at least as big as* $AF|_{Args_1}$ *iff* $Args_1 \subseteq Args_2$.

Proposition 3. *Let* $AF = (Ar, att)$ *be an argumentation framework and* $Args \subseteq Ar$. *The following two statements are equivalent:*

1. $Args$ *is a conflict-free set of* AF
2. $Args$ *is a stable extension of* $AF|_{Args \cup Args^+}$

Theorem 4. *Let* $AF = (Ar, att)$ *be an argumentation framework and* $Args \subseteq Ar$. *The following two statements are equivalent.*

1. $Args$ *is a conflict-free set of* AF *where* $Args \cup Args^+$ *is maximal (w.r.t. set inclusion) among all conflict-free sets (that is,* $Args$ *is a stage extension of* AF*).*
2. $Args$ *is a stable extension of a maximal subframework of* AF *that has at least one stable extension.*

Proof. "from 1 to 2": Let $Args$ be a conflict-free set of AF where $Args \cup Args^+$ is maximal. From Proposition 3 it follows that $Args$ is a stable extension of $AF|_{Args \cup Args^+}$. So $Args$ is a stable extension of a subframework of AF that has at least one stable extension. We now prove that $AF|_{Args \cup Args^+}$ is also a *maximal* subframework that has at least one stable extension. Let $Args'_{range} \supsetneq Args \cup Args^+$ be such that $AF|_{Args'_{range}}$ has at least one stable extension, and let $Args'$ be such a stable extension. It then follows that $Args' \cup Args'^+ = Args'_{range}$. From Proposition 3 it then follows that $Args'$ is a conflict-free set of AF. However, since $Args' \cup Args'^+ \supsetneq Args \cup Args^+$, it follows that $Args$ does not have a maximal range. Contradiction.

"from 2 to 1": Let $Args$ be a stable extension of a maximal subframework that has at least one stable extension. It follows that this maximal subframework is $AF|_{Args \cup Args^+}$. Then from Proposition 3 it follows that $Args$ is a conflict-free set of AF. We now prove that it is also a conflict-free set with a maximal range. Let $Args'$ be a conflict-free set of AF such that $Args \cup Args^+ \subsetneq Args' \cup Args'^+$. Then from Proposition 3 it follows that $Args'$ is a stable extension of $AF|_{Args' \cup Args'^+}$. But this means that $AF|_{Args \cup Args^+}$ is not a *maximal* subframework that has at least one stable extension. Contradiction. $\square$

In order to understand the difference between stage semantics and the admissibility based semantics, it is useful to make an analogy with classical logic. In the presence of a potentially inconsistent knowledge base one could do two things:

1. Take the maximal consistent subsets of the knowledge base, and examine what is entailed by all of these (the "maximal consistency approach"). That is, take the (classical) models of the maximal subsets of the knowledge base that have classical models.
2. Define a new semantics such that the entire knowledge base will have models (the "new semantics approach"). This is the approach that is, for instance, taken in the field of paraconsistent logic [1,9].

Solution 1 (applying the original semantics to maximal subsets of the original problem description) is comparable to stage semantics, whereas solution 2 (redefining the semantics so that it can meaningfully be applied to a bigger class of knowledge bases) is comparable with the admissibility based semantics.

To understand the difference between solution 1 (the maximal consistency approach) and solution 2 (the new semantics approach), it helps to study the following labelling-based definition of stable semantics.

Definition 9. *Let* $AF = (Ar, att)$ *be an argumentation framework. A stable labelling is a function that assigns each argument* $A \in Ar$ *either the label* in *or* out, *such that:*

1. *A is labelled* in *iff all its attackers are labelled* out, *and*
2. *A is labelled* out *iff it has at least one attacker that is labelled* in.

The innovation of complete semantics[5] can be described as adding a third kind of label (undec) to the existing labels (in and out), while keeping the two clauses in the above definition the same [4,8]. A similar approach has been stated in the field of logic programming, where complete semantics is known as the *three-valued stable model semantics* [18]. In either case, the result is that under the new semantics (complete or 3-valued stable) solutions (models or extensions) exist, even for situations where solutions did not exist under the old semantics (2-valued stable). A similar trend can be observed in the field of paraconsistent logic, where some approaches try to warrant the existence of solutions (models) by implementing additional truth values [1,9].

An alternative approach would be not to come up with a fundamentally new semantics, but instead to apply the "traditional" semantics on the maximal part of the knowledge base that has "traditional" solutions. In the domain of classical logic, for instance, one could examine what is entailed by all maximal consistent subsets of formulas in the knowledge base, which in essence is the same as considering the classical models of all maximal subsets of formulas that have classical models. Similarly, in the context of logic programming, one could apply stable model semantics to the maximal subsets of a logic program that have stable models, or in the context of abstract argumentation, one could apply stable semantics to maximal subframeworks that have stable extensions, as is implemented by stage semantics.

5. Discussion

In the current paper, we have re-examined the concept of stage semantics and studied some of its properties. Apart from that, we have provided an algorithm that computes

---

[5]Recall that other admissibility-based semantics (like grounded, preferred, ideal or semi-stable) in essence select particular subsets of the complete extensions (labelings).

all stage labellings, and therefore also all stage extensions. This algorithm starts with the all-in labelling and then performs a sequence of transition steps in which the set of in-labelled arguments decreases and the set of undec-labelled arguments increases. This approach allows one to prune the search space, a possibility that would not be available if one would, for instance, start with the all-undec labelling, and then perform an alternative type of transition steps which increase the sets of in and out-labelled arguments. Nor would pruning be available when one uses the extensions approach (instead of the labellings approach) starting with the empty set while subsequently adding arguments such that the set remains conflict-free.

Although for the extensions approach it would also be possible to allow for pruning by starting with the set of all arguments, and then subsequently removing arguments until the set becomes conflict-free, such an approach would require the computation of the range of the set after every removal. This computation is relatively expensive, because it is essentially a global recomputation from scratch. With the labellings approach, on the other hand, no such global recomputation is needed. Instead of removing an argument (say A) from the set, we perform a transition step on an in-labelled argument. We do this by relabelling the argument from in to out (which is similar to removing the argument from the set) and by subsequently relabelling the out-labelled arguments in $\{A\} \cup A^+$ that have now become illegally out to undec (which serves the same purpose as recalculating the range of the new set). However, while recalculating the range of the new set is a global operation, based on the entire argumentation framework, relabelling any illegally out-labelled arguments in $\{A\} \cup A^+$ to undec only requires a local operation on a restricted part of the argumentation framework. This is one of the main advantages of the labellings approach above the sets approach.

Like was mentioned before, stage semantics forms one of the foundations of Verheij's DEFLOG system [16,17], which can be seen as a generalisation of Dung's notion of an argumentation framework by providing a full logical formalism of justification and attack. Where various recent work in abstract argumentation theory has been driven to implement things like higher order attacks [2] and extended argumentation frameworks [12,13], these concepts have been implemented in DEFLOG already ten years ago, in the context of stage semantics, as well as in the context of other semantics. Apart from this, the concept of semi-stable semantics can be traced back to [15], where it was described in terms of *admissible stage extensions*. Although differences in basic formalisation do not make it immediately obvious (Verheij for instance does not use the standard extensions approach) it can be proved that Verheij's approach is equivalent to that of Caminada, who independently from Verheij rediscovered the same concept, this time under the name of semi-stable semantics [5]. In addition, Caminada has proved various additional properties (like the fact that each semi-stable extension is also a complete extension [5]) and provided an algorithm [6].

One of the more fundamental issues that were treated in this paper is the difference between the "maximal consistency" approach and the "new semantics" approach. For instance, scholars in the field of paraconsistent logic had to justify their often more elaborate new semantical approaches above the simpler approach of selecting the maximal consistent subsets of a knowledge base. However, in argumentation it appears that we have gone directly to the "new semantics" approach (admissibility) without even considering the "maximal consistency" approach (stage semantics) in any serious way. This is remarkable, especially since the maximal consistency approach turns out to be expressible using the relatively simple notion of a conflict-free set with maximal range, which does not require concepts like acceptability, fixpoints and monotonic functions. This raises the question of what are the fundamental advantages of the admissibility based semantics above what appears to be the simpler approach of stage semantics.

References

[1]   O. Arieli and A. Avron. The value of the four values. *Artificial Intelligence*, 102:97–141, 1998.

[2]   P. Baroni, F. Cerutti, M. Giacomin, and G. Guida. Encompassing attacks to attacks in abstract argumentation frameworks. In *Proc. of ECSQARU 2009, 10th European Conference on Symbolic and Quantitative Approaches to Reasoning with Uncertainty*, pages 83–94, 2009.

[3]   P. Baroni, M. Giacomin, and G. Guida. SCC-recursiveness: a general schema for argumentation semantics. *Artificial Intelligence*, 168(1-2):165–210, 2005.

[4]   M.W.A. Caminada. On the issue of reinstatement in argumentation. In M. Fischer, W. van der Hoek, B. Konev, and A. Lisitsa, editors, *Logics in Artificial Intelligence; 10th European Conference, JELIA 2006*, pages 111–123. Springer, 2006. LNAI 4160.

[5]   M.W.A. Caminada. Semi-stable semantics. In P.E. Dunne and T.J.M. Bench-Capon, editors, *Computational Models of Argument; Proceedings of COMMA 2006*, pages 121–130. IOS Press, 2006.

[6]   M.W.A. Caminada. An algorithm for computing semi-stable semantics. In *Proceedings of the 9th European Conference on Symbolic and Quantitalive Approaches to Reasoning with Uncertainty (ECSQARU 2007)*, number 4724 in Springer Lecture Notes in AI, pages 222–234, Berlin, 2007. Springer Verlag.

[7]   M.W.A. Caminada. A labelling approach for ideal and stage semantics. submitted, 2010.

[8]   M.W.A. Caminada and D.M. Gabbay. A logical account of formal argumentation. *Studia Logica*, 93(2-3):109–145, 2009. Special issue: new ideas in argumentation theory.

[9]   W. Carnielli, M.E. Coniglio, and J. Marcos. Logics of formal inconsistency. In D.M. Gabbay and F. Guenthner, editors, *Handbook of Philosophical Logic, second edition*, volume 14, pages 15–114. Springer Verlag, 2002.

[10] P. M. Dung. On the acceptability of arguments and its fundamental role in nonmonotonic reasoning, logic programming and n-person games. *Artificial Intelligence*, 77:321–357, 1995.

[11] P. M. Dung, P. Mancarella, and F. Toni. Computing ideal sceptical argumentation. *Artificial Intelligence*, 171(10-15):642–674, 2007.

[12] S. Modgil. An abstract theory of argumentation that accommodates defeasible reasoning about preferences. In *Proc. ECSQARU 2007*, pages 648–659, 2007.

[13] S. Modgil. Reasoning about preferences in argumentation frameworks. *Artificial Intelligence*, 173:901–1040, 2009.

[14] S. Modgil and M.W.A. Caminada. Proof theories and algorithms for abstract argumentation frameworks. In I. Rahwan and G.R. Simari, editors, *Argumentation in Artificial Intelligence*, pages 105–129. Springer, 2009.

[15] B. Verheij. Two approaches to dialectical argumentation: admissible sets and argumentation stages. In J.-J.Ch. Meyer and L.C. van der Gaag, editors, *Proceedings of the Eighth Dutch Conference on Artificial Intelligence (NAIC'96)*, pages 357–368, Utrecht, 1996. Utrecht University.

[16] B. Verheij. DEFLOG - a logic of dialectical justification and defeat. Technical report, Department of Metajuridica, Universiteit Maastricht, 2000.

[17] B. Verheij. DEFLOG: on the logical interpretation of prima facie justified assumptions. *Journal of Logic and Computation*, 13:319–346, 2003.

[18] Y. Wu, M.W.A. Caminada, and D.M. Gabbay. Complete extensions in argumentation coincide with 3-valued stable models in logic programming. *Studia Logica*, 93(1-2):383–403, 2009. Special issue: new ideas in argumentation theory.

Computational Models of Argument
P. Baroni et al. (Eds.)
IOS Press, 2010
© *2010 The authors and IOS Press. All rights reserved.*
doi:10.3233/978-1-60750-619-5-159

Dialectical Proofs
for Constrained Argumentation

Caroline DEVRED [a] Sylvie DOUTRE [b] Claire LEFÈVRE [a] and Pascal NICOLAS [a]

[a] *LERIA, University of Angers, France*
[b] *IRIT, University of Toulouse, France*

Abstract. Constrained argumentation frameworks (CAF) generalize Dung's frameworks by allowing additional constraints on arguments to be taken into account in the definition of acceptability of arguments. These constraints are expressed by means of a logical formula which is added to Dung's framework. The resulting system captures several other extensions of Dung's original system. To determine if a set of arguments is credulously inferred from a CAF, the notion of dialectical proof (alternating pros and cons arguments) is extended for Dung's frameworks in order to respect the additional constraint. The new constrained dialectical proofs are computed by using Answer Set Programming.

Keywords. Formal models for argumentation, dialogue, implementation, ASP.

Introduction

Argumentation is an approach to nonmonotonic reasoning, based on the notions of argument, and interactions between arguments. Among all the frameworks which have been proposed for argumentation (see [2,16] for a survey), the one by Dung [8] has received a lot of attention. Actually, the high level of abstraction of this framework and its simplicity make it encompass many approaches to nonmonotonic inference and logic programming, and generalize several other approaches to argumentation.

Concretely, [8]'s framework consists of a set of arguments and of an attack relation between arguments. Nothing is said neither on the nature of the arguments, nor on the nature of the attack relation.

Several notions of acceptable sets, namely extensions, are defined as sets of arguments that satisfy some properties. In [8]'s framework, these properties are always defined in terms of attacks between arguments. Some works propose to refine this definition of acceptability by taking into account a notion of preference between arguments, or of values (e.g. [22]). However, it may be necessary to express constraints between arguments which are neither attack-based nor preference-based. An attempt in this sense has been proposed in [21,23]: these works allow the possibility for some arguments to belong to extensions only if necessary. However, these works do not offer the possibility for either an argument x, or an argument y (x and y not attacking each other), to belong to extensions; or the possibility for an argument z to belong to extensions only if x and y both belong to them (z not being attack-related to x and y).

[5] have proposed an extension of Dung's framework with a notion of constraint, which, without taking into account preferences between arguments, offers a way to specify further, non attack-based, requirements which have to be satisfied by the acceptable sets of arguments. The resulting constrained argumentation framework encompasses Dung's framework and several of its existing extensions. For instance, as shown in [5], it captures Dung's preferred extensions and the weakly preferred semantics defined for bipolar systems. The constrained argumentation framework has been applied to practical reasoning in [1].

A crucial problem in argumentation is the derivability (or acceptance) of arguments: is a set of arguments included in at least one, or into every extension of an argumentation framework? In other words, is it credulously, or sceptically acceptable? An answer to the credulous acceptance problem for one argument has been proposed by, for example, [20,4] for Dung's framework. Such an answer takes the form of a dialogue (or argument game) between two players, the one trying to show why the argument is acceptable, the other one in turn trying to show why it is not. Such dialectical proofs not only answer the problem, but also explain why the answer is so, in terms of arguments attacking and defending the argument on stage. Another kind of answer, based on a labeling of arguments, has been proposed by [19]. This approach builds minimal answers, but it does not exhibit dialogues which explain the answer as in the previous approaches. [7] has recently exhibited a unified framework which aims at capturing several dialectical approaches, among which the last two ones, but the approach is limited to Dung's framework. In this paper, we propose an extension of [4]'s dialectical proofs to the credulous acceptance problem for a set of arguments, in a constrained argumentation framework.

Another important issue about argumentation is computation. Some programs exist (e.g. [24,19,25,26,9]), among which some of them compute a kind of dialectical proofs, different from [4]. Furthermore, none of them takes into account the additional notion of constraint presented here. In this paper, we present not only a formal model for these proofs, but also a program which computes them. This program is written using a high level language which makes it rather easy to read and understand. This language is Answer Set Programming (ASP), a paradigm which has already been applied with success in many areas of knowledge representation and reasoning, and for which efficient solvers are available [6,10]. [9] has recently applied ASP to the computation of extensions in Dung's framework. The ASP program we propose here computes the dialectical proofs for credulous acceptance in a constrained argumentation framework.

The paper is organised as follows: we start with presenting Dung's argumentation framework and constrained argumentation frameworks. Then we define the dialectical proofs for the constrained argumentation frameworks. Finally, we present ASP and the program which computes the proofs, before concluding.

1. Argumentation frameworks

This section start s with briefly presenting [8]'s argumentation framework (Def. 1 and 2).

Definition 1 *An* argumentation framework *is a pair* $\langle A, R \rangle$ *where* A *is a set of so-called* arguments *and* R *is a binary relation over* A *(*$R \subseteq A \times A$*). Given two arguments* a *and* b*,* $(a, b) \in R$ *means that* a attacks b *(*a *is said to be an* attacker *of* b*).*

An argumentation framework is nothing but a directed graph, whose vertices are the arguments and edges correspond to the elements of R. For computational reasons, we restrict the argumentation frameworks considered in this article to those whose set of arguments is finite.

Example 1 *Let* $AF = \langle A, R \rangle$ *be an argumentation framework with* $A =\{a, b, c, d, e, f, g,$ $h, i, j, k\}$ *and* $R = \{(a, b), (b, d), (d, i), (i, h), (a, c), (c, e), (e, f), (f, e), (f, g), (g, h),$ $(j, k), (k, j)\}$. *The graph for* AF *is depicted on Figure 1.*

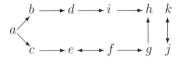

Figure 1. Graphical representation of AF

Definition 2 *Let* $AF = \langle A, R \rangle$ *be an argumentation framework.* $S \subseteq A$ *is a* conflict-free *set of arguments if and only if for every* $a, b \in S$, *we have* $(a, b) \notin R$. *An argument* $a \in A$ *is* acceptable *w.r.t. a subset* S *of* A *if and only if for every* $b \in A$ *s.t.* $(b, a) \in R$, *there exists* $c \in S$ *s.t.* $(c, b) \in R$. $S \subseteq A$ *is* admissible *if and only if* S *is conflict-free and every argument in* S *is acceptable w.r.t.* S. $S \subseteq A$ *is a* preferred extension *if and only if it is maximal w.r.t.* $\subseteq$ *among the set of admissible sets.*

Example 2 (contd.) $\{a, b\}$ *is not a conflict-free set,* $\{a, d\}$ *is.* d *is acceptable w.r.t.* $\{a\}$. $\{a, d, e\}$ *is admissible.* $\{a, d, f, h, j\}$ *and* $\{a, d, e, g, j\}$ *are two of the preferred extensions of* AF.

Dung's argumentation framework has been extended by [5] in order to take into account constraints over arguments (definitions 3, 4 and 5, and proposition 1).

Definition 3 *Let* $PROP_{PS}$ *be a propositional language defined in the usual inductive way from a set* PS *of propositional symbols, the constants* $\top$, $\bot$ *and the connectives* $\neg$, $\wedge$, $\vee$, $\Rightarrow$, $\Leftrightarrow$. *A Constrained Argumentation Framework (CAF) is a triple* $CAF = \langle A, R, \mathcal{C} \rangle$ *where* A *is a finite set of arguments,* R *is a binary relation over* A, *the attack relation, and* $\mathcal{C}$ *is a propositional formula from* $PROP_A$.

Example 3 (contd.) *The argumentation framework* AF *of Figure 1 is extended with a constraint* $\mathcal{C} = (k \Leftrightarrow d) \wedge ((d \Rightarrow (f \vee g)) \vee (\neg d \Rightarrow \neg f))$. *This constraint means, regarding the extensions, that argument* k *belongs to an extension if and only if argument* d *belongs to it, and that, if* d *belongs to an extension, then either* f *or* g *must belong to it, or if* d *does not belong to an extension, then* f *must not belong to it either.*

In the following definitions of this section, we consider that a constrained argumentation framework $CAF = \langle A, R, \mathcal{C} \rangle$ is given. Furthermore, each subset S of A corresponds to an interpretation over A (i.e. a total function from A to {true, false}), given by the completion of S.

Definition 4 *Let* $S \subseteq A$. *S satisfies* C *if and only if the completion* $\widehat{S} = \{a \mid a \in S\} \cup \{\neg a \mid a \in A \setminus S\}$ *of S is a model of* C *(denoted by* $\widehat{S} \models C$).

The notions of admissibility and preferred extensions have been restricted so that the constraint C is satisfied.

Definition 5 *A subset S of A is* C-admissible *if and only if S is admissible for* $\langle A, R \rangle$ *and satisfies* C. *A* C-admissible set $S \subseteq A$ *is a* preferred C-extension *if and only if it is maximal w.r.t.* $\subseteq$ *among the set of* C-*admissible sets.*

Example 4 (contd.) *The set $\{a, d, e\}$ is admissible, but it is not C-admissible, because it does not satisfy the constraint* C. $\{a, e\}$ *is* C-admissible. $\{a, d, e, g, k\}$ *and* $\{a, e, g, j\}$ *are two of the preferred* C-extensions of CAF.

Obviously, a constrained argumentation framework $\langle A, R, C \rangle$ such that $C \equiv \top$ comes down to a Dung's argumentation framework. Its preferred C-extensions are the preferred extensions of $\langle A, R \rangle$.

An important issue in argumentation is to be able to decide, given some definition of acceptability, that is, some semantics, which arguments can be derived from the framework. Usually, an argument is considered as derivable, hence acceptable, when it belongs to one extension (credulous consequence), or to every extension (sceptical consequence) under the semantics.

In this paper, we focus on the credulous derivability of a set of arguments S. Notice that two arguments may be individually derivable, while the set which contains both may not be included in any extension of the framework. Hence, considering the derivability problem for a set of arguments is more general than considering it for a single argument. Notice that it is always possible to come down to a single argument by considering the singleton which contains it. We will say that a set S is *credulously accepted* under the C-preferred semantics if it is included in at least one preferred C-extension of CAF. To answer the credulous acceptance problem, that is, to determine whether a set of arguments is credulously accepted, the following result will be helpful.

Proposition 1 *For each C-admissible set X of CAF, there exists a preferred C-extension E of CAF such that $X \subseteq E$.*

Hence, determining whether a set of arguments is included into a preferred C-extension comes down to determine whether it is included into a C-admissible set.

From a computational point of view, [5] showed that the problem that consists in determining whether a set of arguments S is credulously accepted is NP-complete. To answer this problem, they suggest to use a translation of the constrained argumentation framework into a formula in propositional logic which encodes the preferred C-extensions of the framework. This translation allows the use of SAT provers to answer the problem. However, such provers return a yes/no answer; they do not explain why the answer is so, what are the reasons that make the set of arguments credulously acceptable or not. This is a major drawback of this solution, since the argumentation process aims at explaining the answer in terms of pros and cons, by showing how the arguments on stage are attacked, how they are defended against these attacks, how they respect the constraint.

This process has been captured by [4] and subsequent works, in a dialectical framework for Dung's preferred semantics without constraint.

In the next section, we extend the framework to constrained argumentation frameworks and to the preferred C-extensions, and then we will show how to compute them by using ASP.

2. Defining constrained dialectical proofs

This section starts with introducing a new general dialectical framework, adapted from [4], in the context of which a proof theory for the credulous acceptance problem under the C-preferred semantics is defined.

A dialectical proof is formalised by a dialogue between two players, PRO (the proponent) and OPP (the opponent). The dialogue takes place in a constrained argumentation framework. Its moves are governed by rules expressed in a so-called legal-move function.

Given a set A, A^* denotes the set of finite sequences of elements from A. For a syntactical purpose which will be explained later on, the set of arguments A of the framework is extended with an "empty" argument, denoted by _. The set $A \cup \{\_\}$ is denoted by A^-.

Definition 6 *Let A be a set of arguments. A* dialogue *is a finite sequence $d = \langle a_0.a_1.a_2 \ldots a_n \rangle$ of arguments from A^-. The* player *of a_i, $i \in \{0 \ldots n\}$, in d is* PRO *if i is even and is* OPP *if i is odd.*

Notation 1 *Let $d = \langle a_0 \ldots a_i \ldots a_n \rangle$ be a dialogue.* PRO(d) *(resp.* OPP(d)) *denotes the set of arguments played by* PRO *(resp.* OPP*) in d.*
$\forall i, 1 \leq i \leq n+1, d_i = \langle a_0 \ldots a_{i-1} \rangle$ *is the length i prefix of d. If $i = 0$, $d_0 = \langle \rangle$ is the empty dialogue. For a non empty dialogue $d = \langle a_0 \ldots a_n \rangle$, a_n is denoted by* last(d).

Definition 7 *Let $\langle A, R, C \rangle$ be a constrained argumentation framework and $\phi : A^{-*} \to 2^{A^-}$ a function called* legal-move function. *A ϕ-dialogue for a set of arguments $S \subseteq A$ is a dialogue d such that $\forall i \geq 0, a_i \in \phi(d_i)$ and $S \subseteq$ PRO(d).*

ϕ defines the moves of the dialogue; when it returns an empty set, it means that the dialogue cannot be continued.

We define now a specific legal-move function ϕ_C in order to answer the credulous acceptance problem under the C-preferred semantics. Our proposal follows Proposition 1 that shows that determining whether a set of arguments S is included in at least one preferred C-extension comes down to find a C-admissible set in which S is included.

The set of arguments S, the arguments that defend this set, and the ones necessary to satisfy the constraint, will be played by PRO; the attackers will be played by OPP. If the dialogue successfully shows that S is credulously accepted, then the set of arguments played by PRO is a model of the constraint: its arguments are the positive elements of the model, the arguments played by OPP are negative elements, and the rest of the arguments of A not played in the dialogue are also negative elements of the model. The legal-move function ϕ_C is formally introduced in Definition 8. It is defined by respecting the following general principles.

The first move is played by PRO and follows the same rules as if it replies to an empty argument (see below). A move by OPP contains either an argument which attacks an argument played by PRO in a previous move, if such an argument exists (2), or the empty argument otherwise (1) to indicate that there is no argument in this case. The value of this empty argument is purely syntactical. This argument will be played each time OPP will be in such a case.

A move by PRO replies to the last move by OPP. As long as this move is not the empty argument, the argument played by PRO should attack OPP's argument and should respect a number of constraints defined later in the set CPOSS(d) (6), in order to show that PRO can defend itself against the attacker exhibited by OPP. If there is no such argument, then it means that the set of arguments played so far by PRO cannot be included in any C-admissible set. The dialogue ends; the construction of a C-admissible set which contains S fails.

If OPP's argument is the empty argument, then the set of arguments played so far by PRO is admissible. However, it is not guaranteed that it contains S. If it is not the case, PRO should go on playing the dialogue by moving an argument that belongs to S and to CPOSS(d) (3). If there is no such argument, then it means that S cannot be included in any C-admissible set. The dialogue ends, the construction of such a set fails.

Now if $S \subseteq \text{PRO}(d)$, it is not guaranteed that PRO(d) satisfies the constraint (and hence is C-admissible). If it is not the case, PRO should go on playing the dialogue by moving an argument from CPOSS(d) (4). If there is no such argument, that is, if CPOSS(d) is empty, then PRO cannot continue the dialogue; the dialogue ends. The construction of a C-admissible set which contains S fails.

Now if OPP's argument is the empty argument, if the constraint is satisfied and if S is included in PRO(d), then PRO does not have any more argument to play (5): the set of arguments played by PRO is C-admissible and contains S. The dialogue ends, the construction succeeds.

In order to present the set CPOSS(d) and the legal-move function ϕ_C, several notations are introduced:

Notation 2 *Let $\langle A, R, C \rangle$ be a constrained argumentation framework. Let $x \in A$ and $S \subseteq A$. Refl $= \{x \in A \mid (x, x) \in R\}$. $R^+(S) = \{y \in A \mid \exists x \in S \text{ such that } (x, y) \in R\}$. $R^-(S) = \{y \in A \mid \exists x \in S \text{ such that } (y, x) \in R\}$. $R^\pm(S) = R^+(S) \cup R^-(S)$.*

If a dialogue d would lead to a C-admissible set, then the set of arguments played by PRO should be conflict-free, that is, it should not contain any self-attacking argument (i.e. in Refl), nor any argument attacked or which attacks an argument already played by PRO (i.e. in $R^\pm(\text{PRO}(d))$). Moreover, PRO should not have to repeat an argument it has already played (i.e. in PRO(d)). The set :

$$\text{POSS}(d) = A \setminus (\text{PRO}(d) \cup \text{Refl} \cup R^\pm(\text{PRO}(d)))$$

formalizes these rules.

Moreover, we also want to play an argument that does not prevent us from satisfying the constraint. But, when we consider a C-admissible set, the semantics of C is given by evaluating as *true* all arguments in the set and as *false* all the other ones. But, during the building of a dialogue, this approach is quite too strong because the status (PRO or OPP) of some arguments (outside the dialogue) is not yet determined. That is why we introduce the Kleene's three-valued logic in order to deal with C more precisely. Let us recall that a *Kleene-interpretation* is a mapping ι from the propositional symbols to the set of truth values $\{f, t, u\}$ meaning *false*, *true* and *undetermined*. The truth tables are:

A	$\neg A$		$A \wedge B$	f	t	u		$A \vee B$	f	t	u
f	t		f	f	f	f		f	f	t	u
t	f		t	f	t	u		t	t	t	t
u	u		u	f	u	u		u	u	t	u

and, as in classical logic, $\iota(A \Rightarrow B) = \iota(\neg A \vee B)$.

Proposition 2 *Let φ be a formula, $\{a_1, \ldots, a_n\}$ the set of propositional symbols occurring in φ and ι a Kleene-interpretation such that $\exists k \in \{1, \ldots, n\}, \iota(a_k) = u$.*
Let $k_0 \in \{1, \ldots, n\}$ such that $\iota(a_{k_0}) = u$, we define ι_f and ι_t two Kleene-interpretations
by $\begin{cases} \iota_f(a_i) = \iota_t(a_i) = \iota(a_i), \forall i \neq k_0, i \in \{1, \ldots, n\} \\ \iota_f(a_{k_0}) = f \\ \iota_t(a_{k_0}) = t \end{cases}$
Then, we have $\begin{cases} \iota(\varphi) = f \Rightarrow \iota_f(\varphi) = \iota_t(\varphi) = f \\ \iota(\varphi) = t \Rightarrow \iota_f(\varphi) = \iota_t(\varphi) = t \end{cases}$

Let d be a ϕ-dialogue. It defines a Kleene-interpretation ι_d: $\begin{cases} \iota_d(x) = t \Leftrightarrow x \in \text{PRO}(d) \\ \iota_d(x) = f \Leftrightarrow x \in \text{OPP}(d) \\ \iota_d(x) = u \text{ otherwise} \end{cases}$.

By proposition 2, if for a given ϕ-dialogue d the constraint $\mathcal{C}$ is satisfied, $\iota_d(\mathcal{C}) = t$, (resp. not satisfied, $\iota_d(\mathcal{C}) = f$) then $\mathcal{C}$ is satisfied (resp. not satisfied) by $\iota_{d'}$ for every ϕ-dialogue d' extending d.

Let d be a ϕ_C-dialogue whose last move is by OPP. When we want to extend it with a PRO argument, we have to play some x from $\text{POSS}(d)$ that does not prevent us from satisfying the constraint[1], i.e. $\iota_{d.\langle x \rangle}(\mathcal{C}) \neq f$.

To sum up, the set :
$$\text{CPOSS}(d) = \text{POSS}(d) \cap \{x \mid \iota_{d.\langle x \rangle}(\mathcal{C}) \neq f\}$$
expresses all these elements. Note that, for an even-length dialogue d, $\text{CPOSS}(d) = \emptyset$ means that $\text{PRO}(d)$ cannot be extended into a larger $\mathcal{C}$-admissible set.

The following legal-move function is going to be used to define the dialogues for the credulous acceptance problem.

Definition 8 *Given a constrained argumentation framework $\langle A, R, \mathcal{C} \rangle$, a set $S \subseteq A$, let $\phi_C : A^{-*} \to 2^{A^-}$ be the function defined by:*

- *if d is an odd-length dialogue (next move is by OPP),*
$$\phi_C(d) = \begin{cases} \{\_\} \text{ if } R^-(\text{PRO}(d)) \setminus R^+(\text{PRO}(d)) = \emptyset \ (1) \\ R^-(\text{PRO}(d)) \setminus R^+(\text{PRO}(d)) \text{ otherwise } \ (2) \end{cases}$$

- *if d is an even-length dialogue (next move is by PRO),*
$$\phi_C(d) = \begin{cases} \text{If } d = \langle \rangle \text{ or last}(d) = \_ \\ \quad \text{then if } S \not\subseteq \text{PRO}(d) \\ \quad\quad \text{then CPOSS}(d) \cap S \quad (3) \\ \quad\quad \text{else if } \widehat{\text{PRO}(d)} \not\models \mathcal{C} \\ \quad\quad\quad \text{then CPOSS}(d) \quad (4) \\ \quad\quad\quad \text{else } \emptyset \quad (5) \\ \text{else CPOSS}(d) \cap R^-(\text{last}(d)) \ (6) \end{cases}$$

---

[1] $d.\langle x \rangle$ denotes the dialogue d extended with argument x.

Definition 9 *Let* $\langle A, R, C \rangle$ *be a constrained argumentation framework and* $S \subseteq A$ *be a set of arguments. A* ϕ_C-*proof for* S *is a* ϕ_C-*dialogue* d *for* S *such that*

$$(d = \langle \rangle \vee \text{last}(d) = \_) \wedge \widehat{\text{PRO}(d)} \models C.$$

We say that d *is won by* PRO.

The following result[2] establishes the correctness and the completeness of ϕ_C-proofs.

Proposition 3 *Let* $CAF = \langle A, R, C \rangle$ *be a constrained argumentation framework. If* d *is a* ϕ_C-*proof for a set of arguments* $S \subseteq A$*, then* $\text{PRO}(d)$ *is a* C-*admissible set of* CAF *that contains* S*. If a set of arguments* S *is included in a* C-*admissible set of* CAF *then there exists a* ϕ_C-*proof for* S*.*

Notice that in the case where the constraint is a tautology, the dialectical proofs come down to the dialectical proofs defined in [4].

Example 5 (contd.) *Consider the set* $S = \{e, k\}$*. A* ϕ_C-*dialogue for* S *is:*
$d_0 = \langle \rangle$, $\phi_C(d_0) = \{e, k\}$;
$a_0 = e$, $d_1 = \langle e \rangle$, $\phi_C(d_1) = \{c\}$;
$a_1 = c$, $d_2 = \langle e.c \rangle$, $\phi_C(d_2) = \{a\}$;
$a_2 = a$, $d_3 = \langle e.c.a \rangle$, $\phi_C(d_3) = \{\_\}$;
$a_3 = \_$, $d_4 = \langle e.c.a.\_ \rangle$, $S \not\subseteq \text{PRO}(d_4)$, $\phi_C(d_4) = \{k\}$;
$a_4 = k$, $d_5 = \langle e.c.a.\_.k \rangle$, $\phi_C(d_5) = \{\_\}$;
$a_5 = \_$, $d_6 = \langle e.c.a.\_.k.\_ \rangle$, $S \subseteq \text{PRO}(d_6)$, $\widehat{\text{PRO}(d_6)} \not\models C$, $\phi_C(d_6) = \{d, i, h, g\}$;
$a_6 = g$, $d_7 = \langle e.c.a.\_.k.\_.g \rangle$, $\phi_C(d_7) = \{\_\}$;
$a_7 = \_$, $d_8 = \langle e.c.a.\_.k.\_.g.\_ \rangle$, $S \subseteq \text{PRO}(d_8)$, $\widehat{\text{PRO}(d_8)} \not\models C$, $\phi_C(d_8) = \{d, i\}$;
$a_8 = d$, $d_9 = \langle e.c.a.\_.k.\_.g.\_.d \rangle$, $\phi_C(d_9) = \{\_\}$;
$a_9 = \_$, $d_{10} = \langle e.c.a.\_.k.\_.g.\_.d.\_ \rangle$, $S \subseteq \text{PRO}(d_{10})$, $\widehat{\text{PRO}(d_{10})} \models C$, $\phi_C(d_{10}) = \emptyset$;
d_{10} *is a* ϕ_C-*dialogue won by* PRO*.* $\text{PRO}(d_{10}) = \{e, a, k, g, d\}$ *is a* C-*admissible set. Thus* $\{e, k\}$ *is included into at least one preferred* C-*extension; it is then credulously accepted.*

3. Computing constrained dialectical proofs by ASP

Answer Set Programming (ASP) is a declarative paradigm having its root in the stable model semantics [12] for normal logic programs. It has already been applied with success in many areas of knowledge representation and reasoning in Artificial Intelligence (default reasoning, semantic web, planification, causal reasoning,...). Furthermore, because of the availability of efficient solvers as Clasp [11], Smodels [17] or DLV [14], ASP is also a very good framework to encode and solve combinatorial problems coming from various domains (graph theory, configuration, bio informatics,...). We invite the reader to consult [6] and [10] for a recent, theoretical and practical overview of ASP and we recall in the following the main theoretical notions that we use in this work.

A *normal logic program* is a set of rules like

$$c \leftarrow a_1, \ \ldots, \ a_n, \ not \ b_1, \ \ldots, \ not \ b_m., n \geq 0, m \geq 0,$$

---

[2]The proof of Proposition 3 can be downloaded at http://www.info.univ-angers.fr/pub/claire/asperix/Argumentation

where $c, a_1, \ldots, a_n, b_1, \ldots, b_m$ are ground atoms and *not* represents a default negation. For a rule r (or by extension for a rule set), we note $head(r) = c$ its *head*, $body^+(r) = \{a_1, \ldots, a_n\}$ its *positive body*, $body^-(r) = \{b_1, \ldots, b_m\}$ its *negative body*.

The Gelfond-Lifschitz reduct of a program P by an atom set X is the program $P^X = \{head(r) \leftarrow body^+(r). \mid body^-(r) \cap X = \emptyset\}$. Since it has no default negation, such a program is definite and then it has a unique minimal Herbrand model denoted with $Cn(P)$. By definition, an *answer set* (originally called a *stable model* [12]) of P is an atom set S such that $S = Cn(P^S)$.

As usual in ASP, a rule with an empty body $x \leftarrow .$ is called a *fact* and is simplified as x. and a headless rule is called a *constraint*. For instance, $\leftarrow x, not\ y.$ is a shortcut for the rule $new \leftarrow x, not\ y, not\ new.$, where new is an atom appearing nowhere else in the program. Such a rule forbids to any atom set containing x and not containing y to be an answer set of the program. The use of constraints in a program illustrates the declarative nature of ASP. We just have to describe the situations that we reject in order to exclude them from the potential solutions.

As it is the case in our work, many problems are firstly encoded in ASP by means of a first order logic program containing atoms like $p(X, 3, f(Y))$. Since answer set definition is given for propositional programs, P has to be seen as an intensional version of the propositional program $ground(P)$ defined as follows. Given a rule r, $ground(r)$ is the set of all fully instantiated rules that can be obtained by substituting every variable in r by every constant of the Herbrand universe of P and then, $ground(P) = \bigcup_{r \in P} ground(r)$.

The relationships between argumentation frameworks and ASP have been studied in some previous works. For instance, considering that $att(X, Y)$ stands for "*argument X attacks argument Y*", $acc(X)$ for "*argument X is acceptable*" and $def(X)$ for "*argument X is defeated*", [8] shows that the program

$$
\left\{
\begin{array}{l}
att(a_1, a_2). \ldots, att(a_m, a_n). \\
acc(X) \leftarrow not\ def(X). \\
def(X) \leftarrow att(Y, X),\ acc(Y).
\end{array}
\right\}
$$

has a stable model iff the corresponding argumentation framework has a stable extension. Moreover, the atoms $acc(X)$ occuring in the stable model represent the set of acceptable arguments. Pursuing this line, [9] presents an ASP system able to compute the extensions of a Dung's argumentation framework under various notions of acceptability.

But, up to our knowledge no system has already been developed in order to answer the credulous acceptance problem with constraints. Furthermore, one goal of the framework of dialectical proofs is to exhibit explicitly the argumentative fight between pros and cons arguments and again this point has not already been studied via ASP.

In our present work, ASP is also used to deal with the constraint of the argumentation framework. The links between classical logic and ASP as already been studied in [15,18] whose goals are to compute (if it exists) a model of a formula by means of a normal logic program. In our setting, given an interpretation, we are concerned by the computation of the truth-value (in classical logic or in 3-valued logic) of a formula. Clearly this is a polynomial problem when the previous one, computing a model, is an NP-hard one.

Because of lack of space we give only the main lines of the program that we have written in order to compute the dialectical proofs of a given constrained argumentation framework. The whole program is available at http://www.info.univ-angers.fr/

`pub/claire/asperix/Argumentation`. We mention that our program contains symbolic functions, in particular lists, and then only two ASP solvers, `ASPeRiX` [13] and `DLV-complex` [3], can be used to compute its answer sets.

The ASP program consists of facts encoding an argumentation system and of rules encoding what a ϕ_C-proof is: the legal-move function, POSS and CPOSS sets... The models of the program (the answer sets), if there are, are all the ϕ_C-proofs of the given argumentation system.

The argumentation system is represented via predicates `argu(X)` for the arguments, and `att(X,Y)` for attacks. The set S, for which we want to prove its acceptability, is represented by extension of predicate `inS(X)`, and the constraint by `constraint(C)`. The constraint is expressed by a functional term where the logic constants $\top$ and $\bot$ are `true` and `false`, the logical connectives $\neg, \wedge, \vee, \Rightarrow, \Leftrightarrow$ are unary functor `neg` and binary functors `and`, `or`, `imp`, `equ`. The argumentation system from the example developed in previous sections is encoded by the following facts.

```
argu(a). argu(b). argu(c). ... argu(k).
att(a,b). att(a,c). att(b,d). ... att(k,j).
inS(e). inS(k).
constraint(and(or(imp(d, or(f,g)), impl(neg(d),neg(f))), equ(k,d))).
```

A dialectical proof is represented by a set of atoms of the form `rank(X,N)` meaning that argument X is played at rank N in the dialogue. Term `empty` encodes the special empty argument _. For instance, the dialogue $\langle e.c.a.\_\rangle$ is represented by the set of atoms `{rank(e,0), rank(c,1), rank(a,2), rank(empty,3)}`.

The dialogue can be seen as built incrementally, one rank after another. When several arguments can be played at a rank, one of them is chosen in a non deterministic way. Predicate `nrank` prevents to play more that one argument at a rank: when an argument is chosen for rank N, all other are prohibited for the same rank. The construction of the dialogue begins by choosing an argument for rank 0. Then the dialogue continues until no move can be played at a step. If some final conditions are realized, a model of the program has been built, which represents a dialogue, and which is the output of the solver. Otherwise, the solver tries to built another dialogue.

The legal-move function ϕ_C is represented in the program by rules that define arguments that can be played at each rank of the dialogue. For instance, rules for cases (1), (2) and (6) of Definition 8 are given below. In these rules, `strongAttack(X,N)` means that X attacks the proof but is not attacked by the proof, that is $X \in R^-(\text{PRO}(d)) \setminus R^+(\text{PRO}(d))$ and `imposs(X,N)` represents the complementary set of POSS(d).

```
% X is played by PRO, next move is played by OPP (1)
rank(empty,N+1) :- rank(X,N), N mod 2==0, not weak(N).
weak(N) :- strongAttack(X,N).
% X is played by PRO, next move is played by OPP (2)
rank(Y,N+1) :- rank(X,N), N mod 2==0, strongAttack(Y,N), not nrank(Y,N+1).
...
% X is played by OPP, next move is played by PRO (6)
rank(Y,N+1) :- rank(X,N), X!=empty, N mod 2==1, att(Y,X),
               not imposs(Y,N+1), not nrank(Y,N+1).
% only one argument is played at a rank
nrank(Y,N) :- rank(X,N), argu(Y), X!=Y.
nrank(empty,N) :- rank(X,N), X!=empty.
```

But this program builds too many dialogues: some of them do not correspond to $\mathcal{C}$-admissible sets and thus must be rejected. First, when PRO is playing, he has to play an argument from CPOSS(d) and not only from POSS(d) as we do. So we have to discard the dialogues for which a PRO move makes the constraint false. Second, a dialogue is a successful proof only if some final conditions are realized: the dialogue ends with the empty argument (unless the dialogue is empty), the set S is included in PRO's arguments, and the constraint is satisfied. The "wrong" dialogues are excluded from the models of the program by adding some constraints (headless rules) that prohibit them. In these rules, `false3(C,N)` means that propositional formula C is false in the 3-valued interpretation defined by the dialogue at rank N, i.e. $\iota_d(\mathcal{C}) = f$. `non_satisfiedC(N)` means that the constraint is not satisfied in the 2-valued interpretation defined by the dialogue at rank N, i.e. $\widehat{\text{PRO}(d)} \not\models C$. And `non_includedS(N)` means that $S \not\subseteq \text{PRO}(d)$ at rank N of the dialogue.

```
% the constraint must not be false after a move by PRO
:- constraint(C), false3(C,N).
% last(X) is the last argument of the proof
last(X) :- rank(X,N), not position(N+1).
position(N) :- rank(X,N).
% a proof is empty or ends with the empty argument
:- position(0), not last(empty).
% a proof must satisfy the constraint
:- non_satisfiedC(N), not position(N+1).
% a proof must contain all arguments from S
:- non_includedS(N), not position(N+1).
```

Recall that the constraint is represented as a functional term. The truth values, in 2 and 3-valued logics, of arguments are inferred from the part of the dialogue already built. Then a simple propagation suffices to deduce the value of the whole constraint.

4. Conclusion

In this paper, we propose a new notion of dialectical proofs for constrained argumentation frameworks. These proofs allow to verify the credulous acceptability of a set of arguments under the $\mathcal{C}$-preferred semantics. Such proofs explain why and how the set of arguments is inferred. Thus, it is very easy and natural to associate to the theoretical framework an effective computation of the proof. This last part is realized in ASP. These two contributions can be used to develop any automated reasoning system based on the $\mathcal{C}$-preferred semantics of a constrained argumentation framework (e.g., as pointed out in [5], Dung's preferred semantics, bipolar systems' weakly preferred semantics...).

Another conclusion to draw is that, once again, ASP has proved its very good flexibility to represent and solve a reasoning problem. On one side, we see that the notion of rules is very well adapted to encode the iterating and alternating roles of pros and cons in the building of the proof. On another side, the ASP constraints are a very convenient way to discard unwanted potential solutions.

As a future work, we plan to compare the recent approach by [28] with the one presented in this paper.

References

[1]   Amgoud, L.; Devred, C.; and Lagasquie-Schiex, M.-C. 2008. A constrained argumentation system for practical reasoning. In *AAMAS*, 429–436.

[2]   Besnard, P., and Hunter, A. 2008. *Elements of Argumentation*. The MIT Press.

[3]   Calimeri, F.; Cozza, S.; Ianni, G.; and Leone, N. 2008. Computable functions in ASP: Theory and implementation. In de la Banda and Pontelli, 407–424.

[4]   Cayrol, C.; Doutre, S.; and Mengin, J. 2003. On decision problems related to the preferred semantics for argumentation frameworks. *Journal of Logic and Computation* 13(3):377–403.

[5]   Coste-Marquis, S.; Devred, C.; and Marquis, P. 2006. Constrained argumentation frameworks. In *KR*, 112–122.

[6]   de la Banda, M. G., and Pontelli, E., eds. 2008. *ICLP'08*, volume 5366 of *LNCS*. Springer.

[7]   Dung, P. M., and Thang, P. M. 2009. A unified framework for representation and development of dialectical proof procedures in argumentation. In *IJCAI*, 746–751.

[8]   Dung, P. M. 1995. On the acceptability of arguments and its fundamental role in nonmonotonic reasoning, logic programming and n-person games. *Artificial Intelligence* 77(2):321–358.

[9]   Egly, U.; Gaggl, S. A.; and Woltran, S. 2008. ASPARTIX: Implementing argumentation frameworks using ASP. In de la Banda and Pontelli, 734–738.

[10]   Erdem, E.; Lin, F.; and Schaub, T., eds. 2009. *LPNMR*, volume 5753 of *LNCS*. Springer.

[11]   Gebser, M.; Kaufmann, B.; Neumann, A.; and Schaub, T. 2007. Conflict-driven answer set solving. In *IJCAI'07*, 386–392.

[12]   Gelfond, M., and Lifschitz, V. 1988. The stable model semantics for logic programming. In Kowalski, R. A., and Bowen, K., eds., *ICLP'88*, 1070–1080. The MIT Press.

[13]   Lefèvre, C., and Nicolas, P. 2009. The first version of a new ASP solver : ASPeRiX. In Erdem et al., 522–527.

[14]   Leone, N.; Pfeifer, G.; Faber, W.; Eiter, T.; Gottlob, G.; Perri, S.; and Scarcello, F. 2006. The DLV system for knowledge representation and reasoning. *ACM Transactions on Computational Logic* 7(3):499–562.

[15]   Niemelä, I. 1999. Logic programs with stable model semantics as a constraint programming paradigm. *Annals of Mathematics and Artificial Intelligence* 25(3-4):241–273.

[16]   Rahwan, I., and Simari, G. R. 2009. *Argumentation in Artificial Intelligence*. Springer Publishing Company, Inc.

[17]   Simons, P.; Niemelä, I.; and Soininen, T. 2002. Extending and implementing the stable model semantics. *Artificial Intelligence* 138(1-2):181–234.

[18]   Stéphan, I.; Da Mota, B.; and Nicolas, P. 2009. From (quantified) boolean formulae to answer set programming. *Journal of Logic and Computation* 19(4):565–590.

[19]   Verheij, B. 2007. A labeling approach to the computation of credulous acceptance in argumentation. In *IJCAI*, 623–628.

[20]   Vreeswijk, G.; and Prakken, H. 2000. Credulous and Sceptical Argument Games for Preferred Semantics. In *JELIA*, 239–253.

[21]   Cayrol, C.; Doutre, S.; Lagasquie-Schiex, M.-Ch.; and Mengin, J. 2002. "Minimal defence": a refinement of the preferred semantics for argumentation frameworks. In *NMR*, 408–415.

[22]   Bench-Capon, T. J. M. 2002. Value-based argumentation frameworks. In *NMR*, 443–454.

[23]   Bench-Capon, T. J. M.; Doutre, S.; and Dunne, P. E. 2007. Audiences in argumentation frameworks. In *Artif. Intell., vol. 171*, 42–71.

[24]   Bryant, D.; Krause, P. J.; and Vreeswijk, G. 2006. Argue tuProlog: A Lightweight Argumentation Engine for Agent Applications. In *COMMA*, 27–32.

[25]   South, M.; Vreeswijk G.; and Fox, J. 2008. Dungine: A Java Dung Reasoner. In *COMMA*, 360–368.

[26]   Gaertner, D.; and Toni, F. 2008. Hybrid argumentation and its properties. In *COMMA*, 183–195.

[27]   Dung, P. M.; Kowalski, R. A.; and Toni, F. 2006. Dialectic proof procedures for assumption-based, admissible argumentation In *Artif. Intell., vol. 170, issue 2*, 114–159.

[28]   Brewka, G.; and Woltran, S. 2010. Abstract Dialectical Frameworks. In *KR*, in press.

Computational Models of Argument
P. Baroni et al. (Eds.)
IOS Press, 2010
doi:10.3233/978-1-60750-619-5-171

Towards (Probabilistic) Argumentation for Jury-based Dispute Resolution

Phan Minh DUNG [1], Phan Minh THANG

Department of Computer Science, Asian Institute of Technology, Thailand

Abstract. We propose an argumentation framework for modelling jury-based dispute resolution where the dispute parties present their arguments before a judge and a jury. While the judge as the arbiter of law determines the legal permissibility of the presented arguments the jurors as triers of facts determine their probable weights. Such a framework is based on two key components: classical argumentation frameworks containing legally permissible arguments and probabilistic spaces assigning probable weights to arguments. A juror's probability space is represented by a set of possible worlds coupled with a probabilistic measure computed by assumption-based argumentation framework using grounded semantics.

Keywords. Probabilistic argumentation, jury-based dispute resolution

Introduction

In villages throughout Asia, Africa and Latin America, disputes are often resolved by councils of elders. In modern-day population centers, much of the functions of such elder councils are practiced by trials in legal courts or various kinds of mediation bodies. There are other similar though less formal ways for dispute resolutions like debates between presidential candidates (e.g. Obama and McCain) in an election where the candidates exchange arguments and ultimately the members of audience decide the winner and loser. Committees, task forces are also common forms of dispute resolution. All of these forms of dispute resolution are arguably instances of what we will refer to in this paper as jury-based dispute resolution where the jury members weigh the credibilities of the presented arguments and collectively make their decisions. Though it seems to be recognized widely that argumentation is a key mechanism in jury-based dispute resolution, a formal model of how it is deployed is still to be developed. To clarify the problems, let us start with a simple example whose story line is borrowed from Riveret,Rotolo,Sartor,Prakken and B.Roth[8].

Example 0.1 *John sued Henry for the damage caused to him when he drove off the road to avoid hitting Henry's cow. John's argument is:*

J: Henry should pay damage because Henry is the owner of the cow and the cow caused the accident

---

[1]Corresponding Author: Phan Minh Dung, Department of Computer Science, Asian Institute of Technology, Thailand.

Henry countered by two arguments:

H: John was negligent as evidences at the accident location show that John was driving fast on the hilly road. Hence the cow was not the cause of the accident

H′: The cow was mad and the madness of the cow should be viewed as a force-majeure

Could John win the case ? Suppose that Henry could not put forward any evidence "proving" the madness of his cow. The judge dismisses the second argument H′ as irrelevant. Hence the probability for John to win depends on how likely the judge (as the sole juror) considers fast driving as a cause of the accident.

Note that John's argument J is based on a common norm (or law) that owners are responsible for the damages caused by their animals while Henry's argument H is based on a causal relation between John's fast driving and the accident.

Example 0.2 *We give a bare-bone sketch of the argumentation at the infamous trial of OJ Simpson for the murder of his wife [10]. In a nutshell, the main argument of the prosecutor linking Simpson directly to the murder is based on DNA tests of blood found at the murder scene and on two socks and a glove found in Simpson's house. It could be presented in an informal way as follows:*

P: Based on DNA tests showing that there is Simpson's blood at the murder scene and the victim's blood on the socks and glove, Simpson is the murder.

The defence countered in two ways:

D_1: By introducing Henry Lee, a respectable forensic expert who testifies that the results of DNA tests are not normal

D_2: By pointing out that (1) Mark Fuhrman, the police officer collecting most of the evidences at the crime scene and Simpson's house is a liar and racist who has admitted of planting evidence to help prosecutors convicting defendants in the past and (2) there are other irregularities in the evidence collecting process and (3) the glove does not fit Simpson's hand, the defence puts forwards the claim that there is a police conspiracy to frame Simpson by planting evidences against him.

At the criminal trial, where a conviction must be beyond reasonable doubt, Simpson is not convicted though at the following civil trial where a conviction could be based on preponderance, Simpson is found guilty of murdering his wife and her guest. Interestingly, at the civil trial, "argument" D_2 of the defence is not allowed by the trial judge. Further, the jury at the criminal trial is mostly black while it is mostly white at the civil one. It is generally accepted [10] that racial bias played a key role in the outcomes of both trials.

The purpose of this paper is to offer an agument-based model to shed some light on these kinds of applications. The paper is structured as follows. We first introduce the notion of abstract argumentation for jury-based dispute resolution and two criteria for adjudication: beyond reasonable doubts and majority voting with preponderance. We then introduce probabilistic assumption-based argumentation as a methodolody for representing probability spaces. We illustrate the applicablity of the new framework by applying it to the infamous OJ Simpson trials. We then conclude.

1. Abstract Argumentation For Jury-Based Dispute Resolution (AAJ)

An abstract argumentation framework [3] is a pair $\mathcal{AF} = (AR, att)$, where AR is a set of arguments, and att is a binary relation over AR representing the attack relation between the arguments with $(A, B) \in att$ meaning A attacks B. For simplicity, we restrict ourself on frameworks with finite sets of arguments. A set S of arguments attacks an argument A if some argument in S attacks A; S attacks another set S' if S attacks some argument in S'. A set S of arguments is *conflict-free* iff it does not attack itself. Argument A is *acceptable* with respect to S iff S attacks each argument attacking A. S is *admissible* iff S is conflict-free and each argument in S is acceptable with respect to S. The semantics of argumentation could be characterized by a fixpoint theory of the characteristic function $F(S) = \{A \in AR \mid A \text{ is acceptable wrt } S\}$. It is easy to see that S is admissible iff S is conflict free and $S \subseteq F(S)$. As F is monotonic, the least fixed point of F exists and is defined as the *grounded extension* of AF.

A **finite probability space** is a pair $\Pi = (\mathcal{W}, P)$ where $\mathcal{W}$ a finite set of all possible worlds and P is a mapping from $\mathcal{W}$ into the interval $[0, 1]$ such that $\Sigma_{w \in \mathcal{W}} P(w) = 1$.

There are many forms of jury-based adjudication. In a single judge trial or a three-judges appelate courts, the jury consisting of the judges themself is fully capable to introduce new legal arguments not presented by the parties in their debate. On the other hand, as lay jurors may have only the most basic education and not well-versed in the laws and norms, they should not be allowed to introduce new legal or norm-based arguments in their consideration apart from those presented by the dispute parties. In contrast, the members of audiences in presidential debates have complete freedom to introduce whatever arguments they consider fit in their "adjudication" of the debate. Understanding the fundamentals of jury-based adjudication is an enormous challenge for the research on argument-based dispute resolution. In this paper, we limit ourself to the case where the jurors are restricted to consider the probabilities of causal arguments. We follow evidence law in modeling the judge as the arbiter of law and the jurors as the triers of facts [2] [5,6,11]. In other words, the judge determines the admissibility of evidences while the jurors determine the probable weights of the evidences.

Definition 1.1 *An Abstract Argumentation framework for Jury-based dispute resolution (AAJ) is a tuple*

$$(AF, \Pi_1, \ldots, \Pi_n, \vdash_1, \ldots, \vdash_n), \qquad n \geq 1$$

satisfying following conditions:

1. *$AF = (AR, att)$ is an abstract argumentation framework with a distinct subset of arguments $AR_c \subseteq AR$ representing intuitively the set of arguments that are based on some causal relationships [3].*
   Abusing the notations, arguments in AR_c are called causal arguments while arguments in $AR - AR_c$ are called norm-based arguments.
   Note that the construction of AF is under the arbitration of the judge.

---

[2] This is not saying that jury members are not influenced by their biases in making their decision

[3] Note that an argument could be based on both legal norms and causal relations. Such a argument also belongs to AR_c.

2. $\Pi_i = (\mathcal{W}_i, P_i)$, $1 \leq i \leq n$ *are probability spaces where* $\mathcal{W}_i$ *consists of possible worlds of the juror i.*
   Relations $\vdash_i \subseteq \mathcal{W}_i \times AR$, $1 \leq i \leq n$ *specify the legitimacy of the arguments wrt possile worlds of the jurors where for each* $A \in AR - AR_c$, *for each* $w \in \mathcal{W}_i$:, $w \vdash_i A$ *holds*[4]

Intuitively, probability spaces Π_i assign weights to the arguments allowed for consideration by the judge. The condition $w \vdash_i A$ for $A \in AR - AR_c$ captures the intuition that jurors only determine the probable weights of the arguments, but do not challenge the legality of arguments.

Definition 1.2 *Let* $(AF, \Pi_1, \ldots, \Pi_n, \vdash_1, \ldots, \vdash_n)$ *be an AAJ and* $w \in \mathcal{W}_i$.

- *The argumentation framework wrt* w, *denoted by* $AF_w = (AR_w, att_w)$, *consists of the set of all arguments permissible wrt* w *and the attack relation between them, i.e.*

$$AR_w = \{A \in AR \mid w \vdash_i A\} \qquad att_w = att \cap AR_w \times AR_w$$

  The grounded extension of AF_w *is denoted by* GE_w.
- *We define the grounded probability of argument A* [5] *for juror i, denoted by* $Prob_i(A)$, *as follows*

$$Prob_i(A) = \sum_{w \in \mathcal{W}_i : A \in GE_w} P(w)$$

For illustration, consider the AAJ $(AF, \Pi, \vdash)$ in example 0.1 where $AF = (AR, att)$ with $AR = \{J, H\}$, $AR_c = \{H\}$ and $att = \{(H, J)\}$ and $\Pi = (W, P)$ with $W = \{w_1, w_2\}$ where $w_1 = \{J, H\}$, $w_2 = \{J\}$. Define $w_i \vdash A$ if $A \in w_i$. Suppose $P(w_1) = 0.6$, $P_1(w_2) = 0.4$. As $GE_{w_1} = \{H\}$ and $GE_{w_2} = \{J\}$, the grounded probability of J is: $Prob(J) = 0.4$.

1.1. Protocol for Adjudication

How could a decision be reached in an jury-based adjudication ? There are at least two criteria: Beyond reasonable doubt and majority voting with preponderance.

An argument A is **accepted beyond reasonable doubt** by a juror i if $Prob_i(A) = 1$. A is accepted beyond reasonable doubt by the jury if A is accepted beyond reasonable doubt by each juror.

An argument A is **accepted with preponderance** by a juror i if $Prob_i(A) > 0.5$. A is accepted by majority voting with preponderance if A is accepted with preponderance by a majority of the jurors.

In example of John and Henry, as the probability of John's argument J is only 0.4, the judge would decide the case for Henry. Note that in this case, as the jury consists of only the judge, both protocols give the same result. In later chapter, we will elaborate the case of Simpson's trials for further illustrations.

---

[4]i.e. juror i considers all norm-based arguments legitimate in all of his possible worlds
[5]To be precise, it should be: the probability of A wrt grounded semantics

2. Assumption-based Argumentation For Jury-Based Dispute Resolution (ABAJ)

In general, definition 1.1 puts no restriction on the way probability spaces $\mathcal{W}$ are defined. It could be for example presented using statistical, probabilistic theories or calculus. But at the top level, where the audience (e.g. judges, juries or the general TV audience at large in a presidential debate) should not be expected to have formal technical knowledge, specialized theories (like theories about the probability of the outcome of a DNA test) should be encapsulated in modules whose input-output will be presented to the audience. Further lay jurors almost always employ commonsense reasoning to "compute" the probabilities of the arguments. Let us consider again example 0.1.

Example 2.1 *Argument J is represented by the following rules[6]:*

r_1: *henryPay* $\leftarrow$ *henryOwnerOfCow, cowCauseAccident,* $\sim$ *forceMajeure*
r_2: *cowCauseAccident* $\leftarrow\sim$ *johnNegligent*
r_3: *henryOwnerOfCow* $\leftarrow$

Argument H is represented by the following rules:

r_4: *johnNegligent* $\leftarrow$ *drivingFast,* p_o
r_5: *drivingFast* $\leftarrow p_1$

where p_0, p_1 are probabilistic assumptions with p_0 representing the probability of the accident caused by John's fast driving while p_1 representing the probability of the event that John was driving fast. Note that rules r_1, r_2, r_3 do not contain any probabilistic assumptions. It implies that argument J is norm-based.

The possible worlds in the probabilistic space of the judge when he (acting as the sole juror) reflects on the case before making a decision are represented by maximally consistent subsets of the set of probabilistic assumptions $\{p_0, \neg p_0, p_1, \neg p_1\}$ where $\neg$ is the classical negation operator. Assuming the independence of the assumptions p_0, p_1, a probability measure could be given by clauses

r_6: $[p_0 : 0.8] \leftarrow$
r_7: $[\neg p_0 : 0.2] \leftarrow$
r_8: $[p_1 : 0.75] \leftarrow$
r_9: $[\neg p_1 : 0.25] \leftarrow$

An assumption-based argumentation (ABA) framework [2,4] is a triple $(\mathcal{R}, \mathcal{A}, ^{-})$ where $\mathcal{R}$ is set of inference rules of the form $\alpha \leftarrow \sigma_1, \ldots \sigma_n$ (for $n \geq 0$) over a language $\mathcal{L}$, and $\mathcal{A} \subseteq \mathcal{L}$ is a set of assumptions, and $^{-}$ is a (total) mapping from $\mathcal{A}$ into $\mathcal{L}$, where $\overline{x}$ is referred to as the *contrary* of x. Assumptions do not appear in the heads of rules in $\mathcal{R}$.

A *(backward) deduction* of a conclusion α based on (or supported by) a set of premises Q is a sequence of sets $S_1, \ldots, S_m$, where $S_i \subseteq \mathcal{L}$, $S_1 = \{\alpha\}$, $S_m = Q$, and for every i, where σ is the selected sentence in S_i: $\sigma \notin Q$ and $S_{i+1} = S_i - \{\sigma\} \cup S$ for some inference rule of the form $\sigma \leftarrow S \in \mathcal{R}$.

An *argument* for $\alpha \in \mathcal{L}$ supported by a set of assumptions Q is a (backward) deduction δ from α to Q and denoted by (Q, δ, α). An argument (Q, δ, α) attacks an argument (Q', δ', α') if α is the contrary of some assumption in Q'.

For simplicity, we often refer to an argument (Q, δ, α) by (Q, α) if there is no possibility for mistake.

---

[6]$\sim l$ is a negation-as-failure assumption whose contrary is l.

Given an ABA framework $\mathcal{F}$, a proposition π is said to be a *grounded consequence* of $\mathcal{F}$, denoted by $\mathcal{F} \vdash_{gr} \pi$ if there is an argument supporting π in the grounded extension.

Probabilistic spaces could be represented by probabilistic assumption-based argumentation introduced in the following definition.

Definition 2.1 *A probabilistic assumption-based argumentation (PABA) framework is a triple $\mathcal{P} = (\mathcal{A}_p, \mathcal{R}_p, \mathcal{F})$ satisfying following properties:*

1. $\mathcal{A}_p = \{p_0, \ldots, p_n\}$ *is a set of probabilistic parameters. A* **possible world** *of $\mathcal{P}$ is defined as a maximal (wrt set inclusion) consistent subset of the set $\mathcal{A}_p \cup \neg.\mathcal{A}_p$ where $\neg.\mathcal{A}_p = \{\neg p \mid p \in \mathcal{A}_p\}$ and $\neg$ is the classical negation operator.*

2. $\mathcal{R}_p$ *is a set of probabilistic rules of the form*

$$[\alpha : x] \leftarrow \sigma_1, \ldots \sigma_n {}^{7} \quad n \geq 0$$

where α is a probabilistic parameter or the negation of a probabilistic parameter and $0 \leq x \leq 1$ is a real number such that

   (a) *If a rule of the form $[p : x] \leftarrow \sigma_1, \ldots \sigma_n$ appears in $\mathcal{R}_p$ then $\mathcal{R}_p$ also contains the complementary rule $[\neg p : 1 - x] \leftarrow \sigma_1, \ldots \sigma_n$*

   (b) *For each probabilistic parameter p, $\mathcal{R}_p$ contains a rule of the form*

$$[p : x] \leftarrow$$

   giving the default probability of p.

   (c) *If two rules of the form $[p : x] \leftarrow \sigma_1, \ldots \sigma_n$, $[p : y] \leftarrow \sigma'_1, \ldots \sigma'_m$ appear in $\mathcal{R}_p$ and $x \neq y$ then $\{\sigma_1, \ldots \sigma_n\} \subset \{\sigma'_1, \ldots \sigma'_m\}$ or $\{\sigma'_1, \ldots \sigma'_m\} \subset \{\sigma_1, \ldots \sigma_n\}$* [8] [9]

3. $\mathcal{F}$ *is an ABA framework of the form $(\mathcal{R}, \mathcal{A}, {}^{-})$ where*

   (a) *For each $\alpha \in \mathcal{A}_p$, neither α nor $\neg\alpha$ belongs to $\mathcal{A}$, and*

   (b) *No rules in $\mathcal{R}$ contain probabilistic parameters in their heads*

4. *Probabilistic sentences of the form $[l : x]$ do not appear in the bodies of rules in both $\mathcal{R}$ and $\mathcal{R}_p$.*

For illustration, consider again the example 2.1 where the PABA is defined by $\mathcal{A}_p = \{p_0, p_1\}$, $\mathcal{R}_p = \{r_6, r_7, r_8, r_9\}$ and $\mathcal{F} = (\mathcal{R}, \mathcal{A}, {}^{-})$ with $\mathcal{R} = \{r_1, r_2, r_3, r_4, r_5\}$ and $\mathcal{A} = \{\sim johnNegligent, \sim forceMajeure\}$.

To define the probability measures of probability spaces associated to probabilistic argumentation, we need first to define the semantics of probabilistic argumentation.

Let $\mathcal{P} = (\mathcal{A}_p, \mathcal{R}_p, \mathcal{F})$ be an PABA framework with $\mathcal{F} = (\mathcal{R}, \mathcal{A}, {}^{-})$. Let S be a consistent subset of $\mathcal{A}_p \cup \neg.\mathcal{A}_p$. Define $\mathcal{F}_S$ to be the ABA framework $\mathcal{F}_S = (\mathcal{R}_S, \mathcal{A}, {}^{-})$ where $\mathcal{R}_S = \mathcal{R} \cup \mathcal{R}_p \cup \{\alpha \leftarrow \mid \alpha \in S\}$. An argument of $\mathcal{P}$ wrt S is defined as an argument of the ABA $\mathcal{F}_S$.

---

[7] stating that the probability of α is x if $\sigma_1, \ldots, \sigma_n$ hold

[8] Note that $X \subset Y$ implies that $X \neq Y$

[9] In general, we could also allow the case of $\{\sigma_1, \ldots \sigma_n\} \cup \{\sigma'_1, \ldots \sigma'_m\}$ being inconsistent without causing any problem apart from a somewhat more complicated notion of attack between probabilitic arguments. But to get the conceptual idea across to the readers, we restrict ourself to the simpler case.

Arguments with conclusion of the form $[\alpha : x]$ are referred to as *probabilistic arguments*.

Definition 2.2 *Let* $A = (Q, \delta, [\alpha : x])$, $A' = (Q', \delta', [\beta : y])$ *be probabilistic arguments of* $\mathcal{P}$ *wrt possible world* w *of* $\mathcal{P}$ *and* $\delta = S_1, \ldots, S_m$ *and* $\delta' = S'_1, \ldots, S'_n$. *Further let the probabilistic rules used to derive* S_2 *from* S_1 *and* S'_2 *from* S'_1 *are* r_1, r'_1 *respectively. We say that* A **attacks** A' *by* **specificity** *if* r_1, r'_1 *are respectively of the form*

$$[\alpha : x] \leftarrow \sigma_1, \ldots \sigma_k, \sigma_{k+1}, \ldots, \sigma_{k+j}$$
$$[\beta : y] \leftarrow \sigma_1, \ldots \sigma_k$$

such that $j > 0$ *and* α, β *contain the same probabilistic parameter.*

Definition 2.3 *Let* $A = (Q, \alpha)$, $A' = (Q', \alpha')$ *be arguments of a PABA* $\mathcal{P}$ *wrt a possible world* w *of* $\mathcal{P}$. *We say* A **attacks** A' *if one of the following conditions is satisfied:*

1. *A is a non-probabilistic argument and α is the contrary of some assumption in Q'. This attack is called type 1 attack.*
2. *A, A' are probabilistic arguments and A attacks A' by specificity. This attack is called type 2 attack.*
3. *α is a probabilistic parameter, $A = (\emptyset, \alpha)$ [10] and A' is a probabilistic argument with $\alpha' = [\neg\alpha : x]$ for some x. This attack is called type 3 attack.*

Note that probabilistic arguments do not attack non-probabilistic ones.

Intuitively, the probability of a possible world w of a PABA $\mathcal{P} = (\mathcal{A}_p, \mathcal{R}_p, \mathcal{F})$ is determined by $P(w) = \prod\limits_{(Q,[\alpha:x]) \in GE} x$ where GE is the grounded extension of the ABA framework $\mathcal{F}_w$. Unfortunately this idea does not work in general as the following example illustrates.

Example 2.2 *Consider a PABA* $(\mathcal{A}_p, \mathcal{R}_p, \mathcal{F})$ *with* $\mathcal{A}_p = \{p\}$ *and* $\mathcal{R}_p$ *consisting of the following rules:*

$$[p : 0.5] \leftarrow$$
$$[\neg p : 0.5] \leftarrow$$
$$[p : 0.1] \leftarrow \sim a$$
$$[\neg p : 0.9] \leftarrow \sim a$$

and $\mathcal{F}$ *is represented by*

$$a \leftarrow \sim a$$

where $\sim a$ *is the only assumption in* $\mathcal{F}$ *whose contrary is a. Let* $w = \{p\}$. $\mathcal{F}_w$ *contains the rules in* $\mathcal{R}_p$, $\mathcal{F}$ *and the extra rule* $p \leftarrow$. *The arguments of* $\mathcal{F}_w$ *are* $\{a_0, a_1, a_2, a_3, a_4, a_5\}$ *where* $a_0 = (\emptyset, [p : 0.5])$, $a_1 = (\emptyset, [\neg p : 0.5])$, $a_2 = (\{\sim a\}, [p : 0.1])$, $a_3 = (\{\sim a\}, [\neg p : 0.9])$, $a_4 = (\{\sim a\}, a)$ *and* $a_5 = (\emptyset, p)$. *The attack relation is: i)* a_5 *attacks* a_1, a_3, *ii)* a_2, a_3 *attack* a_0, a_1 *by specificity, iii)* a_4 *attacks itself and attacks also* a_2, a_3. *The grounded extension GE of* $\mathcal{F}_w$ *contains exactly one argument* $(\emptyset, p)$. *Hence* $P(w) = 1$. *Similarly* $P(w') = 1$ *for* $w' = \{\neg p\}$. *Hence* $(\{w, w'\}, P)$ *is not a probability space.*

We introduce now a natural condition guaranteeing the probabilistic coherence of PABA generalizing the idea of acyclic logic programming and also of Baysian nets.

---

[10] i.e. $\alpha \in w$. Note that A is not a probabilistic argument

The **dependency graph** of a PABA $\mathcal{P} = (\mathcal{A}_p, \mathcal{R}_p, \mathcal{F})$ consists of atoms as nodes and there is a link from atom α to atom β if there is a rule in $\mathcal{R}_p$ or in $\mathcal{F}$ containing α in its head and β in its body. A PABA framework is said to be **probabilistic acyclic** if there is no infinite path starting from a probabilistic parameter in its dependency graph.

It is not difficult to see that the PABA frameworks in example 2.2 is not probabilistic acyclic while the PABA in example 2.1 is. Note that each PABA framework with empty set of probabilistic rules is probabilistic acyclic.

Lemma 2.1 *Let* $\mathcal{P} = (\mathcal{A}_p, \mathcal{R}_p, \mathcal{F})$ *be a probabilistic acyclic PABA framework and* W *be the set of all possible worlds of* $\mathcal{P}$. *For* $w \in W$, *let* GE_w *be the grounded extension of the ABA* $\mathcal{F}_w$. *Further define*

$$P(w) = \prod_{(Q,[\alpha:x]) \in GE_w} x$$

Then $\sum_{w \in W} P(w) = 1$.

Proof We prove the lemma by induction on n.

1. Base Case: n = 0. Obvious.
2. Inductive Step: Suppose the lemma holds for $n - 1$. We first prove a couple of support propositions.

    Let $\mathcal{A}_p = \{p_1, \ldots, p_n\}$ such that there is no path from p_i to p_j in the dependency graph for any pair $i < j$. Such enumeration exists due to the probabilistic acyclicity of $\mathcal{P}$.

    From definition 2.3, there are three types of attacks denoted by att_1, att_2, att_3. Let the set of arguments of $\mathcal{P}$ wrt w be denoted by AR_w. Let the grounded extension of AR_w wrt att_1 be GE_1. Further let the grounded extension of (GE_1, att_2) be GE_2 and the grounded extension of (GE_2, att_3) be GE_3.

    Proposition 1 $GE_w = GE_3$.

    Proof As probabilistic arguments do not attack non-probabilistic arguments, the set of non-probabilistic arguments in GE_3 and GE_w coincide. Let this set be NG. It is not difficult to see that GE_1 is the set of all arguments acceptable wrt NG wrt att_1. It follows that GE_2 is the set of arguments acceptable wrt NG wrt $att_1 \cup att_2$. Therefore there are no probabilistic arguments in GE_2 that are more specific than other probabilistic arguments in GE_2. Applying att_3 eliminate arguments with head $[\neg\alpha : x]$ if $\alpha \in w$. Hence $GE_3 = GE_w$.

    From the existence of rules assigning default values to for probabilistic parameters and proposition 1, it follows

    Proposition 2 For each probabilistic parameter p, there exists exactly one argument of the form $(Q, \delta, [p : x])$ (resp $(Q, \delta, [\neg p : 1 - x])$) in GE_w if $p \in w$ (resp $\neg p \in w$).

    From the structures of rules in $\mathcal{R}_p$, it follows:

    Proposition 3 For each probabilistic parameter p, there are exactly two arguments of the form $(Q, \delta, [p : x])$ and $(Q, \delta', [\neg p : 1 - x])$ in GE_2 where δ, δ' differ only in their first elements.

Let $v = w \setminus \{p_n, \neg p_n\}$. Let GE_v be the grounded extension of $\mathcal{F}_v$. From the probabilistic acyclicity of $\mathcal{P}$, it follows

Proposition 4 For each probabilistic literal $\alpha \in v$, each probabilistic argument of the form $A = (Q, [\alpha : x])$, $A \in GE_v$ iff $A \in GE_w$.

Let $w_0 = w \cup \{\beta\}$ where $\beta \in \{p_n, \neg p_n\} \setminus w$.

Proposition 5 Let $(Q, \delta, [\alpha : x])$ with $\alpha \in \{p_n, \neg p_n\}$ be a probabilistic argument belonging to GE_w. Then the complementatry argument $(Q, \delta', [\neg p : 1 - x])$[11] belongs to GE_{w_0}.

From propositions 4,5, it follows: $P(v) = P(w) + P(w_0)$. Hence the lemma follows from the induction hypothesis.

We can now introduce the notion of assumption-based argumentation for jury-based dispute resolution.

Definition 2.4 *An assumption-based argumentation framework for jury-based dispute resolution (ABAJ) is a tuple*

$$(\mathcal{F}, \mathcal{P}_1, \ldots, \mathcal{P}_n), \qquad n \geq 1$$

satisfying following conditions:

1. *$\mathcal{F}$ is an ABA of the form $(\mathcal{R}, \mathcal{A}, \overline{})$ where $\mathcal{A}$ contains a special subset $\mathcal{A}_p$ of positive probabilistic assumptions such that for each $\alpha \in \mathcal{A}_p$, $\neg \alpha \in \mathcal{A}$ and $\overline{\alpha} = \neg \alpha$ and $\overline{\neg \alpha} = \alpha$.*
   Arguments in $\mathcal{F}$ containing no probabilistic assumptions are norm-based arguments while causal arguments are represented by arguments containing probabilistic assumptions.
2. *$\mathcal{P}_i = (\mathcal{A}_p, \mathcal{R}_{i,p}, \mathcal{F}_i)$ are PABA frameworks with $\mathcal{F}_i = (\mathcal{R}_i, \mathcal{A}_i, \overline{})$ such that $\mathcal{R} \subseteq \mathcal{R}_i$ and $\mathcal{A} \setminus \mathcal{A}_p \subseteq \mathcal{A}_i$ [12].*
   Note that the probabilistic assumptions in $\mathcal{F}$ are probabilistic parameters in $\mathcal{P}_i$.

Given a probabilistic assumption-based argumentation framework for jury-based dispute resolution $(\mathcal{F}, \mathcal{P}_1, \ldots, \mathcal{P}_n)$, $n \geq 1$ with $\mathcal{A}_p$ denoting the set of probabilistic assumptions in $\mathcal{F}$, the corresponding abstract argumentation framework for jury-based dispute resolution is $(AF, \Pi_1, \ldots, \Pi_n, \vdash_1, \ldots, \vdash_n)$, $n \geq 1$ where

1. AF is the argumentation framework defined by $\mathcal{F}$ and
2. $\Pi_i = (W_i, P_i)$ where W_i is the set of possible worlds of $\mathcal{P}_i$ and P_i is the associated probability measure, and
3. for each possible world $w \in W_i$, each argument $A = (Q, \alpha)$ in AF, define $w \vdash_i A$ iff $Q \cap (\mathcal{A}_p \cup \neg.\mathcal{A}_p) \subseteq w$ where $\neg.\mathcal{A}_p = \{\neg p \mid p \in \mathcal{A}_p\}$.

One may ask what happens in the case where the set of probabilistic assumptions in $\mathcal{F}$ in an ABAJ is empty. Hence each PABA $\mathcal{P}_i$ has only one possible world, the emptyset. Therefore for each i, $Prob_i(A) = 1$ iff A belongs to the grounded extension of $\mathcal{F}$. This

---

[11]i.e. δ' differs from δ only in its first element

[12]It follows immediately that norm-based arguments from $\mathcal{F}$ are also arguments in each $\mathcal{F}_i$.

implies that all arguments in $\mathcal{F}$ are norm-based. In this case, the judge will simply decide the case without giving it to the jurors. An argument $\mathcal{F}$ is then accepted if it belongs to the grounded extension of $\mathcal{F}$.

Jury's decisions are often biased. Such bias may have deep historical roots and constitute parts of the social fabric. The juries in OJ Simpson trials made their decisions along social lines where black jurors favored Simpson. In PABA frameworks representing the probability spaces of jurors, their biases are captured by the probabilitic rules together with norm-based rules that are not contained in the ABA framework representing the arguments of the dispute parties.

2.1. OJ Simpson again

For illustration, consider again the OJ Simpson example 0.2. For simplification, let us focus only on the blood sample collected at the murder scene. Argument P is simplified to argument P' stating that Simpson is the murder as the DNA test of blood sample collected at the murder scene show that it is Simpson's blood. Argument P' is based on the following rules:

r_0: $simpsonMurder \leftarrow bloodSample(B), SimpsonBlood(B),$
$\qquad\qquad\qquad CollectedAtMurderScence(B), p_1$

r_1: $bloodSample(B) \leftarrow$

r_2: $collectedAtMurderScene(B) \leftarrow p_2$

r_3: $simpsonBlood(B) \leftarrow dnaTest(B) \sim improperDNATest$

where B is the blood sample shown as physical evidence at the trial. The probabilistic assumption p_1 specifies the causal probability to jump from the premises to the conclusion of rule r_0. Prosecutor needs to *convince the jury* that p_1 is very high, basically equivalent to 1.0 to be able to convict Simpson. This is often done by producing evidences showing that Simpson has the motivation and capability to carry out the murder. We will discuss more about how to influence this probability later.

Probabilistic assumption p_2 specifies the probability that the blood sample used for DNA test is collected at the murder scene. Rule r_3 intuitively means that if the DNA test is carried out properly then the blood sample used in such tests is indeed Simpson's blood.

The defence strategy is based on two tracks. First attacking the trustability of the DNA test by using expert's testimony to raise doubts about the way it is conducted. This argument (D_1) is based on the following rules:

r_4: $improperDNATest \leftarrow drHenryTesttimony, p_3$

r_5: $drHenryTesttimony \leftarrow$

where probabilistic assumption p_3 specifies the probability that Henry is right in his testimony.

The second line of defence is to raise reasonable doubt in prosecutor's argument P' by producing evidences to establish that the probabilities of assumptions p_1, p_2 are well below 1.

Imagine the time point during the trial where the prosecution had presented their arguments and evidences but the defence had not started their defence yet. As there is in general no reason to doubt the integrity of the police and the precision of DNA tests, it is sensible to expect that the jury is impressed by the prosecution's presentation. Their impression could be represented by following probabilistic rules:

pr_1: $[p_1 : 1.0] \leftarrow$
pr_2: $[p_2 : 1.0] \leftarrow$ [13]

As it turned out that Dr Henry Lee was quite an influence to the jury in his testimony about the improperity of the DNA tests. The PABA frameworks of black jury members could sensibly contain the rule:

pr_3: $[p_3 : 0.4] \leftarrow$

Further, by exposing police officer Fuhrman as a liar and racist who could go to any length to convict black defendants, the defence managed to reduce the probability of pa_2 in the eyes of the black jurors to an important degree. We could sensibly represent this by a rule like:

pr_4: $[p_2 : 0.95] \leftarrow fuhrman Liar Racist$

Adding other irregularities in evidence collection and the "fact" that the glove does not fit, we could sensibly imagine yet another rule:

pr_5: $[p_2 : 0.9] \leftarrow fuhrman Liar Racist, other Irregularities, glove Not Fit$

To summarize, we can sensibly model the probability spaces of black jurors by a PABA framework $(\mathcal{A}_p, \mathcal{R}_p, \mathcal{F})$ with $\mathcal{F} = (\mathcal{R}, \mathcal{A}, \overline{})$ where $\mathcal{R} = \{r_0, \dots, r_5, r_6, r_7, r_8\}$ with r_6, r_7, r_8 representing facts introduced by the defence:

r_6: $fuhrman Liar Racist \leftarrow$ r_7: $other Irregularities \leftarrow$ r_8: $glove Not Fit \leftarrow$

$\mathcal{A} = \{\sim improper DNATest\}$, with $\mathcal{A}_p = \{p_1, p_2, p_3\}$ and $\mathcal{R}_p = \{pr_1, \dots, pr_5\}$ together with complementary rules.

The ABA framework representing arguments presented by both parties is $(\mathcal{R}, \mathcal{A}, \overline{})$.

Suppose the probability spaces of the black jurors are represented by the above PABA framework. The only possible world of these PABAs in which Simpson is a murder is $w = \{p_1, p_2, \neg p_3\}$. It follows $P(w) = 1.0 \times 0.9 \times 0.6 = 0.54$. It is obvious that black jurors have serious "reasonable doubt" about the conclusion that Simpson is a murder. Hence using the criteria of beyond reasonable doubt, Simpson is acquitted.

In the civil trial both probabilistic rules pr_4, pr_5 are not included in the PABA frameworks of the jury members as Fuhrman is not called as witness and the plaintiff's lawyer does not make the mistake of trying the glove. Testimony about the improper conduct of DNA tests did not raise much doubts. So rule pr_3 could sensibly be replaced by something with a probability of say 0.2.

It is not difficult to see that the probability of "Simpson is the murder" for a whie juror is now 0.8, much higher than 0.5. As most jurors in the civil trial of OJ are white, this explains his conviction by majority vote using preponderance.

2.2. Modelling Rhetoric and Emotional Arguments

Rhetorics and emotions play key roles in trials and decision makings of humans. A good lawyer is often one who could play to the emotions and biases of the jury. This could also be seen at the Simpson's trial. For example, to demonstrate that Simpson is a caring family man, the defence had put a spin on Simpson's life during a visit to his house by the jury, judge and the media by putting a Bible and pictures of his mum and other black people on his table [10]. This seemed to have a good effect at reducing the probability of pa_1, i.e. weakening the conclusive force of the DNA test results. The effects of rhetorics

---

[13]For short, we do not write down explicitly the complementary rules

could be naturally represented in our PABA by probabilistic rules like some rule stating that seeing the Bible reduces the probability of probabilistic parameter p_1.

3. Conclusion and Discussion

We have proposed an argumentation framework for jury-based dispute resolution by incorporating probabilistic reasoning into abstract argumentation as well as assumption-based argumentation. We in fact have provided a theory to measure the strength of arguments and their "accrual". The separation between argumentation and probabilities spaces in probabilitic argumentation offers a very high degree of modularity and encapsulation. There is for example no constraints that the different components of the framework must be based on the same language.

Though our notion of PABA is related the independent choice logic of Poole [7] and the probabilistic logic programming of Baral,Gelfond and Rushton [1], the conceptual idea underlying our work is different to theirs. Unlike in [7,1], we do not consider the (stable or preferred or some other kind of) extensions as possible worlds of the probability spaces represented by a PABA. Note that a PABA with emptyset of probabilistic rules may have many stable extensions but only one possible world consisting of the emptyset of probabilistic parameters. Further, as we use the PABA with grounded semantics as a vehicle to "compute" the probability measure of possible worlds that are defined externally to the PABA, it does not matter whether the concerned PABA has stable semantics or not. In difference to [7,1,9], we are not interested in the probabilities of queries concerning the PABA of the jurors. We are interested in the probabilities of the queries concerning the "non-probabilistic" knowledge base set up by the judge.

References

[1]   C. Baral, M. Gelfond, N. Rushton: Probabilistic reasoning with answer sets, *TPLP* **9**(1), 57-144, 2009.
[2]   A Bondarenko, P M Dung, R A Kowalski, F Toni: An Abstract, Argumentation-Theoretic Approach to Default Reasoning, *Artificial Intelligence* **93**(1-2), 63-101, 1997.
[3]   Phan Minh Dung: On the acceptability of arguments and its fundamental role in nonmonotonic reasoning, logic programming and n-person games, *Artificial Intelligence* **77**(2), 321-357, 1995.
[4]   Phan Minh Dung, Paolo Mancarella, and Francesca Toni: Computing ideal sceptical argumentation, *Artificial Intelligence* **107**(10-15), 642-674, 2007.
[5]   A. Keane, The Modern Law of Evidence, *Oxford University Press*, 2008.
[6]   G.C. Lilly, An Introduction to the Law of Evidence, *West Group*, 1996
[7]   D. Poole: Abducing through Negation as Failure, Stable models within independent choice logic, *The Journal of Logic Programming* **44**(1-3), 5-35, 1998.
[8]   R.Riveret, N. Rotolo, G.Sartor, H.Prakken, B.Roth: Success chances in argument games, A probabilistic approach to legal disputes, *Proc. Jurix*, 2007.
[9]   J. Vennekens, M. Denecker, M. Bruynooghe: CP-logic, A language of causal probabilistic events and its relation to logic programming, *TPLP* **9**(3), 245-308, 2009.
[10]   O.J.Simpson Murder Case *Wikipedia*.
[11]   C.R. Williams, Burdens and Standards in Civil Litigation, *Sydney Law Review*, 2003, 25, 165-188

Computational Models of Argument
P. Baroni et al. (Eds.)
IOS Press, 2010
© 2010 The authors and IOS Press. All rights reserved.
doi:10.3233/978-1-60750-619-5-183

Some design guidelines for practical argumentation systems

Phan Minh DUNG [a] Francesca TONI [b,1] Paolo MANCARELLA [c]

[a] *AIT, Bangkok, Thailand*
[b] *Department of Computing, Imperial College London, UK*
[c] *Dipartimento di Informatica, Università di Pisa, Italy*

Abstract. We give some design guidelines for argumentation systems. These guidelines are meant to indicate essential features of argumentation when used to support "practical reasoning". We express the guidelines in terms of postulates. We use a notion of redundancy to provide a formal counterpart of these postulates. We study the satisfaction of these postulates in two existing argumentation frameworks: assumption-based argumentation and argumentation in classical logic.

Keywords. Formal and informal models for argumentation

Introduction

Argumentation is widely recognised as an important mechanism to support "practical reasoning", e.g. in support of debate [6,3] and for legal reasoning [1]. As an example of the kind of "practical reasoning" we have in mind, consider the following situation: *You are presenting your case of why you should become the president of your country to your voters. These will form a mixed audience, in that some may be of basic education and simple professions, others will be educated or highly-educated. You will have to face one or more opponents, who would also like to become president and will attack your case. How should you conduct and participate in such a debate so as to have a chance to win it?* We believe that the answer lies in the following cardinal principles:

Principle 1 : Your arguments must be simple so that people of all backgrounds can follow them easily. It does not make sense to deliver some sophisticated arguments that only experts can understand, possibly after spending considerable effort. You should make clear the contrast between you and your opponents by attacking their arguments in a simple, transparent way, immediately obvious to the audience.

Principle 2 : Deliver your arguments in full to make your points explicitly, but avoid repetitions and irrelevant details that could be a distraction and a point of attack by your opponents.

Principle 3 : Do not disregard or dismiss any arguments by your opponents, unless you are certain that you can rebate them at any time. Do not disregard or dismiss any argument against the opponents, to avoid losing your edge and be perceived as the loser.

---

[1]Corresponding Author

We explore how these principles can be formalised as guidelines for *generic argumentation systems*, in the form of *postulates*. These systems are given in terms of arguments, viewed as defeasible proofs in some (unspecified) logic, and an attack relation, meant to be used to capture those defeasible proofs that can be deemed acceptable by parties engaged in practical reasoning. We do not prescribe any notion of acceptability of arguments. We allow for some defeasible proofs not to be deployed as arguments in practical reasoning tasks. Thus, not every defeasible proof is an argument in general.

Several well-known argumentation frameworks can be seen as instances of our generic argumentation systems. We analyse the fulfilment of these postulates in the context of some existing logic-based argumentation systems, focusing on assumption-based argumentation (ABA) [8] and argumentation in classical logic (ArCL) [3]. This analysis relies upon a formal understanding of the postulates in terms of a notion of redundancy of arguments, that we provide, in part, in the context of abstract argumentation [6].

The paper is organised as follows. In section 1 we give some background on abstract argumentation, ABA and ArCL. In section 2 we give our postulates for generic argumentation frameworks. In section 3 we reformulate (two of) these postulates in terms of a "less redundant" relation. In sections 4 and 5 we analyse these postulates in ArCL and ABA, respectively. In section 6 we conclude.

1. Background

Abstract argumentation [6]
An **abstract argumentation framework** is a pair $\langle Arg, att \rangle$ where Arg is a finite set, whose elements are referred to as *arguments*, and $att \subseteq Arg \times Arg$ is a binary relation over Arg. Given $\alpha, \beta \in Arg$, α **attacks** β iff $(\alpha, \beta) \in att$. Given sets $X, Y \subseteq Arg$ of arguments, X **attacks** Y iff there exists $x \in X$ and $y \in Y$ such that $(x, y) \in att$. A set of arguments is referred to as *extension*. An extension $X \subseteq Arg$ is

- **acceptable wrt** a set $Y \subseteq Arg$ of arguments iff for each β that attacks an argument in X, there exists $\alpha \in Y$ such that α attacks β;
- **admissible** iff X does not attack itself and X is acceptable wrt itself;
- **preferred** iff X is (subset) maximally admissible;
- **complete** iff X is admissible and X contains all arguments x such that $\{x\}$ is acceptable wrt X;
- **grounded** iff X is (subset) minimally complete;
- **ideal** iff X is admissible and it is contained in every preferred set of arguments.

For $AF = \langle Arg, att \rangle$, the **characteristic function** $\mathcal{F}_{AF}$ is such that $\mathcal{F}_{AF}(X)$ is the set of all acceptable arguments wrt X. Then X that does not attack itself is 1) an admissible extension iff $X \subseteq \mathcal{F}_{AF}(X)$, 2) a complete extension iff it is a fix-point of $\mathcal{F}_{AF}$, and 3) a grounded extension iff X is the least fix-point of $\mathcal{F}_{AF}$.

Assumption-based argumentation (ABA) [4,7,9,8]
An **ABA framework** is a tuple $\langle \mathcal{L}, \mathcal{R}, \mathcal{A}, \bar{} \rangle$ where

- $(\mathcal{L}, \mathcal{R})$ is a *deductive system*, with $\mathcal{L}$ a language and $\mathcal{R}$ a set of inference rules,
- $\mathcal{A} \subseteq \mathcal{L}$, referred to as the set of *assumptions*,
- $\bar{}$ is a (total) mapping from $\mathcal{A}$ into $\mathcal{L}$, where $\bar{x}$ is referred to as the *contrary* of x.

We will assume that inference rules have the syntax $\frac{s_1,\ldots s_n}{s_0}$ (for $n \geq 0$) where $s_i \in \mathcal{L}$.

An *argument* in favour of a sentence c in $\mathcal{L}$ supported by a set of assumptions A is a (defeasible) proof of c from A and (some of) the rules in $\mathcal{R}$. We will provide a formal definition of argument in section 5 (see definition 5.2). For the purposes of defining semantics and computational mechanisms for ABA, the notation $\langle A, c \rangle$ is used, to stand for an argument for c supported by A. This notation can be seen as a shorthand for the notation $\langle A, P, c \rangle$, where P is the proof used to construct the argument. The (short) notation does not distinguish arguments with the same support and conclusion but using different proofs. E.g. $\langle \{a\}, p \rangle$ may represent an argument using inference rule $\frac{a}{p}$ as well as an argument using inference rules $\frac{q}{p}$, $\frac{a}{q}$ (see [9] for a discussion of this issue). The short notation suffices to define semantics and computational mechanisms for ABA, as the only form of defeasibility in ABA is given by assumptions.

All notions of extensions for abstract argumentation can be used in ABA, by using a notion of "attack" amongst arguments whereby $\langle X, x \rangle$ **attacks** $\langle Y, y \rangle$ iff $x = \overline{\alpha}$ for some $\alpha \in Y$. As shown in [9], theorem 2.2, there is a one-to-one correspondence between semantics in terms of extensions (sets of arguments), as presented here, and semantics in terms of sets of assumptions, as presented in the original definition of ABA in [4].

Argumentation based on classical logic (ArCL) [3]
In ArCL, given a (possibly inconsistent) set of (first-order) sentences Δ, an *argument* for a (first-order) sentence c is a pair $\langle S, c \rangle$ such that
  (i) S is consistent
  (ii) $S \vdash c$, where $\vdash$ is the classical consequence relation
  (iii) S is a minimal subset of Δ fulfilling conditions (i), (ii).
An argument $\langle S_1, c_1 \rangle$ is a **canonical undercut for** an argument $\langle S_2, c_2 \rangle$ iff
  (a) $c_1 = \neg(s_1 \wedge \ldots \wedge s_n)$, for $S_2 = \{s_1, \ldots, s_n\}$
  (b) $s_1, \ldots, s_n$ is the canonical enumeration of S_2 (according to some ordering of the elements of Δ given a-priori, without loss of generality).
An *argument tree* for a sentence s is a tree whose nodes are arguments such that
  (I) the root is an argument for s
  (II) for no node $\langle S, c \rangle$, S is a subset of the union of the supports of the node's ancestors
  (III) the children of a node N are all canonical undercuts for N obeying (II).
Nodes of a tree can be marked as undefeated (U) or defeated (D) as follows: for all nodes N, if there is a child of N marked U, then N is marked D; otherwise, N is marked U. Then, an argument tree is **warranted** iff the root of the tree is marked U.

As for ABA, we will see an argument $\langle S, c \rangle$ in ArCL as a shorthand for $\langle S, P, c \rangle$ where P is a proof (e.g. using natural deduction) for c using the sentences in S.

2. Postulates for practical argumentation

In this section we consider generic argumentation frameworks, equipped with notions of

- *legitimate arguments*, as defeasible proofs in some (possibly implicit) underlying logic; each legitimate argument consists of a support, a proof and a claim;
- *"deployed" arguments*, namely (legitimate) arguments that can be deployed in practical argumentation;

- *attack* between arguments, as a binary relation that may be primitive or derived (from primitive notions);
- "dialectical" *semantics* for accepting sets of legitimate arguments.

We will use the terminology *"illegitimate" argument* for any argument that is not legitimate. Illegitimate arguments may be anything, e.g. unsupported claims or supported claims with invalid or without proofs. They may be introduced by any parties involved in the exchange of arguments, e.g., a witness with an incoherent account of past events.

Several existing argumentation frameworks could be seen as providing notions of legitimate arguments in our generic sense, e.g. ABA, ArCL, DeLP [10], just to mention some. These various concrete frameworks differ in the underlying logic (e.g. any deductive system in ABA and standard notions of logical deduction in first-order logic for ArCL), in how their choice of deployed arguments (e.g. ABA requires that deployed arguments can be constructed backwards and ArCL requires minimality and consistency of their support), and in how they define the attack relation as a derived notion (e.g. from a primitive notion of contrary of assumptions in ABA). Finally, the concrete frameworks differ in their choice of dialectical semantics (e.g. ABA uses notions of extensions, ArCL uses a notion of warranted argument trees and DeLP uses a notion of warranted literals).

Our generic argumentation frameworks, for specific choices of "dialectical" semantics, with the set of deployed arguments coinciding with the set of legitimate arguments, can be seen as instances of abstract argumentation frameworks.

We give postulates, intended as design guidelines for generic argumentation systems *when these are used for practical reasoning* (as understood in this paper).

Postulate 2.1 (**Transparency**) Deployed arguments and attacks should be *transparent* in the sense of being computationally tractable, as follows:

1. the computational cost of verifying that deployed arguments are legitimate should be at most polynomial (in the size of the arguments);
2. the computational cost of verifying that an argument attacks another should be at most linear (in the size of the claim of the argument).

The size of an argument is the size of its support and proof. Intuitively, this postulate guarantees that arguments can be understood by any parties, independently of their level of sophistication (cf. principle 1 in the introduction). Note that the construction of deployed arguments could be highly complex, as for example in the case of legal proceedings. However, once these arguments are constructed, the verification that they are so, e.g. by other parties, should be tractable (i.e. polynomial). Proofs in propositional logic, using for example natural deduction or resolution, can be checked in polynomial time. So arguments as proofs in propositional logic can be deemed to fulfil this postulate.

Also, this postulate forces attacks to be directly inspectable (linear time). This is again in line with principle 1 in the introduction. As attacks need to be immediately recognisable, without any "reasoning" by the spectators in a debate. Attacks defined in terms of inconsistency (namely by sanctioning that the claim of the attacking argument is inconsistent with the support of the attacked argument) would not satisfy this postulate.

Postulate 2.2 (**Relevance**) The support of deployed arguments should be *relevant* to the claim of the arguments, to some degree.

Intuitively, this postulate amounts to forcing proponents and opponents of arguments to focus and avoid digressions not contributing to the important points they want to make and possibly opening up attacks from their counterparts (cf. principle 2 in the introduction). In the strongest sense this postulate 2.2 can be interpreted to mean that the support should be necessary to establish the claim, in the sense that the removal of any part of this support would render the arguments illegitimate. In a weaker sense this can be interpreted to mean that the argument is a defeasible proof of its claim from its support, without any obvious redundancy of any parts of the support.

The first two postulates focus on the inner workings of legitimate, deployed arguments and attacks. The third and final postulate instead considers the use of arguments in "debate", namely in the context of "dialectical" semantics.

Postulate 2.3 (No dismissal) No legitimate argument should be dismissed without reason. If, for any reason, some legitimate arguments are dismissed (not deployed), their dismissal should not change the semantics of the given argumentation framework.

This postulate amounts to avoiding leaving any stone unturned (cf. principle 3).

In the remainder we will refer to legitimate arguments simply as arguments. An argument with proof P from support S for a claim c will be represented as a triple $\langle S, P, c \rangle$ or simply as a pair $\langle S, c \rangle$, leaving the proof implicit, if clear from the context.

3. Redundancy

We can formally restate postulates 2.2 and 2.3 in terms of a notion of "redundancy" of arguments, defined in terms of a "less redundant" preference relation:

Postulate 3.1 If a relation $\prec$ represents a *less redundant* relation between arguments, then the following properties should be satisfied:

1. $\prec$ is transitive (i.e., for arguments α, β, γ, if $\alpha \prec \beta$ and $\beta \prec \gamma$, then $\alpha \prec \gamma$) reflexive (i.e. for any argument α, $\alpha \prec \alpha$) and antisymmetric (i.e. for arguments α, β, if $\alpha \prec \beta$ and $\beta \prec \alpha$, then $\alpha = \beta$)
2. given arguments α, β, γ, if $\alpha \prec \beta$ then

   (a) if β attacks γ then α attacks γ;
   (b) if γ attacks α then γ attacks β.

3. for each argument α there is an argument β such that

   (a) $\beta \prec \alpha$, and
   (b) there is no argument γ such that $\gamma \prec \beta$ and $\gamma \neq \beta$.

Intuitively, condition 2a says that α has a stronger conclusive force than β, and condition 2b says that α is less exposed to attacks than β (e.g. because its support is narrower). Condition 3 says that each argument has a "non-redundant" version (possibly itself). Depending on the context, different instances of the "less redundant" relation could be introduced. For example, one could define an argument α as "less redundant than" an argument β (with both arguments supporting the same claim) if the support of α is a subset of the support of β, namely, for $\alpha = \langle S_\alpha, c \rangle$ and $\beta = \langle S_\beta, c \rangle$: $\alpha \prec \beta$ iff $S_\alpha \subseteq S_\beta$ Below, we will refer to this notion of $\prec$ as $\prec_\subseteq$.

We will see, in section 5, another notion of $\prec$ where arguments with proof that can be arranged as trees are "less redundant" than arguments with proofs that cannot.

An example of a relation over pairs of arguments that is *not* a suitable notion of "less redundant" is $\prec$ such that $\alpha \prec \beta$ iff the cardinality of the support of α is strictly smaller than that of the support of β. Indeed, this notion will typically not fulfil condition 2b.

3.1. Redundancy and relevance postulate

Definition 3.1 Given a "less redundant" relation $\prec$, the support of an argument α is *relevant* if α is minimal wrt $\prec$.

For example, given $\prec_\subseteq$ given earlier, relevant arguments are arguments with a subset-minimal support. In the context of the presidential debate considered in the introduction, this subset-minimality-based definition of relevance does not seem to be useful. Indeed, its adoption may violate postulate 2.1 in that, for example, the cost of verifying that arguments as proofs in propositional logic have a subset-minimal support may be non-polynomial. Instead, if arguments are proofs built from Horn clauses, then subset-minimality is acceptable, in that the cost of verifying that arguments in Horn logic have a subset-minimal support is polynomial [2].

3.2. Redundancy and no dismissal postulate

Arguments can be deemed to be *redundant* if there exist other arguments that are "less redundant" than them.

Definition 3.2 Given a "less redundant" relation $\prec$, an argument α is *redundant* (wrt $\prec$) if there exists an argument $\beta \neq \alpha$ such that $\beta \prec \alpha$. The set NR of all *non-redundant* arguments (wrt $\prec$) is such that for each argument α there is $\beta \in NR$ such that $\beta \prec \alpha$.

Theorem 3.1 below states that redundant arguments can be dismissed without affecting (some) "dialectical" semantics. Thus, non-redundant arguments, in the sense of definition 3.2, can be seen as fulfilling postulate 2.3 (for these semantics).

Theorem 3.1 considers (some of) the semantics that have been studied for abstract argumentation frameworks [6,9]. Thus, for the purposes of this theorem, we treat (legitimate) arguments as abstract and assume an abstract argumentation framework $\langle Arg, att \rangle$ where att is the attack relation. The theorem is formulated using the following notion of "$\prec$-trimmed" versions of abstract argumentation framework:

Definition 3.3 Let $\langle Arg, att \rangle$ be an abstract argumentation framework. Let $\prec$ be a "less redundant" relation between arguments in Arg and $NR \subseteq Arg$ the set of all non-redundant arguments (wrt $\prec$). Further, let att_{NR} be the restriction of att on NR, i.e. $att_{NR} = att \cap NR \times NR$. The argumentation framework $\langle NR, att_{NR} \rangle$ is referred to as the *$\prec$-trimmed version of* $\langle Arg, att \rangle$.

Theorem 3.1 follows directly from the following lemmas (see appendix A for all proofs):

Lemma 3.1 Let $\langle NR, att_{NR} \rangle$ be the *$\prec$-trimmed version of* $\langle Arg, att \rangle$. Then

1. If $\beta \in NR$ is acceptable wrt $B \subseteq NR$ in $\langle NR, att_{NR} \rangle$ then β is acceptable wrt B in $\langle Arg, att \rangle$

2. Each admissible set of arguments in $\langle \mathcal{NR}, att_{\mathcal{NR}} \rangle$ is also admissible in $\langle Arg, att \rangle$.
3. If $\alpha \in Arg$ is acceptable wrt $B \subseteq Arg$ in $\langle Arg, att \rangle$ then each $\beta \in Arg$ such that $\beta \prec \alpha$ is acceptable wrt B in $\langle Arg, att \rangle$.
4. If $\alpha \in Arg$ is acceptable wrt $B \subseteq \mathcal{NR}$ in $\langle Arg, att \rangle$ then each $\beta \in \mathcal{NR}$ such that $\beta \prec \alpha$ is acceptable wrt B in $\langle \mathcal{NR}, att_{\mathcal{NR}} \rangle$.

Lemma 3.2 Let $\langle \mathcal{NR}, att_{\mathcal{NR}} \rangle$ be the $\prec$-*trimmed version of* $\langle Arg, att \rangle$. Also, let $\mathcal{C}$ and $\mathcal{C}_{\mathcal{NR}}$ be the sets of complete extensions of $\langle Arg, att \rangle$ and $\langle \mathcal{NR}, att_{\mathcal{NR}} \rangle$ respectively. Further, let $AF = \langle Arg, att \rangle$. Then, $\mathcal{F}_{AF}(X)$ is a monotonic (wrt set inclusion) bijection from $\mathcal{C}_{\mathcal{NR}}$ onto $\mathcal{C}$ such that

1. For each $X \in \mathcal{C}_{\mathcal{NR}}$: $\mathcal{F}_{AF}(X) \cap \mathcal{NR} = X$.
2. For each $X \in \mathcal{C}$: $\mathcal{F}_{AF}(X \cap \mathcal{NR}) = X$.

Theorem 3.1 Let $\langle \mathcal{NR}, att_{\mathcal{NR}} \rangle$ be the $\prec$-*trimmed version of* $AF = \langle Arg, att \rangle$. Then

1. Let X be a complete or preferred or grounded or ideal extension in $\langle Arg, att \rangle$. Then $X \cap \mathcal{NR}$ is a complete or preferred or grounded or ideal extension, respectively, in $\langle \mathcal{NR}, att_{\mathcal{NR}} \rangle$.
2. Let X be a complete or preferred or grounded or ideal extension in $\langle \mathcal{NR}, att_{\mathcal{NR}} \rangle$. Then $\mathcal{F}_{AF}(X)$ is a complete or preferred or grounded or ideal extension, respectively, in $\langle Arg, att \rangle$.

This theorem shows that removing or adding redundant arguments (for any notion of $\prec$) does not change the semantics (of complete, preferred, grounded, and ideal extensions for abstract argumentation) of the underlying argumentation framework. Hence the issue of whether to work with an argumentation framework with less or more redundant arguments is purely of computational efficiency nature.

Consider instead dismissing arguments that are self-attacking. The dismissal of these arguments would violate postulate 2.3 if, for example, the chosen dialectical semantics is that of admissible extensions. Indeed, consider an argumentation framework with arguments α, β such that α attacks β and α attacks itself. Then, $\{\beta\}$ is not an admissible extension in conventional abstract argumentation but would be an admissible extension if self-attacking arguments were dismissed.

4. Postulates for practical argumentation in ArCL

ArCL can be seen as an instance of our generic argumentation frameworks where legitimate arguments are of the (abbreviated) form $\langle S, c \rangle$ such that $S \vdash c$, deployed arguments are arguments in the sense of section 1, attacks are canonical undercuts, and the "dialectical" semantics is given by the notion of warranted trees.

According to this understanding of ArCL, this fulfils the relevance postulate 2.2 in the sense that it uses relevant arguments wrt $\prec_{\subseteq}$ (see section 3).

As far as the transparency postulate 2.1 is concerned, in ArCL:

1. checking consistency of arguments' support cannot be done in polynomial time;
2. both conditions (a) and (b) of the definition of attack (canonical undercut) can be checked in linear time (in the size of the claim of the attacking argument).

Thus, overall, ArCL does not fulfil this postulate.

Finally, ArCL can be deemed not to fulfil the no dismissal postulate 2.3, in the sense that, by disregarding legitimate arguments on the ground that their support is "not new" within a given argument tree (namely, this support is a subset of the support of previously used arguments), one obtains different warranted argument trees. For example, consider $\Delta = \{p, q, \neg p \vee \neg q\}$ (with canonical enumeration $1 : p$, $2 : q$, $3 : \neg p \vee \neg q$). The only argument tree for p has root $\langle \{p\}, p \rangle$ with a single child $N = \langle \{q, \neg p \vee \neg q\}, \neg p \rangle$. The argument tree is unwarranted. Here, the legitimate argument $N' = \langle \{p, q\}, \neg (\neg p \vee \neg q) \rangle$, attacking N, is not allowed as a child of N as its support is "not new". However, If N' had been considered, as a child of N, then the tree would have been warranted.

5. Postulates for practical argumentation in ABA

In this section, unless otherwise specified, we assume as given a generic $\langle \mathcal{L}, \mathcal{R}, \mathcal{A}, \overline{} \rangle$.

Three kinds of arguments have been defined for ABA: forward arguments, as given in definition 5.1 below (adapted from [4,7]); backward arguments, as given in definition 5.2 below (adapted from [7,9]); and tree-arguments, as given in definition 5.3 below (adapted from [8]). As discussed in [8], backward arguments can be seen as constructing, in a top-down manner, tree-arguments. All these kinds of arguments can be seen as legitimate arguments in ABA, but the deployed arguments are backward arguments.

Definition 5.1 A *forward argument* for $c \in \mathcal{L}$ supported by $A \subseteq \mathcal{A}$ is a sequence $\beta_1, \ldots, \beta_m$, of sentences in $\mathcal{L}$, where $m > 0$ and $c = \beta_m$, such that, for all $i = 1, \ldots, m$,

- $\beta_i \in A$, or
- there exists $\frac{s_1, \ldots, s_n}{\beta_i} \in \mathcal{R}$ such that $s_1, \ldots, s_n \in \{\beta_1, \ldots, \beta_{i-1}\}$.

We use the notation $\langle A, [\beta_1, \ldots, \beta_m], c \rangle_f$ for a forward argument for c supported by A with proof $\beta_1, \ldots, \beta_m$. We use the shorthand $\langle A, c \rangle_f$ when the proof is irrelevant.

Definition 5.2 Given a selection function f[2], a *backward argument* for $c \in \mathcal{L}$ supported by $A \subseteq \mathcal{A}$ is as sequence of multi-sets $S_1, \ldots, S_m$, where $S_1 = \{c\}$, $S_m = A$, and for every $1 \leq i < m$, where σ is the sentence occurrence in S_i selected by f:

1. If $\sigma \notin \mathcal{A}$ then $S_{i+1} = S_i - \{\sigma\} \cup S$ for some $\frac{S}{\sigma} \in \mathcal{R}$.
2. If $\sigma \in \mathcal{A}$ then $S_{i+1} = S_i$.

We use the notation $\langle A, [S_1, \ldots, S_m], c \rangle$ for a backward argument for c supported by A with proof $S_1, \ldots, S_m$. We use the shorthand $\langle A, c \rangle$ when the proof is irrelevant.

Definition 5.3 A *tree-argument* for $c \in \mathcal{L}$ supported by $A \subseteq \mathcal{A}$ is a tree $\mathcal{T}$ with nodes labelled by sentences in $\mathcal{L}$ or by τ,[3] such that

- the root is labelled by c
- for every node N

---

[2] A selection function takes in input a sequence of multi-sets and returns as output a sentence occurring in the last multi-set in the sequence [7].

[3] The symbol τ intuitively stands for "true". It allows to distinguish between facts, namely inference rules with an empty set of premises, and assumptions.

* if N is a leaf then N is labelled either by an assumption or by τ;
* if N is not a leaf and l_N is the label of N, then there is an inference rule
  $l_N \leftarrow b_1, \ldots, b_m$ ($m \geq 0$) and
  either $m = 0$ and the child of N is τ
  or $m > 0$ and N has m children, labelled by $b_1, \ldots, b_m$ (respectively)

- A is the set of all assumptions labelling the leaves.

We use the notation $\langle A, \mathcal{T}, c \rangle_t$ for a tree-argument for c supported by A with proof $\mathcal{T}$. We use the shorthand $\langle A, c \rangle_t$ when the proof is irrelevant.

It is easy to see that

- there is a backward argument $\langle A, c \rangle$ iff there is a tree-argument $\langle A, c \rangle_t$

Namely, the notions of backward argument and tree-argument are equivalent. Moreover, by theorem 4.1 in [7]:

- for every backward argument $\langle A, c \rangle$ (or tree-argument $\langle A, c \rangle_t$) there is a forward argument $\langle A, c \rangle_f$
- for every forward argument $\langle A, c \rangle_f$ there is a backward argument $\langle A', c \rangle$ (and tree-argument $\langle A', c \rangle_t$) for some $A' \subseteq A$

In other words, forward arguments may have "redundancies" in their support. We can thus define a notion $\prec_{tree}$ of "less redundant" as follows:

Definition 5.4 Given forward arguments $\langle A_1, c \rangle_f$ and $\langle A_2, c \rangle_f$, $\langle A_1, c \rangle_f \prec_{tree} \langle A_2, c \rangle_f$ iff either there exist tree arguments $\langle A_1, c \rangle_t$ and $\langle A_2, c \rangle_t$ or there exists a tree-argument $\langle A_1, c \rangle_t$ but there exists no tree-argument $\langle A_2, c \rangle_t$.

Lemma 5.1 $\prec_{tree}$ is a "less redundant" relation, in the sense of postulate 3.1.

Note that it may be the case that $\langle A_1, c \rangle_f \prec_{\subseteq} \langle A_2, c \rangle_f$ but $\langle A_1, c \rangle_f \not\prec_{tree} \langle A_2, c \rangle_f$. For example, let $\mathcal{R}$ be $\{\frac{a}{p}\}$ and $\mathcal{A} = \{a, b, e\}$. Then $\langle \{a, b\}, p \rangle_f \prec_{\subseteq} \langle \{a, b, e\}, p \rangle_f$ but $\langle \{a, b\}, p \rangle_f \not\prec_{tree} \langle \{a, b, e\}, p \rangle_f$. However, given a relevant (wrt $\prec_{\subseteq}$) argument $\langle A_1, c \rangle_f$, if $\langle A_1, c \rangle_f \prec_{\subseteq} \langle A_2, c \rangle_f$ then $\langle A_1, c \rangle_f \prec_{tree} \langle A_2, c \rangle_f$. In the earlier example, $\langle \{a\}, p \rangle_f$ is (the only) relevant argument (wrt $\prec_{\subseteq}$), $\langle \{a\}, p \rangle_f \prec_{\subseteq} \langle \{a, b, e\}, p \rangle_f$ and indeed $\langle \{a\}, p \rangle_f \prec_{tree} \langle \{a, b, e\}, p \rangle_f$.

The relevance postulate 2.2 and no dismissal postulate 2.3 hold for all instances of ABA, for the notion $\prec_{tree}$ of "less redundant". In particular, postulate 2.2 holds since:

Property 5.1 Backward arguments are arguments with relevant support in the sense of definition 3.1, wrt $\prec_{tree}$.

Moreover, postulate 2.3 holds because, by focusing on backward arguments, ABA solely dismisses forward arguments that are redundant.

Property 5.2 The set of all non-redundant arguments wrt $\prec_{tree}$, in the sense of definition 3.2, is the set of all backward arguments.

Theorem 3.1 then holds for the $\prec_{tree}$-trimmed version of (the abstract argumentation framework corresponding to) any ABA framework. Theorem 4.2 in [7] is a corollary of lemma 3.1 used to prove our theorem 3.1.

We analyse postulate 2.1 in two of of the existing instances of ABA, studied in [4].

5.1. ABA for logic programming

A *(normal) logic program* [4] is a set of rules of the form $p \leftarrow l_1, \ldots, l_n$ where p is an atom, $l_1, \ldots, l_n$ are literals, and $n \geq 0$. Negative literals, *not q*, are the *negation as failure* of atoms, q. Logic programs P can be represented as ABA frameworks where

- $\mathcal{R} = \{\frac{B}{p} | p \leftarrow B \in P\}$
- $\mathcal{A} = \{not\ p | p \text{ is an atom in the Herbrand base of } P\}$
- $\overline{not\ p} = p$ for all *not* $p \in \mathcal{A}$

This instance of ABA fulfils the transparency postulate 2.1 since

1. the computational cost of verifying that deployed arguments (namely backward arguments) are legitimate arguments (namely proofs) is linear in the size of the argument (number of rules and assumptions used in the argument);
2. the computational cost of verifying that an argument attacks another is constant (a syntactical check on the atom that is the conclusion of the first argument) and thus linear.

5.2. ABA for default logic

A *default theory* [14] is a pair (T, D) where

- $T \subseteq \mathcal{L}_0$, where $\mathcal{L}_0$ is a first-order language
- D is a set of rules $\frac{s_0, Ms_1, \ldots, Ms_n}{s}$ where $s_0, \ldots, s_n, s \in \mathcal{L}_0$, and $n \geq 0$.

Default theories (T, D) can be represented as ABA frameworks $\langle \mathcal{L}, \mathcal{R}, \mathcal{A}, \overline{} \rangle$ where, given some deductive system $(\mathcal{L}_0, \mathcal{R}_0)$ for classical first-order logic:

- $\mathcal{L} = \mathcal{L}_0 \cup \{M\alpha | \alpha \in \mathcal{L}_0\}, \mathcal{R} = \mathcal{R}_0 \cup D$
- $\mathcal{A} = \{M\ s | s \in \mathcal{L}_0\}$
- $\overline{M\ s} = \neg s$ for all $M\ s \in \mathcal{A}$

For example, $\mathcal{R}_0$ may be the set of inference rules for natural deduction, including (all instances of the schemes) $\frac{A, B}{A \wedge B}$ $(\wedge I)$, $\frac{A, A \rightarrow B}{B}$ $(\rightarrow E)$, etc, and all tautologies (as inference rules with empty premises).

This instance of ABA fulfils the transparency postulate 2.1, since

1. the computational cost of verifying that deployed arguments (namely backward arguments) are legitimate arguments (namely proofs) is linear in the size of the argument (number of rules and assumptions used in the argument);
2. the computational cost of verifying that an argument attacks another is linear (since this verification is a syntactical test requiring to scan a sentence s, and is thus linear in the size of s).

---

[4] We focus here on propositional logic programs.

6. Conclusions

We have identified a number of postulates for generic argumentation systems. These postulates are meant to assess the suitability of argumentation systems to support practical reasoning, e.g. of the form needed in debate in front of audiences of mixed expertise. This suitability amounts to transparency (of arguments and attacks), relevance (of the support of arguments) and no dismissal of arguments that may make a difference. We have analysed the fulfilment of these postulates in (two instances of) assumption-based argumentation (ABA) and in argumentation in classical logic (ArCL). Our analysis is solely in the context of the form of practical reasoning we envisage, and does not determine the usability of argumentation frameworks in other settings (e.g. for non-monotonic reasoning, or in support of decision-making, or as a mechanism for resolving inconsistencies).

Other authors have considered postulates for argumentation, notably [5]. However, their focus is on *rationality* postulates for rule-based argumentation systems with strict and defeasible rules, whereas our focus is on any argumentation system when used in support of practical reasoning.

For lack of space, we have omitted to consider other argumentation frameworks: we plan to do so in the future. As an example, it would be interesting to consider DeLP [10] (also an instance of our generic argumentation frameworks, as mentioned in section 2): we envisage that this will not fulfil transparency (because attacks in DeLP cannot be detected in constant time) and no dismissal (in the same sense that ArCL does not). Other argumentation frameworks we plan to study include Prakken and Sartor's [13] and Carneades [11].

Our list of postulates is not exhaustive. It would be interesting to consider other postulates, e.g. concerning the avoidance of obvious repetitions in debate and, as in [12], the relevance of all arguments put forward in the debate to the starting point of the debate.

References

[1]   T. Bench-Capon, H. Prakken, and G. Sartor. Argumentation in legal reasoning. In I. Rahwan and G. Simari, editors, *Argumentation in AI: The Book*, pages 363–382. Springer, 2009.

[2]   J. Bentahar and Z. Maamar. Complexity results for argumentation-based agent communication. In *Proc. of the 4th IEEE Int. Conf. on Innovations in Information Technology*, pages 506–510, 2008.

[3]   P. Besnard and A. Hunter. *Elements of Argumentation*. MIT Press, 2008.

[4]   A. Bondarenko, P.M. Dung, R.A. Kowalski, and F. Toni. An abstract, argumentation-theoretic approach to default reasoning. *Artif. Intell.*, 93(1-2):63–101, 1997.

[5]   M. Caminada and L. Amgoud. On the evaluation of argumentation formalisms. *Artif. Intell.*, 171(5-6):286–310, 2007.

[6]   P.M. Dung. On the acceptability of arguments and its fundamental role in non-monotonic reasoning, logic programming and n-person games. *Artif. Intell.*, 77:321–357, 1995.

[7]   P.M. Dung, R.A. Kowalski, and F. Toni. Dialectic proof procedures for assumption-based, admissible argume ntation. *Artif. Intell.*, 170:114–159, 2006.

[8]   P.M. Dung, R.A. Kowalski, and F. Toni. Assumption-based argumentation. In I. Rahwan and G. Simari, editors, *Argumentation in AI: The Book*, pages 199–218. Springer, 2009.

[9]   P.M. Dung, P. Mancarella, and F. Toni. Computing ideal sceptical argumentation. *Artif. Intell., Special Issue on Argumentation in Artificial Intelligence*, 171(10–15):642–674, 2007.

[10] A. Garcia and G. Simari. Defeasible logic programming: An argumentative approach. *Journal of Theory and Practice of Logic Programming*, 4(1-2):95–138, 2004.

[11] T. F. Gordon, H. Prakken, and D. Walton. The Carneades model of argument and burden of proof. *Artif. Intell.*, 171(10-15):875–896, 2007.

[12] S. Parsons, P. McBurney, E. Sklar, and M. Wooldridge. On the relevance of utterances in formal inter-agent dialogues. In *AAMAS*, page 240, 2007.

[13] H. Prakken and G. Sartor. Argument-based extended logic programming with defeasible priorities. *Journal of Applied Non-Classical Logics*, 7(1):25–75, 1997.

[14] R. Reiter. A logic for default reasoning. *Artif. Intell.*, 13(1-2):81–132, 1980.

A. Proofs

Proof of lemma 3.1

1. Let $\alpha \in Arg$ attack β. Hence there is $\alpha' \in \mathcal{NR}$ such that $\alpha' \prec \alpha$. Hence α' attacks β in $\langle \mathcal{NR}, att_{\mathcal{NR}} \rangle$. Therefore there is $\gamma \in B$ such that γ attacks α'. Hence γ attacks α.
2. Follows directly from item 1 of this lemma.
3. Let $\beta \prec \alpha$ and $\gamma \in Arg$ such that γ attacks β. Therefore γ attacks α. Hence there is $\sigma \in B$ attacking γ.
4. Follows directly from item 3 of this lemma.

Proof of lemma 3.2

The monotonicity of $\mathcal{F}_{AF}(X)$ wrt set inclusion is obvious.

1. We show that $\mathcal{F}_{AF}(X)$ is indeed a function from $\mathcal{C}_{\mathcal{NR}}$ into $\mathcal{C}$ such that $\mathcal{F}_{AF}(X) \cap \mathcal{NR} = X$ by showing that $\mathcal{F}_{AF}(X)$ is a complete extension in $\langle AF, att \rangle$ if X is a complete extension in $\langle \mathcal{NR}, att_{\mathcal{NR}} \rangle$.

   Let X be a complete extension in $\langle \mathcal{NR}, att_{\mathcal{NR}} \rangle$. Hence, by lemma 3.1, item 2, X is admissible in $\langle AF, att \rangle$. Further, by lemma 3.1, item 4, for each $\alpha \in \mathcal{F}_{AF}(X)$, each "non-redundant version of α" is acceptable wrt X in $\langle \mathcal{NR}, att_{\mathcal{NR}} \rangle$. Thus, as X is complete in $\langle \mathcal{NR}, att_{\mathcal{NR}} \rangle$, each "non-redundant version of α" belongs to X. Therefore, $(\mathcal{F}_{AF}(X) - X) \cap \mathcal{NR} = \emptyset$. Hence $\mathcal{F}_{AF}(X) \cap \mathcal{NR} = X$.

   To prove that $\mathcal{F}_{AF}(X)$ is a complete extension, let β be acceptable wrt $\mathcal{F}_{AF}(X)$ and let γ attack β. Hence, there is $\sigma \in \mathcal{F}_{AF}(X)$ attacking γ. Hence, any "non-redundant version of σ" is in X and attacking γ. Hence, X attacks γ. Thus, β is acceptable wrt X, and therefore $\beta \in \mathcal{F}_{AF}(X)$. As a consequence, $\mathcal{F}_{AF}(X)$ is complete.

2. Let C be a complete extension in $\langle AF, att \rangle$. We show that $C' = C \cap \mathcal{NR}$ is complete in $\langle \mathcal{NR}, att_{\mathcal{NR}} \rangle$. From lemma 3.1, item 3, and the fact that C is complete in $\langle AF, att \rangle$, each "non-redundant version of arguments" in C belongs to C.

   Let $\gamma \in \mathcal{NR}$ attack C'. Hence, there is $\alpha \in C$ attacking γ. Let α' be a "non-redundant version of α". Therefore, $\alpha' \in C'$. Hence, α' attacks γ. Hence C' is admissible. Each non-redundant argument acceptable wrt C' is acceptable wrt C and hence belongs to C and hence to C'. C' is therefore complete.

   As $C' \subseteq C$, it is clear that $\mathcal{F}_{AF}(C') \subseteq \mathcal{F}_{AF}(C) = C$. We show now that each argument acceptable wrt C is also acceptable wrt C'. Let β be an argument acceptable wrt C in $\langle AF, att \rangle$ and let σ be an argument attacking β. Hence, there is an argument $\delta \in C$ attacking σ. Hence, there is a "non-redundant version" $\delta' \in C$ of δ attacking σ. Hence C' attacks σ. Thus β is acceptable wrt C' in $\langle AF, att \rangle$. We have shown that $\mathcal{F}_{AF}(C') \supseteq \mathcal{F}_{AF}(C) = C$, i.e. $\mathcal{F}_{AF}(C \cap \mathcal{NR}) = C$.

Proof of theorem 3.1

Let $\mathcal{C}$ and $\mathcal{C}_{\mathcal{NR}}$ be the sets of complete extensions of $\langle Arg, att \rangle$ and $\langle \mathcal{NR}, att_{\mathcal{NR}} \rangle$, respectively.

From lemma 3.2, it follows immediately that for each $X \in \mathcal{C}_{\mathcal{NR}}$, $\mathcal{F}_{AF}(X)$ is minimal or maximal wrt set inclusion in $\mathcal{C}$ iff X is minimal or maximal respectively in $\mathcal{C}_{\mathcal{NR}}$. Hence X is grounded or preferred in $\langle \mathcal{NR}, att_{\mathcal{NR}} \rangle$ iff $\mathcal{F}_{AF}(X)$ is grounded or preferred in $\langle Arg, att \rangle$, respectively.

Similarly, X is contained in every preferred extension of $\langle \mathcal{NR}, att_{\mathcal{NR}} \rangle$ iff $\mathcal{F}_{AF}(X)$ is contained in every preferred extension of $\langle Arg, att \rangle$. Hence X is ideal in $\langle \mathcal{NR}, att_{\mathcal{NR}} \rangle$ iff $\mathcal{F}_{AF}(X)$ is ideal in $\langle Arg, att \rangle$.

Computational Models of Argument
P. Baroni et al. (Eds.)
IOS Press, 2010
doi:10.3233/978-1-60750-619-5-195

Tractability in Value-based Argumentation

Paul E. DUNNE

Department of Computer Science, The University of Liverpool, U.K.

Abstract. Value-based argumentation frameworks (VAFs) have proven to
be a useful development of Dung's seminal model of argumentation in
providing a rational basis for distinguishing mutually incompatible yet
individually acceptable sets of arguments. In classifying argument status within value-based frameworks two main decision problems arise:
subjective acceptance (SBA) and *objective acceptance* (OBA). These problems have proven to be somewhat resistant to efficient algorithmic approaches (the general cases being NP–complete and coNP–complete) even
when very severe limitations are placed on the structure of the supporting Dung-style framework. Although using the number of *values*
(k) represented within a given VAF leads to fixed parameter tractable
(FPT) methods, these are not entirely satisfactory: the rate of growth
of the parameter function ($k!$) making such methods unacceptable in
cases where k is moderately large, e.g. $k \geq 20$. In this paper we consider
an alternative approach to the development of practical algorithms in
value-based argumentation. In particular cases this leads to polynomial
(in $|\mathcal{X}|$) methods, i.e. *irrespective of the value of k*. More general exam-
ples are shown to be decidable in $O(f(k)|\mathcal{X}|^2)$ steps where $f(k) = o(k!)$
resulting in worst-case run times that significantly improve upon enumerating all value orderings.

Keywords. Computational properties of argumentation; value-based
argumentation frameworks; subjective and objective acceptance;

Introduction

The standard argumentation framework (AF) approach of Dung [8] models argu-
mentation via a directed graph, $\langle \mathcal{X}, \mathcal{A} \rangle$, wherein $\mathcal{X}$ is a finite set of atomic *arguments* and $\mathcal{A} \subseteq \mathcal{X} \times \mathcal{X}$ defines the *attack* relation over these: thus $\langle x, y \rangle \in \mathcal{A}$ (read
as "x attacks y") provides an abstract representation of the property that the
arguments x and y are incompatible. Dung's model has been augmented to the
concept of *value-based* argumentation frameworks (VAF) by Bench-Capon [2] so
that the structure $\langle \mathcal{X}, \mathcal{A} \rangle$ becomes $\langle \mathcal{X}, \mathcal{A}, \mathcal{V}, \eta \rangle$. Here $\mathcal{V}$ is a finite set of k abstract
values[1] and $\eta : \mathcal{X} \to \mathcal{V}$ associates each argument with the value underlying it.

Although VAFs provide a number of powerful semantic benefits, as discussed
in [3], [4], there are non-trivial computational problems. In particular, the fact

---

[1]The notion of "value" is qualitative – describing, e.g, ethical, social, political, etc. values –
rather than quantitative.

that the two important decision questions in VAFs – subjective (SBA) and objective (OBA) acceptance – concern properties of *orderings* of $\mathcal{V}$, as opposed to properties of *subsets* of $\mathcal{X}$ has been shown to raise significant algorithmic issues. While restricting the structure of $\langle \mathcal{X}, \mathcal{A} \rangle$ by various means is known to lead to efficient methods for all of the semantics proposed within Dung's model, similar restrictions have proven less effective within VAFs. Thus it is known that requiring $\langle \mathcal{X}, \mathcal{A} \rangle$ to be *acyclic* or *symmetric* or *bipartite* suffices to yield polynomial time decision methods as shown in Dung [8], Coste-Marquis *et al.* [6], and Dunne [9]. In contrast even if $\langle \mathcal{X}, \mathcal{A} \rangle$ is a binary tree (a subset of those frameworks that are both bipartite and acyclic) no reduction in complexity results [9].

Of course within the framework of *fixed parameter tractable* (FPT) methods, [7], it would appear that VAF computations are efficiently dealt with: problems are computable in $O(k!|\mathcal{X}|)$ steps so that both SBA and OBA are fixed parameter tractable with respect to the parameter $k = |\mathcal{V}|$. Such an approach – enumerate all possible value orderings, testing each in turn for the property of interest – fails, however, to be entirely satisfactory. This is not (solely) on account of the $k!$ growth rate for the parameter function - many feasible FPT methods involve significantly faster growing functions – but rather because the parameter itself ($|\mathcal{V}|$) may, in many cases, be moderately large. Ideally, FPT methods exploit parameters whose value is small in typical instances. In contrast there are natural settings of VAFs in which $|\mathcal{V}| \geq 15$ rendering algorithms with $15!|\mathcal{X}|$ steps unreasonable.

Our aim in this paper is to consider the following questions.

A. Are there classes of VAF, in addition to systems in which $\langle \mathcal{X}, \mathcal{A} \rangle$ is symmetric, for which SBA and OBA are polynomial time decidable (in $|\mathcal{X}|$) irrespective of $|\mathcal{V}|$?

B. To what extent can the $k!$ term be improved (possibly by limiting the structure of $\langle \mathcal{X}, \mathcal{A}, \mathcal{V}, \eta \rangle$) to yield FPT methods with run-time $O(f(k)|\mathcal{X}|^r)$ (where r is some small constant) and $f(k)$ is significantly smaller than $k!$?

We obtain positive answers to both questions. In particular we describe a general category of restricted forms for $\langle \mathcal{X}, \mathcal{A}, \mathcal{V}, \eta \rangle$ and algorithms on these having run-time $O(k|\mathcal{X}|^2)$ for both of the principal decision questions. We further describe approaches guaranteeing worst-case run-time of $O(2^{ck} \times |\mathcal{X}|^2)$, where $c \leq 1$ is constant. Although 2^{ck} still imposes unrealistic requirements for very large numbers of values, it compares favourably with, and significantly improves upon, $k!$ (which is asymptotically $2^{O(k \log k)}$).

An important feature of the conditions leading to improved methods is that these combine structural restrictions on $\langle \mathcal{X}, \mathcal{A} \rangle$ *together with* restrictions on the *mapping* $\eta : \mathcal{X} \to \mathcal{V}$. In other words, the class of systems are not defined using purely graph-theoretic forms of the type analysed in [9].

We review background concepts in Section 1 and in Section 2 describe the main results of this paper, introducing the concept of *value graphs* in Sect. 2.1 and showing how, under certain conditions, these lead to polynomial time methods in Section 2.2. The properties of value graphs and the cases considered in Section 2.2 motivate consideration of the extent to which such improvements may result for more general classes of value graph. We consider natural developments of this type in Section 3. Conclusions are given in Section 4. Full proofs are omitted, however, these may be found in [11].

1. Preliminaries: AFs and VAFs

The following concepts were introduced in Dung [8].

Definition 1 *An* argumentation framework *(AF) is a pair* $\mathcal{H} = \langle \mathcal{X}, \mathcal{A} \rangle$*, in which* $\mathcal{X}$ *is a finite set of* arguments *and* $\mathcal{A} \subseteq \mathcal{X} \times \mathcal{X}$ *is the* attack relationship *for* $\mathcal{H}$*. A pair* $\langle x, y \rangle \in \mathcal{A}$ *is referred to as 'y is attacked by x' or 'x attacks y'.* $x \in \mathcal{X}$ *is* acceptable *with respect to* S *if for every* $y \in \mathcal{X}$ *that attacks* x *there is some* $z \in S$ *that attacks* y*;* S *is* conflict-free *if no argument in* S *is attacked by any other argument in* S*. A conflict-free set* S *is* admissible *if every* $y \in S$ *is acceptable w.r.t* S*;* S *is a* preferred extension *if it is a maximal (with respect to* $\subseteq$*) admissible set; An argument* x *is* credulously accepted *if there is some preferred extension containing it;* x *is* sceptically accepted *if it is a member of every preferred extension.*

Bench-Capon [2] develops the concept of "attack" from Dung's model to take account of values.

Definition 2 *A* value-based argumentation framework *(VAF), is defined by a triple* $\mathcal{H}^{(V)} = \langle \mathcal{H}(\mathcal{X}, \mathcal{A}), \mathcal{V}, \eta \rangle$*, where* $\mathcal{H}(\mathcal{X}, \mathcal{A})$ *is an* AF*,* $\mathcal{V} = \{v_1, v_2, \ldots, v_k\}$ *a set of* k values*, and* $\eta : \mathcal{X} \rightarrow \mathcal{V}$ *a mapping that associates a value* $\eta(x) \in \mathcal{V}$ *with each argument* $x \in \mathcal{X}$*. An* audience *for a VAF* $\langle \mathcal{X}, \mathcal{A}, \mathcal{V}, \eta \rangle$*, is a binary relation* $\mathcal{R} \subset \mathcal{V} \times \mathcal{V}$ *whose (irreflexive) transitive closure,* $\mathcal{R}^*$*, is asymmetric, i.e. at most one of* $\langle v, v' \rangle$*,* $\langle v', v \rangle$ *are members of* $\mathcal{R}^*$ *for any distinct* v*,* $v' \in \mathcal{V}$*. We say that* v_i *is preferred to* v_j *in the audience* $\mathcal{R}$*, denoted* $v_i \succ_{\mathcal{R}} v_j$*, if* $\langle v_i, v_j \rangle \in \mathcal{R}^*$*. We say that* α *is a* specific audience *if* α *yields a total ordering of* $\mathcal{V}$*. The notation* $\mathcal{U}$ *is used for the set of all specific audiences over* $\mathcal{V}$*.*

A standard assumption from [2] which we retain in our subsequent development is the following:
Multivalued Cycles Assumption (MCA)
For any *simple cycle* of arguments in a VAF, $\langle \mathcal{X}, \mathcal{A}, \mathcal{V}, \eta \rangle$, – i.e. a finite sequence of arguments $y_1 y_2 \ldots y_i y_{i+1} \ldots y_r$ with $y_1 = y_r$, $|\{y_1, \ldots, y_{r-1}\}| = r - 1$, and $\langle y_j, y_{j+1} \rangle \in \mathcal{A}$ for each $1 \leq j < r$ – there are arguments y_i and y_j for which $\eta(y_i) \neq \eta(y_j)$.

In less formal terms, this assumption states every simple cycle in $\mathcal{H}^{(V)}$ uses at least two distinct values.

Using VAFs, ideas analogous to those introduced in Defn. 1 are given by relativising the concept of "attack" using that of *successful* attack with respect to an audience. Thus,

Definition 3 *Let* $\langle \mathcal{X}, \mathcal{A}, \mathcal{V}, \eta \rangle$ *be a VAF and* $\mathcal{R}$ *an audience. For arguments* x*,* y *in* $\mathcal{X}$*,* x *is a* successful attack *on* y *(or* x defeats y*) with respect to the audience* $\mathcal{R}$ *if:* $\langle x, y \rangle \in \mathcal{A}$ *and it is not the case that* $\eta(y) \succ_{\mathcal{R}} \eta(x)$*.*

Replacing "attack" by "successful attack w.r.t. the audience $\mathcal{R}$", in Defn. 1 yields definitions of "conflict-free", "admissible set" etc. relating to value-based systems, e.g. S is conflict–free w.r.t. to the audience $\mathcal{R}$ if for each x, y in S it is not the case that x successfully attacks y w.r.t. $\mathcal{R}$. It may be noted that a conflict-free set in this sense is not necessarily a conflict-free set in the sense of Defn. 1: for x and y in S we may have $\langle x, y \rangle \in \mathcal{A}$, provided that $\eta(y) \succ_{\mathcal{R}} \eta(x)$, i.e. the value promoted by y is preferred to that promoted by x for the audience $\mathcal{R}$.

Bench-Capon [2] proves that every specific audience, α, induces a unique preferred extension within its underlying VAF: for a given VAF, $\mathcal{H}^{(\mathcal{V})}$, we use $P(\mathcal{H}^{(\mathcal{V})}, \alpha)$ to denote this extension: that $P(\mathcal{H}^{(\mathcal{V})}, \alpha)$ is unique and can be constructed efficiently, is an easy consequence of the following fact, implicit in [2].

Fact 1 For any VAF, $\mathcal{H}^{(\mathcal{V})}(\langle \mathcal{X}, \mathcal{A}, \mathcal{V}, \eta \rangle)$ (satisfying MCA) and specific audience α, the framework induced by including only attacks in the set $\mathcal{B} = \mathcal{A} \setminus \{\langle x, y \rangle : \eta(y) \succ_{\alpha} \eta(x)\}$ is acyclic.

Analogous to the concepts of credulous and sceptical acceptance, in VAFs the ideas of *subjective* and *objective* acceptance arise.

Subjective Acceptance (SBA)
Instance: $\mathcal{H}(\mathcal{X}, \mathcal{A}, \mathcal{V}, \eta)$ and $x \in \mathcal{X}$.
Question: Is there a specific audience, α, for which $x \in P(\langle \mathcal{X}, \mathcal{A}, \mathcal{V}, \eta \rangle, \alpha)$?
Objective Acceptance (OBA)
Instance: $\mathcal{H}(\mathcal{X}, \mathcal{A}, \mathcal{V}, \eta)$ and $x \in \mathcal{X}$.
Question: Is $x \in P(\langle \mathcal{X}, \mathcal{A}, \mathcal{V}, \eta \rangle, \alpha)$ for *every* specific audience α?

The complexity of SBA (NP–complete) and OBA (coNP–complete) is known to be unchanged under quite extreme restrictions on the form of instances as shown in Dunne [9].

2. Algorithms for Subjective and Objective Acceptance

We now describe a general approach by which improvements to the $O(k!|\mathcal{X}|)$ upper bounds on SBA and OBA may be obtained. Underpinning these is the concept of the *value graph* obtained from a VAF. We describe these and their role in algorithms for the decision problems of interest in Section 2.1. In certain cases value graphs allow the set, $\mathcal{U}$, of all specific audiences to be treated in terms of a partition resulting from, what we term, the set of *relevant audiences* with respect to a particular value. Thus, instead of the $k!$ coefficient qualifying algorithmic behaviour, the number of distinct relevant audiences becomes the important factor. In Section 2.2 we establish some upper bounds on this for some special classes of value graph.

2.1. Value graphs

Given $\mathcal{H}^{(\mathcal{V})}(\mathcal{X}, \mathcal{A}, \mathcal{V}, \eta)$ the *value graph* of $\mathcal{H}^{(\mathcal{V})}$, denoted $\mathcal{G}_{\mathcal{H}}(\mathcal{V}, \mathcal{B})$, is the *directed* graph with vertices $\mathcal{V}$ and edges

$$\mathcal{B} = \{\langle v_i, v_j \rangle : \exists \langle x, y \rangle \in \mathcal{A} \text{ s.t. } \eta(x) = v_i \text{ and } \eta(y) = v_j\} \setminus \{\langle v_i, v_i \rangle : v_i \in \mathcal{V}\}$$

It should be noted that value graphs exclude so-called self-loops, i.e. directed edges of the form $\langle x, x \rangle$, although in general there will be attacks involving arguments with the same value. To simplify the notation, where no ambiguity arises, we omit the subscript $\mathcal{H}$ and write $\mathcal{G}(\mathcal{V}, \mathcal{B})$.

The idea behind our improved algorithms is to consider structural properties of the *value graph* rather than structural properties of the Dung-style framework described by $\langle \mathcal{X}, \mathcal{A} \rangle$: in view of [9] the latter approach appears unpromising.

Before introducing these forms, it will be helpful to introduce the following notation which aids in relating properties of value graphs to properties of subsets of arguments in $\langle \mathcal{X}, \mathcal{A}, \mathcal{V}, \eta \rangle$.

Definition 4 *Given* $\langle \mathcal{X}, \mathcal{A}, \mathcal{V}, \eta \rangle$ *with* $\mathcal{V} = \{v_1, v_2, \ldots, v_k\}$, *the* AF *induced by* v_j, *denoted* $\mathcal{H}_j(\mathcal{X}_j, \mathcal{A}_j)$ *has* $\mathcal{X}_j = \{ x \in \mathcal{X} : \eta(x) = v_j \}$ *and* $\mathcal{A}_j = \{\langle x, y \rangle : \eta(x) = \eta(y) = v_j\} \cap \mathcal{A}$. *More generally, the* AF *induced by a subset,* W *of* $\mathcal{V} - \mathcal{H}_W(\mathcal{X}_W, \mathcal{A}_W)$ *has*

$$\mathcal{X}_W = \{x \in \mathcal{X} : \eta(x) \in W\}$$
$$\mathcal{A}_W = \{\langle x, y \rangle : \{\eta(x), \eta(y)\} \subseteq W\} \cap \mathcal{A}$$

The two principal forms of value graph we consider are *strict trees* and *chains* the latter being a subclass of the former.

Definition 5 *A value graph,* $\mathcal{G}(\mathcal{V}, \mathcal{B})$ *is a* strict tree *if the undirected graph formed by replacing each directed edge* $\langle v_i, v_j \rangle$ *with the undirected edge* $\{v_i, v_j\}$ *is acyclic, i.e. defines a tree. A value graph,* $\mathcal{G}(\mathcal{V}, \mathcal{B})$ *is a* chain *if it satisfies:*

a. $\mathcal{G}(\mathcal{V}, \mathcal{B})$ *is a strict tree.*
b. *The undirected graph resulting from* $\mathcal{G}(\mathcal{V}, \mathcal{B})$ *(as described in Defn. 5) forms a simple path joining all vertices in* $\mathcal{V}$.

Figure 1 gives examples of strict trees and chains defined over the value set $\mathcal{V} = \{A, B, C, D, E, F\}$. For a vertex v in a strict tree the set of vertices

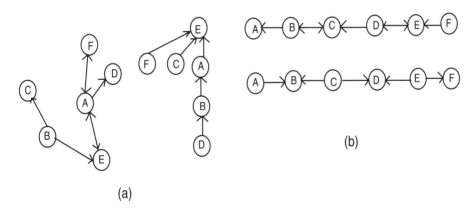

Figure 1. (a) Strict tree examples. (b) Two Chain graphs.

$\{ w_i : \langle w_i, v \rangle \in \mathcal{B}\}$ are referred to as the *children* of v (similarly v is called the *parent* of w_i). The notation $ch(v)$ will be used for the set of children of v and $par(w)$ for the parent of w.

The *sub-tree* of $\mathcal{G}$ *rooted at* v, denoted $\langle W_v, F_v \rangle$, is recursively defined by:

a. If v has no children, i.e. $ch(v) = \emptyset$, then $W_v = \{v\}$ and $F_v = \emptyset$.

b. Otherwise, let $ch(v) = \{w_1, \ldots, w_r\}$. In this case,

$$W_v = \{v\} \cup \bigcup_{u \in ch(v)} W_u \quad ; \quad F_v = \bigcup_{u \in ch(v)} \{\langle u, v \rangle\} \cup F_u$$

The *height* of $w \in \langle W_v, F_v \rangle$ is denoted $ht(v)$. This is defined to be 0 when $ch(v) = \emptyset$ and $1 + \max_{w \in ch(v)} ht(w)$ otherwise.

We note the following, easily proven, property of the sub-tree $\langle W_v, F_v \rangle$ arising from the strict tree $\mathcal{G}(\mathcal{V}, \mathcal{B})$: given a value graph, $\mathcal{G}(\mathcal{V}, \mathcal{B})$ defining a strict tree, the sub-tree rooted at v induces a partial order, $\sqsubseteq_F$ over W_v defined via $v_i \sqsubseteq_F v_j$ if $i = j$ or there is a sequence $v_i = v_0 v_1 \cdots v_r = v_j$ of *distinct* values such that $\langle v_t, v_{t+1} \rangle \in F_v$ for each $0 \le t < r$.

Let μ_F denote the set of *minimal* elements in this partial order. The second example from Fig 1(a) gives rise to the partial order

$$C \sqsubseteq E \quad ; \quad D \sqsubseteq B \sqsubseteq A \sqsubseteq E \quad ; \quad F \sqsubseteq E$$

With the sets of minimal elements being $\{C, D, F\}$

It is not hard to show that,

a. $w \in W_v$ if and only if $w \sqsubseteq_F v$.

b. The root vertex v is the unique maximal element w.r.t. $\sqsubseteq_F$ among the vertices W_v.

c. If w is not the root vertex than $par(w)$ contains exactly one vertex (in $\langle W_v, F_v \rangle$), otherwise $par(w) = \emptyset$.

Finally we note the following important property of (strict) trees: given any $u \in W_v$ there is a unique sequence, $\delta(u, v)$, of *distinct* directed edges in F_v with

$$\delta(u, v) = \langle u, u_1 \rangle \cdot \langle u_1, u_2 \rangle \cdot \langle u_2, u_3 \rangle \cdots \langle u_{r-1}, u_r \rangle \cdot \langle u_r, v \rangle$$

That is, there is a unique path from u to v within F_v. When $u = v$ this is the empty sequence.

A key idea underpinning our improved algorithms is the concept of the set of *relevant audiences* for a sub-tree rooted at v. We give the definition below and discuss its application subsequently.

Definition 6 *Let* $\langle W_v, F_v \rangle$ *be the sub-tree rooted at* v *of a strict tree* $\mathcal{G}(\mathcal{V}, \mathcal{B})$. *Let* $R \subseteq \mathcal{V} \times \mathcal{V}$ *be an audience. We say that R is* relevant *with respect to* v *if*

$$p \succ_R q \implies \langle q, p \rangle \in F_v \quad and \quad \forall \langle x, y \rangle \in W_q \times W_q \; \neg(x \succ_{R^*} y)$$

The strict tree induced in $\langle W_v, F_v \rangle$ *by* R, *denoted* $\langle \mathcal{V}_R, \mathcal{E}_R \rangle$, *has*

$$\mathcal{V}_R = \{ u \in W_v : \forall \langle p, q \rangle \in \delta(u, v) \; \neg(q \succ_R p) \}$$

$$\mathcal{E}_R = F_v \cap \{\langle p, q \rangle : p \in \mathcal{V}_R, q \in \mathcal{V}_R\}$$

Informally, the concept of "relevant audience" w.r.t. v *captures the idea that, as regards determining the acceptability status of arguments,* x *having* $\eta(x) = v$, *instead of considering all $k!$ specific audiences we can associate each such audience* *with exactly one relevant audience. Thus, it will suffice to consider acceptability status w.r.t relevant audiences only.*

For $w \in \mathcal{V}_R$ of the strict tree induced by R, we use $ch(w, R)$ to denote the set of children of w in the strict tree $\langle \mathcal{V}_R, \mathcal{E}_R \rangle$, i.e.

$$ch(w, R) \ = \ \{ u \ : \ \langle u, w \rangle \in \mathcal{E}_R \}$$

We note that $ch(w, R)$ while always a subset of $ch(w)$, the children of w in the strict tree $\langle W_v, F_v \rangle$, the containment may be proper. The height *of w in $\langle \mathcal{V}_R, \mathcal{E}_R \rangle$, $ht(w, R)$, is defined as*

$$ht(w, R) \ = \ \begin{cases} 0 & \text{if } ch(w, R) = \emptyset \\ 1 + \max_{u \in ch(w,R)} \ ht(u, R) & \text{otherwise} \end{cases}$$

For example, in the case of the first example from Fig. 1(a) there are exactly 6 relevant audiences with respect to E. These are shown in Fig. 2

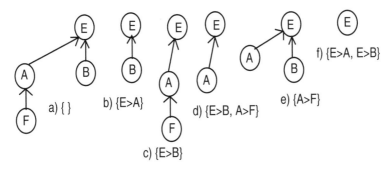

Figure 2. Strict trees induced by relevant audiences

Notice that the values C and D do not appear in these: for this value graph, arguments whose value is C are only attacked by those whose value is B; similarly those whose value is D are only attacked by those with value A. Among the relevant audiences w.r.t E, however, the status of arguments with value E is unaffected whether $B \succ C$ or $C \succ B$ (hence the the ordering of these values is not *relevant* to the status of arguments with value E).

For a value $v \in \mathcal{V}$ we denote by $\mathcal{R}_v$ the set of relevant audiences with respect to v, i.e.

$$\mathcal{R}_v \ = \ \{ R \subset W_v \times W_v \ : \ R \text{ is relevant w.r.t. } v \}$$

Given $R \in \mathcal{R}_v$ with $\langle \mathcal{V}_R, \mathcal{E}_R \rangle$ the strict tree induced in $\langle W_v, F_v \rangle$ by R we define the *framework associated with R*, denoted $\langle \mathcal{Z}_R, \mathcal{D}_R \rangle$, as the AF with

$$\mathcal{Z}_R \ = \ \bigcup_{w \in \mathcal{V}_R} \{ x \ : \ \eta(x) = w \}$$

$$\mathcal{D}_R \ = \ (\mathcal{A} \cap \{ \langle x, y \rangle \ : \ x \in \mathcal{Z}_R, \ y \in \mathcal{Z}_R \}) \setminus \{ \langle x, y \rangle \ : \ \eta(y) \succ_R \eta(x) \}$$

It may be noted that $\langle \mathcal{Z}_R, \mathcal{D}_R \rangle$ is a *sub-graph* of AF induced by $\mathcal{V}_R$.

Lemma 1 *Let* $\mathcal{H}^{(\mathcal{V})}(\mathcal{X}, \mathcal{A}, \mathcal{V}, \eta)$ *be a* VAF *whose value graph,* $\mathcal{G}(\mathcal{V}, \mathcal{B})$ *defines a strict tree. For every* $v \in \mathcal{V}$ *and every* $R \in \mathcal{R}_v$ *the framework,* $\langle \mathcal{Z}_R, \mathcal{D}_R \rangle$*, associated with* R *is acyclic and has a unique preferred extension,* $P(\mathcal{Z}_R, \mathcal{D}_R) \neq \emptyset$.

Definition 7 *Let* R *be a relevant audience w.r.t.* v *in* $\langle W_v, F_v \rangle$*, and* $\langle \mathcal{V}_R, \mathcal{E}_R \rangle$ *the strict tree induced by* R*. A specific audience,* α*, is said to be* R*-compatible if*

S1. $\forall \langle p, q \rangle \in \mathcal{E}_R \quad p \succ_\alpha q$.
S2. $\forall \langle p, q \rangle \in F_v \quad (q \succ_R p) \quad \Rightarrow \quad (q \succ_\alpha p)$

We denote by $\chi(R, v)$ *the set of specific audiences that are* R*-compatible.*

   For α *a specific audience, we say that a relevant audience w.r.t.* v *is* α*-compatible if*

R1. $\forall \langle p, q \rangle \in F_v \quad (q \succ_\alpha p) \quad \Rightarrow \quad q \succ_R p \quad$ *and* $\forall \langle x, y \rangle \in W_p \times W_p \; \neg(x \succ_{R^*} y)$
R2. $\forall \langle p, q \rangle \in \mathcal{E}_R \; p \succ_\alpha q$.

   We use $\rho(\alpha, v)$ *to denote the set of relevant audiences w.r.t.* v *that are* α*-compatible.*

It is straightforward to show $\forall \alpha \in \mathcal{U}, \; \forall R \in \mathcal{R}_v \; \alpha \in \chi(R, v) \Leftrightarrow R \in \rho(\alpha, v)$.

For example, for the cases illustrate in Fig. 2, of the 120 specific audiences over $\mathcal{V} = \{A, B, C, D, E, F\}$ those compatible with the (relevant) audience $\{E \succ A, E \succ B\}$ of Fig. 2(f) include $\{C \succ E \succ D \succ B \succ A \succ F\}$. The specific audience $A \succ E \succ B \succ F \succ C \succ D$ fails to be compatible with $\{E \succ A, E \succ B\}$ (due to the conflicting ordering of E and A): this specific audience is, however, compatible with the relevant audience $\{E \succ B, A \succ F\}$ of Fig. 2(d).

We need two key properties of the set of relevant audiences w.r.t. v to obtain improved algorithms. The first – Thm. 1 – shows that $\mathcal{R}_v$ induces a partition of $\mathcal{U}$; the second, presented in Thm. 2, establishes that it suffices to consider only the *partial* (i.e. not specific) audiences represented in $\mathcal{R}_v$ when considering acceptance properties of arguments with value v.

Theorem 1 *For* $\langle W_v, F_v \rangle$ *the sub-tree of* $\mathcal{G}(\mathcal{V}, \mathcal{B})$ *with root* $v \in \mathcal{V}$*, the set of relevant audiences w.r.t.* v*,* $\mathcal{R}_v$*, satisfies all of the following properties:*

   a. $\forall R \in \mathcal{R}_v \; \chi(R, v) \neq \emptyset$*, i.e. there is at least* *one* R*-compatible specific audience for each* $R \in \mathcal{R}_v$*.*
   b. *For every* $\alpha \in \mathcal{U}$ *there is some* $R \in \mathcal{R}_v$ *for which* α *is* R*-compatible. Formally* $\bigcup_{R \in \mathcal{R}_v} \chi(R, v) = \mathcal{U}$*.*
   c. *Given* R *and* S *in* $\mathcal{R}_v$*, the sets of* R*-compatible specific audiences are disjoint from the set of* S*-compatible specific audiences, i.e.* $\forall R, S \in \mathcal{R}_v \; \chi(R, v) \cap \chi(S, v) \neq \emptyset \Leftrightarrow R = S$*.*
   d. *For all strict trees* $\langle W_v, F_v \rangle$*,* $\mathcal{R}_v$*, the set of relevant audiences w.r.t.* v *satisfies,* $R \in \mathcal{R}_v$ *if and only if there is some subset* $S = \{s_1, s_2, \ldots, s_q\}$ *of* $ch(v)$ *and, for each* $s_i \in S$*, a relevant audience,* $S_i \in \mathcal{R}_{s_i}$ *w.r.t. to* s_i *in* $\langle W_{s_i}, F_{s_i} \rangle$ *so that*

$$R = \bigcup_{i=1}^{q} S_i \; \cup \bigcup_{t \in ch(v) \setminus S} \{v \succ_R t\}$$

Corollary 1 *Given* $\mathcal{H}^{(\mathcal{V})}(\mathcal{X}, \mathcal{A}, \mathcal{V}, \eta)$ *whose value graph is a strict tree, let* $\langle W_v, F_v \rangle$ *be the sub-tree with root* v. *For all specific audiences,* α, $\rho(\alpha, v)$ *contains* exactly *one* relevant audience w.r.t. v.

Recalling that $\langle \mathcal{X}_v, \mathcal{A}_v \rangle$ is the AF induced by arguments with value v, we now establish the second key property of relevant audiences w.r.t. v.

Theorem 2 *For all* $v \in \mathcal{V}$, $R \in \mathcal{R}_v$ *and* $\alpha \in \chi(R, v)$

$$\mathcal{X}_v \cap P(\mathcal{Z}_R, \mathcal{D}_R) = \mathcal{X}_v \cap P(\mathcal{H}^{(\mathcal{V})}, \alpha).$$

Proof: (Outline) The proof is by induction on $ht(v)$, to prove $Q(t)$, where $Q(t)$ is the statement "*If* $ht(v) = t$ *then for all* $R \in \mathcal{R}_v$ *and* $\alpha \in \chi(R, v)$, $\mathcal{X}_v \cap P(\mathcal{Z}_R, \mathcal{D}_R) = \mathcal{X}_v \cap P(\mathcal{H}^{(\mathcal{V})}, \alpha)$" We omit the detailed argument.   □

Corollary 2 *Let* $\mathcal{H}^{(\mathcal{V})}(\mathcal{X}, \mathcal{A}, \mathcal{V}, \eta)$ *be a* VAF *whose value graph defines a strict tree. Let* $x \in \mathcal{X}$ *be any argument and* $\eta(x) = v \in \mathcal{V}$.

   a. SBA$(\mathcal{H}^{(\mathcal{V})}, x)$ *if and only if there exists some* $R \in \mathcal{R}_v$, *i.e. a relevant audience with respect to* $\eta(x)$, *for which* $x \in P(\mathcal{Z}_R, \mathcal{D}_R)$
   b. OBA$(\mathcal{H}^{(\mathcal{V})}, x)$ *if and only if for every,* $R \in \mathcal{R}_v$, $x \in P(\mathcal{Z}_R, \mathcal{D}_R)$.

Hence, given $\mathcal{H}^{(\mathcal{V})}(\mathcal{X}, \mathcal{A}, \mathcal{V}, \eta)$ meeting the conditions of Corollary 2, one can determine if $x \in \mathcal{X}$ with $\eta(x) = v$ is subjectively (resp. objectively) accepted as follows: form the value graph $\langle W_v, F_v \rangle$ rooted at v; determine the set $\mathcal{R}_v$ of relevant audiences w.r.t. the value v; for each $R \in \mathcal{R}_v$, form the AF, $\langle \mathcal{Z}_R, \mathcal{D}_R \rangle$, associated with R (this being *acyclic*); test if $x \in P(\mathcal{Z}_R, \mathcal{D}_R)$. If this test is positive for some (resp. every) $R \in \mathcal{R}_v$ then x is subjectively (resp. objectively) accepted.

In total, Thms. 1, 2 and Corollary 2 suggest the approach of Algorithm 1 for deciding SBA and OBA. in which each $v \in \mathcal{V}$ is assigned a label (called its *orientation level*) denoted $\omega(v)$. We note that as a consequence of Thm. 1(d), the set of relevant audiences – $\mathcal{R}_w$ – required in l. 20 of Algorithm 1 is easily determined from the sets $\mathcal{R}_t$ for $t \in ch(w)$: these need only be determined *once*.

The run-time of Algorithm 1 is bounded above by $O(|\mathcal{R}_v| \times |\mathcal{X}|)$. Hence in structures for which $|\mathcal{R}_v|$ can be guaranteed to be polynomial in $|\mathcal{V}|$, Algorithm 1 provides a polynomial time decision process.

2.2. Bounding the number of relevant audiences

In this section we consider the behaviour of the function $r : \langle \mathcal{X}, \mathcal{A}, \mathcal{V}, \eta \rangle \rightarrow \mathbb{N}$ with $|\mathcal{V}| = k$, $\mathcal{G}(\mathcal{V}, \mathcal{B})$ defining a strict tree, and

$$r(\langle \mathcal{X}, \mathcal{A}, \mathcal{V}, \eta \rangle) = \max_{v \in \mathcal{V}} |\mathcal{R}_v|$$

In terms of Algorithm 1, we obtain algorithms with run-time $O(r(\langle \mathcal{X}, \mathcal{A}, \mathcal{V}, \eta \rangle)|\mathcal{X}|^2)$. We first show that when the value graph is a strict tree we always obtain an improvement on k!

Lemma 2 *For any* VAF *whose value graph is a strict tree,* $r(\langle \mathcal{X}, \mathcal{A}, \mathcal{V}, \eta \rangle) \leq 2^{k-1}$.

Algorithm 1 Deciding argument status in strict tree VAFs

1: **function** STATUS($\langle \mathcal{X}, \mathcal{A}, \mathcal{V}, \eta \rangle$, $x \in \mathcal{X}$)
2:     $\langle W_{\eta(x)}, F_{\eta(x)} \rangle := $ strict tree with root $\eta(x)$
3:     **for** $v \in \mu_F$ **do**
4:         $\omega(v) := 0$
5:     **end for**
6:     **for** $v \in \mathcal{V} \setminus \mu_F$ **do**
7:         $\omega(v) := \perp$
8:     **end for**
9:     **while** $\exists\, w \in \mathcal{V} : \omega(w) := \perp$ **do**
10:         Choose any such w having $\omega(v) \neq \perp$ for all $v \in ch(w)$.
11:         $\omega(w) := 1 + \max_{v \in ch(w)} \omega(v)$
12:     **end while**
13:     Mark each $u \in W_{\eta(x)}$ as **unprocessed**.
14:     **while** $\exists\, u \in W_{\eta(x)} : u$ *is* **unprocessed do**
15:         **while** $\exists\, w \in W_{\eta(x)} : \omega(w) = 0$ *and* w *is* **unprocessed do**
16:             Compute $P(\mathcal{X}_w, \mathcal{A}_w)$
17:             Mark w as **processed**.
18:         **end while**
19:         Choose any w which is **unprocessed** and $\forall\, u \in ch(w)\ u$ is **processed**.
20:         **for** $R \in \mathcal{R}_w$ **do**
21:             Compute $P(\mathcal{Z}_R, \mathcal{D}_R)$
22:         **end for**
23:         Mark w as **processed**
24:     **end while**
25:     if $x \in P(\mathcal{Z}_R, \mathcal{D}_R)$ for every $R \in \mathcal{R}_{\eta(x)}$ report OBA(x)
26:     if $x \in P(\mathcal{Z}_R, \mathcal{D}_R)$ for some $R \in \mathcal{R}_{\eta(x)}$ report SBA(x)
27:     else report x is indefensible.

Any $R \in \mathcal{R}_v$ maps to a subset of F_v so $|\mathcal{R}_v|$ cannot exceed the total number of such sets. There are, however, cases where this bound cannot be improved.

Lemma 3 *If $\langle W_v, F_v \rangle$ is a root vertex v with $ch(v) = \mathcal{V} \setminus \{v\}$ then $|\mathcal{R}_v| = 2^{k-1}$.*

Let $e(k, t, d)$ be defined as

$$\max_{\langle W_v, F_v \rangle} \{ |\mathcal{R}_v| : |W_v| = k,\ \max_{w \in W_v} |ch(w)| = d,\ |\{w \in W_v : |ch(w)| > 1\}| = t \}$$

Our aim is not to prove exact bounds on $e(k, t, d)$ but rather to give an indication when polynomial time algorithms for SBA and OBA result.

Theorem 3

a. $e(k, 0, 1) = e(k, 0, d) = k$

b. $e(k, t, d) \leq \dfrac{(t(d-2) + k + 1)^{td}}{(k-t)^{t-1} \times (t(d-1) + 1)^{t(d-1)+1}}$

Proof: (outline) Part (a) is an easy induction on $k \geq 1$. For part(b), $e(k, t, d)$ is maximised when $\langle W_v, F_v \rangle$ is formed as a t vertex d-ary tree in which each leaf is replaced by a chain of $(k-t)/(t(d-1)+1)$ values, so leading to the recurrence relation, $e(k,t,d) \leq \alpha(r)$ where $r = \log_d(t(d-1)+1)$ and $\alpha(r)$ satisfies

$$\alpha(0) = \frac{k-t}{t(d-1)+1} \quad ; \quad \alpha(r) = (1 + \alpha(r-1))^d$$

For space reasons we omit the detailed analysis of $\alpha(r)$ which leads to the bound

$$e(k,t,d) \leq \frac{(t(d-2)+k+1)^{td}}{(k-t)^{t-1} \times (t(d-1)+1)^{t(d-1)+1}}$$

$\square$

Corollary 3 *For* $\langle \mathcal{X}, \mathcal{A}, \mathcal{V}, \eta \rangle$ *whose value graph is a strict tree* $\langle W_v, F_v \rangle$ *and* x *such that* $\eta(x) = v$, $\mathrm{SBA}(\langle \mathcal{X}, \mathcal{A}, \mathcal{V}, \eta \rangle, x)$ *and* $\mathrm{OBA}(\langle \mathcal{X}, \mathcal{A}, \mathcal{V}, \eta \rangle, x)$ *are*

a. *polynomial time decidable when* $\langle W_v, F_v \rangle$ *has* t *vertices with more than 1 child, no vertex with more than* d *children and* $d \times t$ *is constant.*

b. *decidable by an algorithm taking at most* $\left(\frac{k+d-1}{d}\right)^d \times O(|\mathcal{X}|)$ *steps when* $\langle W_v, F_v \rangle$ *has exactly one vertex* (v) *with* $|ch(v)| > 1$ *(so that* $|ch(v)| = d$*).*

Proof: Both cases are immediate from the general upper bound given in Thm. 3(b). We note that $t = 1$ and $d = 2$ covers the case of chains. $\square$

3. Beyond trees and chains

The fact that, in some circumstances, the structure of the value graph yields polynomial time solutions for SBA and OBA, as demonstrated by Corollary 3(a) and (b) (when d is constant) motivates considering forms other than the trees and chains considered in Section 2. We note that our analysis of the preceding section easily extends to value graphs which are *acyclic*.[2]

A natural development would be to find analogous construction for "tree-like" structures, i.e. value graphs with *bounded treewidth*, see e.g [5,1]. For many problems that are computationally hard in general, polynomial time algorithms exist when instances are restricted to those whose treewidth is constant. Given the results of Section 2, which can be interepreted as dealing with value graphs whose treewidth is 1, it seems reasonable to look for related constructions for value graphs whose treewidth is constant (but greater than 1). In fact bounded tree-width (even when the form of the "tree decomposition" is limited) fails to lead to improved methods.

Theorem 4 *The decision problem* SBA *(*OBA*) is* NP*–complete (*coNP*–complete) even when restricted to instances* $\langle \mathcal{X}, \mathcal{A}, \mathcal{V}, \eta \rangle$ *whose value graph* $\langle \mathcal{V}, \mathcal{B} \rangle$ *has* $tw(\langle \mathcal{V}, \mathcal{B} \rangle) = 2$ *and a witnessing tree decomposition* $\langle \mathcal{I}, \mathcal{F} \rangle$ *which is a chain.*

Proof: (Outline) Both parts follow from the reductions given in [9, Thm. 23]. $\square$

---

[2]Value graphs which are trees in the sense used earlier may contain cycles, e.g. when the underlying VAF contains arguments $\{x, y, z\}$ with $\eta(x) = \eta(y)$, and $\langle x, z \rangle, \langle z, y \rangle \in \mathcal{A}$.

4. Conclusions

This paper has considered the question of identifying tractable special cases for the decision problems Subjective and Objective Acceptance (SBA, OBA) in value-based argumentation. In contrast to acceptability concepts in standard Dung style argumentation frameworks, only the case of symmetric AFs had been known to lead to polynomial time approaches for these problems. By considering properties of the so-called *value graph* – the directed graph structure defined by considering the *values* involved in conflicting arguments – we have identified an extensive, further, class of systems for which SBA and OBA admit polynomial time solutions: specifically those whose value graph is a tree in which the product of t – the number of vertices with more than one child – and d – the maximum number of children of any vertex in the tree – is constant, i.e. indepedent of the number of values. Unfortunately, and providing a further indication of the extent to which value-based argumentation has proven resistant to tractable solution methods, attempts to extend these ideas from value graphs which are trees, equivalent to the class of graphs whose *treewidth* equals 1, to value graphs with bounded treewidth encounter difficulties: even if the value graph has treewidth 2 and the structure of the witnessing tree decomposition is a chain, SBA and OBA remain NP–complete, resp. coNP–complete. Nevertheless despite the failure of bounded treewidth to yield effective solutions in general, given that some progress can be made with restricted structures on the value graph, a natural development would be to consider other graph-theoretic restrictions: a possible candidate structure, and the subject of current investigation is the class of *bipartite* value graphs.

References

[1] S. Arnborg, J. Lagergren, and D. Seese. Easy problems for tree-decomposable graphs. *Jnl. of Algorithms*, 12:308–340, 1991.
[2] T. J. M. Bench-Capon. Persuasion in Practical Argument Using Value-based Argumentation Frameworks. *Journal of Logic and Computation*, 13(3):429–448, 2003.
[3] T. J. M. Bench-Capon and K. Atkinson. Abstract argumentation and values. In I. Rahwan and G. Simari, editors, *Argumentation in AI*, chapter 3, pages 45–64. Springer, 2009.
[4] T. J. M. Bench-Capon and P. E. Dunne. Argumentation in artificial intelligence. *Artificial Intelligence*, 171:619–641, 2007.
[5] H. L.. Bodlaender. A partial k-arboretum of graphs with bounded treewidth. *Theoretical Computer Science*, 209:1–45, 1998.
[6] S. Coste-Marquis, C. Devred, and P. Marquis. Symmetric argumentation frameworks. In L. Godo, editor, *Proc.* 8th *ECSQARU*, volume 3571 of *LNAI*, pages 317–328. Springer-Verlag, 2005.
[7] R. G. Downey and M. R. Fellows. Fixed parameter tractability and completeness I: basic results. *SIAM Jnl. on Computing*, 24:873–921, 1995.
[8] P. M. Dung. On the acceptability of arguments and its fundamental role in nonmonotonic reasoning, logic programming and n-person games. *Artificial Intelligence*, 77:321–357, 1995.
[9] P. E. Dunne. Computational properties of argument systems satisfying graph-theoretic constraints. *Artificial Intelligence*, 171:701–729, 2007.
[10] P. E. Dunne, A. Hunter, P. McBurney, S. Parsons, and M. Wooldridge. Inconsistency tolerance in weighted argument systems. In *Proc. 8th AAMAS*, pages 851–858, 2009.
[11] P. E. Dunne. Tractability in Value-based Argumentation Technical Report, ULCS-10-001, Dept. of Comp. Sci., Univ. of Liverpool, January 2010

Computational Models of Argument
P. Baroni et al. (Eds.)
IOS Press, 2010
doi:10.3233/978-1-60750-619-5-207

Computation with varied-strength attacks in abstract argumentation frameworks

Paul E. DUNNE [a], Diego C. MARTÍNEZ [b] Alejandro J. GARCÍA [b]
Guillermo R. SIMARI [b]

[a] *Department of Computer Science, The University of Liverpool, U.K.*
[b] *Dept. of Computer Science and Engineering, Universidad Nacional del Sur,
Bahia Blanca, Argentina*

Abstract. In abstract frameworks with varied strength attacks (AFV),
arguments may attack each other with different strength. An admissible scenario is an admissible set of arguments fulfilling certain strength
conditions about defences. In this work we analyze the computational
complexity of some decision problems related to the quality of admissible scenarios: checking the property of being top-admissible and the
property of being equilibrated. These problems are implying an exhaustive comparison between scenarios, and both of them are shown to be
coNP–complete.

Keywords. Computational properties of argumentation; varied-strength
attacks; abstract argumentation frameworks; computational complexity;

Introduction

The established view of abstract argumentation promoted by Dung [6] uses a di-
rected graph structure, $\langle \mathcal{X}, \mathcal{A} \rangle$, (called an argumentation framework –AF) wherein
$\mathcal{X} = \{x_1, \ldots, x_n\}$ defines a finite set of *arguments* and $\mathcal{A} \subseteq \mathcal{X} \times \mathcal{X}$ describes
a so-called *attack* relationship between arguments so that $\langle x, y \rangle \in \mathcal{A}$ indicates
"the argument x attacks the argument y": therefore not only can no "consistent"
rational viewpoint accept both x and y but also any such viewpoint endorsing
y can only convincingly do so by providing a counterattack to the argument y.
The sense of [6] is entirely abstract: arguments are neither assumed to have nor
endowed with any particular structure and thus may range from simple atomic
propositions to more intricate schemes, e.g. of the type formulated in the work of
Toulmin [14]. Similarly, the nature of what constitutes an attack is left abstract so
encapsulating the gamut of possibilities from classical logical inconsistency (x asserts a proposition p, y asserts the proposition $\neg p$) through templates denying the
applicability of given deductive claims, e.g. y might correspond to an argument
of the form "p since p follows from q and q is the case" might be attacked by x
asserting $\neg q$ (disputing the basis for deducing p) or by x asserting that $\neg(q \rightarrow p)$
(disputing the validity of the rule itself).

By abstracting away the precise nature of attack, Dung's model focuses on
divers criteria by which subsets of the arguments may be deemed collectively

justified. Thus sets of mutually compatible arguments are described by those satisfying given predicates $\sigma : 2^{\mathcal{X}} \to \langle \top, \bot \rangle$, choices for σ varying from conditions as simple as "$\sigma(S)$ holds whenever no two arguments in S attack each other" (the so-called "naive semantics") through stronger constraints requiring that for any argument in S attacked by $y \notin S$ there is some argument in S that attacks y (the so-called "admissibility semantics") to more recent proposals imposing further conditions, e.g. the ideal semantics of Dung et al. [7,8], semi-stable semantics of Caminada [5], etc. An overview of the principal approaches may be found in the survey of Baroni and Giacomin [3].

As has been observed by a number of researchers, the focus on justifiable stances in terms of subsets of *arguments* ignores issues that result from situations where *attacks* may be interpreted as having distinct characteristics. So, as is recognized in other argumentation scenarios, some attacks on arguments carry less force than others. Such viewpoints have led to a variety of proposals whereby the nature of "the argument x *attacks* the argument y" is explored using formalisms of greater sophistication than merely a binary relationship over arguments. While such methods perforce lose the purely abstract interpretation effected in [6] in compensation they admit a rather more fine-tuned (and, arguably, more practicable) analysis of argumentation processes. Among the earliest proposals recognising the varied nature of attacks are the *preference-based frameworks* of Amgoud and Cayrol [1] and the *value-based* argumentation frameworks of Bench-Capon [4]. Both of these methods consider formalisms by which particular attacks are viewed as "weaker" than others to the extent that such attacks may be disregarded: in [1] the rationale by which $\langle x, y \rangle \in \mathcal{A}$ is discounted is via a preorder $\succ$ over $\mathcal{X}$ under which $y \succ x$ expresses a *preference* for the argument y over the argument x; in [4], arguments are viewed as endorsing (qualitative) *values* so that an attack by x on y has no force for audiences to whom the value endorsed by y is more important than that promoted by x. Recent work of Modgil [13] describes how the approaches of [1,4] may be interpreted in terms of (extended) frameworks which, in contrast to [6], make explicit provision for attacks themselves to be attacked by arguments, i.e. [13] adds a component $\mathcal{D} \subseteq \mathcal{X} \times \mathcal{A}$ to the basis directed graph structure.

Although the structures described in [1,4,13] provide a richer treatment of attack semantics than envisaged in [6], these treatments are still predominantly grounded in interpretations of $\mathcal{X}$ rather than $\mathcal{A}$ explicitly, i.e. the potentially differing natures of $\langle x, y \rangle \in \mathcal{A}$ are provided in terms of views of the *arguments* (x and y) rather than the *attack* ($\langle x, y \rangle$). Recently, however, methods by which treatments based on properties of attacks have been proposed, e.g. [2,10]. One such approach – the AFs with *varied-strength attack* (AVF) of Martínez, García and Simari [12] forms the principal focus of the current article. We note the model studied in [10] (and to a large extent that of [2]) treat the concept of "attack strength" in quantitative terms: in contrast AVFs use a rather more abstract qualitative comparison. We present the formal background to AVFs in Section 1, however, a key innovation of AVFs is in the concept of partitioning $\mathcal{A}$ into sets describing the "relative strength" of attack (an early – non AF based - view of relative strength may be found in Kakas et al. [11]). By considering four distinct relations between attack – $\{\gg, \ll, \approx, ?\}$ – [12] extends the classical admissibility semantics of [6] (defined via subsets of $\mathcal{X}$) into, what are termed, *admissible scenarios*. An admissible scenario is formed by a pairing, $[S, P]$ of $S \subseteq \mathcal{X}$ together with a *defence condition* (specified by $P \subseteq \{\gg, \ll, \approx, ?\}$). Admissible scenarios provide a foundation for comparing different defences of particular arguments so that informal notions of "$[S, P]$ is a *stronger defence* that $[T, Q]$" can be described formally. Such formalisms, however, raise questions concerning the ease with which questions such as "is there a better defence available for an argument?" can be addressed.

This paper is organized as follows. In Section 1, we present formal definitions of abstract frameworks and the chosen decision problems are established. The complexity of these problems is analyzed in Section 2. Conclusions and future work is discussed in Section 3.

1. Background and Definitions

We briefly review the basic forms introduced by Dung [6] below.

Definition 1 *An* argumentation framework *(AF) is a pair* $\mathcal{H} = \langle \mathcal{X}, \mathcal{A} \rangle$, *in which* $\mathcal{X}$ *is a finite set of arguments and* $\mathcal{A} \subseteq \mathcal{X} \times \mathcal{X}$ *is the attack relationship for* $\mathcal{H}$. *A pair* $\langle x, y \rangle \in \mathcal{A}$ *is referred to as 'y is attacked by x' or 'x attacks y'. The convention of excluding "self-attacking" arguments is assumed, i.e. for all* $x \in \mathcal{X}$, $\langle x, x \rangle \notin \mathcal{A}$. *For R, S subsets of arguments in the* AF $\mathcal{H}(\mathcal{X}, \mathcal{A})$, *we say that* $s \in S$ *is attacked by R – written* $attacks(R, s)$ *– if there is some* $r \in R$ *such that* $\langle r, s \rangle \in \mathcal{A}$. *For subsets R and S of* $\mathcal{X}$ *we write* $attacks(R, S)$ *if there is some* $s \in S$ *for which* $attacks(R, s)$ *holds;* $x \in \mathcal{X}$ *is acceptable with respect to S if for every* $y \in \mathcal{X}$ *that attacks x there is some* $z \in S$ *that attacks y;*

For $S \subset \mathcal{X}$ *and argument x acceptable w.r.t. x, the* direct defenders *of x (in S) are*

$$def(x, S) = \{ y \in S : \exists z \in \mathcal{X} \text{ s.t. } \langle z, x \rangle \in \mathcal{A} \ \& \ \langle y, z \rangle \in \mathcal{A}\}$$

S is conflict-free *if no argument in S is attacked by any other argument in S. A conflict-free set S is admissible if every* $y \in S$ *is acceptable w.r.t S; S is a* preferred extension *if it is a maximal (with respect to* $\subseteq$) *admissible set; S is a* stable extension *if S is conflict free and every* $y \notin S$ *is attacked by S;*

For $S \subseteq \mathcal{X}$,

$$S^- =_{\text{def}} \{ p : \exists q \in S \text{ such that } \langle p, q \rangle \in \mathcal{A}\}$$
$$S^+ =_{\text{def}} \{ p : \exists q \in S \text{ such that } \langle q, p \rangle \in \mathcal{A}\}$$

An argument x is credulously accepted *if there is some* preferred extension *containing it; x is* sceptically accepted *if it is a member of every* preferred extension.

In [12] the basic form of [6] is extended by adding a component encapsulating categories of *attack strength*.

Definition 2 *An* argumentation framework with varied strength attacks *(AFV) is a triple* $\langle \mathcal{X}, \langle \mathcal{A}_1, \ldots, \mathcal{A}_n \rangle, \mathcal{R} \rangle$ *where* $\mathcal{A}_i \subseteq \mathcal{X} \times \mathcal{X}$ *(with* $\mathcal{A}_i \cap \mathcal{A}_j = \emptyset$ *whenever* $i \neq j$) *and, with* $\mathcal{A} = \cup_{i=1}^n \mathcal{A}_i$, $\langle \mathcal{X}, \mathcal{A} \rangle$ *describes an* AF; $\mathcal{R} \subseteq \{1, \ldots, n\} \times \{1, \ldots, n\}$ *is a reflexive binary relation. For brevity we write* $\langle \mathcal{X}, \{\mathcal{A}\}_n, \mathcal{R} \rangle$ *for an arbitrary* AFV.

Given $\langle x, y \rangle \in \mathcal{A}_i$ *and* $\langle u, z \rangle \in \mathcal{A}_j$ *we distinguish four interactions between (attacks in)* $\mathcal{A}_i$ *and (attacks in)* $\mathcal{A}_j$ *as follows:*

$\gg$ *We say that* $\mathcal{A}_i \gg \mathcal{A}_j$ *if* $\langle i, j \rangle \in \mathcal{R}$ *and* $\langle j, i \rangle \notin \mathcal{R}$. *In this case* $\mathcal{A}_i$ *is said to provide* stronger attacks *than* $\mathcal{A}_j$.

$\ll$ *We say that* $\mathcal{A}_i \ll \mathcal{A}_j$ *if* $\mathcal{A}_j \gg \mathcal{A}_i$. *In this case* $\mathcal{A}_i$ *is said to provide* weaker attacks *than* $\mathcal{A}_j$.

$\approx$ *We say that* $\mathcal{A}_i \approx \mathcal{A}_j$ *if both* $\langle i, j \rangle \in \mathcal{R}$ *and* $\langle j, i \rangle \in \mathcal{R}$. *Here,* $\mathcal{A}_i$ *and* $\mathcal{A}_j$ *are said to have* equivalent force.

? *We say that* $\mathcal{A}_i$? $\mathcal{A}_j$ *if neither* $\langle i, j \rangle \in \mathcal{R}$ *nor* $\langle j, i \rangle \in \mathcal{R}$. *Here* $\mathcal{A}_i$ *and* $\mathcal{A}_j$ *are referred to as having* unknown difference in force.

For an AVF, $\langle \mathcal{X}, \{\mathcal{A}\}_n, \mathcal{R} \rangle$ *given* $\{x, y, z\} \subseteq \mathcal{X}$ *with* $\langle x, y \rangle \in \mathcal{A}_i$ *and* $\langle y, z \rangle \in \mathcal{A}_j$ *we say that*

a. *x is a* strong defender *of z against y if* $\mathcal{A}_i \gg \mathcal{A}_j$.
b. *x is a* weak defender *of z against y if* $\mathcal{A}_i \ll \mathcal{A}_j$.
c. *x is a* normal defender *of z against y if* $\mathcal{A}_i \approx \mathcal{A}_j$.
d. *x is an* unqualified defender *of z against y if* $\mathcal{A}_i ? \mathcal{A}_j$.

An attack scenario *in* $\langle \mathcal{X}, \{\mathcal{A}\}_n, \mathcal{R} \rangle$ *is a pair* $[S, P]$ *with* $S \subseteq \mathcal{X}$ *and* $P \subseteq \{\gg, \ll, \approx, ?\}$. *An argument* $x \in \mathcal{X}$ *is* acceptable *w.r.t.* $[S, P]$ *if for any y such that* $\langle y, x \rangle \in \mathcal{A}_i$ *there is some* $z \in S$ *with* $\langle z, y \rangle \in \mathcal{A}_j$ *and* $\mathcal{A}_j \rho \mathcal{A}_i$ *for some* $\rho \in P$. *The* direct defenders *of x for x acceptable w.r.t.* $[S, P]$ – *denoted* $def(x, [S, P])$ *are, by analogy with Defn. 1,*

$$\{ y \in S \ : \ \exists z \in \mathcal{X} \text{ s.t. } \langle z, x \rangle \in \mathcal{A}_j, \ \langle y, z \rangle \in \mathcal{A}_i \ \& \ \mathcal{A}_i \rho \mathcal{A}_j \text{ for some } \rho \in P \}$$

The attack scenario $[S, P]$ *is an* admissible scenario *if S is* conflict-free *and* every $x \in S$ *is acceptable w.r.t.* $[S, P]$.

The concepts of admissible scenario and defence conditions provide a mechanism for comparing different defences of specific arguments.

Definition 3 *Let* $\langle \mathcal{X}, \{\mathcal{A}\}_n, \mathcal{R} \rangle$ *be an* AFV *and* $\{u, x, y, z\} \subset \mathcal{X}$ *for which* $\langle u, x \rangle \in \mathcal{A}_i$, $\langle y, u \rangle \in \mathcal{A}_j$ *and* $\langle z, u \rangle \in \mathcal{A}_k$. *We say that the argument y* dominates *the argument z as a defender if* $\mathcal{A}_j \gg \mathcal{A}_k$.

Given attack scenarios $[S_1, P]$ *and* $[S_2, Q]$ *and* $x \in \mathcal{X}$ *for which x is acceptable w.r.t.* $[S_2, Q]$ *we say that* $[S_1, P]$ *is a* stronger collective defence *of* $x \in \mathcal{X}$ *than* $[S_2, Q]$ *if all of the following hold,*

SD1. *x is acceptable w.r.t* $[S_1, P]$.
SD2. $\forall \ y \in S_1$, $z \in S_2$ *z does not* dominate *y (as a defender of x)*
SD3. $\exists \ y \in S_1$, $z \in S_2 \setminus S_1$, $u \in \mathcal{X}$ *such that* $\langle u, x \rangle \in \mathcal{A}_i$, $\langle y, u \rangle \in \mathcal{A}_j$ *and* $\langle z, u \rangle \in \mathcal{A}_k$ *and y dominates z (as a defender of x).*

An AFV can be depicted as a graph with labeled arcs, where the nodes are arguments. In Figure 1 a simple AFV is shown.

Example 1 *Consider the* AFV $\langle \mathcal{X}, \{\mathcal{A}_1, \mathcal{A}_2\}, \mathcal{R} \rangle$ *of Figure 1, where* $\mathcal{X} = \{a, b, c, d, e\}$ *and* $\mathcal{A}_1 \gg \mathcal{A}_2$. *The pairs* $P_1 = [\{e\}, \{\approx\}]$, $P_2 = [\{a, c\}, \{\gg\}]$ *and* $P_3 = [\{a, d\}, \{\approx\}]$ *are admissible scenarios.*

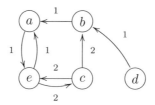

Figure 1. AN AFV

The concept of stronger collective defence of an argument implicitly yields a partial ordering over *all* attack scenarios with respect to which an argument is acceptable. This ordering can be exploited to formulate notions of "best" admissible set as follows.

Definition 4 *Given* $\langle \mathcal{X}, \{\mathcal{A}\}_n, \mathcal{R} \rangle$, *an attack scenario* $[S, P]$ *is* top–admissible *if,*

TA1. $[S, P]$ *is an admissible scenario.*
TA2. $\forall\, x \in S$, *if* $[T, Q]$ *is admissible scenario with* $x \in T$ *then* $[T, Q]$ *is not a stronger collective defence of* x *than* $[S, P]$.

For an admissible scenario $[S, P]$ *given* $x \in S$ *for which* $[T, P]$ *is a stronger defence than* $[S, P]$ *the* upgraded defence of x by $[T, P]$ in $[S, P]$ *is the scenario*

$$upgd(x, S, T, P) \;=\; [S \setminus def(x, [S, P]) \cup def(x, [T, P]),\ P]$$

Finally an admissible scenario, $[S, P]$ *is said to be* equilibrated *if no argument in* S *can be upgraded without weakening the defence of some other argument, i.e.* $\forall\, x \in S$ *if* $[T, P]$ *is a stronger defence of* x *then either* $upgd(x, S, T, P)$ *is not admissible or there is some* $y \in S \cap upgd(x, S, T, P)$ *whose defence is weaker in* $upgd(x, S, T, P)$.

We note a number of properties of top-admissible scenarios, upgraded defences and equilibria. Firstly, while admissible scenarios are always admissible in the sense of Definition 1 it is not necessarily the case that *top*-admissible scenarios are *preferred extensions* in the standard sense. Additionally, it is *not* guaranteed to be the case that $upgd(x, S, T, P)$ is an admissible scenario (although x will be acceptable w.r.t. $upgd(x, S, T, P)$).

Our principal interest in this paper is to consider issues arising from a number of decision problems specific to AFVs. In particular:

- **Top–admissible Scenario** (TAS)
  Instance: AVF $\langle \mathcal{X}, \{\mathcal{A}\}_n, \mathcal{R} \rangle$; $[S, P]$ an admissible scenario.
  Question: Is $[S, P]$ top–admissible in $\langle \mathcal{X}, \{\mathcal{A}\}_n, \mathcal{R} \rangle$?
- **Admissible upgrade** (AU)
  Instance: AVF $\langle \mathcal{X}, \{\mathcal{A}\}_n, \mathcal{R} \rangle$; $[S, P]$ an admissible scenario; $x \in S$.
  Question: Is there any $[T, P]$ such that $[T, P]$ is a stronger defence of x than $[S, P]$ *and* for which $upgd(x, S, T, P)$ is admissible?
- **Equilibrated scenario** (ES)
  Instance: AVF $\langle \mathcal{X}, \{\mathcal{A}\}_n, \mathcal{R} \rangle$; $[S, P]$ an admissible scenario.
  Question: Is $[S, P]$ an equilibrated scenario?

In the following section we address the analysis of computational complexity for these problems.

2. Complexity of admissible scenario related problems

All of the above-mentioned decision problems on admissible scenarios are inquiring about the existence of alternative (stronger,better) defences. As a basis for the results of this section we use the following problem:

MORE-THAN-ONE-SAT (MTOS)
Instance: CNF formula $\varphi(z_1, \ldots, z_n)$ in which for each literal $y_i \in \{z_i, \neg z_i : 1 \leq i \leq n\}$ there is at least one clause, C_j^i with $y_i \in C_j^i$ and $\langle \alpha_1, \ldots, \alpha_n \rangle$ a *satisfying* assignment of $\varphi(z_1, \ldots, z_n)$.
Question: Is there any assignment, $\beta \in \langle \bot, \top \rangle^n$ such that $\beta \neq \alpha$ *and* β satisfies $\varphi(z_1, \ldots, z_n)$?

The MTOS decision problem is NP–complete, as stated in the following Lemma.

Lemma 1 MTOS *is* NP*–complete.*

Proof: Membership in NP is trivial. We prove MTOS is NP–hard by reducing from standard satisfiability restricted to formulae in CNF (with each literal occurring in some clause). Let $\psi(z_1, \ldots, z_n)$ be an instance of CNF-SAT. Without loss of generality it may be assumed that (for some k) $\neg z_1 \vee \neg z_2 \vee \ldots \neg z_k$ is a clause defining ψ.[1] With $Z_n = \{z_1, \ldots, z_n\}$, consider a CNF formula, $\varphi(Z_n)$ that is logically equivalent to

$$\psi(Z_n) \vee \bigwedge_{i=1}^{n} z_i$$

Notice that such a formula is obtained as

$$\varphi(Z_n) = \bigwedge_{C_j \in \psi} \bigwedge_{i=1}^{n} (z_i \vee C_j)$$

---

[1]If this is not the case, then we can relabel literals of ψ without altering its satisfiability properties.

where $\{C_1, \ldots, C_m\}$ are the clauses defining $\psi(Z_n)$. It follows that $\varphi(Z_n)$, as defined above, is only polynomially larger than that $\psi(Z_n)$. The instance of MTOS is formed by $\langle \varphi(Z_n), \langle \top, \top, \ldots, \top \rangle \rangle$. Note that since $\varphi(Z_n) \equiv \psi(Z_n) \vee \bigwedge_{i=1}^{n} z_i$, $\langle \varphi, \langle \top, \ldots, \top \rangle \rangle$ does define a valid instance of MTOS: $\varphi(\top, \ldots, \top) = \top$.

We now argue that $\langle \varphi, \langle \top, \ldots, \top \rangle \rangle$ is accepted as an instance MTOS if and only if ψ is satisfiable.

Suppose that $\langle \beta_1, \ldots, \beta_n \rangle$ is such that $\varphi(\beta_1, \ldots, \beta_n) = \top$ and $\langle \beta_1, \ldots, \beta_n \rangle \neq \langle \top, \ldots, \top \rangle$. Then, from the construction of φ,

$$\varphi(\beta_1, \ldots, \beta_n) \equiv \psi(\beta_1, \ldots, \beta_n) \vee \left(\bigwedge_{i=1}^{n} z_i \right) (\beta_1, \ldots, \beta_n)$$

So that, since $\beta_i = \bot$ for at least one β_i, and $\varphi(\beta_1, \ldots, \beta_n) = \top$ from the premise,

$$\psi(\beta_1, \ldots, \beta_n) \equiv \top$$

That is ψ is satisfiable as claimed.

On the other hand suppose ψ is satisfied by some assignment $\langle \alpha_1, \ldots, \alpha_n \rangle$: from the assumption that $\neg z_1 \vee \ldots \vee \neg z_k$ is a clause within ψ, at least one of $\{\alpha_1, \alpha_2, \alpha_3\}$ is $\bot$. It follows that $\langle \alpha_1, \ldots, \alpha_n \rangle \neq \langle \top, \ldots, \top \rangle$ and

$$\varphi(\alpha_1, \ldots, \alpha_n) \equiv \psi(\alpha_1, \ldots, \alpha_n) \vee \left(\bigwedge_{i=1}^{n} z_i \right) (\alpha_1, \ldots, \alpha_n)$$

so that

$$\varphi(\alpha_1, \ldots, \alpha_n) = \top$$

Thus, if ψ is satisfiable then $\langle \varphi(Z_n), \langle \top, \top, \ldots, \top \rangle \rangle$ is accepted as an instance of MTOS. $\square$

In the following subsections we analyze the complexity of TAS, AU and ES.

2.1. Top-admissibility

The simplest quality notion for admissible scenarios is *top-admissibility*. A top-admissible scenario offers the strongest collective defence for any of its members. In order to prove that TAS is coNP–complete, the reduction constructs an AFV which intuition is the following. Let $\varphi(Z_n)$ be a CNF. In the AFV, there is an argument representing every literal y_i, every clause C_j and φ. If a literal $y_i \in \{z_i, \neg z_i\}$ appears in a clause C_j, then $y_i = \top$ makes C_j satisfiable. The formula φ is unsatisfiable if no C_j is satisfiable. These relations are all translated as attacks, and then φ is defended against C_j by literals included in C_j. The theorem and its proof follows.

Theorem 1 TAS *is coNP–complete.*

Proof: That TAS $\in$ coNP follows from the fact that its complement is in NP as is immediate from the NP algorithm which given $\langle \langle \mathcal{X}, \{\mathcal{A}\}_n, \mathcal{R} \rangle, [S, P] \rangle$ guesses an

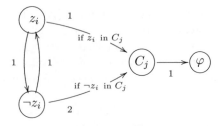

Figure 2. Schematic AFV=$\langle \mathcal{X}_\varphi, \langle \mathcal{A}_1^\varphi, \mathcal{A}_2^\varphi \rangle, \mathcal{R}_\varphi \rangle$ of Theorem 1

attack scenario $[T, Q]$ and accepts the instance if and only if $[T, Q]$ is a stronger defence than $[S, P]$. Since this test is polynomial-time decidable we have coTAS∈NP so that TAS∈coNP.

Let $\langle \varphi(z_1, \ldots, z_n), \langle \alpha_1, \ldots, \alpha_n \rangle \rangle$ be an instance of MTOS and $\{C_1, C_2, \ldots, C_m\}$ be the clauses defining φ. Without loss of generality it is assumed that $\alpha_i = \top$ for all $1 \le i \le n$.

Form the AFV $\langle \mathcal{X}_\varphi, \langle \mathcal{A}_1^\varphi, \mathcal{A}_2^\varphi \rangle, \mathcal{R}_\varphi \rangle$ whose arguments are

$$\{z_i, \neg z_i \ : \ 1 \le i \le n\} \ \cup \ \{C_j \ : \ 1 \le j \le m\} \ \cup \{\varphi\}$$

and with

$$\mathcal{A}_1^\varphi = \{ \ \langle z_i, \neg z_i \rangle, \ \langle \neg z_i, \ z_i \rangle \ : \ 1 \le i \le n\} \ \cup$$
$$\{\langle z_i, C_j \rangle \ : \ z_i \text{ occurs in } C_j\} \ \cup \ \{\langle C_j, \varphi \rangle \ : \ 1 \le j \le m\}$$

The set $\mathcal{A}_2^\varphi$ is

$$\mathcal{A}_2^\varphi = \{\langle \neg z_i, C_j \rangle \ : \ \neg z_i \text{ occurs in } C_j\}$$

Finally $\mathcal{R}_\varphi = \{\langle 1, 1 \rangle, \langle 2, 1 \rangle, \langle 2, 2 \rangle\}$ so that $\mathcal{A}_2^\varphi \gg \mathcal{A}_1^\varphi$. The schematic of the framework is depicted in Figure 2. Note that this is a simplified graph of a complex AFV, since several arguments are subsumed in a single node. The attacks between z_i and C_j and between $\neg z_i$ and C_j may or may not exist; these attacks are annotated with the required condition.

The instance is completed by setting

$$[S_\varphi, P] = [\{\varphi\} \cup \{ \ z_i \ : \ 1 \le i \le n \ \}, \ \{\gg, \approx\}]$$

Notice that $[S_\varphi, P]$ is an admissible scenario: z_i is attacked by $\neg z_i$, however, $\langle z_i, \neg z_i \rangle \in \mathcal{A}_1^\varphi$ provides a defence; φ is attacked by each C_j, however, from the fact that $\langle \top, \ldots, \top \rangle$ satisfies φ the counterattack $\langle z_i, C_j \rangle \in \mathcal{A}_1^\varphi$ again provides a defence.

We claim that $[S_\varphi, P]$ is *not* a top-admissible scenario if and only if $\langle \varphi(z_1, \ldots, z_n), \langle \alpha_1, \ldots, \alpha_n \rangle \rangle$ is accepted as an instance of MTOS. To see this first observe that the only possible argument within S_φ for which a stronger defence might exist is φ: the only argument attacking z_i is $\neg z_i$ and both $\langle z_i, \neg z_i \rangle$ and $\langle \neg z_i, z_i \rangle$ belong to $\mathcal{A}_1^\varphi$. Suppose that $[S_\varphi, P]$ is not top-admissible letting $[T, Q]$ be an admissible scenario in which T contains a stronger collective defence of φ. Let $\{y_1, \ldots, y_n\} = T \cap \{z_i, \neg z_i \ : \ 1 \le i \le n\}$. Since $[T, Q]$ is admissible,

$\varphi \in T$ and provides a stronger collective defence of φ it must be the case that for some C_j and z_i, $\neg z_k \in T$ dominates z_i as a defender of φ (against C_j): i.e. $C_j = z_i \vee \neg z_k \vee \ldots, \langle z_i, C_j \rangle \in \mathcal{A}_1^\varphi, \langle \neg z_k, C_j \rangle \in \mathcal{A}_2^\varphi$. Notice that we may still have $z_i \in T$ but (from $z_k \in S_\varphi$) we do *not* have $\neg z_k \in S_\varphi$ (nor $z_k \in T$). Now since $\{y_1, \ldots, y_n\}$ is a (conflict-free) stronger collective defence of φ it follows that φ is acceptable w.r.t. $[\{y_1, \ldots, y_n\}, \{\gg, \approx\}]$ the assignment $z_i = \bot$ if $y_i = \neg z_i$ and $z_i = \top$ otherwise will satisfy $\varphi(Z_n)$ and differs from $\langle \top, \ldots, \top \rangle$.

Conversely suppose that $\langle \beta_1, \ldots, \beta_n \rangle \neq \langle \top, \ldots, \top \rangle$ satisfies $\varphi(Z_n)$. In this case the attack scenario $[T_\beta \cup \{\varphi\}, \{\gg, \approx\}]$ in which

$$T_\beta = \{z_i : \beta_i = \top\} \cup \{\neg z_i : \beta_i = \bot\}$$

is admissible and is such that $T_\beta \cap \{\neg z_1, \ldots, \neg z_n\} \neq \emptyset$. Furthermore from the requirement that each literal occurs in some clause, there is some C_j for which $\neg z_k \in T_\varphi$ provides a stronger defence. □

By definition, if $[S, P]$ is a top-admissible scenario, no other admissible scenario can offer a stronger defence for arguments in S. In other words, if there is an upgrade for the defence of an argument $x \in S$ such that this upgrade yields to an admissible scenario with a stronger defence of x than $[S, P]$, then $[S, P]$ is not top-admissible. Hence, inquiring about such an upgrade is the same as asking if an admissible scenario is *not* top-admissible. Theorem 1 then leads to the classification of the *Admissible Update* (AU) decision problem.

Corollary 1 AU *is* NP–*complete.*

Proof: Immediate from Theorem 1. □

2.2. Equilibrated scenario

The third decision problem addressed in this article is the determination of the *equilibrated* property for admissible scenarios. The classification of the computational complexity of this problem requires the construction of an AFV, which basic intuition is the same as in Theorem 1, but an argument is added to the framework in order to provide an alternative defence. The theorem follows.

Theorem 2 ES *is* coNP–*complete.*

Proof: For membership in coNP it suffices to note that the complementary problem is in NP via the algorithm that, given, $\langle \langle \mathcal{X}, \{\mathcal{A}\}_n, \mathcal{R} \rangle, [S, P] \rangle$ guesses $x \in S$ and scenario $[T, P]$, accepting if and only if $x \in T$, $[T, P]$ is an admissible scenario, $[T, P]$ is a stronger defence of x, and for each $y \in S \cap T$, the defence of y in the $upgd(x, S, T, P)$ is *at least as strong* as the defence of y in $[S, P]$. These can all be performed in polynomial time.

To establish coNP–hardness we use a reduction from CNF unsatisfiability (without the variations required in Thm. 1). Given $\varphi(z_1 \ldots, z_n)$ an instance of UNSAT form the AVF, $\langle \mathcal{X}_\varphi, \{\mathcal{A}_1^\varphi, \mathcal{A}_2^\varphi\}, \mathcal{R}_\varphi \rangle$ in which $\mathcal{X}_\varphi$ contains

$$\{ z_i, \neg z_i : 1 \leq i \leq n \} \cup \{C_j : 1 \leq j \leq m\} \cup \{\varphi, q\}$$

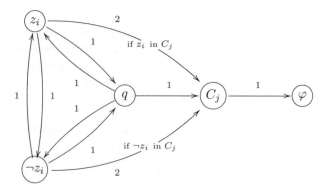

Figure 3. Schematic AFV $\langle \mathcal{X}_\varphi, \langle \mathcal{A}_1^\varphi, \mathcal{A}_2^\varphi \rangle, \mathcal{R}_\varphi \rangle$ of Theorem 2

with

$$\mathcal{A}_1^\varphi = \{ \langle z_i, \neg z_i \rangle, \langle \neg z_i, z_i \rangle : 1 \leq i \leq n \} \cup$$
$$\{ \langle q, z_i \rangle, \langle q, \neg z_i \rangle, \langle z_i, q \rangle, \langle \neg z_i, q \rangle : : 1 \leq i \leq n \} \cup$$
$$\{ \langle q, C_j \rangle, \langle C_j, \varphi \rangle : 1 \leq j \leq m \}$$

and $\mathcal{A}_2^\varphi$ is

$$\{ \langle y_i, C_j \rangle : y_i \text{ is a literal of } C_j \}$$

As before $\mathcal{R}_\varphi$ is $\{ \langle 1, 1 \rangle, \langle 2, 1 \rangle, \langle 2, 2 \rangle \}$ so that $\mathcal{A}_2^\varphi \gg \mathcal{A}_1^\varphi$. The instance is complete by choosing $S_\varphi = \{ \varphi, q \}$ and $P = \{ \gg, \approx \}$.

The schematic framework is shown in Figure 3. We claim $[\{\varphi, q\}, \{\gg, \approx\}]$ is *not* an equilibrated scenario if and only if $\varphi(Z_n)$ is satisfiable.

First notice that $[\{\varphi, q\}, \{\gg, \approx\}]$ is admissible: the attacks on φ (from C_j) are countered by $\langle q, C_j \rangle$ and q is unattacked.

Suppose now that $\varphi(Z_n)$ is satisfiable using, without loss of generality, the assignment $z_i = \top$ for $1 \leq i \leq n$. In this case we have an admissible scenario given by

$$[\{\varphi, z_1, \ldots, z_n\}, \{\gg, \approx\}]$$

Notice that the defenders of φ in this scenario are (a subset of) $\{z_1, \ldots, z_n\}$, i.e. attackers of each clause C_j. Furthermore since $\langle z_i, C_j \rangle \in \mathcal{A}_2^\varphi$ whereas the defender of φ in $\{\varphi, q\}$ is q with $\langle q, C_j \rangle \in \mathcal{A}_1^\varphi$ it follows that the defence of φ in $\{\varphi, z_1, \ldots, z_n\}$ is stronger than the defence of φ in $\{\varphi, q\}$. Consider now the scenario resulting by upgrading the defence of φ in $\{\varphi, q\}$ via the admissible scenario $[\{\varphi, z_1, \ldots, z_n\}, \{\gg, \approx\}]$. We get

$$[\{\varphi, q\} \setminus \{q\} \bigcup \{z_1, \ldots, z_n\}, \{\gg, \approx\}]$$

which is $[\{\varphi, z_1, \ldots, z_n\}, \{\gg, \approx\}]$. Since φ is the only argument common to both scenarios it is immediate that no argument has its defence no weakened. Hence if φ is satisfiable there is an upgraded defence of φ in $[\{\varphi, q\}, \{\gg, \approx\}]$ that does not weaken the defence of any other argument, i.e. $[\{\varphi, q\}, \{\gg, \approx\}]$ is not an equilibrated scenario.

Conversely suppose that $[\{\varphi, q\}, \gg, \approx]$ is not an equilibrated scenario. By definition there must be some argument in $x \in \{\varphi, q\}$ and admissible scenario $[T, P]$ providing a stronger defence of it for which $upgd(x, \{\varphi, q\}, T, \{\gg, \approx\})$ will not weaken the defence of any argument in $S \cap T$. It is easily seen that the only possibility for such a choice is the argument $\{\varphi\}$ and only the defence of φ is (potentially) upgradeable. To see this simply note that

$$
\begin{aligned}
def(\varphi, \{\varphi, q\}) &= \{q\} \\
def(q, \{\varphi, q\}) &= \{q\}
\end{aligned}
$$

It follows that if $[\{\varphi, q\}, \gg, \approx]$ is not an equilibrated scenario then there must be some upgraded defence of φ Such a defence, however, must be formed by a subset of $\{z_i, \neg z_i \; : \; 1 \leq i \leq n\}$ (to counter attacks on φ from $\{C_1, \ldots, C_m\}$). It is immediate that any such subset induces a satisfying assignment of $\varphi(Z_n)$. We deduce that if $[\{\varphi, q\}, \gg, \approx]$ is not an equilibrated scenario then $\varphi(Z_n)$ is satisfiable and, hence, ES is coNP–complete. $\qquad\square$

3. Conclusions and future work

Top-admissible scenarios and equilibrated scenarios are two formalizations about quality of defences in an abstract framework with attacks of varied-strength. The first one captures a scenario with the best defence for its arguments, while the second one captures a scenario in which the defence of an argument is "as good as it gets", given the defences of other arguments in the same scenario. From the computational point of view, the verification of these properties about admissible scenarios requires an extensive comparison of attacks and defences. In this work, we have investigated the computational complexity of two main decision problems inquiring on the quality of defences, known as TAS (top-admissible scenario) and ES (equilibrated scenario). Both of them are proved to be coNP–complete. This is consistent with the general argumentation environment, where many natural questions about arguments and its relationships are computationally intractable [9]. The TAS and ES decision problems are closely related to a third problem, named here AU (admissible upgrade). The AU decision problem is focused on the existence of an admissible upgrade leading to stronger defences, and it is proved to be NP–complete.

Generally speaking, these results show that the determination of sets of arguments with good defences is *hard* to achieve. Nevertheless, in this model of argumentation it is important to grade admissible sets according to inner defences, and then the study of approximation techniques is interesting. For instance, in a dialectical process of argumentation, as in inter-agent dialogues, the definition of heuristic algorithms may guide the selection of arguments according to its defences. When searching for an equilibrated set of arguments, this selection is not necessarily an argument with the strongest defence.

It is also interesting to analyze the computational complexity of decision problems related to AFVs under graph-theoretic restrictions. For example, in a bipartite VAF $\langle \mathcal{X}, \langle \mathcal{A}_1, \ldots, \mathcal{A}_n \rangle, \mathcal{R} \rangle$ where $\mathcal{X} = \mathcal{X}_1 \cup \mathcal{X}_2$, any upgrade of an argument $x \in \mathcal{X}_1$ implies a stronger incoming attack in $\mathcal{X}_2$, because there is a dominant defender in $\mathcal{X}_1$. Credulous and skeptical acceptance in classic bipartite frameworks are proved to be polynomial time decidable [9], but the inclusion of attacks of different strength allows the selection of strong defences. Naturally, the searching for quality requires a deeper analysis.

Another interesting graph restriction is related to the number of attackers that an argument may have. Since there is a finite number of attacks of varied strength, the complexity of the previous decision problems may be reduced.

References

[1] L. Amgoud and C. Cayrol. A reasoning model based on the production of acceptable arguments. *Annals of Math. and Artificial Intelligence*, 34:197–215, 2002.
[2] H. Barringer, D. M. Gabbay, and J. Woods. Temporal dynamics of support and attack networks: From argumentation to zoology. In *Mechanizing Mathematical Reasoning (LNCS Volume 2605)*, pages 59–98. Springer-Verlag: Berlin, Germany, 2005.
[3] P. Baroni and M. Giacomin. Semantics of abstract argument systems. In I. Rahwan and G. Simari, editors, *Argumentation in AI*, chapter 2, pages 25–44. Springer-Verlag, 2009.
[4] T. J. M. Bench-Capon. Persuasion in Practical Argument Using Value-based Argumentation Frameworks. *Journal of Logic and Computation*, 13(3):429–448, 2003.
[5] M. Caminada. Semi-stable semantics. In *Proc. 1st Int. Conf. on Computational Models of Argument*, volume 144 of *FAIA*, pages 121–130. IOS Press, 2006.
[6] P. M. Dung. On the acceptability of arguments and its fundamental role in nonmonotonic reasoning, logic programming and n-person games. *Artificial Intelligence*, 77:321–357, 1995.
[7] P. M. Dung, P. Mancarella, and F. Toni. A dialectical procedure for sceptical assumption-based argumentation. In *Proc. 1st Int. Conf. on Computational Models of Argument*, volume 144 of *FAIA*, pages 145–156. IOS Press, 2006.
[8] P. M. Dung, P. Mancarella, and F. Toni. Computing ideal sceptical argumentation. *Artificial Intelligence*, 171:642–674, 2007.
[9] P. E. Dunne. Computational properties of argument systems satisfying graph-theoretic constraints. *Artificial Intelligence*, 171(10-15):701 – 729, 2007.
[10] P. E. Dunne, A. Hunter, P. McBurney, S. Parsons and M. Wooldridge, Inconsistency tolerance in weighted argument systems, In *Proc. AAMAS 2009*, pages 851–858, 2009
[11] A. Kakas, P. Mancarella, and P. M. Dung. The acceptability semantics for logic programs. In Proc. ICLP, pages 504–515, 1994
[12] D. Martínez, A. García, and G. Simari. An abstract argumentation framework with varied-strength attacks. In *Proceedings of the 11th International Conference on Principles of Knowledge Representation and Reasoning (KR'08)*, 2008.
[13] S. Modgil. Reasoning about preferences in argumentation frameworks. *Artificial Intelligence*, 173(9–10):901–934, 2009.
[14] S. Toulmin. *The uses of argument*. Cambridge University Press, 1959.

Computational Models of Argument
P. Baroni et al. (Eds.)
IOS Press, 2010
doi:10.3233/978-1-60750-619-5-219

Reasoning in Argumentation Frameworks of Bounded Clique-Width [1]

Wolfgang DVOŘÁK, Stefan SZEIDER and Stefan WOLTRAN
Institut für Informationssysteme,
Technische Universität Wien, A-1040 Vienna, Austria.

Abstract. Most computational problems in the area of abstract argumentation are
intractable, thus identifying tractable fragments and developing efficient algorithms
for such fragments are important objectives towards practically efficient argumentation systems. One approach to tractability is to view abstract argumentation frameworks (AFs) as directed graphs and bound certain graph parameters. In particular, Dunne showed that many problems can be solved in linear time for AFs of
bounded treewidth. In this paper we consider the graph-parameter clique-width,
which is more general than treewidth. An additional advantage of clique-width
over treewidth is that it applies well to directed graphs and takes the orientation of
edges into account. We first give theoretical tractability results for AFs of bounded
clique-width and then introduce dynamic-programming algorithms for credulous
and skeptical reasoning.

Keywords. Computational Properties of Argumentation, Clique-Width, Fixed-
Parameter Tractability

1. Introduction

Starting with the seminal work by Dung [14] the area of argumentation has evolved to
one of the most active research branches within Artificial Intelligence (see, e.g., [2]).
Dung's abstract argumentation frameworks, where arguments are seen as abstract entities which are just investigated with respect to their inter-relationship in terms of "attacks", are nowadays well understood and different semantics (i.e. the selection of sets of
arguments which are jointly acceptable) have been proposed. However, most computational problems studied for such frameworks are intractable (see, e.g. [13,16]), while the
importance of efficient algorithms for tractable fragments is evident. Symmetric [6] and
bipartite argumentation frameworks [15] are such examples of fragments, where certain
problems, although intractable in general, can efficiently be solved.

An interesting approach to dealing with intractable problems comes from parameterized complexity theory and is based on the fact, that many hard problems become
polynomial-time tractable if some problem parameter is bounded by a fixed constant. In
case the order of the polynomial bound on the runtime is independent of the parameter
one speaks of *fixed-parameter tractability* (FPT). Since abstract argumentation frame-

---

[1]Dvořák's and Woltran's work was supported by the Vienna Science and Technology Fund (WWTF) under
grant ICT08-028 and Szeider's work was supported by the European Research Council, grant reference 239962.

works are naturally represented as directed graphs, understanding the complexity of argumentation problems with respect to graph parameters is of high importance.

Clique-width is such a graph parameter that measures in a certain sense the structural complexity of a directed or undirected graph [9,10,12]. The parameter is defined via a graph construction process where only a limited number of vertex labels is available; vertices that share the same label at a certain point of the construction process must be treated uniformly in subsequent steps. Clique-width is related to the popular graph parameter *treewidth* [4]. Clique-width can be considered to be more general than treewidth since there are classes of graphs with constant clique-width but arbitrarily high treewidth (complete graphs, for instance). In contrast, graphs with bounded treewidth also have bounded clique-width [5,12].

Many NP-hard problems are tractable for graphs of bounded treewidth or clique-width. By means of a meta-theorem due to Courcelle, Makowsky, and Rotics [11] one can solve any graph problem that can be expressed in Monadic Second Order Logic with second-order quantification on vertex sets (MSO_1) in linear time for graphs of clique-width bounded by some fixed constant k. This result is similar to Courcelle's meta-theorem [7,8] for graphs of bounded treewidth.

First FPT results for argumentation used treewidth as parameter. While Dunne [15] was the first to give the necessary MSO characterizations, recent work [17] turned this theoretical tractability results (which follow from Courcelle's meta-theorem) into efficient dynamic programming algorithms. Moreover, [17] showed that for several other parameters (in particular, directed treewidth) bounding the parameter does not render the argumentation problems tractable.

In this work, we focus on argumentation frameworks of bounded clique-width, which will lead us to a larger class of tractable argumentation frameworks. We emphasize that the MSO characterizations in [15] already yield tractability results for bounded clique-width (the involved MSO formulas are all from MSO_1). Thus, the main contribution in our paper is to introduce novel dynamic programming algorithms which put these theoretical results to work. For this purpose we establish particular succinct data structures (which we shall call (guarded) k-quadruples) characterizing the extensions of an argumentation framework. Due to the different nature of treewidth and clique-width these data structures differ significantly form those introduced in [17].

2. Argumentation Frameworks

In this section we introduce (abstract) argumentation frameworks [14], recall the preferred semantics for such frameworks, and highlight some known complexity results.

An *argumentation framework (AF)* is a pair $\mathcal{F} = (A, R)$ where A is a set of arguments and $R \subseteq A \times A$ is the attack relation. We sometimes write $a \rightarrowtail b$ instead of $(a, b) \in R$, in case no ambiguity arises. Further, for $S \subseteq A$ and $a \in A$, we write $S \rightarrowtail a$ (resp. $a \rightarrowtail S$) iff there exists $b \in S$, such that $b \rightarrowtail a$ (resp. $a \rightarrowtail b$). An argument $a \in A$ is *defended* by a set $S \subseteq A$ iff for each $b \in A$, such that $b \rightarrowtail a$, also $S \rightarrowtail b$ holds.

Example 1. Let $\mathcal{F} = (A, R)$ with $A = \{a, b, c, d\}$ and $R = \{(a, b), (c, b), (c, d), (d, c)\}$. Thus, AFs can be represented as directed graphs. For instance, $\mathcal{F}$ looks like as follows:

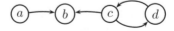

Definition 1. *Let* $\mathcal{F} = (A, R)$ *be an AF. A set* $S \subseteq A$ *is* conflict-free *(in* $\mathcal{F}$*) if there are no* $a, b \in S$*, such that* $(a, b) \in R$*. A set* $S \subseteq A$ *is* admissible *for* $\mathcal{F}$ *if* S *is conflict-free in* $\mathcal{F}$ *and each* $a \in S$ *is defended by* S *in* $\mathcal{F}$*.* S *is a* preferred extension *of* $\mathcal{F}$ *if* S *is a maximal (wrt. subset inclusion) admissible set for* $\mathcal{F}$*. We denote the collection of all preferred extensions of* $\mathcal{F}$ *by* $pref(\mathcal{F})$*.*

For the AF $\mathcal{F}$ in Example 1, we get as admissible sets $\{\}, \{a\}, \{c\}, \{d\}, \{a, c\}$ and $\{a, d\}$. Consequently, $pref(\mathcal{F}) = \{\{a, c\}, \{a, d\}\}$.

Next, we recall the complexity of reasoning over preferred extensions. To this end, we define the decision problems of credulous and skeptical acceptance, which have as input an AF $\mathcal{F} = (A, R)$ and a set $S \subseteq A$ of arguments:

- CA: is there an extension $E \in pref(\mathcal{F})$, such that $S \subseteq E$;
- SA: does $S \subseteq E$ hold, for each $E \in pref(\mathcal{F})$?

It is known that CA is NP-complete, while SA is Π_2^P-complete (see [13,16]). The reason why CA is located on a lower level of the polynomial hierarchy compared to SA is the fact that it is sufficient to check whether S is part of at least one admissible set for the given AF $\mathcal{F}$. Then $S \subseteq E$ also holds for a preferred extension E of $\mathcal{F}$.

3. Clique-Width of Argumentation Frameworks

Let k be a positive integer. A k-*graph* is a graph whose vertices are labeled by integers from $\{1, \ldots, k\} =: [k]$. The labeling of a graph $G = (V, E)$ is formally denoted by a function $\mathcal{L} : V \rightarrow [k]$. We consider an arbitrary graph as a k-graph with all vertices labeled by 1. We call the k-graph consisting of exactly one vertex v (say, labeled by $i \in [k]$) an *initial* k-*graph* and denote it by $i(v)$.

Graphs can be constructed from initial k-graphs by means of repeated application of the following three operations.

- *Disjoint union* (denoted by $\oplus$);
- *Relabeling*: changing all labels i to j (denoted by $\rho_{i \rightarrow j}$);
- *Edge insertion*: connecting all vertices labeled by i with all vertices labeled by j (denoted by $\eta_{i,j}$ or $\eta_{j,i}$); already existing edges are not doubled.[2]

A construction of a k-graph G using the above operations can be represented by an algebraic term composed of $i(v)$, $\oplus$, $\rho_{i \rightarrow j}$, and $\eta_{i,j}$, $(i, j \in [k]$, and v a vertex). Such a term is then called a *cwd-expression defining* G. A k-*expression* is a cwd-expression in which at most k different labels occur. The set of all k-expressions is denoted by CW_k.

Definition 2. *The* clique-width *of a graph* G*,* cwd(G)*, is the smallest integer* k *such that* G *can be defined by a* k*-expression.*

For instance, trees have clique-width 3 and co-graphs have clique-width 2 (co-graphs are exactly given by the graphs which are P_4-free , i.e. whenever there is a path (a, b, c, d) in the graph then $\{a, c\}, \{a, d\}$ or $\{b, d\}$ is also an edge of the graph).

---

[2]Some authors postulate that $i \neq j$ for the edge insertion $\eta_{i,j}$ to prohibit loops, but as AFs may have self-attacking arguments we do not.

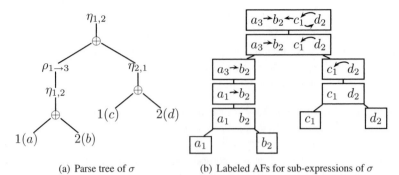

(a) Parse tree of σ (b) Labeled AFs for sub-expressions of σ

Figure 1. Example cwd-expression $\sigma = \eta_{1,2}(\rho_{1\to3}(\eta_{1,2}(1(a) \oplus 2(b))) \oplus \eta_{2,1}(1(c) \oplus 2(d)))$

One can use k-expressions also to construct directed graphs (and thus argumentation frameworks), interpreting $\eta_{i,j}$ as the operation that inserts directed edges that are oriented from vertices labeled i to vertices labeled j. Courcelle and Olariu [12] define the clique-width of a directed graph G as the smallest integer k such that G can be constructed by a k-expression.

Example 2. The parse-tree of a cwd-expression $\sigma \in CW_3$ for the framework $\mathcal{F}$ from Example 1 is given in Figure 1(a). Figure 1(b) illustrates the labeled graphs associated to sub-expressions rooted in a node of the parse-tree. Here the index of a node denotes the current label, i.e. for a such that $\mathcal{L}(a) = 3$ we write a_3. Actually one can show that $\mathrm{cwd}(\mathcal{F}) = 2$, but for demonstrating our algorithms the above 3-expression is appropriate.

There are also classes of dense directed graphs which have low clique-width. As an example, we mention the class of transitive tournaments $\mathcal{T} = \{T_n : n \geq 1\}$ with $T_n = (\{a_1, \ldots, a_n\}, \{(a_i, a_j) : 1 \leq i < j \leq n\})$. For an arbitrary T_n we can give a cwd-expression that only uses two different labels. For illustration, we give such an expression defining the graph T_5 (see Figure 2):

$$\eta_{1,2}(\rho_{2\to1}(\eta_{1,2}(\rho_{2\to1}(\eta_{1,2}(\rho_{2\to1}(\eta_{1,2}(1(a_1) \oplus 2(a_2))) \oplus 2(a_3))) \oplus 2(a_4))) \oplus 2(a_5))$$

Similar 2-expressions exist for each tournament T_n, thus we obtain that the clique-width for each graph in $\mathcal{T}$ is bounded by 2.

Modularity is a further aspect of clique-width that makes it attractive in the context of abstract argumentation. Consider an AF $\mathcal{F} = (A, R)$. A subset $M \subseteq A$ is a *module* of $\mathcal{F}$ if any two arguments in M are "indistinguishable from the outside," i.e., for any $x, x' \in M$ and $y \in A \setminus M$ we have $(x, y) \in R$ iff $(x', y) \in R$, and $(y, x) \in R$ iff $(y, x') \in R$. The AF $\mathcal{F}$ is called *prime* if all its modules are of size 1 or $|A|$. For instance, the AF T_5 of Figure 2 has a large module $\{a_2, \ldots, a_5\}$ and is therefore not prime. In AFs that model real-world situations one would expect to find large modules, for instance, formed by groups of people that share the same beliefs and opinions regarding the world outside the group (but possibly attack each other for some "internal" reason). One can handle AFs that contain large modules efficiently with clique-width based algorithms. Intuitively[3], from the cwd-expression of an AF $\mathcal{F}$ with a large module M we can first find a cwd-expression for the subframework induced by M. Then we give all arguments in M

---

[3]This can be made precise: the clique-width of an AF equals the maximum clique-width of its prime subframeworks [12].

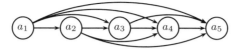

Figure 2. Tournament T_5

the same label and treat them for subsequent considerations as one single argument a_M. Consequently, for solving reasoning problems on $\mathcal{F}$ we can then strongly benefit from the "compression" of M to a_M when we use the clique-width based dynamic programming methods as described in Section 5.

Finally we summarize the properties that make clique-width an appealing parameter for abstract argumentation:

- There are both, sparse (e.g. tree-like AFs or AFs of bounded tree-width, see below) and dense AFs (e.g. transitive tournaments) that possess small clique-width.
- Clique-width incorporates the orientation of attacks.
- Clique-width offers an efficient handling for modular structures.

4. Fixed-Parameter Tractability

As we have already mentioned, clique-width is related to the popular graph parameter *treewidth* [4], therefore it is useful to review known results for the two parameters side by side. Clique-width can be considered to be more general than treewidth since there are graphs of constant clique-width but arbitrarily high treewidth (complete graphs, for instance), but graphs of bounded treewidth also have bounded clique-width [12,5]. An additional advantage of clique-width over treewidth is that it applies well to directed graphs and takes the orientation of edges into account.

By means of a meta-theorem due to Courcelle, Makowsky, and Rotics [11] one can solve any graph problem that can be expressed in Monadic Second Order Logic with second-order quantification on vertex sets (MSO_1) in linear time for graphs of clique-width bounded by some constant k. This result is similar to Courcelle's meta-theorem [7,8] which applies to a more general class of problems (problems expressible in Monadic Second Order Logic with second-order quantification on vertex sets and edge sets, MSO_2) on less general classes of graphs (graphs of bounded treewidth).

Treewidth and clique-width are both NP-hard to compute (as shown in [1] and [18], respectively). However, one can check in polynomial time whether the width of a given graph is bounded in terms of a fixed k. For treewidth this can be accomplished even exactly in linear time via Bodlaender's algorithm [3]. For clique-width, the known algorithms involve an additive approximation error that is bounded in terms of k: as shown by Oum and Seymour [20], there is a function f such that one can find in polynomial time (of order independent of k) an $f(k)$-expression for an undirected graph of clique-width k. As shown by Kanté [19], a similar result holds also for directed graphs.

Dunne [15] already provided MSO_2 characterizations to show the fixed-parameter tractability of reasoning problems for argumentation frameworks of bounded treewidth. We observe that these MSO_2 characterizations do not make use of quantification over edge sets and so are in fact MSO_1 characterizations. Together with the meta-theorem for clique-width, we thus can immediately give the following result.

Proposition 1. *For AFs of clique-width bounded by a constant, the problems* CA *and* SA *are decidable in linear time.*

5. Algorithms

In this section we provide our dynamic-programming algorithms for credulous and skeptical acceptance. In fact, we start with credulous acceptance which relies on a simpler data structure (since we only have to characterize admissible sets), and then extend our ideas to skeptical acceptance. However, both algorithms follow the same basic principles by making use of a k-expression σ defining an argumentation framework $\mathcal{F}$ in the following way: we assign certain objects (e.g. for CA we use k-quadruples as defined in Definition 3 below) to each subexpression of σ. We manipulate these objects in a bottom-up traversal of the parse tree of the k-expression such that the objects in the root of the parse tree then provide the necessary information to decide the problem under consideration. The size of these objects is bounded in terms of k (and independent of the size of $\mathcal{F}$) and the number of such objects required is linear in the size of $\mathcal{F}$. Most importantly, we will show that these objects can also be efficiently computed for bounded k. Thus, we obtain the desired linear running time for AFs of bounded clique-width.

In what follows, we consider (unless stated otherwise) an AF $\mathcal{F} = (A, R)$ as a labeled directed graph, where the labeling is given by $\mathcal{L} : A \to [k]$ with appropriate k.

5.1. Credulous Acceptance

Definition 3. *A tuple $Q = (I, A, O, D)$ with $I, A, O, D \subseteq [k]$ is called a k-quadruple, and we refer to its parts using $Q_{in} = I$, $Q_{att} = A$, $Q_{out} = O$ and $Q_{def} = D$. The set of all k-quadruples is given by $\mathcal{Q}_k$.*

The "semantics" of a k-quadruple Q with respect to a given AF $\mathcal{F}$ is given as follows.

Definition 4. *Let $Q \in \mathcal{Q}_k$ and $\mathcal{F} = (A, R)$ be an AF labeled by $\mathcal{L} : A \to [k]$. An $\mathcal{F}$-extension of Q is a conflict-free set $E \subseteq A$ satisfying:*

$$Q_{in} = \{\mathcal{L}(a) : a \in E\}$$
$$Q_{att} = \{\mathcal{L}(a) : a \in A \setminus E, a \rightarrowtail E, E \not\rightarrowtail a\}$$
$$Q_{out} = \{\mathcal{L}(a) : a \in A \setminus E, E \not\rightarrowtail a, b \not\rightarrowtail E \text{ or } E \rightarrowtail b \text{ for all } b \text{ with } \mathcal{L}(b)=\mathcal{L}(a)\}$$
$$Q_{def} = \{\mathcal{L}(a) : a \in A \setminus E, E \rightarrowtail a, E \rightarrowtail b \text{ for all } b \text{ with } \mathcal{L}(b)=\mathcal{L}(a)\}$$

The set of all $\mathcal{F}$-extensions of Q is denoted by $\mathcal{E}_{\mathcal{F}}(Q)$. If $\mathcal{E}_{\mathcal{F}}(Q) \neq \emptyset$ we call the k-quadruple Q valid for $\mathcal{F}$.

Informally speaking, for a given AF $\mathcal{F}$, a k-quadruple Q characterizes sets E such that for each $l \in Q_{in}$, at least one argument with $\mathcal{L}(a) = l$ is contained in E. Moreover, for arguments not contained in E, the sets $Q_{att}, Q_{out}, Q_{def}$ provide some further information about the relationship between arguments with respect to their labels. Let us mention here that for a valid k-quadruple Q, a label $l \in [k]$ may be contained in Q_{in} and also in one of $Q_{att}, Q_{out}, Q_{def}$; however, Q_{att}, Q_{out} and Q_{def} are pairwise disjoint. It is important to observe that for each k there is only a finite number of k-quadruples. With this finite number of k-quadruples we are able to represent an unbounded number of different sets E.

To further illustrate the idea behind k-quadruples, consider the AF $\mathcal{F}$ from Example 1 with labels $\mathcal{L}(a) = 3$, $\mathcal{L}(b) = \mathcal{L}(d) = 2$ and $\mathcal{L}(c) = 1$ as depicted in the root of the tree in Figure 1(b). Consider $Q = (\{1, 3\}, \emptyset, \emptyset, \{2\})$ and let us construct a set E such that $E \in \mathcal{E}_{\mathcal{F}}(Q)$. We have only a single argument with label 1 and resp. with label 3, thus $E = \{a, c\}$. Moreover, both arguments with label 2, b and d, satisfy the condition for Q_{def}, i.e. we have $E \rightarrowtail b$ and $E \rightarrowtail d$. Hence, $E \in \mathcal{E}_{\mathcal{F}}(Q)$ holds. As a second example, consider $Q' = (\{2\}, \{1, 3\}, \{2\}, \emptyset)$. Since there are two arguments with label 2, we have three candidates for being an $\mathcal{F}$-extension E' of Q', namely $\{b\}$, $\{d\}$ and $\{b, d\}$ (all of them are conflict-free in $\mathcal{F}$). However, since $1 \in Q'_{att}$, $c \rightarrowtail E'$ and $E' \not\rightarrow c$ has to hold. Thus, d cannot be contained in an $\mathcal{F}$-extension of Q'. Checking the remaining properties, one can show that $\mathcal{E}_{\mathcal{F}}(Q') = \{\{b\}\}$. Finally, consider $Q'' = (\{1, 2\}, \{2, 3\}, \emptyset, \emptyset)$ and suppose an $E'' \in \mathcal{E}_{\mathcal{F}}(Q'')$. Then $c \in E''$, since c is the only argument with label 1. However, also b or d has to be contained in E'' since $2 \in Q''_{in}$. But then, E'' is not conflict-free in $\mathcal{F}$. Thus $\mathcal{E}_{\mathcal{F}}(Q'') = \emptyset$, i.e. Q'' is not valid for $\mathcal{F}$.

The following definition assigns k-quadruples (and certain relations between them) to the nodes of the parse-tree of a given k-expression. In what follows, we denote the AF defined by a k-expression σ as $\mathcal{F}_{\sigma}$.

Definition 5. *A full k-quadruple assignment for a k-expression σ is a function that maps each subexpression θ of σ to a relation L_{θ} over k-quadruples in the following way:*

- *$L_{\theta}(Q, R, S)$ iff $\theta = \theta_1 \oplus \theta_2$, Q, R, S are valid k-quadruples for $\mathcal{F}_{\theta}$, $\mathcal{F}_{\theta_1}$, and resp. $\mathcal{F}_{\theta_2}$, and for each $E_1 \in \mathcal{E}_{\mathcal{F}_{\theta_1}}(R)$, $E_2 \in \mathcal{E}_{\mathcal{F}_{\theta_2}}(S)$, also $E_1 \cup E_2 \in \mathcal{E}_{\mathcal{F}_{\theta}}(Q)$;*
- *$L_{\theta}(Q, Q')$ iff either $\theta = \rho_{i \to j}(\theta')$ or $\theta = \eta_{i,j}(\theta')$, Q and Q' are valid k-quadruples for $\mathcal{F}_{\theta}$ and resp. $\mathcal{F}_{\theta'}$, and for each $E \in \mathcal{E}_{\mathcal{F}_{\theta'}}(Q')$, also $E \in \mathcal{E}_{\mathcal{F}_{\theta}}(Q)$;*
- *$L_{l(v)}(Q)$ iff Q is a valid k-quadruple of $\mathcal{F}_{l(v)}$.*

The following theorem reveals the benefits of full k-quadruple assignments for our algorithmic purposes. Indeed, the desired dynamic programming algorithm for CA is used within the proof of that result. We bound the running time of our algorithms in terms of the length of the given cwd-expression (which is linear in the size of the given AF).

Theorem 1. *Let k be a constant.*

1. *Given a k-expression σ for an AF $\mathcal{F}$, we can compute the full k-quadruple assignment for σ in linear time.*
2. *Given the full k-quadruple assignment for σ and a set S of arguments, we can decide in linear time whether some preferred extension of $\mathcal{F}$ contains S.*

In the remainder of the subsection, we sketch a proof of this result and illustrate the central concepts using Example 1.

For the first part of the theorem we have to establish valid k-quadruples for all subexpressions θ of σ and the respective relations L_{θ} without an explicit computation of $\mathcal{F}$-extensions. Instead, we use a bottom-up computation along the parse tree of σ. To this end, we recursively define a function F_{CA} which associates to each subexpression of σ the set of k-quadruples which are valid for the respective subframework.

Definition 6. *The function $F_{CA} : CW_k \to 2^{\mathcal{Q}_k}$ is recursively defined along the structure of k-expressions as follows.*

- *$F_{CA}(i(v)) = \{(\{i\}, \emptyset, \emptyset, \emptyset), (\emptyset, \emptyset, \{i\}, \emptyset)\}$*
- *$F_{CA}(\sigma_1 \oplus \sigma_2) = \{Q \oplus^{CA} Q' : Q \in F_{CA}(\sigma_1), Q' \in F_{CA}(\sigma_2)\}$ where*

$$Q \oplus^{CA} Q' = (Q_{in} \cup Q'_{in}, Q_{att} \cup Q'_{att}, (Q_{out} \cup Q'_{out}) \setminus (Q_{att} \cup Q'_{att}), Q_{def} \cap Q'_{def})$$

- $F_{\mathsf{CA}}(\rho_{i\to j}(\sigma)) = \{\rho_{i\to j}^{\mathsf{CA}}(Q') : Q' \in F_{\mathsf{CA}}(\sigma)\}$ where $\rho_{i\to j}^{\mathsf{CA}}(Q') = Q$ holds iff the following conditions are jointly satisfied:

  * $Q_{in} = \begin{cases} Q'_{in} \setminus \{i\} \cup \{j\} & \text{if } i \in Q'_{in} \\ Q'_{in} & \text{otherwise} \end{cases}$

  * $Q_{att} = \begin{cases} Q'_{att} \setminus \{i\} \cup \{j\} & \text{if } i \in Q'_{att} \\ Q'_{att} & \text{otherwise} \end{cases}$

  * $Q_{out} = \begin{cases} Q'_{out} \setminus \{i\} \cup \{j\} & \text{if } i \in Q'_{out} \text{ and } j \notin Q'_{att} \\ Q'_{out} \setminus \{i, j\} & \text{if } i \in Q'_{att} \\ Q'_{out} \setminus \{i\} & \text{otherwise} \end{cases}$

  * $Q_{def} = \begin{cases} Q'_{def} \setminus \{i\} \cup \{j\} & \text{if } i \in Q'_{def} \text{ and } j \notin Q'_{att} \cup Q'_{out} \\ Q'_{def} \setminus \{j\} & \text{otherwise} \end{cases}$

- $F_{\mathsf{CA}}(\eta_{i,j}(\sigma)) = \{\eta_{i,j}^{\mathsf{CA}}(Q) : Q \in F_{\mathsf{CA}}(\sigma), \{i, j\} \not\subseteq Q_{in}\}$ where

$$\eta_{i,j}^{\mathsf{CA}}(Q) = \begin{cases} (Q_{in}, Q_{att} \setminus \{j\}, Q_{out} \setminus \{j\}, Q_{def} \cup \{j\}) & \text{if } i \in Q_{in} \\ (Q_{in}, Q_{att} \cup \{i\}, Q_{out} \setminus \{i\}, Q_{def} \setminus \{i\}) & \text{if } j \in Q_{in}, i \in Q_{out} \\ Q & \text{otherwise} \end{cases}$$

By definition, F_{CA} provides the necessary relations for the desired full k-quadruple assignment. Figure 3 illustrates the function F_{CA} for the cwd-expression used in Example 2 to define the AF $\mathcal{F}$. Each table in Figure 3 shows the valid k-quadruples for the subframeworks of $\mathcal{F}$ (the tree of tables mirrors the tree of subframeworks as given in Figure 1(b)). For a better understanding, we provide in Figure 3 also the extension[4] $\mathcal{E}$ of the k-quadruples; however, those extensions are not required for computing F_{CA}.

Let us have a look at a few aspects of the computation of F_{CA}. We start at the leaf nodes. For instance, in the leaf of the left branch, we consider the subframework defined by the expression $\sigma_1 = 1(a)$, i.e. the framework $\mathcal{F}_1 = (\{a\}, \emptyset)$ with a labeled by 1. By definition of F_{CA}, two k-quadruples are assigned to σ_1, viz. $Q_1 = (\{1\}, \emptyset, \emptyset, \emptyset)$ and $Q_1' = (\emptyset, \emptyset, \{1\}, \emptyset)$ representing the two conflict-free sets of $\mathcal{F}_1$, $\{a\}$ and $\emptyset$. Similar k-quadruples (see the rhs sibling) are assigned to the framework $(\{b\}, \emptyset)$ defined by $\sigma_2 = 2(b)$. Then, $F_{\mathsf{CA}}(\sigma_1 \oplus \sigma_2)$ combines these k-quadruples according to Definition 6. In the next step we have to deal with an edge-insertion, i.e. we compute $F_{\mathsf{CA}}(\eta_{1,2}(\sigma_1 \oplus \sigma_2))$; observe that the k-quadruple $Q = (\{1, 2\}, \emptyset, \emptyset, \emptyset)$ thus drops out by definition, since $\{1, 2\} \subseteq Q_{in}$. Also observe that the status of the arguments which have been "out" changes accordingly to the direction of the introduced edge. Due to space restrictions, we cannot give a discussion about the entire bottom-up computation of F_{CA} here, but we mention that each k-quadruple as computed by F_{CA} in Figure 3 is indeed valid for the respective subframework. As well, all the relations from Definition 5 are established by computing F_{CA}. The general result is as follows.

Lemma 1. *Let σ be a k-expression defining an AF $\mathcal{F}$. Then, $F_{\mathsf{CA}}(\sigma)$ coincides with the set of valid k-quadruples for $\mathcal{F}$. Further, the valid k-quadruples together with the operators $\oplus^{\mathsf{CA}}, \rho_{i\to j}^{\mathsf{CA}}, \eta_{i,j}^{\mathsf{CA}}$ give the full k-quadruple assignment for σ.*

---

[4]In this example, there is always exactly one such extension for the depicted valid k-quadruples; hence $\emptyset$ refers to the empty extension and not to the empty set of extensions.

Figure 3. The function F_{CA} for the k-expression in Example 2

The time to compute $F_{CA}(\sigma)$ depends (heavily) on k but is linear in the size of σ (and thus in the size of $\mathcal{F}_\sigma$). This concludes the proof sketch for (1).

To prove the second part of Theorem 1, we require an appropriate connection between admissible sets and k-quadruples.

Lemma 2. *Let $\mathcal{F}$ be an AF and E be conflict-free in $\mathcal{F}$. Then there is a unique valid k-quadruple Q with $E \in \mathcal{E}_\mathcal{F}(Q)$. Further, E is an admissible extension of $\mathcal{F}$ iff $Q_{att} = \emptyset$.*

Given the full k-quadruple assignment for σ, we are now able to efficiently decide whether an argument set S is contained in at least one admissible extension of $\mathcal{F}$: For each node of the parse-tree, i.e. each subexpression σ', we mark the valid k-quadruples that represent at least one admissible extension E of the subframework $\mathcal{F}_{\sigma'} = (A', R')$ such that $S \cap A' \subseteq E$. This can be done as follows: First, for each cwd-expression $i(v)$, $(\{i\}, \emptyset, \emptyset, \emptyset)$ is marked in case $v \in S$; otherwise, both $(\{i\}, \emptyset, \emptyset, \emptyset)$ and $(\emptyset, \emptyset, \{i\}, \emptyset)$ are marked. Hence, quadruples without a mark indicate that some element from S is missing. In the $\eta_{i,j}$ and $\rho_{i \to j}$ nodes of the parse tree, a quadruple is marked if it is in relation with a marked quadruple in the child node. For a $\oplus$-node (i.e. for a subexpression θ with $\oplus$ as main connective), we mark the quadruple Q if $L_\theta(Q, Q_1, Q_2)$ holds for some marked quadruples Q_1, Q_2. If we have a marked quadruple Q in the root and this quadruple represents an admissible extension, i.e. $Q_{att} = \emptyset$ holds, then S is credulously accepted.

This marking algorithm is obviously running in linear time w.r.t. to the size of the full k-quadruple assignment of $\mathcal{F}$. This shows the second part of the theorem.

5.2. Skeptical Reasoning

For skeptical acceptance we augment each k-quadruple by a so-called guard which stores quadruples representing larger (wrt. $\subseteq$) extensions. This will allow us to characterize not only admissible but also preferred extensions.

Definition 7. A guarded k-quadruple is a pair (Q, Γ) where $Q \in \mathcal{Q}_k$ and $\Gamma \subseteq \mathcal{Q}_k$ is the guard for Q. The set of all guarded k-quadruples is given by $G\mathcal{Q}_k$.

Definition 8. Let $(Q, \Gamma) \in G\mathcal{Q}_k$ and $\mathcal{F} = (A, R)$ be an AF. An $\mathcal{F}$-extension of (Q, Γ) (in $\mathcal{F}$), is a conflict-free set $E \subseteq A$ in $\mathcal{F}$ satisfying: (1) $E \in \mathcal{E}_\mathcal{F}(Q)$; (2) for each conflict-free set E' of $\mathcal{F}$ with $E \subset E'$, there is a $Q' \in \Gamma$ such that $E' \in \mathcal{E}_\mathcal{F}(Q')$; and (3) for each $Q' \in \Gamma$ there exists an E' with $E \subset E'$, such that $E' \in \mathcal{E}_\mathcal{F}(Q')$.

The set of all $\mathcal{F}$-extensions of (Q, Γ) (in $\mathcal{F}$) is denoted by $\mathcal{E}_\mathcal{F}(Q, \Gamma)$. If $\mathcal{E}_\mathcal{F}(Q, \Gamma) \neq \emptyset$ we call (Q, Γ) valid for $\mathcal{F}$.

Replacing in Definition 5 k-quadruples by guarded k-quadruples and $\mathcal{E}(Q)$ by $\mathcal{E}(Q, \Gamma)$ gives us the concept of a full guarded k-quadruple assignment.

Theorem 2. Let k be a constant.

1. Given a k-expression σ for an AF $\mathcal{F}$, we can compute the full guarded k-quadruple assignment for σ in linear time.
2. Given the full guarded k-quadruple assignment for σ and a set S of arguments, we can decide in linear time whether all preferred extensions of $\mathcal{F}$ contain S.

As before, we now provide a function, which recursively establishes the full guarded k-quadruple assignment without an explicit computation of extensions (for $\Gamma, \Gamma' \subseteq \mathcal{Q}_k$, we below use the operator $\Gamma \oplus^{\text{SA}} \Gamma' = \{Q \oplus^{\text{CA}} Q' : Q \in \Gamma, Q' \in \Gamma'\}$).

Definition 9. The function $F_{\text{SA}} : CW_k \to 2^{G\mathcal{Q}_k}$ is recursively defined as follows.

- $F_{\text{SA}}(i(v)) = \{(\{i\}, \emptyset, \emptyset, \emptyset), \emptyset), \ (\emptyset, \emptyset, \{i\}, \emptyset), \{(\{i\}, \emptyset, \emptyset, \emptyset)\})\}$
- $F_{\text{SA}}(\sigma_1 \oplus \sigma_2) = \{(Q_1 \oplus^{\text{CA}} Q_2, (\Gamma_1 \oplus^{\text{SA}} \Gamma_2) \cup (\{Q_1\} \oplus^{\text{SA}} \Gamma_2) \cup (\Gamma_1 \oplus^{\text{SA}} \{Q_2\})) :$
  $(Q_1, \Gamma_1) \in F_{\text{SA}}(\sigma_1), (Q_2, \Gamma_2) \in F_{\text{SA}}(\sigma_2)\}$
- $F_{\text{SA}}(\rho_{i \to j}(\sigma)) = \{(\rho_{i \to j}^{\text{CA}}(Q), \{\rho_{i \to j}^{\text{CA}}(Q') : Q' \in \Gamma\}) : (Q, \Gamma) \in F_{\text{SA}}(\sigma)\}$
- $F_{\text{SA}}(\eta_{i,j}(\sigma)) = \{(\eta_{i,j}^{\text{CA}}(Q), \{\eta_{i,j}^{\text{CA}}(Q') : Q' \in \Gamma, \{i, j\} \nsubseteq Q'_{in}\}) :$
  $(Q, \Gamma) \in F_{\text{SA}}(\sigma), \{i, j\} \nsubseteq Q_{in}\}$

Roughly speaking, for $(Q, \Gamma) \in G\mathcal{Q}_k$ we apply here the already defined function F_{CA} not only to Q but also to each element in Γ. It can be shown that $F_{\text{SA}}(\sigma)$ coincides with the set of valid guarded k-quadruples for $\mathcal{F}_\sigma$. Further the valid guarded k-quadruples together with the operators $\oplus^{\text{SA}}$, $\rho_{i \to j}^{\text{SA}}$, $\eta_{i,j}^{\text{SA}}$ give the full guarded k-quadruple assignment for σ. We note that due to the use of guards, computing $F_{\text{SA}}(\sigma)$ is more involved compared to $F_{\text{CA}}(\sigma)$, for a given k-expression σ. However, the size of the tables for each node in the parse-tree of σ still remains bound by k and is independent from the actual size of σ. This guarantees a linear-running time with respect to the size of AFs defined by σ also for $F_{\text{SA}}(\sigma)$ as long as the AFs have their clique-width bounded by k.

To show (2) we give a certain link between preferred sets and guarded k-quadruples.

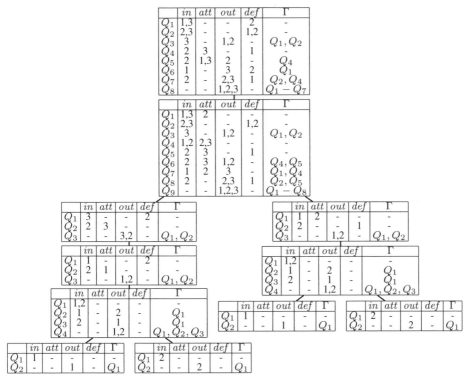

Figure 4. The function F_{SA} for Example 2

Lemma 3. *Let $\mathcal{F}$ be an AF and let E be conflict-free in $\mathcal{F}$. Then there exists a unique valid guarded k-quadruple (Q, Γ) such that $E \in \mathcal{E}_{\mathcal{F}}(Q, \Gamma)$. Moreover, E is a preferred extension of $\mathcal{F}$ iff $Q_{att} = \emptyset$ and there is no $Q' \in \Gamma$ such that $Q'_{att} = \emptyset$.*

Figure 4 illustrates the function F_{SA} for our running example. Compared to Figure 3 we now give also the guard for each k-quadruple. Due to space restrictions, a detailed discussion of this example has to be omitted. We just note that there are four valid guarded k-quadruples (Q, Γ) in the root which match the condition that there is no $Q' \in \Gamma$ such that $Q'_{att} = \emptyset$, namely $G_1 = ((\{1, 3\}, \emptyset, \emptyset, \{2\}), \emptyset)$, $G_2 = ((\{2, 3\}, \emptyset, \emptyset, \{1, 2\}), \emptyset)$, $G_4 = ((\{2\}, \{3\}, \emptyset, \{1\}), \emptyset)$ and $G_5 = ((\{2\}, \{1, 3\}, \{2\}, \emptyset), \{(\{2\}, \{3\}, \emptyset, \{1\})\})$, with their extensions $\mathcal{E}_{\mathcal{F}}(G_1) = \{\{a, c\}\}$, $\mathcal{E}_{\mathcal{F}}(G_2) = \{\{a, d\}\}$, $\mathcal{E}_{\mathcal{F}}(G_4) = \{\{b, d\}\}$ and $\mathcal{E}_{\mathcal{F}}(G_5) = \{\{b\}\}$. G_1, G_2 and G_4 thus characterize maximal conflict-free sets of $\mathcal{F}$, but G_4 is identified to be not preferred since $(G_4)_{att} = \{3\} \neq \emptyset$. We also have selected G_5, since there is no superset of $\{b\}$ admissible in $\mathcal{F}$; however, we also have $(G_5)_{att} = \{1, 3\} \neq \emptyset$. Thus, G_1 and G_2 are the only ones fulfilling all necessary conditions for characterizing preferred extensions of $\mathcal{F}$, which indeed are $\{a, c\}$ and $\{a, d\}$.

The algorithm for skeptical acceptance is similar to the one for CA discussed above. The only pairs marked in leafs $i(v)$ are $((\emptyset, \emptyset, \{i\}, \emptyset), \{(\{i\}, \emptyset, \emptyset, \emptyset)\})$ for $v \in S$. In the other nodes, a guarded k-quadruple is marked if it is in relation with at least one marked pair in its child(ren). Now, there is a marked pair for the root representing a preferred extension (cf. Lemma 3) exactly if S is *not* skeptically accepted, since in this case we have found a preferred extension where at least one argument from S was left out.

6. Conclusion

In this paper, we turned some theoretical tractability results (which implicitly follow from previous work [15]) for argumentation frameworks of bounded clique-width into efficient algorithms. These algorithms are applicable to arbitrary frameworks, whenever a defining k-expression is given, but the runtime heavily depends on k, rather than the size of the AF. Thus the algorithms are expected to run efficiently in particular for small k.

We restricted ourselves here to the problem of acceptance with respect to the preferred semantics, which relies on maximal admissible sets. However, admissibility and maximality are prototypical properties common in many other argumentation semantics. Hence, we expect that the methods developed here can also be extended to other semantics and reasoning tasks, which is left for future work.

References

[1] S. Arnborg, D. G. Corneil, and A. Proskurowski. Complexity of finding embeddings in a k-tree. *SIAM J. Algebraic Discrete Methods*, 8(2):277–284, 1987.
[2] T. J. M. Bench-Capon and P. E. Dunne. Argumentation in artificial intelligence. *Artificial Intelligence*, 171(10-15):619–641, 2007.
[3] H. L. Bodlaender. On linear time minor tests with depth-first search. *J. Algorithms*, 14(1):1–23, 1993.
[4] H. L. Bodlaender. A tourist guide through treewidth. *Acta Cybernetica*, 11:1–21, 1993.
[5] D. G. Corneil and U. Rotics. On the relationship between clique-width and treewidth. *SIAM J. Comput.*, 34(4):825–847, 2005.
[6] S. Coste-Marquis, C. Devred, and P. Marquis. Symmetric argumentation frameworks. In *Proc. EC-SQARU'05*, volume 3571 of *LNCS*, pages 317–328. Springer, 2005.
[7] B. Courcelle. Recognizability and second-order definability for sets of finite graphs. Technical Report I-8634, Université de Bordeaux, 1987.
[8] B. Courcelle. Graph rewriting: an algebraic and logic approach. In *Handbook of Theoretical Computer Science, Vol. B*, pages 193–242. Elsevier Science Publishers 1990.
[9] B. Courcelle, J. Engelfriet, and G. Rozenberg. Context-free handle-rewriting hypergraph grammars. In *Proc. Graph Grammars 1990*, volume 532 of *LNCS*, pages 253–268. Springer, 1991.
[10] B. Courcelle, J. Engelfriet, and G. Rozenberg. Handle-rewriting hypergraph grammars. *J. of Computer and System Sciences*, 46(2):218–270, 1993.
[11] B. Courcelle, J. A. Makowsky, and U. Rotics. Linear time solvable optimization problems on graphs of bounded clique-width. *Theory Comput. Syst.*, 33(2):125–150, 2000.
[12] B. Courcelle and S. Olariu. Upper bounds to the clique-width of graphs. *Discr. Appl. Math.*, 101(1-3):77–114, 2000.
[13] Y. Dimopoulos and A. Torres. Graph theoretical structures in logic programs and default theories. *Theoret. Comput. Sci.*, 170(1-2):209–244, 1996.
[14] P. M. Dung. On the acceptability of arguments and its fundamental role in nonmonotonic reasoning, logic programming and n-person games. *Artificial Intelligence*, 77(2):321–358, 1995.
[15] P. E. Dunne. Computational properties of argument systems satisfying graph-theoretic constraints. *Artificial Intelligence*, 171(10-15):701–729, 2007.
[16] P. E. Dunne and T. J. M. Bench-Capon. Coherence in finite argument systems. *Artificial Intelligence*, 141(1/2):187–203, 2002.
[17] W. Dvořák, R. Pichler, and S. Woltran. Towards fixed-parameter tractable algorithms for argumentation. In *Proc. KR'10*, pages 112-122. AAAI Press, 2010
[18] M. R. Fellows, F. A. Rosamond, U. Rotics, and S. Szeider. Clique-width is NP-complete. *SIAM J. Discrete Math.*, 23(2):909–939, 2009.
[19] M. M. Kanté. The rank-width of directed graphs. *CoRR*, abs/0709.1433, 2007.
[20] S. Oum and P. Seymour. Approximating clique-width and branch-width. *J. Combin. Theory Ser. B*, 96(4):514–528, 2006.

Computational Models of Argument
P. Baroni et al. (Eds.)
IOS Press, 2010
© 2010 The authors and IOS Press. All rights reserved.
doi:10.3233/978-1-60750-619-5-231

Two-Agent Conflict Resolution with Assumption-Based Argumentation

Xiuyi FAN, Francesca TONI, Adil HUSSAIN

Department of Computing, Imperial College London,
South Kensington Campus, London SW7 2AZ, UK

Abstract. Conflicts exist in multi-agent systems. Agents have different interests and desires. Agents also hold different beliefs and may make different assumptions. To resolve conflicts, agents need to better convey information between each other and facilitate fair negotiations that yield jointly agreeable outcomes. In this paper, we present a two-agent conflict resolution scheme developed under Assumption-Based Argumentation (ABA). Agents represent their beliefs and desires in ABA. Conflicts are resolved by merging conflicting arguments. We also discuss the notion of fairness and the use of argumentation dialogue in conflict resolution.

Keywords. Multi-Agent Systems, Argumentation, Conflict Resolution

1. Introduction

Complex multi-agent systems are composed of heterogeneous agents with different beliefs and desires. Agents usually perform tasks in a joint manner so as to promote high common welfare. In this paper, we consider conflicts arising for two reasons during a collaboration among two agents. Firstly, agents reason with different assumptions to fill gaps in their beliefs. Since some assumptions may be incorrect, agents may be misinformed and decide on incompatible actions that lead to conflict. Secondly, even if agents share the same information, they may still disagree if they have different desires.

We use Assumption-Based Argumentation (ABA) [BTK93,BDKT97,DKT09] for conflict resolution, as beliefs and desires can be represented in ABA. In this setting, to resolve conflicts between *two agents* is to merge two ABA frameworks because the merge eliminates misunderstanding between agents and considers desires from both agents. To eliminate misunderstanding, an agent's assumptions are updated by considering beliefs from the other agent. Therefore, incorrect assumptions are invalidated. To satisfy desires from both agents, we propose the mechanism of *concatenation* to merge rules. Upon a successful concatenation merge, both agents' desires may be satisfied. We also briefly consider cases where a concatenation merge is not possible, and define *fair compromise* for these cases.

Research merits of this paper are: (1) the partition of rules in ABA in belief rules and desire rules, (2) the definition of a merge operator for rules about desires to resolve conflicts between agents, (3) the consideration of fairness for cases where not all agents' desires are satisfiable, and (4) the exploration of the use of argumentation dialogues to resolve conflicts.

The paper is organized as follows. Section 2 reviews the ABA framework, serving as the ground for our work. Section 3 presents a number of examples that motivate our approach. Section 4 describes the merge operator. Section 5 explains how conflict resolution can be performed in a distributed and progressive manner. It further explores the concept of fairness as making similar compromise between agents. Section 6 reviews some related work in conflict resolution among agents. We conclude at section 7 with a summary and a discussion about possible future directions.

2. Assumption-Based Argumentation (ABA)

An ABA framework [BTK93,BDKT97,DKT09] is a tuple $\langle \mathcal{L}, \mathcal{R}, \mathcal{A}, \mathcal{C} \rangle$ where

- $\langle \mathcal{L}, \mathcal{R} \rangle$ is a deductive system, with a *language* $\mathcal{L}$ and a set of inference *rules* $\mathcal{R}$ of the form $s_0 \leftarrow s_1, \ldots, s_m (m \geq 0)$,
- $\mathcal{A} \subseteq \mathcal{L}$ is a (non-empty) set, whose elements are referred to as *assumptions*,
- $\mathcal{C}$ is a total mapping from $\mathcal{A}$ into $2^{\mathcal{L}}$, where each $c \in \mathcal{C}(\alpha)$ is a *contrary* of α.[1]

Given a rule $s_0 \leftarrow s_1, \ldots, s_m$, s_0 is referred as the *head* and $s_1, \ldots, s_m$ as the *body* of the rule. We will use the following notation: $Head(s_0 \leftarrow s_1, \ldots, s_m) = s_0$ and $Body(s_0 \leftarrow s_1, \ldots, s_m) = s_1, \ldots, s_m$.

Basically, ABA frameworks can be defined for any logic specified by means of inference rules. Sentences in the underlying language include assumptions. *Arguments* are deductions of claims supported by sets of assumptions. *Attacks* are directed at the assumptions in the support of arguments.

In an ABA framework $\langle \mathcal{L}, \mathcal{R}, \mathcal{A}, \mathcal{C} \rangle$, an argument can be formally defined in terms of $\mathcal{R}$ and $\mathcal{A}$ in several ways [BDKT97,DKT06,DKT09]. Here, we adopt the definition of [DKT09]: *an argument for (the claim) $c \in \mathcal{L}$ supported by $S \subseteq \mathcal{A}$ ($S \vdash c$ in short) is a tree with nodes labelled by sentences in $\mathcal{L}$ or by the symbol τ,[2] such that*

1. the root is labelled by c;
2. for every node N

   - if N is a leaf then N is labelled either by an assumption or by τ;
   - if N is not a leaf and l_N is the label of N, then there is an inference rule $l_N \leftarrow b_1, \ldots, b_m (m \geq 0)$ and either $m = 0$ and the child of N is τ or $m > 0$ and N has m children, labelled by $b_1, \ldots, b_m$ (respectively);

3. S is the set of all assumptions labelling the leaves.

The notion of attack in ABA is formally defined as follows:

- *an argument $S_1 \vdash c_1$ attacks an argument $S_2 \vdash c_2$ iff the claim c_1 of the first argument is a contrary of one of the assumptions in the support S_2 of the second argument ($\exists \alpha \in S_2$ such that $c_1 \in \mathcal{C}(\alpha)$);*
- *a set of arguments Arg_1 attacks a set of arguments Arg_2 iff an argument in Arg_1 attacks an argument in Arg_2.*

---

[1]Here, as in [GT08], we define the contrary of an assumption as a total mapping from an assumption to a set of sentences, instead of a mapping from an assumption to a sentence as in the original ABA [BDKT97].

[2]Here, as in [DKT09], $\tau \notin \mathcal{L}$ intuitively represents "true".

Attacks between (sets of) arguments correspond in ABA to attacks between sets of assumptions:

- *a set of assumptions A attacks a set of assumptions B* iff an argument supported by a subset of A attacks an argument supported by a subset of B.

With argument and attack defined, commonly used argumentation semantics such as conflict-free, admissible, complete, grounded, preferred, ideal and stable semantics can be applied in ABA [BTK93,BDKT97,DKT06,DMT07]. In this work, we focus on the conflict-free semantics, defined as follows:

- *a set of assumptions is conflict-free* iff it does not attack itself;
- *a set Args of arguments is conflict-free* iff the union of all sets of assumptions that support arguments in $Args$ does not attack itself.

Throughout the paper, we use the following terminology: *a sentence s belongs to a conflict-free extension with respect to an argument arg iff s is the claim of arg and arg* belongs to a conflict-free set of arguments.

3. Examples

Imagine a scenario such as the following. Two agents, Jenny and Amy, are planning a film night together. They want to decide the movie to watch.

Example 3.1. Jenny wants to pick a movie that is entertaining. She finds action movies entertaining. *Spider Man* and *Terminator* are both screening at the moment. Jenny believes *Terminator* is an action movie. She does not have much information about *Spider Man*. Hence she believes it is not an action movie. Jenny then concludes she wants to watch *Terminator*. Represented in ABA, Jenny's beliefs and desires are[3]:

Rules:
watchMovie(X) ← selectMovie(X), entertainingMovie(X)
entertainingMovie(X) ← actionMovie(X)
actionMovie(*Terminator*)
Assumptions:
selectMovie(X)
¬actionMovie(X)
Contraries:
C(selectMovie(X)) = {¬ selectMovie(X), selectMovie(Y)| Y ≠ X }
C(¬ actionMovie(X)) = {actionMovie(X)}

Here, Jenny's goal watch(*Terminator*) is supported by the argument in Figure 1 and belongs to a conflict-free extension.

---

[3]In presenting ABA frameworks we use the following conventions:
- constants are in *italic*;
- X, Y etc. are variables; inference rule/assumptions/contrary schemata (with variables) are used to stand for the set of all their ground instances with respect to constants. E.g., selectMovie(X) stands for select-Movie(*Terminator*) and selectMovie(*Spider Man*);
- $s \leftarrow$ is represented simply as s, for any sentence $s \in \mathcal{L}$.

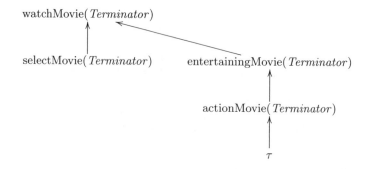

Figure 1. Jenny's argument about watching *Terminator* in Example 3.1 (and Example 3.2).

Amy also wants to watch an action movie that is entertaining. However, she has watched *Terminator* before hence does not want to watch it again. Amy has watched the trailer of *Spider Man* and believes it also is an action movie. Amy concludes she wants to watch *Spider Man*. After exchanging their preferences and reasoning, Amy realized that Jenny mistakenly held an incorrect assumption, as *Spider Man* is an action movie. Jenny hence learns this new information and agrees to watch *Spider Man* with Amy. In ABA, Amy's beliefs and desires are:

Rules:
watchMovie(X) ← selectMovie(X), entertainingMovie(X)
entertainingMovie(X) ← actionMovie(X)
¬selectMovie(*Terminator*)
actionMovie(*Spider Man*)
Assumptions and Contraries:
as for Jenny

In this example, agreement can be reached simply by information exchange of actionMovie(*SpiderMan*), resulting in a merged ABA framework with:

watchMovie(*Spider Man*) ← selectMovie(*Spider Man*),
                            entertainingMovie(*Spider Man*)
entertainingMovie(*Spider Man*) ← actionMovie(*Spider Man*)
actionMovie(*Spider Man*)

Example 3.2. Similarly to the previous example, Jenny wants to watch an action movie that is entertaining. She believes two films, *Terminator* and *Harry Potter*, are screening at the moment. She believes *Harry Potter* is a fantasy movie and *Terminator* is an action movie. She then decides to watch *Terminator*. In ABA, Jenny's beliefs and desires are:

Rules:
watchMovie(X) ← selectMovie(X), entertainingMovie(X)
entertainingMovie(X) ← actionMovie(X)
actionMovie(*Terminator*)
fantasyMovie(*Harry Potter*)
Assumptions:
selectMovie(X)
¬actionMovie(X)

¬fantasyMovie(X)
Contraries:
$\mathcal{C}$(selectMovie(X)) = { ¬ selectMovie(X), selectMovie(Y)| Y ≠ X }
$\mathcal{C}$(¬ actionMovie(X)) = {actionMovie(X)}
$\mathcal{C}$(¬ fantasyMovie(X)) = {fantasyMovie(X)}

Instead of watching an action movie, Amy wants to watch an entertaining fantasy movie. In addition to the two movies Jenny knows of, Amy also knows that *Lord of the Rings* (*LoR* in short), an action and a fantasy movie, is screening. She is uncertain between *Harry Potter* and *LoR*. After exchanging information, Jenny becomes aware of the extra piece of information about *LoR* and both agree to watch this movie. In ABA, Amy's beliefs and desires are :

Rules:
watchMovie(X) ← selectMovie(X), entertainingMovie(X)
entertainingMovie(X) ← fantasyMovie(X)
actionMovie(*Terminator*)
fantasyMovie(*Harry Potter*)
fantasyMovie(*LoR*)
actionMovie(*LoR*)
Assumptions and Contraries:
as for Jenny

In this example, agreement is reached by information exchange of actionMovie(*LoR*) and the creation of a new rule that a movie is entertaining if it is both an action movie and a fantasy movie. The resulting merged ABA framework contains:

watchMovie(*LoR*) ← selectMovie(*LoR*), entertainingMovie(*LoR*)
entertainingMovie(*LoR*) ← actionMovie(*LoR*), fantasyMovie(*LoR*)
actionMovie(*LoR*)
fantasyMovie(*LoR*)

Figure 2 gives the argument for watching *LoR* in the merged framework.

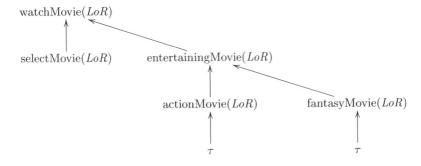

Figure 2. Argument for watching *Lord of the Rings* in the merged belief base in Example 3.2.

These examples demonstrate the two main aspects of our approach: (1) beliefs can be communicated to update incorrect assumptions; (2) when there is a conflict between agents' desires, we try to reach an agreement satisfying both agents by merging rules.

4. Conflict Resolution as Merge of Beliefs

Inspired by the examples presented in section 3, we resolve conflicts between two agents with a merge of conflicting arguments/ABA frameworks. Conceptually, conflict resolution can be understood as follows. Two agents share the same high level *goal*, $\mathcal{G}$. Each agent i has its own mean, δ_i, to realize $\mathcal{G}$. Hence $\mathcal{G}$ is realizable by each agent independently. Conflict arises as the two means, δ_1 and δ_2, of deriving $\mathcal{G}$ are different. Resolving conflict between two agents means detecting a commonly acceptable mean, δ, to realize $\mathcal{G}$. As an illustration, in example 3.1 $\mathcal{G}$ is watchMovie(X) (where X is implicitly existentially quantified), $\delta_1 = \{X/Terminator\}$, $\delta_2 = \{X/Spider\ Man\}$ and $\delta = \{X/Spider\ Man\}$ (namely, realizations are variable instantiations). Our approach is to construct a joint ABA framework by extracting information from both agents' ABA frameworks. The joint ABA framework supports a conflict-free realization $\mathcal{G}\delta$ of $\mathcal{G}$.

4.1. Belief Rules vs. Desire Rules

Before we formally define conflict resolution, there is one classification we need to make. When describing agents with an ABA framework $\langle \mathcal{L}, \mathcal{R}, \mathcal{A}, \mathcal{C} \rangle$, there are two types of rules in $\mathcal{R}$: (1) *belief rules*, $\mathcal{BR}$, and (2) *desire rules*, $\mathcal{DR}$. In previous examples,

    actionMovie(*Terminator*)
    fantasyMovie(*Harry Potter*)

  are belief rules. Agents with different desires can be modelled by different desire rules. In previous examples,

    entertainingMovie(X) ← actionMovie(X)
    entertainingMovie(X) ← fantasyMovie(X)

  are desire rules. Intuitively, desire rules are directly relevant to goals and can be used to build arguments for goals. Instead, belief rules may contribute to undermining arguments for goals.

  Note that rules may be defeasible (e.g. an agent desire to select and watch a movie that is entertaining) or not (e.g. an agent believes an action movie is entertaining). Defeasibility, as conventional in ABA, is given by the presence of assumptions [DKT09].

4.2. Formal Definition of Conflict and Conflict Resolution

Formally, we have $Agent_1$ with ABA framework $AF_1 = \langle \mathcal{L}, \mathcal{R}_1, \mathcal{A}_1, \mathcal{C}_1 \rangle$ and $Agent_2$ with ABA framework $AF_2 = \langle \mathcal{L}, \mathcal{R}_2, \mathcal{A}_2, \mathcal{C}_2 \rangle$. In each framework, the set of rules $\mathcal{R}_i$ is composed of belief rules $\mathcal{BR}_i$ and desire rules $\mathcal{DR}_i$, such that $\mathcal{R}_i = \mathcal{BR}_i \cup \mathcal{DR}_i$, and $\mathcal{BR}_i \cap \mathcal{DR}_i = \emptyset$. The agents share the same language $\mathcal{L}$ while having potentially different rules, assumptions and contraries of assumptions. The agents share the same goal $\mathcal{G}$ while having different instantiations $\mathcal{G}\delta_1$ and $\mathcal{G}\delta_2$ thereof.

Definition 4.1. Conflict. A *conflict between $Agent_1$ and $Agent_2$ with ABA frameworks AF_1 and AF_2 (respectively) with respect to a goal $\mathcal{G}$ is a pair of goals $(\mathcal{G}\delta_1, \mathcal{G}\delta_2)$ such that $\mathcal{G}\delta_i \in \mathcal{L}$, $\mathcal{G}\delta_i$ belongs to a conflict-free extension of AF_i ($i = 1,2$) and $\mathcal{G}\delta_1 \neq \mathcal{G}\delta_2$.*

Definition 4.2. Conflict Resolution. A *conflict resolution* $\mathcal{G}\delta$ *for a conflict* $(\mathcal{G}\delta_1, \mathcal{G}\delta_2)$ *with respect to* $\mathcal{G}$ is such that $\mathcal{G}\delta$ belongs to conflict-free extensions of AF_1' and AF_2' defined as $AF_1' = \langle \mathcal{L}, \mathcal{R}_1 \cup \mathcal{BR}_2, \mathcal{A}, \mathcal{C} \rangle$ and $AF_2' = \langle \mathcal{L}, \mathcal{R}_2 \cup \mathcal{BR}_1, \mathcal{A}, \mathcal{C} \rangle$, where

- $\mathcal{A} = \mathcal{A}_1 \cup \mathcal{A}_2$;
- $\mathcal{C}$ is defined as $\mathcal{C}(\alpha) = \mathcal{C}_1(\alpha) \cup \mathcal{C}_2(\alpha)$ (for any $\alpha \in \mathcal{A}$).

4.3. The Merge Operator

The merge of two ABA frameworks, AF_1 and AF_2, can be reduced to the merge of the two sets of rules, $\mathcal{R}_1$ and $\mathcal{R}_2$, sets of assumptions, $\mathcal{A}_1$ and $\mathcal{A}_2$, and contrary mappings, $\mathcal{C}_1$ and $\mathcal{C}_2$. We define the merge of two sets of assumptions as their union. Since ABA does not have any requirement on assumptions being consistent, the union of two sets of assumptions to produce another set is always a valid operation.

Then we define the merge of two contrary mappings as the union of the two individual contrary mappings. This can be justified as follows: if any of the agents knows a sentence is contrary with an assumption, then jointly both agents know the sentence is contrary with the assumption.

The merge of the rules goes one step beyond a simple union. Recall Example 3.2, where $Agent_1$ has the rule:

entertainingMovie(X) ← actionMovie(X)

whereas $Agent_2$ has a different rule with the same head:

entertainingMovie(X) ← fantasyMovie(X)

The final merged rule is:

entertainingMovie(X) ← actionMovie(X), fantasyMovie(X)

This merge corresponds with our intuition. It suggests that when two rules are used to describe agents' desires, the resolution is to create a win-win situation by satisfying both agents' desires at the same time. We define this as the *concatenation merge*.

Definition 4.3. Concatenation Merge. The merge operator between two ABA frameworks, $AF_1 = \langle \mathcal{L}, \mathcal{R}_1, \mathcal{A}_1, \mathcal{C}_1 \rangle$ and $AF_2 = \langle \mathcal{L}, \mathcal{R}_2, \mathcal{A}_2, \mathcal{C}_2 \rangle$, is defined as $AF_1 \oplus AF_2 = AF = \langle \mathcal{L}, \mathcal{R}, \mathcal{A}, \mathcal{C} \rangle$, such that:

- $\mathcal{A} = \mathcal{A}_1 \cup \mathcal{A}_2$
- $\mathcal{C}(\alpha) = \mathcal{C}_1(\alpha) \cup \mathcal{C}_2(\alpha)$
- $\mathcal{R} = \mathcal{R}_1 \oplus_R \mathcal{R}_2$, where $\oplus_R$ is defined as follows, given that $\mathcal{DR}_1 = \{r_1{}^1, r_1{}^2, \ldots, r_1{}^n\}$ and $\mathcal{DR}_2 = \{r_2{}^1, r_2{}^2, \ldots, r_2{}^m\}$ $(n, m \geq 0)$:

  * $\mathcal{R} = \mathcal{BR} \cup \mathcal{DR}$ where

    * $\mathcal{BR} = \mathcal{BR}_1 \cup \mathcal{BR}_2$
    * $\mathcal{DR}$ is such that, for $i = 1, \ldots, n$ and $j = 1, \ldots, m$:

      · if $Head(r_1{}^i) \neq Head(r_2{}^j)$ then $r_1{}^i, r_2{}^j \in \mathcal{DR}$;
      · if $r_1{}^i = r_2{}^j = r$, then $r \in \mathcal{DR}$;
      · if $Head(r_1{}^i) = Head(r_2{}^j) = h$, then $r \in \mathcal{DR}$, where $Head(r) = h$ and $Body(r) = Body(r_1{}^i), Body(r_2{}^j)$;

· nothing else is in $\mathcal{DR}$.

We refer to AF as the *merged ABA framework (resulting from AF_1 and AF_2)*.

Theorem 4.1. When there exists a conflict $(\mathcal{G}\delta_1, \mathcal{G}\delta_2)$ between $Agent_1$ and $Agent_2$ with respect to some goal $\mathcal{G}$, if

- $\mathcal{G}\delta$ belongs to a conflict-extension of $AF = AF_1 \oplus AF_2$ with respect to an argument $S \vdash \mathcal{G}\delta$, and
- there exist arguments $S_1 \vdash \mathcal{G}\delta$, $S_2 \vdash \mathcal{G}\delta$ in AF'_1 and AF'_2, respectively, such that $S_i \subseteq S$ $(i = 1, 2)$

then $\mathcal{G}\delta$ is a conflict resolution for $(\mathcal{G}\delta_1, \mathcal{G}\delta_2)$ with respect to $\mathcal{G}$.

Proof. We know that $\mathcal{G}\delta$ is the claim of $S_i \vdash \mathcal{G}\delta$ in AF'_i hence $\mathcal{G}\delta$ is supported by S_i in AF'_i. We also know $S_i \subseteq S$ and S is conflict-free in AF. We need to prove that S_i is conflict-free in AF'_i. By contradiction, suppose S_i is not conflict-free in AF'_i, and there exists $A \subseteq Si$ and $A \vdash c$ with respect to AF'_i such that $c = \mathcal{C}(\alpha)$ for some $\alpha \in S_i$. This implies that $A \vdash c$ attacks α in AF, since AF contains the union of all belief rules in AF'_1 and AF'_2. Therefore S is not conflict-free in AF: contradiction. $\square$

It is worth noticing that the reverse of this theorem does not hold. Hence, if a conflict resolution $\mathcal{G}\delta$ exists with respect to $\mathcal{G}$, it may not the case that $\mathcal{G}\delta$ belongs to a conflict-free extension of the merged AF, as demonstrated by the following example.

Example 4.1. Assume the conflict is (p(2),p(3)), for some constants 2 and 3. The ABA frameworks are given below (here, all rules are desire rules):

	AF_1:	AF_2:	$AF = AF_1 \oplus AF_2$:
Rules:	p(X) ← a(X)	p(X) ← q(X)	p(X) ← a(X),q(X)
		q(X) ← b(X)	q(X) ← b(X)
Assumptions:	a(1); a(2)	b(1); b(3)	a(1); a(2); b(1); b(3)
Contraries:	$\mathcal{C}(a(X)) = \{q(X)\}$	$\mathcal{C}(b(X)) = \{r(X)\}$	$\mathcal{C}(b(X)) = \{r(X)\}$
			$\mathcal{C}(a(X)) = \{q(X)\}$

Then, p(1) is a conflict resolution as {a(1)} is conflict-free and supports p(1) in $AF_1 = AF'_1$ and {b(1)} is conflict-free and supports p(1) in $AF_2 = AF'_2$. However, p(1) does not belong to a conflict-free extension in AF, since p(X)← a(X),q(X) is in AF and q(X) is the contrary of a(X). So p(X) cannot belong to a conflict-free extension in AF.

It is also worth noticing that Theorem 4.1 holds under the condition that $\mathcal{G}\delta$ has to exist in both AF'_1 and AF'_2. The follow counter-example justifies this condition.

Example 4.2. Assume $(\mathcal{G}\delta_1, \mathcal{G}\delta_2)$ is the conflict and (again, all rules are desire rules):

	AF_1:	AF_2:	$AF = AF_1 \oplus AF_2$:
Rules:	$\mathcal{G}\delta \leftarrow a$	$\mathcal{G}\delta_2 \leftarrow c$	$\mathcal{G}\delta \leftarrow a$; $\mathcal{G}\delta_1 \leftarrow b$
	$\mathcal{G}\delta_1 \leftarrow b$		$\mathcal{G}\delta_2 \leftarrow c$
Assumptions:	$a; b$	c	$a; b; c$
Contraries:	$\mathcal{C}(a) = \{w\}$	$\mathcal{C}(c) = \{w\}$	$\mathcal{C}(a) = \{w\}; \mathcal{C}(b) = \{w\}$
	$\mathcal{C}(b) = \{w\}$		$\mathcal{C}(c) = \{w\}$

Then, $\{a\}$, which supports $\mathcal{G}\delta$, belongs to a conflict-free extension of AF. However, since there is no argument for $\mathcal{G}\delta$ in $AF_2=AF'_2$, there is no conflict-free set of assumptions that supports $\mathcal{G}\delta$. Hence, $\mathcal{G}\delta$ is not a conflict resolution for $(\mathcal{G}\delta_1, \mathcal{G}\delta_2)$.

5. Discussion

5.1. Relevance of Arguments and Interactive Argumentation

The merge operation presented in Section 4 is a generic solution. It solves conflicts between two argumentation frameworks by statically merging them. While performing conflict resolution dynamically between two agents, we can adopt a goal-driven approach by performing the merge interactively and progressively from the claim. Conflict resolution with ABA can be performed interactively. Unlike some other argumentation frameworks, ABA ensures all arguments that support a claim are relevant [DKT09]. While resolving conflicts, each agent only discloses beliefs and desires that are relevant to the claim.

A distributed dispute derivation can be conducted by agents presenting beliefs and desires that support the claim interactively and progressively. Such derivation can be carried out in a top-down fashion. For instance, Example 3.2 can be modelled as followings:

Step 1:
Jenny: watchMovie(X) ← selectMovie(X), entertainingMovie(X)
Amy: watchMovie(X) ← selectMovie(X), entertainingMovie(X)
Joint: watchMovie(X) ← selectMovie(X), entertainingMovie(X)
Step 2:
Jenny: entertainingMovie(X) ← actionMovie(X)
Amy: entertainingMovie(X) ← fantasyMovie(X)
Joint: watchMovie(X) ← selectMovie(X), entertainingMovie(X)
        entertainingMovie(X) ← actionMovie(X),fantasyMovie(X)
Step 3:
Jenny: actionMovie(*Terminator*)
        fantasyMovie(*Harry Potter*)
Amy: actionMovie(*Terminator*)
        fantasyMovie(*Harry Potter*)
        fantasyMovie(*LoR*)
        actionMovie(*LoR*)
Joint: watchMovie(X) ← selectMovie(X), entertainingMovie(X)
        entertainingMovie(X) ← actionMovie(X),fantasyMovie(X)
        actionMovie(*Terminator*)
        fantasyMovie(*Harry Potter*)
        fantasyMovie(*LoR*)
        actionMovie(*LoR*)

This example shows exchange of rules. Assumptions and contraries of assumptions can be exchanged in a similar manner. Communicating information progressively has the advantage that only necessary and sufficient information is disclosed. It hence avoids possible unnecessary disclosure and computation. Agents have the freedom to control the type and content of the information they disclose. This feature is useful to address privacy concerns that agents may have.

5.2. On Failure Cases of the Concatenation Merge

The concatenation merge fails in certain cases. In particular, the body of rules to be concatenated may be in conflict with each other (as in Example 4.1). Furthermore, there may be no jointly satisfactory argument (as in Example 3.2 without the constant *LoR*). In these cases, only "biased" solution may exist, e.g., either watch *Harry Potter* or *Terminator*. These solutions impose a compromise on one of the agents.

When compromises are inevitable, and when there are multiple compromises to make, fairness can be interpreted to mean that both agents make an equivalent amount of compromise. An example scenario is the following. Jenny and Amy are planning for a film night, and also want to have a dinner together. Two movies are screening, *Terminator* and *Harry Potter*. Based on their individual reasoning, Jenny wants to watch *Terminator* and Amy wants to watch *Harry Potter*. As for the choice of food, Jenny wants to have *Italian food* whereas Amy wants to have *Thai food*. Due to budget constrains, they can only watch one movie and have one dinner.

Intuitively, the fair outcome in this example is that Jenny and Amy either watch *Terminator* and have *Thai food* or watch *Harry Potter* and have *Italian food*. Indeed, any other settlement, e.g. *Terminator* and *Italian food* or *Harry Potter* and *Thai food*, favors one agent while compromising the other agent. To map the intuition into a formal mechanism, we can take the following approach.

Step 1: Employ a score keeping system such that if a desire is fulfilled for an agent, the agent gets a score of 1; if a desire is not fulfilled for an agent, it gets a score of 0.
Step 2: The fair selections are ones that maximize the total score of all agents and minimize the difference between scores obtained by each individual agent.

The maximization is used to ensure agents' desires are satisfied as much as possible. The minimization is used to ensure both agents make a similar amount of compromise. This approach assumes that all desires have the same value and values of desires are perceived equally by all agents. Alternatively, we can consider desires having different values, e.g. as in value-based argumentation [BC03]. As a further alternative, we can consider desires of agents as resources. Hence, satisfying desires becomes an issue of maximizing social welfare in the context of resources allocation. In this view, well-defined utility functions and social welfare criteria, such as *Utilitarian, Egalitarian, Envy-freeness* [CDE+06] can be used.

6. Related Work

Multi-agent conflict resolution has been a much studied area in AI. Tessier et. al [TCM01] presents a collection of papers that study various aspects of conflicts between agents, such as the definition and categorization of conflicts [TLFC01], conflicts in the view of sociology [Han01,MW01], and conflicts among collaborative agents [JT01,Cha01]. At a high level view, [TLFC01] categorizes conflicts as *physical conflicts* and *knowledge conflicts*. Physical conflicts are resource conflicts, where agents' interests are hindered by insufficient resources. Effective resource sharing or operational coordination in multi-agent systems have hence been studied [TPS98,RH03,LS08]. Knowledge conflicts are epistemic conflicts, where agents have different views towards the environment and their own desires. To resolve knowledge conflicts, agents can merge potentially conflicting beliefs. Research in this area includes [Rev93,Cho98,KP98,BDKP02]. Our work is within the realm of resolving knowledge conflicts.

More recent development in argumentation [CnMS06,BH08,RS09,BCPS09] have demonstrated the versatility of various argumentation frameworks for conflict resolution.

Amgoud et. al. [AP02,AK05,AK07] have explored how argumentation dialogues can be used as a process for resolving conflicts between agents. In their approach, conflicts are potentially conflicting arguments. As stated in [AK07], argumentation has the unique advantage that knowledge bases from different agents do not need to be merged statically. Rather, an interactive and progressive procedure is taken by agents interchangeably uttering their beliefs. Our approach is to aim at merging "relevant" part of the belief base of agents, defined as argumentation frameworks. We plan to further study how this "relevant" merge can be supported by dialogue.

In the context of belief revision in argumentation, [FKIS09] has surveyed a number of works that investigate the relation between belief revision and argumentation, thus setting the stage for the research presented in this paper. [CDLS08] has presented a study for revising a Dung-style abstract argumentation system by adding a new argument that interacts with one previous argument. The authors have studied how a single operation may affect various extensions of a set of arguments. [CMDK05,CMDK$^+$07] have presented a framework for merging argumentation systems from Dung's theory of argumentation. Their approach is composed of two steps. Firstly, all argumentation systems are expanded so every single argument is known by all argumentation systems. Then a voting mechanism is used to determine attacks that are recognized by all argumentation systems. [PC04] has presented a comparison between argumentation and belief revision. Our merge is based on focusing solely on the source of conflict (a goal) and does not result in a belief revision except for joining up all beliefs.

7. Conclusion and Future Work

In this paper, we have presented a two-agent conflict resolution mechanism based on merging ABA frameworks. We recognize two sources of conflicts between agents: agents being misinformed or bearing incomplete information, and agents having different desires. We have explored the merge operator, that takes two ABA frameworks and produces a single one. Information is shared during the merge and the resulting joint arguments satisfy both agents' desires as much as possible. We have considered the issue of fairness when resolving a conflict. We have also discussed how to resolve conflicts with argumentation dialogues, in the ABA context.

Future work includes further investigating properties of the merge operator proposed in this paper. This includes investigation of the merge operation with respect to some other argumentation semantics and investigation on performing the merge via dialogues. We also plan to further explore strategies for resolving conflicts when no mutually agreeable solution exists and a fair solution needs to be found.

References

[AK05]   L. Amgoud and S. Kaci. An argumentation framework for merging conflicting knowledge bases: The prioritized case. In *Proc. ECSQARU*, pages 527–538. Springer, 2005.

[AK07]   L. Amgoud and S. Kaci. An argumentation framework for merging conflicting knowledge bases. *International Journal Approximate Reasoning*, 45(2):321–340, 2007.

[AP02]   L. Amgoud and S. Parsons. An argumentation framework for merging conflicting knowledge bases. In *Proc. JELIA*, pages 27–37. Springer, 2002.

[BC03]   T. J. M. Bench-Capon. Persuasion in practical argument using value-based argumentation
             frameworks. *Journal of Logic and Computation*, 13(3):429–448, 2003.
[BCPS09]   T. Bench-Capon, H. Prakken, and G. Sartor. Argumentation in legal reasoning. In Rahwan and
             Simari [RS09], pages 363–382.
[BDKP02]   S. Benferhat, D. Dubois, S. Kaci, and H. Prade. Possibilistic merging and distance-based fusion
             of propositional information. *Annals of Mathematics and AI*, 34(1–3):217–252, 2002.
[BDKT97]   A. Bondarenko, P. M. Dung, R. Kowalski, and F. Toni. An abstract, argumentation-theoretic
             approach to default reasoning. *Artificial Intelligence*, 93(1–2):63–101, 1997.
[BH08]   P. Besnard and A. Hunter. *Elements of Argumentation*. MIT Press, 2008.
[BTK93]   A. Bondarenko, F. Toni, and R. A. Kowalski. An assumption-based framework for non-
             monotonic reasoning. In *Proc. LPNMR*, pages 171–189. MIT Press, 1993.
[CDE$^+$06] Y. Chevaleyre, P. E. Dunne, U. Endriss, J. Lang, M. LeLemaitre, N. Maudet, J. Padget,
             S. Phelps, J. A. Rodriguez-aguilar, and P. Sousa. Issues in multiagent resource allocation.
             Informatica, 30(1):3–31, 2006.
[CDLS08]   C. Cayrol, F. Dupin de St-Cyr, and M. Lagasquie-Schiex. Revision of an argumentation system.
             In *Proc. KR*, pages 124–134. AAAI Press, 2008.
[Cha01]   F. Chantemargue. Conflicts in collective robotics. In Tessier et al. [TCM01], pages 203–222.
[Cho98]   L. Cholvy. Reasoning about merging information. In D. Gabbay and P. Smets, editors, *Hand-
             book of Def. Reas. and Unc. Management Systems*, volume 3, pages 233–263. Springer, 1998.
[CMDK05]   S. Coste-Marquis, C. Devred, and S. Konieczny. Merging argumentation systems. In *Proc.
             AAAI*, pages 614–619. AAAI Press, 2005.
[CMDK$^+$07] S. Coste-Marquis, C. Devred, S. Konieczny, M. Lagasquie-Schiex, and P. Marquis. On the
             merging of Dung's argumentation systems. *Artificial Intelligence*, 171(10–15):730–753, 2007.
[CnMS06]   C. Chesñevar, A. G. Maguitman, and G. R. Simari. Argument-based critics and recommenders:
             a qualitative perspective on user support systems. *Data Knowledge Eng.*, 59(2):293–319, 2006.
[DKT06]   P.M. Dung, R.A. Kowalski, and F. Toni. Dialectic proof procedures for assumption-based,
             admissible argume ntation. *Artificial Intelligence*, 170:114–159, 2006.
[DKT09]   P. M. Dung, R. A. Kowalski, and F. Toni. Assumption-based argumentation. In Rahwan and
             Simari [RS09], pages 25–44.
[DMT07]   P.M. Dung, P. Mancarella, and F. Toni. Computing ideal sceptical argumentation. *Artificial
             Intellgence*, 171(10–15):642–674, 2007.
[FKIS09]   M. Falappa, G. Kern-Isberner, and G. Simari. Belief revision and argumentation theory. In
             Rahwan and Simari [RS09], pages 341–360.
[GT08]   D. Gaertner and F. Toni. Hybrid argumentation and its properties. In *Proc. COMMA*, pages
             183–195. IOS Press, 2008.
[Han01]   M. Hannebauer. Their problems are my problems. In Tessier et al. [TCM01], pages 63–100.
[JT01]   H. Jung and M. Tambe. Conflicts in agent teams. In Tessier et al. [TCM01], pages 153–169.
[KP98]   S. Konieczny and R. P. Perez. On the logic of merging. In *Proc. KR*, pages 488–498. Morgan
             Kaufmann, 1998.
[LS08]   J. Lian and S. M. Shatz. A modeling methodology for conflict control in multi-agent systems.
             Int. Journal of Software Engineering and Knowledge Engineering, 18(3):263–303, 2008.
[MW01]   T. Malsch and G. Weiss. Conflicts in social theory and MAS. In Tessier et al. [TCM01], pages
             101–152.
[PC04]   F. Paglieri and C. Castelfranchi. Revising beliefs through arguments: Bridging the gap between
             argumentation and belief revision in MAS. In *Proc. ArgMAS*, pages 78–94. Springer, 2004.
[Rev93]   P. Z. Revesz. On the semantics of theory change: arbitration between old and new information.
             In *Proc. PODS*, pages 71–82. ACM, 1993.
[RH03]   S. Resmerita and M. Heymann. Conflict resolution in multi-agent systems. In *Proc. 42nd IEEE
             Conference on Decision and Control*, pages 2537–2572. IEEE, 2003.
[RS09]   I. Rahwan and G. R. Simari, editors. *Argumentation in Artificial Intelligence*. Springer, 2009.
[TCM01]   C. Tessier, L. Chaudron, and H. Müller, editors. *Conflicting agents: conflict management in
             multi-agent systems*. Kluwer Academic Publishers, 2001.
[TLFC01]   C. Tessier, M. Laurent, H. Fiorina, and L. Chaudron. Agents' conflicts: new issues. In Tessier
             et al. [TCM01], pages 1–32.
[TPS98]   C. Tomlin, G. J. Pappas, and S. Sastry. Conflict resolution for air traffic management: A study
             in multiagent hybrid systems. *IEEE Transactions on Automatic Control*, 43:509–521, 1998.

Computational Models of Argument
P. Baroni et al. (Eds.)
IOS Press, 2010
doi:10.3233/978-1-60750-619-5-243

cf2 Semantics Revisited [1]

Sarah Alice GAGGL and Stefan WOLTRAN

Institute of Information Systems 184, Vienna University of Technology,
A-1040 Vienna, Austria

Abstract. Abstract argumentation frameworks nowadays provide the most popular formalization of argumentation on a conceptual level. Numerous semantics for this paradigm have been proposed, whereby *cf2* semantics has shown to nicely solve particular problems concernend with odd-length cycles in such frameworks. In order to compare different semantics not only on a theoretical basis, it is necessary to provide systems which implement them within a uniform platform. Answer-Set Programming (ASP) turned out to be a promising direction for this aim, since it not only allows for a concise representation of concepts inherent to argumentation semantics, but also offers sophisticated off-the-shelves solvers which can be used as core computation engines. In fact, many argumentation semantics have meanwhile been encoded within the ASP paradigm, but not all relevant semantics, among them *cf2* semantics, have yet been considered. The contributions of this work are thus twofold. Due to the particular nature of *cf2* semantics, we first provide an alternative characterization which, roughly speaking, avoids the recursive computation of sub-frameworks. Then, we provide the concrete ASP-encodings, which are incorporated within the ASPARTIX system, a platform which already implements a wide range of semantics for abstract argumentation.

Keywords. Abstract Argumentation. Implementation.

1. Introduction

Abstract argumentation frameworks (AFs), introduced by Dung [4], represent the most popular approach for formalizing and reasoning over argumentation problems on a conceptual level. Dung already introduced different extension-based semantics (preferred, complete, stable, grounded) for such frameworks. In addition, recent proposals tried to overcome several shortcomings observed for those original semantics. For instance, the semi-stable semantics [2] handles the problem of the possible non-existence of stable extensions, while the ideal semantics [5] is proposed as a unique-status approach (each AF possesses exactly one extension) less skeptical than the grounded extension.

Another family of semantics, the so-called SCC-recursive semantics [1], has been introduced in order to solve particular problems arising for AFs with odd-length cycles. Hereby, a recursive decomposition of the given AF along strongly connected components (SCCs) is necessary to obtain the extensions. A particular instance of the SCC-recursive semantics, the *cf2* semantics, satisfies many requirements such as the symmetric treatment of odd- and even-length cycles, and ensures that attacks from self-defeating

---
[1] This work was supported by the Vienna Science and Technology Fund (WWTF) under grant ICT08-028.

arguments have no influence on the selection of other arguments to be included in an extension.

This leads us to the fact that abstract argumentation actually offers an ever growing number of different semantics, and thus a uniform implementation is necessary to compare them not only on a theoretical level. Answer-Set Programming (ASP, for short) is a promising approach towards this direction, since this paradigm [9,10] allows a concise representation of concepts as Guess and Check (guess a set of arguments and check whether this set satisfies the semantics' properties) and transitive closure (important to formulate reachability). Moreover, sophisticated ASP-systems such as Smodels, DLV, Cmodels, Clasp, or ASSAT are able to deal with large problem instances [3]. Finally, the data complexity of evaluating ASP programs ranges (depending from different syntactical classes) from complexity classes P, NP, coNP up to Σ_2^P and to Π_2^P. It is thus possible to provide ASP queries which are on the same complexity level as the encoded argumentation problem (see [6] for such complexity results). Previous work [7,11,13,14] already addressed this issue and gave ASP-encodings for several argumentation semantics. In particular, the system ASPARTIX [7] provides queries for the most important types of extensions including preferred, stable, semi-stable, complete, grounded and ideal.

In this paper, we focus on the theoretical foundations towards an ASP-encoding for the *cf2* semantics, which has been neglected in the literature so far. In particular, it turns out to be rather cumbersome to represent *cf2* semantics directly within ASP. This is due the fact that the original definition involves a recursive computation of different subframeworks. Our aim here is, roughly speaking, to shift the need of recursion from generating subframeworks to the concept of recursively component defeated arguments. Having computed this set $\mathcal{RD}_F(S)$ for a given AF F and a set S of arguments, we construct from F an *instance* of F with respect to $\mathcal{RD}_F(S)$ such that the *cf2* extensions of F are given by the sets S which are maximal conflict-free in their instance with respect to $\mathcal{RD}_F(S)$. As a second result, we show that the set $\mathcal{RD}_F(S)$ can be captured via a fixed-point operator; in other words, this allows to characterize *cf2* semantics using linear recursion only. This novel characterization is then captured by a corresponding ASP-encoding, where we now are able to directly (i) guess a set S and then (ii) check whether S is maximal conflict-free in the respective instance of the given AF F. Our encodings are incorporated to the ASPARTIX system and are available on the web[2].

The remainder of the paper is organized as follows. In the next section we recall the necessary basics of argumentation frameworks and give the definition of *cf2* semantics. In Section 3 we introduce our alternative characterization for *cf2* semantics and in Section 4 we put this characterization to work and sketch our ASP-encodings for the *cf2* semantics. Finally, in Section 5 we conclude with a brief discussion of related and future work.

2. Preliminaries

We first recall some basic definitions for abstract argumentation frameworks and introduce some further notations which are relevant for the rest of the paper.

---

[2]www.dbai.tuwien.ac.at/research/project/argumentation/systempage/

Definition 1 *An argumentation framework (AF) is a pair $F = (A, R)$, where A is a finite set of arguments and $R \subseteq A \times A$. The pair $(a, b) \in R$ means that a attacks b. A set $S \subseteq A$ of arguments* **defeats** *b (in F), if there is an $a \in S$, such that $(a, b) \in R$. An argument $a \in A$ is* **defended** *by $S \subseteq A$ (in F) iff, for each $b \in A$, it holds that, if $(b, a) \in R$, then S defeats b (in F).*

A minimal criterion for an acceptable set of arguments is to not contain an argument attacking another argument in the set. Such acceptable sets are called conflict-free, and maximal (wrt. set-inclusion) such sets will play an important role for *cf2* semantics.

Definition 2 *Let $F = (A, R)$ be an AF. A set $S \subseteq A$ is said to be* **conflict-free** *(in F), if there are no $a, b \in S$, such that $(a, b) \in R$. We denote the collection of sets which are conflict-free (in F) by $cf(F)$. $S \subseteq A$ is* **maximal conflict-free**, *if $S \in cf(F)$ and for each $T \in cf(F)$, $S \not\subset T$. We denote the collection of all maximal conflict-free sets of F by $mcf(F)$. For the empty AF $F_0 = (\emptyset, \emptyset)$, we set $mcf(F_0) = \{\emptyset\}$.*

For our purposes, we require some further formal machinery. By $SCCs(F)$, we denote the set of strongly connected components of an AF $F = (A, R)$ which identify the maximal strongly connected[3] subgraphs of F; $SCCs(F)$ is thus a partition of A. Moreover, for an argument $a \in A$, we denote by $C_F(a)$ the component of F where a occurs in, i.e. the (unique) set $C \in SCCs(F)$, such that $a \in C$. AFs $F_1 = (A_1, R_1)$ and $F_2 = (A_2, R_2)$ are called *disjoint* if $A_1 \cap A_2 = \emptyset$. Moreover, the union between (not necessarily disjoint) AFs is defined as $F_1 \cup F_2 = (A_1 \cup A_2, R_1 \cup R_2)$.

It turns out to be convenient to use two different concepts to obtain sub-frameworks of AFs. Let $F = (A, R)$ be an AF and S a set of arguments. Then, $F|_S = ((A \cap S), R \cap (S \times S))$ is the *sub-framework* of F wrt S and we also use $F - S = F|_{A \setminus S}$. We note the following relation (which we use implicitly later on), for an AF F and sets S, S': $F|_{S \setminus S'} = F|_S - S' = (F - S')|_S$. In particular, for an AF F, a component $C \in SCCs(F)$ of F and a set S we thus have $F|_{C \setminus S} = F|_C - S$.

We now give the definition of *cf2* semantics. Our definition slightly differs from (but is equivalent to) the original definition in [1].[4]

Definition 3 *Let $F = (A, R)$ be an AF and $S \subseteq A$. An argument $b \in A$ is* **component-defeated** *by S (in F), if there exists an $a \in S$, such that $(a, b) \in R$ and $a \notin C_F(b)$. The set of arguments component-defeated by S in F is denoted by $D_F(S)$.*

Definition 4 *Let $F = (A, R)$ be an argumentation framework and S a set of arguments. Then, S is a cf2 extension of F, i.e. $S \in cf2(F)$, iff*

- *in case $|SCCs(F)| = 1$, then $S \in mcf(F)$,*
- *otherwise, $\forall C \in SCCs(F)$, $(S \cap C) \in cf2(F|_C - D_F(S))$.*

In words, the recursive definition $cf2(F)$ is based on a decomposition of the AF F into its $SCCs$ depending on a given set S of arguments. We illustrate the behavior of this procedure in the following example.

---

[3]A directed graph is called *strongly connected* if there is a path from each vertex in the graph to every other vertex of the graph.

[4]$D_F(S)$, as introduced next, replaces the set "$D_F(S, E)$" and $F|_C - D_F(S)$ replaces "$F_{\downarrow UP_F(S,E)}$"; moreover, the set of undefeated arguments "$U_F(S, E)$" as used in the general schema from [1], is not required here, because the base function for *cf2* semantics does make use of this set.

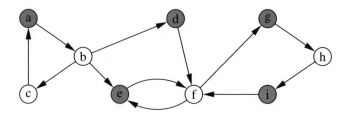

Figure 1. The argumentation framework F from Example 1.

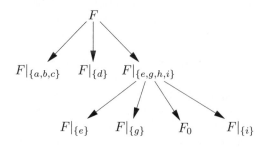

Figure 2. Tree of recursive calls for computing $cf2(F)$.

Example 1 *Consider the AF* $F = (A, R)$ *with* $A = \{a, b, c, d, e, f, g, h, i\}$ *and* $R = \{(a, b), (b, c), (c, a), (b, d), (b, e), (d, f), (e, f), (f, e), (f, g), (g, h), (h, i), (i, f)\}$ *as illustrated in Figure 1. We want to check whether* $S = \{a, d, e, g, i\}$ *is a cf2 extension of* F *(the arguments of the set* S *are highlighted in Figure 1). Following Definition 4, we first identify the SCCs of* F, *namely* $C_1 = \{a, b, c\}$, $C_2 = \{d\}$ *and* $C_3 = \{e, f, g, h, i\}$. *Moreover, we have* $D_F(S) = \{f\}$. *This leads us to the following checks (see also Figure 2 which shows the involved subframeworks).*

1. $(S \cap C_1) \in cf2(F|_{C_1})$: $F|_{C_1}$ *consists of a single SCC; hence, we have to check whether* $(S \cap C_1) = \{a\} \in mcf(F|_{C_1})$, *which indeed holds.*

2. $(S \cap C_2) \in cf2(F|_{C_2})$: $F|_{C_2}$ *consists of a single argument* d *(and thus of a single SCC);* $(S \cap C_2) = \{d\} \in mcf(F|_{C_2})$ *thus holds.*

3. $(S \cap C_3) \in cf2(F|_{C_3} - \{f\})$: $F|_{C_3} - \{f\} = F|_{\{e,g,h,i\}}$ *consists of four SCCs, namely* $C_4 = \{e\}$, $C_5 = \{g\}$, $C_6 = \{h\}$ *and* $C_7 = \{i\}$. *Hence, we need a second level of recursion for* $F' = F|_{\{e,g,h,i\}}$ *and* $S' = S \cap C_3$. *Note that we have* $D_{F'}(S') = \{h\}$. *The single-argument AFs* $F'|_{C_4} = F|_{\{e\}}$, $F'|_{C_5} = F|_{\{g\}}$, $F'|_{C_7} = F|_{\{i\}}$ *all satisfy* $(S' \cap C_i) \in mcf(F'|_{C_i})$; *while* $F'|_{C_6 \setminus \{h\}}$ *yields the empty AF. Therfore,* $(S' \cap C_6) = \emptyset \in cf2(F|_{C_6 \setminus \{h\}})$ *holds as well.*

We thus conclude that S *is a cf2 extension of* F. *Further cf2 extensions of* F *are* $\{b, f, h\}$, $\{b, g, i\}$ *and* $\{c, d, e, g, i\}$.

3. An Alternative Characterization for the $cf2$ Semantics

In this section, we provide an alternative characterization for the $cf2$ semantics. In particular, our aim is to avoid the recursive computation of sub-frameworks (as, for instance, depicted in Figure 2) and instead collect the different sets of component-defeated arguments by a recursively defined set of arguments.

To avoid splitting an AF into sub-frameworks, we introduce the following concept.

Definition 5 *An AF $F = (A, R)$ is called* **separated** *if for each $(a, b) \in R$, $C_F(a) = C_F(b)$. We define $[[F]] = \bigcup_{C \in SCCs(F)} F|_C$ and call $[[F]]$ the* **separation** *of F.*

In words, an AF is separated if there are no attacks between different strongly connected components. Thus, the separation of an AF always yields a separated AF. The following technical lemma will be useful later.

Lemma 1 *For any AF F and set S of arguments, $\bigcup_{C \in SCCs(F)}[[F|_C - S]] = [[F - S]]$.*

Proof. We first note that for disjoint AFs F and G, $[[F]] \cup [[G]] = [[F \cup G]]$ holds. Moreover, for a set S of arguments and arbitrary AFs F and G, $(F - S) \cup (G - S) = (F \cup G) - S$ is clear. Using these observations, we obtain

$$\bigcup_{C \in SCCs(F)} [[F|_C - S]] = [[\bigcup_{C \in SCCs(F)} (F|_C - S)]] = [[(\bigcup_{C \in SCCs(F)} F|_C) - S]] = [[[[F]] - S]].$$

It remains to show that $[[[[F]] - S]] = [[F - S]]$. Obviously, both AFs possess the same arguments A. Thus let R be the attacks of $[[[[F]] - S]]$ and R' the attacks of $[[F - S]]$. $R \subseteq R'$ holds by the fact that each attack in $[[F]]$ is also contained in F. To show $R' \subseteq R$, let $(a, b) \in R'$. Then $a, b \notin S$, and $C_{F-S}(a) = C_{F-S}(b)$. From the latter, $C_F(a) = C_F(b)$ and thus (a, b) is an attack in $[[F]]$ and also in $[[F]] - S$. Again using $C_{F-S}(a) = C_{F-S}(b)$, shows $(a, b) \in R$. $\qquad\square$

Next, we define the level of recursiveness a framework shows with respect to a set S of arguments and then the aforementioned set of recursively component defeated arguments (by S) in an AF.

Definition 6 *For an AF $F = (A, R)$ and a set S of arguments, we recursively define the* **level** $\ell_F(S)$ *of F wrt S as follows:*

- *if $|SCCs(F)| = 1$ then $\ell_F(S) = 1$;*
- *otherwise, $\ell_F(S) = 1 + max(\{\ell_{F|_C - D_F(S)}(S \cap C) \mid C \in SCCs(F)\})$.*

Definition 7 *Let $F = (A, R)$ be an AF and S a set of arguments. We define the set of arguments* **recursively component defeated** *by S (in F) as follows:*

- *if $|SCCs(F)| = 1$ then $\mathcal{RD}_F(S) = \emptyset$;*
- *otherwise, $\mathcal{RD}_F(S) = D_F(S) \cup \bigcup_{C \in SCCs(F)} \mathcal{RD}_{F|_C - D_F(S)}(S \cap C)$.*

We are now prepared to give our first alternative characterization, which establishes a $cf2$ extension S of a given AF F by checking whether S is maximal conflict-free in a certain separated framework constructed from F using S.

Lemma 2 *Let $F = (A, R)$ be an AF and S be a set of arguments. Then,*

$$S \in cf2(F) \text{ iff } S \in mcf([[F - \mathcal{RD}_F(S)]]).$$

Proof. We show the claim by induction over $\ell_F(S)$.

Induction base. For $\ell_F(S) = 1$, we have $|SCCs(F)| = 1$. By definition $\mathcal{RD}_F(S) = \emptyset$ and we have $[[F - \mathcal{RD}_F(S)]] = [[F]] = F$. Thus, the assertion states that $S \in cf2(F)$ iff $S \in mcf(F)$ which matches the original definition for the $cf2$ semantics in case the AF has a single strongly connected component.

Induction step. Let $\ell_F(S) = n$ and assume the assertion holds for all AFs F' and sets S' with $\ell_{F'}(S') < n$. In particular, we have by definition that, for each $C \in SCCs(F)$, $\ell_{F|_C - D_F(S)}(S \cap C) < n$. By the induction hypothesis, we thus obtain that, for each $C \in SCCs(F)$, the following holds:

$$(S \cap C) \in cf2(F|_C - D_F(S)) \text{ iff } (S \cap C) \in mcf\left([[(F|_C - D_F(S)) - \mathcal{R}'_{F,C,S}]]\right) \quad (1)$$

where $\mathcal{R}'_{F,C,S} = \mathcal{RD}_{F|_C - D_F(S)}(S \cap C)$. Let us fix now a $C \in SCCs(F)$. Since for each further $C' \in SCCs(F)$ (i.e. $C \neq C'$), no argument from $\mathcal{RD}_{F|_{C'} - D_F(S)}(S \cap C')$ occurs in $F|_C$, we have

$$(F|_C - D_F(S)) - \mathcal{R}'_{F,C,S} =$$

$$\left((F|_C - D_F(S)) - \mathcal{R}'_{F,C,S}\right) - \bigcup_{C' \in SCCs(F); C \neq C'} \mathcal{RD}_{F|_{C'} - D_F(S)}(S \cap C') =$$

$$\left(F|_C - D_F(S)\right) - \bigcup_{C \in SCCs(F)} \mathcal{RD}_{F|_C - D_F(S)}(S \cap C) =$$

$$F|_C - \left(D_F(S) \cup \bigcup_{C \in SCCs(F)} \mathcal{RD}_{F|_C - D_F(S)}(S \cap C)\right) = F|_C - \mathcal{RD}_F(S).$$

Thus, for any $C \in SCCs(F)$, relation (1) amounts to

$$(S \cap C) \in cf2(F|_C - D_F(S)) \text{ iff } (S \cap C) \in mcf([[F|_C - \mathcal{RD}_F(S)]]). \quad (2)$$

We now prove the assertion. Let $S \in cf2(F)$. By definition, for each $C \in SCCs(F)$, $(S \cap C) \in cf2(F|_C - D_F(S))$. Using (2), we get that for each $C \in SCCs(F)$, $(S \cap C) \in mcf([[F|_C - \mathcal{RD}_F(S)]])$. By the definition of components and the semantics of being maximal conflict-free, the following relation thus follows:

$$\bigcup_{C \in SCCs(F)} (S \cap C) \in mcf\left(\bigcup_{C \in SCCs(F)} [[F|_C - \mathcal{RD}_F(S)]]\right).$$

Since $S = \bigcup_{C \in SCCs(F)} (S \cap C)$ and, by Lemma 1, $\bigcup_{C \in SCCs(F)} [[F|_C - \mathcal{RD}_F(S)]] = [[F - \mathcal{RD}_F(S)]]$, we arrive at $S \in mcf([[F - \mathcal{RD}_F(S)]])$ as desired. The other direction is by essentially the same arguments. $\qquad \square$

Next, we provide an alternative characterization for $\mathcal{RD}_F(S)$ via a fixed-point operator. In other words, this yields a linearization in the recursive computation of this set. To this end, we require a parameterized notion of reachability.

Definition 8 Let $F = (A, R)$ be an AF, B a set of arguments, and $a, b \in A$. We say that b is **reachable** in F from a modulo B, in symbols $a \Rightarrow_F^B b$, if there exists a path from a to b in $F|_B$, i.e. there exists a sequence $c_1, \ldots, c_n$ $(n > 1)$ of arguments such that $c_1 = a$, $c_n = b$, and $(c_i, c_{i+1}) \in R \cap (B \times B)$, for all i with $1 \leq i < n$.

Definition 9 For an AF $F = (A, R)$, $D \subseteq A$, and a set S of arguments,

$$\Delta_{F,S}(D) = \{a \in A \mid \exists b \in S : b \neq a, (b, a) \in R, a \nRightarrow_F^{A \backslash D} b\}.$$

The operator is clearly monotonic, i.e. $\Delta_{F,S}(D) \subseteq \Delta_{F,S}(D')$ holds for $D \subseteq D'$. As usual, we let $\Delta_{F,S}^0 = \Delta_{F,S}(\emptyset)$ and, for $i > 0$, $\Delta_{F,S}^i = \Delta(\Delta_{F,S}^{i-1})$. Furthermore, $\Delta_{F,S}$ is used to denote the lfp of $\Delta_{F,S}(\emptyset)$, which exists due to the monotonicity. We need two more lemmata before showing that $\Delta_{F,S}$ captures $\mathcal{RD}_F(S)$.

Lemma 3 For any AF $F = (A, R)$ and any set $S \subseteq A$, $\Delta_{F,S}^0 = D_F(S)$.

Proof. We have $\Delta_{F,S}^0 = \Delta_{F,S}(\emptyset) = \{a \in A \mid \exists b \in S : b \neq a, (b, a) \in R, a \nRightarrow_F^A b\}$. Hence, $a \in \Delta_{F,S}^0$, if there exists a $b \in S$, such that $(b, a) \in R$ and a does not reach b in F, i.e. $b \notin C_F(a)$. This meets exactly the definition of $D_F(S)$. $\qquad\square$

Lemma 4 For any AF $F = (A, R)$ and any set $S \in cf(F)$,

$$\Delta_{F,S} = D_F(S) \cup \bigcup_{C \in SCCs(F)} \Delta_{F|_C - D_F(S),(S \cap C)}.$$

Proof. Let $F = (A, R)$. For the $\subseteq$-direction, we show by induction over $i \geq 0$ that $\Delta_{F,S}^i \subseteq D_F(S) \cup \bigcup_{C \in SCCs(F)} \Delta_{F|_C - D_F(S),(S \cap C)}$. To ease notation, we write $\bar{\Delta}_{F,S,C}$ as a shorthand for $\Delta_{F|_C - D_F(S),(S \cap C)}$, where $C \in SCCs(F)$.

Induction base. $\Delta_{F,S}^0 \subseteq D_F(S) \cup \bigcup_{C \in SCCs(F)} \bar{\Delta}_{F,S,C}$ follows from Lemma 3.

Induction step. Let $i > 0$ and assume $\Delta_{F,S}^j \subseteq D_F(S) \cup \bigcup_{C \in SCCs(F)} \bar{\Delta}_{F,S,C}$ holds for all $j < i$. Let $a \in \Delta_{F,S}^i$. Then, there exists a $b \in S$, such that $(b, a) \in R$ and $a \nRightarrow_F^D b$, where $D = A \setminus \Delta_{F,S}^{i-1}$. If $b \notin C_F(a)$, we have also $a \nRightarrow_F^A b$ and thus $a \in D_F(S)$. Hence, suppose $b \in C_F(a)$. Then, $a \notin D_F(S)$ and, since $S \in cf(F)$ and $b \in S$, also $b \notin D_F(S)$. Thus, both a and b are contained in the framework $F|_C - D_F(S)$ (and so is the attack (b, a)) for $C = C_F(a)$. Moreover, $b \in (S \cap C)$. Towards a contradiction, assume now $a \notin \bar{\Delta}_{F,S,C}$. This yields that $a \Rightarrow_{F|_C - D_F(S)}^{D'} b$ for $D' = A \setminus \bar{\Delta}_{F,S,C}$, i.e. there exist arguments $c_1, \ldots, c_n$ $(n > 1)$ in $F|_C - D_F(S)$ but not contained in $\bar{\Delta}_{F,S,C}$, such that $c_1 = a$, $c_n = b$, and $(c_i, c_{i+1}) \in R$, for all i with $1 \leq i < n$. Obviously all the c_i's are contained in F as well, but since $a \nRightarrow_F^D b$ (recall that $D = A \setminus \Delta_{F,S}^{i-1}$), it must hold that at least one of the c_i's, say c, has to be contained in $\Delta_{F,S}^{i-1}$. By the induction hypothesis, we get $c \in \bar{\Delta}_{F,S,C}$, a contradiction.

For the $\supseteq$-direction of the claim we proceed as follows. By Lemma 3, $D_F(S) = \Delta^0_{F,S}$ and thus $D_F(S) \subseteq \Delta_{F,S}$. It remains to show $\bigcup_{C \in SCCs(F)} \Delta_{F|_C - D_F(S), (S \cap C)} \subseteq \Delta_{F,S}$. We show by induction over i that $\Delta^i_{F|_C - D_F(S), (S \cap C)} \subseteq \Delta_{F,S}$ holds for each $C \in SCCs(F)$. Thus, let us fix a $C \in SCCs(F)$ and use $\bar{\Delta}^i_{F,S,C}$ as a shorthand for $\Delta^i_{F|_C - D_F(S), (S \cap C)}$.

Induction base. Let $a \in \bar{\Delta}^0_{F,S,C}$. Then, there is a $b \in (S \cap C)$, such that b attacks a in $F' = F|_C - D_F(S)$ and $a \not\Rightarrow^{A'}_{F'} b$, where A' denotes the arguments of F', i.e. $A' = C \setminus D_F(S)$. Since $F|_C$ is built from a SCC C of F, it follows that $a \not\Rightarrow^{A \setminus D_F(S)}_F b$. Since $b \in S$, $(b, a) \in R$, and $D_F(S) = \Delta^0_{F,S}$ (Lemma 3), we get $a \in \Delta^1_{F,S} \subseteq \Delta_{F,S}$.

Induction step. Let $i > 0$ and assume $\bar{\Delta}^j_{F,S,C} \subseteq \Delta_{F,S}$ for all $j < i$. Let $a \in \bar{\Delta}^i_{F,S,C}$. Then, there is a $b \in (S \cap C)$, such that b attacks a in F' and $a \not\Rightarrow^{D'}_{F'} b$, where $D' = A' \setminus \bar{\Delta}^{i-1}_{F,S,C}$. Towards a contradiction, suppose $a \notin \Delta_{F,S}$. Since $b \in S$ and $(b, a) \in R$, it follows that there exist arguments $c_1, \ldots, c_n$ $(n > 1)$ in $F \setminus \Delta_{F,S}$, such that $c_1 = a$, $c_n = b$, and $(c_i, c_{i+1}) \in R$, for all i with $1 \leq i < n$. All these c_i's are thus contained in the same component as a, and moreover these c_i's cannot be contained in $D_F(S)$, since $D_F(S) \subseteq \Delta_{F,S}$. Thus, they are contained in $F|_C - D_F(S)$, but since $a \not\Rightarrow^{D'}_{F'} b$, there is at least one such c_i, say c, contained in $\bar{\Delta}^{i-1}_{F,S,C}$. By the induction hypothesis, $c \in \Delta_{F,S}$, a contradiction. $\qquad\square$

We now are able to obtain the desired relation.

Lemma 5 *For any AF $F = (A, R)$ and any set $S \in cf(F)$, $\Delta_{F,S} = \mathcal{RD}_F(S)$.*

Proof. The proof is by induction over $\ell_F(S)$.

Induction base. For $\ell_F(S) = 1$, $|SCCs(F)| = 1$ by Definition 6. From this and Definition 7, we obtain $\mathcal{RD}_F(S) = D_F(S) = \emptyset$. By Lemma 3, $\Delta^0_{F,S} = D_F(S) = \emptyset$. By definition, $\Delta_{F,S} = \emptyset$ follows from $\Delta^0_{F,S} = \emptyset$.

Induction step. Let $\ell_F(S) = n$ and assume the claim holds for all pairs $F', S' \in cf(F')$, such that $\ell_{F'}(S') < n$. In particular, this holds for $F' = F|_C - D_F(S)$ and $S' = (S \cap C)$, with $C \in SCCs(F)$. Note that $(S \cap C)$ is indeed conflict-free in $F|_C - D_F(S)$. By definition, $\mathcal{RD}_F(S) = D_F(S) \cup \bigcup_{C \in SCCs(F)} \mathcal{RD}_{F|_C - D_F(S)}(S \cap C)$ and by Lemma 4, $\Delta_{F,S} = D_F(S) \cup \bigcup_{C \in SCCs(F)} \Delta_{F|_C - D_F(S), S \cap C}$. Using the induction hypothesis, i.e. $\Delta_{F|_C - D_F(S), S \cap C} = \mathcal{RD}_{F|_C - D_F(S)}(S \cap C)$, the assertion follows. $\qquad\square$

We finally reached our main result in this section, i.e. an alternative characterization for *cf2* semantics, where the need for recursion is delegated to a fixed-point operator.

Theorem 1 *For any AF F, $cf2(F) = \{S \mid S \in cf(F) \cap mcf([[F - \Delta_{F,S}]])\}$.*

Proof. The result holds by the following observations. By Lemma 2, $S \in cf2(F)$ iff $S \in mcf([[F - \mathcal{RD}_F(S)]])$. Moreover, from Lemma 5, for any $S \in cf(F)$, $\Delta_{F,S} = \mathcal{RD}_F(S)$. Finally, $S \in cf2(F)$ implies $S \in cf(F)$ (see [1], Proposition 47). $\qquad\square$

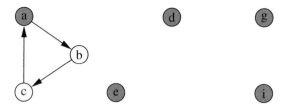

Figure 3. Graph of instance $[[F - \Delta_{F,S}]]$ of Example 2.

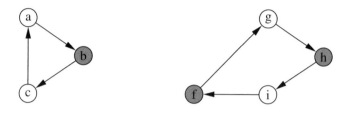

Figure 4. Graph of instance $[[F - \Delta_{F,S'}]]$ of Example 2.

Example 2 *To exemplify the behavior of $\Delta_{F,S}$ and $[[F - \Delta_{F,S}]]$, we consider the AF F and $S = \{a, d, e, g, i\}$ from Example 1. In the first iteration of computing the lfp of $\Delta_{F,S}$, we have $\Delta_{F,S}(\emptyset) = \{f\}$ because the argument f is the only one which is attacked by S but its attacker d is not reachable by f in F. In the second iteration, we obtain $\Delta_{F,S}(\{f\}) = \{f, h\}$, and in the third iteration we reach the lfp with $\Delta_{F,S}(\{f, h\}) = \{f, h\}$. Hence, $[[F - \Delta_{F,S}]]$ of the AF F wrt S is given by*

$$[[F - \Delta_{F,S}]] = \big(\{a, b, c, d, e, g, i\}, \{(a, b), (b, c), (c, a)\}\big).$$

Figure 3 shows the graph of $[[F - \Delta_{F,S}]]$. As is easily checked $S \in mcf([[F - \Delta_{F,S}]])$ as expected, since $S \in cf2(F)$. For comparison, Figure 4 shows the graph of $[[F - \Delta_{F,S'}]]$ wrt the cf2 extension $S' = \{b, f, h\}$ consisting of two SCCs.

4. ASP-Encodings

In this section, we first give a brief overview of ASP (to be more precise, logic programming under the answer-set semantics [8]). Then, we use our novel characterization to implement the *cf2* semantics under this paradigm. To this end, we provide a fixed program π_{cf2} which, augmented with an input database representing a given AF F, has its answer sets in a one-to-one correspondence to the *cf2* extensions of F. For more background on ASP, we refer to [9].

An *atom* is an expression $p(t_1, \ldots, t_n)$, where p is a *predicate* of arity $n \geq 0$ and each t_i is either a variable or a constant from a domain $\mathcal{U}$. We suppose that a total order $<$ over the domain elements is available.[5] An atom is *ground* if it is free of variables. By $B_{\mathcal{U}}$ we denote the set of all ground atoms over $\mathcal{U}$. A *rule* r is of the form

---

[5] ASP-solvers as DLV [9], which is underlying our system ASPARTIX, usually provide such an order for the domain elements of the currently given program.

$$a :\text{-} b_1, \ldots, b_k, \; not \, b_{k+1}, \ldots, \; not \, b_m,$$

with $m \geq k \geq 0$, and where $a, b_1, \ldots, b_m$ are atoms, and "*not*" stands for *default negation*. We identify the *head* of such a rule r as $H(r) = a$ and also use $B^+(r) = \{b_1, \ldots, b_k\}$ and $B^-(r) = \{b_{k+1}, \ldots, b_m\}$ to denote the positive, and resp., negative body of r. A rule r is *ground* if no variable occurs in r. An *(input) database* is a set of ground rules with empty body. A program is a finite set of rules. For a program $\mathcal{P}$ and an input database D, we write $\mathcal{P}(D)$ instead of $D \cup \mathcal{P}$. $Gr(\mathcal{P})$ is the set of rules $r\sigma$ obtained by applying, to each rule $r \in \mathcal{P}$, all possible substitutions σ from the variables in $\mathcal{P}$ to the constants in $\mathcal{P}$.

An *interpretation* $I \subseteq B_\mathcal{U}$ *satisfies* a ground rule r iff $H(r) \in I$ whenever $B^+(r) \subseteq I$ and $B^-(r) \cap I = \emptyset$. A program $\mathcal{P}$ is satisfied by an interpretation I, iff I satisfies each rule in $Gr(\mathcal{P})$. $I \subseteq B_\mathcal{U}$ is an *answer set* of $\mathcal{P}$ iff it is a subset-minimal set satisfying

$$\mathcal{P}^I = \{H(r) :\text{-} B^+(r) \mid I \cap B^-(r) = \emptyset, r \in Gr(\mathcal{P})\}.$$

For a program $\mathcal{P}$, we denote the set of its answer sets by $\mathcal{AS}(\mathcal{P})$.

We now turn to our encoding π_{cf2} which computes *cf2* extension along the lines of Theorem 1. For a better understanding, we split π_{cf2} into several modules which we explain in an informal manner. These modules implement the following steps, given an AF $F = (A, R)$:

1. *Guess* the conflict-free sets $S \subseteq A$ of F.
2. For each S, compute the set $\Delta_{F,S}$.
3. For each S, derive the *instance* $[[F - \Delta_{F,S}]]$.
4. *Check* whether S is maximal conflict-free in $[[F - \Delta_{F,S}]]$.

To start with, let us first fix that a given AF $F = (A, R)$ is presented to π_{cf2} as a database

$$\widehat{F} = \{ \, \text{arg}(a) \mid a \in A \} \cup \{\text{att}(a, b) \mid (a, b) \in R \, \}.$$

1. The guessing module. The following rules guess, when augmented by $\widehat{F}$ for an AF $F = (A, R)$, any subset $S \subseteq A$ (to be precise, for an argument $a \in A$, atom $\text{in}(a)$ indicates that $a \in S$; while atom $\text{out}(a)$ indicates that $a \notin S$) and then check whether the represented guess S is conflict-free in F:

$$\pi_{cf} = \{ \, \text{in}(X) :\text{-} \, not \, \text{out}(X), \text{arg}(X);$$

$$\text{out}(X) :\text{-} \, not \, \text{in}(X), \text{arg}(X);$$

$$:\text{-} \, \text{in}(X), \text{in}(Y), \text{att}(X, Y) \, \}.$$

2. The fixed-point module. Here we use the auxiliary predicates $\inf(\cdot)$, $\text{succ}(\cdot, \cdot)$ and $\sup(\cdot)$ which identify an infimum, a successor function and a supremum for arguments with respect to the previously mentioned order $<$.[6] We exploit this order to iterate over the operator $\Delta_{F,S}(\cdot)$. Given $F = (A, R)$, by definition of $\Delta_{F,S}$ it is sufficient to compute at most $|A|$ such iterations to reach the fixed-point. Let us now present the module and then explain its behavior in more detail.

---

[6] For more details, we refer to [7], where a module $\pi_<$ is given which defines these predicates.

$$\pi_{\text{reach}} = \{\ \text{arg\_set}(N, X) :\text{-} \ \text{arg}(X), \inf(N); \tag{3}$$

$$\text{reach}(N, X, Y) :\text{-} \ \text{arg\_set}(N, X), \text{arg\_set}(N, Y), \text{att}(X, Y); \tag{4}$$

$$\text{reach}(N, X, Y) :\text{-} \ \text{arg\_set}(N, X), \text{att}(X, Z), \text{reach}(N, Z, Y); \tag{5}$$

$$\text{d}(N, X) :\text{-} \ \text{arg\_set}(N, Y), \text{arg\_set}(N, X), \text{in}(Y), \text{att}(Y, X),$$
$$not\ \text{reach}(N, X, Y); \tag{6}$$

$$\text{arg\_set}(M, X) :\text{-} \ \text{arg\_set}(N, X), not\ \text{d}(N, X), \text{succ}(N, M)\ \}. \tag{7}$$

Rule (3) first copies all arguments into a set indexed by the infimum which initiates the computation. The remaining rules are applicable to arbitrary indices, whereby rule (7) copies (a subset of the) arguments from the currently computed set into the "next" set using the successor function $\text{succ}(\cdot, \cdot)$. This guarantees a step-by-step computation of $\text{arg\_set}(i, \cdot)$ by incrementing the index i. The functioning of rules (4)–(7) is as follows. Rules (4) and (5) compute a predicate $\text{reach}(n, x, y)$ indicating that there is a path from argument x to argument y in the given framework *restricted* to the arguments of the current set n. In rule (6), $\text{d}(n, x)$ is obtained for all arguments x which are component-defeated by S in this restricted framework. In other words, if n is the i-th argument in the order $<$, $\text{d}(n, x)$ carries exactly those arguments x which are contained in $\Delta_{F,S}^i$. Finally, rule (7) copies arguments from the current set which are *not* component-defeated to the successor set.

3. The instance module. As already outlined above, if the supremum m is reached in π_{reach}, we are guaranteed that the derived atoms $\text{arg\_set}(m, x)$ characterize exactly those arguments x from the given AF which are not contained in $\Delta_{F,S}$. It is thus now relatively easy to obtain the instance $[[F - \Delta_{F,S}]]$ which is done below via predicates $\text{arg\_new}(\cdot)$ and $\text{att\_new}(\cdot, \cdot)$.

$$\pi_{inst} = \{\ \text{arg\_new}(X) :\text{-} \ \text{arg\_set}(M, X), \sup(M);$$
$$\text{att\_new}(X, Y) :\text{-} \ \text{arg\_new}(X), \text{arg\_new}(Y), \text{att}(X, Y),$$
$$\text{reach}(M, Y, X), \sup(M)\ \}.$$

4. The checking module. It remains to verify whether the initially guessed set S is a *cf2* extension. To do so, we need to check whether S is maximal conflict-free in the instance $[[F - \Delta_{F,S}]]$. The following module does this job by checking whether only those arguments are not contained in S, for which an addition to S would yield a conflict.

$$\pi_{mcf} = \{\ \text{conflicting}(X) :\text{-} \ \text{att\_new}(Y, X), \text{out}(X), \text{in}(Y);$$
$$\text{conflicting}(X) :\text{-} \ \text{att\_new}(X, Y), \text{out}(X), \text{in}(Y);$$
$$\text{conflicting}(X) :\text{-} \ \text{att\_new}(X, X);$$
$$:\text{-} \ not\ \text{conflicting}(X), \text{out}(X), \text{arg\_new}(X)\ \}.$$

We now have our entire encoding $\pi_{cf2} = \pi_{cf} \cup \pi_< \cup \pi_{\text{reach}} \cup \pi_{inst} \cup \pi_{mcf}$ available (recall that we have not given here the definition of $\pi_<$; see [7] for the details). The desired correspondence between answer-sets and *cf2* extensions is as follows.

Theorem 2 *Let F be an AF. Then, (i) for each $S \in cf2(F)$, there is an $I \in \mathcal{AS}(\pi_{cf2}(\widehat{F}))$ with $S = \{a \mid \text{in}(a) \in I\}$; (ii) for each $I \in \mathcal{AS}(\pi_{cf2}(\widehat{F}))$, $\{a \mid \text{in}(a) \in I\} \in cf2(F)$.*

5. Discussion and Conclusions

In this paper, we introduced an alternative characterization for the $cf2$ semantics which is based on a certain fixed-point operator in order to avoid the more involved recursions from the original definition [1]. This new characterization allowed us to provide a relatively succinct ASP-encoding for computing $cf2$ extensions which has been incorporated to the ASP-based argumentation system ASPARTIX. Extending our techniques to other SCC-recursive semantics [1] is ongoing work.

Previous work [12] has shown that $cf2$ extensions can be characterized using a different (however, not implemented) semantics for logic programs. In the same paper, complexity results for $cf2$ semantics have been reported, in particular that the verification problem (i.e. checking whether a given set is a $cf2$ extension) can be decided in polynomial time. We note that this result is reflected in our encodings by the fact that (unstratified) negation is only used for guessing a candidate set, while the verification part does not contain any costly programming concepts (in particular, we could avoid the use of disjunction which is necessary to capture more involved semantics; see [7] for details).

References

[1]   P. Baroni, M. Giacomin, and G. Guida. SCC-Recursiveness: A General Schema for Argumentation Semantics. *Artif. Intell.*, 168(1-2):162–210, 2005.

[2]   M. Caminada. Semi-Stable Semantics. *Proc. COMMA'06*, volume 144 of *FAIA*, pages 121–130. IOS Press, 2006.

[3]   M. Denecker, J. Vennekens, S. Bond, M. Gebser, and M. Truszczynski. The Second Answer Set Programming Competition. *Proc. LPNMR'09*, volume 5753 of *LNCS*, pages 637–654. Springer, 2009.

[4]   P. M. Dung. On the Acceptability of Arguments and its Fundamental Role in Nonmonotonic Reasoning, Logic Programming and n-Person Games. *Artif. Intell.*, 77(2):321–358, 1995.

[5]   P. M. Dung, P. Mancarella, and F. Toni. Computing Ideal Sceptical Argumentation. *Artif. Intell.*, 171(10-15):642–674, 2007.

[6]   P. E. Dunne and M. Wooldridge. Complexity of Abstract Argumentation. *Argumentation in Artificial Intelligence*, pages 85–104. Springer, 2009.

[7]   U. Egly, S. A. Gaggl, and S. Woltran. Answer-Set Programming Encodings for Argumentation Frameworks. Accepted for publication in *Argument and Computation*. Available as Technical Report DBAI-TR-2008-62, Technische Universität Wien, 2008.

[8]   M. Gelfond and V. Lifschitz. Classical Negation in Logic Programs and Disjunctive Databases. *New Generation Comput.*, 9(3/4):365–386, 1991.

[9]   N. Leone, G. Pfeifer, W. Faber, T. Eiter, G. Gottlob, Simona Perri, and Francesco Scarcello. The DLV System for Knowledge Representation and Reasoning. *ACM Trans. Comput. Log.*, 7(3):499–562, 2006.

[10] I. Niemelä. Logic Programming with Stable Model Semantics as a Constraint Programming Paradigm. *Ann. Math. Artif. Intell.*, 25(3–4):241–273, 1999.

[11] J. C. Nieves, M. Osorio, and U. Cortés. Preferred Extensions as Stable Models. *Theory and Practice of Logic Programming*, 8(4):527–543, 2008.

[12] J. C. Nieves, M. Osorio, and C. Zepeda. Expressing Extension-Based Semantics Based on Stratified Minimal Models. *Proc. WoLLIC'09*, volume 5514 of *LNCS*, pages 305–319. Springer, 2009.

[13] M. Osorio, C. Zepeda, J. C. Nieves, and U. Cortés. Inferring Acceptable Arguments with Answer Set Programming. *Proc. ENC'05*, pages 198–205. IEEE Computer Society, 2005.

[14] T. Wakaki and K. Nitta. Computing Argumentation Semantics in Answer Set Programming. *Proc. JSAI'08*, volume 5447 of *LNCS*, pages 254–269. Springer, 2008.

Computational Models of Argument
P. Baroni et al. (Eds.)
IOS Press, 2010
© 2010 The authors and IOS Press. All rights reserved.
doi:10.3233/978-1-60750-619-5-255

Probabilistic Semantics for the Carneades Argument Model Using Bayesian Networks

Matthias Grabmair [a] Thomas F. Gordon [b] and Douglas Walton [c]

[a] *Intelligent Systems Program, University of Pittsburgh, USA*
[b] *Fraunhofer FOKUS, Berlin, Germany*
[c] *University of Windsor, Canada*

Abstract. This paper presents a technique with which instances of argument structures in the Carneades model can be given a probabilistic semantics by translating them into Bayesian networks. The propagation of argument applicability and statement acceptability can be expressed through conditional probability tables. This translation suggests a way to extend Carneades to improve its utility for decision support in the presence of uncertainty.

Keywords. Carneades, argumentation and probability, Bayesian Networks

1. Introduction

The *Carneades* argument model [9] was developed with the goal of formalizing *Walton*'s theory of argumentation structure and evaluation. The acceptability of a proposition at issue is determined by aggregating pro and con arguments using proof standards. Several proof standards in the legal domain have been formally modeled, including preponderance of the evidence, clear and convincing evidence and beyond a reasonable doubt [8,9]. A Carneades argument graph is a bipartite, directed, acyclic graph, with statement nodes and argument nodes. Each statement node represents two literals, an atomic proposition, P, and its logical complement, $\neg P$. An argument pro P is an argument con $\neg P$ and vice versa. The acceptability of a literal P is determined by using proof standards to aggregate the applicable arguments pro and con P. An argument is applicable only if, recursively, its premises are acceptable and its negative premises and exceptions are not acceptable.

This paper uses the structural similarities between Carneades argument graphs and Bayesian networks (BN) to demonstrate how the Carneades method of evaluating arguments using proof standards can be simulated with BNs by translating an argument structure into a *Carneades Bayesian Network* (CBN). The translation relies on the Carneades formalism to define a class of BNs which can be instantiated to an autonomous BN given an instance of an argument evaluation structure. The simulation gives Carneades an alternative, potentially useful probabilistic semantics and suggests a way to extend Carneades, by modeling assumptions as probability distributions over possible statuses of literals and inferring probability distributions over the acceptability of arguments and derivability of other literals. The benefit for some applications could be that probabilities seamlessly interface to established decision-support techniques and allow a qualitative model of argument to be extended to support quantitative methods for reasoning about uncertainty.

2. Bayesian Networks

A Bayesian network (BN) is a model of random variables and the conditional probabilities between them based on a directed acyclic graph [17]. BNs allow for a structured representation of probabilistic causal relationships by exploiting conditional independence relations to reduce the number of probabilistic parameters over the full joint distribution, thereby also reducing the computational complexity of the inference calculation. One can compute the probability of a certain variable having a certain status given information about the status of other variables by multiplying the respective Bayesian probabilities.

Definition 1 (Bayesian Network) *A **Bayesian Network (BN)** is an ordered triple $\langle V, D, \mathcal{P} \rangle$, where V is a set of nodes in the network which correspond to random variables. D is the set of directed edges between the nodes represented as ordered pairs (v_1, v_2) where $v_1, v_2 \in V$. $\mathcal{P}$ is a set of probability functions, each mapping a certain node and a configuration of its immediate parent nodes onto a probability value. Further, the Markov assumption needs to be met, i.e. each random variable needs to be conditionally independent of its non-descendant variables given its parent variables.*

3. The Carneades Model

This section gives an introduction to the Carneades argument model as it has been defined in previous work in greater detail, e.g. [9,10]. Our point of departure is the concept of an argument. Put informally, an argument consists of a set of premises which have to hold in order for the argument to be applicable.

Definition 2 (argument) *Let $\mathcal{L}$ be a propositional language. An **argument** is a tuple $\langle P, E, c \rangle$ where $P \subset \mathcal{L}$ are its **premises**, $E \subset \mathcal{L}$ are its **exceptions** and $c \in \mathcal{L}$ is its **conclusion**. For simplicity, c and all members of P and E must be literals, i.e. either an atomic proposition or a negated atomic proposition. Let p be a literal. If p is c, then the argument is an argument **pro** p. If p is the complement of c, then the argument is an argument **con** p.*

Argumentation takes place in a dialogue, which Carneades divides into *states* [10]. Each state contains a "momentary instance" of the arguments brought forth.

Definition 3 (argumentation process) *An **argumentation process** is a sequence of **states** where each state is a set of arguments. In every chain of arguments, $a_1, \ldots a_n$, constructable from the arguments in a state by linking the conclusion of an argument to a premise or exception of another argument, a conclusion of an argument a_i may not be a premise or exception of an argument a_j, if $j < i$. A set of arguments which violates this condition is said to contain a* cycle *and a set of arguments which complies with this condition is called* cycle-free.

Arguments are assessed using the concept of an *audience*, which has certain factual assumptions and a set of subjective weights it assigns to the arguments presented [2,1].

Definition 4 (audience) *An* audience *is a structure* $\langle \Phi, f \rangle$, *where* $\Phi \subset \mathcal{L}$ *is a consistent set of literals assumed to be acceptable by the audience and f is a partial function mapping arguments to real numbers in the range* $0.0 \ldots 1.0$, *representing the relative weights assumed to be assigned by the audience to the arguments.*

The actual evaluation of arguments presented at a given state to an audience takes place in an *evaluation structure*. It assigns a proof standard to each statement in the argument, representing the argumentative threshold for establishing a statement.

Definition 5 (argument evaluation structure) *An* **argument evaluation structure** *is a tuple* $\langle \Gamma, \mathcal{A}, g \rangle$, *where* Γ *is a state in an argumentation process,* $\mathcal{A}$ *is an audience and g is a total function mapping propositions in* $\mathcal{L}$ *to their applicable proof standards in the process. A* **proof standard** *is a function mapping tuples of the form* $\langle p, \Gamma, \mathcal{A} \rangle$ *to the Boolean values true and false, where p is a literal in* $\mathcal{L}$.

In a given evaluation context, a statement is acceptable if its proof standard has been met according to the assessment of the audience.

Definition 6 (acceptability) *Let* $\mathcal{S} = \langle \Gamma, \mathcal{A}, g \rangle$ *be an argument evaluation structure, where* $\mathcal{A} = \langle \Phi, f \rangle$. *A literal p is* **acceptable** *in* $\mathcal{S}$ *if and only if* $g(p)(p, \Gamma, \mathcal{A})$ *is true.*

In addition to the acceptability, we further make use of the derivability of literals as defined in Gordon & Ballnat [11].

Definition 7 (derivability) *Let* $\mathcal{S} = \langle \Gamma, \mathcal{A}, g \rangle$ *be an argument evaluation structure, where* $\mathcal{A} = \langle \Phi, f \rangle$. *A literal p is* **in** S, *denoted* $(\Gamma, \Phi) \vdash_{f,g} p$, *if and only if*

- $p \in \Phi$ *or*
- $(\neg p \notin \Phi$ *and p is acceptable in* $S)$

Otherwise p is **out**, *denoted* $(\Gamma, \Phi) \nvdash_{f,g} p$.

Consequently, an argument is applicable once it has been put forward and each of its premises has either been assumed to be acceptable or is acceptable. Further, none of the exceptions of the argument may be acceptable or assumed to be acceptable.

Definition 8 (argument applicability) *Let* $\langle state, audience, standard \rangle$ *be an argument evaluation structure. An argument* $\langle P, E, c \rangle$ *is* **applicable** *in this argument evaluation structure if and only if*

- *the argument is a member of the arguments of the state,*
- *every proposition* $p \in P$, *the premises, is an assumption of the audience or, if neither p nor* $\overline{p}$ *is an assumption, is acceptable in the argument evaluation structure and*
- *no proposition* $p \in E$, *the exceptions, is an assumption of the audience or, if neither p nor* $\overline{p}$ *is an assumption, is acceptable in the argument evaluation structure.*

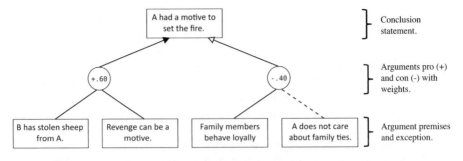

Figure 1. The arson example argument in the current Carneades visualization method.

For reasons of brevity, this paper only explains one proof standard, namely *preponderance of the evidence*. It states that a literal or its complement is acceptable depending on which side has the stronger applicable argument.

Definition 9 (preponderance of the evidence) *Let* $\langle \Gamma, \mathcal{A}, g \rangle$ *be an argument evaluation structure and let* p *be a literal in* $\mathcal{L}$. $pe(p, \Gamma, \mathcal{A}) = true$ *if and only if*

- *there is at least one applicable argument pro* p *in* Γ *and*
- *the maximum weight assigned by the audience* $\mathcal{A}$ *to the applicable arguments pro* p *is greater than the maximum weight of the applicable arguments con* p.

Fig. 1 shows an exemplary Carneades argument graph. Imagine an attorney representing farmer A in a civil proceeding. A has been accused of having set the farm of his brother B on fire and has been sued for compensation. The evidence speaks against A and the only element still at issue is the motive with which A had set the fire. The claimant has the burden of proof and argues (pro-argument, black arrowhead) that A had a motive (Literal M) as it has been established that B had stolen a sheep from A some time ago (Literal S) and revenge is a plausible motive for the arson (Literal R). The defense argument (con-argument, white arrowhead) is that it is less likely that A would commit the arson as they are members of the same family, hence A would likely be loyal to his sibling (Literal L). This argument would be applicable unless the claimant could show that A is not a "family person", i.e. someone who cares about family ties (Literal $\neg F$, exception shown as dashed line). Under the preponderance of evidence standard, one assigns greater weight to the pro-argument (0.6 vs. 0.4, see fig. 1), because one thinks the notion of revenge weighs heavier with the jury than loyalty among siblings. For the pleading to the jury, consequently, one sketches out the (admittedly simplified) argument graph shown in fig. 1. While one could expand each leaf node literal into a subtree of arguments or add additional arguments relating, for example, family loyalty and revenge, we leave the graph at this level of complexity for purposes of the illustration.

4. The Translation

The BN produced by our translation is not functionally equivalent to a Carneades argument structure in that it can be arbitrarily modified and still reflect a valid Carneades argument graph. Instead, the translation produces a BN *conditioned* on a specific configuration of an argument evaluation structure (see def. 5) with a set of probability functions emulating the status propagation of the just presented Carneades formalism. We thereby show how to simulate Carneades using a homomorphic BN. We do not claim that Carneades argument evaluation structures and BNs are isomorphic, which would allow, in the reverse direction, arbitrary BNs to be simulated using Carneades.

We justify the translation by explanation and by presenting an example argument graph and its corresponding BN. We do not have a full formal proof of functional correctness of the translation yet. We expect to be able to publish it in the near future.

We begin by introducing random variables for literals and arguments. Statement variables represent the *in*- or *out*-status of a literal given its proof standard and connecting arguments. Recall that in a Carneades graph structure, p and $\neg p$ are treated as a unit. We do not capture this unity in the BN translation. Instead, for each literal p in the argument structure, the BN contains two variables, one corresponding to p and the other one to $\neg p$. An argument depending on the literal as a premise or exception can then be linked to the respective variables as needed. This also means that every argument variable always connects to two statement variables, namely to one for its conclusion as a pro argument and to another one for its negated conclusion as a con argument. Since statement and argument variables represent two different kinds of random variables, our BN is effectively bipartite. This is distinct from Vreeswijk's interpretation of an existing BN as containing argument subtrees [20] as well as from Muecke & Stranieri [15], who manually translate generic argument graphs into BNs.

Definition 10 (statement and argument variables) *A **statement variable** is a random variable representing the probability of a given literal having a certain derivability status. It can take the values* $\{in, out\}$*. An **argument variable** is a random variable representing the probability of a certain argument being applicable. It can take the values* $\{applicable, not\ applicable\}$*.*

We can now translate an argument evaluation structure into a BN structure of variables, edges and probability functions. We commence by translating literals and arguments into their respective kind of variables. Notice that we need to create a statement variable not only for every literal used in the state, but also for its complement.

Definition 11 (variable translation) *If* $\mathcal{S} = \langle \Gamma, \mathcal{A}, g \rangle$ *is an argumentation evaluation structure, then* $V_{\mathcal{S}} = L \cup A$ *is the set of statement and argument variables corresponding to the literals in* Γ*. Let* $literals(\Gamma)$ *be a set of literals consisting of both positive and negated versions of all literals used by arguments in* Γ*. Let* sv_l *be a statement variable representing literal* l *and* av_a *be an argument variable representing argument* a*.*

- *Literals:* $L = \{sv_l | l \in literals(\Gamma)\}$
- *Arguments:* $A = \{av_a | a \in \Gamma\}$

We can now connect the variables using directed, labeled edges. We create two outgoing edges for arguments, one for its conclusion and one for its complement.

Definition 12 (edge translation) *If* $\mathcal{S} = \langle \Gamma, \mathcal{A}, g \rangle$ *is an argumentation evaluation structure, then* $D_{\mathcal{S}} = D_{Pr} \cup D_X \cup D_C$ *is a set of directed, labeled edges connecting the variables of* $V_{\mathcal{S}}$ *represented as three-element tuples. Let* $v_x \in V_{\mathcal{S}}$ *be the random variable associated with statement/argument* x*.*

- *Premises:* $D_{Pr} = \{(v_p, v_a, premise) | a = \langle P, E, c \rangle \in \Gamma, p \in P\}$
- *Exceptions:* $D_X = \{(v_e, v_a, exception) | a = \langle P, E, c \rangle \in \Gamma, e \in E\}$
- *Conclusions:* $D_C = \{(v_a, v_c, pro) | a = \langle P, E, c \rangle \in \Gamma\}$
  $\cup \{(n_a, n_{\neg c}, con) | a = \langle P, E, \neg c \rangle \in \Gamma\}$

The propagation functionality is added through the set of probability functions, which associates with each variable a function that determines the probability of the given random variable having a certain value conditioned on the values of the immediate parent variables and, as explained above, the elements of the argument evaluation structure: assumptions, proof standards and argument weights. For an argument variable, the parent variables are its premises and exceptions, while the parents of a statement variable represent arguments pro and con the statement. As we simulate the value propagation of the Carneades model, all conditional probabilities assigned are either 0 or 1, making the nodes in the network behave deterministically in accordance with the argument formalism. Notice that all information about the adjudication of competing applicable arguments (i.e. proof standards and argument weights) flows into the probability functions.

Definition 13 (probability functions) *If $S = \langle \Gamma, \mathcal{A}, g \rangle$ is an argument evaluation structure where $\mathcal{A} = \langle \Phi, f \rangle$, $V_S = S \cup A$ consists of a set of statement variables S and a set of argument variables A, and D_S is the set of connecting edges, then $\mathcal{P}_S = \mathcal{P}_a \cup \mathcal{P}_s$ is a set of probability functions defined as follows:*

If $a \in A$ is an argument variable and $s_1, ..., s_n$ are its parent statement variables, then P_a is the probability function for the variable a in the BN.

$$P_a(a = applicable | s_1, ..., s_n) = \begin{cases} 1, & \text{if for every } s_i \text{ it holds that either:} \\ & ((s_i, a, premise) \in D_S \text{ and } s_i = in) \\ & \text{or } ((s_i, a, exception) \in D_S \text{ and } s_i = out) \\ 0, & \text{otherwise} \end{cases}$$

$$P_a(a = not\ applicable | s_1, ..., s_n) = 1 - P_a(a = applicable | s_1, ..., s_n)$$

If $s \in S$ is a statement variable representing literal l and $a_1...a_n$ are its parent argument variables, then P_s is the probability function for the variable s:

$$P_s(s = in | a_1, ..., a_n) = \begin{cases} 1, & \text{if } (\Gamma, \Phi) \vdash_{f,g} p \\ 0, & \text{if } (\Gamma, \Phi) \nvdash_{f,g} p \end{cases}$$

$$P_s(s = out | a_1, ..., a_n) = 1 - P_a(s = in | a_1, ..., a_n)$$

Let $\mathcal{P}_a = \{P_a | a \in A\}$ and $\mathcal{P}_s = \{P_s | s \in S\}$.

By itself, the translation defines a class of BNs conditioned on an argument evaluation structure. One can instantiate a single autonomous CBN (variables, edges, probability functions) given a specific argument evaluation structure.

Definition 14 (Carneades Bayesian network) *A **Carneades Bayesian Network** (CBN) is an ordered tuple $\langle V_S, D_S, \mathcal{P}_S \rangle$, where V_S is a set of statement and argument variables in the network, D_S is a set of directed edges and $\mathcal{P}_S$ is the set of probability functions*

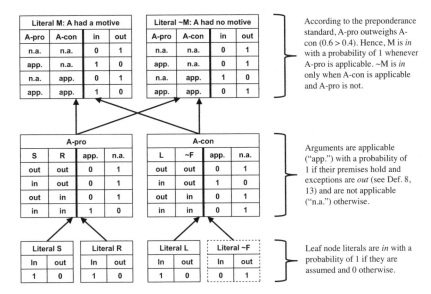

Figure 2. The example argument as a BN. The dashed box represents a negative literal. Negation is shown as ~. Unused literals have been omitted. For the propositions of the abbreviated literals, see end of section 3.

conditioned on the information in a given argument evaluation structure S. Further, the class of CBNs shall be defined as:

$$\mathcal{C} = \{\langle\langle V_S, D_S, \mathcal{P}_S\rangle\rangle | S \text{ is a Carneades argument evaluation structure}\}$$

5. An Example Translation

To give an illustration of a full reduction, we show our Carneades argument in the arson example as a BN in fig. 2 with the conditional probability tables attached to each variable. We begin by assuming that all premises of the two arguments hold, i.e. S, R and L are accepted and F is rejected. Given this configuration, the network behaves like a Carneades argument graph and will conclude that the presence of a motive will be deemed acceptable by the audience with a probability of 1 (i.e. $P(M = in) = 1$), because although both arguments are applicable, the pro-argument trumps the con-argument by virtue of it having a higher weight. This is an example of the patterns of 0s and 1s in the probability tables being contingent on the proof standard of each statement as well as the assumptions and weights attributed to the audience. If one were to change the weights so that the con-argument outweighed the pro-argument, the probability tables for *A-pro* and *A-con* in the depicted BN would change according to the translation.

6. The Characteristics and Utility of Probabilistic Semantics

6.1. Extension for Probability Distributions over Leaf Node Literals

In the example, we have modeled the assumptions about the audience in such a way that both arguments are applicable. The final binary determination of whether it will conclude that there is a motive is a matter of the proof standard and therefore about the weights which the audience is believed to assign to the arguments. However, the much more intuitive approach is to speak of the audience being more or less *likely* to accept or reject a certain statement, thereby introducing a notion of uncertainty into the concept of assumptions. Here, we can benefit from probabilistic semantics and extend the CBN model by introducing probability distributions over the *in-* and *out*-status of leaf literals (i.e. literals without arguments for or against them).

Up to now, we have modeled the literals l and $\neg l$ as distinct nodes in the network. Hence, such an extension conflicts with the consistency requirement for literals assumed by the audience. If both l and $\neg l$ are *in* with a certain nonzero probability each, the product of these probabilities is the probability of the assumptions being inconsistent with regard to that pair of literals. In order to remedy this issue, our extension needs to enforce the exlusiveness of the *in*-status. We achieve this by connecting positive/negated literal leaf pairs to a new common parent leaf variable with three possible values, which we shall refer to as a *probabilistic assumption variable*. If l is *accepted*, it is *in* and $\neg p$ is *out*. l being *rejected* is the inverse case. If l is *questioned*, both l and $\neg l$ are *out*.

Definition 15 (probabilistic assumption variable) *A **probabilistic assumption variable** is a random variable taking the possible values $M = \{accepted, rejected, questioned\}$ representing the probability of a certain literal being accepted, rejected or left undecided by the audience.*

Definition 16 (enhanced probability functions for leaf literals) *Assume $c = \langle V_S, D_S, \mathcal{P}_S \rangle$ is a CBN. Let $P_l \in \mathcal{P}_S$ be the probability function for a literal l's statement variable v_l in V_S and let L be the set of positive leaf literals in the argument. Let B be a set containing a probabilistic assumption variable b_l for each literal l in L. Let $\mathcal{P}_{ass}$ be set of a probability functions $P_{ass}(b_l = m)$ determining the probability with which $b_l \in B$ has status $m \in M$ such that $\sum_{m \in M} P_{ass}(b_l = m) = 1$ for all $b_l \in B$. Then an enhanced CBN $c' = \langle N_S', D_S', \mathcal{P}'_S \rangle$ is constructed from the following components:*

$$V_S' = V_S \cup B$$

$$D_S' = D_S \cup \{(b_l, v_l, ass), (b_l, v_{\neg l}, ass) | b_l \in B; v_l, v_{\neg l} \in V_S'\}$$

$$P_l'(v_l = in | b_l) = \begin{cases} 1, & \text{if } b_l = accepted \\ 0, & \text{otherwise} \end{cases}$$

$$P_l'(v_l = out | b_l) = 1 - P_l'(v_l = in | b_l)$$

$$P_{\neg l}'(v_{\neg l} = in | b_l) = \begin{cases} 1, & \text{if } b_l = rejected \\ 0, & \text{otherwise} \end{cases}$$

$$P_{\neg l}'(v_{\neg l} = out | b_l) = 1 - P_{\neg l}'(v_{\neg l} = in | b_l)$$

$$\mathcal{P}_{leaf} = \{P_l, P_{\neg l} | l \in L\} \; ; \; \mathcal{P}_l' = \{P_l' | l \in L\} \; ; \; \mathcal{P}_{\neg l}' = \{P_{\neg l}' | \neg l \in L\}$$

$$\mathcal{P}_S' = (\mathcal{P}_S \setminus \mathcal{P}_{leaf}) \cup \mathcal{P}_l' \cup \mathcal{P}_{\neg l}' \cup \mathcal{P}_{ass}$$

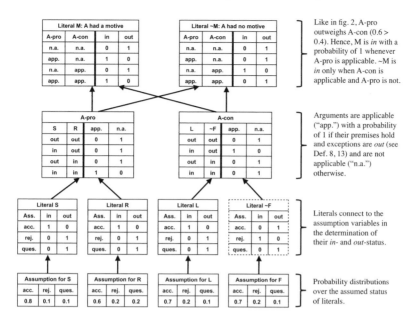

Like in fig. 2, A-pro outweighs A-con (0.6 > 0.4). Hence, M is *in* with a probability of 1 whenever A-pro is applicable. ~M is *in* only when A-con is applicable and A-pro is not.

Arguments are applicable ("app.") with a probability of 1 if their premises hold and exceptions are *out* (see Def. 8, 13) and are not applicable ("n.a.") otherwise.

Literals connect to the assumption variables in the determination of their *in*- and *out*-status.

Probability distributions over the assumed status of literals.

Figure 3. The example BN with extended literals and some possible probability distribution over assumed statements. Literals not used as premises or exceptions have been omitted.

This functionality connects Carneades to tasks of practical reasoning and planning. In the example, the claimant has the burden of proof and must show that $M = in$. The defendant's attorney does not need to establish $\neg M = in$, but only that $M = out$. She cannot tell for certain that the jury is going to accept a certain statement, but she can formulate her intuition about whether it is more likely to accept than to reject it. We extend the example BN and assign some probability distribution to the assumptions as shown in fig. 3. The diagram shows a distribution where the audience is likely to accept literals S (stolen sheep), L (loyalty among siblings) and F (A cares about family ties), but only moderately likely to accept R (revenge as a plausible motive), because burning the farm as revenge for a stolen sheep appears to be disproportionate. One can calculate the probability of successfully arguing that a motive has not been established: $P(M = out) = 0.52$. Modifying the assumption distributions or argument weights and recalculating the probabilities will yield insight into how best to persuade the jury and improve the chances. For example, the attorney can try to further weaken the jury's belief in revenge as a plausible motive (decrease of the probability the assumption for R to, for example, $P(\text{Assumption for R} = acc.) = 0.4$), thereby decreasing the probability of A-pro being applicable and achieving an overall success chance of $P(M = out) = 0.68$. Alternatively, she can try to convince the audience that A-con should weigh more heavily than A-pro (alteration of the conditional probability tables of M and $\neg M$ so that A-con wins over A-pro if both are applicable). This would increase her probability of success to $P(M = out) = 0.79$. Based on the calculations, it appears to be strategically better to plead for the family loyalty argument to have a higher weight than the revenge argument versus arguing that revenge is not a plausible motive.

We can see that this probabilistic form of Carneades allows some argumentation strategy decisions like the ones illustrated in the example to be cast into a modification of either the argument weights (thereby altering the probability functions) or the probabilistic assumption variables. After the modification, the network needs to be reinstantiated because of the change in the probability tables. The new BN can then be used to calculate the probability of successfully establishing the conclusion, which will improve, stay the same or worsen, thereby spreading open a space of possible actions, each associated with a certain payoff in argumentative certainty. We plan to pursue this possible utility of the BN translation in future work, specifically with regard to goal selection (see Gordon & Ballnat [11]) and dialogue games. Concerning the latter, our extension is similar to Riveret et al. [18], where probabilities were attached to premises of arguments to reflect the chance that a judge would accept the premise.

6.2. Probabilities, Proof Standards and Weights

In previous work on Carneades [10], it was argued that proof standards should not be modeled probabilistically because of (1) the difficulty in quantifying the necessary probabilities in argumentation scenarios, and (2) because multiple arguments can not typically be assumed to be independent of each other. The latter makes it difficult to generalize (conditional) independence between literals as one does not know whether they semantically connect to each other in a way not represented in the argument graph. In this paper, we use BNs to model the probability of a literal being accepted by the audience or satisfying its proof standard, i.e. the probability of the literal being *in* our *out*, not the probability of it being true given the evidence. The probability of a proof standard being satisfied does not depend on an assumption that the arguments are independent.

Our model distinguishes between the strength of an argument by virtue of its weight in the eyes of the audience and the strength of an argument by virtue of its premises being highly likely to be fulfilled (i.e. the argument being applicable). The former is taken into account by the conditional probability tables which simulate the Carneades model. The latter is determined via propagating the probability distributions of the assumptions across the BN. Eventually, both quantities are synthesized into a single probability value representing how likely it is that the conclusion is successfully established through the given argumentation. A strong-weighted argument with unlikely premises may have less of an impact on the probability of success than a weaker-weighted argument which is applicable with a high probability. The new probabilistic semantics hence add an additional functional dimension to argument weights and proof standards as they allow the probabilities to reveal and quantify the tradeoffs involved in assessing the *value* of a certain argument a given context.

7. Computational Complexity

Despite the benefits of BNs over full joint distributions, exact inference of probabilities from a BN is NP-hard [5]. To remedy this, well-performing iterative sampling-based (so-called *Monte-Carlo*) approximation methods are commonly used. More efficient methods may be possible which exploit the structure of Carneades argument graphs. This is not the focus of this paper and we hence leave it for future work. Notice that computational complexity issues are only relevant when Carneades is extended as described in Section 6.1. Computational complexity issues are irrelevant for the general conceptual aspects of a probabilistic interpretation of existing argument models and for the main result of this paper, i.e. providing Carneades with a probabilistic semantics (section 4).

8. Further Related Work

Williams & Williamson have experimented with inferring argument weights for a model graph from existing data using BN learning methods [19]. By contrast, our approach constructs BNs from an existing model graph. Also, our model does not interpret argument weights in a probabilistic fashion. Freeman's transferral [8] of Cohen's concept of ampliative probability [4] to the Toulmin model is distinct in that it infers argument strength from the probability of its premises being fulfilled. Our model perceives argument strength as the weight assigned to an argument by a subjective audience given the fulfillment of its premises, the latter of which is computed probabilistically. This is conceptually similar to distinguishing different notions of argument strength as done by Krause et al.[14] to produce a confidence measure with regard to a proposition. The argumentation system of Zukerman et al. [21] distinguishes between an argument being normatively strong according to domain knowledge and it being persuasive to an audience by mapping two separate BNs onto each other. By contrast to our work, the probability measure of the BN is again per se equated with strength of belief in a goal proposition.

Carofiglio [3] proposes a multi-partite BN version of a Toulmin-like model with which probability distributions over the beliefs can be calculated. While this approach is similar to ours with regard to the translation, our translation handles the richer Carneades model, including proof standards. A quantitative probabilistic representation for belief in uncertain facts (explored in detail by Kadane & Schum [13]) has been criticized by Parsons [16]. He distinguishes different kinds of uncertainty and argues for the greater adequacy of qualitative methods in dealing with problems of uncertainty. We present a probabilistic interpretation of an existing argument model and hence do not take a substantive position with regard to these issues but intend to address them in future research.

Howard & Matheson [12] have abstracted BNs into *influence diagrams*, integrating both probabilistic inferences and decision problems into a graphical model. In influence diagrams, deterministic nodes are used to represent certain outcomes, similar to our approach of simulating the deterministic Carneades model through conditional probabilities. Also in the decision-theory context, Druzdzel & Suermondt [7] surveyed methods to identify random variables in a network relevant to a query given some evidence, thereby also relying on deterministic nodes. GeNIe & SMILE [6] provide a solid implementation of graphical decision-theoretic models including functionality for deterministic nodes.

9. Conclusions and Future Work

We have simulated Carneades argument evaluation structures using a specially constructed class of BNs and instances thereof. The translation centers around argument- and statement-specific probability functions which are used to compute conditional probability tables. The translation into BNs suggests a way to extend the Carneades model to handle argumentation with uncertain premises, where the premises are assigned a priori probabilities. Future research will focus on evaluating the utility of the extended Carneades model for quantitative decision support systems, reducing inference complexity, as well as on the implications for argumentation theory of viewing claims and decisions as having probabilities.

10. Acknowledgments

The authors thank Prof. Kevin Ashley, Collin Lynch and Saeed Amizadeh (Intelligent Systems Program, University of Pittsburgh) as well as Prof. Henry Prakken (Computer Science Department, Utrecht University; Law Faculty, University of Groningen) for very helpful suggestions and feedback during the process of writing this paper.

References

[1]   T. J. Bench-Capon, S. Doutre, and P. E. Dunne. Audiences in argumentation frameworks. *Artificial Intelligence*, 171(42-71), 2007.

[2]   T. Bench-Capon. Persuasion in practical argument using value-based argumentation frameworks. *Journal of Logic and Computation*, 13(3):429–448, 2003.

[3]   V. Carofiglio. Modelling Argumentation with Belief Networks. 4th Workshop on Computational Models of Natural Argument, ECAI 2004.

[4]   L. J. Cohen. An Introduction to the Philosophy of Induction and Probability. Clarendon Press, 1989.

[5]   G. F. Cooper. Probabilistic Inference using Belief Networks is Np-Hard. Paper No. SMI-87-0195, Knowledge Systems Laboratory, Stanford University. Stanford, CA, USA, 1987.

[6]   See the GeNIe & SMILE software: http://genie.sis.pitt.edu

[7]   M. J. Druzdzel and H. J. Suermondt. Relevance in Probabilistic Models: "Backyards" in a "Small World". Working notes of the AAAI–1994 Fall Symposium Series: Relevance, 60-63, 1994.

[8]   J. B. Freeman. Argument Strength, the Toulmin Model, and Ampliative Probability. In: van Eemeren, Garssen, B. (eds.), Pondering on Problems of Argumentation, 2009.

[9]   T. F. Gordon, H. Prakken, and D. Walton. The Carneades model of argument and burden of proof. Artificial Intelligence 171, 10-11, 875-896, 2007.

[10] T. F. Gordon and D. Walton. Proof Burdens and Standards. Argumentation in Artificial Intelligence, I. Rahwan and G. Simari, Eds. Springer-Verlag, Berlin, Germany, 2009.

[11] T.F. Gordon and S. Ballnat. Goal Selection in Argumentation Processes. Proceedings of COMMA 2010.

[12] R. A. Howard and J. E. Matheson. Influence diagrams. Readings on the Principles and Applications of Decision Analysis, pages 721-762. Strategic Decisions Group, 2003.

[13] J. B. Kadane and D. A. Schum. A Probabilistic Analysis of the Sacco and Vanzetti Evidence. Wiley & Sons, 1996.

[14] P. Krause, S. Ambler, M. Elvang-Goransson, and J. Fox. A Logic of Argumentation for Reasoning under Uncertainty. Computational Intelligence 11, 113-131, 1995.

[15] N. Muecke and A. Stranieri. An argument structure abstraction for bayesian belief networks: just outcomes in on-line dispute resolution. Proceedings of the fourth Asia-Pacific Conference on Conceptual Modeling, pp. 35-40, 2007.

[16] S. Parsons. Qualitative Methods for Reasoning under Uncertainty. MIT Press, 2009.

[17] J. Pearl. Bayesian Networks: A Model of Self-Activated Memory for Evidential Reasoning. (UCLA Technical Report CSD-850017). Proceedings of the 7th Conference of the Cognitive Science Society, 1985.

[18] R. Riveret, H. Prakken, A. Rotolo and G. Sartor. Heuristics in Argumentation: A Game-Theoretical Investigation. Proceedings of COMMA 2008, pp. 324-335, 2008.

[19] M. Williams and J. Williamson. Combining Argumentation and Bayesian Nets for Breast Cancer Prognosis. Journal of Logic, Language and Information 15: 155-178, 2006.

[20] G. A. Vreeswijk. Argumentation in Bayesian Belief Networks. Argumentation in Multi-Agent Systems, LNAI 3366, pp. 111-129, 2005.

[21] I. Zukerman, R. Mcconachy, and K. B. Korb. Bayesian Reasoning in an Abductive Mechanism for Argument Generation and Analysis. Proceedings of the Fifteenth National Conference on Artificial Intelligence, pp. 833-838, 1998.

Computational Models of Argument
P. Baroni et al. (Eds.)
IOS Press, 2010
doi:10.3233/978-1-60750-619-5-267

How Argumentation can Enhance Dialogues in Social Networks

Stella HERAS [a,1], Katie ATKINSON [b], Vicente BOTTI [a], Floriana GRASSO [b],
Vicente JULIAN [a], and Peter MCBURNEY [b]

[a] *Dep. de Sistemas Informáticos y Computación, Univ. Politécnica de Valencia, Spain*
[b] *Dep. of Computer Science, University of Liverpool, UK*

Abstract. Many websites nowadays allow social networking between their users
in an explicit or implicit way. In this work, we show how the theory of argumentation schemes can provide a valuable help to formalize and structure on-line discussions and user opinions in decision support and business oriented websites that
hold social networks among their users. A real study case is considered and analysed. Then, guidelines for website and system design are provided to enhance social decision support and recommendations with argumentation.

Keywords. Social Networks, Customer Support, Argumentation Schemes

Introduction

The current incarnation of the Web as a platform for computing and collaborative interaction, supported by the development of so-called Web 2.0 technologies and standards, has resulted in the fast proliferation of web-based communities and on-line social networks. Social networking is encouraged ever more often, in an explicit or implicit way. Together with declared leisure oriented social networking sites, like Face-
book (www.facebook.com), Flickr (www.flickr.com) or MySpace (www.myspace.com),
many more decision support or business oriented sites allow users to interact, share their
preferences and profiles, form communities and give advice, recommendations and feedback about their experiences. This is the case of Amazon (www.amazon.com) or eBay
(www.ebay.com) and consumer review sites, like Tripadvisor (www.tripadvisor.com) or
Epinions (www.epinions.com).

Regardless of the purpose of the social networking, in all of these communities discussions arise from the difference of opinion between users, and individual views are
mixed in the tangle of user-generated content posted in discussion boards, wikis and
blogs. Mostly, this information is unstructured, and gives little opportunity for complex
knowledge elicitation. When on the other hand information *is* structured, as in the typical
recommender systems, usually there is no explanation of the reasoning process behind
the recommendation, which is simply presented as the result of the application of the
recommending algorithm. However, it has been shown that people trust recommenda-

[1]Corresponding Author: Information Systems and Computing Department, Universidad Politécnica de
Valencia, Camino de Vera s/n. 46022 Valencia, Spain, email: sheras@dsic.upv.es

tions more when the engine can explain their rationale [10] and currently the notion of a "good" recommendation has changed from the one that minimises some error evaluation measure about the output of content, collaborative filtering or hybrid recommendation methods, to the one that really makes people more satisfied.

In this work, we discuss how Argumentation Schemes Theory [14] could help formalise and structure on-line discussions and user opinions. Although not directly applied to social networks, the work most relevant to our purposes is perhaps the work on recommender systems [1][7][4]. Here, research has investigated the impact of the social network dynamics on the recommendation, typically based on the notion of "social trust" [5,12]. The work in the present paper contributes to this area but from the different perspective of structuring and clarifying the reasoning process followed by users to provide pieces of advice and recommendations to other users of their social network.

We focus in particular business oriented websites that allow a social interaction among their users. We leave out of our analysis for the time being decision support, leisure or ethics oriented social networking sites, as the scope and target of on-line business websites makes them more suitable to define tools to analyse opinions and elicit knowledge from their users. In this paper, we formalise our notion of social network, and we show how this definition fits to Amazon, probably best epitomize how implicit social networks emerged from business websites. Finally, we discuss how argumentation schemes could be best utilised to improve social networking features.

1. Definition of a Social Network Model

We studied a number of social networks, focusing in particular to the argumentation activities that, either implicitly or explicitly, users would engage in. In particular, following the typology of argumentative dialogue in [13], we assessed how different social networks compare with this feature. From this analysis, we extrapolated a general abstraction of social network.

For our purposes, we consider a social network as an abstraction to represent social structures that link individuals or organisations. Links can stand for different types of interdependency, such as friendship, trade, shared knowledge, common hobbies, etc. We distinguish between **explicit social networks**, which openly represent users and links among them, so that users can, for instance, search their *contact list* to interact with other users, and **implicit social networks**, which may or may not store information about social relationships among users, but which usually do not make this information accessible to users, who cannot access their contact lists to retrieve previous partners or do not have an easy way of searching reports about previous exchanges. For both types, we identify the following features that define a social network in our model:

- Overall **purpose** of the network: e.g. friendship, business, shared hobbies.
- Permitted **tasks**: e.g. recommend, provide opinions, evaluate others' opinions.
- **Nodes** representing individuals or organisations.
- **Roles** that individuals or organisations can play in the social network.
- **Knowledge databases**: individual or shared knowledge databases associated with each node and representing information about the issues related with each role.
- **Ties**, or links, between nodes, which can be of different sorts, depending on the overall purpose of the network (e.g. values, visions, ideas, financial exchange,

friendship, personal relationships, kinship, dislikes, conflict, trade). Ties can be directed or not. Undirected links represent social relations that are present in the network, but whose related information is not stored nor explicitly supported.

- Social network **analysis measures**, used to evaluate the relations that a tie represents. Values of trust and reputation are common examples of these measures.
- Types of **argumentative dialogues** that can be held in the network.

In what follows we concentrate on a study case, analyzing arguably one of the most popular business oriented websites that allow social interaction among users, despite this not being their primary purpose: Amazon. We analyse the features that make it considered *de facto* social network, and we represent it in the light of the model we defined above.

1.1. Amazon

Amazon (www.amazon.com) is possibly the largest on-line retailer offering, either directly or via "marketplace" associated sellers, a very wide range of products, from books, to groceries, from furniture to clothes and shoes, and so on. Social networking features allow users to interact in different ways. Amazon's users can:

- write reviews about products, whether purchased or not. As part of their review, users can rate products. Reviews can be annotated with the nickname of the reviewer or his popularity as reviewer ("reviewer rank"), based on both positive and negative votes received, as well as the time when the review was published. In addition, other users can write comments on reviews, rate them as useful/unuseful, and report them to the company if they consider them offensive or inappropriate.
- leave feedback about "marketplace" sellers after a purchase, with a comment. Seller ratings are computed using the votes received over the transactions performed in a specific period of time. Sellers have the opportunity to respond to the comment/rating and rate the transaction, but they cannot rate buyers (only feedback submitted by buyers is considered to compute a seller rating).
- join customer communities: users can create a profile and share it with other users, join different communities, participate in forum, create *Listmania* lists with the Amazon products they like or recommend and *Wish* lists with the products they are interested in, suggest products to their communities by adding a tag, write *So You'd Like to...* guides to directly recommend products. Posts can be replied to, rated and reported, but these ratings are not used to compute customer ranks.

On top of this, Amazon website runs a powerful recommendation algorithm that matches each customer's purchased and rated item to similar items, and outputs a personalised recommendation list [9]. This algorithm follows an *item-to-item collaborative filtering* approach that scales to massive data, producing recommendations in real time with a brief explanation (e.g. "N% customers buying X also bought Y").

1.1.1. Amazon Social Network Models

Explicit social networks are formed by the users joining communities, while implicit social networks emerge from the activity of writing reviews and from sales and their subsequent feedback. In the spirit of our analysis, we focus here on the latter, and we analyse the social networks emerging from reviews and sales according to our model.

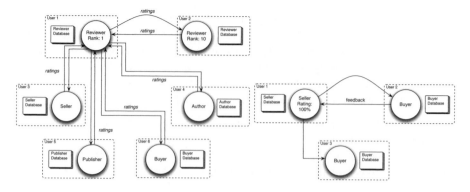

Figure 1. a: Amazon Social Network of Reviews; b: Amazon Social Network of Sales

Social Network of Reviews

Reviews that Amazon users write give rise to social relations from which emerges an *Amazon Social Network of Reviews*, with the **purpose** of sharing information on the products, and with **nodes** representing buyers, sellers, reviewers, authors (of books for example) and publishers/manufacturers. The **tasks** permitted are: writing reviews on Amazon products, writing comments on reviews, rating reviews or reporting reviews. The main type of **dialogue** enabled by this social networking activity is information seeking and sharing, but persuasion is also enabled by means of free comments and responses to them. Figure 1a is an example of a network of reviews with six Amazon customers playing each role that is involved in the activity of writing reviews. Arrows stand for **social ties** implicitly created from users' activity. In the example, User 1 reviewed a product related with other users (because they are sellers, authors, publishers or buyers of the product). Users 3, 4, 5 and 6 rated or reported the review of User 1, while Users 1 and 2 commented, rated or reported the same review, or each other's review. **Knowledge databases** are attached to each role, denoting the information that the website stores for each role, e.g. the reviews made by a reviewer and how they were rated, though not always the information is accessible to a user (e.g. there is no obvious way for users to check their list of reviews). **Analysis measures** evaluate users' performance in the social network, e.g. the reviewer's rank can be used as a reputation measure to evaluate the importance of a reviewer. Measures can also label ties, e.g. individual reviewers' trust measures could be computed from the usefulness ratings assigned over a certain period of time.

Social Network of Sales

The overall **purpose** of the *Amazon Social Network of Sales* is to run commercial transactions between its members and to inform about them. Therefore, the **tasks** permitted on the network are sell and buy products and leave feedback about these commercial transactions, while **nodes** are simply buyers and sellers (as feedback cannot be left unless a transaction has occurred). The main type of **dialogue** that these tasks enable is that of information seeking and sharing, by leaving feedback, and persuasion, by supporting this feedback and responding to it. Figure 1b shows an example of an Amazon social network of sales with one seller (User 1) and two buyers (Users 2 and 3) and their respective **knowledge databases**. As before, arrows show **social ties**: User 1 sold a product to Users 2 and 3, while User 2 provided feedback about his sale with User 1. Amazon aggregates reviews to compute a seller rating, which can also be used as a reputation **measure** to label nodes that represent customers playing the role of sellers. The seller can also leave comments about the transaction and the feedback received, represented in the figure by the arrow from User 1 to User 2, but cannot rate the transaction (no label on the arrow).

2. Argumentation Schemes to Support On-line Dialogues in Social Networks

In this section, we concentrate on how argumentation could enhance the performance of the emergent activities carried out by the users of a social network, with a preliminary step towards the application of argumentation schemes to formalise the underlying reasoning shown in the dialogues held among the users of the networks in our cases of study. Argumentation schemes [14] are characterised by a set of premises and their underlying conclusion, and are associated with a set of critical questions (CQs) that stand for potential attacks that could refute the conclusion drawn from the scheme. This feature is very useful to guide argumentation dialogues. Thus, if a proponent of a position uses a pattern of reasoning that matches with an argumentation scheme, an opponent can try to pose one of its critical questions to attack that position. We analysed a number of typical dialogues held in the situation described in the Amazon study case, and we identify the following advantages of applying argumentation schemes to social networked business: 1) *to provide a formal structure to opinions and recommendations*, allowing for explanations and justifications that clarify the position of the reviewer; 2) *to provide a way of evaluating user opinions and recommendations*, by looking at their associated reasoning patterns, with critical questions as a way to show weaknesses and possible attacks and 3) *to provide a formal structure to the dialogue as a whole*, clarifying the dynamics of each individual contribution in terms of the overall argument.

To illustrate these advantages, consider for example the conversation extract (inspired by real posts on Amazon) shown in figure 2 reviewing book B. The argumentation can be summarised as:

- *User1* provides an argument in favour of the book:
  - **A1:** I am a scholar in the area of AI; I strongly recommend the reading of the book; THEREFORE this is a good reading
- *User2* replies with two arguments: an opinion about the topic and an attack to A1:
  - **A2:** I have read the 2nd book of the series of B; This wasn't a good reading; THEREFORE book B couldn't be a good reading either.
  - **A3:** *User1* says that book B and its series are good; *User1* posted a hard criticism and discouraged the reading of the book B in a previous review; THEREFORE the review of *User1* is inconsistent with what he said previously
- Finally, *User3* replies to *User2* with an argument that supports the argument of *User1*:
  - **A4:** *User1* is a scholar in the area of AI; *User1* discourages the reading for non-scholars of the 2nd book of the series of B; THEREFORE the 2nd book of the series of B isn't a good reading for non-scholars

Following [14], these arguments could be translated into argumentation schemes as:

A1: Argument From Expert Opinion
  Major Premise: Source *User1* is an expert in subject domain *AI* containing proposition

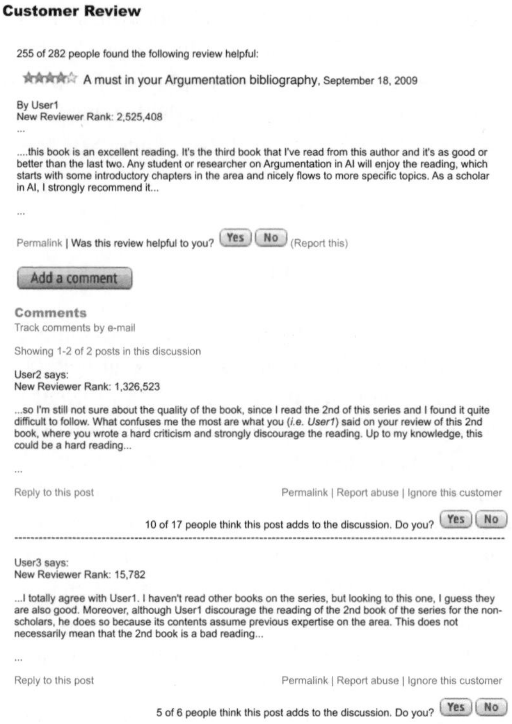

Customer Review

255 of 282 people found the following review helpful:

★★★★☆ A must in your Argumentation bibliography, September 18, 2009

By User1
New Reviewer Rank: 2,525,408
...

....this book is an excellent reading. It's the third book that I've read from this author and it's as good or better than the last two. Any student or researcher on Argumentation in AI will enjoy the reading, which starts with some introductory chapters in the area and nicely flows to more specific topics. As a scholar in AI, I strongly recommend it...

...

Permalink | Was this review helpful to you? [Yes] [No] (Report this)

[Add a comment]

Comments
Track comments by e-mail

Showing 1-2 of 2 posts in this discussion

User2 says:
New Reviewer Rank: 1,326,523

...so I'm still not sure about the quality of the book, since I read the 2nd of this series and I found it quite difficult to follow. What confuses me the most are what you (i.e. User1) said on your review of this 2nd book, where you wrote a hard criticism and strongly discourage the reading. Up to my knowledge, this could be a hard reading...

...

Reply to this post   Permalink | Report abuse | Ignore this customer

10 of 17 people think this post adds to the discussion. Do you? [Yes] [No]

User3 says:
New Reviewer Rank: 15,782

...I totally agree with User1. I haven't read other books on the series, but looking to this one, I guess they are also good. Moreover, although User1 discourage the reading of the 2nd book of the series for the non-scholars, he does so because its contents assume previous expertise on the area. This does not necessarily mean that the 2nd book is a bad reading...

...

Reply to this post   Permalink | Report abuse | Ignore this customer

5 of 6 people think this post adds to the discussion. Do you? [Yes] [No]

Figure 2. An example on Amazon reviews

book B is a good reading
Minor Premise: *User1* asserts that *book B is a good reading* is true
Conclusion: *book B is a good reading* is true
CQ1: How credible is *User1* as an expert source?
CQ2: Is *User1* an expert in the field *AI* for which *book B is a good reading*?
CQ3: What did *User1* assert that implies that *book B is a good reading*?
CQ4: Is *User1* personally reliable as a source?
CQ5: Is the proposition *book B is a good reading* consistent with other experts assert?
CQ6: Is *User1*'s assertion based on evidence?

A2: Argument From Position to Know
Major Premise: Source *User2* is in position to know about things in a certain subject domain *books on B series* containing proposition *book B is a good reading*
Minor Premise: *User2* asserts that *book B is a good reading* is false
Conclusion: *book B is a good reading* is false
CQ1: Is *User2* in position to know whether *book B is a good reading* is true of false?
CQ2: Is *User2* an honest source?
CQ3: Did *User2* assert that the *book B is a good reading* is true or false?

A3: Argument From Inconsistent Commitment
Initial Commitment Premise: *User1* has claimed that he is committed to proposition *book B and its series are a good reading*
Opposed Commitment Premise: Other evidence shows that *User1* is not committed to proposition *book B and its series are a good reading* since he discouraged the reading of the book *B* in a previous review

Conclusion: *User1's* commitments are inconsistent
CQ1: What is the evidence supposedly showing that *User1* is committed to proposition *book B and its series are a good reading*?
CQ2: What further evidence in the case is alleged to show that *User1* is not committed to proposition *book B and its series are a good reading*?
CQ3: How does the evidence from premise 1 and premise 2 prove that there is a conflict of commitments?

A4: Argument From Expert Opinion
    Major Premise: Source *User1* is an expert in subject domain *AI* containing proposition *book B is a good reading*
    Minor Premise: *User1* asserts that *the 2nd book of the series isn't a good reading for non-scholars* is true
    Conclusion: *the 2nd book of the series isn't a good reading for non-scholars* is true
    (CQs as in A1)

By associating a scheme to each argument, opinions are given, obviously enough, a formal structure, which makes the pattern of reasoning explicit. Users could be asked to explain their arguments by using the critical questions of a schema. For instance, in the example above, A3 attacks A1 in fact by instantiating its CQ4. Or, A4 attacks A3 instantiating its CQ2. Moreover, users could be encouraged to clarify their position better: we have often found negative ratings of a product where the free text reveals that the bad experience was in fact related to the transaction (e.g. late shipment, item broken, etc.).

Of course for this situation to be realistic, users need to find the use of argumentation natural enough not to be discouraged to use it. Recent developments have introduced Web 2.0 standards to support on-line debate. Some contributions of this type are Cope_it! [8], which encourages collaboration by sharing opinions and resources; the semantic web-based argumentation system ArgDF [11]; Cohere [2], a web tool for social bookmarking, idea-linking and argument visualisation; the Argument Blogging project [15], which intends to harvest textual resources from the Web and organise them into distributed argumentative dialogues and the On-line Visualisation of Argument (OVA at ARG:dundee: www.arg.dundee.ac.uk) tools, which facilitate argument analysis and manipulation in on-line environments. Some examples of tools that are of a more formal and structured nature include the Parmenides system [3] and the Carneades system [6]. Despite the proliferation of these tools, their uptake by business oriented websites like Amazon is questionable, as their main interest is not to alienate users from their site by providing a seamless and natural interaction.

3. Conclusions: Desiderata for Argumentation enhanced Social Networks

In this work we showed how argumentation theory can provide valuable insights in formalising and structuring on-line discussions and user opinions in business oriented websites. We gave a model of social network, and we provided a case study of a commercial website, Amazon, fitting this model. Finally, we demonstrated how typical interactions in these environments could be seen as argumentation dialogues, and could in fact be enhanced by such features. Several conditions need to be verified before a more widespread uptake of argumentation techniques could be possible, however.

First, sites like Amazon should make each underlying social network explicit, so that users could exploit all information resources available in the website, in turn enhancing trust and reputation by providing public and transparent measures. Secondly, sites should provide easy-to-use tools for the quick and seamless identification of argumentation schemes in the line of reasoning that a user is following in a post. Although this aspect is more related to the advancement of the state of the art on argumentation and computation research, websites which decide for the uptake of a particular tool could grant some reward (e.g. positive feedback) to the users of these tools. Third, sites should provide tools to represent the dynamics of dialogues among users, so that attack and defense statements can be easily identified. Again, this comes at a considerable cost to the users (who would not necessarily be prepared to engage in a dialogue each time they want to leave a review for a product), so reward mechanisms should be used. Finally, sites should provide tools for summarising and analysing the information gathered from the schemes and attacks identification. A "summary" showing statistics and a graphical representation of debate on a product would represent a concrete added value for users, and an effective motivation to engage in argumentative activities. This it would allow, for instance, users to understand at a glance which is the most prominent view of a particular product they want to purchase, without having to read all reviews.

We believe that argumentation *can* make business driven social networking more rewarding, and we see this as one of the most promising application areas for research in argument and computation.

References

[1]   G. Adomavicious and A. Tuzhilin: Toward the Next Generation of Recommender Systems: A Survey of the State-of-the-Art and Possible Extensions. IEEE Transactions on Knowledge and Data Engineering, Vol. 17, No. 6, pp. 734-749, 2005.

[2]   S. Buckingham Shum: Cohere: Towards Web 2.0 Argumentation. Proceedings of the 2nd Int. Conf. on Computational Models of Argument, COMMA, pp. 28-30, 2008.

[3]   D. Cartwright and K. Atkinson. Political engagement through tools for argumentation. In Proceedings of the 2nd Int. Conf. on Computational Models of Argument, COMMA, pp. 116-127, 2008.

[4]   C.I. Chesñevar, A.G. Maguitman and M.P. GonzÃąlez: Empowering Recommendation Technologies Through Argumentation. Argumentation in Artificial Intelligence, pp. 403-422, Springer, 2009.

[5]   J. Golbeck: Generating Predictive Movie Recommendations from Trust in Social Networks. Proceedings of the Fourth International Conference on Trust Management, LNCS, Vol. 3986, pp. 93-104, 2006.

[6]   T. Gordon, H. Prakken, and D. Walton. The Carneades model of argument and burden of proof. Artificial Intelligence, Vol. 171, No. 10-15, pp. 875-896, 2007.

[7]   S. Heras, M. Navarro, Vicente Botti and V. Julián: Applying Dialogue Games to Manage Recommendation in Social Networks. Proc. of the 6th Int. Workshop on Argumentation in MAS, ArgMAS, 2009.

[8]   N. Karacapilidis and M. Tzagarakis: Web-based collaboration and decision making support: A multidisciplinary approach. Web-Based Learning and Teaching Technologies, Vol. 2, No. 4, pp. 12-23, 2007.

[9]   G. Linden, B. Smith and J. York: Amazon.com Recommendations: Item-to-Item Collaborative Filtering. IEEE Internet Computing, Vol. 7, No, 1, pp. 76-80, 2003.

[10] G. Linden, J. Hong, M. Stonebraker and M. Guzdial: Recommendation Algorithms, Online Privacy and More. Communications of the ACM, Vol. 52, No. 5, 2009.

[11] I. Rahwan, F. Zablith and C. Reed: Laying the Foundations for a World Wide Argument Web. Artificial Intelligence, Vol. 171, No. 10-15, pp. 897-921, 2007.

[12] J. Sabater and C. Sierra: Reputation and Social Network Analysis in Multi-Agent Systems. Proceedings of AAMAS 2002, No. 1, pp. 475-482, 2002.

[13] D. Walton and E. Krabbe: Commitment in Dialogue: Basic Concepts of Interpersonal Reasoning. State University of New York Press, 1995.

[14] D. Walton, C. Reed and F. Macagno: Argumentation Schemes. Cambridge University Press, 2008.

[15] S. Wells, C. Gourlay and C. Reed: Argument Blogging. Proceedings of Computational Models of Natural Argument, CMNA 2009.

Computational Models of Argument
P. Baroni et al. (Eds.)
IOS Press, 2010
doi:10.3233/978-1-60750-619-5-275

Base Logics in Argumentation

Anthony HUNTER

Department of Computer Science,
University College London,
Gower Street, London WC1E 6BT, UK
a.hunter@cs.ucl.ac.uk

Abstract. There are a number of frameworks for modelling argumentation in logic. They incorporate a formal representation of individual arguments and techniques for comparing conflicting arguments. A common assumption for logic-based argumentation is that an argument is a pair $\langle \Phi, \alpha \rangle$ where Φ is a minimal subset of the knowledgebase such that Φ is consistent and Φ entails the claim α. We call the logic used for consistency and entailment, the base logic. Different base logics provide different definitions for consistency and entailment and hence give us different options for argumentation. This paper discusses some of the commonly used base logics in logic-based argumentation, and considers various criteria that can be used to identify commonalities and differences between them.

Keywords. logic-based argumentation, logical argument systems, consequence relations, defeasible logic, classical logic

1. Introduction

Proposals for logic-based argumentation rely on an underlying logic, which we call a *base logic*, for generating logical arguments and for defining the counterargument relationships (using inference of conflict or existence of inconsistency). For logic-based argumentation, we assume that an argument is a pair $\langle \Phi, \alpha \rangle$ where Φ entails the claim α. Let $\vdash_x$ be the consequence relation of the base logic, and so Φ entails the claim α means $\Phi \vdash_x \alpha$. Many proposals for logic-based argumentation also stipulate that for $\langle \Phi, \alpha \rangle$ to be an argument, Φ is minimal (i.e. there is no $\Phi' \subset \Phi$ such that $\Phi' \vdash_x \alpha$), and/or Φ is consistent (which in most proposals for argumentation systems means that it is not the case that $\Phi \vdash_x \alpha$ and $\Phi \vdash_x \neg\alpha$ for any atom α).

The choice of base logic is an important design decision for a logic-based argumentation system. This then raises the questions of what are the minimal requirements for a base logic and what are the factors that need to be considered for a base logic? In this paper, we consider these questions in terms of general properties and in terms of the base logics that arise in key approaches to logic-based argumentation. The net result is that we can see some useful properties holding for all the key approaches (including the important properties of cut, monotonicity, and a restricted form of reflexivity), and some useful properties that differentiate approaches. We also suggest that given the wide range of logics being developed in the knowledge representation field, there are further interesting opportunities for using different base logics in argumentation.

2. Examples of base logics in argument systems

To help us explore the nature of base logics, we consider some key proposals for logic-based argumentation, and draw out the base logics used. We start with simple proposals that use classical logic $\vdash_c$ as base logic [10,3,5], and for which $\langle \Phi, \alpha \rangle$ is an argument iff $\Phi \vdash_c \alpha$ and there is no $\Phi' \subset \Phi$ such that $\Phi' \vdash_c \alpha$ and $\Phi \not\vdash_c \bot$.

Example 1. *Let* $\Delta = \{\neg\neg a, \neg b \rightarrow \neg a, \neg b \vee (c \wedge d), b \wedge c \wedge \neg b, \neg f \rightarrow g \vee h\}$. *So according to the above,* $\langle \{\neg\neg a, \neg b \rightarrow \neg a, \neg b \vee (c \wedge d)\}, e \rightarrow d \rangle$ *is an argument.*

The most common kind of base logic is a form of defeasible logic such as used in defeasible logic programming [16], defeasible argumentation with specificity-based preferences [27], the ASPIC system [9], and argument-based extended logic programming [24]. For a general coverage of defeasible logics in argumentation see [11,25,26].

The language for defeasible logic is based on rules of the following form where $\beta_1, \ldots, \beta_j, \beta_{j+1}$ are literals and $\rightarrow_k$ is an implication symbol.

$$\beta_1 \wedge \ldots \wedge \beta_j \rightarrow_k \beta_{j+1}$$

For the defeasible logic approaches to argumentation, such as [16], there can be more than one type of implication symbol $\rightarrow_k$, and the proof theory for the base logic is given by a derivation using modus ponens as defined next. Note, the consequence relation ignores any differences between the different types of implication symbol that may appear in the knowledgebase[1].

Definition 1. *Let* Δ *be the union of a set of rules and a set of literals. The defeasible logic consequence relation* $\vdash_d$ *is defined as follows.*

$$\Delta \vdash_d \psi \text{ iff there is a sequence of literals } \alpha_1, \ldots, \alpha_n$$
such that ψ *is* α_n *and for each* $\alpha_i \in \{\alpha_1, \ldots \alpha_n\}$
either α_i *is a literal in* Δ
or there is a $\beta_1 \wedge \ldots \wedge \beta_j \rightarrow_k \alpha_i \in \Delta$
and $\{\beta_1, \ldots, \beta_j\} \subseteq \{\alpha_1, \ldots, \alpha_{i-1}\}$

In the following example, $\rightarrow_1$ denotes a strict rule and $\rightarrow_2$ denotes a defeasible rule, though, as defined above, this denotation is ignored by the $\vdash_d$ consequence relation.

Example 2. *Let* $\Delta = \{p, \neg q, p \rightarrow_1 \neg r, \neg q \wedge \neg r \rightarrow_2 s, s \rightarrow_1 t, p \wedge t \rightarrow_2 u\}$. *Therefore* $\Delta \vdash_d u$ *where the sequence of literals in the derivation is* $p, \neg r, \neg q, s, t, u$.

For defeasible logic programming [16], $\langle \Phi, \alpha \rangle$ is an argument iff $\Phi \vdash_d \alpha$ and there is no $\Phi' \subset \Phi$ such that $\Phi' \vdash_d \alpha$ and it is not the case that there is a β such that $\Phi \vdash_d \beta$ and $\Phi \vdash_d \neg\beta$ (i.e. Φ is a minimal consistent set entailing α), whereas for assumption-based argumentation [12], $\langle \Phi, \alpha \rangle$ is an argument iff $\Phi \vdash_d \alpha$. Note, in [16] only the defeasible rules are explicitly represented in the support of the argument, and in [12] only the literals are explicitly represented in the support of the argument, but in both cases it is a trivial change (as we do here) to explicitly represent both the rules and literals used in the derivation in the support of the argument.

---

[1]The type of implication appearing in each formula in the support of an argument is used for determining the relative preference of the argument when compared with other arguments.

Example 3. *Continuing Example 2, the following is an argument in defeasible logic programming [16].*

$$\langle \{p, \neg q, p \rightarrow_1 \neg r, \neg q \wedge \neg r \rightarrow_2 s, s \rightarrow_1 t, p \wedge t \rightarrow_2 u\}, u\rangle$$

Example 4. *For $\Delta = \{p, \neg q, s, p \rightarrow \neg r, \neg q \wedge \neg r \wedge s \rightarrow t, t \wedge p \rightarrow u, v\}$, the following is an argument in assumption-based argumentation [12].*

$$\langle \{p, \neg q, s, p \rightarrow \neg r, \neg q \wedge \neg r \wedge s \rightarrow t\}, t\rangle$$

Also note that in [12], there is the notion of a backward argument which is an argument that can be constructed by backward chaining reasoning: This means that the derivation is constructed starting from the goal, which generates subgoals, and which are addressed by recursion. If $\langle \Phi, \alpha\rangle$ is a backward argument, then $\langle \Phi, \alpha\rangle$ is an argument, and so $\Phi \vdash_d \alpha$. Furthermore, this backward reasoning will avoid some unnecessary formulae appearing in the support of the argument, but it is not guaranteed that the support is minimal (i.e. it is possible that there is a $\Phi' \subset \Phi$ such that $\Phi' \vdash_d \alpha$).

Clearly, classical logic has a richer language and proof theory than defeasible logic. Even if we restrict classical logic to the same language as defeasible logic, then we see many simple situations where classical logic gives an intuitive inference and defeasible logic fails to give the inference, such as in the following example.

Example 5. *Let $\Delta = \{a \rightarrow b, \neg a \rightarrow b\}$. Hence, $\Delta \vdash_c b$, but $\Delta \nvdash_d b$.*

However, we should not regard classical logic as better than defeasible logic, or vice versa. Rather, there is a range of logics available as base logics, and that we should choose the base logic according to the needs of the application. Moreover, we should not restrict consideration to those base logics already considered in the literature on argumentation. There are many other candidates in the literature on artificial intelligence that could be harnessed as base logics.

In some approaches to defeasible logic, such as argument-based extended logic programming [24], a more complex defeasible rule is used that is based on two types of negation (strong $\neg$ and weak $\sim$). For an atom γ, both γ and $\neg\gamma$ are strong literals, and for a strong literal δ, $\sim\delta$ is a weak literal. An enhanced defeasible rule is a formula of the following form where $\alpha_0, \ldots, \alpha_m$ are strong literals, $\beta_0, \ldots, \beta_n$ are weak literals, and δ is a strong literal and $\rightarrow_k$ is an implication symbol.

$$\alpha_0 \wedge \ldots \wedge \alpha_m \wedge \beta_0 \wedge \ldots \wedge \beta_n \rightarrow_k \delta$$

Using this language, we can obtain a refined form of a defeasible consequence relation, which we call the enhanced consequence relation $\vdash_e$ as follows. In this, the antecedent of a defeasible rule is satisfied when the strong literals can be obtained earlier in the derivation. The meaning of the weak literals is that they are assumed to not hold, and if there is evidence to the contrary in Δ, this will be manifested in the existence of a counterargument.

Definition 2. *Let Δ be the union of a set of enhanced defeasible rules and a set of strong literals. The enhanced consequence relation $\vdash_e$ is defined as follows.*

$\Delta \vdash_e \psi$ *iff there is a sequence of literals* $\alpha_1, \ldots, \alpha_n$
such that ψ *is* α_n *and for each* $\alpha_i \in \{\alpha_1, \ldots \alpha_n\}$
either α_i *is a strong literal in* Δ
or there is a $\gamma_0 \wedge \ldots \wedge \gamma_m \wedge \beta_0 \wedge \ldots \wedge \beta_n \rightarrow_k \delta \in \Delta$
and $\{\gamma_0, \ldots, \gamma_m\} \subseteq \{\alpha_1, \ldots, \alpha_{i-1}\}$

In the following example, $\rightarrow_1$ denotes a strict rule and $\rightarrow_2$ denotes an enhanced defeasible rule, though as before, this differentiation does not affect the consequence relation.

Example 6. *Let* $\Delta = \{p, p \rightarrow_1 \neg r, \neg r \wedge \sim q \rightarrow_2 s, s \rightarrow_1 t, p \wedge t \rightarrow_1 u\}$. *Therefore* $\Delta \vdash_d u$ *where the sequence of literals in the derivation is* $p, \neg r, s, t, u$.

For argument-based extended logic programming [24], we can define $\langle \Phi, \alpha \rangle$ as an argument iff $\Phi \vdash_e \alpha$ and there is no $\Phi' \subset \Phi$ such that $\Phi' \vdash_e \alpha$.

Example 7. *Continuing Example 6, the following is an argument in argument-based extended logic programming [24].*

$$\langle \{p, p \rightarrow_1 \neg r, \neg r \wedge \sim q \rightarrow_2 s, s \rightarrow_1 t, p \wedge t \rightarrow_1 u\}, u \rangle$$

In [8,9], various proposals for argumentation based on defeasible logic were criticized for violating some postulates that they proposed for acceptable argumentation. They suggested introducing contraposition into the reasoning of the base logic offered a way to address this problem. We introduce contraposition by defining a consequence relation as follows where Contrapositives(Δ) is the set of contrapositives formed from the rules in Δ.

Definition 3. *Let* Δ *be a set of rules and literals. The defeasible logic consequence relation* $\vdash_f$ *is defined as follows.*

$\Delta \vdash_f \psi$ *iff there is a sequence of literals* $\alpha_1, \ldots, \alpha_n$
such that ψ *is* α_n *and for each* $\alpha_i \in \{\alpha_1, \ldots \alpha_n\}$
either α_i *is a literal in* Δ
or there is a $\beta_1 \wedge \ldots \wedge \beta_j \rightarrow_k \alpha_i \in \Delta \cup$ Contrapositives(Δ)
and $\{\beta_1, \ldots, \beta_j\} \subseteq \{\alpha_1, \ldots, \alpha_{i-1}\}$

Example 8. *Let* $\Delta = \{q, \neg r, p \wedge q \rightarrow r, \neg p \rightarrow u\}$. *So* Contrapositives($\Delta$) $= \{\neg r \wedge q \rightarrow \neg p, p \wedge \neg r \rightarrow \neg q, \neg u \rightarrow p\}$. *Therefore,* $\Delta \vdash_f u$, *where the sequence of literals in the derivation is* $q, \neg r, \neg p, u$.

Further base logics considered for logic-based argumentation include (i) variants of defeasible logic with annotations for lattice-theoretic truth values (such as for Belnap's four-valued logic) [28] and for possibility theory [1], (ii) temporal reasoning calculi used with defeasible logic [4] and with classical logic [21], (iii) minimal logic (which is intuitionistic logic without the $\bot \rightarrow \phi$ axiom) [18], and (iv) a form of modal logic [13].

A more general approach to logic-based argumentation is to leave the logic for deduction as a parameter. This was proposed in abstract argumentation systems [29], and developed in assumption-based argumentation (ABA) [12]. However, since a substantial part of the development of the theory and implementation of ABA is focused on defeasible logic (e.g. [15]), we have considered the base logic of ABA as being given by the $\vdash_d$ consequence relation.

$\Delta \cup \{\alpha\} \vdash_x \alpha$ (Reflexivity)

$\Delta \cup \{\alpha\} \vdash_x \alpha$ if α is a literal   (Literal reflexivity)

$\Delta \cup \{\beta\} \vdash_x \gamma$ if $\Delta \cup \{\alpha\} \vdash_x \gamma$ and $\vdash \alpha \leftrightarrow \beta$ (Left logical equivalent)

$\Delta \vdash_x \alpha$ if $\Delta \vdash_x \beta$ and $\vdash \beta \rightarrow \alpha$ (Right weakening)

$\Delta \vdash_x \alpha \wedge \beta$ if $\Delta \vdash_x \alpha$ and $\Delta \vdash_x \beta$ (And)

$\Delta \cup \{\alpha\} \vdash_x \beta$ if $\Delta \vdash_x \beta$ (Monotonicity)

$\Delta \vdash_x \beta$ if $\Delta \vdash_x \alpha$ and $\Delta \cup \{\alpha\} \vdash_x \beta$ (Cut)

$\Delta \vdash_x \alpha \rightarrow \beta$ if $\Delta \cup \{\alpha\} \vdash_x \beta$ (Conditionalization)

$\Delta \cup \{\alpha\} \vdash_x \beta$ if $\Delta \vdash_x \alpha \rightarrow \beta$ (Deduction)

$\Delta \cup \{\alpha\} \vdash_x \beta$ if $\Delta \cup \{\neg\beta\} \vdash_x \neg\alpha$ (Contraposition)

$\Delta \cup \{\alpha \vee \beta\} \vdash_x \gamma$ if $\Delta \cup \{\alpha\} \vdash_x \gamma$ and $\Delta \cup \{\beta\} \vdash_x \gamma$ (Or)

Figure 1. Some properties of a consequence relation $\vdash_x$ adapted from [20].

3. Properties of base logics

We have defined a base logic as the logic for defining entailment in constructing arguments. Given that many logics have been proposed in philosophy, linguistics, and artificial intelligence, a natural question to ask is what are the required properties of a consequence relation. The list of properties of a consequence relation given in Figure 1 provides a good starting point for considering this question. These properties have been proposed as desirable conditions of a consequence relation. Furthermore, according to Gabbay [14] and Makinson [20], the minimal properties of a consequence relation are reflexivity, monotonicity (or a variant of it) and cut, and the need for each of them can be justified as follows:

- Reflexivity captures the idea of "transparency"; If a formula α is assumed (i.e. $\alpha \in \Delta$), then α can be declared (i.e $\Delta \vdash_x \alpha$).
- Monotonicity captures the idea of "irreversibility"; Once a formula α is declared (i.e $\Delta \vdash_x \alpha$), then there is no assumption that can cause α to be withdrawn (i.e. there is no β such that $\Delta \cup \{\beta\} \nvdash_x \alpha$).
- Cut captures the idea of "equitability" of assumptions and inferences. Once a formula α is declared (i.e $\Delta \vdash_x \alpha$), it can be used for further reasoning.

These three properties can be seen equivalently in terms of the following three properties based on the consequence closure C_x of a logic x [20], where $C_x(\Delta) = \{\alpha \mid \Delta \vdash \alpha\}$: (inclusion) $\Delta \subseteq C_x(\Delta)$; (idempotence) $C_x(\Delta) = C_x(C_x(\Delta))$; and (monotony) $C_x(\Delta') \subseteq C_x(\Delta)$ whenever $\Delta' \subseteq \Delta$.

Classes of base logic can be identified using properties of the consequence relation, and then argument systems can be developed in terms of them. For instance, to instantiate abstract argumentation, in [2], the class of Tarskian logics has been used. This is the class defined by inclusion, idempotence, finiteness (i.e. $C_x(\Delta)$ is the union of $C_x(\Gamma)$ for all finite subsets Γ of Δ), absurdity (i.e. $C_x(\{\phi\}) = \mathcal{L}$ for some ϕ in the language $\mathcal{L}$), and coherence (i.e. $C_x(\emptyset) \neq \mathcal{L}$). Classical logic is an example of a Tarskian logic.

We now consider the base logics $\vdash_c$, $\vdash_d$, $\vdash_e$, and $\vdash_f$, reviewed in the previous section, in terms of the properties of the consequence relation given in Figure 1.

Proposition 1. *Each property holding for each of $\vdash_c$, $\vdash_d$, $\vdash_e$ and $\vdash_f$ is denoted by $\times$ in the following table.*

	$\vdash_c$	$\vdash_d$	$\vdash_e$	$\vdash_f$
Reflexivity	×			
Literal reflexivity	×	×	×	×
Left logical equivalence	×			
Right weakening	×			
And	×			
Monotonicity	×	×	×	×
Cut	×	×	×	×
Conditionalization	×			
Deduction	×			
Contraposition	×			×
Or	×			

The good news from the above proposition is that the base logics $\vdash_c$, $\vdash_d$, $\vdash_e$, and $\vdash_f$, that appear in the main proposals for logic-based argumentation, satisfy the properties of monotonicity and cut. Furthermore, by a trivial adaptation of the $\vdash_d$, $\vdash_e$, and $\vdash_f$ consequence relations, they could also all satisfy reflexivity. For instance, for $\vdash_d$ if we add the meta-rule that "if ψ is a rule in Δ, then $\Delta \vdash_d \psi$", then reflexivity also holds. This means that we can say that the main base logics used in argumentation meet the minimal requirements for being consequence relations. Furthermore, if we add the above meta-rule, then we will also get the deduction property holding.

We can also compare base logics according to inferential strength of their consequence relations as follows.

Definition 4. *For $\vdash_x$ and $\vdash_y$, $\vdash_x$ is at **least as strong** as $\vdash_y$ iff for all knowledgebases Δ, and all formulae α, if $\Delta \vdash_y \alpha$, then $\Delta \vdash_x \alpha$. Furthermore, $\vdash_x$ is **stronger** than $\vdash_y$ iff $\vdash_x$ is at least as strong as $\vdash_y$ and it is not the case that $\vdash_y$ is at least as strong as $\vdash_x$. Finally, $\vdash_x$ and $\vdash_y$ are **equally strong** iff $\vdash_x$ is at least as strong as $\vdash_y$ and $\vdash_y$ is at least as strong as $\vdash_x$.*

Proposition 2. *Let Δ be the union of a set of rules (excluding enhanced defeasible rules) and a set of literals (excluding weak literals): (1) $\vdash_c$ is stronger than $\vdash_d$, $\vdash_e$, and $\vdash_f$; (2) $\vdash_f$ is stronger than $\vdash_d$ and $\vdash_e$; and (3) $\vdash_d$ and $\vdash_e$ are equally strong.*

Another way that we can compare the consequence relations is with how they deal with inconsistent assumptions. For this, we consider the trivializable and the purity properties. The former characterizes the situations where any formula of the language follows from an inconsistent set of premises, and the later characterizes a notion of relevancy between premises and consequences.

Definition 5. *The consequence relation $\vdash_x$ is trivializable iff for all Δ, there is an atom α such that if $\Delta \vdash \alpha$ and $\Delta \vdash \neg\alpha$ then $\Delta \vdash_x \beta$ for all atoms β.*

Definition 6. *Let $\mathsf{Atoms}(\Gamma)$ give the atoms appearing in a set of formulae Γ. A formula α is pure with respect to Δ iff $\mathsf{Atoms}(\Delta) \cap \mathsf{Atoms}(\{\alpha\}) \neq \emptyset$. A consequence relation $\vdash_x$ is pure iff for all α and Δ, if $\Delta \vdash_x \alpha$, then α is pure with respect to Δ.*

Proposition 3. *If a consequence relation $\vdash_x$ is pure, then $\vdash_x$ is not trivializable. However, the converse does not necessarily hold.*

Proposition 4. *The $\vdash_c$ consequence relation is trivializable and not pure, whereas the $\vdash_d$, $\vdash_e$, and $\vdash_f$ consequence relations are not trivializable and they are pure.*

The trivialization and lack of purity of classical logic does not appear to be a shortcoming in argumentation since for $\langle \Phi, \alpha \rangle$ to be an argument, most proposals have that Φ is consistent.

Another dimension for comparing base logics is with respect to computational complexity. For $\vdash_c$, it is well-known that the decision problem for entailment is co-NP complete and for satisfiability it is NP complete [17]. This results in the problem of deciding whether a tuple $\langle \Phi, \alpha \rangle$ is an argument (i.e. the support entails the claim, it is minimal for this, and it is consistent) being Σ_2^p complete [23]. We can also regard $\vdash_f$ as being co-NP complete for entailment and NP complete for satisfiability since generating the contrapostives for each defeasible rule can equivalently be captured by treating each rule as a clause (i.e. a disjunction of literals) and with the proof rule being disjunctive syllogism instead of modus ponens. Hence, we can formalize the $\vdash_f$ decision problems as decision problems of Boolean satisfiability and its complement. In contrast, the $\vdash_d$ and $\vdash_e$ consequence relations are much more efficient for entailment and consistency checking (where $\Delta \not\vdash_x \bot$ is an abbreviation for $\Delta \not\vdash_x \alpha$ and $\Delta \not\vdash_x \neg\alpha$). For these, we can define a polynomial algorithm (adapting an algorithm by Mahler [19]) to decide whether $\Delta \vdash_x \alpha$ holds and whether $\Delta \not\vdash_x \bot$ holds.

In this section, we have considered how we can compare base logics used in argumentation. We see that the key properties of cut and monotonicity that have been proposed as being essential properties for a logic, together with the restricted form of reflexivity (called literal reflexivity), hold for the base logics for a number of key proposals. We also see that a number of key proposals are essentially equivalent in terms of the base logic, and that differences between the proposals can be identified in terms of these properties. We do not suggest that any particular proposal is superior to others because of its properties. Rather, different applications call for different base logics. See for instance the discussion of when contraposition is desirable [8] and undesirable [7].

4. Framework for combined base logics

An approach to defining a base logic is to compose it from two other logics. Before we define this idea, we consider an example taken from a proposal for ontology-based argumentation with the base logic $\vdash_\Gamma$ as follows [30]. The essential idea is that a set of defeasible rules can be used with an ontology so that the ontology contains the information that is certain and the defeasible rules contain the information that is uncertain. In the prototype system presented in [30], a specialized description logic software was harnessed for the ontology. See also [22] for a similar proposal.

Definition 7. *Let Δ be a set of defeasible rules of the form $\beta_1 \wedge \ldots \beta_j \rightarrow \beta_{j+1}$ and let Γ be an ontology in classical logic or description logic.*

$$\Delta \vdash_\Gamma \psi \text{ iff } \text{ there is a sequence of literals } \alpha_1, \ldots, \alpha_n$$
$$\text{such that } \psi \text{ is } \alpha_n \text{ and for each } \alpha_i \in \{\alpha_1, \ldots \alpha_n\}$$
$$\text{either } \Gamma \cup \{\alpha_1, \ldots, \alpha_{i-1}\} \vdash_c \alpha_i$$
$$\text{or there is a } \beta_1 \wedge \ldots \wedge \beta_j \rightarrow \alpha_i \in \Delta$$
$$\text{such that } \{\beta_1, \ldots, \beta_j\} \subseteq \{\alpha_1, \ldots, \alpha_{i-1}\}$$

Example 9. $\{a \to b, c \to \neg d\} \vdash_{\{a, b \to c\}} \neg d$ *because of the sequence* $a, b, c, \neg d$.

An alternative to this definition would be to only allow for the ontology to be called for literal inferences, and no inferences from the defeasible reasoning could be passed back to the ontology for further inferences (i.e. we have $\Gamma \vdash_c \alpha_i$ instead of $\Gamma \cup \{\alpha_1, \ldots, \alpha_{i-1}\} \vdash_c \alpha_i$). This is a more cautious form of reasoning.

Definition 8. *Let Δ be a set of defeasible rules of the form $\beta_1 \wedge \ldots \beta_j \to \beta_{j+1}$ and let Γ is an ontology in classical/description logic.*

$$\Delta \vdash'_\Gamma \psi \text{ iff } \text{ there is a sequence of literals } \alpha_1, \ldots, \alpha_n$$
$$\text{such that } \psi \text{ is } \alpha_n \text{ and for each } \alpha_i \in \{\alpha_1, \ldots \alpha_n\}$$
$$\text{either } \Gamma \vdash_c \alpha_i$$
$$\text{or there is a } \beta_1 \wedge \ldots \wedge \beta_j \to \alpha_i \in \Delta$$
$$\text{such that } \{\beta_1, \ldots, \beta_j\} \subseteq \{\alpha_1, \ldots, \alpha_{i-1}\}$$

Example 10. *Continuing Example 9, for $\Delta = \{a \to b, c \to \neg d\}$, and $\Gamma = \{a, b \to c\}$, we get $\Delta \vdash_\Gamma b$, but $\Delta \not\vdash_\Gamma c$, and $\Delta \not\vdash_\Gamma \neg d$,*

Now we generalize Definition 7 into a form of combined base logic, in what we call a bilogic, as follows.

Definition 9. *Let $\vdash_x$ be the consequence relation for a logic x, and let $\vdash_y$ be the consequence relation for a logic y. Also let $\Delta \subseteq \mathcal{L}_x$ be a knowledgebase in the language x, and let $\Gamma \subseteq \mathcal{L}_y$ be a knowledgebase in the language y. The consequence relation for the* **bidirectional bilogic** $\vdash_{x \oplus y}$, *is defined as follows.*

$$(\Delta, \Gamma) \vdash_{x \oplus y} \alpha \text{ iff } \text{ either } \Delta \cup \{\beta_1, \ldots, \beta_n\} \vdash_x \alpha \text{ or } \Gamma \cup \{\beta_1, \ldots, \beta_n\} \vdash_y \alpha$$
$$\text{where } (\Delta, \Gamma) \vdash_{x \oplus y} \beta_1 \text{ and } \ldots \text{ and } (\Delta, \Gamma) \vdash_{x \oplus y} \beta_n$$

Using the notion of the bidirectional bilogic, we see in the following proposition that we can define the consequence relation $\vdash_\Gamma$ (i.e. Definition 7) equivalently just using the $\vdash_d$ and $\vdash_c$ consequence relations.

Proposition 5. *For a set of defeasible rules and literals Δ and a set of formulae Γ, $\Delta \vdash_\Gamma \psi$ iff $(\Delta, \Gamma) \vdash_{c \oplus d} \psi$.*

We can also see that other base logics can be captured as bidirectional bilogics, as illustrated next, and this may help us better understand existing definitions.

Proposition 6. *If Δ is a set of defeasible rules and literals, and Γ is a set of strict rules and literals, then $(\Delta, \Gamma) \vdash_{d \oplus d} \psi$ iff $\Delta \cup \Gamma \vdash_d \psi$.*

Now, we consider an alternative notion of bilogic, generalizing Definition 8, that lets one of the constituent logics be used as a service for providing formulae without conditional reasoning.

Definition 10. *Let $\vdash_x$ be the consequence relation for a logic x, and let $\vdash_y$ be the consequence relation for a logic y. Also let $\Delta \subseteq \mathcal{L}_x$ be a knowledgebase in the language x, and let $\Gamma \subseteq \mathcal{L}_y$ be a knowledgebase in the language y. The consequence relation for the* **unidirectional bilogic** $\vdash_{x \ominus y}$, *is defined as follows.*

$$(\Delta, \Gamma) \vdash_{x \ominus y} \alpha \; iff \;\; either \; \Delta \vdash_{x} \alpha \; or \; \Gamma \cup \{\beta_1, \ldots, \beta_n\} \vdash_y \alpha$$
$$where \; (\Delta, \Gamma) \vdash_{x \ominus y} \beta_1 \; and \; \ldots \; and \; (\Delta, \Gamma) \vdash_{x \ominus y} \beta_n$$

Using unidirectional bilogic, we can define the consequence relation $\vdash'_\Gamma$ equivalently just using the $\vdash_d$ and $\vdash_c$ consequence relations.

Proposition 7. *For a set of defeasible rules and literals Δ and a set of formulae Γ, $\Delta \vdash'_\Gamma \psi$ iff $(\Delta, \Gamma) \vdash_{c \ominus d} \psi$.*

We can also consider new proposals for combining existing base logics. For instance, if Δ is a set of strict rules and literals and Γ is a set of defeasible rules and literals, then $(\Delta, \Gamma) \vdash_{d \ominus d}$ is a cautious defeasible logic (as opposed to the $\vdash_{d \oplus d}$ considered in Proposition 6) that is cautious with its use of strict rules (i.e. those in Δ).

Example 11. *Let $\Delta = \{a, b, c \to e, d \to \neg e\}$ be a set of strict rules, and let $\Gamma = \{a \to c, b \to d\}$ be a set of defeasible rules. Using $\vdash_d$, with $\Delta \cup \Gamma$, we get e and $\neg e$ as inferences (i.e. $\Delta \cup \Gamma \vdash_d e$ and $\Delta \cup \Gamma \vdash_d \neg e$), which may be regarded as unacceptable, since a contradiction follows from the strict rules). As an alternative, we can use $\vdash_{d \ominus d}$, and we do not get a contradiction since $(\Delta, \Gamma) \nvdash_{d \ominus d} e$ and $(\Delta, \Gamma) \nvdash_{d \ominus d} \neg e$.*

In general, a unidirectional bilogic is more cautious than its bidirectional bilogic counterpart, and hence, it gives fewer inferences. Therefore, the bidirectional bilogic is stronger for a given choice of base logics x and y.

Proposition 8. *For any base logics x and y, if $(\Delta, \Gamma) \vdash_{x \ominus y} \alpha$, then $(\Delta, \Gamma) \vdash_{x \oplus y} \alpha$.*

Considering existing base logics as bilogics allows us to decompose existing, perhaps complex, definitions and consider them in terms of the simpler constituent logics. Furthermore, combining base logics in the form of bilogics gives us the possibility for designing and implementing new base logics more quickly. It also raises opportunities for using existing technology (e.g. description logic reasoners, defeasible logic reasoners, logic programming systems, database systems, etc) for implementing base logics, and then combining them as bilogics to give systems appropriate for applications.

5. Impact of choice of base logic

The choice of base logic has a significant impact on the arguments generated by an argument system. For instance, if we use $\vdash_c$ as our base logic, then $\langle \{a \to b, \neg a \to b\}, b \rangle$ is an argument, whereas if we use $\vdash_d$ as our base logic, then $\langle \{a \to b, \neg a \to b\}, b \rangle$ is not an argument. There are many examples where it is debatable whether an inference is intuitive or not, and it seems that whether to choose a logic that permits or prohibits certain inferences depends on the application.

So far we have focused our discussion on propositional logics as base logics. But, there are first-order logics that we can use as base logics [6]. By choosing a first-order logic, we get further choices for defining arguments. Consider the knowledgebase $\Delta = \{p(a), \forall x.(p(x) \to q(x))\}$. We can let $\langle \{p(a), \forall x.(p(x) \to q(x))\}, q(a) \rangle$ be an argument since the support is a minimal consistent set of formulae that entails the claim. However, we may also want to let $\langle \{p(a), p(a) \to q(a)\}, q(a) \rangle$ be an argument since we may regard forming a ground version of the premises as being an acceptable step in forming the argument [21]. In other words, if Δ is a knowledgebase, and Ground(Δ) is formed from Δ by universal specialization (i.e. grounding of universally quantified formulae), then we may allow $\langle \Phi, \alpha \rangle$ as an argument when Φ is a minimal consistent subset of Ground(Δ). This definition seems intuitive. Furthermore, it allows for arguments to be formed for a claim when it is not possible to do so from the original knowledgebase as illustrated in the next example.

Example 12. *Consider* $\Phi = \{\forall x.p(x) \rightarrow q(x), p(a) \wedge p(b) \wedge p(c) \wedge \neg q(b)\}$. *Since* $\Phi \vdash_c \perp$, $\langle \Phi, q(a) \rangle$ *is not an argument. However, there is a* $\Psi \subseteq$ Ground(Φ) *such that* $\langle \Psi, q(a) \rangle$ *is an argument, namely* $\Psi = \{p(a) \rightarrow q(a), p(a) \wedge p(b) \wedge p(c) \wedge \neg q(b)\}$.

Richer logics also lead to more possibilities for counterarguments. For example, using defeasible logic as a base logic, a counterargument $\langle \Phi, \alpha \rangle$ for an argument $\langle \Psi, \beta \rangle$ is often defined as being such that α is the negation of a literal occurring in the derivation of β from Ψ. In other words, there is a γ such that $\Psi \vdash_d \gamma$ and γ is the complement of α (for instance, $\langle \{p, p \rightarrow q, q \rightarrow r\}, r \rangle$ is an argument and $\langle \{s, s \rightarrow \neg q, \}, \neg q \rangle$ is a counterargument to it). Now, if we consider a richer logic as a base logic, such as classical logic, then we see we have more counterarguments (as illustrated in the following example).

Example 13. *Consider* $\Delta = \{a, b, a \rightarrow c, b \rightarrow d, \neg a \vee \neg b\}$. *used to generate the following arguments using* $\vdash_c$ *as the base logic.*

$$A_1 = \langle \{a, b, a \rightarrow c, b \rightarrow d\}, c \wedge d \rangle \qquad A_2 = \langle \{a, \neg a \vee \neg b\}, \neg b \rangle$$
$$A_3 = \langle \{a, \neg a \vee \neg b\}, \neg a \rangle \qquad\qquad A_4 = \langle \{\neg a \vee \neg b\}, \neg a \vee \neg b \rangle$$

Here, we see that A_2 *and* A_3 *are counterarguments to* A_1 *as discussed above. However, we see that the claim of* A_4 *also contradicts some of the support of* A_1. *It does not contradict an individual literal, but rather contradicts a conjunction of literals. It is a weaker counterargument than* A_2 *and* A_3 *in the sense it has a subset of the support and the claim is implied by the claim of each of* A_2 *and* A_3.

In [5], the nature of counterarguments in a rich logic such as classical logic was explored, and the proposal made that only the maximally conservative counterarguments (the arguments with the weakest claim necessary for contradicting the argument) need to be considered since they subsume the other counterarguments. The value of maximally conservative counterarguments can even be seen with a language of defeasible rules as illustrated next.

Example 14. *Consider* $\Delta = \{a, b, a \wedge b \rightarrow c, a \rightarrow \neg b\}$. *used to generate the following arguments using* $\vdash_d$ *as the base logic. Here, we see that* A_2 *is a counterargument to* A_1 *as discussed above. However, we may have preferred to have* $\langle \{a \rightarrow \neg b\}, a \rightarrow \neg b \rangle$ *as the counterargument since it is based on fewer premises.*

$$A_1 = \langle \{a, b, a \wedge b \rightarrow c\}, c \rangle \qquad A_2 = \langle \{a, a \rightarrow \neg b\}, \neg b \rangle$$

When dealing with richer logics, the need to avoid unnecessary counterarguments is important. Richer logics can create many more inferences, and therefore they can create many more counterarguments. Often, it seems there is much redundancy, and so selecting a subset of counterarguments can render the use of argumentation more manageable by eliminating potentially many redundant counterarguments.

One issue that we have conflated so far in this paper is the dichotomy identified between assumption-based and derivation-based approaches to the definition of arguments. In the former, the support of an argument is a set of premises that proves the claim (as we have considered in this paper), and in the later, the support of an argument is a proof resulting in the claim. For defining individual arguments, the assumption-based approach seems sufficient since the proof can be generated from the assumptions: Given an argument $\langle \Phi, \alpha \rangle$ and a base logic x, there is a function $\mathsf{Proofs}_x(\langle \Phi, \alpha \rangle)$ which returns the set of proofs of α from Φ. The reason that proofs become important is that some approaches to comparing arguments take into account the sequence in which formulae are brought into the proof and the relative "strength" of those premises. For instance, consider the following arguments.

$$A_1 = \langle \{a, a \to_1 b, b \to_2 c\}, c \rangle \qquad A_2 = \langle \{a, a \to_2 \neg b, \neg b \to_1 \neg c\}, \neg c \rangle$$

So A_1 and A_2 rebut each other, and furthermore each has a subargument that undercuts the other: $A_3 = \langle \{a, a \to_1 b\}, b \rangle$ undercuts A_2 and $A_4 = \langle \{a, a \to_2 \neg b\}, \neg b \rangle$ undercuts A_1. Now, suppose $\to_1$ denotes strict implication, and $\to_2$ denotes defeasible implication, then we may regard A_3 as sufficient to defeat A_2, in which case A_1 has no counterargument. For more discussion of these issues, see [25].

6. Discussion

There are a number of proposals for logic-based formalizations of argumentation. Often these proposals are quite complex in that they are based on number of defined notions (e.g. definition of an argument, counterargument, preference criteria, acceptability or warrant criteria, etc), and as a result they become difficult to compare. Therefore, attempts to draw out features of logic-based argument systems, in order to find commonalities and differences, is potentially valuable.

In this paper, we have seen how base logics are an important part of a logic-based argument system. By considering the base logic, we can identify properties to compare and contrast the base logics. There are some properties of the consequence relation in common for all the key approaches (including the important properties of cut, monotonicity, and a restricted form of reflexivity), and there are properties of the consequence relation to differentiate base logics (e.g. and, or, left logical equivalence, etc). But, obviously, increasing the strength of the consequence relation can affect the computational complexity of decision problems (such as validity and consistency) for the logic. Also, increasing the strength of the consequence relation, and the language over which it operates, can also lead to an increasing range of options for how to define notions such as argument, counterargument, attack, and defeat.

References

[1] T Alsinet, C Chesñevar, L Godo, and G Simari. A logic programming framework for possibilistic argumentation: Formalization and logical properties. *Fuzzy Sets and Systems*, 159(10):1208–1228, 2008.

[2]   L Amgoud and Ph Besnard. Bridging the gap between argumentation systems and logic. In *Scalable Uncertainty Management*, volume 5785 of *LNCS*, pages 12–27. Springer, 2009.

[3]   L. Amgoud and C. Cayrol. On the acceptability of arguments in preference-based argumentation. In G. Cooper and S. Moral, editors, *Proceedings of the 14th Conference on Uncertainty in Artificial Intelligence (UAI 1998)*, pages 1–7. Morgan Kaufmann, 1998.

[4]   J Augusto and G Simari. Temporal defeasible reasoning. *Knowl. Inf. Syst.*, 3(3):287–318, 2001.

[5]   Ph. Besnard and A. Hunter. A logic-based theory of deductive arguments. *Artificial Intelligence*, 128:203–235, 2001.

[6]   Ph Besnard and A Hunter. *Elements of Argumentation*. MIT Press, 2008.

[7]   M Caminada. On the issue of contraposition of defeasible rules. In *Computational Models of Argument: Proceedings of COMMA 2008*, pages 109–115. IOS Press, 2008.

[8]   M. Caminada and L. Amgoud. An axiomatic account of formal argumentation. In *Proceedings of the 20th National Conference on Artificial Intelligence (AAAI 2005)*, pages 608–613, 2005.

[9]   M Caminada and L Amgoud. On the evaluation of argumentation formalisms. *Artificial Intelligence*, 171(5-6):286–310, 2007.

[10] C Cayrol. On the relationship between argumentation and non-monotonic coherence-based entailment. In *Proceedings IJCAI'95*, pages 1443–1448, 1995.

[11] C. Chesñevar, A. Maguitman, and R. Loui. Logical models of argument. *ACM Computing Surveys*, 32:337–383, 2000.

[12] P. Dung, R. Kowalski, and F. Toni. Dialectical proof procedures for assumption-based admissible argumentation. *Artificial Intelligence*, 170:114–159, 2006.

[13] J Fox and S Das. *Safe and Sound: Artificial Intelligence in Hazardous Applications*. MIT Press, 2000.

[14] D Gabbay. Theoretical foundations for nonmonotonic reasoning in expert systems. In K Apt, editor, *Logic and Models of Concurrent Systems*. Springer, 1985.

[15] D Gaertner and F Toni. Computing arguments and attacks in assumption-based argumentation. *IEEE Intelligent Systems*, 22(6):24–33, 2007.

[16] A. García and G. Simari. Defeasible logic programming: An argumentative approach. *Theory and Practice of Logic Programming*, 4:95–138, 2004.

[17] M. Garey and D. Johnson. *Computers and Intractability*. W. H. Freeman, 1979.

[18] P Krause, S Ambler, M Elvang-Gøransson, and J Fox. A logic of argumentation for reasoning under uncertainty. *Computational Intelligence*, 11:113–131, 1995.

[19] M. Maher. Propositional defeasible logic has linear complexity. *Theory and Practice of Logic Programming*, 1(6):691Ű711, 2001.

[20] D Makinson. General patterns in nonmonotonic reasoning. In D Gabbay, C Hogger, and J Robinson, editors, *Handbook of Logic in Artificial Intelligence and Logic Programming, Volume 3: Nonmonotonic Reasoning and Uncertainty Reasoning*, pages 35–110. Oxford University Press, 1994.

[21] N Mann and A Hunter. Argumentation using temporal knowledge. In *Computational Models of Argument: Proceedings of COMMA'08*, pages 204–215. IOS Press, 2008.

[22] A Munoz and Juan A. Botia. Asbo: Argumentation system based on ontologies. In *Cooperative Information Agents XII (CIA'08)*, volume 5180 of *LNCS*, pages 191–205. Springer, 2008.

[23] S Parsons, M Wooldridge, and L Amgoud. Properties and complexity of some formal inter-agent dialogues. *Journal of Logic & Computation*, 13(3):347–376, 2003.

[24] H. Prakken and G. Sartor. Argument-based extended logic programming with defeasible priorities. *Journal of Applied Non-classical Logic*, 7:25–75, 1997.

[25] H. Prakken and G. Vreeswijk. Logical systems for defeasible argumentation. In D. Gabbay, editor, *Handbook of Philosophical Logic*, pages 219–318. Kluwer, 2002.

[26] I Rahwan and G Simari, editors. *Argumentation in Artificial Intelligence*. Springer, 2009.

[27] G. Simari and R. Loui. A mathematical treatment of defeasible reasoning and its implementation. *Artificial Intelligence*, 53:125–157, 1992.

[28] T Takahashi and H Sawamura. A logic of multiple-valued argumentation. In *Proceedings of the Third International Joint Conference on Autonomous Agents and Multiagent Systems (AAMAS'04)*, pages 800–807. IEEE Computer Society, 2004.

[29] G. Vreeswijk. Abstract argumentation systems. *Artificial Intelligence*, 90:225–279, 1997.

[30] M Williams and A Hunter. Ontological-based argumentation. In *Proceedings of the International Conference on Tools with AI*. IEEE Press, 2007.

Computational Models of Argument
P. Baroni et al. (Eds.)
IOS Press, 2010
doi:10.3233/978-1-60750-619-5-287

287

Qualitative Evidence Aggregation using Argumentation

Anthony HUNTER [a] and Matthew WILLIAMS [b]

[a] *UCL Department of Computer Science,*
Gower Street, London, WC1E 6BT, UK
[b] *Royal Free Hospital,*
Pond Street, London, NW3 2QG, UK

Abstract Evidence-based decision making is becoming increasingly important in many diverse domains, including healthcare, environmental management, and government. This has raised the need for tools to aggregate evidence from multiple sources. For instance, in healthcare, much valuable evidence is in the form of the results from clinical trials that compare the relative merits of treatments. For this, in a previous paper [5], we have proposed a general language for encoding, capturing and synthesizing knowledge from clinical trials and a framework that allows the construction and evaluation of arguments from such knowledge. Now, in this paper, we consider a specific version of the general framework for aggregating qualitative information about trials, and undertake an evaluation of this qualitative framework by comparing the results we obtain with those that are published in the biomedical literature. Whilst the results from our qualitative system are inferior, we show that they do offer a quick and useful aggregation of the evidence, and furthermore, we suggest that it could be coupled with information extraction technology to provide a valuable automated solution.

1. Introduction

The systematic use of evidence is already established in healthcare, and is being increasingly advocated in other domains, such as education and environmental management. However, the rapidly increasing amount of evidential knowledge on a subject means that it is difficult for a decision maker to locate, or even be aware of, new research that is relevant to their needs. Even if the decision maker locates the necessary evidence, it is difficult for them to effectively and efficiently assimilate and fully exploit it. In addition to the difficulty presented by the sheer volumes of information, the evidence is often conceptually complex, heterogeneous, incomplete and inconsistent. Not least, is the imperative to abstract away from the details of individual items of evidential knowledge, and to aggregate the evidence in a way that reduces the volume, complexity, inconsistency and incompleteness.

One important kind of evidence comes from superiority-testing clinical trials which compare the efficacy of two or more treatments in a particular class of patients. In order to have a global view of the relative merits of treatments for a particular condition, a potentially large number of publications needs to be reviewed. To address this, syntheses of the evidence on particular treatments are routinely produced using systematic search and statistical aggregation techniques (e.g., systematic reviews and meta-analyses). Often such syntheses involve groups of clinicians and statisticians. Such syntheses require significant time and effort, and they can quickly become out of date as new results are frequently being published.

Therefore, getting a quick, up-to-date review of the state of the art on treatment efficacy for a particular condition is not always feasible. Thus, it would be helpful to have a method for automatically analyzing and presenting the clinical trial results and the possible ways to aggregate those in an intuitive form, highlighting agreement and conflict present within the literature. Our proposal in [6,5] aims to suggest such a method. The first part of our proposal is a language that can be used to encode the published results in a semantically appropriate way, and methods for constructing a knowledge base from the encoded results. The second part of our framework allows the construction of arguments on the basis of evidence as well as their syntheses, published or generated on-the-fly. The evidence available is then presented and organized according to the agreement and conflict inherent. In addition, users can encode preferences for automatically ruling in favour of the preferred arguments in a conflict.

In this paper, we go beyond what we have done in [6,5] by presenting a specific set of inference rules and preference rules for qualitative evidence aggregation. The motivation for doing this is two-fold. First, with this very simple version of our general framework, we can investigate the quality with respect to published meta-analyses. Since meta-analyses are undertaken by clinicians, and medical statisticians, using standard techniques from statistics, for aggregating evidence, we see them as providing a "gold standard" for the aggregated evidence. So in this paper, we present some results comparing our approach with 15 meta-analyses obtained from three National Institute of Clinical Excellence (NICE) Guidelines (www.nice.org.uk).

The second reason we want to present the qualitative version of our framework is that it only requires a minimal amount of information from the published clinical trials. Indeed, the information we require can often be obtained from the abstract of the published paper covering the clinical trial. This then raises the possibility of using information extraction technology with the abstracts obtained from PubMed (www.pubmed.org) which catalogues all published clinical trials. The coupling of information extraction technology with argument-based aggregation could then be used for providing an automated and immediate abstract view on the relevant literature (highlighting where the evidence is in agreement and where there are key conflicts), and for generating rough drafts of meta-analysis, guidelines, and systematic review.

2. Representing clinical trials

Our focus will be on 2-arm superiority trials, i.e., clinical trials whose purpose is to determine whether, given two treatments, one is superior to the other (strictly speaking, such a trial tries to disprove the hypothesis that the two treatments are identical). This is an extremely common trial design.

We assume a set of trials TRIALS where each trial is just an atomic name for which we associate information about the trial. We give an example in Table 1, and explain the attributes as follows. The first attribute is the **patient class** involved. In this example, it is

Table 1. Two results obtain from the NICE Glaucoma Guideline (Appendix pages 70-72) where PGA is an abbreviation for prostaglandin analogue and BB is an abbreviation for beta-blocker. The first row corresponds to a trial performed by Pfeifer *et al* in 2002 (Pfe02) and the second row corresponds to a trial performed by Felman *at al* in 2002 (Fel02).

Trial name	Patient class	Leftarm	Rightarm	Outcome indicator	Risk ratio	Statistically significant
Pfe02	glaucoma	PGA	BB	safe IOP	1.43	no
Fel02	glaucoma	PGA	BB	safe IOP	1.29	yes

patients who have glaucoma (a problem resulting from increased pressure in the eye causing damage to the optic nerve and retina). The patient class may involve a conjunction and/or disjunction of terms from a medical ontology and description logics can be used to provide inferencing (see [2]). See [16,6] for proposals for using a medical ontology in argumentation about clinical trials. However, in this paper, for simplicity we assume that the set of results in TRIALS concerns a particular, sensible patient class, and so we do not consider this aspect further here.

The next component of our representation concerns treatments. Again, medical ontologies cater for this task by providing categories and relationships on treatments, substances used, and other characteristics. We use the attributes **leftarm** and **rightarm** to signify the treatments compared in each trial in TRIALS.

A trial comparing two treatments will do so with respect to a particular outcome, which we call the **outcome indicator** e.g., in the case of the trials above, it is the proportion of patients for whom IOP (i.e. intra ocular pressure) is reduced to a safe level. As another example, for evaluating cancer treatments, it can be the proportion of patients who survive after 5 years.

A trial uses a statistical method to compare the two treatments. There is a range of methods, each appropriate to specific trial designs and outcomes. Here, **risk ratio** is used which in general means the measure of the outcome indicator obtained from the leftarm divided by measure of the outcome indicator obtained from the rightarm. For these trials, specifically it means the proportion of patients in the leftarm (i.e. those treated with prostaglandin) who during the trial period had the IOP reduced to a safe level divided by the proportion of patients in the rightarm (i.e. those treated with betablocker) who during the trial period had the IOP reduced to a safe level. So for both Pfe02 and Fel02, the risk ratio is greater than 1, which means that in both trials, prostaglandin is associated with more patients having a safe IOP than betablocker.

The final attribute is **statistical significance** for which if the entry is "yes" means that it is unlikely that the risk ratio result could have been obtained by chance (using a conventional cut-off such as 0.05), whereas if it is "no" then it means that it is quite likely to have been obtained by chance.

The set of attributes we have discussed here is only indicative. Often other attributes are useful for assessing and aggregating evidence (e.g. the number of patients involved in each trial, the geographical location for each trial, the drop-out rate for the trial, the methods of randomization for ensuring patients and clinician do not know which arm a patient is in, etc), and it is straightforward to accommodate these extra attributes in our framework. For a general introduction to the nature of clinical trials, and a discussion of a wider range of attributes, see [7].

3. General framework

In this section, we review the general framework presented in [5] for constructing and comparing arguments based on the kind of information presented in the previous section.

For a superiority clinical trial comparing treatments τ_1 and τ_2 with respect to the outcome indicator μ, there are three possible interpretations of its results: (1) $\tau_1 >_\mu \tau_2$, meaning that we believe that the result supports the claim that treatment τ_1 is superior to τ_2 with respect to μ; (2) $\tau_1 <_\mu \tau_2$, meaning that we believe that the result supports the claim that treatment τ_1 is inferior to τ_2 with respect to μ; And (3) $\tau_1 \sim_\mu \tau_2$, meaning that we believe the result as supporting the claim that neither τ_1 nor τ_2 is superior to each other with respect to μ; Any formula of the form $\tau_1 >_\mu \tau_2$, $\tau_1 \sim_\mu \tau_2$ and $\tau_1 <_\mu \tau_2$ we will call a **claim**, denoted by ϵ, possibly subscripted. Note, we treat $\tau_1 > \tau_2$ as equivalent to $\tau_2 < \tau_1$ and $\tau_1 \sim \tau_2$ as equivalent to $\tau_2 \sim \tau_1$.

Given a set of results TRIALS one can informally think of an argument comprising of a set of evidence (i.e. a subset of TRIALS), an inferential rule and a conclusion or claim. For example, a plausible interpretation of Fel02 is that since the value for risk ratio is greater than 1, the first treatment is better than the second with respect to obtaining a safe IOP, i.e., that PGA $>_{\text{safeIOP}}$ BB. We define this process by an inference rule.

Definition 1. *An **inference rule**, λ, is a rule with conditions (employing set-theoretic expressions and equations utilizing attributes over the reals) on a set of results $\Phi \subseteq$ TRIALS and a claim ϵ.*

Example 1. *For TRIALS, let τ_1 be the leftarm, let τ_2 be the rightarm, let μ be the outcome indicator, and let $\gamma \in$ TRIALS.*

(λ_s) *For $\Phi = \{\gamma\}$, if γ is statistically significant*
and the risk ratio is greater than 1, then $\tau_1 >_\mu \tau_2$.

Example 2. *For TRIALS, let τ_1 be the leftarm, let τ_2 be the rightarm, let μ let the outcome indicator, and let $\gamma \in$ TRIALS.*

(λ_n) *For $\Phi = \{\gamma\}$, if γ is not statistically significant, then $\tau_1 \sim_\mu \tau_2$*

Definition 2. *An **argument** is a triple $\langle \Phi, \lambda, \epsilon \rangle$ where $\Phi \subseteq$ TRIALS is a set of results, λ is an inference rule, Φ satisfies the conditions of λ and ϵ is the claim of λ applied to Φ.*

Example 3. *Using the data in the previous section concerning Fel02 and Pfe02, we obtain the following arguments.*

$\langle \{\text{Fel02}\}, \lambda_s, \text{PGA} >_{\text{safeIOP}} \text{BB} \rangle$ $\langle \{\text{Pfe02}\}, \lambda_n, \text{PGA} \sim_{\text{safeIOP}} \text{BB} \rangle$

In the above example, we see that the two arguments are in conflict. We capture this kind of conflict with the following definition. Note that this definition is symmetric, i.e., if A conflicts with B then B conflicts with A.

Definition 3. *If $A = \langle \Phi_A, \lambda_A, \epsilon_A \rangle$ and $B = \langle \Phi_B, \lambda_B, \epsilon_B \rangle$ are two arguments then we say that A **conflicts** with B whenever:*

1. *$\epsilon_A = \tau_1 >_\mu \tau_2$, and either $\epsilon_B = \tau_1 \sim_\mu \tau_2$ or $\epsilon_B = \tau_1 <_\mu \tau_2$.*
2. *$\epsilon_A = \tau_1 \sim_\mu \tau_2$, and either $\epsilon_B = \tau_1 >_\mu \tau_2$ or $\epsilon_B = \tau_1 <_\mu \tau_2$.*

3. $\epsilon_A = \tau_1 <_\mu \tau_2$, and either $\epsilon_B = \tau_1 >_\mu \tau_2$ or $\epsilon_B = \tau_1 \sim_\mu \tau_2$.

We organize the arguments into a graph. To do this, we first consider the conflict relation given above. It is easy to see that the graph induced is tripartite, and its independent sets are given by those arguments with claim $\tau_1 >_\mu \tau_2$, those arguments with claim $\tau_1 \sim_\mu \tau_2$, and those arguments with claim $\tau_1 <_\mu \tau_2$. In our example, this graph is as follows.

$$\langle \{\text{Fel02}\}, \lambda_s, \text{PGA} >_{\text{safeIOP}} \text{BB} \rangle \rightleftarrows \langle \{\text{Pfe02}\}, \lambda_n, \text{PGA} \sim_{\text{safeIOP}} \text{BB} \rangle$$

Since the argument graph is by definition symmetric (if we use the conflict relation), it would be beneficial to allow breaking the symmetry with user-defined preferences. We do this by defining preference rules.

Definition 4. *A preference rule is a set of conditions on an ordered pair of conflicting arguments A, B. When the conditions are satisfied, A is said to be preferred to B otherwise, we say that A is not preferred to B.*

Example 4. *For $A = \langle \{\gamma_a\}, \lambda_a, \epsilon_A \rangle$ and $B = \langle \{\gamma_b\}, \lambda_b, \epsilon_B \rangle$ such that A conflicts with B, A is preferred to B iff γ_a is statistically significant and γ_b is not statistically significant.*

Preference rules are not required to be infallible in any sense. Indeed the above example embodies one of the aspects of *publication bias*, where by preferring significant results to non-significant ones, one may miss evidence that supports the claim that the significant results are a chance occurrence.

We use the preference rules chosen by the user in breaking the symmetry present in the conflict relation, as developed by Amgoud and Cayrol [1], and capture the attack relation as follows.

Definition 5. *For any pair of arguments A and B, A **attacks** B iff A conflicts with B and A is preferred to B and it is not the case that B is preferred to A.*

The motivation here is that if A and B conflict with each other and A is preferred to B then B's conflict with A is cancelled. However, this wording leads to problems when A is preferred to B according to a preference rule and B is preferred to A according to a preference rule. In this case, cancelling both attacks will give the misleading impression that A and B are consistent together. For this reason we give the above, more complicated definition, which only cancels an attack if exactly one argument is preferred to the other.

Now we combine these components by defining an argument graph based on a set of trial results, a set of inference rules, and a set of preference rules as follows.

Definition 6. *Given a pair of treatments τ_1, τ_2 and an outcome indicator μ, and a set* TRIALS *concerning these treatments and outcome indicator, an **argument graph** is a graph where the set of nodes is the set of arguments formed using a set of inference rules as given by Definition 1 and the set of arcs is the attacks relation given by Definition 5.*

We can directly use the dialectical semantics given by Dung [4] to decide extensions of argument graphs. We regard a preferred set of arguments as an interpretation of a TRIALS (i.e. an aggregation of the evidence in TRIALS. So if X is an extension of the argument graph, and $A \in X$, and ϵ is the claim of A, then ϵ is a possible aggregation of the evidence.

4. Qualitative framework

Now we present a specific version of the framework including inference rules and pre-ference rules. We start with a set of trials TRIALS = $\{t_1, .., t_n\}$ each of which uses the same outcome indicator and compares the same pair of treatments τ_1 and τ_2. We partition TRIALS into three sets SUPERIOR, EQUITABLE, and INFERIOR. Those in SUPERIOR are the trials for which τ_1 was shown to be superior to τ_2, those in EQUITABLE are the trials for which τ_2 was shown to equitable with τ_1, and those in INFERIOR are the trials for which τ_2 was shown to be superior to τ_1. We also partition TRIALS into two sets SIGNIFI-CANT and NONSIGNIFICANT. Those in SIGNIFICANT are the trials for which the result is significant, and those in NONSIGNIFICANT are the trials for which the result is not signi-ficant. In this paper, we focus on qualitative aggregation based solely on the distribution of trials in SUPERIOR, EQUITABLE, INFERIOR, SIGNIFICANT and NONSIGNIFICANT.

The inference rules we use for the qualitative framework are given in Table 2. From these inference rules, we get four types of argument as follows.

- $\langle \text{SUPERIOR}, R_x, \tau_1 > \tau_2 \rangle$ where $R_x \in \{R_1, ..., R_{12}\}$
- $\langle \text{INFERIOR}, R_x, \tau_1 < \tau_2 \rangle$ where $R_x \in \{R_1, ..., R_{12}\}$
- $\langle \text{EQUITABLE}, R_x, \tau_1 \sim \tau_2 \rangle$ where $R_x \in \{R_{13}, .., R_{15}\}$
- $\langle \text{NONSIGNIFICANT}, R_{16}, \tau_1 \sim \tau_2 \rangle$

Note, the items of evidence in INFERIOR state that τ_1 is inferior to τ_2 which is equivalent to stating that τ_2 is superior to τ_1. Furthermore, as we specified earlier, $\tau_1 < \tau_2$ is equivalent to $\tau_2 > \tau_1$. Hence, by this correspondence, we may be able to apply the rules in $R_x \in \{R_1, ..., R_{12}\}$ to generate an argument $\langle \text{INFERIOR}, R_x, \tau_1 < \tau_2 \rangle$ where $R_x \in \{R_1, ..., R_{12}\}$.

Given a set TRIALS, we let Args(TRIALS) denote the set of arguments that can be generated by this set of rules. Also, for an argument A, let Rule(A) be the inference rule used in the argument, and let Claim(A) be the claim of the argument (i.e. for $A = \langle \Phi, \lambda, \epsilon \rangle$, Rule($A$) = λ and Claim(A) = ϵ).

Example 5. *For prostaglandin v beta-blocker (see Table 4), for obtaining a safe IOP, we have* |TRIALS| = 12, |SUPERIOR| = 12, *and* |SIGNIFICANT| = 7. *Hence, we get the argument* $\langle \text{SUPERIOR}, R_2, \text{PGA} >_{\text{safeIOP}} \text{BB} \rangle$.

We motivate the inference rules as follows. First, $R_1, .., R_4$ are for when all the trials show superiority (of the leftarm over the rightarm), $R_5, .., R_8$ are for when the majority of the trials show superiority, and $R_9, .., R_{12}$ are for when a minority of the trials show superiority. Then each of these three groups is broken down according to the proportion of the trials that show superiority are also significant, i.e., $\frac{|\text{SUPERIOR} \cap \text{SIGNIFICANT}|}{|\text{SUPERIOR}|}$. So for instance, for R_1, all trials are significant, for R_2, it is the majority that are signifi-cant, for R_3, it is a minority that are significant, and for R_4, none are significant. Then, $R_{13}, .., R_{15}$ are for when some trials show equality (of the left and right arms). So R_{13} is when a minority show equality, R_{14} is when a majority show equality, and R_{15} is when all show equality. Note, $R_{13}, .., R_{15}$ are not broken down by significance since techni-cally, when a trial shows equality it is a failure to show a difference, whereas significance is for showing whether a difference occurred by chance. Hence, for equality, significance is not meaningful. Finally, R_{16} is for when the proportion of trials that are nonsignificant is greater than or equal to 1/2.

Table 2. Inference rules for qualitative framework. Given TRIALS, let ρ_1 = |SUPERIOR/TRIALS|, ρ_2 = |SIGNIFICANT∩SUPERIOR/SUPERIOR|, ρ_3 = |SIGNIFICANT/TRIALS|, and ρ_4 = |EQUITABLE/TRIALS|.

Rule	Condition	Explanation	Claim
R_1	(1) $\rho_1 = 1$ (2) $\rho_2 = 1$	all trials show superiority of which all are significant	$\tau_1 > \tau_2$
R_2	(1) $\rho_1 = 1$ (2) $0.5 < \rho_2 < 1$	all trials show superiority of which a majority are significant	$\tau_1 > \tau_2$
R_3	(1) $\rho_1 = 1$ (2) $0 < \rho_2 \leq 0.5$	all trials show superiority of which a minority are significant	$\tau_1 > \tau_2$
R_4	(1) $\rho_1 = 1$ (2) $\rho_2 = 0$	all trials show superiority of which none are significant	$\tau_1 > \tau_2$
R_5	(1) $0.5 < \rho_1 < 1$ (2) $\rho_2 = 1$	a majority of trials show superiority of which all are significant	$\tau_1 > \tau_2$
R_6	(1) $0.5 < \rho_1 < 1$ (2) $0.5 < \rho_2 < 1$	a majority of trials show superiority of which a majority are significant	$\tau_1 > \tau_2$
R_7	(1) $0.5 < \rho_1 < 1$ (2) $0 < \rho_2 \leq 0.5$	a majority of trials show superiority of which a minority are significant	$\tau_1 > \tau_2$
R_8	(1) $0.5 < \rho_1 < 1$ (2) $\rho_2 = 0$	a majority of trials show superiority of which none are significant	$\tau_1 > \tau_2$
R_9	(1) $0 < \rho_1 \leq 0.5$ (2) $\rho_2 = 1$	a minority of trials show superiority of which all are significant	$\tau_1 > \tau_2$
R_{10}	(1) $0 < \rho_1 \leq 0.5$ (2) $0.5 < \rho_2 < 1$	a minority of trials show superiority of which the majority are significant	$\tau_1 > \tau_2$
R_{11}	(1) $0 < \rho_1 \leq 0.5$ (2) $0 < \rho_2 \leq 0.5$	a minority of trials show superiority of which a minority are significant	$\tau_1 > \tau_2$
R_{12}	(1) $0 < \rho_1 \leq 0.5$ (2) $\rho_2 = 0$	a minority of trials show superiority of which none are significant	$\tau_1 > \tau_2$
R_{13}	$0 < \rho_4 \leq 0.5$	a minority of trials show equality of τ_1 and τ_2	$\tau_1 \sim \tau_2$
R_{14}	$0.5 < \rho_4 < 1$	a majority of trials show equality of τ_1 and τ_2	$\tau_1 \sim \tau_2$
R_{15}	$\rho_4 = 1$	all trials show equality of τ_1 and τ_2	$\tau_1 \sim \tau_2$
R_{16}	$0.5 \leq \rho_3 \leq 1$	half or more trials are statistically nonsignificant	$\tau_1 \sim \tau_2$

Given a set TRIALS comparing τ_1 and τ_2, the inference rules R_1 to R_{16} impose constraints on what combinations of arguments are possible together in Args(TRIALS).

Proposition 1. *If there is an argument $A_i \in$ Args(TRIALS) where Claim$(A_i) = \tau_1 > \tau_2$, then there is at most one argument $A_j \in$ Args(TRIALS) where Claim$(A_j) = \tau_2 > \tau_1$, and there is at most two arguments $A_k \in$ Args(TRIALS) where Claim$(A_k) = \tau_1 \sim \tau_2$,*

So the above says that there is at most one argument showing superiority, at most two showing equivalence, and at most one showing inferiority, and the following says that there is always argument with at least one of these claims.

Proposition 2. *If TRIALS $\neq \emptyset$, then there is an argument $A_i \in$ Args(TRIALS) where* Claim$(A_i) = \tau_1 > \tau_2$ *or* Claim$(A_i) = \tau_1 \sim \tau_2$ *or* Claim$(A_i) = \tau_2 > \tau_1$.

Being able to use rules R_5 to R_{12} means that conflicting arguments can be generated from R_5 to R_{15} as captured by the following proposition.

Table 3. For arguments A_i and A_j, A_i is preferred to A_j iff one of P_2 to P_{11} holds for $\text{Rule}(A_i)$ and $\text{Rule}(A_j)$.

Preference rule	$\text{Rule}(A_i)$	$\text{Rule}(A_j)$
P_2	R_2	$\{R_{16}\}$
P_3	R_3	$\{R_{16}\}$
P_4	R_4	$\{R_{16}\}$
P_5	R_5	$\{R_{11}, R_{12}, R_{13}, R_{16}\}$
P_6	R_6	$\{R_{11}, R_{12}, R_{13}, R_{16}\}$
P_7	R_7	$\{R_{12}, R_{13}, R_{16}\}$
P_8	R_8	$\{R_{12}, R_{13}, R_{16}\}$
P_9	R_9	$\{R_8, R_{11}, R_{12}, R_{13}, R_{16}\}$
P_{10}	R_{10}	$\{R_8, R_{11}, R_{12}, R_{13}, R_{16}\}$
P_{11}	R_{11}	$\{R_8, R_{13}\}$

Proposition 3. *If there is an argument $A_i \in \text{Args}(\text{TRIALS})$ s.t. $\text{Rule}(A_i) \in \{R_5, ..., R_{12}\}$ and $\text{Claim}(A_i) = \tau_1 > \tau_2$, then there is an argument $A_j \in \text{Args}(\text{TRIALS})$ where $\text{Rule}(A_j) \in \{R_5, ..., R_{15}\}$ and either $\text{Claim}(A_j) = \tau_1 < \tau_2$ or $\text{Claim}(A_j) = \tau_1 \sim \tau_2$.*

However, being able to use rules R_1 to R_4 means that no conflicting arguments can be generated by using rules R_5 to R_{15}.

Proposition 4. *If there is an argument $A_i \in \text{Args}(\text{TRIALS})$ where $\text{Rule}(A_i) \in \{R_1, ..., R_4\}$ and $\text{Claim}(A_i) = \tau_1 > \tau_2$, then there is no argument $A_j \in \text{Args}(\text{TRIALS})$ where $\text{Rule}(A_j) \in \{R_5, ..., R_{15}\}$ and either $\text{Claim}(A_j) = \tau_1 < \tau_2$ or $\text{Claim}(A_j) = \tau_1 \sim \tau_2$.*

Being able to use rules R_{13} or R_{14} also means that conflicting arguments can be generated as captured by the following propositions.

Proposition 5. *If there is an argument $A_i \in \text{Args}(\text{TRIALS})$ s.t. $\text{Claim}(A_i) = \tau_1 \sim \tau_2$ and either $\text{Rule}(A_i) = R_{13}$ or $\text{Rule}(A_i) = R_{14}$, then there is an argument $A_j \in \text{Args}(\text{TRIALS})$ where $\text{Rule}(A_j) \in \{R_5, ..., R_{12}\}$ and either $\text{Claim}(A_j) = \tau_1 > \tau_2$ or $\text{Claim}(A_j) = \tau_1 < \tau_2$.*

However, being able to use rule R_{15} means that no conflicting arguments can be generated by using rules R_1 to R_{15}.

Proposition 6. *If there is an argument $A_i \in \text{Args}(\text{TRIALS})$ where $\text{Rule}(A_i) = R_{15}$ then there is no argument $A_j \in \text{Args}(\text{TRIALS})$ where $\text{Rule}(A_j) \in \{R_1, ..., R_{14}\}$.*

The preference rules are given in Table 3. Note, we do not consider R_1 because if it applies, no other rule could apply, and for $R_2, .., R_4$, the only other rule that can fire is R_{16}. Also, we do not consider $R_{12}, .., R_{16}$ since any argument based on them is not preferred to any other argument.

Example 6. *For prostaglandin v beta-blocker (m_3 in Table 4), for lower risk of respiratory problems as a side-effect, there are 2 trials, of which 1 shows superiority significantly and 1 shows superiority non-significantly (and so all the trials say that prostaglandin is superior to beta-blocker). By preference rule P2, the attack from the right* *argument to the left argument is suppressed. Therefore, we have the following argument graph, and we obtain the left argument in the resulting grounded extension.*

$$\langle \text{SUPERIOR}, R_3, \text{PGA} >_{\text{respiratory}} \text{BB} \rangle \rightarrow \langle \text{EQUITABLE}, R_{16}, \text{PGA} \sim_{\text{respiratory}} \text{BB} \rangle$$

Example 7. *For prostaglandin v beta-blocker (m_4 in Table 4), for lower risk of cardio-logical problems as a side-effect, there are 5 trials, of which 1 shows superiority signifi-cantly, 2 show superiority non-significantly and 2 show inferiority non-significantly. So by preference rule P7, the attack from the right argument to the left argument is sup-pressed, and the attack from the lower argument to the left argument is also suppressed. Therefore, we have the following argument graph, and we obtain the left argument in the resulting grounded extension.*

$$\langle \text{SUPERIOR}, R_7, \text{PGA} >_{\text{cardio}} \text{BB} \rangle \rightarrow \langle \text{INFERIOR}, R_{12}, \text{PGA} <_{\text{cardio}} \text{BB} \rangle$$
$$\searrow \qquad \swarrow \nearrow$$
$$\langle \text{NONSIGNIFICANT}, R_{16}, \text{PGA} \sim_{\text{cardio}} \text{BB} \rangle$$

With the qualitative framework, we have a simple set of inference rules and prefe-rence rules, that given a set of trial results TRIALS produces a small set of arguments and attack relationships. It allows for highlighting key conflicts in possible aggregations of the evidence, and as we show in the next section, it appears to perform well with real data.

5. Case study

In order to evaluate the qualitative framework, we have taken 14 meta-analyses from 3 NICE Guidelines (www.nice.org.uk), and we compare the results they obtained with the results that our qualitative evidence aggregation produced. We give a summary of this comparison in Tables 4, 5, and 6.

In these tables, each row is a based on a meta-analysis in the NICE guide-line where $n_1 = |\text{SUPERIOR} \cap \text{SIGNIFICANT}|$, $n_2 = |\text{SUPERIOR} \cap \text{NONSIGNIFICANT}|$, $n_3 = |\text{EQUITABLE}|$, $n_4 = |\text{INFERIOR} \cap \text{NONSIGNIFICANT}|$, and $n_5 = |\text{INFERIOR} \cap \text{SIGNIFICANT}|$. The column "Their result" is the weighted average presented in the meta-analysis in the guideline where sup (respectively eq and inf) denotes superior (respecti-vely equal and inferior) and sig (respectively non-sig) denotes significant (respectively non-significant). The column "Rule used" gives the rules that appear in the arguments we generate from the data in $n_1, .., n_5$, and "Our result" is the form of the claims of the arguments in the union of the preferred extensions. So for example, in Table 4, the first row labelled m_1, concerns a meta-analysis based on 12 clinical trials, of which 7 were statistically significant, and their weighted average result showed the leftarm was significantly superior to the rightarm, and our result showed leftarm was superior to the rightarm, and this was based on an argument involving inference rule R_2.

- From the NICE Glaucoma Guideline (CG85), we have investigated 6 meta-analyses, and give the data and results in Table 4. In each case where their result is superior significantly (respectively inferior significantly), we obtain $\tau_1 > \tau_2$ (respectively $\tau_1 < \tau_2$). For the cases where the their result is superior non-significantly, we obtain $\tau_1 > \tau_2$. For the case where their result is inferior non-

Table 4. Comparison of qualitative argument-based evidence aggregation with meta-analyses from NICE Glaucoma Guideline (CG85, Appendix, pp 218-221). Each row is a meta-analysis where the left arm is a prostaglandin analogue and the right arm is a beta-blocker. The treatment is intended to lower intraocular pressure (IOP). The outcome indicator for each meta-analysis is as follows: m_1 Decrease of IOP; m_2 Acceptable (safe) IOP; m_3 Respiratory problems; m_4 Cardiological problems; m_5 Allergic problems; m_6 Hyperaemia problems.

	n_1	n_2	n_3	n_4	n_5	Their result	Rules used	Our result
m_1	7	5	0	0	0	sup sig	R_2	$\tau_1 > \tau_2$
m_2	6	1	0	0	0	sup sig	R_2	$\tau_1 > \tau_2$
m_3	1	1	0	0	0	sup non-sig	R_2, R_{16}	$\tau_1 > \tau_2$
m_4	1	2	0	2	0	sup non-sig	R_7, R_{12}, R_{16}	$\tau_1 > \tau_2$
m_5	0	1	0	1	0	inf non-sig	R_8, R_{16}	$\tau_1 > \tau_2, \tau_1 \sim \tau_2, \tau_1 < \tau_2$
m_6	0	0	0	4	6	inf sig	R_2	$\tau_1 < \tau_2$

significantly, we obtain the vaguer result of a disjunction of $\{\tau_1 > \tau_2, \tau_1 \sim \tau_2, \tau_1 < \tau_2\}$ instead of $\tau_1 < \tau_2$. So overall, in 5 out of 6 cases, we get the same superiority/inferiority relation as their result, and in 1 out of 6 cases, we get a vaguer result (i.e. disjunction of $\{\tau_1 > \tau_2, \tau_1 \sim \tau_2, \tau_1 < \tau_2\}$).

- From the NICE Hypertension Guideline (CG34), we have investigated 5 meta-analyses, and give the data and results in Table 5. In each case where their result is superior significantly (respectively inferior significantly), we obtain $\tau_1 > \tau_2$ (respectively $\tau_1 < \tau_2$). There are 2 cases where their result is inferior non-significant, for which we obtain $\tau_1 > \tau_2$ in one case and $\tau_1 < \tau_2$ in the other case. Also there is 1 case where their result is superior non-significant, for which we obtain $\tau_1 < \tau_2$. So overall, in 3 out of 5 cases, we get the same as their result, and for 2 out of 5 cases, we get the opposite (i.e. either $\tau_1 > \tau_2$ instead of $\tau_1 < \tau_2$ or $\tau_1 < \tau_2$ instead of $\tau_1 > \tau_2$).

- From the NICE Type 2 Diabetes Guideline (CG66), we have investigated 3 meta-analyses, and give the data and results in Table 6. In the case where their result is superior significantly, we obtain $\tau_1 > \tau_2$. In the case where their result is superior non-significantly, we obtain $\tau_1 > \tau_2$. And in the case where their result is inferior non-significantly, we obtain the disjunction of $\{\tau_1 > \tau_2, \tau_1 \sim \tau_2, \tau_1 < \tau_2\}$.

From this consideration of 14 meta-analyses, it would appear that the qualitative evidence aggregation performs well. In 10 out of 14 meta-analyses, we get the same result (i.e. superiority or inferiority), in 2 out of 14 meta-analyses, we get a vaguer result (i.e. a disjunction), and in 2 out of 14 meta-analyses, we get the opposite result (i.e. the incorrect result) to the meta-analysis.

6. Discussion

We have presented a qualitative framework for argumentation on treatment efficacy. Using these components along with standard argumentation tools, users can describe their preferences and analyze the available evidence in terms of agreement and conflict.

The advantage of qualitative evidence aggregation is that it allows for abstraction from details of a meta-analysis, and it allows for modularity of analysis (thereby facilitating the aggregation according to multiple outcome indicators). Obviously such qualitative evidence aggregation is not able to replace statistical evidence aggregation. Ra-

Table 5. Comparison of qualitative argument-based evidence aggregation with meta-analysis data and results taken from NICE Hypertension Guideline (CG34, pp 36-43). Each row is a meta-analysis where the left arm is a calcium channel blocker and the right arm is a thiazide. The treatment is intended to lower blood pressure. The outcome indicator for each meta-analysis is as follows: m_7 Mortality; m_8 Myocardial infarction; m_9 Stroke; m_{10} Heart failure; and m_{11} Diabetes.

	n_1	n_2	n_3	n_4	n_5	Their result	Rules used	Our result
m_7	0	2	0	3	0	sup non-sig	R_8, R_{12}, R_{16}	$\tau_1 < \tau_2$
m_8	0	1	0	4	0	inf non-sig	R_8, R_{12}, R_{16}	$\tau_1 < \tau_2$
m_9	0	3	0	2	0	inf non-sig	R_8, R_{12}, R_{16}	$\tau_1 > \tau_2$
m_{10}	0	1	0	2	2	inf sig	R_7, R_{12}, R_{16}	$\tau_1 < \tau_2$
m_{11}	2	1	0	0	0	sup sig	R_2	$\tau_1 > \tau_2$

Table 6. Comparison of qualitative argument-based evidence aggregation with meta-analysis data and results taken from NICE Type 2 Diabetes Guideline (CG66, Appendix, p 18). Each row is a meta-analysis where the outcome indicator is the lowering of HbA1c (a protein involved in diabetes). For m_{13}, the leftarm is biphasic insulin and the rightarm is human insulin; for m_{14}, the leftarm is glargin insulin and the rightarm is human insulin; and for m_{15}, the leftarm is biphasic insulin and the rightarm is glargin insulin.

	n_1	n_2	n_3	n_4	n_5	Their result	Rules used	Our result
m_{12}	0	4	1	1	0	sup non-sig	$R_8, R_{12}, R_{13}, R_{16}$	$\tau_1 > \tau_2$
m_{13}	0	1	0	1	0	inf non-sig	R_8, R_{16}	$\tau_1 > \tau_2, \tau_1 \sim \tau_2, \tau_1 < \tau_2$
m_{14}	3	0	0	0	0	sup sig	R_1	$\tau_1 > \tau_2$

ther it is meant to complement it by addressing some of the shortcomings of statistical evidence aggregation including statistics suppresses conflict by using averages (whereas argumentation highlights conflict), statistics hides issues such as problems with particular sources of evidence (whereas in argumentation this can be made explicit by use of appropriate preference rules and/or further types of inference rule), and statistics is based on assumptions that either might be hidden or debatable.

Little work exists that aims to address the problem in focus here. Medical informatics and bioinformatics research does not address the reasoning aspects inherent in the analysis of evidence of primary nature, especially from clinical trials. Previous interesting work ([9,14,15] and others) exists that uses argumentation as a tool in medical decision support, but as such, assumes the existence of a hand-crafted knowledgebase.

We believe that the work presented here is a step towards an automated system for aggregating qualitative evidence. It is straightforward to implement the inference rules for generating arguments and the preference rules for generating the attack relation. Furthermore, given that there is only a small number of arguments generated per set TRIALS, a naive algorithm that considers each subset of arguments for calculating preferred extensions is viable.

For developing information extraction of clinical trials, it may be possible to build on a set of open source tools and resources for clinical text mining that are available as part of the well-established GATE framework [3]. These resources include the CLEF corpus of annotated clinical documents [12], terminological resources such as the Unified Medical Language System (UMLS) [8], and machine learning methods (such as SVMs) that have been tailored to statistical named entity recognition (NER) and relationship extraction. Using GATE, Roberts and co-workers have recently developed and evaluated hybrid methods (combining terminological resources with statistical methods) for recognizing a set of entity types (medical condition, drug, intervention, etc.) relevant to our research [10], and statistical methods for the extraction of clinical relationships between these entities [11]. Also, there is the Trial Bank Project which is concerned with extracting detailed information about the patient class from published clinical trials [13].

References

[1] L Amgoud and C Cayrol. Inferring from inconsistency in preference-based argumentation frameworks. *Journal of Automated Reasoning*, 29:125–169, 2002.

[2] F Baader, D Calvanese, D McGuinness, D Nardi, and P Patel-Schneider, editors. *The description logic handbook: theory, implementation, and applications*. Cambridge University Press, New York, NY, USA, 2003.

[3] H Cunningham, D Maynard, K Bontcheva, and V Tablan. Gate: A framework and graphical development environment for robust NLP tools and applications. In *Proceedings of the 40th Anniversary Meeting of the Association for Computational Linguistics (ACL'02)*, 2002.

[4] P Dung. On the acceptability of arguments and its fundamental role in nonmonotonic reasoning, logic programming, and n-person games. *Artificial Intelligence*, 77:321–357, 1995.

[5] N Gorogiannis, A Hunter, V Patkar, and M Williams. Argumentation about treatment efficacy. In *Knowledge Representation for Healthcare (KR4HC)*, LNCS. Springer, 2010.

[6] N Gorogiannis, A Hunter, and M Williams. An argument-based approach to reasoning with clinical knowledge. *International Journal of Approximate Reasoning*, 51(1):1 – 22, 2009.

[7] A Hackshaw. *A Concise Guide to Clinical Trials*. WileyBlackwell, 2009.

[8] D Lindberg, B Humphreys, and A McCray. Unified medical language system. *Methods of Information in Medicine*, 32(4), 1993.

[9] V Patkar, C Hurt, R Steele, S Love, A Purushotham, M Williams, R Thomson, and J Fox. Evidence-based guidelines and decision support services: adiscussion and evaluation in triple assessment of sus-pectedbreast cancer. *British Journal of Cancer*, 95(11):1490–1496, 2006.

[10] A Roberts, R Gaizasukas, M Hepple, and Y Guo. Combining terminology resources and statistical methods for entity recognition: an evaluation. In *Proc. of the Sixth International Language Resources and Evaluation (LREC'08)*, 2008.

[11] A Roberts, R Gaizasukas, M Hepple, and Y Guo. Mining clinical relationships from patient narratives. *BMC bioinformatics*, 9, 2008. Suppl 11,S3.

[12] A Roberts, R Gaizauskas, M Hepple, N Davis, G Demetriou, Y Guo, J Kola, I Roberts, A Setzer, A Ta-puria, and B Wheeldin. The clef corpus: semantic annotation of clinical text. In *Proceedings of the Annual Symposium of American Medical Informatics Association (AMIA'07)*, pages 625–629, 2007.

[13] I Sim, D Owens, P Lavori, and G Rennels. Electronic trial banks: A complementary method for reporting randomized trials. *Medical Decision Making*, 20(4):440–450, 2000.

[14] P Tolchinsky, U Cortés, S Modgil, and F Caballeroand A López-Navidad. Increasing human-organ transplant availability:argumentation-based agent deliberation. *IEEE Intelligent Systems*, 21(6):30–37, 2006.

[15] R Walton, C Gierl, P Yudkin, H Mistry, M Vessey, and J Fox. Evaluation of computer support for prescribing (CAPSULE). *British Medical Journal*, 315:791–795, 1997.

[16] M Williams and A Hunter. Harnessing ontologies for argument-based decision-making in breast cancer. In *Proceedings of the 19th IEEE International Conference on Tools with Artificial Intelligence (ICTAI 2007)*, volume 2, pages 254–261. IEEE Computer Society Press, 2007.

Computational Models of Argument
P. Baroni et al. (Eds.)
IOS Press, 2010
© 2010 The authors and IOS Press. All rights reserved.
doi:10.3233/978-1-60750-619-5-299

Refined Preference-based Argumentation Frameworks

Souhila KACI [a,1]

[a] *CRIL, CLLE-LTC, France*

Abstract. Argumentation is a reasoning model based on constructing arguments, determining potential conflicts between arguments and determining acceptable arguments. Dung's argumentation theory is an abstract framework based on a binary defeat relation between arguments. Due to this abstract representation, it has been instantiated in different ways. In particular, preference-based argumentation frameworks take into account a preference relation over arguments together with a (non necessarily symmetric) attack relation. We show that preference-based argumentation frameworks faithfully instantiate Dung's framework only when the attack relation is symmetric. Moreover the latter condition prevents undesirable results. We also promote a higher impact of preferences in preference-based argumentation frameworks and propose different ways to rank-order sets of acceptable arguments.

Keywords. Argumentation, Preferences

Introduction

Argumentation is a reasoning model based on constructing arguments, determining potential conflicts between arguments and determining acceptable arguments. Dung's argumentation theory is an abstract framework based on a set of arguments and a binary defeat (called attack by Dung) relation defined over the set of arguments [9].

The output of an argumentation framework are sets of acceptable arguments called acceptable extensions (sometimes we simply speak about extensions). The latter should satisfy two basic requirements: (1) an extension is conflict-free i.e. there is no defeat relation between two arguments in the extension, and (2) an extension should defend its arguments against any defeat.

Conflicts between arguments have better chance to be solved in the presence of preferences over arguments. Dung's argumentation framework has been instantiated to take into account such a possibility giving birth to preference-based argumentation frameworks, where a preference relation over arguments is used together with an attack relation over arguments [1,5,10]. The preference relation over arguments can be computed from the strength of knowledge on which they are built [2] or in a more abstract way from an ordering on values they promote [5]. A value may be a goal, a criterion, a viewpoint, etc. Dung's argumentation framework is then derived where an argument a defeats an argument b if and only if a attacks b and b is not strictly preferred to a w.r.t. the underly-

---

[1]Corresponding Author: Souhila Kaci, CRIL, CNRS UMR 8188, IUT de Lens F-62307, France,
CLLE-LTC, CNRS UMR 5263, 5 Allées Machado 31058 Toulouse Cedex 9, France; E-mail: kaci@cril.fr

ing preference relation. We say that the preference-based argumentation framework represents the derived Dung's argumentation framework. Extensions of a preference-based argumentation framework are the extensions of Dung's argumentation framework it represents.

However the use of preferences (even in the most elaborate way) in preference-based argumentation frameworks has been done in a limited way in the sense that preferences over arguments are only used to permit an attack relation to succeed or not. Once the defeat relation is computed from an attack relation and a preference relation, preferences over arguments are no longer used. Moreover it seems that the use of preferences in argumentation framework recently became rather a source of confusion. In particular, it has been argued in [3] that preference-based argumentation frameworks induce undesirable results as they may violate conflict-freeness of acceptable extensions. We show that this flaw is not due to the use of preferences but to a more fundamental problem regarding the attack relation. In fact existing preference-based argumentation frameworks rely on an attack relation which is not necessarily symmetric. This is because researchers define preference-based argumentation frameworks as an extension of Dung's framework (in which the defeat relation is not necessarily symmetric) and not as an instantiation of that framework. Since acceptable extensions of a preference-based argumentation framework are acceptable extensions of the Dung's framework it represents, we should rather speak about an instantiation. This remark is much deeper than a simple problem of a terminology since an instantiation implicitly requires that a preference-based argumentation framework should faithfully preserve minimal requirements of Dung's framework namely defense and, more importantly, conflict-freeness. In fact, a preference-based argumentation framework faithfully instantiates Dung's framework only when the attack relation is symmetric.

In addition, we promote a higher impact of preferences on the output of preference-based argumentation frameworks. So far the agent is provided with different acceptable extensions considered as equally preferred. The authors of [8] have advocated this problem and defined new extensions that only return the most preferred acceptable extensions. We believe that returning the most preferred acceptable extensions and excluding the other ones is not suitable. This is because all acceptable extensions satisfy minimal requirements of Dung's framework namely defense and conflict-freeness so no reason is valid to exclude some of them. Instead, we keep all acceptable extensions but propose different more or less strong ways to rank-order them.

The remainder of this paper is organized as follows. After notations and necessary definitions, we recall in Section 2 Dung's argumentation framework and preference-based argumentation frameworks. In Section 3 we review the critics of Dung's framework and flaws of existing preference-based argumentation frameworks. We comment them and give the way we intend to solve these flaws. In Section 4 we propose different ways to rank-order acceptable extensions. Lastly we conclude.

1. Notations and definitions

A preference relation $\succeq$ on $\mathcal{X} = \{x, y, z, \cdots\}$ is a reflexive binary relation such that $x \succeq y$ stands for x is at least as preferred as y. x and y are equally preferred when both $x \succeq y$ and $y \succeq x$ hold. Lastly x and y are incomparable when neither $x \succeq y$ nor $y \succeq x$

holds. A strict preference relation over $\mathcal{X}$ is an irreflexive binary relation such that $x \succ y$ means that x is strictly preferred to y. We also say that x dominates y. A strict preference relation $\succ$ can be defined from a preference relation $\succeq$ as $x \succ y$ if $x \succeq y$ holds but $y \succeq x$ does not.

$\succeq$ (resp. $\succ$) is a preorder (resp. order) on $\mathcal{X}$ if and only if $\succeq$ (resp. $\succ$) is transitive, i.e., if $x \succeq y$ and $y \succeq z$ then $x \succeq z$ (if $x \succ y$ and $y \succ z$ then $x \succ z$). $\succeq$ (resp. $\succ$) is a complete preorder (resp. order) if and only if $\forall x, y \in \mathcal{X}$, we have either $x \succeq y$ or $y \succeq x$ (resp. either $x \succ y$ or $y \succ x$).

A complete preorder $\succeq$ over a set Σ can also be represented by a well ordered partition of Σ. This is an equivalent representation, in the sense that each preorder corresponds to one ordered partition and vice versa.

Definition 1 (Partition) *A sequence of subsets of Σ of the form $(E_1, \ldots, E_n)$ is a partition of Σ if and only if (i) $\forall i$, $E_i \neq \emptyset$, (ii) $E_1 \cup \cdots \cup E_n = \Sigma$, and (iii) $\forall i, j$, $E_i \cap E_j = \emptyset$ for $i \neq j$.*

A partition of Σ is ordered if and only if it is associated with a preorder $\succeq$ over Σ such that $(\forall t, t' \in \Sigma$ with $t \in E_i, t' \in E_j$ we have $i \leq j$ if and only if $t \succeq t')$.

A complete preorder $\succeq$ over Σ is consistent with a partial preorder $\succeq'$ over Σ iff $(\forall t, t' \in \Sigma$, if $t \succeq' t'$ then $t \succeq t')$.

Given a (complete or partial) preorder $\succeq$ over a set Σ, the best (resp. worst) elements of Σ w.r.t. $\succeq$ are those which are not dominated by (resp. which do not dominate) any element of Σ. Formally, we write:
$$\max(\Sigma, \succeq) = \{t | t \in \Sigma, \nexists t' \in \Sigma, t' \succ t\}$$
(resp. $\min(\Sigma, \succeq) = \{t | t \in \Sigma, \nexists t' \in \Sigma, t \succ t'\}$).

2. Argumentation theory

Argumentation is a reasoning model based on constructing arguments, determining potential conflicts between arguments and determining acceptable arguments.

2.1. Dung's argumentation framework

Dung's framework [9] is based on a binary *defeat* relation. In that framework, an argument is an abstract entity whose role is determined only by its relation to other arguments. Its structure and its origin are not known. We restrict ourselves to *finite* argumentation frameworks, i.e., in which the set of arguments is *finite*.

Definition 2 (Argumentation framework) *An argumentation framework is a tuple $\langle \mathcal{A}, Def \rangle$ where $\mathcal{A}$ is a finite set of arguments and Def is a binary (defeat) relation defined on $\mathcal{A} \times \mathcal{A}$.*

The output of $\langle \mathcal{A}, Def \rangle$ is derived from the sets of selected acceptable arguments, called acceptable extensions, with respect to some acceptability semantics. We need the following definitions before we recall the most widely used acceptable extensions given in the literature.

Definition 3 *Let $\langle \mathcal{A}, Def \rangle$ be an argumentation framework. Let $A \subseteq \mathcal{A}$.*

- *A defends a if $\forall b \in \mathcal{A}$ such that b Def a, $\exists c \in A$ such that c Def b.*
- *$A \subseteq \mathcal{A}$ is conflict-free if and only if there are no $a, b \in A$ such that a Def b.*

The following definition summarizes the well-known acceptable extensions.

Definition 4 (Acceptable extensions) *[9]*
Let $\langle \mathcal{A}, Def \rangle$ be an argumentation framework.

- *A subset $A \subseteq \mathcal{A}$ is an admissible extension iff it is conflict-free and it defends all elements in A.*
- *A subset $A \subseteq \mathcal{A}$ is a preferred extension iff it is a maximal (for set inclusion) admissible extension.*
- *A subset $A \subseteq \mathcal{A}$ is a stable extension iff it is a preferred extension that attacks any argument in $\mathcal{A} \setminus A$.*
- *A subset $A \subseteq \mathcal{A}$ is a complete extension iff it is conflict-free and $A = \{a \mid a \in \mathcal{A}, A \text{ defends } a\}$.*
- *A subset $A \subseteq \mathcal{A}$ is a grounded extension iff it is the smallest (for set inclusion) complete extension of $\langle \mathcal{A}, Def \rangle$.*

2.2. Preference-based argumentation framework

Preference-based argumentation framework [1] is an instantiation of Dung's framework where the defeat relation is derived from a binary attack relation between arguments and a preference relation over the set of arguments.

Definition 5 (Preference-based argumentation framework) *A preference-based argumentation framework is a 3-tuple $\langle \mathcal{A}, Att, \succeq \rangle$ where $\mathcal{A}$ is a set of arguments, Att is a binary attack relation defined on $\mathcal{A} \times \mathcal{A}$ and $\succeq$ is a (complete or partial) preorder on $\mathcal{A} \times \mathcal{A}$.*

A preference-based argumentation framework can represent an argumentation framework.

Definition 6 *A preference-based argumentation framework $\langle \mathcal{A}, Att, \succeq \rangle$ represents $\langle \mathcal{A}, Def \rangle$ if and only if $\forall a, b \in \mathcal{A}$, we have a Def b iff $(a \ Att \ b \ and \ not(b \succ a))$.*

The extensions of a preference-based argumentation framework are simply the extensions of the unique argumentation framework it represents.

3. Critical analysis of argumentation frameworks

Thanks to the abstract representation of Dung's framework [9], it has been used in different ways. In particular different preference-based argumentation frameworks have been proposed to instantiate Dung's framework. However in spite of these advances, both Dung's framework and its instantiated preference-based argumentation frameworks have been recently criticized. In the next subsections, we review these criticisms and comment them.

3.1. Strength of arguments

In [3] it has been argued that Dung's framework does not faithfully model some situations.

Example 1 *(Borrowed from [3])*
An agent wants to buy a violin. An expert says that the violin is produced by Stradivari (s), that's why it is expensive. So the agent has an argument a_1 whose conclusion is "e: the violin is expensive". The agent has a 3-years old son who says that the violin was not produced by Stradivari ($\neg s$). Thus, the agent has an argument a_2 whose conclusion is $\neg s$. The agent has two arguments a_1 and a_2 with $a_1 = \langle \{s, s \rightarrow e\}, e \rangle$ and $a_2 = \langle \{\neg s\}, \neg s \rangle$. An argument "a" has the form $\langle H, h \rangle$ where H is a set of formulas and h is logically induced from H. H and h are called the support and the conclusion of "a" respectively. The conclusion of a_2 contradicts an element in the support of a_1.

The authors of [3] model Example 1 by a Dung's argumentation framework $\langle \mathcal{A}, Def \rangle$ defined by $\mathcal{A} = \{a_1, a_2\}$ and a_2 *Def* a_1. Thus a_2 is the only acceptable argument. However they criticized this result arguing that an argument given by an expert is stronger than an argument given by a 3-years old children. So a_1 should be accepted instead of a_2. Note that if we consider a third argument $a_3 = \langle \{s\}, s \rangle$ then the grounded extension is empty while it should be equal to $\{a_1, a_3\}$.

While the above problem seems intuitively correct we think that it is rather due to a misunderstanding of Dung's framework. In fact the conflict relation between the two arguments $a_1 = \langle \{s, s \rightarrow e\}, e \rangle$ and $a_2 = \langle \{\neg s\}, \neg s \rangle$ is modelled by a defeat relation a_2 *Def* a_1 in [3]. We believe that this modeling is the source of undesirable results. In fact we should not omit that Dung's argumentation framework is an "abstract" framework which is defined by a set of abstract arguments and a binary relation over arguments representing defeat relations between arguments. Indeed Dung proposed a general and abstract framework and left is to us to define the set of arguments and, more importantly, fix the defeat relation. Indeed if we believe that the source of an argument should play a role in the definition of the defeat relation then we define accordingly this relation. This turns out to have a_1 *Def* a_2 instead of a_2 *Def* a_1 which faithfully models the problem and returns the intended result, namely a_1.
By the above observation, we aim to say that Dung's framework does not fail to take into account preferences but should be suitably instantiated for this purpose.

3.2. Conflict-free acceptable extensions

In order to take into account the strength of arguments in the above example, the authors of [3] model Example 1 by a preference-based argumentation framework $\langle \mathcal{A}, Att, \succeq \rangle$ with $a_1 \succ a_2$ and a_2 *Att* a_1. Dung's argumentation framework associated to $\langle \mathcal{A}, Att, \succeq \rangle$ is $\langle \mathcal{A}, Def \rangle$ with $Def = \emptyset$ since a_2 *Att* a_1 but $a_1 \succ a_2$. Again the authors of [3] criticized this result as both a_1 and a_2 are accepted. Therefore the acceptable extension is not conflict-free.
Example 1 can also be modelled in value-based argumentation framework [5] and Modgil's preference-based argumentation framework [10] in which we also recover the problem raised above. Due to the lack of space, we do not recall these frameworks.

Here again we believe that undesirable results are due to the way the example is modelled. In preference-based argumentation framework, the sources providing arguments are considered leading to a preference relation over arguments, $a_1 \succ a_2$ in our example. However the trouble comes from the attack relation modelled by a_2 Att a_1. Since $a_1 \succ a_2$ then a_2 Att a_1 fails and we conclude that neither a_1 Def a_2 nor a_2 Def a_1 holds. It is worth noticing that in Dung's argumentation framework extensions are conflict-free and any arguments related by Def cannot appear in the same extension. This means that the existence of an argument in an extension implies the exclusion of any argument with which it is related by a defeat relation. This crucial principle is not faithfully reported in preference-based argumentation framework. In fact a_1 and a_2 are conflicting which means that they cannot appear in the same extension. However since the attack relation is "asymmetric" (we only have a_2 Att a_1) then having $a_1 \succ a_2$ makes that a_1 and a_2 are not related by Def. Indeed they both belong to acceptable extensions. In Example 1, and preference-based argumentation frameworks in general, a faithful modeling of the idea that two conflicting arguments, let's say a_1 and a_2, should not appear in the same extension (thus ensuring the conflict-freeness of extensions) is to exclude one of them from an extension as soon as they are related by the attack relation whatever in which sense it is, i.e., a_1 Att a_2 or a_2 Att a_1 or both. The preference relation is then used to determine the sense of the defeat relation between the two arguments, i.e., a_1 Def a_2 or a_2 Def a_1 or both. Therefore we ensure that both arguments will not belong to the same acceptable extension since they are related by the defeat relation. This idea can be recovered by a "symmetric" attack relation in preference-based argumentation frameworks. Since an attack is intuitively not necessarily symmetric we will speak about a conflict relation. Therefore we define preference-based argumentation frameworks with a symmetric conflict relation. We denote such frameworks by $\langle \mathcal{A}, C, \succeq \rangle$. We represent C by a set of pairs, i.e., $C = \{(a_i, a_j)\}$. Therefore when (a_i, a_j) belongs to C then (a_j, a_i) necessarily belongs to C too. Dung's argumentation framework represented by $\langle \mathcal{A}, C, \succeq \rangle$ is defined in the standard way, i.e., a Def b if and only if $(a, b) \in C$ and $not(b \succ a)$.

Example 2 *(Example 1 continued) The problem is modelled by $\langle \mathcal{A}, C, \succeq \rangle$ with $\mathcal{A} = \{a_1, a_2\}$, $C = \{(a_1, a_2), (a_2, a_1)\}$ and $a_1 \succ a_2$. Then Dung's argumentation framework represented by $\langle \mathcal{A}, C, \succeq \rangle$ is $\langle \mathcal{A}, Def \rangle$ with $a_1 Def a_2$. The only acceptable extension is $\{a_1\}$ which is the intended result.*

Note that Example 1 can also be modelled by a preference-based argumentation framework $\langle \mathcal{A}, Att, \succeq \rangle$ where $\mathcal{A} = \{a_1, a_2, a_3\}$ with $a_3 = \langle \{s\}, s \rangle$, a_2 Att a_1, a_2 Att a_3, a_3 Att a_2 and $a_3 \succ a_2$. Then the set of acceptable arguments is $\{a_1, a_3\}$. However this only works on the example but not in general. Just consider two abstract arguments a_1 and a_2 such that a_1 Att a_2 but $a_2 \succ a_1$. Then the attack does not succeed and the set of acceptable arguments is $\{a_1, a_2\}$.

3.3. Preferences & acceptable extensions

So far preferences in preference-based argumentation frameworks have been used in a limited way in the sense that they only serve to compute the defeat relation from a conflict relation. In [8], it has been argued that preferences can be used to refine the selection of acceptable extensions.

Example 3 *Let* $\langle \mathcal{A}, C, \succeq \rangle$ *be a preference-based argumentation framework with* $\mathcal{A} = \{a_1, a_2, a_3, a_4\}$, *and* $C = \{(a_1, a_2), (a_2, a_1), (a_1, a_4), (a_4, a_1), (a_3, a_2), (a_2, a_3), (a_3, a_4), (a_4, a_3)\}$. $\succeq$ *is defined by* $a_2 \succ a_1$ *and* $a_4 \succ a_3$. *Dung's argumentation framework associated to* $\langle \mathcal{A}, C, \succeq \rangle$ *is* $\langle \mathcal{A}, Def \rangle$ *with* $a_2 Def a_1$, $a_4 Def a_3$, $a_1 Def a_4$, $a_4 Def a_1$, $a_2 Def a_3$ *and* $a_3 Def a_2$. *Stable extensions of* $\langle \mathcal{A}, Def \rangle$ *(thus of* $\langle \mathcal{A}, C, \succeq \rangle$*) are* $E_1 = \{a_2, a_4\}$ *and* $E_2 = \{a_1, a_3\}$.

Due to the preference relation, the authors of [8] claim that only E_1 should be considered as stable extension since $a_2 \succ a_1$ and $a_4 \succ a_3$, so E_1 is preferred to E_2. Consequently, they define super-stable extensions which return E_1 only in Example 3.

While we agree that the role of preferences should be greater in preference-based argumentation frameworks we do not think that returning only the most preferred extensions (and excluding the other ones) is the right way to further incorporate preferences in preference-based argumentation frameworks. In fact all acceptable extensions satisfy basic requirements of Dung's framework (and its instantiations), namely conflict-freeness and defense so excluding some of them is not intuitively plausible. Rather rank-ordering these extensions is more helpful as it not only provides all extensions but also a preference relation over them. Therefore the agent is aware about all acceptable extensions and is free to select the most preferred ones. Moreover the most preferred extensions may no longer be feasible (for example achieving all arguments of an extension is too costly) then the agent will select the immediately less preferred extensions and so on. This idea is already at work in representing and reasoning about preferences where alternatives are rank-ordered w.r.t. agent's preferences instead of returning the most preferred ones only. In the next section, we propose different ways to rank-order acceptable extensions.

4. Comparing sets of arguments

Comparing sets of arguments may raise some difficulties mainly for two reasons: (1) the "kind" of the preference relation over arguments from which sets of arguments are compared and (2) different preference semantics between sets of arguments can be considered.

4.1. Complete preorders over arguments

Let us consider the following example.

Example 4 *Let* $\langle \mathcal{A}, C, \succeq \rangle$ *with* $\mathcal{A} = \{a_1, a_2, a_3, a_4, a_5, a_6\}$, $C = \{(a_1, a_4), (a_4, a_1), (a_2, a_3), (a_3, a_2), (a_2, a_6), (a_6, a_2), (a_4, a_5), (a_5, a_4), (a_1, a_6), (a_6, a_1), (a_3, a_5), (a_5, a_3), (a_1, a_5), (a_5, a_1), (a_3, a_6), (a_6, a_3), (a_3, a_4), (a_4, a_3), (a_4, a_6), (a_6, a_4), (a_2, a_5), (a_5, a_2)\}$. $\succeq$ *is defined by* $a_5 \succ a_2 \succ a_1$ *and* $a_6 \succ a_4$. *We have three stable extensions* $S_1 = \{a_1, a_3\}$, $S_2 = \{a_2, a_4\}$ *and* $S_3 = \{a_5, a_6\}$. *The associated Dung's argumentation framework is defined by* $a_5 Def a_1$, $a_5 Def a_2$, $a_6 Def a_4$ *and* $a_i Def a_j$ *and* $a_j Def a_i$ *for all other* (a_i, a_j) *in* C. *Figure 1 depicts stable extensions and the partial preorder* $\succeq$. *An arrow from* a_i *to* a_j *stands for* $a_i \succ a_j$.

Figure 1. Stable extensions of $\langle \mathcal{A}, \mathcal{C}, \succeq \rangle$ and the partial preorder $\succeq$.

Let us first compare S_1, S_2 and S_3 w.r.t. the partial preorder $\succeq$. We consider one possible preference semantics between sets and state that "S_i is preferred to S_j if and only if any argument in S_j is strictly less preferred w.r.t. $\succeq$ to at least one argument in S_i". Let $>_1$ be the preference relation over $2^{\mathcal{A}}$ w.r.t. this semantics. We have that $S_3 >_1 S_2$ since $a_5 \succ a_2$ and $a_6 \succ a_4$. On the other hand, S_1 is incomparable with both S_2 and S_3. However one may consider that S_3 is preferred to S_1 as $a_5 \succ a_1$ and a_6 and a_3 are incomparable. Similarly S_2 is preferred to S_1 since $a_2 \succ a_1$ and a_4 and a_3 are incomparable. Therefore we have $S_3 >_1 S_2 >_1 S_1$. The transitivity of $>_1$ is intuitively meaningful since there is only one "step" from a_5 to a_2 while there are two steps from a_5 to a_1 in the partial preorder $\succeq$.

Counting the length of preferences path and ignoring incomparability in a partial preorder is known in preference representation (and AI in general) as a linearisation of the partial preorder which means that a complete preorder consistent with the partial preorder is computed. Different complete preorders can be associated to a partial preorder. It is nevertheless possible to distinguish a unique complete preorder on the basis of insights from non-monotonic reasoning. Let $\succeq$ be a partial preorder and $\succeq_* = (E_1, \cdots, E_n)$ be its unique associated complete preorder. Recall that the lowest is k, the most preferred are arguments in E_k. We distinguish two ways to compute $\succeq_*$ from $\succeq$ [11].

1. each argument is put as *high* as possible in the preorder, i.e., in the lowest possible rank k. This way is based on the principle that an argument is satisfactory unless the contrary is stated. The resulting preorder is denoted $\succeq_h$.
2. each argument is put as *low* as possible in the preorder, i.e., in the greatest possible rank k. This way is based on the principle that an argument is not satisfactory unless the contrary is stated. The resulting preorder is denoted $\succeq_l$.

Algorithm 1 (resp. Algorithm 2) gives the way $\succeq_h$ (resp. $\succeq_l$) is constructed from a partial preorder $\succeq$ [11].

Example 5 *(Example 4 continued) We have* $\succeq = \{a_5 \succ a_2, a_2 \succ a_1, a_6 \succ a_4\}$. *So* $\succ = \succeq$.
Let us first apply Algorithm 1. We put in E_1 *arguments that are not dominated w.r.t.* $\succ$. *We have* $E_1 = \{a_3, a_5, a_6\}$. *We remove* $a_5 \succ a_2$ *and* $a_6 \succ a_4$ *from* $\succ$ *then* $\succ = \{a_2 \succ a_1\}$. *We update* $\mathcal{A}$ *so* $\mathcal{A} = \{a_1, a_2, a_4\}$. *We repeat the same reasoning and get* $E_2 = \{a_2, a_4\}$ *and* $E_1 = \{a_1\}$. *So* $\succeq_h = (\{a_3, a_5, a_6\}, \{a_2, a_4\}, \{a_1\})$. *We can check that each argument has been put as high as possible in the preorder. For example, if we put* a_2 *higher we get* $\succeq' = (\{a_2, a_3, a_5, a_6\}, \{a_4\}, \{a_1\})$ *which is not consistent with* $\succeq$ *since* $a_5 \succ a_2$ *is not true in* $\succeq'$.
Let us now apply Algorithm 2. We put in E_1 *arguments which do not dominate any*

Algorithm 1:

Data: A partial preorder $\succeq = \{a_i \succeq a_j\}$ over $\mathcal{A}$

Result: A complete preorder $\succeq_h$ over $\mathcal{A}$

begin

    $k = 0, \succ = \{a_i \succ a_j | a_i \succeq a_j, not(a_j \succeq a_i)\}$

    while $\mathcal{A} \neq \emptyset$ **do**

        $k = k + 1$

        $E_k = \{a | a \in \mathcal{A}, \nexists b \in \mathcal{A}, b \succ a\}$

        if $E_k = \emptyset$ **then** $E_k = \mathcal{A}$

        - remove $a \succ a_j$ from $\succ$, where $a \in E_k$

        - $\mathcal{A} = \mathcal{A} \backslash E_k$

    return $\succeq_h = (E_1, \cdots, E_k)$

end

Algorithm 2:

Data: A partial preorder $\succeq = \{a_i \succeq a_j\}$ over $\mathcal{A}$

Result: A complete preorder $\succeq_l$ over $\mathcal{A}$

begin

    $k = 0, \succ = \{a_i \succ a_j | a_i \succeq a_j, not(a_j \succeq a_i)\}$

    while $\mathcal{A} \neq \emptyset$ **do**

        $k = k + 1$

        $E_k = \{a | a \in \mathcal{A}, \nexists b \in \mathcal{A}, a \succ b\}$

        if $E_k = \emptyset$ **then** $E_k = \mathcal{A}$

        - remove $a_i \succ a$ from $\succ$, where $a \in E_k$

        - $\mathcal{A} = \mathcal{A} \backslash E_k$

    return $\succeq_l = (E'_1, \cdots, E'_k)$ with $E'_m = E_{k-m+1}$

end

other argument so $E_1 = \{a_1, a_3, a_4\}$. We remove $a_2 \succ a_1$ and $a_6 \succ a_4$ from $\succ$ then $\succ = \{a_5 \succ a_6\}$. We update $\mathcal{A}$ so $\mathcal{A} = \{a_2, a_5, a_6\}$. We repeat the same reasoning and get $E_2 = \{a_2, a_6\}$ and $E_3 = \{a_5\}$. Indeed $\succeq_l = (\{a_5\}, \{a_2, a_6\}, \{a_1, a_3, a_4\})$.

4.2. Preference semantics

Before presenting further results, we summarize how we proceed to rank-order acceptable extensions. Our approach follows three steps:

1. We first compute acceptable extensions of a preference-based argumentation framework $\langle \mathcal{A}, C, \succeq \rangle$. Let $\mathcal{E}$ be this set.
2. We compute a complete preorder $\succeq_*$ ($\succeq_h$ or $\succeq_l$) consistent with $\succeq$ following Algorithm 1 or Algorithm 2.
3. We rank-order sets of $\mathcal{E}$ given $\succeq_*$.

Item 3 involves the comparison of sets of arguments. We present in the following different ways to compare sets of arguments used in preference representation.

Let Σ_1 and Σ_2 be two sets of arguments. The most natural way to state a preference for Σ_1 over Σ_2 is when any argument in Σ_1 is preferred to any argument in Σ_2 given a complete preorder over $\mathcal{A}$. However this way to compare sets of arguments may lead to unwished drastic results. Let us consider the following example.

Example 6 *Consider a preference-based argumentation framework* $\langle \mathcal{A}, C, \succeq \rangle$ *with* $\mathcal{A} = \{a_1, a_2, a_3, a_4\}$, $C = \{(a_2, a_4), (a_4, a_2)\}$ *and* $a_1 \succ a_4$, $a_2 \succ a_3$. *Dung's argumentation framework* $\langle \mathcal{A}, Def \rangle$ *represented by* $\langle \mathcal{A}, C, \succeq \rangle$ *is defined by* a_2 *Def* a_4 *and* a_4 *Def* a_2. *We have two preferred extensions* $P_1 = \{a_1, a_2, a_3\}$ *and* $P_2 = \{a_1, a_3, a_4\}$. *We have that* $\succeq_h = \succeq_l = (\{a_1, a_2\}, \{a_3, a_4\})$. P_1 *and* P_2 *are incomparable since no argument in* P_1 *is strictly preferred to any argument in* P_2 *and vice versa. However this is rather an undesirable result since the incomparability here is due to the fact that* P_1 *and* P_2 *share some arguments. If we only focus on non common arguments i.e.* $P_1 \backslash P_2$ *and* $P_2 \backslash P_1$ *then we have that* P_1 *is preferred to* P_2 *since* $P_1 \backslash P_2 = \{a_2\}$, $P_2 \backslash P_1 = \{a_4\}$ *and* $a_2 \succ_h a_4$ *(also* $a_2 \succ_l a_4$).

The idea of focusing on non common elements is already at work in preference representation [12] where a formula (let's say p) is preferred to another formula (let's say q) is interpreted as $p \wedge \neg q$-worlds are preferred to $\neg p \wedge q$-worlds w.r.t. a given semantics.

The preference semantics given in Example 6 is formally defined as follows:

Definition 7 (Strong semantics) *[13]*
Let Σ_1 *and* Σ_2 *be two subsets of* $\mathcal{A}$. *Let* $\succeq$ *be a complete preorder over* $\mathcal{A}$. Σ_1 *is at least as strongly preferred as* Σ_2, *denoted* $\Sigma_1 \geq_{st} \Sigma_2$, *iff* $\Sigma_2 \subseteq \Sigma_1$, *or*
$$\forall a \in \Sigma_1 \backslash \Sigma_2, \forall b \in \Sigma_2 \backslash \Sigma_1, a \succeq b.$$
Σ_1 *and* Σ_2 *are strongly equally preferred, denoted* $\Sigma_1 =_{st} \Sigma_2$, *iff* $\Sigma_1 \geq_{st} \Sigma_2$ *and* $\Sigma_2 \geq_{st} \Sigma_1$.
Σ_1 *is strongly preferred to* Σ_2, *denoted* $\Sigma_1 >_{st} \Sigma_2$, *iff* $\Sigma_1 \geq_{st} \Sigma_2$ *and* $not(\Sigma_2 \geq_{st} \Sigma_1)$.

Example 7 *(Example 4 continued)*
We first consider $\succeq_h$. *We have* $S_3 >_{st} S_2$. *On the other hand,* S_1 *and* S_2 *(also* S_1 *and* S_3) *are incomparable w.r.t.* $\geq_{st}$. *Let us now consider* $\succeq_l$. *We have* $S_3 >_{st} S_1$ *while* S_2 *and* S_3 *(also* S_1 *and* S_2) *are incomparable w.r.t.* $\geq_{st}$.

Note that $\geq_{st}$ is not transitive. Let $\Sigma_1 = \{a, b\}$, $\Sigma_2 = \{b\}$ and $\Sigma_3 = \{c\}$ with $b \succ c \succ a$. We have $\succeq_h = \succeq_l = \succ$. Then we have $\Sigma_1 >_{st} \Sigma_2$ and $\Sigma_2 >_{st} \Sigma_3$ but $not(\Sigma_1 >_{st} \Sigma_3)$. Note however that the non-transitivity is due to the fact that $\Sigma_2 \subseteq \Sigma_1$. This is not the case of extensions that are maximal, i.e., preferred/stable extensions (cf. Definition 4). Indeed $\geq_{st}$ is transitive when acceptable extensions are compared.

Proposition 1 *Let* $\mathcal{E}$ *be the set of preferred/stable extensions of a preference-based argumentation framework. Let* $\succeq$ *be a complete preorder on* $\mathcal{A}$. *Let* $\geq_{st}$ *be the preference relation over* $\mathcal{E}$ *following strong semantics w.r.t.* $\succeq$. *Then* $\geq_{st}$ *is a* partial preorder *over* $\mathcal{E}$.

Super-stable extensions defined in [8] correspond to the best stable extensions w.r.t. $>_{st}$. In our example, they correspond to S_1 and S_3 when we consider $\succeq_h$.

Strong semantics, as indicated by its name, is too strong since it may induce an incomparability while we can argue for a strict preference. Consider again Example 4 and the complete preorder $\succeq_h$ over $\mathcal{A}$. S_1 and S_2 are incomparable w.r.t. $\geq_{st}$. One may weaken the preference semantics and state that S_1 is preferred to S_2 because the best-ranked argument in S_1 w.r.t. $\succeq_h$ is a_3 which is preferred w.r.t. $\succeq_h$ to the best-ranked atguments in S_2 w.r.t. $\succeq_h$ namely a_2 and a_4. One may also argue for the converse preference i.e. S_2 is preferred to S_1 since the worst-ranked argument in S_2 w.r.t. $\succeq_h$, namely

a_2 and a_4, are preferred w.r.t. $\succeq_h$ to the worst-ranked argument in S_1 namely a_1. This gives birth to two additional preference semantics.

Definition 8 (Optimistic semantics) *[7]*
Let Σ_1 and Σ_2 be two subsets of $\mathcal{A}$. Let $\succeq$ be a complete preorder over $\mathcal{A}$. Σ_1 is at least as optimistically preferred as Σ_2, denoted $\Sigma_1 \geq_{opt} \Sigma_2$, iff $\Sigma_2 \subseteq \Sigma_1$, or
$$\forall a \in \max(\Sigma_1 \backslash \Sigma_2, \succeq), \forall b \in \max(\Sigma_2 \backslash \Sigma_1, \succeq), a \succeq b.$$
Σ_1 and Σ_2 are optimistically equally preferred, denoted $\Sigma_1 =_{opt} \Sigma_2$, iff $\Sigma_1 \geq_{opt} \Sigma_2$ and $\Sigma_2 \geq_{opt} \Sigma_1$.
Σ_1 is optimistically preferred to Σ_2, denoted $\Sigma_1 >_{opt} \Sigma_2$, iff $\Sigma_1 \geq_{opt} \Sigma_2$ and $not(\Sigma_2 \geq_{opt} \Sigma_1)$.

Example 8 *(Example 1 continued)*
Let us first consider $\succeq_h$. We have $S_3 >_{opt} S_2$, $S_1 >_{opt} S_2$ and $S_1 =_{opt} S_3$. Let us now consider $\succeq_l$. We have $S_3 >_{opt} S_2 >_{opt} S_1$. We can also check that $S_3 >_{opt} S_1$ holds.

Proposition 2 *Let $\mathcal{E}$ be the set of acceptable extensions of a preference-based argumentation framework. Let $\succeq$ be a complete preorder on $\mathcal{A}$. Let $\geq_{opt}$ be the preference relation over $\mathcal{E}$ following optimistic semantics w.r.t. $\succeq$. Then $\geq_{opt}$ is a complete preorder over $\mathcal{E}$.*

Definition 9 (Pessimistic semantics) *[6]*
Let Σ_1 and Σ_2 be two subsets of $\mathcal{A}$. Let $\succeq$ be a complete preorder over $\mathcal{A}$. Σ_1 is at least as pessimistically preferred as Σ_2, denoted $\Sigma_1 \geq_{pes} \Sigma_2$, iff $\Sigma_2 \subseteq \Sigma_1$, or
$$\forall a \in \min(\Sigma_1 \backslash \Sigma_2, \succeq), \forall b \in \min(\Sigma_2 \backslash \Sigma_1, \succeq), a \succeq b.$$
Σ_1 and Σ_2 are pessimistically equally preferred, denoted $\Sigma_1 =_{pes} \Sigma_2$, iff $\Sigma_1 \geq_{pes} \Sigma_2$ and $\Sigma_2 \geq_{pes} \Sigma_1$.
Σ_1 is pessimistically preferred to Σ_2, denoted $\Sigma_1 >_{pes} \Sigma_2$, iff $\Sigma_1 \geq_{pes} \Sigma_2$ and $not(\Sigma_2 \geq_{pes} \Sigma_1)$.

Example 9 *(Example 1 continued)*
Let us first consider $\succeq_h$. We have $S_3 >_{pes} S_2 >_{pes} S_1$. We can also check that $S_3 >_{pes} S_1$ holds. Let us now consider $\succeq_l$. We have $S_3 >_{pes} S_2$, $S_3 >_{pes} S_1$ and $S_1 =_{pes} S_2$.

Proposition 3 *Let $\mathcal{E}$ be the set of acceptable extensions of a preference-based argumentation framework. Let $\succeq$ be a complete preorder on $\mathcal{A}$. Let $\geq_{pes}$ be the preference relation over $\mathcal{E}$ following pessimistic semantics w.r.t. $\succeq$. Then $\geq_{pes}$ is a complete preorder over $\mathcal{E}$.*

One may also imagine other preferences semantics. Due to the lack of space we restricted ourselves to the most well-known ones. As illustrated by our running example, they rank-order the acceptable extensions in different ways. In fact, S_i is strongly preferred to S_j w.r.t. $\succeq$ when any argument in S_i is preferred w.r.t. $\succeq$ to any argument in S_j while optimistic (resp. pessimistic) semantics compares only the most (resp. least) preferred arguments in S_i and S_j w.r.t. $\succeq$. Therefore the different semantics reflect how much the user is "requiring".

The following corollary states that strong semantics is "stronger" than both optimistic and pessimistic semantics, as one would expect.

Corollary 1 *Let $\mathcal{E}$ be the set of extensions of a preference-based argumentation framework. Let $\succeq$ be a complete preorder on $\mathcal{A}$. $\forall S_i, S_j \in \mathcal{E}$,*
$$\text{if } S_i \geq_{st} S_j \text{ then } (S_i \geq_{opt} S_j \text{ and } S_i \geq_{pes} S_j).$$

5. Conclusion

So far preference-based argumentation frameworks with symmetric conflict relation have been considered as a special case of preference-based argumentation frameworks. Recently, it has been argued that existing preference-based argumentation frameworks suffer from flaws as they may violate conflict-freeness of acceptable extensions. We have shown that a symmetric conflict relation should not be considered as a special case of attack relation in preference-based argumentation frameworks but as the right way to model incompatibility between arguments in order to faithfully represent Dung's argumentation framework. It allows to satisfy conflict-freeness of acceptable extensions.

We also argued for a higher use of preferences in the output of preference-based argumentation frameworks and proposed different ways to rank-order acceptable extensions. In the future we intend to investigate other preference semantics over acceptable extensions and study their properties. We also intend to relate the ranking of subsets of arguments in our framework to that proposed in [4].

References

[1] L. Amgoud and C. Cayrol: Inferring from Inconsistency in Preference-Based Argumentation Frameworks, IJAR, 29(2), 2002, 125-169.
[2] L. Amgoud and C. Cayrol and D. LeBerre: Comparing arguments using preference orderings for argument-based reasoning, ICTAI, 1996, 400-403.
[3] L. Amgoud and S. Vesic: Repairing Preference-Based Argumentation Frameworks, IJCAI, 2009, 665-670.
[4] P. Baroni and M. Giacomin: Resolution-based argumentation semantics, COMMA'08, 2008, 25-36.
[5] T.J.M. Bench-Capon: Persuasion in Practical Argument Using Value-based Argumentation Frameworks, Journal of Logic and Computation, 13(3), 2003, 429-448.
[6] S. Benferhat and D. Dubois and S. Kaci and H. Prade: Bipolar representation and fusion of preferences in the possibilistic logic framework, KR, 2002, 421-432.
[7] C. Boutilier: Toward a logic for qualitative decision theory, KR, 1994, 75-86.
[8] Y. Dimopoulos and P. Moraitis and L. Amgoud: Extending argumentation to make good decisions, ADT, 2009, 225-236.
[9] P. M. Dung: On the acceptability of arguments and its fundamental role in non-monotonic reasoning, logic programming and n-person games, Artificial Intelligence, 77, 1995, 321-357.
[10] S. Modgil: Reasoning about preferences in argumentation frameworks, Artificial Intelligence, 173(9-10), 2009, 901-934.
[11] J. Pearl: System Z: A natural ordering of defaults with tractable applications to default reasoning, TARK, 1990, 121-135.
[12] G. H. von Wright: The Logic of Preference, University of Edinburgh Press, 1963.
[13] N. Wilson: Extending CP-Nets with Stronger Conditional Preference Statements, AAAI, 2004, 735-741.

Computational Models of Argument
P. Baroni et al. (Eds.)
IOS Press, 2010
doi:10.3233/978-1-60750-619-5-311

Algorithms and Complexity Results for Persuasive Argumentation [1]

Eun Jung KIM [a], Sebastian ORDYNIAK [b] and Stefan SZEIDER [b]

[a] *Department of Computer Science, Royal Holloway, University of London, UK*
[b] *Institute of Information Systems, Vienna University of Technology, Austria*

Abstract. Value-based argumentation frameworks, as introduced by Bench-Capon, allow the abstract representation of persuasive argumentation. This formalism takes into account the relative strength of arguments with respect to some ordering which represents an audience. Deciding subjective or objective acceptance (i.e., acceptance with respect to at least one or with respect to all orderings) are intractable computational problems.

In this paper we study the computational complexity of testing the subjective or objective acceptance for problem instances that obey certain restrictions. We consider structural restrictions in terms of the underlying graph structure of the value-based argumentation framework and in terms of properties of the equivalence relation formed by arguments with the same relative strength. We identify new tractable fragments where subjective and objective acceptance can be tested in polynomial time. Furthermore we show the intractability of some fragments that are located at the boundary to tractability. Our results disprove two conjectures of Dunne (*Artificial Intelligence* 171, 2007).

Keywords. Value-based argumentation frameworks, treewidth, NP-hardness, polynomial-time tractability, subjective and objective acceptance.

1. Introduction

The study of arguments as abstract entities and their interaction in form of *attacks* as introduced by Dung [8] has become one of the most active research branches within Logic, Artificial Intelligence, and Reasoning [4]. The key concept in this study is the notion of an abstract argumentation system or *argumentation framework* that can be considered as a directed graph whose nodes represent arguments, a directed edge that runs from an argument x to an argument y represents that "x attacks y."

Extending Dung's concept, Bench-Capon [2] introduced *value-based argumentation frameworks* (*VAFs*, for short) where arguments are ranked with respect to their strength, and an argument cannot attack another argument of higher rank. The ranking is specified by the combination of an assignment of values to arguments, and a (total) ordering of the values; the latter is called a (specific) *audience*. As explained by Bench-Capon [2], the role of arguments in this setting is to *persuade* rather than to prove, demonstrate or refute. An argument is said to be *subjectively accepted* in a value-based argumentation

---

[1] Ordyniak and Szeider's research was supported by the European Research Council, grant reference 239962.

framework if it is accepted for at least one specific audience; it is *objectively accepted* if it is accepted for all specific audiences. Here acceptance refers to the standard semantics of *preferred extensions* [8].

Most computational problems that arise in the context of abstract argumentation are intractable [11]. In particular, as shown by Dunne and Bench-Capon [10], the problem SUBJECTIVE ACCEPTANCE (deciding whether an argument is subjectively accepted in a VAF) is NP-complete, and the problem OBJECTIVE ACCEPTANCE (deciding whether an argument is objectively accepted in a VAF) is co-NP-complete. In view of the intractability of these problems, it is a natural and relevant research question to ask for tractable fragments, and to carve out the boundaries between tractability and intractability.

In this paper we study the computational complexity of the problems SUBJECTIVE/OBJECTIVE ACCEPTANCE for VAFs that satisfy certain restrictions in terms of the following notions.

- Bounds on the largest number of arguments that share the same value; we call this parameter the *value-width* of the VAF under consideration.
- Bounds on the number of attacks (x, y) such that x and y share the same value; we call this parameter the *attack-width* of the VAF under consideration.
- Structural restrictions on the *graph structure* of the VAF under consideration; the graph structure is the graph whose vertices are arguments and where two distinct arguments are adjacent if and only if one attacks the other.
- Bounds on the *treewidth* of the *extended graph structure* of the VAF under consideration; the extended graph structure is obtained from the graph structure by adding edges between any two arguments that share the same value.

The parameters value-width and attack-width were first considered by Dunne [9] (using a different terminology). VAFs with a bipartite graph structure generalize the VAFs whose graph structure is a tree. To consider the treewidth of the extended graph structure is motivated by the fact that testing for subjective or objective acceptance is already intractable for VAFs whose graph structure is a tree [9].

Dunne [9] showed that SUBJECTIVE ACCEPTANCE remains NP-hard for instances of value-width 3 and whose graph structure is a tree. Furthermore, he stated the following two conjectures:

Conjecture 1 ([9]). SUBJECTIVE ACCEPTANCE *is polynomial-time decidable for VAFs of value-width* 2.

Conjecture 2 ([9]). SUBJECTIVE ACCEPTANCE *is fixed-parameter tractable when parameterized by the attack-width.*

A decision problem is called *fixed-parameter tractable* if an instance of size n and parameter k can be decided in time $O(f(k)n^c)$ where f is an arbitrary computable function and c is a constant independent of k [7]. Note that if a problem is fixed-parameter tractable, then each "slice" of the problem (obtained by fixing k to a constant) is decidable in polynomial time [12].

New Results

We have obtained positive and negative complexity results for SUBJECTIVE/OBJECTIVE ACCEPTANCE.

Theorem 1. (A) SUBJECTIVE ACCEPTANCE remains NP-hard for instances of value-width 2 and attack-width 1.

(B) OBJECTIVE ACCEPTANCE remains co-NP-hard for instances of value-width 2 and attack-width 1.

As a consequence of (A), Conjectures 1 and 2 do not hold unless P = NP. It is easy to see that SUBJECTIVE/OBJECTIVE ACCEPTANCE become trivial if we further restrict the value-width to 1 or if we further restrict the attack-width to 0 [9], hence the bounds in Theorem 1 are tight.

On the positive side we show that Conjecture 1 is true if we restrict ourselves to VAFs with a bipartite graph structure.

Theorem 2. (A) SUBJECTIVE ACCEPTANCE can be decided in polynomial time for instances with a bipartite graph structure and of value-width 2.

(B) OBJECTIVE ACCEPTANCE can be decided in polynomial time for instances with a bipartite graph structure and of value-width 2.

Since trees are bipartite, it follows that both problems can be decided in polynomial time for VAFs of value-width 2 if the graph structure is a tree.

Finally, we consider VAFs with value-width ≥ 2 and an *extended graph structure* of bounded treewidth.

Theorem 3. SUBJECTIVE/OBJECTIVE ACCEPTANCE *can be decided in linear time for instances whose extended graph structure has bounded treewidth. This remains true even for instances whose value-width is greater than two.*

We obtain this result by expressing the problems within the formalism of monadic second-order (MSO) logic on finite structures, and using Courcelle's meta-theorem [6,12].

2. Preliminaries

In this section we introduce the objects of our study more formally.

An *abstract argumentation system* or *argumentation framework* (*AF*, for short) is a pair (X, A) where X is a finite set of elements called *arguments* and $A \subseteq X \times X$ is a binary relation called the *attack relation*. If $(x, y) \in A$ we say that x *attacks* y.

An AF $F = (X, A)$ can be considered as a directed graph, and therefore it is convenient to borrow notions and notation from graph theory. For example, if $(x, y) \in A$ then we say that x is an in-neighbor of y and that y is an out-neighbor of x. We write $N_F^-(x)$ and $N_F^+(x)$ for the sets of in- respectively out-neighbors of x in F, and we omit the subscript if F is clear from the context.

Next we define commonly used semantics of AFs as introduced by Dung [8] (for the discussion of other semantics and variants, see e.g., Baroni and Giacomin's survey [1]). Let $F = (X, A)$ be an AF and $S \subseteq X$.

1. S is *conflict-free* in F if there is no $(x, y) \in A$ with $x, y \in S$.
2. S is *acceptable* in F if for each $x \in S$ and $y \in N^-(x)$ we have $N^-(y) \cap S \neq \emptyset$.
3. S is *admissible* in F if it is conflict-free and acceptable.
4. S is a *preferred extension* of F if S is admissible in F and there is no admissible set S' of F that properly contains S.

Let $F = (X, A)$ be an AF and $x_1 \in X$. The argument x_1 is *credulously accepted* in F if x_1 is contained in some preferred extension of F, and x_1 is *skeptically accepted* in F if x_1 is contained in all preferred extensions of F. In this paper we are especially interested in finding preferred extensions in acyclic AFs. It is well known that every acyclic AF $F = (X, A)$ has a unique preferred extension S_F, and that S_F can be found in polynomial time (S_F coincides with the "grounded extension" [8]). In fact, S_F can be found via a simple labeling procedure that repeatedly applies the following two rules to the arguments in X until each of them is either labeled IN or OUT: (1) An argument x is labeled IN if all in-neighbors of x are labeled OUT. (2) An argument x is labeled OUT if there exists an in-neighbor of x with label IN. The unique preferred extension S_F is then the set of all arguments that are labeled IN.

A *value-based argumentation framework* (VAF) is a tuple $F = (X, A, V, \eta)$ where (X, A) is an argumentation framework, V is a set of *values* and η is a mapping $X \to V$ such that the graph $(\eta^{-1}(v), \{ (x, y) \in A \mid x, y \in \eta^{-1}(v) \})$ is acyclic for all $v \in V$. An *audience* $\leq$ for a VAF is a partial ordering $\leq$ on the set of values of F. Given a VAF $F = (X, A, V, \eta)$ and an audience $\leq$ for F, we define the AF $F_\leq = (X, A_\leq)$ by setting $A_\leq = \{ (x, y) \in A \mid \neg(\eta(x) < \eta(y)) \}$. An audience $\leq$ is *specific* if it is a total ordering on V. For an audience $\leq$ we also define $<$ in the obvious way, i.e., $x < y$ if and only if $x \leq y$ and $x \neq y$. Note that if $\leq$ is a specific audience, then $F_\leq = (X, A_\leq)$ is an acyclic digraph and thus, has a unique preferred extension [4]. For a VAF $F = (X, A, V, \eta)$ and a value $v \in V$ we denote by $F - v$ the VAF obtained from F by deleting all arguments with value v and all attacks involving these arguments.

Let $F = (X, A, V, \eta)$ be a VAF. We say that an argument $x_1 \in X$ is *subjectively accepted* in F if there exists a specific audience $\leq$ such that x_1 is in the unique preferred extension of $F_\leq$. Similarly, we say that an argument $x_1 \in X$ is *objectively accepted* in F if x_1 is contained in the unique preferred extension of $F_\leq$ for every specific audience $\leq$.

We consider the following decision problems.

SUBJECTIVE ACCEPTANCE
Instance: A VAF $F = (X, A, V, \eta)$ and an argument $x_1 \in X$.
Question: Is x_1 subjectively accepted in F?

OBJECTIVE ACCEPTANCE
Instance: A VAF $F = (X, A, V, \eta)$ and an argument $x_1 \in X$.
Question: Is x_1 objectively accepted in F?

Considering an instance (F, x_1) of SUBJECTIVE/OBJECTIVE ACCEPTANCE, we shall refer to the argument x_1 as the *initial argument*.

Let $F = (X, A, V, \eta)$ be a VAF. We define the *value-width* of F as the largest number of arguments with the same value, i.e., $\max_{v \in V} |\eta^{-1}(v)|$, and the *attack-width* as the cardinality of the set $\{ (x, y) \in A \mid \eta(x) = \eta(y) \}$. The *graph structure* of F is the undirected graph $G_F = (X, E)$ where $E := \{ \{u, v\} \mid (u, v) \in A \}$. We say that a VAF F is a *tree* if G_F is a tree. Similarly we say that F is *bipartite* if G_F is a bipartite graph.

3. Certifying Paths

In this section we introduce the notion of a certifying path that is key for the proofs of Theorems 1 and 2.

Let $F = (X, A, V, \eta)$ be a VAF of value-width 2. We call an odd-length sequence $C = (x_1, z_1, \ldots, x_k, z_k, t)$, $k \geq 0$, of distinct arguments a *certifying path for $x_1 \in X$ in F* if it satisfies the following conditions:

C1 For every $1 \leq i \leq k$ it holds that $\eta(z_i) = \eta(x_i)$.
C2 For every $1 \leq i \leq k$ there exists a $1 \leq j \leq i$ such that $(z_i, x_j) \in A$.
C3 For every $2 \leq i \leq k$ it holds that $(x_i, z_{i-1}) \in A$ and $N_F^+(x_i) \cap \{z_i, x_1, \ldots, x_{i-1}\} = \emptyset$.
C4 $(t, z_k) \in A$ and $N_F^+(t) \cap \{x_1, \ldots, x_k\} = \emptyset$.
C5 If there exists a $z \neq t$ with $\eta(z) = \eta(t)$ then either $(t, z) \in A$ or $N_F^+(z) \cap \{x_1, \ldots, x_k, t\} = \emptyset$.

Lemma 1. *Let $F = (X, A, V, \eta)$ be a VAF of value-width 2 and $x_1 \in X$. Then x_1 is subjectively accepted in F if and only if there exists a certifying path for x_1 in F.*

Proof. Let $C = (x_1, z_1, \ldots, x_k, z_k, t)$ be a certifying path for x_1 in F. Take a specific audience $\leq$ such that $\eta(x_1) < \cdots < \eta(x_k) < \eta(t)$ and all other values in V are smaller than $\eta(x_1)$. We claim that the unique preferred extension P of $F_\leq$ includes $\{x_1, \ldots, x_k, t\}$ and excludes $\{z_1, \ldots, z_k\}$, which means that x_1 is subjectively accepted in F. It follows from C5 that t is not attacked by any other argument in $F_\leq$ and hence $t \in P$ (see also Section 2 for a description of an algorithm to find the unique preferred extension of an acyclic AF). From C4 it follows that $z_k \notin P$. Furthermore, if there exists an argument $z \neq t$, $\eta(t) = \eta(z)$ then either $(t, z) \in A_\leq$ or there is no arc from z to an argument in $\{x_1, \ldots, x_k, t\}$. In the first case $z \notin P$ and does not influence the membership in P for any other arguments in X. In the second case $z \in P$ but there are no arcs to any argument in $\{x_1, \ldots, x_k, t\}$. In both cases it follows that $x_k \in P$. Using C3 it follows that $z_{k-1} \notin P$ and since we already know that $z_k \notin P$ it follows that $x_{k-1} \in P$. A repeated application of the above arguments establishes the claim, and hence $x_1 \in P$ follows.

Conversely, suppose that there exists a specific audience $\leq$ such that x_1 is contained in the unique preferred extension P of $F_\leq$. We will now construct a certifying path C for x_1 in F. Clearly, if there is no $z_1 \in X \setminus \{x_1\}$ with $\eta(z_1) = \eta(x_1)$ and $(z_1, x_1) \in A$, then (x_1) is a certifying path for x_1 in F. Hence, it remains to consider the case where such a z_1 exists. Since $x_1 \in P$ it follows that $z_1 \notin P$. The sequence (x_1, z_1) clearly satisfies properties C1–C3. We now show that we can always extend such a sequence until we have found a certifying path for x_1 in F. Hence, let $S = (x_1, z_1, \ldots, x_l, z_l)$ be such a sequence satisfying conditions C1–C3, and in addition assume S satisfies the following two conditions:

S1 It holds that $\eta(x_1) < \cdots < \eta(x_l)$.
S2 For every $1 \leq i \leq l$ we have $x_i \in P$ and $z_i \notin P$.

Clearly, the sequence (x_1, z_1) satisfies S1 and S2, hence we can include these conditions in our induction hypothesis. It remains to show how to extend S to a certifying path. Let $Z := \{ x' \in P \mid (x', z_l) \in A \land \eta(x') > \eta(x_l) = \eta(z_l) \}$. Then $Z \neq \emptyset$ because

$z_\ell \notin P$ by condition S2 and the assumption that P is a preferred extension. If there is a $t \in Z$ such that $(x_1, z_1, \ldots, x_l, z_l, t)$ is a certifying path for x_1 in F we are done. Hence assume there is no such $t \in Z$.

We choose $x_{l+1} \in Z$ arbitrarily. Note that C' satisfies the condition C4; $(x_{l+1}, z_l) \in A$ (as $x_{l+1} \in Z$) and $(x_{l+1}, x_i) \notin A$ for $1 \le i \le l$ (as $x_{l+1}, x_i \in P$ and P is conflict-free). Since we assume that C' is not a certifying path, C' must violate C5.

It follows that there exists some $z_{l+1} \in X$ with $\eta(z_{l+1}) = \eta(x_{l+1})$ such that $(x_{l+1}, z_{l+1}) \notin A$ and $(z_{l+1}, x_i) \in A$ for some $1 \le i \le l + 1$. We conclude that $S' = (x_1, z_1, \ldots, x_l, z_l, x_{l+1}, z_{l+1})$ satisfies conditions C1–C3 and S1–S2. Hence, we are indeed able to extend S and will eventually obtain a certifying path for x_1 in F. $\quad\square$

Lemma 2. *Let* $F = (X, A, V, \eta)$ *be a VAF of value-width 2 and* $x_1 \in X$. *Then* x_1 *is objectively accepted in* F *if and only if for every* $p \in N_F^-(x_1)$ *it holds that* $\eta(p) \ne \eta(x_1)$ *and* p *is not subjectively accepted in* $F - \eta(x_1)$.

Proof. Assume that x_1 is objectively accepted in F. Suppose there is a $p \in N_F^-(x)$ with $\eta(p) = \eta(x_1)$. If we take a specific audience $\le$ where $\eta(x_1)$ is the greatest element, then x_1 is not in the unique preferred extension of $F_\le$, a contradiction to the assumption that x_1 is objectively accepted. Hence $\eta(p) \ne \eta(x_1)$ for all $p \in N_F^-(x_1)$. Next suppose there is a $p \in N_F^-(x_1)$ that is subjectively accepted in $F - \eta(x_1)$. Let $\le$ be a specific audience such that p is in the unique preferred extension of $(F - \eta(x_1))_\le$. We extend $\le$ to a total ordering of V ensuring $\eta(x_1) \le \eta(p)$. Clearly x_1 is not in the unique preferred extension of $F_\le$, again a contradiction. Hence indeed for all $p \in N_F^-(x_1)$ we have $\eta(p) \ne \eta(x_1)$ and p is not subjectively accepted in $F - \eta(x_1)$

We establish the reverse direction by proving its counter positive. Assume that x_1 is not objectively accepted in F. We show that there exists some $p \in N_F^-(x_1)$ such that either $\eta(p) = \eta(x_1)$ or p is subjectively accepted in $F - \eta(x_1)$. Let $\le$ be a specific audience of F such that x_1 is not in the unique preferred extension P of $F_\le$. In view of the labeling procedure for finding P as sketched in Section 2, it follows that there exists some $p \in N_F^-(x_1) \cap P$ with $\eta(x_1) \le \eta(p)$. If $\eta(x_1) = \eta(p)$ then we are done. On the other hand, if $\eta(p) \ne \eta(x_1)$, then p is in the unique preferred extension of $(F - \eta(x_1))_\le$, and so p is subjectively accepted in $F - \eta(x_1)$. $\quad\square$

4. Proof of Hardness Results

Proof of Theorem 1(A). We devise a polynomial reduction from 3-SAT. Let Φ be a 3-CNF formula with clauses $C_1, \ldots, C_m$ and $C_j = x_{j,1} \vee x_{j,2} \vee x_{j,3}$ for every $1 \le j \le m$. We construct a VAF $F = (X, A, V, \eta)$ of value-width 2 and attack-width 1 such that the initial argument $x_1 \in X$ is subjectively accepted in F if and only if Φ is satisfiable. See Figure 1 for an example.

The set X contains: (i) two vertices x_j, z_j for every clause C_j; (ii) two vertices x_j^i, z_j^i for every clause C_j and $1 \le i \le 3$; (iii) one vertex t.

The set A contains: (i) one arc from z_1 to x_1; (ii) one arc from x_j^i to z_j and one arc from z_j^i to x_j for every $1 \le j \le m$ and $1 \le i \le 3$; (iii) one arc from x_{j+1} to z_j^i and one arc from z_{j+1} to x_j^i for every $1 \le j < m$ and $1 \le i \le 3$; (iv) one arc from t to z_m^i for every $1 \le i \le 3$; (v) one arc from x_j^i to $x_{j'}^{i'}$ for every $1 \le j' < j \le m$ and $1 \le i, i' \le 3$ such that $x_{j,i}$ and $x_{j',i'}$ are complementary literals.

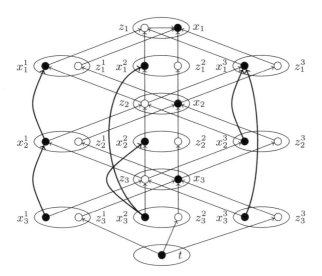

Figure 1. The instance F in the proof of Theorem 1 for the 3-CNF Formula $(x_1 \lor x_2 \lor x_3) \land (\neg x_1 \lor x_2 \lor \neg x_3) \land (x_1 \lor \neg x_2 \lor \neg x_3)$.

Let $V = \{ v_j \mid 1 \leq j \leq m \} \cup \{ v_j^i \mid 1 \leq j \leq m \land 1 \leq i \leq 3 \} \cup \{v_t\}$ be the set of values, $|V| = 4m + 1$, and let x_1 be the initial argument. The mapping η is defined such that $\eta(x_j) = \eta(z_j) = v_j$, $\eta(x_j^i) = \eta(z_j^i) = v_j^i$ for every $1 \leq j \leq m$ and $1 \leq i \leq 3$, and $\eta(t) = v_t$. It is easy to see that F has attack-width 1 and value-width 2 and can be constructed from Φ in polynomial time. It remains to show that Φ is satisfiable if and only if x_1 is subjectively accepted in F.

To see this note that every certifying path for x_1 in F must have the form $(x_1, z_1, x_1^{i_1}, z_1^{i_1}, x_2, z_2, x_2^{i_2}, z_2^{i_2}, x_3, z_3, \ldots, x_m, z_m, x_m^{i_m}, z_m^{i_m}, t)$ such that $i_j \in \{1, 2, 3\}$ for every $1 \leq j \leq m$ and for every pair $1 \leq j < j' \leq m$ there is no arc from a vertex $x_{j'}^{i_{j'}}$ to a vertex $x_j^{i_j}$. Hence there exists a certifying path for x_1 in F if and only if there exists a set L of literals that corresponds to a satisfying truth assignment of Φ (i.e., L contains a literal of each clause of Φ but does not contain a complementary pair of literals). $\square$

Proof of Theorem 1(B). Let F be the VAF as constructed in the proof of part (A) of this theorem. Let $F' = (X', A', V', \eta')$ be the VAF such that $X' := X \cup \{x_0\}$, $A' := A \cup \{(x_1, x_0)\}$, $V' := V \cup \{v_0\}$, $\eta'(x_0) = v_0$ and $\eta'(x) = \eta(x)$ for every $x \in X$. Then it is easy to see that x_0 is objectively accepted in F' if and only if Φ is not satisfiable. $\square$

5. Polynomial-Time Algorithm for Bipartite VAFs

This subsection is devoted to prove Theorem 2. Throughout this section, we assume that we are given a bipartite VAF $F = (X, A, V, \eta)$ together with an initial argument x_1. Furthermore, let X_{even} and X_{odd} be the subsets of X containing all arguments x such that the length of a shortest directed path in F from x to x_1 is even respectively odd.

Lemma 3. *Let* $C = (x_1, z_1, \ldots, x_k, z_k, t)$ *be a certifying path for* x_1 *in* F. *Then* $(\{ x_i \mid 1 \leq i \leq k \} \cup \{t\}) \subseteq X_{\text{even}}$ *and* $\{ z_i \mid 1 \leq i \leq k \} \subseteq X_{\text{odd}}$.

Proof. The claim follows easily via induction on k by using the properties of a certifying path and the fact that F is bipartite. □

Based on the observation of Lemma 3, we construct an auxiliary directed graph $H_F := (V, E)$ as follows. The vertex set of H_F is the set of values V of F and there is an arc from $v_i \in V$ to $v_j \in V$ if there is an argument $x \in X_{\text{even}}$ with $\eta(x) = v_i$ and an argument z with $\eta(z) = v_j$ such that $(x, z) \in A$. Note that $z \in X_{\text{odd}}$ since F is bipartite.

Lemma 4. *If* $C = (x_1, z_1, \ldots, x_k, z_k, t)$ *is a certifying path for* x_1 *in* F, *then* $(\eta(t), \eta(x_k), \ldots, \eta(x_1))$ *is a directed path from* $\eta(t)$ *to* $\eta(x_1)$ *in* H_F.

Proof. By the definition of a certifying path, we have $(t, z_k) \in A$ and for every $2 \leq i \leq k$ it holds that $(x_i, z_{i-1}) \in A$. Lemma 3 implies that t and x_i for every $1 \leq i \leq k$ are contained in X_{even} and hence $(\eta(t), \eta(x_k)) \in E$ and $(\eta(x_i), \eta(x_{i-1})) \in E$ for every $1 < i \leq k$. □

Lemma 4 tells us that we can limit ourselves in searching for a directed path in H_F in order to find a certifying path for x_1 in F. We want to know exactly what kind of directed path will correspond to a certifying path. To this end, we consider a subgraph $H_F^{-v_i}$ of H_F for each $v_i \in V$ obtained as follows: if there is an argument $z_i \in X_{\text{odd}}$ with $\eta(z_i) = v_i$ and there is no argument $x_i \in \eta^{-1}(v_i) \setminus \{z_i\}$ with $(x_i, z_i) \in A$, then remove every vertex $\eta(y_i)$ from H_F such that $y_i \in N_F^+(z_i)$ and $y_i \in X_{\text{even}}$. Note that if there is a $y_i \in N_F^+(z_i)$ with $\eta(y_i) = \eta(z_i)$, then we remove the vertex v_i itself from H_F.

Lemma 5. *Consider an odd-length sequence* $C = (x_1, z_1, \ldots, x_k, z_k, t)$ *of distinct arguments of a bipartite VAF* F *of value width* 2. *Then* C *is a certifying path for* x_1 *in* F *if and only if the following conditions hold:*

(1) $\eta(x_i) = \eta(z_i)$ *for* $1 \leq i \leq k$.
(2) $(\eta(t), \eta(x_k), \ldots, \eta(x_1))$ *is a directed path from* $\eta(t)$ *to* $\eta(x_1)$ *in* $H_F^{-\eta(t)}$.
(3) *None of the sub-sequences* $\eta(x_i), \ldots, \eta(x_1)$ *is a directed path from* $\eta(x_i)$ *to* $\eta(x_1)$ *in* $H_F^{-\eta(x_i)}$ *for* $1 \leq i \leq k$.

Proof. Assume $C = (x_1, z_1, \ldots, x_k, z_k, t)$ is a certifying path for x_1 in F. Property (1) follows from condition C1 of a certifying path, property (2) follows from condition C5 and Lemma 4. Property (3) follows from conditions C2 and C3.

To see the reverse assume that C satisfies properties (1)–(3). Condition C1 follows from property (1). Conditions C3, C4 and C5 follow from property (2) and the assumption that F is bipartite. Condition C2 follows from property (3). Hence C is a certifying path for x_1 in F. □

Lemma 5 suggests a simple strategy to find a certifying path for x_1 in F, if one exists. If for some $v_t \in V$ there exists a directed path P from v_t to $\eta(x_1)$ in $H_F^{-v_t}$ and v_t is the closest value to $\eta(x_1)$ with this property, then the sequence of arguments in X whose values form P is a certifying path for x_1 in F. On the other hand, if there is no such value, then there is no certifying path for x_1 in F.

We call this algorithm DETECT CERTIFYING PATH, summarized below.

1. For each $v \in V$, we check whether there is a directed path from v to $v_1 = \eta(x_1)$ in H_F^{-v}. Find a shortest path, if one exists.

2. If there exists a vertex v which has a shortest directed path $v, v_k, \ldots, v_1$ in H_F^{-v}, then among such vertices choose one with minimum k. Take the total ordering $<$ as $v_1 < \cdots < v_k < v$ and $v' < v_1$ for every $v' \in V \setminus \{v, v_1, \ldots, v_k\}$.
3. If there is no such vertex, return NO.

Proposition 1. *The algorithm* DETECT CERTIFYING PATH *correctly returns a certifying path for x_1 if one exists and returns NO otherwise in time $O(|V| \cdot (|V| + |E|))$.*

Proof. The correctness of DETECT CERTIFYING PATH follows from Lemma 5. For each $v \in V$, building H_F^{-v} and finding a shortest directed path from v to $v_1 = \eta(x_1)$, if one exists, takes $O(|V| + |E|)$ time. As we iterate over all vertices of V, the claimed running time follows. □

Proof of Theorem 2. Statement (A) of the theorem follows from Lemma 1 and Proposition 1. Statement (B) follows from Statement (A) and Lemma 2. □

6. Linear-Time Algorithm for VAFs of Bounded Treewidth

As mentioned above, it is known that SUBJECTIVE/OBJECTIVE ACCEPTANCE are intractable even when the given VAF is a tree. This is perhaps not surprising since two arguments of a tree-like VAF can be considered as linked with each other because they have the same value. In fact, such links may form cycles in an otherwise tree-like VAF. Therefore we propose to consider the *extended graph structure* of a VAF that takes such links into account. We show that SUBJECTIVE/OBJECTIVE ACCEPTANCE are easy for VAFs whose extended graph structure is a tree, and more generally, the problem can be solved in linear-time for VAFs with an extended graph structure of bounded treewidth (treewidth is a popular graph parameter that indicates in a certain sense how similar a graph is to a tree; we give a definition of treewidth below).

Let $F = (X, A, V, \eta)$ be a VAF. We define the *extended graph structure* of F as the graph $G = (X, E)$ where E contains an edge between two distinct arguments $x, y \in X$ if and only if $(x, y) \in A$ or $(y, x) \in A$ or $\eta(x) = \eta(y)$. We define the treewidth of a VAF as the treewidth of its extended graph structure.

The treewidth of a graph is defined using the following notion of a tree decomposition [5]: a *tree decomposition* of $G = (V, E)$ is a pair (T, χ) where T is a tree and χ is a labeling function with $\chi(t) \subseteq V$ for every tree node t such that the following conditions hold: (i) Every vertex of G occurs in $\chi(t)$ for some tree node t. (ii) For every edge $\{u, v\}$ of G there is a tree node t such that $u, v \in \chi(t)$. (iii) For every vertex v of G, the tree nodes t with $v \in \chi(t)$ induce a connected subtree of T. The *width* of a tree decomposition (T, χ) is the size of a largest set $\chi(t)$ minus 1 among all nodes t of T. A tree decomposition of smallest width is *optimal*. The *treewidth* of a graph G is the width of an optimal tree decomposition of G.

We are going to show Theorem 3 which states that the problems SUBJECTIVE/OBJECTIVE ACCEPTANCE can be decided in linear time for VAFs of bounded treewidth. The proof of this theorem requires some preparation. Let S denote a finite relational structure and φ a sentence in monadic second-order logic (MSO logic) on S. That is, φ may contain quantification over atoms (elements of the universe) of S and over sets of atoms of S. Furthermore, we associate with the structure S its *Gaifman graph*

$G(S)$, whose vertices are the atoms of S, and where two distinct vertices are joined by an edge if and only if they occur together in some tuple of a relation of S. The treewidth of S is the treewidth of its Gaifman graph $G(S)$.

We shall use Courcelle's celebrated result [6] that for a fixed MSO sentence φ and a fixed integer w, one can check in linear time whether φ holds for a graph (or more generally, for a relational structure) of treewidth at most w. We use Courcelle's result as laid out in Flum and Grohe's book [12].

First we explain how we represent an instance (F, x_1) of SUBJECTIVE/OBJECTIVE ACCEPTANCE as a relational structure S_F. Let $F = (X, A, V, \eta)$ be a VAF, $x_1 \in X$, and $<$ an arbitrary but fixed linear ordering of V. For every pair of values (u, v) such that $u < v$ and A contains an arc (x, x') with $\eta(x) = u$ and $\eta(x') = v$ or $\eta(x) = v$ and $\eta(x') = u$, we take a new atom $w_{(u,v)}$; let $R_<$ be the set of all such atoms. The universe of S_F is the set $X \cup V \cup R_<$. Furthermore, S_F has one unary relation U_a^* and four binary relations $H_{R_<}, T_{R_<}, B_a$ and B_η that are defined as follows:

1. $U_a^*(x)$ if and only if $x = x_1$ (used to "mark" the initial argument).
2. $T_{R_<}(t, w_{(u,v)})$ if and only if $t = u$ (used to represent the tail relation for $R_<$)
3. $H_{R_<}(h, w_{(u,v)})$ if and only if $h = v$ (used to represent the head relation for $R_<$)
4. $B_a(x, y)$ if and only if $(x, y) \in A$ (used to represent the attack relation).
5. $B_\eta(x, v)$ if and only if $\eta(x) = v$ (used to represent the mapping η).

We shall define two MSO sentences φ_s and φ_o such that φ_s is true for S_F if and only if x_1 is subjectively accepted in F, and φ_o is true for S_F if and only if x_1 is objectively accepted in F.

Before doing so, we establish that the treewidth of S_F is bounded in terms of the treewidth of F. Note that the Gaifman graph for S_F is the graph $G(S_F) = (V_{S_F}, E_{S_F})$ with $V_{S_F} = X \cup V \cup R_<$ and $E_{S_F} = \{ \{u, v\} \mid (u, v) \in T_{R_<} \cup H_{R_<} \cup B_a \cup B_\eta \}$.

Lemma 6. *The treewidth of S_F is at most twice the treewidth of F plus 1.*

Proof. Let $G'(S_F)$ be the graph obtained from $G(S_F)$ after replacing every path of the form $(t, w_{(t,h)}, h)$ by an edge $\{t, h\}$; i.e., $G'(S_F) = (X \cup V, (E_{S_F} \cap \{ \{u, v\} \mid u, v \in (X \cup V) \}) \cup \{ \{t, h\} \mid (t, h) \in R_< \}$. Conversely one can obtain $G(S_F)$ from $G'(S_F)$ by sub-dividing all edges of the form $\{t, h\}$ with a vertex $w_{(t,h)}$. However, subdividing edges does not change the treewidth of a graph [5], hence it suffices to show that the treewidth of $G'(S_F)$ is at most twice the treewidth of F plus 1. Let $\mathcal{T} = (T, \chi)$ be a tree decomposition of the extended graph structure of F. We observe that $\mathcal{T}' = (T, \chi')$ where $\chi'(t) = \chi(t) \cup \{ \eta(v) \mid v \in \chi(t) \}$ is a tree decomposition for $G'(S_F)$ where $|\chi'(t)| \leq 2 \cdot |\chi(t)|$ for all nodes t of T; hence the width of $\mathcal{T}'$ is at most twice the width of $\mathcal{T}$ plus 1. $\qquad\square$

For our subsequent considerations it is convenient to introduce the following concepts and notation. Let $D^< = (V, E^<)$ be the directed graph where V is the set of values of F and $E^< := \{ (u, v) \mid w_{(u,v)} \in R_< \}$. Furthermore, for a subset $Q \subseteq E^<$ let $D_Q^< = (V, E_{Q}^<)$ be the directed graph obtained from $D^<$ by reversing all arcs in Q, i.e., $E_Q^< := \{ (u, v) \mid (u, v) \in E^< \setminus Q) \} \cup \{ (v, u) \mid (u, v) \in E^< \cap Q \}$. We also define the AF $F_Q^< := (X, A_Q^<)$ as the AF obtained from F such that $A_Q^< := \{ (u, v) \in A \mid (\eta(u), \eta(v)) \notin E_Q^<) \}$.

Every audience $\leq$ can be represented by some subset $Q \subseteq E^<$ for which the directed graph $D_Q^\leq$ is acyclic, and conversely every set $Q \subseteq E^<$ such that $D_Q^\leq$ is acyclic represents a specific audience $\leq$. This is made precise in the following lemma whose easy proof is omitted due to space limitations.

Lemma 7. *An argument x_1 is subjectively accepted in F if and only if there exists a set $Q \subseteq E^<$ such that $D_Q^\leq$ is acyclic and x_1 is in the unique preferred extension of $F_Q^\leq$. An argument x_1 is objectively accepted in F if and only if for every set $Q \subseteq E^<$ such that $D_Q^\leq$ is acyclic it holds that x_1 is in the unique preferred extension of $F_Q^\leq$.*

We are now in the position to state the main lemma of this section.

Lemma 8. *There exists an MSO sentence φ_s such that φ_s is true for S_F if and only if x_1 is subjectively accepted in F. Similarly, there exists an MSO sentence φ_o such that φ_o is true for S_F if and only if x_1 is objectively accepted in F.*

Proof. In order to define φ_s and φ_o we need the following auxiliary formulas:

The formula $\mathrm{TH}(t, h, a)$ holds if and only if t is the tail and h is the head of $a \in R_<$:

$$\mathrm{TH}(t, h, a) := \mathrm{T}_{R_<}(t, a) \wedge \mathrm{H}_{R_<}(h, a)$$

The formula $\mathrm{E}(t, h, Q)$ holds if and only if the arc (t, h) is contained in $E_Q^\leq$:

$$\mathrm{E}(t, h, Q) := \exists a \left[(\neg Qa \wedge \mathrm{TH}(t, h, a)) \vee (Qa \wedge \mathrm{TH}(h, t, a)) \right]$$

The formula $\mathrm{ACYC}(Q)$ checks whether $D_Q^\leq$ is acyclic[2]:

$$\mathrm{ACYC}(Q) := \neg \exists C \, (\exists x Cx \wedge \forall t \exists h [Ct \rightarrow (Ch \wedge \mathrm{E}(t, h, Q))])$$

The formula $\mathrm{B}_a'(t, h, Q)$ holds if and only if t attacks h in $F_Q^\leq$:

$$\mathrm{B}_a'(t, h, Q) := \mathrm{B}_a(t, h) \wedge \exists v_h \exists v_t \left[\mathrm{B}_\eta(t, v_t) \wedge \mathrm{B}_\eta(h, v_h) \wedge \neg \mathrm{E}(v_h, v_t, Q) \right]$$

The formula $\mathrm{ADM}(S, Q)$ checks whether a set $S \subseteq X$ is admissible in $F_Q^\leq$:

$$\mathrm{ADM}(S, Q) := \forall x \forall y \left[(\mathrm{B}_a'(x, y, Q) \wedge Sy) \rightarrow (\neg Sx \wedge \exists z (Sz \wedge \mathrm{B}_a'(z, x, Q))) \right]$$

Now φ_s can be defined as follows:

$$\varphi_s := \exists Q \left[\mathrm{ACYC}(Q) \wedge (\exists S (\forall x (\mathrm{U}_a^*(x) \rightarrow Sx) \wedge \mathrm{ADM}(S, Q))) \right]$$

It follows from Lemma 7 that φ_s is true for S_F if and only if x_1 is subjectively accepted in F. A trivial modification of φ_s gives us the desired sentence φ_o as follows:

$$\varphi_o := \forall Q \left[\mathrm{ACYC}(Q) \rightarrow (\exists S (\forall x (\mathrm{U}_a^*(x) \rightarrow Sx) \wedge \mathrm{ADM}(S, Q))) \right]$$

It follows from Lemma 7 that φ_o is true for S_F if and only if x_1 is objectively accepted in F and the result follows. $\square$

Proof of Theorem 3. In view of Lemmas 6 and 8 the result now follows by Courcelle's Theorem. $\square$

---

[2] We use the well-known fact that a directed graph contains a directed cycle if and only if there is a nonempty set C of vertices each having an out-neighbor in C.

7. Conclusion

We have studied the computational complexity of persuasive argumentation for value-based argumentation frameworks under structural restrictions. We have established the intractability of deciding subjective or objective acceptance for VAFs with value-width 2 and attack-width 1, disproving conjectures stated by Dunne. It might be interesting to note that our reductions show that intractability even holds if the attack relation of the VAF under consideration forms a directed acyclic graph. On the positive side we have shown that VAFs with value-width 2 whose graph structure is bipartite are solvable in polynomial time. These results establish a sharp boundary between tractability and intractability of persuasive argumentation for VAFs with value-width 2. Furthermore we have introduced the notion of the *extended graph structure* of a VAF and have shown that subjective and objective acceptance can be decided in linear-time if the treewidth of the extended graph structure is bounded (that is, the problems are *fixed-parameter tractable* when parameterized by the treewidth of the extended graph structure). This result suggests that the extended graph structure is indeed an appropriate graphical model for studying the computational complexity of persuasive argumentation. It might be interesting for future work to extend this study to other graph-theoretic properties or parameters of the extended graph structure.

References

[1]   P. Baroni and M. Giacomin. Semantics of abstract argument systems. In I. Rahwan and G. Simari, editors, *Argumentation in Artificial Intelligence*, pages 25–44. Springer Verlag, 2009.

[2]   T. J. M. Bench-Capon. Persuasion in practical argument using value-based argumentation frameworks. *J. Logic Comput.*, 13(3):429–448, 2003.

[3]   T. J. M. Bench-Capon, S. Doutre, and P. E. Dunne. Audiences in argumentation frameworks. *Artificial Intelligence*, 171(1):42–71, 2007.

[4]   T. J. M. Bench-Capon and P. E. Dunne. Argumentation in artificial intelligence. *Artificial Intelligence*, 171(10-15):619–641, 2007.

[5]   H. L. Bodlaender. A tourist guide through treewidth. *Acta Cybernetica*, 11:1–21, 1993.

[6]   B. Courcelle. Recognizability and second-order definability for sets of finite graphs. Technical Report I-8634, Université de Bordeaux, 1987.

[7]   R. G. Downey and M. R. Fellows. *Parameterized Complexity*. Monographs in Computer Science. Springer Verlag, 1999.

[8]   P. M. Dung. On the acceptability of arguments and its fundamental role in nonmonotonic reasoning, logic programming and n-person games. *Artificial Intelligence*, 77(2):321–357, 1995.

[9]   P. E. Dunne. Computational properties of argument systems satisfying graph-theoretic constraints. *Artificial Intelligence*, 171(10-15):701–729, 2007.

[10]   P. E. Dunne and T. J. M. Bench-Capon. Complexity in value-based argument systems. In J. J. Alferes and J. A. Leite, editors, *Logics in Artificial Intelligence, 9th European Conference, JELIA 2004, Lisbon, Portugal, September 27-30, 2004, Proceedings*, volume 3229 of *Lecture Notes in Computer Science*, pages 360–371. Springer Verlag, 2004.

[11]   P. E. Dunne and M. Wooldridge. Complexity of abstract argumentation. In L. Rahwan and G. R. Simari, editors, *Argumentation in Artificial Intelligence*, pages 85–104. Springer Verlag, 2009.

[12]   J. Flum and M. Grohe. *Parameterized Complexity Theory*, volume XIV of *Texts in Theoretical Computer Science. An EATCS Series*. Springer Verlag, 2006.

Computational Models of Argument
P. Baroni et al. (Eds.)
IOS Press, 2010
© 2010 The authors and IOS Press. All rights reserved.
doi:10.3233/978-1-60750-619-5-323

Pitfalls in Practical Open Multi Agent Argumentation Systems: Malicious Argumentation

Andrew KUIPERS [a,1], Jörg DENZINGER [a]

[a] *University of Calgary, Canada*

Abstract. When an interaction mechanism such as argumentation is considered for use in open multi agent domains, such as E-Commerce or other business applications, it is necessary to consider the possibility of agents performing malicious actions. Common themes when studying malicious actions in communication protocols are that of withholding information and misrepresenting information. In argumentation, however, the use of a complex underlying formal logic allows for the possibility of another type of malicious action: the introduction of superfluous complexity into information, designed to overwhelm the reasoning capacity of another agent. We examine a malicious strategy in open multi agent systems based on exploiting the complexity of the formal logic underlying argumentation in order to manipulate the outcome of argument acceptability evaluation. Further, we briefly discuss the general problem of defensive strategies against this type of malicious argumentation, and the inherent difficulty in detecting occurrences of it.

Keywords. argumentation, open multi-agent systems, malicious agents

1. Introduction

Argumentation offers many advantages as a method of interaction in multi agent systems. In exchanges such as negotiation or deliberation, argumentation allows agents to offer formalized reasons supporting their proposed solutions, as well as specific reasons behind their rejection of solutions proposed by other agents. The expressive advantage of argumentation is dependent on an expressive underlying formal logic, which is required not only for representing solutions, but also for the reasons supporting solutions. However, logics which are sufficiently expressive, such as the first-order BDI logic used by Parsons et al. [12], are often undecidable. While this property of the underlying logic may only pose a technical difficulty in cooperative multi agent argumentation systems, in open multi agent argumentation systems [1], the undecidability of the underlying logic opens the possibility for exploitation by malicious agents.

Due to the intractable complexity of determining consequence relations in sufficiently expressive formal logics, it is often necessary to impose resource bounds on automated reasoning components used by agents in multi agent systems, in order for these

---

[1]Corresponding Author: Department of Computer Science, University of Calgary, Calgary, Canada; E-mail: amkuiper@cpsc.ucalgary.ca.

agents to make decisions in a timely fashion. What little attention has been paid to resource bounds in argumentation [10] has been focused on resource bounds as a termination condition for dialogues, particularly in situations where agents execute sequentially on a single serializable resource. Further, resource bounds placed on agents during their individual turns are dealt with by a fairness mechanism designed to distribute resources appropriately between agents. However, this conception of resource bounded argumentation fails to adequately address the situation of distributed open multi agent systems, wherein agents execute simultaneously on private resources, and protocol is insufficient for guaranteeing an equitable consumption of resources by both sides. While agents' automated reasoning procedures must still be resource bounded due to the intractability of the underlying logic, it is possible that one agent may employ resources far superior to those of another.

In a distributed open multi agent argumentation system, this resource disparity may be exploited by malicious agents towards their own interests. By employing superior resources, an agent may attempt to overwhelm the reasoning capacity of another. In this way, an agent's argument acceptability evaluation procedure may be targeted by a malicious strategy, as acceptability evaluation relies primarily on deciding the attack relation between arguments, which in turn is dependent on performing deduction in the underlying formal logic. If an argument can be modified in such a way that the resources allocated to determining attack relations onto the argument are exhausted before these relations can be decided, the argument may be attributed a higher justification status than would be warranted by an agent using an unbounded reasoning component. Using such a malicious strategy, without explicitly lying an agent may force a desired outcome from the dialogue which would not occur if the other agent had sufficient resources to thoroughly evaluate incoming arguments.

Argumentation has recently been explored as a means of interaction in Electronic Commerce and Business applications [5,4,16], and even for rights management in general open multi agent systems [1]. In such scenarios, it is imperative to consider the possibility of malicious actions performed by adversarial or self-interested agents. Similar security concerns have been studied at length in other areas such as Peer-to-Peer file sharing [9] and the constant battle against malware [14]. However, little attention has been paid to malicious agent strategies in multi agent argumentation, such as Rahwan et al.'s investigation into argumentative agents withholding information to gain an advantage [15] and Dunne's research of strategic delay tactics [8]. Before argumentation can be considered a viable means of interaction in open multi agent systems, it is necessary to study malicious argumentation strategies such as the ones presented in this paper, in order to develop adequate defenses against them.

2. Argumentation in Multi Agent Systems

We are interested in examining argumentative dialogues between agents in a multi agent system. In such systems, arguments generally represent solutions (and reasons supporting these solutions), and so arguments are taken to be structures of formulae in an underlying logical language rather than abstract entities. Further, we consider agents possessing separate knowledge bases, such that relations between arguments must be decided dynamically, as foreknowledge of all possible arguments by any one agent is impossible.

From a general perspective, such a multi agent argumentation system can be viewed as a hierarchy of five structural components:

Dialogue Game - Defines the locutions agents may utter during their interaction, and the protocol governing the interaction

Argument Evaluation - Uses acceptability semantics to evaluate arguments, the result of which is used by the agent to determine its next move in the dialogue

Argumentation Framework - Abstractly defines arguments and relations between arguments, upon which the acceptability semantics are based

Relational Semantics - Concrete definitions of relations between arguments, such as the *attack* relation, often expressed in terms of relations between formulae in the underlying logic

Underlying Logic - The formal logical language from which arguments are constructed

An argumentation framework represents arguments as abstract entities [7], which then have relations defined between them. While it is useful for theoretical purposes to abstract away from the content of arguments, argumentation systems implemented as dialogue games between agents require arguments to have content and structure, based on the underlying logic. Commonly, an argument is structured as an ordered pair (S, p), where S is a set of formulae in the underlying logical language $\mathcal{L}$ supporting a conclusion formula $p \in \mathcal{L}$. Further, the following conditions are generally imposed on this structure, and we denote the set of all arguments constructible from a knowledge base $\Sigma \subseteq \mathcal{L}$ which satisfy these conditions as $\mathcal{A}(\Sigma)$.

1. p is a logical consequence of $S : S \vdash p$
2. S is consistent : $S \nvdash \bot$
3. S is minimal with respect to set inclusion : $\neg \exists\, S' \subset S \mid S' \vdash p \wedge S' \nvdash \bot$

A common feature in all argumentation frameworks, beginning with the seminal framework of P.M. Dung [7], is the binary *attack* relation between arguments. While this relation is an abstraction away from the content of arguments from the perspective of the acceptability semantics, it is commonly realized as a relation defined between formulae in the underlying logic [12,2]. Argumentation is primarily concerned with the two attack relations introduced by J. Pollock [13], the *undercut* and *rebuttal* attack relations, which may be generally expressed as follows: Let A_1, A_2 be arguments.

$A_1 = (S_1, p_1)$ is an *undercut* of $A_2 = (S_2, p_2)$ iff $\exists s \in S_2$ such that p_1 and s conflict.
$A_1 = (S_1, p_1)$ is a *rebuttal* of $A_2 = (S_2, p_2)$ iff p_1 and p_2 conflict.

Both the *undercut* and *rebuttal* attack relations are based on the notion of *conflict* between formulae. The definition of conflict depends on the underlying logic used, yet is generally based on the property of contradiction. A contradiction in a boolean logic occurs when every interpretation maps a formula onto the truth value false, which is decided by a deductive procedure, as will be discussed in Section 3.

In an argumentative dialogue game between agents in a multi agent system, argument evaluation is needed by agents to determine which locutions to utter at each step of the dialogue. When an agent receives an argument from its opponent, the argument must be tested for acceptability with respect to the agent's knowledge base. Further, when building arguments to transmit to its opponent, an agent also employs acceptability semantics to test the viability of the arguments it constructs. We are primarily concerned with the former case, although the two are not fundamentally very different.

Argumentation has primarily focused on defining acceptability semantics in terms of computing *extensions* of the set of all arguments [7], whereby an argument's acceptability status is defined by its membership in these extensions. While there are many different extension definitions available, they are generally based on the following properties:

Conflict Free: A set of arguments S is *conflict free* iff $\forall A, B \in S : \neg attacks(A, B)$

Acceptable: An argument A is *acceptable with respect to* a set of arguments S iff for every argument B such that $attacks(B, A)$, $\exists C \in S$ such that $attacks(C, B)$

Admissible: A set of arguments S is *admissible* iff S is conflict free, and $\forall A \in S$, A is acceptable with respect to S

Computing an extension of a set of arguments then relies on computing the attack relation decision procedure between numerous arguments. When agents have disjoint knowledge bases, the set of arguments from which the extensions are computed changes during the dialogue due to argument exchange, and so these extensions must be dynamically computed by agents at each step of the dialogue.

Due to either time constraints imposed by the dialogue game protocol, or the intractability of deduction in the underlying logic, it is often necessary to impose resource bounds on the argument evaluation procedure. While it may be the case that the argument being evaluated is attacked by an argument which would result in its exclusion from the particular extension used by the agent's acceptability semantics, if the resource bounds of the argument evaluation procedure are exhausted before this attack relation can be decided, the argument may be determined to be acceptable where otherwise it would not. An agent may therefore construct arguments designed to exhaust the resource bounds of its opponents argument evaluation procedure, in order to manipulate the arguments' acceptability status, ultimately affecting the outcome of the dialogue as a whole. Towards this end, in Section 5 we examine strategies for this form of malicious argumentation, in Section 6 we present a concrete example of such malicious argumentation, and in Section 7 we discuss defense strategies against this form of malicious argumentation.

3. Deduction Systems

On a high level, a *logic* can be seen as a triple $(\mathcal{L}, \mathcal{W}, \mathcal{I})$, where $\mathcal{L}$ is the set of correctly formed formulae used by the logic, usually recursively defined using function and predicate symbols, variable symbols, logical operators and quantifiers, $\mathcal{W}$ is a set of truth values, and $\mathcal{I}$ is a set of interpretations where each interpretation links terms in formulae to some objects in a domain of interest to the user of the logic, predicate symbols to predicates in the domain using the values in $\mathcal{W}$ and formulae to truth values in $\mathcal{W}$. For most usages of a logic, a user is interested in determining if a particular formula is interpreted by all interpretations in $\mathcal{I}$ to a particular truth value $w \in \mathcal{W}$. For example, in first-order predicate logic, the set $\mathcal{I}$ contains all possible interpretations (that interpret the logical operators and quantifiers in the usual way) over the set $\mathcal{W} = \{\text{true},\text{false}\}$. And the interest of users are tautologies, i.e. formulae that are interpreted to true by every $I \in \mathcal{I}$.

While the use of interpretations to identify the interests of users is convenient from a theoretical perspective, especially when looking at creating logics with symbols that should be specially interpreted, like the higher-order predicates in BDI-logics, this use is not exactly helpful in creating practical reasoning systems. For this, appropriate calculi and deduction systems are needed. A *calculus* is a pair $(\mathcal{R}, Ax)$, where $\mathcal{R}$ is a set of inference rules and $Ax \subseteq \mathcal{L}$ a set of formulae that are used to ground the deduction process. Depending on the calculus, the axioms in Ax either define a starting point or end conditions for a search in the search space defined by the inference rules, and the formulae forming the problem instance define end conditions or the starting point (whatever is not defined by the axioms). For example, the resolution calculus (as used by Prover9, see [11]) has two inference rules, resolution and factorization, the set Ax contains only the empty clause, signalling the end condition of the search (i.e. if the empty clause has been generated), and the initial formula that is attempted to be proven as a tautology is negated and then transformed into a set of clauses that forms the start state of the search. For very simple logics, a calculus can also be just looking up formulae from Ax and adding them to the search state, with an end criterion that stops the search when the formula of interest is in the current search state. A calculus for a logic needs to be at least correct, i.e. if a particular search ends up fulfilling the end condition then the problem instance is indeed interpreted by all interpretations of the logic to the particular truth value.

For a given problem instance, most calculi allow for many possible ways how the search is performed, because usually many different applications of inference rules are possible in a search state. So, a *deduction system* uses a calculus and adds to it a *search control* that decides which of the many inference rule applications is performed to create the next search state. Different search controls usually result in very different sequences of search states that often are of quite different length. Therefore many deduction systems, like Prover9, offer users quite a variety of search controls using quite different types of knowledge (see, for example, [6]). As an example, the primitive calculus looking up axioms can have a search control that simply goes through the list of possible (pre-computed) axioms one after the other, but another search control could use a hash table to just go through the conflict set for the hash table entry that corresponds to the formula(e) to the problem instance.

4. Resource Bounded Argumentation

As already stated, it is often necessary to impose resource bounds on the computations performed by agents in a multi agent system. In argumentative multi agent dialogues, this may be realized as resource constraints imposed on turns in the dialogue, as well as constraints on the dialogue overall, as seen in [10]. Here, we are primarily concerned with the former situation, whereby agents have a limited amount of resources to decide the locution to utter during their turn in the dialogue.

Given that deciding attack relations between arguments is a component procedure of argument evaluation, which in turn is a component procedure of locution decision, the resource limit of the attack relation decision procedure is maximally bounded by the resource limit of the locution decision procedure. If determining conflict between formulae in arguments tested by the attack relation requires greater resources than are allocated to locution decision, then whatever resources are allocated to the attack relation will be insufficient to establish the conflict.

For simplicity's sake, we describe the resource limit of the attack relation decision procedure as a limit on the number of inference steps performed in deduction, as in [10]. We use the notation $\vdash_k$ to denote practical deductive inference limited to at most k inference rule applications, such that if the deduction system can generate a proof for $\phi \vdash \psi$ in k or less inference steps, then $\phi \vdash_k \psi$, otherwise $\phi \nvdash_k \psi$. The conflict relation between formulae, and therefore the attack relation between arguments, can now be defined as resource bounded relations limited by the number of inference steps involved. For instance, a resource bounded undercut relation can be defined as:

An argument $A_1 = (S_1, p_1)$ is an *undercut*$_k$ of an argument $A_2 = (S_2, p_2)$ iff $\exists s \in S_2$ such that $\{p_1, s\} \vdash_k \bot$

Abstracting away from the specific implementation of the attack relation as undercut and/or rebuttal, we denote an attack relation decision procedure limited to at most k inference steps as $attacks_k$. Note that if the deduction system cannot establish a contradiction between p_1 and s in k or less inference steps, it is assumed p_1 and s do not contradict, and so A_1 does not attack A_2. We could assume instead that two formulae contradict in the case that the resource bounds are exhausted before the contradiction is found, in order to deal with the malicious strategies presented in Section 6.3. Such an approach would be practically infeasible, however, as determining that $\{p_1, s\} \nvdash \bot$ requires the exhaustion of all possible applications of inference rules (without coming to a contradiction). The resource bounds of the prover will often be exhausted before this can be established, and so such an approach would lead to many false positives identifying attack relations between arguments where none exist.

5. Malicious Argumentation Strategies

We are concerned with malicious argumentation strategies in which agents modify the content of their arguments in order to exploit the computational complexity of decision procedures in their adversaries to affect the outcome of these decision procedures. This is notably distinct from other cases of malicious argumentation, where agents may withhold information [15], employ delay tactics [8] or explicitly lie in order to affect the outcome of the interaction. Further, we specifically focus on malicious strategies designed to overwhelm the deduction component used to determine conflict between formulae in arguments, with the goal of affecting the outcome of the attack relation decision procedure used in argument evaluation.

Determining conflict amongst a set of formulae, such as contradiction, requires a procedure of deductive inference, as discussed in Section 3. Knowledge of the deduction component employed for this purpose by an agent's adversary will allow an agent to simulate this procedure and determine a minimal bound for the number of inference steps required to deduce a conflict. Given knowledge of the maximal resource bound of the adversary's automated reasoning component[2] k, an agent may construct an argument A_1 for which its adversary has an argument A_2 such that $attacks(A_2, A_1)$, yet given the adversary's resource limit k, $\neg attacks_k(A_2, A_1)$.

---

[2]which can, for instance, be determined using knowledge of the resource limit imposed on locution decision by the protocol, as discussed in Section 4, or approximated by other means

6. An Example of Malicious Argumentation

We consider now an example situation in which malicious argumentation can occur. After a description of the system, we shall first consider a "normal" interaction wherein an agent presents an unacceptable argument, and the other agent responds with an attack on the argument. We then describe modifications to the argument's support that could be used to exhaust the resource bounds of the other agent's automated reasoner before it can deduce the existence of the attack relation on the argument, in order to render the unacceptable argument acceptable under the given resource limitations.

6.1. Example System

In this example, a company uses a task postings board to list requests for certain components to be designed and constructed by outside contractors. The items listed on this board contain the functional requirements of the components to be designed, written as formal specifications in first-order logic, and possibly other requirements, also in first-order logic. A manager agent a_m is then responsible for testing the acceptability of design arguments proposed by a contractor agent a_c, responding with an attacking argument if the design is found to be unacceptable.

6.1.1. Example Semantics

The specifications, as well as the design proposed by contractor agents, make use of a shared catalogue language Σ_{cat} based on a common ontology of symbols and concepts Γ_{cat}, which describes myriad parts, properties and functionalities available to the company and their contractors. Along with the design specification $\Theta_{spec} \subset \Sigma_{cat}$, the company also publishes a set of conditions $\Theta_{int} \subset \Sigma_{cat}$, which describes internal corporate policies or other knowledge apart from the design specifications that may be used to attack design proposal arguments. Designs proposed by contractors then must have a conclusion that satisfies Θ_{spec}, and be acceptable with relation to $\Theta_{spec} \cup \Theta_{int}$.

The following predicates are used by a_m to describe design specifications and other internal conditions, and also by a_c in the design proposal.

$$
\begin{array}{ll}
UseC(X) & : \text{design uses component X} \\
HasP(X,Y) & : \text{component X has property Y} \\
ProvF(X,Y) & : \text{component X provides function Y} \\
Conn(X,Y) & : \text{component X connected to component Y}
\end{array}
$$

6.1.2. Testing Acceptability

Rather than describing a full dialogue between the agents, we shall focus here on the initial assert locution in which a_c proposes a design argument $A_D = (S_D, p_D)$, and a_m tests the acceptability of this argument, responding with an attacking argument if one is found. Due to resource constraints, a_m will impose an inference count limit k on the process of determining argument acceptance, as described in Section 4; we do not, however, consider any resource constraints placed on a_c, as we are concerned here only with the process of resource bound acceptance used by a_m which may be exploited by malicious agents.

In order to determine the acceptability of A_D with respect to its internal knowledge Θ_{int} and the design specifications Θ_{spec}, agent a_m will attempt to construct an argument $A_A = (S_A, p_A)$ from the formulae in $\Theta_{spec} \cup \Theta_{int}$ such that $attacks(A_A, A_D)$. We will herein focus on the undercut attack relation described in Section 2, which is limited by the resource bound k, such that a_m will need to test the resource bounded attack relation decision procedure $undercut_k(A_A, A_D)$. To accomplish this, a_m will need to employ its automated reasoner to determine whether $\exists(S_A, p_A) \in \mathcal{A}(\Theta_{spec} \cup \Theta_{int})$ such that $S_D \cup \{p_A\} \vdash_k \perp$. While argument evaluation as described in Section 2 is more complicated than simply testing a single attack relation, for the sake of brevity we focus on a single attack relation decision, which will nonetheless be a component of argument evaluation. In the case that an argument A_A cannot be found such that $undercut_k(A_A, A_D)$, then A_D will be considered acceptable.

6.1.3. Automated Reasoning Component

In this example, we make use of first-order predicate logic for the underlying logic of the argumentation system, similar to the approaches found in [12,3,1]. For experimental purposes, we make use of the Prover9 automated theorem prover [11]. While Prover9 allows the use of several variants of the resolution calculus, to keep our example simple, we configure it to use only the binary resolution inference rule (and factorization). Further, we have modified the Prover9 system to impose a limit on the number of inference steps performed during the search for a proof, which we use as the resource limit of the deduction component.

6.2. "Normal" Interaction Scenario

In this example, the manager agent a_m has posted a request for a design of a component which can produce fixed amplitude waveforms of 20mA at a frequency of 30Hz, represented by *amp20mA* and *genFreq30Hz* respectively. This is represented in the formal semantics defined above as :

$$\exists x : ProvF(x, genFreq30Hz) \wedge HasP(x, amp20mA). \tag{C_1}$$

6.2.1. The Design Proposal

An external contractor agent a_c analyzes this request and uses it's knowledge of various electric components to construct a design which incorporates the WG3000 wave generator. However, it's knowledge of this component specifies that the WG3000 must be connected to an adequate power supply in order to function, which is represented as:

$$HasP(wg3000, amp20mA). \tag{C_2}$$

$$\exists x : (UseC(wg3000) \wedge Conn(x, wg3000) \wedge ProvF(x, power20mA)) \\ \rightarrow ProvF(x, genFreq30Hz). \tag{C_3}$$

Agent a_c also has knowledge of a specific power supply which can be used for this purpose, the PSU423, which provides the necessary 20mA output required for use with the WG3000.

$$UseC(psu423) \rightarrow ProvF(psu423, power20mA). \tag{C_4}$$

Along with the specifications of the components described in $C_2, ..., C_4$, agent a_c must include design specifications on their use and interconnections, expressed as:

$$UseC(wg3000) \wedge UseC(psu423) \wedge Conn(psu423, wg3000). \qquad (C_5)$$

The design is expressed by agent a_c as the argument $A_D = (S_D, p_D) = (\{C_2, ..., C_5\}, C_1)$[3]. Upon receipt of the proposal from a_c, agent a_m can verify the argument's validity as described in Section 2, by testing that $C_2 \wedge ... \wedge C_5 \vdash C_1$ using it's automated reasoner, as well as the conditions that $C_2 \wedge ... \wedge C_5 \nvdash \bot$ and $\neg \exists S' \subset \{C_2, ..., C_5\} : S' \nvdash \bot \wedge S' \vdash C_1$.

6.2.2. The Attacking Argument

However, let us assume that a_m has a further condition in Θ_{int} which specifies that the component must be compliant with the Restriction of Hazardous Substances (RoHS) directive, which agent a_c has not taken into account in its design:

$$\forall x : UseC(x) \leftrightarrow HasP(x, rohsCompliant). \qquad (C_6)$$

Included in this directive is a restriction on the use of various toxic substances, including the use of lead:

$$\forall x : HasP(x, rohsCompliant) \leftrightarrow$$
$$\neg(HasP(x, containsLead) \vee HasP(x, containsCadmium) \qquad (C_7)$$
$$\vee HasP(x, containsHexavalentChromium)).$$

Further, a_m has the knowledge that the PSU423 power supply unit contains lead:

$$HasP(psu423, containsLead). \qquad (C_8)$$

The clauses C_6, C_7 and C_8 can then be used as support for the conclusion:

$$\neg UseC(psu423). \qquad (C_9)$$

This can be formed into the argument $A_A = (S_A, p_A) = (\{C_6, C_7, C_8\}, C_9)$. Through the use of it's automated reasoner, a_m can determine that $p_A \cup S_D \vdash \bot$ due to the conflicting clauses $UseC(psu423)$ and $\neg UseC(psu423)$, and so the argument A_A attacks the argument A_D. To test this example, the Prover9 automated theorem prover was configured to use the standard simple weighted term selection search control. In this configuration, it took the prover a single inference step to prove that $p_A \cup S_D \vdash \bot$, and so the prover could determine that $p_A \cup S_D \vdash_k \bot$ for any $k \geq 1$. Agent a_m can now respond to a_c with the attacking argument A_A.

---

[3]Formulae are entered into the theorem prover in the order they appear here

6.3. Malicious Argumentation Scenario

Knowing the attack to the argument A_D described above, a_c could make use of a resource exhaustion strategy to overwhelm agent a_m's deductive reasoning capacity before a_m can determine that its argument A_A attacks A_D. This would be of advantage to a_c if, for example, it has a surplus of PSU423 units and needs to get rid of them. Using further knowledge of the automated reasoner used by a_m, such as the resource bounds and the search control[4], a_c can modify the argument A_D so that a_m will not find the contradiction within the given inference limit, in which case a_m will accept the argument (see Section 4).

6.3.1. Implication Chaining

This new argument A'_D can be constructed by modifying the clause C_5 to move the contradicting term $UseC(psu423)$ deep enough in the search space so that it cannot be resolved with the term $\neg UseC(psu423)$ before the inference limit is reached. A simple method of pushing the contradictory term further in the search space is to modify it to be the consequent of a chain of implications. An example of this would be to create a sequence of fake parts, whose use implies the use of the next fake part in the sequence, and finally the part in question. The clause C_5 can then be rewritten as:

$$UseC(wg3000) \wedge UseC(fake_1) \wedge UseC(fake_1) \rightarrow UseC(fake_2) \wedge$$
$$... \wedge UseC(fake_{n-1}) \rightarrow UseC(fake_n) \wedge \qquad (C_5^n)$$
$$UseC(fake_n) \rightarrow UseC(psu423) \wedge Conn(psu423, wg3000).$$

Note that this modification of the argument's support still does not violate the minimality criteria of arguments presented in Section 2, as the removal of any one of these added clauses would violate the condition that $S \vdash p$[5].

To test the attack relation between the new argument A'_D and the attacking argument A_A, agent a_m's resource bounded automated reasoner is used to determine:

$$\{C_2, ..., C_4, C_5^n\} \cup \{\neg UseC(psu423)\} \vdash_k \bot \qquad (P_1)$$

If the resource limit k is exhausted before P_1 can be proven by resolving the terms $UseC(psu423)$ and $\neg UseC(psu423)$ to a contradiction, then it cannot be established that $attacks_k(A_A, A_D)$. To demonstrate the use of this method of resource exhaustion, Prover9 is used to test P_1 with incremental values of k. Values of n for the clause C_2^n were then found which exceed k inferences before P_1 is proven. The results of this can be found in Table 1.

6.3.2. Tautology Injection

A further method of exhausting resource bounds was implemented, by rewriting the contradictory term to be the consequent of an implication whose antecedent is a tautology. After transformation into clauses, the tautology must first be resolved before the consequent can be established, and so the contradictory term can be pushed deeper into the

---

[4]If a_m uses a commercially available argumentation system, knowledge of these factors would not be unreasonable

[5]In general, this minimality criterion is, from a deduction perspective, very questionable.

search space. Similar to the method of implication chaining discussed above, this method can be scaled in order to exceed specific resource bounds by conjoining multiple instances of tautologies (possibly the same one) to form the antecedent of the implication. The clause C_5 in the example can then be rewritten as:

$$UseC(wg3000) \wedge ((((a_1 \rightarrow b_1) \wedge (b_1 \rightarrow c_1)) \rightarrow (a_1 \rightarrow c_1))$$
$$\wedge ... \wedge (((a_n \rightarrow b_n) \wedge (b_n \rightarrow c_n)) \rightarrow (a_n \rightarrow c_n))) \qquad (C_5^{n'})$$
$$\rightarrow UseC(psu423) \wedge Conn(psu423, wg3000).$$

As with the method of implication chaining, experiments were run using Prover9 to determine the value of n necessary to exceed specific inference count limits k. The results of this are shown in Table 2.

inference limit (k)	chain length (n)
100	49
200	99
300	149
400	199
500	249

Table 1. Results for Implication Chains

inference limit (k)	repetitions (n)
100	3
200	3
300	3
400	4
500	4

Table 2. Results for Tautology Injection

7. Possible Defense Strategies

There are several obvious counters to the kind of malicious argumentation that our examples from the last section represent. Similar to anti-virus software, an agent could have stored patterns of commonly used malicious argumentation and check an argument for occurrence of these patterns (see [14]). If a pattern occurs, this would be considered as an attack to this argument, perhaps even as a reason for terminating the whole dialog. Also similar to anti-virus software, there is naturally the danger of false positives, so that we, again, might reject legitimate arguments. And since checking for a pattern is essentially a kind of inference rule (for a new logic that explicitly deals with malicious argumentation), there is again the possibility for resource exhaustion strategies, if the number of patterns is too big. This might require that malicious users set an agent up via a series of dialogues, but this just shows how much danger malicious argumentation represents.

So, just dealing with the ideas behind our two example strategies to avoid malicious argumentation will not result in clear cut solutions. But there are many more possibilities how superfluous information may be added to an argument. Only with an unbound and decidable reasoner would it be possible to determine argument acceptability in general. As this is often impractical, implementations of argumentation systems which have to deal with potentially malicious agents must develop strategies to handle attempts to purposefully exhaust resource bounds, even if these defense strategies must necessarily be imperfect. If no attempt is made to detect malicious argumentation, the simplest methods, like the ones used in our examples, may be used to confound an agent into accepting unacceptable arguments.

In general, from a practical point of view, argumentation needs to join the many other areas that have to deal with malicious agents and has to accept that it will have to participate in an "arms race" to keep its systems from being abused (respectively, to establish enough trust in them by the non-malicious users to really use them). And, similar to these other areas, it has to be the goal to stay a few steps ahead of the amateur malicious users, the analogues to the "script-kiddies" from the virus world.

8. Conclusion and Future Work

In this paper, we provided examples for how malicious agents may construct arguments designed to exhaust the resource bounds of another agent's automated reasoning component, highlighting the danger of malicious argumentation in practical applications. By doing this, arguments which would be otherwise unacceptable (if given sufficient time to complete the deductions) can be made acceptable to that agent, given knowledge of the resource bounds and operation of its automated reasoning component.

By accepting the possibility of malicious argumentation as described above, there are many future research possibilities. As already mentioned, integrating techniques to deal with malicious arguments into the logic and/or the argumentation framework is of interest. Further, collecting all kinds of malicious arguments is obviously a necessary step in trying to establish defenses against them.

References

[1]   E. Alonso. Rights and Argumentation in Open Multi-Agent Systems. *Artificial Intelligence Review* 21, 2004, pp. 3–24.
[2]   L. Amgoud, N. Maudet, and S. Parsons. Modeling Dialogues Using Argumentation. *Proc. ICMAS 2000*, Boston, 2000, pp. 31–38.
[3]   P. Besnard and A. Hunter. Practical First-Order Argumentation. *Proc. AAAI 20*, 2005, pp. 590–595.
[4]   L. Brito and J. Neves. Argument exchange in heterogeneous electronic commerce environments. *Proc. AAMAS-02*, Bologna, 2002, pp. 410–417.
[5]   L. Brito and J. Neves. Properties and Complexity in Feasible Logic-Based Argumentation for Electronic Commerce. *Proc. 8th IBERAMIA*, Seville, 2002, pp. 90–100.
[6]   J. Denzinger and M. Fuchs. A Comparison of Equality Reasoning Heuristics, in W. Bibel, P.H. Schmitt (eds.): Automated Deduction. A basis for applications. Vol. II, Kluwer, 1998, pp. 361–382.
[7]   P.M. Dung. On the Acceptability of Arguments and its Fundamental Role in Nonmonotonic Reasoning and Logic Programming. *Proc. IJCAI-93*, Chamberry, 1993, pp. 852–859.
[8]   P.E. Dunne. Prevarication in Dispute Protocols. *Proc. ICAIL-03*, Edinburgh, 2003, pp. 12–21.
[9]   T. Locher, P. Moor, S. Schmid, and R. Wattenhofer. Free riding in BitTorrent is cheap. *Proc. HotNets-V*, Irvine, 2006, pp. 85–90.
[10] R.P. Loui. Process and Policy: Resource-Bounded Nondemonstrative Reasoning. *Computational Intelligence* 14, 1998, pp. 1–38.
[11] W.   McCune.   Prover9   Manual.   http://www.cs.unm.edu/~mccune/mace4/manual/Aug-2007/, as seen on Oct. 7, 2009.
[12] S. Parsons, C. Sierra and N. Jennings. Agents that Reason and Negotiate by Arguing. *J. Logic Computat.* 8(3), 1998, pp. 261–292.
[13] J. Pollock. Defeasible Reasoning. *Cognitive Science* 11(4), 1987, pp. 481–518.
[14] M.D. Preda, M. Christodorescu, S. Jha, and S.K. Debray. A semantics-based approach to malware detection. *ACM Trans. Program. Lang. Syst.* 30(5), 2008.
[15] I. Rahwan and K. Larson. Mechanism Design for Abstract Argumentation. *Proc. AAMAS 2008*, 2008, pp. 1031–1039.
[16] C. Sierra. Agent-Mediated Electronic Commerce. *JAAMAS* 9(3), 2004, pp. 285–301.

Computational Models of Argument
P. Baroni et al. (Eds.)
IOS Press, 2010
doi:10.3233/978-1-60750-619-5-335

Integrating Dialectical and Accrual Modes of Argumentation

Sanjay Modgil[1], Trevor Bench-Capon

Department of Computer Science, University of Liverpool

Abstract. This paper argues that accrual should be modelled in terms of reasoning about the application of preferences to sets of arguments, and shows how such reasoning can be formalised within metalevel argumentation frameworks. These frameworks adopt the same machinery and level of abstraction as Dung's argumentation framework. We thus provide a dialectical argumentation semantics that integrates accrual, and illustrate our approach by instantiating our framework with the arguments and attacks defined by an object level formalism that accommodates reasoning about priorities over sets of rules.

Keywords. Dialectical, Accrual, Metalevel, Preferences, Abstract Argumentation.

1. Introduction

Many applications of argumentation build on Dung's seminal theory [3] and its various developments. A Dung *argumentation framework* (*AF*) consists of a binary conflict based *attack* relation R on a set A of arguments. A 'dialectical calculus' is then applied to evaluate the justified and rejected arguments. Amongst developments of AFs are those that evaluate arguments only w.r.t successful attacks (*defeats*), where x defeats y only if x attacks y, and y is not stronger than x [1,2,7].

The continuing impact of Dung's theory can be attributed to its level of abstraction, and encoding of intuitive general principles of commonsense reasoning in the dialectical calculus. One defines what constitutes an argument and attack for a logic $\mathcal{L}$, so that an AF can be instantiated by the arguments and attacks defined by a theory in $\mathcal{L}$. The theory's inferences are then defined in terms of the claims of the justified arguments, as has been shown for logic programming formalisms and a number of non-monotonic logics (Dung's theory can therefore be viewed as a *dialectical semantics* for these logics).

However, this dialectical mode of argumentation fails to accommodate the intuition that the strengths of arguments may *accrue*: while an argument x claiming c is justified at the expense of arguments $y1$ and $y2$ independently claiming $\neg c$, the *combined* strength of $y1$ and $y2$ can mean that they should collectively prevail over x. Accrual may apply when evidence for and against is used to establish the truth of the matter. While in some areas it may be sensible to use Bayesian reasoning to come to an overall estimate of the probability of the hypothesis, in other cases this is not appropriate. Consider a witness testifying that P. One does not adduce some quantifiable probability of the truth of P;

---

[1]Corresponding Author: Sanjay Modgil, E-mail: sanjaymodgil@yahoo.co.uk.

rather one presumptively believes P. If another witness testifies the opposite, and neither witness can be discredited, then one must make a *judgement* as to who will be believed. Given several witnesses, then the witness judged to be individually the most credible may be rejected on the basis of the cumulative weight of conflicting testimony from a number of individually less credible witnesses. Accrual may also apply in decision making contexts requiring a subjective judgement or *choice*. Consider arguments supplying reasons for alternative holiday destinations. These do not force a decision, but additionally need a subjective commitment to the relative worth of the reasons they supply. It may be that the ideal destination would have good weather, food and cultural facilities. But if a paradise offering all three cannot be found, one may need to *choose* between a place with good weather and one with culture and food. One may prefer good weather to either culture or food individually, but the *combination* of the latter two may incline one towards the second possibility. We are thus interested in cases involving judgement of evidence for which a probability based treatment is not sensible, and cases requiring a choice, where a decision must be made on the basis of weighing arguments for and against. While techniques such as Multiattribute Utility Theory have been applied to such problems, they have proved problematical in practice, and fail to model actual decision-making which typically takes place in circumstances of relative ignorance. Like [11] we advocate a treatment reflecting 'quick-and-dirty' commonsense reasoning, where people reason under resource limitations and with coarse qualitative approximations to the truth.

In [11], both the *knowledge representation* (*kr*) and *inference* approaches to accrual are reviewed. In the former (e.g. [10,12]) accruals are encoded in the knowledge base, so that as well as distinct rules (and thus arguments) expressing that P is a reason for R and Q is a reason for R, there is an additional rule (and hence argument) for P *and* Q being a reason for R, and the strength of the various accruals is expressed through a priority relation on the rules. In the inference approach (e.g., [5,6,11,13]), that [11] argues has advantages over the *kr* approach, the object level inference rules permit construction of 'super-arguments' that combine individual rules that yield the same conclusion.

This paper argues for and formalises an approach to accrual that is distinct from existing approaches in two important respects. Firstly, accrual is not handled through additional arguments, whether deriving from explicit rules or from the inference mechanism. Rather, we argue that accrual is more properly effected in the (subjective) evaluation of arguments; specifically in the reasoning about and application of preferences. We thus avoid the proliferation of rules required by the *kr* approach, many of which are somewhat artificial given that their premises are entirely independent of one another. In contrast to the inference approach we respect the individuality of the accrued arguments; they continue to provide separate orthogonal reasons for the conclusions rather than a combined super-reason. Secondly, we provide an abstract integration of accrual and dialectical argumentation. We make use of the recently introduced Metalevel Argumentation Frameworks (*MAF*s) [8] to integrate argumentation based reasoning about preferences and their application, with the object level arguments being evaluated. Since *MAF*s adopt the same basic machinery of a Dung AF, we thus integrate accrual within the dialectical mode of argumentation, and therefore provide an abstract dialectical semantics for object level logical formalisms incorporating mechanisms for accrual.

In Section 2 we review background concepts. Section 3 formalises integration of accrual in *MAF*s, and relates the formalisation to [11]'s principles of accrual. In Section 4, we show how our formalism provides both a dialectical and accrual based semantics for an object level logic in which one can reason about priorities over sets of rules. We conclude with a discussion of related and future work in Section 5.

2. Background

A Dung AF is a tuple (A, R), where $R \subseteq (A \times A)$ is an attack relation on arguments A. $x \in A$ is said to be *acceptable* w.r.t. $S \subseteq A$ iff $\forall y \in A$ s.t yRx, implies $\exists z \in S$ s.t. zRy. If S is conflict free (i.e., $\forall x, y \in S$, $(x, y) \notin R$), and all arguments in S are acceptable w.r.t. S, then S is said to be an *admissible* extension. The status of arguments is then evaluated w.r.t. extensions defined under different semantics:

Definition 1 Let S be an admissible extension of (A, R).

• S is *complete* iff S contains all arguments in A which are acceptable w.r.t S; *grounded* iff S is the minimal (w.r.t. set inclusion) *complete* extension; *preferred* iff S is a maximal *complete* extension, and *stable* iff $\forall y \notin S$, $\exists x \in S$ s.t. $(x, y) \in R$

• For $s \in \{\text{complete, preferred, grounded, stable}\}$:
If $x \in A$ is in at least one, respectively all, s extension(s) of (A, R), then x is said to be credulously, respectively sceptically, justified under the s semantics.

For the examples in this paper, we will assume justified arguments as evaluated under the sceptical preferred semantics (although these will always coincide with the grounded semantics), and will also refer to the labelling based evaluation of arguments [9] to assist the reader's processing of the example AFs shown. A legal labelling assigns to $x \in A$: i) 1 iff $\forall y$ s.t. yRx, $y = 0$; ii) 0 iff $\exists y$ s.t. yRx and $y = 1$, and; iii) u (for undecided) iff neither i) or ii) hold. The arguments in a preferred extension are then those labelled 1 in a legal labelling with a maximal set of arguments labelled 1.

More recently, Metalevel Argumentation Frameworks (*MAF*s) [8] categorise meta-arguments according to the claims they make *about* object level arguments and their properties and relations. These meta-arguments are organised into a Dung AF whose meta-attack relation obeys constraints imposed by the claim based characterisation.

Definition 2 A MAF is a tuple $\Delta_\mathcal{M} = (\mathcal{A}, \mathcal{R}, \mathcal{C}, \mathcal{L}, \mathcal{D})$, where $(\mathcal{A}, \mathcal{R})$ is a Dung AF, and:

- $\mathcal{L}$ consists of a countable set of constant symbols and includes the predicates: $\{\, justified, defeat, rejected, preferred \,\}$. The set $wff(\mathcal{L})$ is defined by the following BNF (x, x_i range over constant symbols)[2]:
$$\mathcal{L} : X ::= x, \{x_1, \ldots, x_n\} \mid justified(X) \mid rejected(X) \mid defeat(X, X') \mid preferred(X, X')$$

- The claim function $\mathcal{C}$ is defined as $\mathcal{C} : \mathcal{A} \mapsto 2^{wff(\mathcal{L})}$

- $\mathcal{D}$ is a set of constrains on $\mathcal{R}$ of the form:
   if $l \in \mathcal{C}(\alpha)$ and $l' \in \mathcal{C}(\beta)$ then $(\alpha, \beta) \in \mathcal{R}$

• $\mathcal{R}$ is said to be *defined by* $\mathcal{D}$ if whenever $(\alpha, \beta) \in \mathcal{R}$ then the claims of α and β satisfy the antecedent of some constraint in $\mathcal{D}$.

• The extensions and justified arguments of $\Delta_\mathcal{M}$ are the extensions and justified arguments of $(\mathcal{A}, \mathcal{R})$.

---

[2]In [8] $\mathcal{L}$ also includes *val*, *val_pref*, *audience* and wff constructed from these predicates.

Henceforth, we may use abbreviations j, r, d and p for $justified, rejected, defeat$ and $preferred$ respectively. We may also denote an argument by its claims. E.g, if $\mathcal{C}(\gamma) = \{defeat(preferred(\{a1, a2\}, \{b\}), defeat(b, a1))\}$, we may denote γ by $d(p(\{a1, a2\}, b), d(b, a1))$.

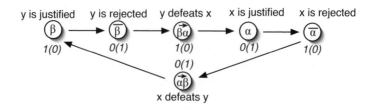

Figure 1. The MAF characterisation of a Dung AF $x \rightleftarrows y$

The basic idea of metalevel argumentation is that given an object level AF, (A, R), then the existence of an argument $x \in A$, constitutes a meta-argument $\alpha \in \mathcal{A}$ of the form 'there is an $x \in A$ that is an admissible extension of (A, R)', supporting the claim that 'x *is justified*'. The existence of an object level attack yRx, constitutes a meta-argument $\overrightarrow{\beta\alpha}$ = 'y successfully attacks x' that supports the claim 'y defeats x'. Since the justified status of x in the object level framework is challenged by a defeat on x, then $\overrightarrow{\beta\alpha}$ attacks α at the metalevel, and so we have the following constraint on the meta-level attack relation $\mathcal{R}$ (V, W, X, Y, Z will henceforth range over wff of $\mathcal{L}$):

D1 : if $d(Y, X) \in \mathcal{C}(\gamma)$ and $j(X) \in \mathcal{C}(\alpha)$ then $(\gamma, \alpha) \in \mathcal{R}$

y does not defeat x if y is rejected, and so $\overrightarrow{\beta\alpha}$ is attacked by a meta-argument $\overline{\beta}$ claiming 'y is rejected'. However, y does defeat x if y is justified, and so β claiming 'y is justified' attacks $\overline{\beta}$. We thus have the following metalevel constraints:

D2 : if $d(Y, X) \in \mathcal{C}(\gamma)$ and $r(Y) \in \mathcal{C}(\beta)$ then $(\beta, \gamma) \in \mathcal{R}$
D3 : if $j(X) \in \mathcal{C}(\alpha)$ and $r(X) \in \mathcal{C}(\beta)$ then $(\alpha, \beta) \in \mathcal{R}$

Fig 1 shows the MAF characterisation of a Dung AF $x \rightleftarrows y$ (together with the two labellings – the second in brackets – identifying the two preferred extensions). In [8] it is shown that:

Let $\Delta = (A, R)$, $\Delta_\mathcal{M}$ its MAF $(\mathcal{A}, \mathcal{R}, \mathcal{C}, \mathcal{L}, \mathcal{D})$, where $x \in A$ iff $j(x), r(y) \in \mathcal{A}$, $(y, x) \in R$ iff $d(y, x) \in \mathcal{A}$, and $\mathcal{R}$ is defined by $\{D1, D2, D3\}$. Then x is a justified argument of Δ iff $j(x)$ is a justified argument of $\Delta_\mathcal{M}$ (under any semantics).

Developments of AFs, including preference based AFs (PAFs) [1], value based AFs [2] and hierarchical extended AFs [7], are also given MAF characterisations. For example, x is a justified argument of a PAF iff $j(x)$ is a justified argument of its MAF characterisation in which object level strict preferences constitute meta-arguments that claim $preferred(x, y)$, and are constrained to meta-level ($\mathcal{R}$) attack arguments claiming $d(y, x)$. These MAF characterisations of object level argumentation allow for application of the full range of results and techniques developed for Dung AFs to be applied to the various object level developments of AFs, and provide for principled integration and extension of object level formalisms. Furthermore, in the same way that a theory's inferences can be identified by instantiating an AF, so MAFs can be instantiated by arguments and attacks defined by a theory, so motivating development of object level logical formalisms whose inferences can thus be identified.

3. Formalising Accrual in *MAF*s

In this section we argue that accrual is properly modelled in terms of reasoning about preferences and their undermining of the success of attacks as defeats. We formalise such reasoning within a *MAF* with metalevel constraints that explicitly obey principles of accrual identified in [11]. We thus define a dialectical argumentation semantics that integrates accrual. In the next section we instantiate such a *MAF* with the arguments and attacks defined by an object level theory, and so identify the theory's inferences as defined through a combination of dialectical and accrual modes of reasoning.

We illustrate how the dialectical mode of argumentation fails to accommodate accrual, by considering a variation on an example in [11]. Suppose an argument b claiming one should go jogging given that it is the appointed time, an argument $a1$ not to go jogging given that it is hot, and an argument $a2$ not to go jogging given that it is raining. b symmetrically attacks $a1$ and $a2$, yielding two preferred extensions $\{b\}$ and $\{a1, a2\}$; hence no argument is sceptically justified. Suppose that b is stronger than (strictly preferred to) $a1$ and stronger than $a2$. Hence the attacks from $a1$ to b and $a2$ to b do not succeed, and we are left with b asymmetrically defeating $a1$ and $a2$, so yielding the single preferred extension $\{b\}$. However, some may consider that the *combined* weight of the two independent arguments not to go jogging, outweighs b. The problem with the dialectical mode is that it considers only pair-wise relationships between arguments so that b continues to asymmetrically defeat $a1$ and $a2$, and so remains sceptically justified.

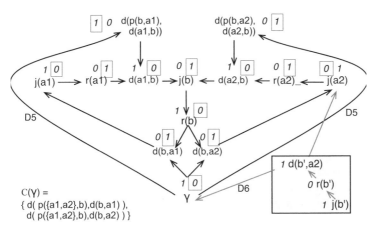

Figure 2. The accrual MAF for the jogging example with the arguments labelled as described in Section 2. The labelling shaded boxes is obtained assuming the additional arguments in the shaded box.

We claim that accrual should be modelled in terms of reasoning about preferences and their undermining of attacks. Not only do the relative strengths of individual arguments constitute reasons for undermining the success of attacks, but intuitively, the combined, or 'accrued' strengths of $a1$ and $a2$ being greater than b constitute a reason for undermining the attacks from b to $a1$ and b to $a2$. Letting upper case letters refer to accruals consisting of sets of arguments:

AC1: *The existence of a preference for accrual X over Y, based on the accrued strength of arguments in X being greater than the accrued strength of arguments in Y, is a reason for an attack from some $y \in Y$ on $x \in X$ failing to succeed as a defeat.*

We thus have meta-arguments γ with claims of the form: $defeat(preferred(X, Y)$, $defeat(y, x)) \in \mathcal{C}(\gamma)$, where $y \in Y$, $x \in X$, and the following constraint:

D4 : if $d(p(X, Y), d(y, x)) \in \mathcal{C}(\gamma)$ and $d(y, x) \in \mathcal{C}(\beta)$ then $(\gamma, \beta) \in \mathcal{R}$

Consider the *MAF* in Figure 2 in which (apart from the argument γ that makes two claims) the arguments are denoted by the claims they make, and set brackets are omitted for singleton sets. The meta-attacks are defined by $D1 \ldots D4$ and relate meta-arguments claiming the justified and rejected status of the object level arguments b, $a1$ and $a2$, and the object level defeats between them. Given object level preferences b over $a1$, b over $a2$, and the joint preference for $a1$ and $a2$ over b, then meta-arguments claiming these preferences undermine attacks.

The preference for $\{a1, a2\}$ over $\{b\}$ preferentially undermines b's attacks on $a1$ and b's attacks on $a2$, rather than b's preference over the accrual's elements $a1$ and $a2$ undermining attacks from $a1$ to b and $a2$ to b. In general:

AC2: *Preferences defined by an accrual take precedence over the preferences defined by elements of the accrual, in that the former preferentially undermine attacks.*

The following constraint *D5* encodes **AC2** since it requires that a meta-argument γ' claiming the undermining of an attack by a preference over accruals, attacks (and so takes precedence over) any γ claiming the undermining of an attack by preferences over elements of the accruals.

D5 : if $d(p(X, Y), d(y, x)) \in \mathcal{C}(\gamma)$ and $d(p(Y', X'), d(x', y')) \in \mathcal{C}(\gamma')$ and $(X, Y) \prec_a (Y', X')$, then $(\gamma', \gamma) \in \mathcal{R}$, where:

$(X, Y) \prec_a (Y', X')$ iff $Y \subseteq Y'$, $X \subseteq X'$, and either $Y \subset Y'$ or $X \subset X'$

For example, we have attacks (labelled D5) from γ to $d(p(b, a1), d(a1, b))$ and $d(p(b, a2), d(a2, b))$ in Figure 2. Now, suppose we also had that $\{b, b1\}$ preferred to $\{a1, a2, a3\}$ (assuming additional object level argument $b1$ and $a3$). Since $(\{a1, a2\}, \{b\})$ $\prec_a (\{b, b1\}, \{a1, a2, a3\})$, this would attack γ and so preferentially undermine attacks from $a1$ and $a2$ to b, rather than b to $a1$ and $a2$.

Analogous to **AC2**, [11] states that: "When an accrual of arguments is applicable, that is, when there are no convincing grounds to reject the accruing elements as individual arguments, then the accrual makes its elements inapplicable." According to this principle, Prakken advocates that neither $a1$ or $a2$ are justified [3], but rather that a 'super-argument' combining $a1$ and $a2$ is justified at the expense of b. However, in our view, $a1$ and $a2$ *should* be justified. They remain individually valid reasons not to go jogging, but their acceptability in the context of a counter-argument b requires that they are jointly acceptable so that their combined weight can be taken into account. To say then, that "the accrual makes its elements inappplicable" is to refer to their applicability in an evaluative context; it is the *preferences* of the individual arguments that should not be considered applicable. Hence, Prakken's qualification – "when there are no convincing

---

[3] Although these arguments for the intermediate labelled versions of the conclusions *are* justified in [11].

grounds to reject the accruing elements" – on the applicability of the accrual (which he states as a separate principle: "flawed arguments may not accrue"), amounts in our view to the defeat of an element of an accrual invalidating the undermining of an attack by a preference involving that accrual. For example, if $a2$ is defeated by some b' contradicting $a2$'s premise that it is raining, then the accrued weight of $a1$ and $a2$ being greater than b should no longer preferentially undermine b's attacks on $a1$ and $a2$ since otherwise $a1$ would inappropriately be justified.

Suppose that instead we preferred $\{b\}$ to $\{a1, a2\}$, preferentially undermining attacks from $a1$ and $a2$ to b, so that b now defeats $a1$ and $a2$. We would similarly want that b''s defeat of $a2$ invalidate the use of the preference in undermining the attacks. This is because $\{a1, a2\}$ may be weaker than $a1$ alone, so that $\{b\}$ may not be preferred to $\{a1\}$. Finally, observe that we would obviously not want b's defeats of $a1$ and $a2$ to invalidate the use of the preference, since it is these defeats that are effectively decided by the preference in the first place. We thus have the following principle (analogous to [11]'s "flawed arguments may not accrue") and constraints:

AC3: *A preference for accrual X over Y undermines an attack from an argument in Y on an argument in X, if no $y \in Y$ is defeated by some $z \notin X$, and no $x \in X$ is defeated by some $z \notin Y$.*

> **D6** : if $d(p(X,Y), d(y,x)) \in \mathcal{C}(\gamma)$, and $d(z,x) \in \mathcal{C}(\beta)$, $z \notin Y$, $x \in X$, then $(\beta, \gamma) \in \mathcal{R}$
>
> **D7** : if $d(p(X,Y), d(y,x)) \in \mathcal{C}(\gamma)$, and $d(z,y) \in \mathcal{C}(\beta)$, $z \notin X$, $y \in Y$, then $(\beta, \gamma) \in \mathcal{R}$ [4]

For the jogging example, given the AF ($a1 \rightleftarrows b \rightleftarrows a2$) and the preferences $\{b\} > \{a1\}$, $\{b\} > \{a2\}$, $\{a1, a2\} > \{b\}$, then the justified arguments of the MAF in Figure 2 include $j(a1)$ and $j(a2)$. We also show the extra meta-arguments and attacks (shaded grey) that characterise the object level attack from b' to $a2$ (where b' contradicts $a2$'s premise that it is raining). Now b rather than $a1$ and $a2$ are justified (as indicated by the labelling in grey).

We alluded above to Prakken's third principle of accrual: "Accruals are sometimes weaker than their elements". It may be that some consider $a1$ and $a2$ to be individually stronger reasons not to go jogging, so that $a1$ and $a2$ asymmetrically defeat b and are sceptically justified. However, some may consider the combination of rain and hot to be less unpleasant, and so the accrued weight of $a1$ and $a2$ is less than b and so is preferentially a reason for undermining $a1$ and $a2$'s attacks on b, so that b now defeats $a1$ and $a2$ and b is sceptically justified. This illustrates that reasoning *about* the strengths of accruals (and more generally preferences) is itself subject to uncertainty and conflict, and so argumentation based semantics integrating accrual should accommodate object level reasoning *about* preferences. Furthermore, note that in the jogging example one could in principle prefer $\{a1, a2, b\}$ to $\{a1, a2\}$, resulting in $a1$ and $a2$ being justified. This would of course be inappropriate given that $\{a1, a2, b\}$ accrues arguments for contradictory conclusions. However, this could be precluded if one allows argumentation about preferences, so accommodating reasoned justifications for preferences over accruals. In the following definition we therefore assume a function P that maps some arguments to

---

[4]Note that $D6$ and $D7$ need only be applied when $|X| > 1$ and $|Y| > 1$ respectively. Space limitations preclude a detailed discussion of why this is the case.

pairwise preferences (over sets of arguments) that these arguments express (note that no commitments are made to how these preferences are defined; they may be based on unitilites, values, etc.). Hence, if $z \in A$ claims a preference for $X \subseteq A$ over $Y \subseteq A$, then we will have meta-arguments α claiming both $j(z)$ *and* $j(p(X, Y))$, and β claiming both $r(z)$ *and* $r(p(X, Y))$, where by D3, α will $\mathcal{R}$ attack β, and by D2 β will $\mathcal{R}$ attack any γ claiming $d(p(X, Y), d(y, x))$. This will be illustrated further in the following section.

Definition 3 An *Accrual MAF* (*A-MAF*) is a tuple $\Delta_\mathcal{M} = (\mathcal{A}, \mathcal{R}, \mathcal{C}, \mathcal{L}, \mathcal{D})$, where $\mathcal{D}$ is the set of constraints $D1 \ldots D7$.

Let Δ be the *AF* (A, R) augmented by a partial function $P : A \mapsto 2^A \times 2^A$. The *A-MAF* $\Delta_\mathcal{M}$ for Δ is defined as follows:

- $\lceil x \rceil^5$ is a constant in $\mathcal{L}$ iff $x \in A$
- $\mathcal{A}$ is the union of the disjoint sets $\mathcal{A}_1 \ldots \mathcal{A}_4$ where:

  1. $\alpha \in \mathcal{A}_1, j(\lceil z \rceil) \in \mathcal{C}(\alpha)$ iff $z \in A$, where $j(p(\lceil X \rceil, \lceil Y \rceil)) \in \mathcal{C}(\alpha)$ iff $P(z) = (X, Y)$.
  2. $\alpha \in \mathcal{A}_2, r(\lceil z \rceil) \in \mathcal{C}(\alpha)$ iff $z \in A$, where $r(p(\lceil X \rceil, \lceil Y \rceil)) \in \mathcal{C}(\alpha)$ iff $P(z) = (X, Y)$.
  3. $\alpha \in \mathcal{A}_3, d(x, y) \in \mathcal{C}(\alpha)$ iff $(x, y) \in R$
  4. $\alpha \in \mathcal{A}_4, d(p(X, Y), d(y, x)) \in \mathcal{C}(\alpha)$ iff $\exists z \in A$ s.t. $P(z) = (X, Y)$, and $\beta \in \mathcal{A}, d(y, x) \in \mathcal{C}(\beta)$, and $y \in Y, x \in X$.

- $\mathcal{R}$ is defined by $\mathcal{D}$.

Then: x is a *justified argument* of Δ iff $j(x)$ is a *justified meta-argument* of $\Delta_\mathcal{M}$.

Note that when an $AF = (A, R)$ is augmented by $> \subseteq 2^A \times 2^A$ (rather than preferences being reasoned about in the domain of argumentation) then one can straightforwardly obtain $(A*, R*)$ where $A*$ is A augmented by arguments that map to preferences $(X, Y) \in >$, and $R* = R \cup \{(z, z') | P(z) = (X, Y), P(z') = (Y, X)\}$. The *A-MAF* of (A, R) and $>$ would then be the *A-MAF* of $(A*, R*)$ and P.

To see that the constraints on an *A-MAF*'s attack relation ensure that the principles of accrual AC1-3 are satisfied, observe that if $j(x)$ is a justified argument of $\Delta_\mathcal{M}$, then for every object level attack $(y, x) \in R$, $d(y, x)$ is attacked by some justified meta-argument $d(p(X, Y), d(y, x))$ and/or some justified $r(y)$. Consider the latter case[6]. For $r(y)$ to be justified there must be some justified $d(z, y)$ that attacks $j(y)$ and so ensures that $r(y)$ is reinstated against the attack by $j(y)$(see Fig.3). We can then state that the following holds (space limitations preclude inclusion of a formal proof in this paper):

Proposition 1 Let $\Delta_\mathcal{M}$ be the *A-MAF* for (A, R) augmented by a partial function P. Let $j(x)$ be a justified meta-argument of $\Delta_\mathcal{M}$ such that $x, y \in A$, $(y, x) \in R$. Then:

If a) $r(y)$ is not justified, or; b) it holds that: $r(y)$ is justified implies that $z = x$ for any $d(z, y)$ that is justified, then:

There are justified meta-arguments $j(p(X, Y))$ and $d(p(X, Y), d(y, x))$ such that $x \in X, y \in Y$, and:

---

[5] Sense quotes $\lceil \ \rceil$ are conventionally used to abbreviate metalevel representations of object level formulae.

[6] Notice that it is not necessarily the case that y is rejected ($r(y)$ is a justified meta-argument) in that y might *asymmetrically* attack x so that if x and x' are both justified, and $\{x, x'\} > \{y\}$, then the asymmetric attack may be undermined and $\{x, x', y\}$ is conflict free and so possibly admissible.

1. $\forall x' \in X$, $j(x')$ is justified;
2. $\forall y' \in Y$, if $r(y')$ is justified, then any meta-argument attacking $j(y')$ (and so reinstating $r(y')$) is of the form $d(x', y)$, where $x' \in X$.
3. There is no justified $d(p(Y', X'), d(x, y))$ such that $(X, Y) \prec_a (Y', X')$ and Y', X' respectively satsify 1 and 2.

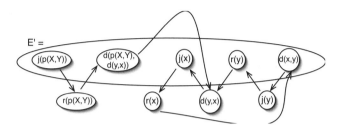

Figure 3. Meta-arguments in some $E' \subseteq E$, where E is the grounded or a preferred extension.

Informally, Proposition 1 states that if x is justified, then for any attack from y to x, if a) y is not rejected, or b) y is rejected given only that it is successfully attacked by x, then: there must be some justified argument expressing a preference for the accrual X over Y ($x \in X, y \in Y$) that undermines the attack from y to x (AC1), and: 1) All arguments in X are justified; 2) if any argument in Y is rejected, it is exclusively because of some attack originating from an argument in X (1, 2, and b equate with satisfaction of AC3); 3) there is no justified undermining of an attack from x to y by a preference for accrual Y' over an accrual X', such that X and Y are subsets of X' and Y' (AC2).

4. Instantiating A-MAFs

In this section we instantiate an A-MAF with arguments built from an object level logic that allows for reasoning about priorities over conjunctions of rules. Arguments concluding such priorities express preferences over sets of arguments, so that the instantiated A-MAF defines the inferences obtained under integration of dialectical and accrual modes of argumentation. In what follows, we assume atomic formulae built from a first order language containing the nullary predicate $pref$, and complex formulae built using the connectives $\Rightarrow \neg$, $\wedge$ and $>$. We distinguish *priority formulae* of the form $X > Y$, where X and Y are conjunctions of atomic formulae.

Definition 4 A theory Γ is a set of rules $r : L_1 \wedge \ldots L_m \Rightarrow L_n$, where:
• Each unique rule name r is an atomic first order formula
• Each L_i is an atomic first order formula or a priority formula, or such a formula preceded by strong negation $\neg$.

As usual, a rule with variables is a scheme standing for all its ground instances. For any atom A or priority formula P, we say that A (P) and $\neg A$ ($\neg P$) are the complement of each other. In the metalanguage, $\overline{L}$ denotes the complement of L. Henceforth, we will refer to rules by their names, and write $head(r)$ and $body(r)$ to respectively denote the consequent and antecedent of the rule named r. We also assume that any Γ contains rules that ensure the priority relation $>$ is closed under transitivity, in the sense that if $r_1, r_2 \in \Gamma$, then $\exists r \in \Gamma$ s.t. $body(r) = body(r_1) \wedge body(r_2)$, where;

i) $head(r_1) = Y > X$, $head(r_2) = Z > Y$, $head(r) = Z > X$, or;
ii) $head(r_1) = Y > X$, $head(r_2) = \neg(Z > X)$, $head(r) = \neg(Z > Y)$, or;
iii) $head(r_1) = Z > Y$, $head(r_2) = \neg(Z > X)$, $head(r) = \neg(Y > X)$.

Definition 5 Given a theory Γ, an argument x is either:

1. a tree of rules s.t. each node $r : L_1 \wedge \ldots L_m \Rightarrow L_n$ has child nodes with rules $r_1 \ldots r_m$, where for $i = 1 \ldots m$, $head(r_i) = L_i$, and $r, r_1 \ldots r_m \in \Gamma$, and each leaf node of x is a rule with an empty antecedent, and no two distinct rules have the same head (so excluding arguments with circular chains of reasoning); or
2. a tree with the special root node '$pref$', each of whose child nodes is the root node r_i of a tree of type 1, where $head(r_i)$ is a priority formula.

Table 1. A theory and its arguments and attack relation

Γ	A'
$r1 :\Rightarrow b, r2 : b \Rightarrow a$	$y1 = [r1, r2]$
$r3 :\Rightarrow c, r4 : c \Rightarrow a$	$y2 = [r3, r4]$
$r5 \Rightarrow d, r6 : d \Rightarrow \neg a$	$z1 = [r5, r6]$
$r7 :\Rightarrow e, r8 : e \Rightarrow \neg a$	$z2 = [r7, r8]$
$r9 :\Rightarrow r6 > r2$	$p1 = [r9, pref], P(p1) = (\{z1\}, \{y1\})$
$r10 :\Rightarrow r8 > r2$	$p2 = [r10, pref], P(p2) = (\{z2\}, \{y1\})$
$r11 :\Rightarrow r2 \wedge r4 > r6 \wedge r8$	$p3 = [r11, pref], P(p3) = (\{y1, y2\}, \{z1, z2\})$
$r12 :\Rightarrow r6 \wedge r8 > r2 \wedge r4$	$p4 = [r12, pref], P(p4) = (\{z1, z2\}, \{y1, y2\})$
$r13 :\Rightarrow f, r14 : f \Rightarrow r11 > r12$	$q1 = [r13, r14, pref], P(q1) = (\{p3\}, \{p4\})$

$$R' = y1 \rightleftarrows z1, y1 \rightleftarrows z2, y2 \rightleftarrows z1, y2 \rightleftarrows z2, p3 \rightleftarrows p4$$

Definition 6 For any argument x, L is a conclusion of x iff L is the head of some rule in x. Let A be the arguments defined by Γ. For any $x, y \in A$:
x and y *attack* each other (i.e., $(x, y), (y, x) \in R$) on (L, L') iff L is a conclusion of x and L' is a conclusion of y, where $L' = \overline{L}$, or if $L = X > Y$ then $L' = Y > X$.

Arguments with root node $pref$ link together arguments concluding priorities over conjunctions of rules names. Thus, one can define pairwise preferences over sets of arguments w.r.t. priorities linked in a single $pref$ argument. Henceforth, $rules(L, Z)$ will denote $\{r|r$ is a rule in $z, z \in Z$, and $head(r) = L\}$, where Z is a set of arguments.

Definition 7 Let A be the arguments defined by Γ, and $X, Y \subseteq A$ s.t. $\{(L_1, L'_1), \ldots, (L_n, L'_n)\}$ is the non-empty set of pairs of conclusions s.t. for $i = 1 \ldots n$, $\exists x \in X, y \in Y$, x and y attack on (L_i, L'_i).
Let z be an argument with root node $pref$. Then $P(z) = (X, Y)$ iff for $i = 1 \ldots n$, $\bigwedge(rules(L_i, X)) > \bigwedge(rules(\overline{L_i}, Y))$ is a conclusion of z.

To enhance readability we henceforth describe propositional examples and write arguments as sequences of paths in a tree. Consider arguments $x1 = [r1 :\Rightarrow b, r2 : b \Rightarrow c]$, $x2 = [r3 :\Rightarrow c]$ and $y1 = [r4 :\Rightarrow \neg b, r5 : \neg b \Rightarrow \neg c]$ which attack each other on the pairs $(b, \neg b)$ and $(c, \neg c)$. Suppose rules $r6 :\Rightarrow r1 > r4$ and $r7 :\Rightarrow r2 \wedge r3 > r5$. Then z with root node $pref$ consists of the two paths $[r6, pref], [r7, pref]$, and $P(z) = (\{x1, x2\}, \{y1\})$.

Example 2 Consider the example Γ in Table 1 in which a subset A' and R' of the arguments and attack relation defined by Γ are shown. The instantiated A-MAF (given by Definition 3 is shown in Figure 4, in which:

$C(\pi 3) = \{d(p(\{y1, y2\}, \{z1, z2\}), d(\alpha, \beta)) \mid \alpha \in \{z1, z2\}, \beta \in \{y1, y2\}\}$;
$C(\pi 4) = \{d(p(\{z1, z2\}, \{y1, y2\}), d(\alpha, \beta)) \mid \alpha \in \{y1, y2\}, \beta \in \{z1, z2\}\}$.

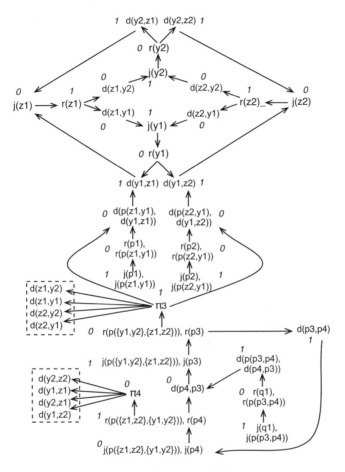

Figure 4. The A-MAF for the theory in Example 2 (to ease readability some arguments – those surrounded by dotted lines – are repeated).

In general, we say that α is an inference of Γ iff α is the conclusion of an argument x defined by Γ, and $j(x)$ is a sceptically justified argument of the A-MAF instantiated by Γ. Thus, the justified arguments of Figure 4's A-MAF (i.e., those labelled 1) identify a rather than $\neg a$ as an inference of Example 2's theory. Although arguments $z1$ and $z2$ concluding $\neg a$ are individually preferred to $y1$ concluding a, $p3$ concludes that the accrual $\{y1, y2\}$ is stronger than $\{z1, z2\}$, and $q1$ justifies a preference for this pairwise comparison over the contrary pairwise comparison concluded by $p4$.

5. Conclusions

We have argued that accrual is more properly effected through reasoning about and application of preferences in meta-argumentation frameworks that adopt the standard dialectical mode of argumentation. By contrast, existing approaches to accrual adopt either
the inference or knowledge representation approach. Furthermore, they either require
somewhat ad-hoc mechanisms to ensure satisfaction of accrual principles (e.g., the labelling mechanism in [11]), or formalise accrual for specific logics (e.g., [6]), or make
commitments to the structure of, and interactions between arguments (e.g., [13] and [4]
in which arguments are *not* evaluated using Dung's dialectical calculus), or do not accommodate dialectical argumentation (e.g., [5]). Our approach is the first to integrate accrual within Dung's dialectical theory, while preserving the theory's level of abstraction
so that the inferences of various instantiating logics can be identified under integration
of the dialectical and accrual modes of reasoning, and where such logics may encode
reasoning about the strengths of accruals. To substantiate this claim we have shown how
the inferences of a theory in such a logic are identified by the justified arguments of the
theory's instantiated A-MAF. One can then apply the results and techniques developed
for Dung AFs, to the instantiated A-MAFs. For example, argument game proof theories
and algorithms for AFs [9] can be applied to A-MAFs. Future work can then investigate
how efficiency gains can be obtained. For example, in an argument game, a player could
in one move play arguments $d(X,Y)$ and $j(X)$, given that his counterpart will always
be able to play $r(X)$ in response to $d(X,Y)$, which in turn can always be countered by
$j(X)$. If played together the counterpart could then either attack $d(X,Y)$ or $j(X)$. One
could thus eliminate unnecessary rounds without impacting on the game's outcome.

References

[1] L. Amgoud and C. Cayrol. A reasoning model based on the production of acceptable arguments. *Annals of Mathematics and Artificial Intelligence*, 34:197–216, 2002.
[2] T. J. M. Bench-Capon. Persuasion in practical argument using value-based argumentation frameworks. *Journal of Logic and Computation*, 13(3):429–448, 2003.
[3] P. M. Dung. On the acceptability of arguments and its fundamental role in nonmonotonic reasoning, logic programming and n-person games. *Artificial Intelligence*, 77:321–357, 1995.
[4] T. Gordon and D. Walton. Proof burdens and standards. In I. Rahwan and G. Simari, editors, *Argumentation in AI*. Springer-Verlag, 2009.
[5] P. Krause, S. Ambler, M. Elvang-Gøransson, and J. Fox. A logic of argumentation for reasoning under uncertainty. *Computational Intelligence*, 11(1):113–131, 1995.
[6] M. J. Gómez Lucero, C. Chesñevar, and G.R. Simari. On the accrual of arguments in defeasible logic programming. In *IJCAI'09: Proc. 21st Int. joint Conf. on Artifical intelligence*, pages 804–809, 2009.
[7] S. Modgil. Reasoning about preferences in argumentation frameworks. *Artificial Intelligence*, 173(9-10):901–934, 2009.
[8] S. Modgil and T.J.M Bench-Capon. Metalevel argumentation. *Technical Report*, page www.csc.liv.ac.uk/research/ techreports/techreports.html, 2009.
[9] S. Modgil and M. Caminada. Proof theories and algorithms for abstract argumentation frameworks. In I. Rahwan and G. Simari, editors, *Argumentation in AI*. Springer-Verlag, 2009.
[10] J. L. Pollock. *Cognitive Carpentry. A Blueprint for How to Build a Person*. MIT Press, 1995.
[11] H. Prakken. A study of accrual of arguments, with applications to evidential reasoning. In *ICAIL '05: Proc. 10th Int. Conf. on Artificial intelligence and law*, pages 85–94, 2005.
[12] H. Prakken and G. Sartor. Modelling reasoning with precedents in a formal dialogue game. *Artificial Intelligence and Law*, 6:231–287, 1998.
[13] Bart Verheij. Accrual of arguments in defeasible argumentation. In *Proc. 2nd Dutch/German Workshop on Nonmonotonic Reasoning*, pages 217–224, 1995.

Computational Models of Argument
P. Baroni et al. (Eds.)
IOS Press, 2010
doi:10.3233/978-1-60750-619-5-347

Reasoning about Preferences in Structured Extended Argumentation Frameworks

Sanjay Modgil[a][1], Henry Prakken[b]

[a]*Department of Computer Science, University of Liverpool,* [b]*Department of
Information and Computing Sciences, Utrecht University & Faculty of Law, University
of Groningen*

Abstract. This paper combines two recent extensions of Dung's abstract argumentation frameworks in order to define an abstract formalism for reasoning about preferences in structured argumentation frameworks. First, extended argumentation frameworks extend Dung frameworks with attacks on attacks, thus providing an abstract dialectical semantics that accommodates argumentation-based reasoning *about* preferences over arguments. Second, a recent extension of the ASPIC framework (ASPIC+) instantiates Dung frameworks with accounts of the structure of arguments, the nature of attack and the use of preferences to resolve attacks. In this paper, ASPIC+ is further developed in order to define attacks on attacks, resulting in a dialectical semantics that accommodates argumentation based reasoning about preferences in structured argumentation. Then, some recently proposed rationality postulates for structured extended argumentation are proven to hold.

Keywords. Abstract Argumentation, Preferences, Postulates.

1. Introduction

A Dung *argumentation framework* (DF) [6] consists of a binary *attack* relation on a set of arguments. The justified arguments are then evaluated under different semantics. The abstract nature of DFs successfully provides for a general and intuitive semantics for the consequence notions of argumentation logics and for nonmonotonic logics in general: a DF can be instantiated by the arguments and attacks defined by a theory in a logic, and the theory's inferences are then defined in terms of the claims of the justified arguments. On the other hand, the abstract nature of DFs precludes giving guidance as to what kinds of instantiation ensure that the instantiating theory's defined inferences satisfy intuitively rational properties. To address this issue, the ASIPC abstract framework for structured argumentation [2] integrated work on rule-based argumentation [12,15,14] with [6]'s abstract approach. ASPIC provides abstract accounts of the structure of arguments, the nature of attack, and the use of a given preference ordering to determine which attacks succeed as *defeats*. [5] then exploited this added expressiveness to formulate several consistency and closure rationality postulates that cannot be formulated at Dung's fully abstract level. These postulates were then proven to be satisfied for a special case of [2]'s ASPIC framework; one in which preference orderings were *not* accounted for.

---

[1]Corresponding Author: Sanjay Modgil, E-mail: sanjaymodgil@yahoo.co.uk.

More recently, [13] generalised the ASPIC framework to develop ASPIC+. The significance of this work is that: 1) ASPIC+ is proven to capture a broader range of systems than ASPIC, e.g., assumption-based argumentation [4] and systems using argument schemes; 2) ASPIC+, and so any existing or new argumentation logic instantiating ASPIC+, is shown to satisfy [5]'s postulates for the more general case in which preferences *are* accounted for. Hence, for example, preferences can be applied to remove attacks defined by an instantiation of ASPIC+, whilst guaranteeing that the claims of the arguments in a complete extension are mutually consistent.

In a parallel development, [7] addressed a limitation of developments of *DF*s that account for the relative strengths of attacking arguments in order to determine which attacks succeed as defeats [1,3]. While [1] and [3] respectively assume *given* preference and value orderings for valuating the relative strengths of arguments, in reality, such valuations are often themselves the outcome of argumentation based reasoning. To model this, [7] extends *DF*s so that arguments expressing preferences attack the attacks between the arguments over which the preferences are expressed. [7] then defines evaluation of the justified arguments of these Extended Argumentation Frameworks (*EAFs*) under each of the Dung semantics. However, while [7] investigates two specific instantiations of *EAFs*, a general principled account of structured argumentation accommodating argumentation about preferences has thus far been lacking.

In this paper we provide such an account. Section 2 reviews Dung's theory, *EAFs*, and ASPIC+. Section 3 then builds on ASPIC+ to allow for arguments that express preferences over other arguments, and which then instantiate a version of [7]'s *EAFs* in the same general way as *DF*s have been instantiated by ASPIC+. We then show that the resulting *structured EAFs* satisfy [5]'s rationality postulates. The significance of this work is that it enables principled development of novel and existing instantiating logics (e.g., [4]) to incorporate reasoning about priorities; principled in the sense that these logics' inferences, defined now through instantiation of *structured EAFs*, are guaranteed to satisfy [5]'s rationality postulates. For example, one can now guarantee that despite the fact that the instantiating logic defines arguments that attack and so remove attacks, the claims of arguments contained in a complete extension of the instantiated *EAF* will be mutually consistent. In Section 3.3 we illustrate this with an example instantiation.

2. Background

2.1. A Review of Abstract Argumentation

A *Dung argumentation framework* (*DF*) [6] is a tuple $(\mathcal{A}, \mathcal{C})$, where $\mathcal{C} \subseteq \mathcal{A} \times \mathcal{A}$ is an attack relation on the arguments in $\mathcal{A}$. An argument $X \in \mathcal{A}$ is then said to be acceptable w.r.t. some $S \subseteq \mathcal{A}$ iff $\forall Y$ s.t. $(Y, X) \in \mathcal{C}$ implies $\exists Z \in S$ s.t. $(Z, Y) \in \mathcal{C}$ (i.e., Z reinstates X). A *DF*'s characteristic function $\mathcal{F}$ is defined such that for any $S \subseteq \mathcal{A}$, $\mathcal{F}(S) = \{X | X$ is acceptable w.r.t. S $\}$. We now recall Dung's definition of extensions under different semantics:

Definition 1 Let $(\mathcal{A}, \mathcal{C})$ be a *DF*, $S \subseteq \mathcal{A}$ be *conflict free* (i.e., $\forall X, Y \in S, (X, Y) \notin \mathcal{C}$): S is an *admissible* extension iff $S \subseteq \mathcal{F}(S)$; S is a *complete* extension iff $S = \mathcal{F}(S)$; S is a preferred extension iff it is a set inclusion maximal complete extension; S is a grounded extension iff it is a set inclusion minimal complete extension (since $\mathcal{F}$ is monotonic there is guaranteed to be a unique grounded extension given by $\mathcal{F}$'s least fixed point); S is a stable extension iff it is preferred and $\forall Y \notin S, \exists X \in S$ s.t. $(X, Y) \in \mathcal{C}$.

For $s \in \{\text{complete, preferred, grounded, stable}\}$, $X \in \mathcal{A}$ is *sceptically* justified under the s semantics, if X belongs to all s extensions, and *credulously* justified if X belongs to at least one s extension.

Extended Argumentation Frameworks (*EAF*s) [7] extend *DF*s to include a second attack (*pref-attack*) relation:

Definition 2 [*EAF*] An *EAF* is a tuple $(\mathcal{A}, \mathcal{C}, \mathcal{D})$, where $(\mathcal{A}, \mathcal{C})$ is a *DF*, $\mathcal{D} \subseteq \mathcal{A} \times \mathcal{C}$, and if $(Z, (X, Y)), (Z', (Y, X)) \in \mathcal{D}$ then $(Z, Z'), (Z', Z) \in \mathcal{C}$.

Note the constraint on any Z, Z', where given that they respectively pref-attack (X, Y) and (Y, X), then they express contradictory preferences (Y is preferred to X, respectively X is preferred to Y) and so themselves symmetrically attack.

Henceforth, we focus on *bounded hierarchical EAF*s that are stratified so that attacks at some level i are only pref-attacked by arguments in the next level up (such *EAF*s have been shown to suffice for many applications of *EAF*s [8,9,10]):

Definition 3 [*bh-EAF*s] $\Delta = (\mathcal{A}, \mathcal{C}, \mathcal{D})$ is a *bounded hierarchical EAF* (*bh-EAF*) iff there exists a partition $\Delta_H = (((\mathcal{A}_1, \mathcal{C}_1), \mathcal{D}_1), \ldots, ((\mathcal{A}_n, \mathcal{C}_n), \mathcal{D}_n))$ such that $\mathcal{D}_n = \emptyset$, and:

- $\mathcal{A} = \bigcup_{i=1}^{n} \mathcal{A}_i, \mathcal{C} = \bigcup_{i=1}^{n} \mathcal{C}_i, \mathcal{D} = \bigcup_{i=1}^{n} \mathcal{D}_i$, and for $i = 1 \ldots n$, $(\mathcal{A}_i, \mathcal{C}_i)$ is a *DF*.
- $(C, (A, B)) \in \mathcal{D}_i$ implies $(A, B) \in \mathcal{C}_i, C \in \mathcal{A}_{i+1}$.

The notion of a successful attack (*defeat*) is then parameterised w.r.t. preferences specified by some given set S of arguments:

Y *defeats*$_S$ X, denoted $Y \rightarrow^s X$, iff $(Y, X) \in \mathcal{C}$ and $\neg \exists Z \in S$ s.t. $(Z, (Y, X)) \in \mathcal{D}$.

An *EAF conflict free* set S is then defined as a set that does not admit arguments that symmetrically attack, but can contain some Y and X such that Y *asymmetrically* attacks X, given a $Z \in S$ that pref-attacks this attack. That is, S is *conflict free* iff :

$\forall X, Y \in S$: if $(Y, X) \in \mathcal{C}$ then $(X, Y) \notin \mathcal{C}$, and $\exists Z \in S$ s.t. $(Z, (Y, X)) \in \mathcal{D}$.

The acceptability of an argument X w.r.t. a set S requires that there is a *reinstatement set* for any reinstating defeat:

Definition 4 [EAF acceptability] Let $S \subseteq \mathcal{A}$ in $(\mathcal{A}, \mathcal{C}, \mathcal{D})$. Let $R_S = \{X_1 \rightarrow^S Y_1, \ldots, X_n \rightarrow^S Y_n\}$ where for $i = 1 \ldots n$, $X_i \in S$. Then R_S is a reinstatement set for $A \rightarrow^S B$, iff $A \rightarrow^S B \in R_S$, and $\forall X \rightarrow^S Y \in R_S$, $\forall Y'$ s.t. $(Y', (X, Y)) \in \mathcal{D}$, $\exists X' \rightarrow^S Y' \in R_S$

X is acceptable w.r.t. $S \subseteq \mathcal{A}$ iff $\forall Y$ s.t. $Y \rightarrow^S X$, there is a *reinstatement set* for some $Z \rightarrow^S Y$.

Given this definition of acceptability, admissible, preferred, complete, grounded and stable extensions are defined in the same way as for *DF*s (except that '$X \rightarrow^S Y$' replaces '$(X, Y) \in \mathcal{C}$' in the definition of stable extensions), and Dung's fundamental lemma [6] is shown to hold for *EAF*s. The domain of an *EAF*s characteristic function $\mathcal{F}$ is limited to conflict free sets and is monotonic for *bh-EAF*s, so that the grounded extension is defined by the least fixed point of $\mathcal{F}^2$.

---

[2]For arbitrary *EAF*s, $\mathcal{F}$ is not monotonic. However [7] shows that iterating $\mathcal{F}$ starting from the empty set does provide a fixed point that identifies the grounded extensions

2.2. A Framework for Structured Argumentation

As stated earlier, the ASPIC+ framework of [13] further develops [2,5]'s instantiation of [6]'s abstract frameworks with accounts of the structure of arguments, the nature of attack and the use of preferences to resolve attacks. The framework instantiates Dung's abstract approach by assuming an unspecified logical language and by defining arguments as inference trees formed by applying strict or defeasible inference rules. The notion of an argument as an inference tree naturally leads to three ways of attacking an argument: attacking an inference, attacking a conclusion and attacking a premise. To resolve such conflicts, preferences may be used, which leads to three corresponding kinds of defeat: undercutting, rebutting and undermining defeat. To characterise them, some minimal assumptions on the logical object language are made; namely that certain well-formed formulas are a contrary or contradictory of certain other well-formed formulas. Apart from this the framework is still abstract: it applies to any set of inference rules divided into strict and defeasible, and to any logical language with a defined contrary relation.

The basic notion of [13]'s framework is that of an argumentation system.

Definition 5 [Argumentation system] An *argumentation system* is a tuple $AS = (\mathcal{L}, ^-, \mathcal{R}, \leq)$ where

- $\mathcal{L}$ is a logical language.
- $^-$ is a contrariness function from $\mathcal{L}$ to $2^{\mathcal{L}}$, such that if $\varphi \in \overline{\psi}$ then if $\psi \notin \overline{\varphi}$ then φ is called a *contrary* of ψ, otherwise φ and ψ are called *contradictory*. The latter case is denoted by $\varphi = -\psi$ (i.e., $\varphi \in \overline{\psi}$ and $\psi \in \overline{\varphi}$).
- $\mathcal{R} = \mathcal{R}_s \cup \mathcal{R}_d$ is a set of strict ($\mathcal{R}_s$) and defeasible ($\mathcal{R}_d$) inference rules such that $\mathcal{R}_s \cap \mathcal{R}_d = \emptyset$.
- $\leq$ is a partial preorder on $\mathcal{R}_d$.

Henceforth, a set $S \subseteq \mathcal{L}$ is said to be consistent iff $\nexists \psi, \varphi \in S$ such that $\psi \in \overline{\varphi}$, otherwise it is *inconsistent*.

Arguments are built by applying inference rules to one or more elements of $\mathcal{L}$. Strict and defeasible rules are of the form $\varphi_1, \ldots, \varphi_n \to \varphi$ and $\varphi_1, \ldots, \varphi_n \Rightarrow \varphi$, interpreted as 'if the *antecedents* $\varphi_1, \ldots, \varphi_n$ hold, then *without exception*, respectively *presumably*, the *consequent* φ holds'. As is usual in logic, inference rules can be specified by schemes in which a rule's antecedents and consequent are metavariables ranging over $\mathcal{L}$. Arguments are constructed from a knowledge base, which is assumed to contain three kinds of formulas.

Definition 6 [Knowledge bases] A *knowledge base* in an argumentation system $(\mathcal{L}, ^-, \mathcal{R}, \leq)$ is a pair $(\mathcal{K}, \leq')$ where $\mathcal{K} \subseteq \mathcal{L}$ and $\leq'$ is a partial preorder on $\mathcal{K} \setminus \mathcal{K}_n$. Here, $\mathcal{K} = \mathcal{K}_n \cup \mathcal{K}_p \cup \mathcal{K}_a$ where these subsets of $\mathcal{K}$ are disjoint and:

- $\mathcal{K}_n$ is a set of (necessary) *axioms*. Intuitively, arguments cannot be attacked on their axiom premises.
- $\mathcal{K}_p$ is a set of *ordinary premises*. Intuitively, arguments can be attacked on their ordinary premises, and whether this results in defeat must be determined by comparing the attacker and the attacked premise (in a way specified below).
- $\mathcal{K}_a$ is a set of *assumptions*. Intuitively, arguments can be attacked on their ordinary assumptions, where these attacks always succeed.

The following definition of arguments is taken from [15], in which for any argument A, the function Prem returns all the formulas of $\mathcal{K}$ (called *premises*) used to build A, Conc returns A's conclusion, Sub returns all of A's sub-arguments, DefRules returns all defeasible rules in A, and TopRule returns the last inference rule used in A.

Definition 7 [Argument] An *argument* A on the basis of a knowledge base $(\mathcal{K}, \leq')$ in an argumentation system $(\mathcal{L}, ^-, \mathcal{R}, \leq)$ is:

1. φ if $\varphi \in \mathcal{K}$ with: $\text{Prem}(A) = \{\varphi\}$; $\text{Conc}(A) = \varphi$; $\text{Sub}(A) = \{\varphi\}$; $\text{Rules}(A) = \emptyset$; $\text{TopRule}(A) = $ undefined.
2. $A_1, \ldots A_n \to/\Rightarrow \psi$ if $A_1, \ldots, A_n$ are arguments such that there exists a strict/defeasible rule $\text{Conc}(A_1), \ldots, \text{Conc}(A_n) \to/\Rightarrow \psi$ in $\mathcal{R}_s/\mathcal{R}_d$.
   $\text{Prem}(A) = \text{Prem}(A_1) \cup \ldots \cup \text{Prem}(A_n)$,
   $\text{Conc}(A) = \psi$,
   $\text{Sub}(A) = \text{Sub}(A_1) \cup \ldots \cup \text{Sub}(A_n) \cup \{A\}$.
   $\text{Rules}(A) = \text{Rules}(A_1) \cup \ldots \cup \text{Rules}(A_n) \cup \{\text{Conc}(A_1), \ldots, \text{Conc}(A_n) \to/\Rightarrow \psi\}$
   $\text{DefRules}(A) = \text{DefRules}(A_1) \cup \ldots \cup \text{DefRules}(A_n)$,
   $\text{TopRule}(A) = \text{Conc}(A_1), \ldots \text{Conc}(A_n) \to/\Rightarrow \psi$

Furthermore, $\text{DefRules}(A) = \text{Rules}(A)/\mathcal{R}_s$. Then A is: *strict* if $\text{DefRules}(A) = \emptyset$; *defeasible* if $\text{DefRules}(A) \neq \emptyset$; *firm* if $\text{Prem}(A) \subseteq \mathcal{K}_n$; *plausible* if $\text{Prem}(A) \not\subseteq \mathcal{K}_n$.

The notion of an argument ordering is used in the notion of an argument theory. The argument ordering is a partial preorder $\preceq$ on arguments (with its strict counterpart $\prec$ defined in the usual way), and is assumed to be 'admissible', i.e., firm-and-strict arguments are strictly better than all other arguments, and a strict inference cannot make an argument strictly better or worse than its weakest proper subargument. Note that [13] investigates two example definitions of $\preceq$ in terms of the orderings on $\mathcal{R}_d$ and $\mathcal{K}$.

Definition 8 [Argumentation theories] An *argumentation theory* is a triple $AT = (AS, KB, \preceq)$ where AS is an argumentation system, KB is a knowledge base in AS and $\preceq$ is an admissible ordering on the set of all arguments that can be constructed from KB in AS.

As indicated above, when arguments are inference trees, three syntactic forms of attack are possible: attacking a premise, a conclusion, or an inference. Below these attacks will be called, respectively, undermining, rebutting and undercutting attack. To model undercutting attacks on inferences, it is assumed that applications of inference rules can be expressed in the object language; the precise nature of this naming convention will be left implicit, unless indicated otherwise in examples.

Definition 9 [Attacks]
• Argument A *undercuts* argument B (on B') iff $\text{Conc}(A) \in \overline{B'}$ for some $B' \in \text{Sub}(B)$ of the form $B''_1, \ldots, B''_n \Rightarrow \psi$.
• Argument A *rebuts* argument B on (B') iff $\text{Conc}(A) \in \overline{\varphi}$ for some $B' \in \text{Sub}(B)$ of the form $B''_1, \ldots, B''_n \Rightarrow \varphi$. In such a case A *contrary-rebuts* B iff $\text{Conc}(A)$ is a contrary of φ.
• Argument A *undermines* B (on φ) iff $\text{Conc}(A) \in \overline{\varphi}$ for some $\varphi \in \text{Prem}(B) \setminus \mathcal{K}_n$. In such a case A *contrary-undermines* B iff $\text{Conc}(A)$ is a contrary of φ or if $\varphi \in \mathcal{K}_a$.

Attacks combined with the preferences defined by an argument ordering yield three kinds of defeat. For undercutting attack no preferences will be needed to make it result in defeat, since otherwise a weaker undercutter and its stronger target might be in the same extension. The same holds for the other two ways of attack as far as they involve contraries (i.e., non-symmetric conflict relations between formulas).

Definition 10 [Successful rebuttal, undermining and defeat]
A successfully rebuts B if A rebuts B on B' and either A contrary-rebuts B' or $A \not\prec B'$.
A successfully undermines B if A undermines B on φ and either A contrary-undermines B or $A \not\prec \varphi$.
A defeats B iff A undercuts or successfully rebuts or successfully undermines B.

The success of rebutting and undermining attacks thus involves comparing the conflicting arguments at the points where they conflict. The definition of successful undermining exploits the fact that an argument premise is also a subargument.

In [13], structured argumentation theories are then linked to Dung frameworks:

Definition 11 An *abstract argumentation framework* DF_{AT} *corresponding to an argumentation theory* AT is a pair $\langle \mathcal{A}, Def \rangle$ such that $\mathcal{A}$ is the set of arguments defined by AT as in Definition 7, and Def is the relation on $\mathcal{A}$ given by Definition 10.

Then any semantics for Dung frameworks can be used to define the acceptability status of arguments and their conclusions.

3. Linking Structured Argumentation Theories to Extended Argumentation Frameworks

3.1. Defining Structured Extended Argumentation Frameworks

We build on the previous section's work in order to link structured argumentation theories to a modified version of [7]'s bounded hierarchical *EAF*s. The idea is that the previous section's reference to the argument ordering $\preceq$ is removed; we instead assume a fully abstract partial function $\mathcal{P}$ that extracts orderings from *sets of* arguments that conclude preferences (over other arguments). These sets of preference arguments then *collectively* pref-attack attacks in order to undermine the success of the latter as defeats. In the following section, we then make $\mathcal{P}$ more specific for an argumentation theory that defines $\preceq$ in terms of the two orderings $\leq$ on defeasible rules and $\leq'$ on the knowledge base.

To motivate the generalisation of [7]'s theory to accommodate collective pref-attacks, consider the following informal example argumentation theory in which rules express priorities over other rules (through the use of rule names as in [14]):

Example 12 Let $A = [r_1 :\Rightarrow p, r_2 : p \Rightarrow q]$, $B = [r_3 :\Rightarrow s, r_4 : s \Rightarrow \neg q]$, $C_1 = [r_5 :\Rightarrow r_1 > r_3]$, $C_2 = [r_6 :\Rightarrow r_2 > r_3]$, $D_1 = [r_7 :\Rightarrow r_3 > r_2]$, $D_2 = [r_8 :\Rightarrow r_4 > r_2]$.

A and B attack each other, and A is preferred to B since rule r_3 in B is strictly less than all rules in A, as concluded by arguments C_1 and C_2. Effectively then, it is the arguments C_1 and C_2 that *in combination* express a preference for A over B. In [7] the object level construction of arguments accounts for the conjoining of such arguments C_1 and C_2, so as to obtain a super-argument '$C_1 + C_2$' that attacks the attack from B

to A. This is somewhat inelegant, so that in this paper we conservatively modify [7]'s extended theory to allow for arguments to *collectively* attack attacks, and re-define the notions of defeat, conflict free, and reinstatements sets accordingly. For arbitrary *EAF*s it can be shown that the results in [7] are preserved under this generalisation. In this paper we are interested in *bh-EAF*s, and thus only present collective attacks on attacks (and other modifications) for such *EAF*s:

Definition 13 [*bh-EAFC*]
- A *bh-EAFC* is a tuple $(\mathcal{A}, \mathcal{C}, \mathcal{D})$, where $(\mathcal{A}, \mathcal{C})$ is a *DF* and $\mathcal{D} \subseteq (2^{\mathcal{A}}/\emptyset) \times \mathcal{C}$, and the hierarchical partition of $(\mathcal{A}, \mathcal{C}, \mathcal{D})$ is defined as in Definition 3, replacing a set ϕ of arguments for the single preference argument C.
- A defeats$_S$ B iff $(A, B) \in \mathcal{C}$ and $\neg \exists \phi \subseteq S$ s.t. $(\phi, (A, B)) \in \mathcal{D}$.
- $S \subseteq \mathcal{A}$ is conflict free iff $\forall A, B \in S$, if $(A, B) \in \mathcal{C}$, then $\exists \phi \subseteq S$ s.t. $(\phi, (A, B)) \in \mathcal{D}$ (i.e., $\forall A, B \in S, A \not\rightarrow^S B$).
- Let $R_S = \{X_1 \rightarrow^S Y_1, \ldots, X_n \rightarrow^S Y_n\}$ where for $i = 1 \ldots n$, $X_i \in S$. R_S is a reinstatement set for $A \rightarrow^S B$, iff $A \rightarrow^S B \in R_S$, and $\forall X \rightarrow^S Y \in R_S$, $\forall \phi$ s.t. $(\phi, (X, Y)) \in \mathcal{D}$, $\exists X' \rightarrow^S Y' \in R_S$ for some $Y' \in \phi$.

Acceptability and extensions of *bh-EAFC*s are then defined as in Section 2.1.

Two other modifications are worth noting in the above definition. Firstly, we have not included what one would expect to be the following generalisation to the collective case: If $(\phi, (A, B)), (\phi', (B, A)) \in \mathcal{D}$, then $\exists Z \in \phi, Z' \in \phi$ s.t. $(Z, Z'), (Z', Z) \in \mathcal{C}$. As will be shown in Section 3.3, this is because when linking structured theories to *bh-EAFC*s one cannot always guarantee that this (or indeed the weaker constraint that an asymmetric attack exists between some Z and Z') follows from the definition of attacks given in Definition 9. The second modification to note is that the definition of conflict free drops the requirement that conflict free sets exclude mutually attacking arguments. We do not want to impose such a constraint at the abstract level; rather we want that it follows from the defined linkage of structured theories to *bh-EAFC*s, that no extension under any of the semantics admits arguments that attack (this will be implied by showing that the linked theories satisfy rationality postulates in Section 3.2). However, it can be shown that despite both these modifications, the key results for the extended theory defined in Definition 13 still hold (proofs of all the results in this paper can be found in [11]):

Proposition 14 [Fundamental lemma and Monotonicity of Characteristic Function]
Let $\Delta = (\mathcal{A}, \mathcal{C}, \mathcal{D})$ be a *bh-EAFC*. Then:

1) If S is an admissible extension of Δ, and A, A' arguments acceptable w.r.t S, then: $S' = S \cup \{A\}$ is admissible; A' is acceptable w.r.t. S'.
2) Let S and S' be conflict free subsets of $\mathcal{A}$ such that $S \subseteq S'$. Then $\mathcal{F}(S) \subseteq \mathcal{F}(S')$.[3]

We are now ready to link structured theories to *bh-EAFC*s.

---

[3]This result is to be expected given that the requirements that contradictory preference arguments symmetrically attack, and that conflict free sets exclude symmetrically attacking arguments, are only required to show (in [7]) that iterating $\mathcal{F}$ from the empty set yields a fixed point and so defines the grounded extension for *arbitrary EAF*s. For *bh-EAFC*s, it follows from 1) that all admissible extensions form a complete partial order w.r.t. set inclusion, and 2) guarantees the existence of a least fixed point for $\mathcal{F}$ that identifies a finitary *bh-EAFC*'s grounded extension.

Definition 15 [Extended Argumentation Theory, Arguments and Preference Function]
- An *extended argumentation system* is a triple $EAS = (\mathcal{L}, ^-, \mathcal{R})$
- An *extended knowledge base* is a set $EKB = \mathcal{K} = \mathcal{K}_n \cup \mathcal{K}_p \cup \mathcal{K}_a$
- An *extended argumentation theory* is a tuple $EAT = (EAS, EKB)$
- Let $\mathcal{A}$ denote the set of arguments defined by EAT as in Definition 7. We say that $\mathcal{P}$ is a partial function defined by EAT, where:

$$\mathcal{P} : X \longrightarrow Pow(\mathcal{A} \times \mathcal{A}) \text{ (for some } X \in \mathcal{A}).$$

When instantiating a *bh-EAFC*, we note that since A may rebut or undermine B on more than one sub-argument, respectively premise, then by Definition 10, A does not defeat B if A does not contrary-rebut/undermine B, and *for all* rebutted sub-arguments B' and undermined premises ϕ of B, $A \prec B'$ and $A \preceq \phi$. This will be made explicit when defining attacks on attacks in the following definition.

Definition 16 [*bh-EAFC* for structured arguments] A *bh-EAFC$_{EAT}$* corresponding to an EAT, henceforth referred to as a *structured EAF*, is a *bh-EAFC* $(\mathcal{A}, \mathcal{C}, \mathcal{D})$ such that:

1. $\mathcal{A}$ is the set of arguments defined by EAT as in Definition 7;
2. $(A, B) \in \mathcal{C}$ iff A undercuts, rebuts or undermines B according to Definition 9;
3. $(\phi, (A, B)) \in \mathcal{D}$ iff $(A, B) \in \mathcal{C}$, and:

    (a) $\forall B' \in \text{Sub}(B)$ s.t. A rebuts or undermines B on B', $\exists \phi' \subseteq \phi$ s.t. $A \prec B' \in \mathcal{P}(\phi')$, and ϕ is a minimal (under set inclusion) set satisfying this condition.
    (b) A does not contrary undermine, contrary rebut or undercut B (since by Definition 10 these attacks succeed as defeats irrespective of preferences).
    (c) it is not the case that A is firm and strict and B is plausible or defeasible (since by the admissibility of argument orderings described prior to Definition 8, it must be that $B \prec A$).

We say that E is an extension of an EAT iff E is an extension of *bh-EAFC$_{EAT}$*.

3.2. Satisfaction of Rationality Postulates by Structured EAFs

In [13], DF_{AT}s are shown to satisfy [5]'s rationality postulates. Structured *EAFs* also satisfy these rationality postulates. Firstly, the sub-argument closure and closure under strict rules postulates are unconditionally satisfied:

Theorem 17 [Sub-argument Closure] Let $(\mathcal{A}, \mathcal{C}, \mathcal{D})$ be a *bh-EAFC$_{EAT}$* and E any of its extensions under a given semantics subsumed by complete semantics. Then for all $A \in E$: if $A' \in \text{Sub}(A)$ then $A' \in E$.

Theorem 18 [Closure under strict rules] Let $(\mathcal{A}, \mathcal{C}, \mathcal{D})$ be a *bh-EAFC$_{EAT}$* and E any of its extensions under a given semantics subsumed by complete semantics. Then $\{\text{Conc}(A)|A \in E\} = Cl_{\mathcal{R}_s}(\{\text{Conc}(A)|A \in E\})$ [4].

In [13] it is shown that DF_{AT}s satisfy the consistency postulates under a number of assumptions that are more fully described in [13]:

---

[4]$Cl_{\mathcal{R}_s}(P)$, where $P \subseteq \mathcal{L}$ is the smallest set containing P and the consequent of any strict rule in $\mathcal{R}_s$ whose antecedents are in $Cl_{\mathcal{R}_s}(P)$

(Ass1) the argumentation system's strict rules are closed under 'transposition'[5].
(Ass2) the closure of $\mathcal{K}_n$ under strict rule application is consistent.
(Ass3) the argumentation theory is 'well-formed'.
(Ass4) the argument ordering is 'reasonable'.

In this paper we refer to assumptions **Ass1-3** straightforwardly applied to the extended argumentation theories of Definition 15. We discuss **Ass4** after first describing an assumption that essentially expresses (at the level of the instantiating EAT) an analogue of the omitted constraint on contradictory sets of preference arguments discussed earlier:

Definition 19 [Ass5] Let $\Delta = (\mathcal{A}, \mathcal{C}, \mathcal{D})$ be a *bh-EAFC$_{EAT}$*, and suppose $\phi, \psi \subseteq \mathcal{A}$ s.t. $B \prec A \in \mathcal{P}(\phi)$, $A \prec B \in \mathcal{P}(\psi)$. Then Δ satisfies **Ass5** if for some $X \in \phi$, $Y \in \psi$, either X and Y have contradictory conclusions, or there exists some set of strict rules extending X to the argument $X+$ s.t. $X+$ and Y have contradictory conclusions.

We informally illustrate **Ass5** with Example 12, in which $(\{C_1, C_2\}, (B, A)) \in \mathcal{D}$ and $(\{D_1, D_2\}, (A, B)) \in \mathcal{D}$. Assume the strict rules contain the axioms of a partial order, including the rule for asymmetry: $o_4 : X > Y \rightarrow \neg(Y > X)$, where X and Y range over rule names. Then D_1 can be extended to $D_1' = [r_7 :\Rightarrow r_3 > r_2, o_4 : r_3 > r_2 \rightarrow \neg(r_2 > r_3)]$ whose conclusion contradicts C_2's conclusion. Hence D_1' asymmetrically attacks C_2. Before discussing **Ass4**, we recall some notation from [13]:

Notation 20 $M(B)$ denotes the maximal fallible sub-arguments of B, where for any $B' \in \text{Sub}(B)$, $B' \in M(B)$ iff: 1) B' final inference is defeasible or B' is a non-axiom premise; and 2) there is no $B'' \in \text{Sub}(B)$ s.t. $B'' \neq B$ and $B' \in \text{Sub}(B'')$ and B'' satisfies 1).

Ass4's reasonable ordering assumption captures the intuition that given arguments A and B, both of which are plausible or defeasible and such that $B \prec A$, then there must be some $B' \in M(B)$ such that:

  i B' is not stronger than any maximal fallible sub-argument in $M(B)$ (i.e., $M(B)$ contains a $\preceq$ minimal element);
  ii $B' \prec A$ (since otherwise it cannot be that $B \prec A$ given that B consists of $M(B)$ extended by strict rules that by the admissibility of $\preceq$ cannot weaken the arguments in $M(B)$)

Articulating a counterpart to the **Ass4** in the context of *structured EAFs*, recall that we are interested in cases where $(\phi, (B, A)) \in \mathcal{D}$, where for each sub-argument A' of A rebutted or undermined by B, there is a subset of ϕ that expresses a preference for A' over B. Also, since contradictory preferences can be expressed, and so the existence of $\preceq$ minimal arguments cannot be guaranteed, we also need to express the assumption in the context of some set of arguments E in which such a minimal argument does exist:

Definition 21 [Ass6] Let $\Delta = (\mathcal{A}, \mathcal{C}, \mathcal{D})$ be a *bh-EAFC$_{EAT}$*, $E \subseteq \mathcal{A}$, $A, B \in E$, and $(\phi, (B, A)) \in \mathcal{D}$. Let there exist at least one argument $X \in M(B)$ that is a $\preceq$ minimal argument in E in the sense that:

$$\text{for all } B'' \in M(B), \neg\exists\psi \subseteq E \text{ s.t. } B'' \prec X \in \mathcal{P}(\psi).$$

Then Δ satisfies **Ass6** if $\forall A'$ s.t. A' is a sub-argument of A and B rebuts or undermines A on A', $\exists B' \in M(B)$ that is $\preceq$ minimal in E, $\exists\phi' \subseteq \phi$ s.t. $B' \prec A' \in \mathcal{P}(\phi')$

---

[5]i.e., $s = \varphi_1, \ldots, \varphi_n \rightarrow \psi \in \mathcal{R}_s$ iff for $i = 1 \ldots n$, $\varphi_1, \ldots, \varphi_{i-1}, -\psi, \varphi_{i+1}, \ldots, \varphi_n \rightarrow -\varphi_i \in \mathcal{R}_s$

Notice that if for a finite $M(B)$ there is no argument in $M(B)$ that is $\preceq$ minimal in E, then $\forall B' \in M(B), \exists B'' \in M(B), \exists \phi \subseteq E$ s.t. $B'' \prec B' \in \mathcal{P}(\phi)$. This in turn implies that for some $B', B'' \in M(B), \exists \phi, \psi \subseteq E$ s.t. $B' \prec B'' \in \mathcal{P}(\phi)$, $B'' \prec B' \in \mathcal{P}(\psi)$. Then by **Ass5**, there must be some $X \in \phi, Y \in \psi$ such that Y, and X or $X+$ extending X with strict rules, have contradictory conclusions. Hence **Ass5** effectively implies that a $\preceq$ minimal $X \in M(B)$ exists in a set free of arguments with contradictory conclusions. We can now state the following theorems:

Theorem 22 Let $(\mathcal{A}, \mathcal{C}, \mathcal{D})$ be a *bh-EAFC$_{EAT}$* satisfying **Ass1-3**, **Ass5**, and **Ass6**. Let E be any of its extensions under a given semantics subsumed by complete semantics. Then $\{\texttt{Conc}(A)|A \in E\}$ is consistent.

Theorem 23 Let $(\mathcal{A}, \mathcal{C}, \mathcal{D})$ be a *bh-EAFC$_{EAT}$* satisfying **Ass1-3**, **Ass5**, and **Ass6**. Let E be any of its extensions under a given semantics subsumed by complete semantics. Then $Cl_{\mathcal{R}_s}(\{\texttt{Conc}(A)|A \in E\})$ is consistent.

3.3. An Example Extended Argumentation Theory

In this section we describe an extended argumentation theory (*EAT*) and its *structured EAF*. As in Example 12 we assume arguments constructed from named rules that may express priorities over other rules. We also assume that any *EAT* contains (in its component *EAS*) strict rules axiomatising a partial order (x,y,z are meta-variables ranging over rule names and $o2$ and $o3$ are the transpositions of $o1$):

- $o_1 : (y > x) \wedge (z > y) \rightarrow (z > x)$ • $o_2 : (y > x) \wedge \neg(z > x) \rightarrow \neg(z > y)$
- $o_3 : (z > y) \wedge \neg(z > x) \rightarrow \neg(y > x)$ • $o_4 : (y > x) \rightarrow \neg(x > y)$

We then assume that $B \prec A \in \mathcal{P}(\phi)$ if the arguments in ϕ conclude rule priorities such that A is stronger than B under the last link principle [2]:

Definition 24 [Conclusion of $\prec_s$ by a set of arguments] Let $\Gamma = \{r_1 : l_1, \ldots, r_n : l_n\}$ be a set of objects named by wff of $\mathcal{L}$, and $\geq$ a partial ordering on Γ (with its strict counterpart $>$ defined in the usual way). Let $\Gamma' \subseteq \Gamma, \Gamma'' \subseteq \Gamma$. Then for some set ϕ of arguments:

ϕ is said to conclude that $\Gamma' \prec_s \Gamma''$, iff $\exists r_i : l_i \in \Gamma'$ s.t. $\forall r : l \in \Gamma'', r > r_i$ is the conclusion of an argument in ϕ.

Definition 25 [$\mathcal{P}$ defined under the last link principle] Let $(\mathcal{A}, \mathcal{C}, \mathcal{D})$ be a *bh-EAFC$_{EAT}$*, $A, B \in \mathcal{A}, \phi \subseteq \mathcal{A}$. Then $B \prec A \in \mathcal{P}(\phi)$ under the last link principle iff

1. ϕ concludes $\texttt{LastDefRules}(B) \prec_s \texttt{LastDefRules}(A)$; or
2. $\texttt{LastDefRules}(B)$ and $\texttt{LastDefRules}(A)$ are empty and ϕ concludes $\texttt{Prem}(B) \prec_s$ $\texttt{Prem}(A)$

Let us now illustrate how a *structured EAF* is instantiated by arguments constructed from an *EAT*. For simplicity, our example is with domain-specific inference rules, mostly with empty antecedents. Consider the following defeasible rules:

$$
\begin{array}{lll}
r_1: \Rightarrow a & p_1: \Rightarrow r_3 > r_1 & m_1: \Rightarrow p_3 > p_1 \\
r_2: \Rightarrow \neg a & p_2: \Rightarrow r_2 > r_3 & m_2: \Rightarrow p_1 \approx p_2 \\
r_3: \Rightarrow b & p_3: \Rightarrow r_1 > r_2 &
\end{array}
$$

Indexing the inferences with the names of the rules applied, we have the mutually rebutting arguments $X_1 : \Rightarrow_{r1} a$, $X_2 : \Rightarrow_{r2} \neg a$, and:

$A_1:$ $\Rightarrow_{p1} r_3 > r_1$	$B_1:$ $\Rightarrow_{p3} r_1 > r_2$	$C:$ $\Rightarrow_{m1} p_1 < p_3$
$A_2:$ $\Rightarrow_{p2} r_2 > r_3$	$B_2:$ $B_1 \rightarrow_{o4} \neg(r_2 > r_1)$	$D:$ $\Rightarrow_{m2} p_1 \approx p_2$
$A_3:$ $A_1, A_2 \rightarrow_{o1} r_2 > r_1$		

Applying the last link principle, $\mathcal{P}(\{A_3\}) = \{X_1 \prec X_2\}$ hence $(\{A_3\}, (X_1, X_2)) \in \mathcal{D}$, and $\mathcal{P}(\{B_1\}) = \{X_2 \prec X_1\}$ hence $(\{B_1\}, (X_2, X_1)) \in \mathcal{D}$, as illustrated in Figure 1.

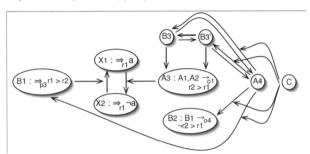

Figure 1. *Structured EAF for example EAT*

Now note that B_1 and A_3 do not attack each other. Furthermore, although B_1 can be extended with a strict rule to B_2, with A_3 and B_2 having contradictory conclusions (illustrating satisfaction of **Ass5**), A_3 and B_2 do not attack each other since both have a strict top rule. However, with transpositions of these strict top rules, both can be extended to attack the other on a defeasible subargument:

$A_4:$	$A_3 \rightarrow_{o4} \neg(r_1 > r_2)$	(rebutting B_1, and so B_2, B_3 and B_3' on B_1)
$B_3:$	$B_2, A_1 \rightarrow_{o2} \neg(r_2 > r_3)$	(rebutting A_2, and so A_3 and A_4 on A_2)
$B_3':$	$B_2, A_2 \rightarrow_{o3} \neg(r_3 > r_1)$	(rebutting A_1, and so A_3 and A_4 on A_1)

Now, $\mathtt{LastDefRules}(A_4) = \{p_1, p_2\}$, $\mathtt{LastDefRules}(B_1) = \{p_3\}$, and for $i = 1, 2, 3, 3'$, $A_4 \prec B_i \in \mathcal{P}(\{C\})$ and so $(\{C\}, (A_4, B_i)) \in \mathcal{D}$. Also, $\mathtt{LastDefRules}(B_3) = \{p_1, p_3\}$ and $\mathtt{LastDefRules}(A_2) = \{p_2\}$. Then it is easy to verify that no ϕ pref-attacks B_3's attack on A_2. Similarly, $\mathtt{LastDefRules}(B_3') = \{p_2, p_3\}$ and $\mathtt{LastDefRules}(A_2) = \{p_1\}$, so no ϕ pref-attacks B_3''s attack on A_2. This means that A_3 will not be in any extension: in grounded semantics this is since neither A_1 nor A_2 is in the grounded extension, while in the other semantics this is since each extension contains either A_1 or A_2 but not both (since each extension contains B_3 or B_3'). So in all extensions X_1's attack on X_2 is successful. Since C and D are not attacked, they will be in all extensions. Hence all attacks from A_4 on B_1, B_2, B_3 and $B3'$ are attacked by C, so that each extension will contain B_1, B_2 and B_3 or B_3'. Hence, in no extension is X_2's attack on X_1 successful, and so for any E under any of [6]'s semantics, $X_1 \rightarrow^E X_2$ but not $X_2 \rightarrow^E X_1$. So all such extensions contain X_1 but not X_2.

Finally, for the *structured EAFs* obtained by the instantiating $EATs$ in this section, the theorems in the previous section imply that all the rationality postulates hold, given that we can show that **Ass5** and **Ass6** hold under the last link principle:

Proposition 26 Let $(\mathcal{A}, \mathcal{C}, \mathcal{D})$ be a *bh-EAFC*$_{EAT}$, where the strict rules in EAT include $o1 \ldots o4$. Let $\mathcal{P}$ be defined under the last link principle. Then $(\mathcal{A}, \mathcal{C}, \mathcal{D})$ satisfies **Ass5** and **Ass6**.

4. Conclusions

In this paper we have presented an abstract formalism for reasoning about preferences in structured extended argumentation frameworks. We motivated modifications to [7]'s extended argumentation, dropping [7]'s constraints on conflict free sets and (sets of) arguments expressing contradictory preferences, and enabling collective pref-attacks on attacks. We showed that the fundamental results that hold for bounded hierarchical *EAF*s also hold for the modified theory. We then instantiated the modified *EAF*s with [13]'s structured argumentation theories modified so as to allow for sets of arguments to express preferences over other arguments. We then showed that the obtained instantiated *structured EAF*s satisfy [5]'s closure and consistency postulates, and described an instantiation by arguments built from rules that can express priorities over other rules. The abstract specification of the instantiating structured argumentation theories means that our work enables principled development of novel and existing systems. In future work we will thus investigate how various existing argumentation systems (e.g. [4]'s assumption based argumentation) that are shown to be a special case of [13]'s instantiaton of *DF*s, can now be extended in a principled way to enable argumentation based reasoning about preferences over other arguments. Future work will also investigate the more general case of non-hierarchical *EAF*s, and application of preference criteria other than the last link principle (such as the weakest link principle).

References

[1]   L. Amgoud and C. Cayrol. A reasoning model based on the production of acceptable arguments. *Annals of Mathematics and Artificial Intelligence*, **34(1-3)**, 197–215, (2002).

[2]   L. Amgoud, L. Bodenstaff, M. Caminada, P. McBurney, S. Parsons, H. Prakken, J. van Veenen, and G.A.W. Vreeswijk. Final review and report on formal argumentation system. Deliverable D2.6, ASPIC IST-FP6-002307, (2006).

[3]   T.J.M. Bench-Capon. Persuasion in practical argument using value-based argumentation frameworks. *Journal of Logic and Computation*, **13**, 429–448, (2003).

[4]   A. Bondarenko, P.M. Dung, R.A. Kowalski, and F. Toni. An abstract, argumentation-theoretic approach to default reasoning. *Artificial Intelligence*, **93**, 63–101, (1997).

[5]   M. Caminada and L. Amgoud. On the evaluation of argumentation formalisms. *Artificial Intelligence*, **171**, 286–310, (2007).

[6]   P.M. Dung. On the acceptability of arguments and its fundamental role in nonmonotonic reasoning, logic programming, and *n*–person games. *Artificial Intelligence*, **77**, 321–357, (1995).

[7]   S. Modgil. Reasoning about preferences in argumentation frameworks. *Artificial Intelligence*, **173**, 901–934, (2009).

[8]   T. J. M. Bench-Capon and S. Modgil. Case law in extended argumentation frameworks. In *ICAIL*, 118–127, (2009).

[9]   S. Modgil. An argumentation based semantics for agent reasoning. In *Proc. Workshop on Languages, methodologies and development tools for multi-agent systems (LADS 07)*, 37–53, UK, (2007).

[10] S. Modgil and M. Luck. Argumentation based resolution of conflicts between desires and normative goals. In *Proc. 5th Int. Workshop on Argumentation in Multi-Agent Systems*, 252–263, (2008).

[11] S. Modgil and H. Prakken. Technical Report: Proofs for *Structured EAF*s. In http://people.cs.uu.nl/henry/ASPIC-EAF-TR.pdf, (2010).

[12] J.L. Pollock. Justification and defeat. *Artificial Intelligence*, **67**, 377–408, (1994).

[13] H. Prakken. An abstract framework for argumentation with structured arguments. To appear in: *Argument and Computation*, **1**, (2010). www.cs.uu.nl/research/techreps/UU-CS-2009-019.html

[14] H. Prakken and G. Sartor. Argument-based extended logic programming with defeasible priorities. *Journal of Applied Non-classical Logics*, **7**, 25–75, (1997).

[15] G.A.W. Vreeswijk. Abstract argumentation systems. *Artificial Intelligence*, **90**, 225–279, (1997).

Computational Models of Argument
P. Baroni et al. (Eds.)
IOS Press, 2010
doi:10.3233/978-1-60750-619-5-359

Argument Theory Change Through Defeater Activation

Martín O. MOGUILLANSKY, Nicolás D. ROTSTEIN[1],
Marcelo A. FALAPPA, Alejandro J. GARCÍA and Guillermo R. SIMARI
National Research Council (CONICET), AI R&D Lab (LIDIA)
Department of Computer Science and Engineering (DCIC)
Universidad Nacional del Sur (UNS), Argentina
e-mail: nico.rotstein@abdn.ac.uk, {mom, maf, ajg, grs}@cs.uns.edu.ar

Abstract. Argument Theory Change (ATC) applies classic belief change concepts to the area of argumentation. This intersection of fields takes advantage of the definition of a Dynamic Abstract Argumentation Framework, in which an argument is either active or inactive, and only in the former case it is taken into consideration in the reasoning process. ATC identifies how the framework has to be modified in order to achieve warrant for a certain argument. The present article copes with this matter by defining a revision operator based on activation of arguments, *i.e.*, recognizing the knowledge that is missing.

1. Introduction and Background

This article presents a new approach to Argument Theory Change (ATC) [9,11], where belief change concepts [1,8] are translated to the field of argumentation. Here we use the Dynamic Abstract Argumentation Framework (DAF) [12], which extends Dung's framework [6] in order to consider (1) subarguments (internal, necessary parts of an argument that are arguments by themselves), and (2) a set of active arguments (those available to perform reasoning). The main contribution provided by ATC is a revision operator at argument level that revises a theory by an argument seeking for its warrant. That is, an argument is activated (begins to be considered by the argumentation machinery) and after its new status is analyzed, the revision theory proposes additional modifications to the set of active arguments in order to finally warrant the argument at issue. The arguments to be activated will be defeaters of those somehow interfering with the warrant of the argument at issue. However, since defeaters might be unavailable to be activated, the activating revision is not always successful.

This article does not pursue a full formalization according to the classical theory of belief revision. Thus, no representation theorems nor characterization postulates are to be defined here. Instead, we look at the process of change from the argumentation standpoint. However, the usual principles of change from belief revision were taken into account, namely, minimal change and success.

---

[1]Employed by the University of Aberdeen (Scotland, UK) for dot.rural Digital Economy Research, under the RCUK Digital Economy Programme, http://www.dotrural.ac.uk

2. A Dynamic Abstract Framework

Arguments, in the usual sense, are interpreted as a reason for a certain claim from a set of premises. In abstract argumentation [5,10], these features are abstracted away; hence we will work with arguments as "black boxes of knowledge" which may be divided in several smaller arguments, referred to as *subarguments*. In the dynamic framework used here we assume a *universal set* of arguments holding every conceivable argument that could be used by the inference machinery, from which a subset of *active arguments* can be distinguished. These arguments represent the current state of the world and are the only ones to be considered to compute warrant. Activation and deactivation of arguments are thus assumed to be determined from an external mechanism. In some domains, an agent might have the capability of de/activating arguments, and therefore the challenge is to decide what kind of change has to be performed, *i.e.*, what to de/activate. This is the point in which ATC enters the scene, allowing to handle de/activation of arguments in a proper manner, seeking for a concrete objective. These changes are performed at a theoretical level, *i.e.*, any inactive argument could be eventually activated.

Definition 1 (DAF) *A **dynamic abstract argumentation framework** (DAF) is a tuple* $\langle \mathbb{U}, \hookrightarrow, \sqsubseteq \rangle [\mathbb{A}]$, *where* $\mathbb{U}$ *is a finite set of arguments called **universal**,* $\mathbb{A} \subseteq \mathbb{U}$ *is called the **set of active arguments**,* $\hookrightarrow \subseteq \mathbb{U} \times \mathbb{U}$ *denotes the **attack relation**, and* $\sqsubseteq \subseteq \mathbb{U} \times \mathbb{U}$ *denotes the **subargument relation**.*

The principle characterizing argument activation is:

(Activeness Propagation) $\mathcal{B} \in \mathbb{A}$ iff $\mathcal{B}' \in \mathbb{A}$ for any $\mathcal{B}' \sqsubseteq \mathcal{B}$.

In this article, we build and evaluate a *dialectical tree* rooted in the argument under study in order to determine whether it is warranted. A dialectical tree is conformed by a set of *argumentation lines*; each of which is a non-empty sequence λ of arguments from a DAF, where each argument in λ attacks its predecessor in the line. The first argument is called the *root*, and the last one, the *leaf* of λ. Different restrictions on the construction of argumentation lines can be defined under the name of *dialectical constraints* (DC) [7]. DCs are useful to determine whether an argumentation line is finally *acceptable*. We assume a DC to avoid constructing circular argumentation lines, keeping them finite.

We call *dynamic argumentation theory* (DAT) to a DAF closed under activeness propagation and enriched with DCs. An operator $C_{ap} : \mathcal{P}(\mathbb{U}) \to \mathcal{P}(\mathbb{U})$ is assumed to implement the *closure under activeness propagation* required by a DAT $\mathsf{T} = \langle \mathbb{U}, \hookrightarrow, \sqsubseteq \rangle [\mathbb{A}]$, where $\mathbb{A} = C_{ap}(\mathbb{A})$. To represent change over the set of active arguments we assume an *activation operator* $\oplus : \mathcal{P}(\mathbb{U}) \times \mathcal{P}(\mathbb{U}) \to \mathcal{P}(\mathbb{U})$ such that $\Psi_1 \oplus \Psi_2 = C_{ap}(\Psi_1 \cup \Psi_2)$, with $(\Psi_1 \cup \Psi_2) \subseteq \mathbb{U}$. The domain of all acceptable argumentation lines in a DAT T, is noted as $\mathfrak{Lines}_{\mathsf{T}}^{\mathbb{U}}$, while $\mathfrak{Lines}_{\mathsf{T}}^{\mathbb{A}} \subseteq \mathfrak{Lines}_{\mathsf{T}}^{\mathbb{U}}$ will be the domain enclosing every acceptable line containing only active arguments. The root argument of a line λ from a DAT T will be identified through the function $\mathrm{root} : \mathfrak{Lines}_{\mathsf{T}}^{\mathbb{U}} \to \mathbb{U}$. From now on, given a DAT T, to refer to an argument $\mathcal{A}$ belonging to a line $\lambda \in \mathfrak{Lines}_{\mathsf{T}}^{\mathbb{A}}$, we will overload the membership symbol and write "$\mathcal{A} \in \lambda$", and will refer to λ simply as argumentation line (or just line) assuming it is acceptable. We identify the *set of pro (resp, con) arguments* containing all arguments placed on odd (resp, even) positions in a line λ, noted as λ^+ (resp, λ^-).

Definition 2 (Upper Segment) *Given a DAT* T *and a line* $\lambda \in \mathfrak{Lines}_T^U$ *such that* $\lambda = [\mathcal{B}_1, \ldots, \mathcal{B}_n]$, *the* **upper segment** *of* λ *wrt.* $\mathcal{B}_i$ $(1 \leq i \leq n)$ *is defined as* $\lambda^\uparrow[\mathcal{B}_i] = [\mathcal{B}_1, \ldots, \mathcal{B}_i]$. *The* **proper upper segment** *of* λ *wrt.* $\mathcal{B}_i$ $(i \neq 1)$ *is* $\lambda^\uparrow(\mathcal{B}_i) = [\mathcal{B}_1, \ldots, \mathcal{B}_{i-1}]$.

We refer to both proper and non-proper upper segments simply as "upper segment" and either usage will be distinguishable through its notation (round or square brackets respectively).

Definition 3 (Dialectical Tree) *Given a DAT* T, *a* **dialectical tree** $\mathcal{T}_T(\mathcal{A})$ *rooted in* $\mathcal{A}$ *is built by a set* $X \subseteq \mathfrak{Lines}_T^U$ *of lines rooted in* $\mathcal{A}$, *such that an argument* $\mathcal{C}$ *in* $\mathcal{T}_T(\mathcal{A})$ *is: (1) a* **node** *iff* $\mathcal{C} \in \lambda$, *for any* $\lambda \in X$; *(2) a* **child** *of a node* $\mathcal{B}$ *in* $\mathcal{T}_T(\mathcal{A})$ *iff* $\mathcal{C} \in \lambda$, $\mathcal{B} \in \lambda'$, *for any* $\{\lambda, \lambda'\} \subseteq X$, *and* $\lambda'^\uparrow[\mathcal{B}] = \lambda^\uparrow(\mathcal{C})$. *A leaf of any line in* X *is a* **leaf** *in* $\mathcal{T}_T(\mathcal{A})$.

However, the acceptability of a dialectical tree will depend on the set X of lines used to build such tree. Hence, an acceptable dialectical tree will be constructed from a *bundle set* $\mathcal{S}_T(\mathcal{A})$ which –given a DAT T– contains all the acceptable and exhaustive argumentation lines from $\mathfrak{Lines}_T^A$ rooted in $\mathcal{A}$. (We refer to a line as exhaustive when no more arguments can be added to it.) Thus, following Def. 3, $\mathcal{T}_T(\mathcal{A})$ is acceptable if it is built from a set $X = \mathcal{S}_T(\mathcal{A})$. The domain of all acceptable dialectical trees from T is noted as $\mathfrak{Trees}_T$. Besides, we will overload the membership symbol and write "$\lambda \in \mathcal{T}_T(\mathcal{A})$" when the line λ belongs to the tree $\mathcal{T}_T(\mathcal{A}) \in \mathfrak{Trees}_T$.

Dialectical trees allow to determine whether the root node of the tree is warranted or not. This evaluation will weigh all the information present in the tree through a *marking criterion* to evaluate each argument in the tree –in particular the root– by assigning them a mark within the domain $\{D, U\}$, where U (resp., D) denotes an undefeated (resp., defeated) argument. We will adopt a skeptical marking criterion: (1) all leaves are marked U; and (2) every inner node $\mathcal{B}$ is marked U iff every child of $\mathcal{B}$ is marked D, otherwise, $\mathcal{B}$ is marked D. Finally, warrant is specified through a function Mark : $\mathfrak{Trees}_T \to \{D, U\}$ returning the mark of the root.

Definition 4 (Warrant) *Given a DAT* T, *an active argument* $\mathcal{A} \in \mathbb{A}$ *is* **warranted** *iff* $\mathrm{Mark}(\mathcal{T}_T(\mathcal{A})) = U$. *Whenever* $\mathcal{A}$ *is warranted, the dialectical tree* $\mathcal{T}_T(\mathcal{A})$ *is called* **warranting tree***; otherwise, it is called* **non-warranting tree**.

3. An Activating Approach to ATC

The core of the change machinery involves the *alteration* of some lines in such dialectical tree when it happens to be non-warranting. Therefore, the objective of altering lines is to change the topology of the tree containing them in order to turn it to warranting. Alteration of lines comes from activation of arguments; that is, arguments cannot be simply added to the tree. Since an argument could appear in different positions in several lines in a tree, an alteration of a line could result in collateral alterations of other lines. This may end up extending the line and even incorporating new lines to the tree.

Definition 5 (Attacking Set) *Given a (not necessarily acceptable) tree* $\mathcal{T}_T(\mathcal{A})$ *built from a set* $X \subseteq \mathfrak{Lines}_T^U$ *of lines rooted in* $\mathcal{A}$; *the* **attacking set** $Att(\mathcal{T}_T(\mathcal{A}))$ *is the minimal subset of* X *if the tree built from the set* $(X \setminus Att(\mathcal{T}_T(\mathcal{A})))$ *warrants* $\mathcal{A}$, *otherwise* $Att(\mathcal{T}_T(\mathcal{A})) = X$.

We refer to the lines included in the attacking set as *attacking lines*. The objective of Def. 5 is to identify attacking lines in a tree. This definition considers any set X, disregarding acceptability of lines and in/active arguments. (This generalization will be useful later.) In particular, when X is a bundle set $\mathcal{S}_\mathsf{T}(\mathcal{A})$, the tree $\mathcal{T}_\mathsf{T}(\mathcal{A})$ is acceptable, however, $(\mathcal{S}_\mathsf{T}(\mathcal{A})\backslash Att(\mathcal{T}_\mathsf{T}(\mathcal{A})))$ is not a bundle set, since it discards lines rooted in $\mathcal{A}$, and thus the tree built from it is not acceptable. That is, the removal of the attacking lines from the bundle set of a non-warranting tree is not intended to conform a change operation, but to pose a hypothetical scenario useful to isolate the causes for a non-warranting tree. Observe that a tree without attacking lines is warranting.

Lemma 1 *A tree $\mathcal{T}_\mathsf{T}(\mathcal{A})$ is warranting* iff $Att(\mathcal{T}_\mathsf{T}(\mathcal{A})) = \emptyset$.

Proposition 1 *Given a line $\lambda \in \mathcal{T}_\mathsf{T}(\mathcal{A})$, if $\lambda \in Att(\mathcal{T}_\mathsf{T}(\mathcal{A}))$ then every $\mathcal{B} \in \lambda^+$ (resp., $\mathcal{B} \in \lambda^-$) is marked D (resp., U).*

The following example (worked throughout the rest of the article) shows the importance of identifying the precise argument –in a line to be altered– for which a defeater needs to be activated. This is addressed by the *argument selection function* (Def. 6). Trees are drawn with gray/white triangles denoting defeated/undefeated arguments.

Example 1 *Consider a DAT* T *yielding the tree $\mathcal{T}_\mathsf{T}(\mathcal{A})$ on the right with lines $\lambda_1 = [\mathcal{A}, \mathcal{B}_1, \mathcal{B}_3]$ and $\lambda_2 = [\mathcal{A}, \mathcal{B}_2, \mathcal{B}_4, \mathcal{B}_5]$. There is a single attacking line within the attacking set $Att(\mathcal{T}_\mathsf{T}(\mathcal{A})) = \{\lambda_2\}$. If we activate a defeater for $\mathcal{B}_2$ in* T*, we would generate a new line within a new tree having no attacking lines. If we instead add a defeater for $\mathcal{B}_5$, the line that was attacking is "extended" and again, in the resulting tree, there would be no attacking lines. On the other hand, if we activate a defeater for $\mathcal{B}_4$, we would generate another attacking line.*

We call *effective alteration* to the alteration of an attacking line that turns it to non-attacking. The alteration of a given attacking line is done by activating a defeater $\mathcal{D}$ for a con argument $\mathcal{B}$ in the line. This would imply $\mathcal{B}$ to end up marked as defeated. Afterwards, from Prop. 1, the resulting altered line would not be attacking. However, a variety of situations may appear: if $\mathcal{D}$ does not exist, the alteration of the line over $\mathcal{B}$ turns out to be unachievable. Later it will be clear that, when this happens for every con argument in the same line, the revision operation cannot succeed. On the other hand, activating a defeater for a con argument may bring not only that argument to the resulting tree, but a whole new subtree. Hence, an effective alteration in the activating approach will require to ensure the new defeater to end up undefeated within the resulting tree.

Definition 6 (Argument Selection) *Given a DAT* T $= \langle \mathbb{U}, \hookrightarrow, \sqsubseteq \rangle[\mathbb{A}]$ *and a line $\lambda \in \mathcal{T}_\mathsf{T}(\mathcal{A})$; the argument selection function $\gamma_\mathsf{T} : \mathfrak{Lines}_\mathsf{T}^\mathbb{A} \rightarrow \mathbb{A}$ is such that $\gamma_\mathsf{T}(\lambda) \in \lambda^-$.*

When selecting a con argument from a line $\lambda \in \mathcal{T}_\mathsf{T}(\mathcal{A})$, a selection criterion could lead the mapping of $\gamma_\mathsf{T}(\lambda)$ to an argument $\mathcal{B} \in \lambda^-$ by setting an ordering among the con arguments in λ. In this article we abstract away from any specific selection criterion.

Definition 7 (Set of Inactive Defeaters) *Let* T $= \langle \mathbb{U}, \hookrightarrow, \sqsubseteq \rangle[\mathbb{A}]$ *be a DAT, the set of inactive defeaters of an argument $\mathcal{B}$ in a line $\lambda \in \mathfrak{Lines}_\mathsf{T}^\mathbb{A}$, is determined by the function*

$\text{idefs}_T : \mathbb{A} \times \mathfrak{Lines}_T^{\mathbb{A}} \to \mathcal{P}(\mathbb{I})$ *such that:*

$\text{idefs}_T(\mathcal{B}, \lambda) = \{\mathcal{D} \in \mathbb{I} \mid \text{for every } \lambda' \in \mathfrak{Lines}_T^{\mathbb{U}}, \text{ such that } \mathcal{D} \in \lambda' \text{ and } \lambda^{\uparrow}[\mathcal{B}] = \lambda'^{\uparrow}(\mathcal{D})\}$

From Def. 7, every inactive defeater $\mathcal{D}$ of $\mathcal{B} \in \lambda$ belongs to a line λ' from $\mathfrak{Lines}_T^{\mathbb{U}}$ which means that λ' is acceptable but contains inactive arguments. Requiring $\lambda'^{\uparrow}(\mathcal{D})$ to coincide with $\lambda^{\uparrow}[\mathcal{B}]$ implies not only the segments from the root to $\mathcal{B}$ in both λ and λ' to be equal, but also $\mathcal{D} \hookrightarrow \mathcal{B}$.

The following notion allows to anticipate the effect of several changes over a DAT T by identifying a *hypothetical tree* $\mathcal{H}_T(\mathcal{A}, \Psi)$, as the tree rooted in $\mathcal{A}$ that would result from T by the hypothetical activation of the arguments in a set $\Psi \subseteq \mathbb{U}$. We refer to these trees as hypothetical given that they do not appear within the domain $\mathfrak{Trees}_T$.

Definition 8 (Hypothetical Tree) *Given a DAT* $T = \langle \mathbb{U}, \hookrightarrow, \sqsubseteq \rangle[\mathbb{A}]$, $\mathcal{A} \in \mathbb{A}$, *and* $\Psi \subseteq \mathbb{U}$; *the* **hypothetical tree** $\mathcal{H}_T(\mathcal{A}, \Psi)$ *is the tree built from the set of lines:*

$\{\lambda^{\uparrow}[\mathcal{B}] \mid \forall \lambda \in \mathfrak{Lines}_T^{\mathbb{U}}, \forall \mathcal{C} \in \lambda^{\uparrow}[\mathcal{B}] : \mathcal{C} \in (\mathbb{A} \oplus \Psi) \text{ holds, where } \text{root}(\lambda) = \mathcal{A} \text{ and}$
either $(\mathcal{B}$ *is the leaf of* λ) *or* $(\exists \mathcal{D} \in \lambda : \lambda^{\uparrow}(\mathcal{D}) = \lambda^{\uparrow}[\mathcal{B}] \text{ and } \mathcal{D} \notin (\mathbb{A} \oplus \Psi))\}$

Example 2 (Ex. 1 cont.) *Given the attacking line* $\lambda_2 = [\mathcal{A}, \mathcal{B}_2, \mathcal{B}_4, \mathcal{B}_5]$ *from Ex. 1, in order to warrant* $\mathcal{A}$ *a selection in* λ *should be performed. Assume that* $\mathcal{B}_2$ *is the most suitable argument according to the selection criterion:* $\gamma_T(\lambda_2) = \mathcal{B}_2$. *Let consider* $\mathcal{D}_1 \in \text{idefs}_T(\mathcal{B}_2, \lambda_2)$ *as a* $\mathcal{B}_2$*'s defeater that could be activated, and assume the activation of* $\mathcal{D}_1$ *determines a new active set of arguments such that* $\{\mathcal{C}_1, \mathcal{C}_2\} \subset \mathbb{A} \oplus \{\mathcal{D}_1\}$. *Assume the collateral activation of* $\mathcal{C}_1$ *as a consequence of the activation of* $\mathcal{D}_1$ *–for instance, we could have that* $\mathcal{C}' \sqsubseteq \mathcal{D}_1, \mathcal{C}' \sqsubseteq \mathcal{C}_1$ *and that the activation of* $\mathcal{C}'$ *activates* $\mathcal{C}_1$. *Additionally, suppose that* $\mathcal{C}_1 \hookrightarrow \mathcal{B}_4$. *Regarding* $\mathcal{C}_2$, *let assume it defeats* $\mathcal{D}_1$, *thus the activation of* $\mathcal{D}_1$ *would provoke* $\mathcal{C}_2$ *to be included in the resulting tree. Hence, from the hypothetical tree* $\mathcal{H}_T(\mathcal{A}, \{\mathcal{D}_1\})$ *on the right,* $\mathcal{A}$ *remains defeated, since the mark of* $\mathcal{B}_2$ *could not be turned to* D.

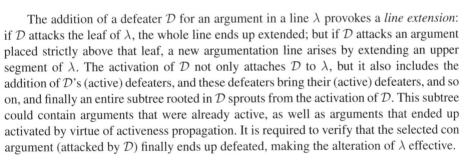

The addition of a defeater $\mathcal{D}$ for an argument in a line λ provokes a *line extension*: if $\mathcal{D}$ attacks the leaf of λ, the whole line ends up extended; but if $\mathcal{D}$ attacks an argument placed strictly above that leaf, a new argumentation line arises by extending an upper segment of λ. The activation of $\mathcal{D}$ not only attaches $\mathcal{D}$ to λ, but it also includes the addition of $\mathcal{D}$'s (active) defeaters, and these defeaters bring their (active) defeaters, and so on, and finally an entire subtree rooted in $\mathcal{D}$ sprouts from the activation of $\mathcal{D}$. This subtree could contain arguments that were already active, as well as arguments that ended up activated by virtue of activeness propagation. It is required to verify that the selected con argument (attacked by $\mathcal{D}$) finally ends up defeated, making the alteration of λ effective.

Definition 9 (Argument Defeating) *Given a DAT* $T = \langle \mathbb{U}, \hookrightarrow, \sqsubseteq \rangle[\mathbb{A}]$ *and a line* $\lambda \in \mathfrak{Lines}_T^{\mathbb{A}}$, *where* $\gamma_T(\lambda) = \mathcal{B}$ *is the selected argument over* $\lambda \in \mathcal{T}_T(\mathcal{A})$ *and* $\mathcal{A} = \text{root}(\lambda)$; *the* **argument defeating function** $\sigma_T : \mathfrak{Lines}_T^{\mathbb{A}} \to \mathbb{U}$ *is:*

$$\sigma_T(\lambda) = \begin{cases} \mathcal{D} \in \text{idefs}_T(\mathcal{B}, \lambda) & \text{if } \mathcal{B} \in \lambda' \text{ is marked } D. \\ \mathcal{A} & \text{otherwise.} \end{cases}$$

where $\lambda' \in \mathcal{H}_T(\mathcal{A}, \{\mathcal{D}\})$, *and* $\lambda'^{\uparrow}[\mathcal{B}] = \lambda^{\uparrow}[\mathcal{B}]$.

The defeating function returns the root argument when either it does not find a defeater, or every defeater found leads to a non-effective alteration. Thus, there would be no plausible inactive defeater for the selection at issue, situation that could be solved by a new selection in the same line. This is addressed by the following principle.

(Effective Alteration) $\sigma_T(\lambda) \neq \mathcal{A}$, for any $\lambda \in \mathcal{T}_T(\mathcal{A})$.

Example 3 (Ex. 2 cont.) *From* $\gamma_T(\lambda_2) = \mathcal{B}_2$ *we have that introducing* $\mathcal{D}_1$ *as a defeater for* $\mathcal{B}_2$ *would not be an effective alteration. Assume there exists a second defeater* $\mathcal{D}_2 \in \mathsf{idefs}_T(\mathcal{B}_2, \lambda_2)$ *whose activation would yield the hypothetical tree* $\mathcal{H}_T(\mathcal{A}, \{\mathcal{D}_2\})$ *on the right. Now the mark of* $\mathcal{B}_2$ *turns to D; nonetheless, by assuming* $\mathcal{C}_3 \in \mathbb{A} \oplus \{\mathcal{D}_2\}$ *and* $\mathcal{C}_3 \hookrightarrow \mathcal{B}_3$, *line* $\lambda_1 = [\mathcal{A}, \mathcal{B}_1, \mathcal{B}_3]$ *is collaterally altered, and even more, such collateral alteration turns the line to attacking. Since this alteration is independent from* λ_2, λ_1 *needs to be treated separately in a way that such collateral alteration does not affect it.*

Definition 10 (Collateral Alterations) *Let* $T = \langle \mathbb{U}, \hookrightarrow, \sqsubseteq \rangle[\mathbb{A}]$ *be a DAT, the* ***set of collateral alterations*** *of a line* $\lambda \in \mathcal{T}_T(\mathcal{A})$, *where* $\mathcal{A} = \mathsf{root}(\lambda)$, *is a function* $\mathsf{coll}(\sigma_T)$: $\mathfrak{Lines}_T^{\mathbb{A}} \to \mathcal{P}(\mathbb{U} \times \mathfrak{Lines}_T^{\mathbb{A}})$ *such that:*
$\mathsf{coll}(\sigma_T)(\lambda) = \{\langle \mathcal{C}, \lambda' \rangle \mid$ *for any* $\lambda' \in \mathcal{T}_T(\mathcal{A})$ *and any* $\mathcal{C} \in \lambda'$ *such that for either* $\lambda \neq \lambda'$ *or* $\mathcal{C} \neq \gamma_T(\lambda)$, *it follows* $\mathsf{idefs}_T(\mathcal{C}, \lambda') \cap (\mathbb{A} \oplus \{\sigma_T(\lambda)\}) \neq \emptyset\}$
A tuple $\langle \mathcal{C}, \lambda' \rangle$ *identifies* $\mathcal{C} \in \lambda'$ *for which an inactive defeater is collaterally activated.*

Example 4 *Collateral alterations occur in Ex. 2, where activating* $\mathcal{D}_1$ *implies the collateral activation of* $\mathcal{C}_1$, *and the collateral alteration of* λ_2. *A similar situation occurs in Ex. 3 with the activation of* $\mathcal{D}_2$ *and the collateral activation of* $\mathcal{C}_3$. *Finally, since* $\sigma_T(\lambda_2) = \mathcal{D}_2$ *we have that* $\langle \mathcal{B}_3, \lambda_1 \rangle \in \mathsf{coll}(\sigma_T)(\lambda_2)$.

Collateral alterations should be controlled to avoid triggering new attacking lines. Since these changes have still not been made to the theory, the selection necessarily needs to map to arguments in the original tree. The selection function in a line that will be collaterally altered should be required to map to an argument in the upper segment of the collateral activation in that line. Thus we would *preserve* the effectivity of alterations achieved through a defeating function.

(Preservation) If $\langle \mathcal{C}, \lambda \rangle \in \mathsf{coll}(\sigma_T)(\lambda')$ then $\gamma_T(\lambda) \in \lambda^{\uparrow}[\mathcal{C}]$ and $\mathcal{C} \neq \mathcal{A}, \forall \lambda' \in \mathcal{T}_T(\mathcal{A})$

Requiring to select in $\lambda^{\uparrow}[\mathcal{C}]$ ensures the mapping of the defeating function to provoke an effective alteration, since the new subtree would appear only below $\mathcal{C}$. This solves having this subtree defeating a pro argument in λ. Collateral alterations may extend the same line more than once. This threat is called *cumulative collateral alteration*.

(Non-Cumulativity) For any $\lambda \in \mathfrak{Lines}_T^{\mathbb{U}}$ and $\lambda' \in \mathcal{T}_T(\mathcal{A})$ such that $\sigma_T(\lambda') = \mathcal{D}$, if $\lambda^{\uparrow}(\mathcal{D}) = \lambda'^{\uparrow}[\mathcal{B}]$ then either $\mathcal{D}$ is a leaf of λ or there is some $\mathcal{C} \in \lambda$ such that $\mathcal{D} \in \lambda^{\uparrow}(\mathcal{C})$ and $\forall \mathcal{B}' \in \lambda^{\uparrow}(\mathcal{C})$ it holds that $\mathcal{B}' \in \mathbb{A} \oplus \{\mathcal{D}\}$ and $\mathcal{C} \notin \mathbb{A} \oplus \bigcup \sigma_T(\lambda''), \forall \lambda'' \in \mathcal{T}_T(\mathcal{A})$

To clarify, consider $\lambda = [\mathcal{A}, \ldots, \mathcal{B}, \mathcal{D}, \ldots, \mathcal{D}', \mathcal{C}, \ldots]$ where $\lambda' = [\mathcal{A}, \ldots, \mathcal{B}]$ is a line in the tree to be altered. Assume a defeating function mapping to $\mathcal{D}$, thus the activation of $\mathcal{D}$ leads to $[\mathcal{A}, \dots, \mathcal{B}, \mathcal{D}, \dots, \mathcal{D}']$ which ends up conforming the new altered line. (Recall that the defeating function ensures this alteration to be effective.) Afterwards, an argument activation from a different line in the tree triggers the collateral activation of $\mathcal{C}$, which ends up altering once more the same line, extending it. In this case, the activation of $\mathcal{D}$ cannot be ensured to be an effective alteration. Therefore, we need to protect the new subtree rooted in $\mathcal{D}$ (attached to $\mathcal{B}$) from collateral alterations like $\mathcal{C}$, which are "invisible" to the preservation principle.

Definition 11 (Warranting Defeating) *A defeating function "σ_T" is said to be **warranting** if it satisfies effective alteration, preservation, and non-cumulativity.*

The *alteration set* of a tree, contains the tree's attacking set along with those collaterally altered lines that end up turned into attacking in the resulting tree.

Definition 12 (Alteration Set) *Given a DAT* $T = \langle \mathbb{U}, \hookrightarrow, \sqsubseteq \rangle [\mathbb{A}]$; *the **alteration set** $\Lambda_T(\mathcal{A})$ of the tree $\mathcal{T}_T(\mathcal{A}) \in \mathfrak{Trees}_T$ is the least fixed point of the operator $\ell_T(\mathcal{A})$:*
$\ell_T(\mathcal{A})^0 = Att(\mathcal{T}_T(\mathcal{A}))$, *and*
$\ell_T(\mathcal{A})^{k+1} = \ell_T(\mathcal{A})^k \cup \{\lambda' \in \mathcal{T}_T(\mathcal{A})|$ *for any* $\lambda \in Att(\mathcal{H}_T(\mathcal{A}, \Psi))$ *there is some* $\mathcal{B} \in \lambda$ *and* $\mathcal{D} \in \lambda$ *such that* $\mathcal{D} \notin \lambda'$ *and* $\lambda^{\uparrow}(\mathcal{D}) = \lambda'^{\uparrow}[\mathcal{B}]$ *where* $\Psi = \bigcup_{\lambda'' \in \ell_T(\mathcal{A})^k} \sigma_T(\lambda'')\}$

Within a step $\ell_T(\mathcal{A})^{k+1}$ we include the lines in $\ell_T(\mathcal{A})^k$ along with every $\lambda' \in \mathcal{T}_T(\mathcal{A})$ that would be collaterally altered (by activating an argument $\sigma_T(\lambda'')$ where $\lambda'' \in \mathcal{T}_T(\mathcal{A})$ and λ'' belongs to $\ell_T(\mathcal{A})^k$) conforming a line λ which would end up being a new attacking line in the hypothetical tree. Finally, if "σ_T" is warranting then it cannot be the case that $\lambda' = \lambda''$ holds. This means that once the mapping $\sigma_T(\lambda'')$ is considered in Ψ, no collateral alteration of λ'' will be included in $Att(\mathcal{H}_T(\mathcal{A}, \Psi))$ for any tree $\mathcal{H}_T(\mathcal{A}, \Psi)$.

Definition 13 (Argument Revision) *An **activating argument revision** operator "$*$" over* $T = \langle \mathbb{U}, \hookrightarrow, \sqsubseteq \rangle [\mathbb{A}]$ *by* $\mathcal{A} \in \mathbb{U}$ *is defined as:*

$$T * \mathcal{A} = \begin{cases} \langle \mathbb{U}, \hookrightarrow, \sqsubseteq \rangle [\mathbb{A}''] & \text{if "σ_T" is warranting, or} \\ T & \text{otherwise,} \end{cases}$$

where $\mathbb{A}'' = \mathbb{A}' \oplus \bigcup_{\lambda \in \Lambda_{T'}(\mathcal{A})} \sigma_T(\lambda)$, $\mathbb{A}' = \mathbb{A} \oplus \{\mathcal{A}\}$, *and* $T' = \langle \mathbb{U}, \hookrightarrow, \sqsubseteq \rangle [\mathbb{A}']$

Example 5 (Ex. 3 cont.) *From* $\sigma_T(\lambda_2) = \mathcal{D}_2$ *we have that* λ_1 *is collaterally altered by the collateral activation of* $\mathcal{C}_3$*. Moreover, since line* $[\mathcal{A}, \mathcal{B}_1, \mathcal{B}_3, \mathcal{C}_3]$ *is in the attacking set of* $\mathcal{H}_T(\mathcal{A}, \{\mathcal{D}_1\})$*, the resulting alteration set ends up being* $\Lambda_T(\mathcal{A}) = \{\lambda_1, \lambda_2\}$*. Note that having* $\langle \mathcal{B}_3, \lambda_1 \rangle \in coll(\sigma_T)(\lambda_2)$*, from preservation* $\gamma_T(\lambda_1) \in \lambda_1^{\uparrow}[\mathcal{B}_3]$ *must hold. Thus, assuming* $\gamma_T(\lambda_1) = \mathcal{B}_1$ *and* $\sigma_T(\lambda_1) = \mathcal{D}_3$*, preservation is guaranteed. Note that the defeating function ends up guaranteeing also both the effective alteration and the non-cumulativity principles. Finally, the warranting tree on the right appears from the revised framework* $T * \mathcal{A} = \langle \mathbb{U}, \hookrightarrow, \sqsubseteq \rangle [\mathbb{A} \oplus \{\mathcal{A}, \mathcal{D}_2, \mathcal{D}_3\}]$*.*

The following results ensure that the revision of a theory through a warranting defeating function is successful and warrants $\mathcal{A}$, as stated by Theorem 1. Corollary 1 states that the revision does not change the original theory either when it already warranted $\mathcal{A}$ or the revision could not be successful.

Lemma 2 *If* $\mathsf{T}*\mathcal{A}$ *uses a warranting defeating function then* $Att(\mathcal{T}_{(\mathsf{T}*\mathcal{A})}(\mathcal{A})) = \emptyset$.

Theorem 1 $\mathsf{T}*\mathcal{A}$ *warrants* $\mathcal{A}$ *iff* $\mathsf{T}*\mathcal{A}$ *uses a warranting defeating function.*

Corollary 1 $\mathsf{T}*\mathcal{A} = \mathsf{T}$ *iff either* T *warrants* $\mathcal{A}$ *or* $\mathsf{T}*\mathcal{A}$ *does not warrant* $\mathcal{A}$.

4. Conclusions, Related and Future Work

We have presented a new approach for argument revision considering activation of arguments. This new approach is comprehended within Argument Theory Change [11] and provides another standpoint to change the status of warrant of an argument.

Regarding related work, in [4] change is studied over the set of extensions of a system after adding an argument. However, they pose a strong restriction: the newly added argument must have at most one interaction (via attack) with an argument in the system. This restriction (which we do not assume) greatly simplifies the revision problem, as multiple interactions with the original system are difficult to handle. Moreover, we consider the complexity added by subarguments.

Revision over an argumentation-based decision making system was defined in [2] through a generalization of the revision technique from [4], which evaluates the warrant status of a newly inserted argument supporting an option. A similar approach was presented in [3]. There, the *abstraction* of a framework (*i.e.,* removal of a set of arguments or attacks) is considered, and principles are proposed to establish conditions under which the semantics remains unchanged, in order to avoid its recomputation.

References

[1] Carlos Alchourrón, Peter Gärdenfors, and David Makinson. *On the Logic of Theory Change: Partial Meet Contraction and Revision Functions. The Journal of Symbolic Logic*, 50:510–530, 1985.
[2] Leila Amgoud and Srdjan Vesic. On revising argumentation-based decision systems. In *ECSQARU*, pages 71–82, 2009.
[3] Guido Boella, Souhila Kaci, and Leendert van der Torre. Dynamics in argumentation with single extensions: Abstraction principles and the grounded extension. In *ECSQARU*, pages 107–118, 2009.
[4] Claudette Cayrol, Florence Dupin de Saint-Cyr, and Marie-Christine Lagasquie-Schiex. Revision of an Argumentation System. In *KR*, pages 124–134, 2008.
[5] Carlos Chesñevar, Ana Maguitman, and Ronald Loui. Logical Models of Argument. *ACM Computing Surveys*, 32(4):337–383, 2000.
[6] Phan Minh Dung. On the Acceptability of Arguments and its Fundamental Role in Nonmonotonic Reasoning, Logic Programming and n-person Games. *AIJ*, 77:321–357, 1995.
[7] Alejandro García and Guillermo Simari. Defeasible Logic Programming: An Argumentative Approach. *TPLP*, 4(1-2):95–138, 2004.
[8] Sven Ove Hansson. Kernel Contraction. *Journal of Symbolic Logic*, 59:845–859, 1994.
[9] Martín Moguillansky, Nicolás Rotstein, Marcelo Falappa, Alejandro García, and Guillermo Simari. Argument Theory Change Applied to Defeasible Logic Programming. In *AAAI*, pages 132–137, 2008.
[10] Henry Prakken and Gerard Vreeswijk. Logical Systems for Defeasible Argumentation. In *Handbook of Philosophical Logic, 2nd ed.* 2000.
[11] Nicolás Rotstein, Martín Moguillansky, Marcelo Falappa, Alejandro García, and Guillermo Simari. Argument Theory Change: Revision Upon Warrant. In *COMMA*, pages 336–347, 2008.
[12] Nicolás Rotstein, Martín Moguillansky, Alejandro García, and Guillermo Simari. An Abstract Argumentation Framework for Handling Dynamics. In *NMR*, pages 131–139, 2008.

Computational Models of Argument
P. Baroni et al. (Eds.)
IOS Press, 2010
doi:10.3233/978-1-60750-619-5-367

Exploring the Role of Emotions in Rational Decision Making

Fahd Saud NAWWAB [1], Paul E. DUNNE, Trevor BENCH-CAPON

Department of Computer Science, The University of Liverpool, U.K.

Abstract. Our focus in this paper is to explore how emotional factors can complement rationality in decision making. Our approach is to develop a model of the situation and use this model to generate arguments for and against the actions that an agent can perform. Actions are then chosen by evaluating this set of arguments according to the subjective preferences and emotional state of the agent concerned. A mechanism to control and balance the extent of emotional effects is also introduced. We illustrate our approach with an extended case study based on an implemented system embodying this approach.

Keywords. practical reasoning, emotion, decision making with argumentation.

1. Introduction

People very often take decisions influenced by emotional factors, and this influence can be beneficial [4,5]. We certainly behave differently to our family and friends, and this difference cannot easily be explained simply in rational terms. Also the goals we choose to give priority to may depend on our mood, and how anxious or encouraged we have become by recent failures and successes [6]. In this paper, we discuss the realisation of the approach to incorporating emotions into the argumentation-based model of decision making described in [7] first sketched in [8]. Our experiments show in practice how the decisions of an agent can be improved if it considers emotional aspects.

We draw extensively on the work of others for our conception of emotions. The underlying model is OCC [9]. We adapt mechanisms for the generation, storage, decay and behavioural effects of emotions from [10]. Our formal structure for representing emotions is based on the formalisation of OCC given in [11]. We extend this body of work to incorporate particular emotions in the decision-making model. By implementing the methodology, we hope to be able to give a better understanding of the work on emotions. The formalisations presented in [7,8] show the applicability of this work to agent systems; and explore different setups and scenarios where conditions and reactions from the environment differ, to allow an analysis of the effects of emotions on the decision-making process and analyse the effect of different setups. Section 2 gives some necessary background, Section 3

---

[1]Corresponding author: Email: fahad@csc.liv.ac.uk

discusses emotions and decision making, Section 4 describes the case study and discusses its results. Section 5 offers some concluding remarks.

2. The Decision-Making Model

The model of agent decision making is based on the approach of [1], which was further developed in [7]. The approach relies on argumentation techniques: candidate actions are identified by providing *prima facie* justifications for them by instantiating a particular argumentation scheme on the basis of an underlying state transition model. This justification can then be critiqued by a set of characteristic counterarguments, and the decision is then made by choosing a defensible set of action justifications, according to the preferences of the decision maker. In [7], which contains full details of the five steps and their formal underpinnings, the following methodology was proposed:

1. *Formulating the Problem*: A representation of the problem scenario in terms of an Action-Based Alternating Transition System (AATS) [12]. A particular feature of the AATS is that the transitions are *joint* actions (a joint action is composed from one action from each agent in the scenario), and so whether the agent will reach the state intended when selecting an action depends on what the other agents present in the scenario do.

2. *Determining the Arguments*: Instantiations of the argument scheme justifying actions in terms of the AATS, and counter arguments based on critical questions appropriate to that scheme are identified. A formal description of the argument scheme and critical questions can be found in [1]. A particular feature of this argument scheme is that it associates arguments with social values, such as equality, liberty and fraternity, for the sake of which the actions are performed. Some social values, like equality, represent common goods and are calculated for the group of agents as a whole, while others, such as happiness, are calculated with respect to each individual agent.

3. *Building the Argumentation Framework*: Using the values associated with the arguments by the argument scheme, the arguments and counter arguments identified in the previous step are formed into a Value Based Argumentation Framework (VAF) [3]. A VAF allows for attacks from one argument to another to succeed or fail according to the relative weight given to the values associated with them by the audience concerned.

4. *Evaluating the Framework*: The particular subjective value ordering of the agent concerned is now used to identify the preferred extension of the VAF for that agent. This identifies the arguments that withstand the critique from the perspective of the decision-making agent, and actions justified by this set are those that the agent will wish to perform.

5. *Sequencing the Actions*: The set of actions justified in the previous step are now sequenced for execution. Actions are sequenced according to the *safety* (the subsequent actions remain possible even when the intended action fails), *threats* (consequences of the joint action not being as expected) and *opportunities* (possible actions they enable) associated with them.

Once the actions have been sequenced, the agent will attempt to execute the sequence. In the absence of emotions, the agent will continue to execute the sequence as long as it is possible to do so, and so will replan only if the joint action reaches a state in which the preconditions for the next action are not satisfied. We further include at this point an emotional response: the particular emotions generated will be according to whether the joint action was such as to reach the state intended or not. Our idea now is that the emotional state will impact the degree to which values are thought worth pursuing, causing the agent to prize some values more and some less. For example, if another agent acts so that the joint action leads to an undesired state, our agent is likely to favour the happiness of that agent less. At some points, these changes in weights of values can lead to a change in the ordering of values. At this point, the subjective preferences of the agent will have changed to an extent which could impact on the arguments justified by the VAF. Such a change thus provides an additional trigger for replanning.

3. Emotions

We take as a starting point a formalisation of the the OCC model of emotions adapted from [11]. We have changed some of the emotions' names so that *love* and *hate* have become *like* and *dislike* to make it clear that our emotional states need not be extreme. We also subscript the goals to make clear which agent they are goals of.

Definition 1 (Emotional Fluents); The set Emotions is the set of emotional fluents, which is defined as follows: Emotions =

$joy_i(k_i)$,	$distress_i(\neg k_i)$,
$hope_i(\pi, k_i)$,	$fear_i(\pi, \neg k_i)$,
$satisfaction_i(\pi, k_i)$,	$disappointment_i(\pi, \neg k_i)$,
$relief_i(\pi, k_i)$,	$fears - confirmed_i(\pi, \neg k_i)$,
$happy - for_i(j, k_j)$,	$resentment_i(j, k_j)$,
$gloating_i(j, \neg k_j)$,	$pity_i(j, \neg k_j)$,
$pride_i(\alpha_i)$,	$shame_i(\alpha_i)$,
$admiration_i(j, \alpha_j)$,	$reproach_i(j, \alpha_j)$,
$like_i(j)$,	$dislike_i(j)$,
$gratification_i(\alpha_i, k_i)$,	$remorse_i(\alpha_i, \neg k_i)$,
$gratitude_i(j, \alpha_j, k_i)$,	$displeasure_i(j, \alpha_j, \neg k_i)$,

Where i and j are distinct agents, α_i and α_j are actions available to these agents, π a plan of agent i expressed as a sequence of actions, and k is a partial state of affairs, so that k_i is a goal of agent i and K_j is a goal of $agent_j$.

Note that these emotions can be directed towards two *agents*, which we shall refer to as *self* and *other* respectively, a *plan*, which in our model relates to the sequence of actions identified in step 5, and a *goal*. Since, however, in our model the agent is only interested in goals because they promote values, we will use values rather than goals in this role. Here we will only consider those emotions relating to the values of self: our model does not yet embrace the identification of the values pursued by the other agents. The emotions form eleven pairs of emotions, each pair comprising one positive and one negative emotion. The emotional response will depend on whether the joint action was such as to promote the value for the sake of which the agent chose its own action. If the value is promoted, positive emotions will be experienced, otherwise negative emotions will be experienced. We will consider the negative emotions: *mutans mutandis* the positive emotions are similar. If the value had not been promoted, one or more agents will have acted other than as was required by the anticipated joint action. Self will feel displeasure and reproach towards them in respect of their action. This in turn will increase the feeling of dislike towards those agents. Since self's choice was not effective, self will feel remorse in respect of that choice, which in turn give rise to feelings of shame. Because the value was not promoted feelings of distress will increase, and because part of the plan has failed disappointment will be experienced. Remember, too, that the action chosen was part of a sequence. Since the failure of the action may threaten the plan, fear is felt in respect of the values to be promoted by the remaining actions. If some actions become impossible, fears-confirmed will be experienced. Thus the various emotions can be generated by comparing the state reached with the state intended.

Emotions can, however, be experienced with varying degrees of intensity. OCC identified a number of variables affecting intensity, but we follow [10] in simplifying the model and consider only two factors, *importance* and *unexpectedness*. The importance of success will reflect the degree of importance associated with the value aimed at. We extend the VAFs of [3] by associating a weight with each value for each agent, reflecting the importance of the value to that agent. The value order is formed by arranging the values according to these weights. The importance of the success of an action will also be calculated on the basis of these weights. Unexpectedness is derived from expectations as to what the other agents will do. In the absence of other information, we could regard each possible joint action as equally likely. Often, however, we can see that the actions in the joint actions would be advantageous to the other agents. In such cases, we would expect them to comply and so would find a failure unexpected. So it can be possible to estimate the probability of the actions being chosen by the other agents and to use this estimate to calculate unexpectedness. The more sophisticated our model of other agents, the more reliable will be the probability, but even poor estimates can be used to determine the intensity of the emotional response. It is after all the subjective estimate of the agent concerned.

We must now consider the storage of emotions. Again we follow the treatment of [10]. Some emotions are momentary: gratitude and displeasure, for example, are experienced with respect to particular events, but others, such as joy, distress, like and dislike, persist through time, subject to a decay factor, but modified by events. Thus the emotion of liking for another agent will reflect the cumulative effect of a series of past actions giving rise to gratitude and displeasure. In order to calculate the effect on values, the various emotions are combined into *behavioural features*, such as general mood, or friendliness towards other agents. Rules to modify the value weights are then expressed in terms of these behavioural features. Definitions relating to the intensity, storage and decay of emotions were given in [8]. We will now illustrate the approach by considering a case study.

4. Case Study

In this section we describe the case study. We will describe the set up of the study and explore some particular executions in detail. Our agent is a head of an academic department (HoD) in a university, and he is faced with a dilemma of choosing how to allocate the department's budget in the light of departmental and individual interests. Our agent (HoD) has requests relating to travel funding to attend two specific conferences. He received requests from three different students and needs to decide which of them to send. Students S_1 and S_2 are new students. S_1 is asking to go to a nearby conference, which will be cheaper financially; S_2 is asking for an overseas conference, which will cost more, but S_2 has prepared a good paper that might help the department's publication rate. Student S_3 is an experienced student asking to be sent to the local conference. Although she did not prepare a paper for submission, she is an excellent networker who is likely to impress other delegates and so promote the reputation of the department. The conferences are on different topics, so S_3's paper would not be suitable for the local conference, but both conferences are of equal standing. The budget only allows two students to be sent. Our first step is to formulate the problem in terms of an AATS.

4.1. AATS

An AATS requires a number of elements. We instantiate each of them for the case study.

- *A set of states.* States are composed of propositions. The propositions of interest are: the available budget, whether each of the three student has been sent to a conference or not, whether each of the three students has written a paper and whether each of the three students has previously attended the conference. We write this as $B-C_1C_2C_3-W_1W_2W_3-A_1A_2A_3$. The initial state where the budget is 3, no students have been sent, only student 2 has written a paper and only student 3 has previously attended a conference is thus: 300-000-010-001. The remaining states can be generated by considering all possible combinations of values for these propositions.
- *A set of agents.* We have four agents: the Head of Department and three students. Thus the set of agents in $\{H, S_1, S_2, S_3\}$.
- *A set of actions for each agent.* These are shown in Table 1, and the joint actions that can be formed from them in Table 2.
- A precondition function. The preconditions for each action are shown in Table 1.
- A transition function giving the result of joint actions. The post conditions of each joint action are shown in Table 2.
- A set of values. We consider the Publication and Esteem of the Department and Happiness and Experience of each of the three students. This the set of values is $\{P, Est, H_1, H_2, H_3, E_1, E_2, E_3\}$.
- A description of how values are promoted and demoted. This is shown in Table 3. The device of increasing A_n to show that a student does well is a workaround to cater for the fact that the value is promoted in virtue of

the action rather than in virtue of moving to the target state. A treatment of such issues can be provided by using the action state semantics of [2].

Agent	Action	Reference	Precondition
HoD	Send Sn to a conference	$\alpha 1(n)$	Cn = 0
HoD	Asks Sn to write a paper	$\alpha 2(n)$	Wn = 0
Sn	Student n does well at the conference	β_n	none
Sn	Student n does poorly at the conference	$\beta_n\prime$	none
Sn	Student n writes a paper	γ_n	Wn = 0
Sn	Student n does not write a paper	$\gamma_n\prime$	Wn = 0

Table 1. All Possible Actions

Joint Ac	Combination	Description	Postcondition
$J1_n$	$\alpha 1(n), \beta_n$	HoD sends Sn to a conference and she does well	If n = 2 then B = B -2 else B = B-1. Cn = 1. An := An + 1
$J2_n$	$\alpha 1(n), \beta_n\prime$	HoD sends Sn to a conference and she does poorly	If n = 2 then B = B -2 else B = B-1. Cn = 1.
$J3_n$	$\alpha 2(n), \gamma_n$	HoD asks Sn to write a paper and she does	Wn = 1
$J4_n$	$\alpha 2(n), \gamma_n\prime$	HoD asks Sn to write a paper and she does not	

Table 2. All Possible Joint Actions

Value	Source State	Target State	Sign
P	Wn = 1, Cn = 0	Cn = 1	+
Est	An ≥ 1, Cn = 0	Cn = 1. An increases	+
Hn	Cn = 0	Cn = 1	+
Hn	Wn = 1, Cn = 0	Cn = 0	-
En	Cn = 1. An = 0	An = 1	+

Table 3. Changes affecting Values

This gives all the information required to construct the AATS and produce the arguments and counterarguments as in [7]. If we ascribe a value order to the HoD we can evaluate the resulting VAF. For example, the Value Order ($VO_0 = Est > P > (E_1 = E_2 = E_3) > (H_1 = H_2 = H_3)$) will justify the set of actions $\{ask(S_3), send(S_3), send(S_2)\}$. This will also be the sequence in which the actions should be performed, since it is better to ask a student to write a paper before sending him, so that there is an incentive to comply, and sending S_3 promotes more values and commits less budget than sending S_2.

4.2. Adding Emotions

We next add the components required for an emotional response. In the implementation, actual numbers are used. The precise numbers, however, are not of much significance: what does matter is their relative values, and different numbers only affect when things happen rather than what can happen, which is our concern here. For a particular application, particular numbers can be chosen and tuned to give the required behaviour, for example whether the agent is very responsive to emotional effects, or relatively impassive. We will therefore attempt to summarise the experiments by talking in qualitative terms, rather than by reporting the numerical outputs. First, we need to produce estimates of the importance of values and the probabilities of the students performing as hoped. Each of the values are assigned degrees of importance reflecting the the value order of the HoD, V_0. For the purposes of our experiments, we assigned probabilities to the various students succeeding in writing a paper and performing well at the conference. In our experiments we ordered the actions as follows, starting with the most probable: $(\beta_1 = \beta_2) > \beta_3 > \gamma_3 > (\gamma_1 = \gamma_2)$. This reflects that it is easier to write a paper than to make an impact at an international conference: that the more independently minded and experienced student is less likely than the new students to write a paper but more likely to perform well at the conference. Of course, other assumptions could have been made. Initially, all the emotions and behavioural features are set to 0. However as emotions will be generated and stored in the scenario we need to consider the rate of decay for each emotion. The rules for decay are shown in Table 4.

Emotion	Decay
Joy(G)	50% with each transition
Distress(G)	50% with each transition
Hope($\underline{j}$,G)	Decays to 0 when a student is sent to a conference and attends
Fear($\underline{j}$,G)	Decays to 0 when the other student S writes and attends a conference
Satisfaction($\underline{j}$,G)	Decays to 0 when Joy(G) becomes 0
Fears-Confirmed($\underline{j}$,G)	Decays to 0 when Distress(G) becomes 0
Pride(α)	50% with each transition
Shame(α)	50% with each transition
Like(S)	30% with every transition
Dislike(S)	30% with every transition
Admiration(S,α)	50% when Pride(α) becomes 0
Reproach(S,α)	50% when Shame(α) becomes 0

Table 4. Decay functions of the Example study

Next, we need to assign weights to the values of the HoD. We gave the HoD the initial Value Order ($VO_0 = Est > Publication > Experience > Happiness$). The weights will have two components, one to reflect the intrinsic worth of the values and one to reflect their relative worth. We want the departmental values of Publication and Esteem to be able change places, but to be always preferred to the student directed values of Experience and Happiness. We also wish to allow quite ready movement between the student directed values, and especially the order in which a particular value is directed towards different students. Thus, Esteem and Publication will be given high intrinsic worth TI_H, and Experience and Happiness medium intrinsic worth (TI_M). To give emotions a moderate influence on the decision-making process, we place a medium threshold (TR) between the different values. TR will be multiplied by a factor indicating the rank of the value in the value order. The weights of values can be given as: $VO_0 = Esteem_{TIL+(3\times TR)} > Publication_{TIL+(2\times TR)} > (E1_{TIM+(1\times TR)} = E2_{TIM+(1\times TR)} = E3_{TIM+(1\times TR)}) > (H1_{TIM+(0\times TR)} = H2_{TIM+(0\times TR)} = H3_{TIM+(0\times TR)}).$

The final part of the set up to accommodate emotions is that we link emotions to values through behavioural features. The connection between the emotional state of the agent (HoD) and the decision-making methodology is made by setting the different behaviorial features and linking them to the Values in the value order. We identify four behavioural features and link them to values using rules. The Behavioural Features are:

1. Mood = (Joy(G) - Distress(G) + Hope(G)) / 2
2. Friendliness(S) = (Mood + (Like(S) - Dislike(S)))/2
3. Defensive(S) = (Dislike(S) + Reproach(S,α_S))/2
4. Worried(G) = (Fears-confirmed(π,G) + Fear(π,G) /2 + Distress(G) - Relief(π,G)

The effect of these features on values is given by the following rules:

- $H_S = H_S$ + Mood + Friendliness(S)
- $E_S = E_S$ - Defensive(S) + (Friendliness(S)/3)
- P = P + Worried(P)
- Est = Est + Worried(Est) + Mood

We are now ready to execute the first action, observe the outcome, and calculate the emotional response.

4.3. Effects of Particular Actions

In the following sub-sections we will consider the possible responses to various actions.

4.3.1. Asking S_3 to Write a Paper

Recall from section 4.1 that the initial plan was {ask(S_3), send(S_3), send(S_2)}. So the HoD wants $J3_3$ to be performed, but it is possible that $J4_3$ will be the actual joint action. Suppose the joint action is $J3_3$. This will give rise to an emotion of admiration (rather than gratitude, since no values are yet promoted) towards S_3, increasing the emotion of like towards S_3. It is also a step in the plan, and gives the possibility of promoting P, and so gives hope with respect to P. Behaviourally the mood of the HoD will improve, and the friendliness towards S_3 will increase. This in turn will raise the weight of the happiness of all students (through mood) and experience in respect of S_3 (through friendliness). Finally the mood will also increase the importance of esteem. The only possible change in the value order than can result (whether it does or not depend on the precise numbers chosen) from this is that the Happiness of students 2 and 3 rises above their experience. This will not affect the plan, since S_3 will still be chosen in the hope of promoting Esteem as well as Publication, and the increased weight of Happiness and Experience relating to S_3 can only reinforce the decision.

Suppose, however, that S_3 fails to produce a paper, so that the actual joint action is $J4_3$. This will mean that the HoD experiences reproach towards S_3, increasing dislike of S_3 and fear with respect to Publication. These emotions decrease the friendliness towards S_3, make the HoD defensive towards S_3 and make him worried with respect to Publication. These behavioural features will not affect the values relating to the other students, but the happiness and experience of S_3 will get less weight. Additionally the worry will cause the weight on the value of Publication to rise. These changes will have an effect on the plan if the increase in the value of Publication is sufficient to push it above that of Esteem. If this is so, then the Hod will ask S_1 to write a paper as this is the best way to promote publication. Sending S_2 will also promote publication, but will be sequenced after asking S_1 to write as sending S_2 remains possible even if S_1 fails. If, however, Esteem remains preferred to publication, the plan will continue. So at the second step, the HoD will either send S_3 or ask S_1 to write a paper.

4.3.2. Sending S_3 to the Conference

Now the Hod wants $J1_3$ to be performed, but it is possible that $J2_3$ will be the actual joint action. Suppose $J1_3$ happens, realising the value of Esteem, and, provided S_3 wrote a paper in the first step, Publication also. Now the HoD will experience both gratitude (since at least one value was promoted) and admiration towards S_3, increasing his liking of S_3. Additionally he will experience joy, hope, and satisfaction with respect to Esteem, and possibly Publication. His mood will improve, as will his friendliness towards S_3. Since Esteem is an important goal and success was less likely than S_3 writing a paper in the previous step, the liking for S_3 will more than compensate for any dislike generated if S_3 failed in the previous step. Thus the happiness and experience of all students will rise in importance, and those in respect of S_3 will move ahead of those in respect of the other students. Esteem will also increase in importance because of the improved mood. None of this should affect the plan, and so in the next step the HoD will complete the plan by sending S_2 to his conference.

Suppose, however, that S_3 does not perform well, so that the joint action is $J2_3$. There are two cases: one where S_3 wrote a paper in the first step and one where she did not. First suppose that she did. Now although Esteem is not promoted, Publication is. Thus the HoD will experience joy with respect to Publication and distress with respect to Esteem. But because it is the more important value that has failed, the distress will outweigh the joy and the mood will become worse. The mood will decrease the weight given to the happiness of all students, and more so in the case of S_3 as friendliness has decreased. The importance of Esteem will rise because the worry in respect of that value will offset the effect of mood. None of this, however, will affect the value order or the plan.

If, however, the paper has not been written, the effect of the failure to achieve esteem will not be ameliorated by the success of Publication. The mood will become worse, the friendliness to S_3 even lower, and the defensiveness towards S_3 higher. Finally, the fears-confirmed with respect to Publication will increase worry with respect to that value. This will depress the happiness and experience of S_3 below that of the other students, and may have the effect of raising Publication above Esteem. This will not, however, change the plan: the budget is now too small to send both S_1 and S_2 and so publication is most safely promoted by sending S_2 who has already written a paper. Note that the worst outcome is where HoD persists with the plan after the first step has failed. If the second step also fails it has become too late to rectify matters. The opportunity to replan given by the emotional response to the failure of the first step, provides a way of avoiding this. Replanning would have led to S_1 being asked to write a paper.

4.3.3. Asking S_1 to Write a Paper

This action is performed when S_3 failed to write a paper and the emotional response moved the value of Publication above that of Esteem. Now the HoD wants $J3_1$ to be performed, but it is possible that $J4_1$ will be the actual joint action. If S_1 succeeds, the situation will be similar to that where S_3 succeeded in step 1. Admiration will be felt towards S_1. Mood will improve, because of the hope with respect to P, and friendliness towards S_1 will increase because of liking increasing. Now within the values of happiness and experience the students are ordered $S_1 > S_2 > S_3$, that of S_1 having risen at this step and that of S_3 having fallen at the previous step. Esteem rises in line with the improved mood while Publication remains unchanged. Note, however, that this will not cause Esteem to return to being preferred to Publication since the relative expectedness of S_1 writing compared to S_3 writing will mean that the hope engendered at this stage does not compensate for the worry at the previous stage. The preference for the happiness and experience of S_1 over S_2 will mean that S_1 is sent. Suppose, however, S_1 fails to write the paper. Now the experience will be similar to that when S_3 failed at step 1. Fear with respect to Publication will increase further, and so to will worry with respect to that value. The weight placed on the happiness and experience of S_1 will fall, and because success was rather expected, will fall below that with respect to S_3. In consequence, the HoD will in this case choose to send S_2 as the next action.

4.3.4. Sending S_1 to the Conference

Suppose that S_1 succeeded and is sent to the conference. $J1_1$ is intended, although it is felt that $J2_1$ is more likely to be the actual joint action. Since S_2 has written a paper either outcome will promote Publication giving a small boost to the relevant emotions (small because with the paper already written it was expected). If the joint action is $J2_1$ there will be a variety of effects, similar to those resulting from the failure of S_3 when sent in step 2, but relatively small, since the HoD did not expect much from S_1. There will be little impact on the value order, except to decrease the relative happiness and experience relative to S_1. As a result, the HoD will press on with his plan and send S_2, which will certainly promote Publication, whereupon his budget will be insufficient to do anything further. Perhaps, however, S_1 will have an unexpected triumph, so promoting Esteem as well as Publication. Because this was not anticipated, it will have a big effect on the emotions, greatly increasing admiration and gratitude towards, and hence liking for, S_1. This will further boost the HoD's preference for his happiness and experience. The joy resulting from the unexpected promotion of Esteem will also improve the mood of the HoD, raising the importance of the happiness of all three students, and also impacting on the weight given to Esteem. Given the intensity of the emotions, and the relief felt with respect to Publication, this may return

Esteem to being the most preferred value. If this is the case, then whereas the original plan was to next send S_2, the renewed importance of esteem, and the cancellation of the effect on the happiness of S_3 consequent on the changed mood, may lead the Hod to send S_3 so as to promote esteem. From the point of view of departmental values, this is certainly the right thing to do, but S_2 may well feel hard done by. The various routes through the scenario are shown in Figure 1.

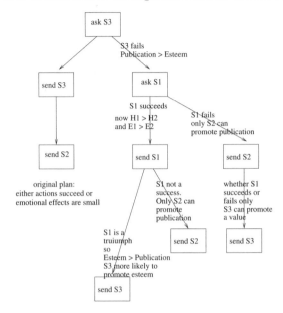

Figure 1. Variations arising from emotional influences

Emotions can influence the decision making at three points in the above scenario: If S_3 fails to write a paper. Worry about Publication may mean that S_1 is asked to write a paper instead of Esteem being pursued by sending S_3. If S_1 writes a paper. Now liking for S_1 will mean that S_1 is sent before S_2. If S_1 succeeds at the conference. Relief with respect to Publication, together with the improved mood after this unexpected bonus may mean that Esteem again becomes the priority and S_3 is sent to pursue this value.

Of particular note is the way in which the emotional response prevented staying with a failing plan and instead sought an alternative way of promoting key values in step 3, and caused a refocus on important departmental goals in response to the unexpected success of S_1 in Section 4.3.4. It may appear that S_2 suffers because he is given no opportunity to impress the HoD. We may think this is appropriate as the aims of the department are furthered. However, if we wish to give the interests of S_2 more weight, we could increase the liking for S_2 in the initial position, to reflect that he already had a paper written.

5. Summary

This paper presented an approach to enable emotions to have an influence on rational decision making, illustrated with a detailed case study. One purpose of providing this example was to give a comprehensive explanation of the mechanisms by using an example relevant to the topic. The key role of emotions in our approach is to trigger replanning through a change in value ordering, either because the performance of a given agent has altered its standing with respect to other agents, or because success (or failure) has led to a change in priorities. These changes are controlled by thresholds representing the volatility of the agent.

Consideration of emotions might also help in developing cooperation amongst agents. This aspect was not implemented nor studied thoroughly in this work, in which the focus was on the decisions of only one of the agents in the scenario, but is a topic for further research using scenarios in which the decision making of all the agents concerned is modelled. If agents considered the emotional impact of their actions on one another when deciding what to do, this might have an influence on their choice of action. When S_3 refused to write a paper at the beginning of the case study scenario, this affected future considerations about whether she should be sent to a conference (not related directly to her failure, but to the emotional response of the HoD). This in turn means that S_3 fails to promote her happiness, which may be presumed to be an important value for her. If S_3 had anticipated that failing to write will have emotional effects to the HoD, she would have had a stronger reason to write the paper. Thus, awareness of the emotional impact and its consequences can help to foster cooperation.

References

[1] K. Atkinson and T. Bench-Capon. Practical reasoning as presumptive argumentation using action based alternating transition systems. *Artificial Intelligence*, 171(10-15):855–874, 2007.
[2] K. Atkinson and T. Bench-Capon. Action-state semantics for practical reasoning. In *AAAI Fall Symposium. Technical Report SS-09-06*, pages 8–13, 2009.
[3] T. Bench-Capon. Persuasion in practical argument using value-based argumentation frameworks. *Journal of Logic and Computation*, 13(3):429–448, 2003.
[4] A. Damasio. *Descartes' Error*. G P Putnams Sons, 1994.
[5] N. Frijda. *The Emotions*. Cambridge University Press, Cambridge, 1986.
[6] N. Frijda, A. Manstead, and S. Bem. *Emotions and beliefs*. Cambridge University press, 2006.
[7] F. S. Nawwab, T. Bench-Capon, and P. E. Dunne. A methodology for action-selection using value-based argumentation. In *Computational Models of Argument: Proceedings of Computational Model of Arguments 2008*, volume 172, pages 264–275. IOS Press, 2008.
[8] F. S. Nawwab, T. Bench-Capon, and P. E. Dunne. Emotions in rational decision making. In *Argumentation in Multi-Agent Systems*, volume 6057 of *Lecture Notes in Computer Science*, pages 273–291. Springer, 2010.
[9] A. Ortony, G. Clore, and A. Collins. *The Cognitive Structure of Emotions*. Cambridge University Press, 1988.
[10] S. Reilly. *Believable social and emotional agents*. PhD thesis, Carnegie Mellon University (CMU), 1996.
[11] B. R. Steunebrink, M. Dastani, and J.-J. C. Meyer. A logic of emotions for intelligent agents. In *Association for the Advancement of Artificial Intelligence (AAAI)*, pages 142–147, 2007.
[12] M. Wooldridge and W. van der Hoek. On obligations and normative ability: Towards a logical analysis of the social contract. *J. Applied Logic*, 3(3-4):396–420, 2005.

Computational Models of Argument
P. Baroni et al. (Eds.)
IOS Press, 2010
doi:10.3233/978-1-60750-619-5-379

Moving Between Argumentation Frameworks

Nir OREN [a,1], Chris REED [b] and Michael LUCK [a]

[a] *Dept. of Computer Science, King's College London, UK*
[b] *Dept. of Computer Science, University of Dundee, Scotland*

Abstract. Abstract argument frameworks have been used for various applications within multi-agent systems, including reasoning and negotiation. Different argument frameworks make use of different inter-argument relations and semantics to identify some subset of arguments as coherent, yet there is no easy way to map between these frameworks; most commonly, this is done manually according to human intuition. In response, in this paper, we show how a set of arguments described using Dung's or Nielsen's argument frameworks can be mapped from and to an argument framework that includes both attack and support relations. This mapping preserves the framework's semantics in the sense that an argument deemed coherent in one framework is coherent in the other under a related semantics. Interestingly, this translation is not unique, with one set of arguments in the support based framework mapping to multiple argument sets within the attack only framework. Additionally, we show how EAF can be mapped into a subset of the argument interchange format (AIF). By using this mapping, any other argument framework using this subset of AIF can be translated into a DAF while preserving its semantics.

Keywords. Argumentation, Abstract Argument Frameworks, Semantics

1. Introduction

Typical applications of argumentation theory represent background knowledge and facts about the world as arguments, and reach some decision (e.g. what price to name in a negotiation) based on the interactions between these arguments. In many cases, reaching a decision depends on identifying which subsets of the entire set of arguments are, in some sense, coherent. Abstract argument frameworks model sets of arguments as atomic entities, ignoring their inner structure, and concerning themselves only with the interactions between arguments. Such argument frameworks then identify a coherent set of arguments according to some semantics, based on the interactions between the arguments.

For example, Dung's argument framework [7] makes use of the notion of an attack between arguments, and identifies a set of arguments as coherent if a sceptical reasoner would believe they are coherent (in the case of the *grounded* extension). Within the argumentation literature, a plethora of argument frameworks have been proposed, capable of modelling not only attacks between arguments, but also support [2,12] and prefer-

---

[1]Corresponding Author: Dept. of Computer Science, King's College London, UK; E-mail: nir.oren@kcl.ac.uk

ence and value orderings [1,3]. Each argument framework, and its associated semantics, claims to capture some novel aspect of argument interaction that other frameworks do not. However, little attention has been paid to the possibility of translating between argument frameworks *at the semantic level*. Yet such translation is critical in an open system where agents make use of argumentation; by translating, entities making use of different underlying argumentation frameworks can agree on the status of an argument, justifying why some decision was taken.

In this paper, we begin addressing this translation problem by describing how arguments represented using Oren et al's Evidential Argument Framework [12] can be translated into Dung's abstract argument framework [7], and vice-versa. This translation is designed to be semantics preserving. That is, given some set of arguments deemed coherent in one framework under some specific semantics, the same set of arguments should be deemed consistent in the other framework under a similar semantics. As an added benefit, this translation procedure allows us to trivially translate from Nielsen's framework [11] to the other two frameworks (Translating from Dung's semantics to Nielsen's is trivial, and we may thus freely translate between the three frameworks).

As an example of the use of translation, we consider the AIF standard [6], which was created in order to allow for the interchange of arguments between different systems, each of which may use a different internal argument representation, and a different framework for reasoning. AIF is RDF based, and is purely representational, therefore not yielding to standard acceptability semantics, and has no defined operational semantics. However, it is capable of representing concepts found in many different frameworks, including attacks, supports and preference, as well as more complex notions such as argument schemes.Evidential argument frameworks (EAFs) provide an intuitively appealing representation of a subset of AIF, and our work thus provides the tantalising suggestion of translating from some argumentation framework into AIF, then from AIF into EAFs, and finally from EAFs into Dung's framework. This translation thus allows for linkages between many different frameworks.

The main contribution of this paper lies in identifying a mapping between Oren's, Dung's and Nielsen's frameworks, and providing an operationalisation of this mapping. As an application of this mapping, we show how EAFs may be represented as a subset of AIF, allowing any other argument framework described using this AIF subset to be mapped into Dung and Nielsen's frameworks.

In the next section, we provide an overview of the frameworks we examine in depth in this paper, namely Dung's argument framework, Nielsen's extensions to it, and Oren's evidential argument framework. Section 3 then describes a simple algorithm to translate between the frameworks, following which refinements to the basic algorithm are introduced. Finally, we show how a mapping from AIF to Oren's framework may be created, after which we discuss related work, and possible paths for future research.

2. Background

Abstract argument frameworks do not concern themselves with the internal structure of an argument, instead focusing on the interactions between sets of arguments. Thus, for example, an argument "Nixon should not invade Vietnam because it would start a war he could never win", could be represented by the argument a. Dung's seminal argument framework consists of a set of arguments, and one possible type of interaction between them, namely by attacking each other.

Definition 1 *(Dung Argument Framework) A Dung argument framework (DAF) is a tuple $DAF = (Args, Attacks)$ where $Args$ is a set of arguments, and $Attacks$: $Args \times Args$ is a binary relation.*

An argument a is said to attack another argument b if $(a, b) \in Attacks$. From this simple representation, we may define a number of notions:

Definition 2 *(Auxiliary Notions for DAFs) Given a DAF $(Args, Attacks)$, a set of arguments $S \subseteq Args$ is* conflict free *iff $\forall a, b \in S, (a, b) \notin Attacks$.*
An argument $a \in Args$ is acceptable *with respect to a set of arguments $S \subseteq Args$ iff $\forall b \in Args$ such that $(b, a) \in Attacks$, $\exists c \in S$ such that c attacks b.*
A conflict free set of arguments S is admissible *iff all its elements are acceptable w.r.t S.*

Definition 3 *(Semantics for DAFs) Given a DAF, a set of arguments is said to be a* preferred extension *if it is a maximal (w.r.t. set inclusion) admissible set of arguments. A set of arguments S is a* stable extension *iff $S = \{a | a \in Args$ and a is not attacked by $S\}$. A set of arguments S is a* grounded extension *if it is the least fixed point of the function $F_{AF}(S) = \{a | a$ is acceptable with respect to $S\}$.*

Nielsen [11] popularised a simple, but important extension to DAFs. Instead of attacks operating between single arguments, an attack may require a set of arguments to take place. While it has been claimed (but not proved) that DAFs can model such cases, Nielsen's framework allows these situations to be represented more compactly, and without the need to introduce additional, *virtual* arguments into the system.

Definition 4 *(Nielsen's Argument Framework) An argument framework in Nielsen's extension to DAF, denoted a NAF, is a tuple $NAF = (Args, NAttacks)$ where $Args$ is a set of arguments, and $NAttacks : 2^{Args} \times Args$ is the attacks relation.*

Concepts such as acceptability, conflict freeness and admissibility, originally defined on DAFs are directly translatable to NAFs. By translating these concepts, extensions can be defined on NAFs which are analogous to DAF extensions.

Oren's[12] evidential argument framework (EAF) is another framework based on Dung's work, which also makes use of Nielsen's extensions to DAFs. Like a DAF, an EAF consists of a graph containing nodes representing arguments. An EAF also contains an additional, special argument η, which represents a default, or some form of unquestionable evidence. Unlike a DAF, two types of edges exist between nodes, the first associated with the attack relation, while the second represents support between arguments (one interpretation of a support edge from η to an argument is that the supported argument is true by default, or that some unassailable evidence for the argument exists. Support between other arguments can imply that an inferential link exists between them).

Definition 5 *(Evidential Argumentation Systems)*
An evidential argumentation system is a tuple (A, R_a, R_e) where A is a set of arguments, R_a and R_e are relations of the form $(2^A \setminus \emptyset) \times A$, and that within the argumentation system, $\nexists x \in 2^A, y \in A$ such that $x R_a y$ and $x R_e y$. We assume the existence

of a "special" argument $\eta \in A$, such that $\nexists(x, y) \in R_a$ where $\eta \in x$; and $\nexists x$ where $(x, \eta) \in R_a$ or $(x, \eta) \in R_e$.

The introduction of the support relation means that concepts such as a successful attack between arguments, acceptability and admissibility, are computed in a different manner to a DAF.

A necessary condition for an argument to appear in an extension is that it is directly, or indirectly supported by some evidence; that is, there is a path from η to the argument, according to the edges of the R_e relation.

Definition 6 *(Evidential Support)* *An argument a has evidential support from a set S iff either $S R_e a$ where $S = \{\eta\}$ or*

$\exists T \subset S$ *such that $T R_e a$ and $\forall x \in T$, x has evidential support from $S \setminus \{x\}$.*

S is a minimum support for a if a has evidential support from S and there is no $T \subset S$ such that a is supported by T.

If a has evidential support from S, we may say that S e-supports a, or that a is e-supported by S. Where obvious, we abbreviate e-support to support. The notion of attack requires the attacking argument to be supported.

Definition 7 *(Evidence Supported Attack)* *A set S carries out an evidence supported attack on an argument a if $X R_a a$ where $X \subseteq S$, and, all elements $x \in X$ are supported by S.*

An evidence supported attack by a set S on a is minimal iff S carries out an evidence supported attack on a, and there is no $T \subset S$ such that T carries out an evidence supported attack on a.

From these basic concepts, we can define a number of auxiliary notions

Definition 8 *(Auxiliary Notions for EAFs)* *An argument a is acceptable with respect to a set S iff S e-supports a, and for any minimal evidence-supported attack by a set $X \subseteq 2^A$ against a, $\exists T \subseteq S$ such that $T R_a x$, where $x \in X$ so that $X \setminus \{x\}$ is no longer an evidence-supported attack on a.*
A set of arguments S is conflict free iff $\forall y \in S$, $\nexists X \subseteq S$ such that $X R_a y$.
A set of arguments S is self supporting iff $\forall x \in S$, S e-supports x.

As in DAFs, a set of arguments is admissible if it acceptable and conflict free. We can then define semantics for EAFs in an identical manner as for DAFs. For example, a maximal admissible set of arguments is a member of the e-preferred extension.

Having provided a brief survey of DAFs, NAFs and EAFs, we proceed to show how a set of arguments can be converted from one framework to another, with arguments found in an extension in the original framework contained in an analogous extension in the new framework.

3. Converting Between Argument Frameworks

In this section, we show how sets of arguments may be represented in different argument frameworks. We show how DAFs may be converted to NAFs, and from there to an EAF, and then show how an EAF may be converted to a DAF.

Figure 1. Some possible mappings from an EAF (left) to an equivalent DAF (right). Solid lines represent support between arguments, dashed lines indicate attacks.

3.1. Converting a DAF/NAF to an EAF

Converting an argument system from a DAF to a NAF is trivial, with the source argument set in the attack relation in the NAF containing only the source attacking argument in the DAF. For example, an attack on b by a in a DAF would be mapped to an attack on b from $\{a\}$ in the analogous NAF.

To convert from a NAF to an EAF is also easy. The EAF contains all arguments and attacks from the NAF, together with argument η. η then supports all other arguments in the NAF. Intuitively, this transformation is possible due to the fact that without any extra information (which cannot be encoded into a NAF), we must assume that all arguments in the original argument system are either true by default, or have some evidence to support them (otherwise, the argument would not have appeared in the original NAF). Conversion from a DAF to an EAF can then take place by first converting the DAF to a NAF, and then converting the NAF to an EAF.

Clearly, any argument attacked in the original argument framework is evidence support attacked in the EAF. Also, if an argument is acceptable in the original framework with respect to a set S, it is acceptable in the EAF with respect to the set $S \cup \eta$. Similarly, the notion of conflict free remains the same, implying that any argument admissible in the DAF or NAF is also admissible in the EAF. Given this, any argument in a preferred/stable/grounded extension is in the e-preferred/e-stable/e-grounded extension, and any argument not in a DAF or NAF extension is not in the EAF extension.

3.2. Converting an EAF to a DAF

The notion of support, as well as the ability of multiple arguments to attack or support a single argument, makes mapping from EAFs and DAFs/NAFs more difficult than mapping from DAFs/NAFs to EAFs. In this section, we show a many to one mapping between EAFs and DAFs. This mapping is many to one in the sense that many different EAFs can be converted to a DAF with identical graph structure. The goal of this conversion is to preserve the EAF's semantics. That is, any argument that is within some extension within the EAF should be in an analogous extension with the DAF.

Our approach centres around the mapping of a set of related arguments — informally arguments taken together with their supporting arguments, recursively back to η — into a single DAF argument[2]. Consider, for example, the EAF and DAF shown on the left of Figure 1. Intuitively, This EAF can be converted into the DAF shown to the right of it[3]; arguments η, a, c from the EAF are grouped into one argument within the DAF, while

---

[2]If viewed as an argument/subargument relationship, then the ideas of [8] are highly applicable.
[3]When drawing EAFs and DAFs, arguments in the DAF are enclosed within ellipses. We omit set notation in the source of support and attack relations in the EAF if the source of the support or attack is a single argument.

Algorithm 1 A simple algorithm to create a DAF with the same semantics as the EAF.

Require: An EAF $(Args, R_a, R_e)$
1: $DARGS = \{\}$ %DAF arguments
2: $DATT = \{\}$ %DAF attacks
3: **for all** $A \in 2^{Args}$ **do**
4:    **if** A is self supporting **then**
5:        Add A to $DARGS$
6:    **end if**
7: **end for**
8: **for all** (X, a) such that $X R_a a$ **do**
9:    **for all** $D \in DARGS$ such that $X \subseteq D$ and $A \in DARGS$ such that $a \in A$ **do**
10:        Add (D, A) to $DATT$
11:    **end for**
12: **end for**
13: **return** (DARGS,DATT)

η, b are grouped into another. This means that if η, b are found in some extension of the EAF, they also appear in an equivalent extension of the DAF, and vice-versa. The same holds for the remaining arguments, and thus, in the DAF, we have a single argument η, a, c composed of the EAF arguments η, a and c. The right hand EAF shown in Figure 1 maps to a DAF with the same structure as the left hand EAF in that figure. Thus, multiple EAFs can be represented as a DAF with identical graph structure.

We begin by describing a simple approach to performing the conversion between EAFs and DAFs. We then examine the properties of this conversion, to show that the semantics of the EAF are preserved when transformed into a DAF. In Section 4, we describe refinements to this simple approach.

Algorithm 1 details the basic approach. This algorithm operates by generating all possible self supporting argument sets (SSAS), and utilises these SSASs as the resultant DAF's atomic arguments. Attacks in the DAF are generated according to whether an attack exists between elements of the two SSASs (Lines 8–12).

We can show two simple, but important properties for the algorithm, namely that attacks carry over between the EAF and DAF, and that admissibility also carries over.

Lemma 1 *If an argument is e-support attacked in the original EAF, any SSAS containing the argument is still attacked in the resultant DAF.*
Proof: *An e-supported attack must be part of a SSAS; since only self supporting sets of arguments are copied into the DAF, all such e-supported attacks are copied (Line 5). Of course, if the attacked argument is not part of a SSAS, the attack against it are not be copied, but in this case, there is no possibility that the argument is acceptable as acceptability within the EAF requires support.* □

Lemma 2 *Given an EAF and the DAF derived from it according to Algorithm 1, a set of SSASs S' is admissible within the DAF if and only if all arguments found within $\bigcup S'$ (i.e. all arguments found in the set of SSASs) are admissible within the EAF.*
Proof: If: *Clearly, since S is admissible, there is some set of SSASs S' within the DAF made up of subsets of S. Since S is conflict free, S' is also conflict free. Thus, to show S' is admissible, we must show that it is acceptable. In other words, given a SSAS that attacks some $s' \in S'$, we must show that there is some SSAS s'', made up of subsets of S, that attacks s'.*

Now, within the EAF, for any attack $X R_a s$ where $X \subseteq Y$ and Y is a minimal self supported set, for s to be acceptable w.r.t S, there must be some $T \subseteq S$ that (e-support) attacks an element of X, or (e-support) attacks an element of Y, thus causing the original attack to no longer be e-supported.

Since, within the EAF, all attacks against $s \in S$ are e-supported, there are sets of SSASs $Y_1 \ldots Y_n$ within the DAF attacking all SSASs containing s.

Since s is acceptable with respect to S, and S is self supporting, there must be some subsets of arguments $T_i \subseteq S$ that carry out an e-supported attack against Y_j for all $j = 1 \ldots n$.

Thus, if a set S is admissible within an EAF, there is a set of SSASs consisting of subsets of S that are admissible within the DAF.

Only if *clearly, S is self supporting. Furthermore, since S' is conflict free, there are no attacks between its elements, and S is thus also conflict free. Finally, since S' is admissible, any attack against its members, say by a SSAS T, is attacked by a member of S'. Since T is self supporting, the attack against T must either directly attack an argument that attacked an argument of S, or render T not self-supporting. Thus, each member of S is acceptable with respect to S, and S is thus admissible.* $\square$

This result means that any semantics based on admissibility (such as the grounded and preferred semantics) are preserved by Algorithm 1 when moving from an EAF to a DAF. The carry over of attacks also means that the stable semantics is preserved by the translation process.

4. Eliminating Redundant Sets of Arguments

Given an EAF containing a minimal self supporting set of n arguments with no attacks against it, it is clear that on the order of 2^n SSASs can be formed when using the simple algorithm described above. All of these 2^n SSASs would not be attacked in the resultant DAF, and if so all appear in the admissible set, with all of their component arguments being admissible in the original EAF. The removal of all but the maximal SSAS (with respect to set inclusion) from the DAF has no impact on the arguments in the final group of admissible sets within the DAF, and thus, no information is lost if all non-maximal SSASs are removed from the DAF. In this section, we examine which SSASs must be kept so as to convey the information found in the original EAF.

Consider a self supporting set of arguments $\{\eta, a, b\}$ found as part of an EAF. If no attacks exist against this argument set, then, when converted into a DAF, it forms part of the (for example) preferred extension, as do the SSASs $\{\eta, a\}$ and $\{\eta\}$. The latter two SSASs are thus, in a sense, redundant. In fact, the only time a subset of the maximal SSAS can be found in an extension while the maximal SSAS may not be is when an argument within the maximal SSAS is attacked. Now instead, consider the argument set $\{\eta, a, b, c\}$, and assume that a, which is supported by η, supports b which in turn supports c. Now assume that an attack exists against argument b. In such a situation only two argument SSASs need be considered, namely the full SSAS (containing η, a, b and c) and the SSAS $\{a, \eta\}$. If the full SSAS is not in the extension, but the latter SSAS is, then $\{\eta\}$ is also in the extension, while $\{\eta, a, b\}$ will not be present. More formally (where by *status*, we mean whether the SSAS is admissible or not):

Algorithm 2 An algorithm for converting from an EAF to a DAF.

Require: An EAF $(Args, R_a, R_e)$
1: AC={all maximal self supporting argument sets of the EAF},Att={}
2: **for all** $(S, t) \in R_a$ **do**
3:    Let $TEAF = (Args\backslash\{t\}, R_a, R_e)$
4:    Add all maximal self supporting chains of $TEAF$ to AC
5: **end for**
6: **for all** $C \in AC$ **do**
7:    **for all** $D \in AC$ **do**
8:       **if** $(S, t) \in R_a$ such that $S \subseteq C, t \in D$ **then**
9:          Add (c, d) to Att
10:      **end if**
11:   **end for**
12: **end for**
13: **return** (AC, Att)

Figure 2. The EAF and the DAF that results from applying Algorithm 2 (left) and Algorithm 3 (right).

Lemma 3 *Given a SSAS $AS = \{a_1, \ldots, a_n\}$ and an attack against a_i,*

1. *All self supporting subsets that can be formed from $AS\backslash\{a_i\}$ have the same status (we label these subsets S_{i-1}).*
2. *All subsets of $AS\backslash S_{i-1}$ have the same status.*

Proof: *The admissibility of a SSAS depends on whether it is attacked or not. Since S_{i-1} are not attacked, their status is identical. Similarly, since all subsets of $AC\backslash S_{i-1}$ are attacked, their status is identical.* □

Thus, a DAF containing only maximal SSASs, as well as subsets of the maximal SSASs, up to the point in which the set is attacked, is sufficient to represent the original EAF system. This result allows us to propose Algorithm 2 for converting from an EAF to a DAF. This algorithm, as with the algorithms proposed later, runs in polynomial time. While correct in the sense that identical arguments appear in admissible sets within both the EAF and DAF, This algorithm does yield some unintuitive results. Consider, for example, the following EAF system:

$$(\{\eta, a, b, c\}, \{(\eta, a), (\eta, b), (a, c)\}, \{(b, a)\}) \tag{1}$$

As shown on the left of Figure 2, applying this algorithm results in the DAF $(\{\alpha, \beta\}, \{(\alpha, \beta), (\beta, \beta)\})$. Here, $\alpha = \{\eta, b\}$ and $\beta = \{\eta, a, b, c\}$. As expected, η and b are admissible in both the DAF and EAF. However, as shown on the right of Figure 2, if $\beta = \{\eta, a, c\}$, we obtain the same set of admissible arguments, and this representation of the interactions between arguments more closely agrees with our intuitions.

The fact that there is initially one maximal argument set, starting at η, is the source of this problem. In order to overcome this issue, we must adapt the manner in which we

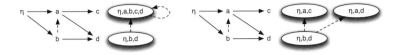

Figure 3.   The EAF and the DAF that results from applying Algorithm 3 (left) and Algorithm 5 (right).

Algorithm 3 An algorithm for computing maximal argument sets.

Require: $AF = (Args, R_a, R_e)$
 1: $MaximalChains = \{\}$
 2: **for all** $a \in Args$ **do**
 3:     $maxChain = computeMaxSupportedSet(a, \{\eta\}, AF)$
 4:     **if** $maxChain \cup \{\eta\}$ is a self supporting chain **then**
 5:         $MaximalChains = MaximalChains \cup maxChain \cup \{\eta\}$
 6:     **end if**
 7: **end for**
 8: **return** $MaximalChains$

---

make use of η. For example, we could allow (conceptually) different versions of η to support different arguments, which in turn would allow for distinct sets of maximal SSASs to appear. In such a situation, each support relation from η to another argument could be replaced by a support from some new, unique, non-attacked, argument to the other argument. To achieve this, we change Lines 1 and 4 of Algorithm 2 to make use of Algorithm 3 when computing the SSASs. Constructing a maximal SSAS according to this algorithm "ignores" η when forming argument sets. However, this is in fact equivalent to making use of a unique η for each SSAS.

When evaluated using the modified form of Algorithm 2, The EAF from Equation 1 results in the DAF $(\{\alpha, \beta\}, \{(\alpha, \beta)\})$. Now, $\alpha = \{\eta, b\}$ and $\beta = \{\eta, a, c\}$ (as shown on the right of Figure 2), agreeing with our intuition. However, this algorithm still yields counter-intuitive results in some situations. For example, given the EAF

$$(\{a, b, c, d\}, \{(\eta, a), (\eta, b), (a, d), (a, c), (b, d)\}, \{(b, a)\}) \tag{2}$$

this algorithm would result in a DAF containing SSASs $\{\eta, a, b, c, d\}$ and $\{\eta, b, d\}$, with attacks between the latter and former, and the first node attacking itself (shown on the left of Figure 3). The independence of support between a, c and a, d means that a, c and a, b, d should appear as separate nodes within the SSAS.

By assuming that a SSAS has a single argument as its conclusion, i.e. that a SSAS ultimately provides support for only a single argument, we can use Algorithm 5 to create a DAF from an EAF in a more intuitive manner. This algorithm computes (using the $computeBackSet()$ described in Algorithm 6) all possible SSASs that have some argument a as their single conclusion, for all arguments in the system. Any SSAS not containing η is removed. Finally, any SSAS that is a subset of another SSAS is removed, leaving maximal SSASs, which can then be used in Lines 1 and 4 of Algorithm 2.

Algorithm 5 returns a DAF containing the SSASs $\{\eta, a, c\}$, $\{\eta, a, d\}$ and $\{\eta, b, d\}$ as arguments when evaluated on the EAF from Equation 2. This, together with the attacks found in the DAF, is illustrated on the right of Figure 3.

Algorithm 4 $computeMaxSupportedSet(a, Visited, AF)$

Require: An argument a, a set of nodes $Visited \subseteq Args$, an EAF $AF = (Args, R_a, R_e)$
 1: $Answer = \{a\}, ToVisit = \{\}, Visited = Visited \cup \{a\}$
 2: **for all** $B \subseteq Args$ such that $(B, a) \in R_e$ **do**
 3:      $ToVisit = ToVisit \cup B$
 4: **end for**
 5: **for all** $c \in Args$ such that $(\{\ldots, a, \ldots\}, c) \in R_e$ **do**
 6:      $ToVisit = ToVisit \cup c$
 7: **end for**
 8: **for all** $d \in ToVisit \backslash Visited$ **do**
 9:      $Answer = Answer \cup computeMaxSupportedSet(d, Visited, AF)$
10: **end for**
11: **return** $Answer$

Algorithm 5 Algorithm to generate a DAF from an EAF.

Require: An EAF $AF = (Args, R_a, R_e)$
 1: **for all** $a \in Args$ **do**
 2:      $Answer = Answer \cup computeBackSet(a, \{\}, AF)$
 3: **end for**
 4: **for all** $AS \in Answer$ **do**
 5:      **if** $\eta \notin AS$ **then**
 6:          $Answer = Answer \backslash \{AS\}$
 7:      **end if**
 8:      **if** $\exists AS' \in Answer$ such that $AS \subseteq AS'$ **then**
 9:          $Answer = Answer \backslash \{AS\}$
10:      **end if**
11: **end for**
12: **return** $Answer$

Algorithm 6 $computeBackSet(a, Visited, AF)$

Require: An argument a, a set of visited edges $Visited \subseteq R_e$, an EAF $AF = (Args, R_a, R_e)$
 1: **for all** $(X, a) \in R_e$ such that $(X, a) \notin Visited$ **do**
 2:      $B = \times_{x_i} computeBackSet(x_i, Visited \cup \{(X, a)\}, AF)$ for $x_i \in X$
 3:      **for all** $b \in B$ **do**
 4:          $b = b \cup \{a\}$
 5:      **end for**
 6:      $Ans = Ans \cup B$
 7: **end for**
 8: **return** Ans

---

5. From AIF to EAF

Having described how translation between DAFs, NAFs and EAFs is possible, we now examine the argument interchange format (AIF), a RDF based ontology for the representation of argument related concepts. As discussed below, a simple mapping exists between a subset of AIF and EAF. By utilising this mapping, we can translate between any argument system using this subset of AIF, and the three argumentation frameworks described in this paper. We begin this section by providing a brief introduction to AIF, following which we show how translations between EAFs and AIFs can take place.

AIF assumes that arguments can be represented as nodes in a directed graph, and makes use of two types of nodes: I-nodes, which hold data, and S-nodes, which represent "the inferential passage associated with an argumentative statement" [13]. S-nodes fall into one of three categories: RA-nodes, which represent the application of a rule of inference; PA-nodes, which represent some preference ordering; and CA-nodes, which represent conflict between information. I-Nodes may not have edges linking them to other I-Nodes, while S-Nodes may link to any node. In this paper, we examine a subset of AIF, considering only RA and CA nodes, and assume that S-Nodes are linked only to I-Nodes. While this restriction appears severe, many natural language oriented argument systems, such as Araucaria [14] make use of such simplified AIF graphs.

From the foregoing discussion, it should be clear that there are strong similarities between RA-nodes and support in an EAF, and CA-nodes and the notion of an attack. Moving between an AIF representation of an argument system and an EAF is thus simple: let the set of arguments be the set of I-Nodes (together with the additional argument η); add an element $(\{a_1, \ldots, a_n\}, b)$ into R_a if there is a set of edges from $a_1, \ldots, a_n$ to a CA-Node c, and another edge from c to b; and add an element $(\{a_1, \ldots, a_n\}, b)$ into R_s if there is a set of edges from $a_1, \ldots, a_n$ to a RA-Node c, and another edge from c to b. Finally, add an edge from η to any I-Node which does not have an edge leading to it that originates at an RA-Node. This last step makes the assumption that the I-Node is either true by default, or has some support from unassailable evidence. If the AIF graph encodes such evidential notions, then this last step is not necessary.

Similarly, it is trivial to represent an EAF in AIF; the set of I-Nodes is derived from the set $Args$; for every element of $(A, b) \in R_a$, create an CA-Node with edges going to the CA-Node from all elements of A, and an edge from the CA-Node to b. Finally, a similar operation can be performed when creating RA-Nodes. Any argument framework that may be mapped to the subset of AIF used here can be mapped to an EAF, and thus to a DAF/NAF, and vice-versa.

6. Discussion and Conclusions

In this paper, we have described semantics preserving translations between DAFs, NAFs and EAFs. We also presented a number of algorithms for performing these translations. Different algorithms made different assumptions about the nature of groups of arguments, and yielding different, but equivalent DAFs. The fact that multiple EAFs may be represented as a single DAF is interesting; this result indicates that the notion of support adds information to an argument system which cannot be captured in a DAF alone, due to the DAF's more abstract nature.

In this work, we focused on the preferred, stable and grounded semantics, due to their widespread use. These semantics are based on the notion of admissibility, and since our results show the equivalence of admissibility between different frameworks, our work is applicable to any other admissibility based semantics. We intend to investigate the effects of translation on additional semantics as part of our future work.

We also intend to extend the translation process to preference and value based argument frameworks [1,3]. Apart from EAFs, bipolar argument frameworks (BAFs) are another approach to including support into abstract argument frameworks [2]. While [5] discusses how EAFs can be translated into BAFs, we hope to investigate how a BAF may be translated into an EAF. Other work that deals with translating between disparate argument frameworks includes [10], which shows how preference type argument frameworks can be represented within his extended argument framework [9]. Finally, in [4], the authors show how a DAF can be directly translated into a bipolar argument framework.

We showed how EAF can be mapped into a subset of AIF. The ability to map an AIF argument structure into an EAF, and then move from there into other frameworks allows translation between many disparate frameworks while preserving the semantics of the argument set. Two related pieces of future work that we intend to investigate involve examining translations between additional frameworks and EAF, and extending the subset of AIF that we can map into an EAF.

Additionally, we intend to examine additional algorithms for performing translation between different systems. As seen here, different approaches make sense when different assumptions are made, and additional algorithms with pleasing intuitive properties may exist for the EAF to DAF case. We would like to see if such algorithms can be identified.

References

[1]   L. Amgoud and C. Cayrol. Integrating preference orderings into argument-based reasoning. In *EC-SQARU/FAPR '97: Proceedings of the First International Joint Conference on Qualitative and Quantitative Practical Reasoning*, pages 159–170, London, UK, 1997. Springer-Verlag.

[2]   L. Amgoud, C. Cayrol, and M.-C. Lagasquie-Schiex. On the bipolarity in argumentation frameworks. In *Proceedings of the 10th International Workshop on Non-monotonic Reasoning*, pages 1–9, Whistler, Canada, 2004.

[3]   T. Bench-Capon. Value based argumentation frameworks. In *Proceedings of the 9th International Workshop on Nonmonotonic Reasoning*, pages 444–453, Toulouse, France, 2002.

[4]   C. Cayrol and M.-C. Lagasquie-Schiex. On the acceptability of arguments in bipolar argumentation frameworks. In *Pro. of the Eighth European Conference on Symbolic and Quantitative Approaches to Reasoning With Uncertainty*, volume 3571 of *LNAI*, pages 378–389. Springer-Verlag, 2005.

[5]   C. Cayrol and M.-C. Lagasquie-Schiex. Bipolar Abstract Argumentation Systems. In I. Rahwan and G. Simari, editors, *Argumentation in Artificial Intelligence*, chapter 4, pages 65–84. Springer, http://www.springerlink.com, 2009.

[6]   C. Chesñevar, J. McGinnis, S. Modgil, I. Rahwan, C. Reed, G. Simari, M. South, G. Vreeswijk, and S. Willmott. Towards an argument interchange format. *Knowl. Eng. Rev.*, 21(4):293–316, 2006.

[7]   P. M. Dung. On the acceptability of arguments and its fundamental role in nonmonotonic reasoning, logic programming and n-person games. *Artificial Intelligence*, 77(2):321–357, 1995.

[8]   D. C. Martínez, A. J. García, and G. R. Simari. Progressive defeat paths in abstract argumentation frameworks. In *Canadian Conference on AI*, pages 242–253, Québec, Canada, 2006.

[9]   S. Modgil. An abstract theory of argumentation that accommodates defeasible reasoning about preferences. In *ECSQARU '07: Proceedings of the 9th European Conference on Symbolic and Quantitative Approaches to Reasoning with Uncertainty*, pages 648–659, Berlin, Heidelberg, 2007. Springer-Verlag.

[10] S. Modgil. Reasoning about preferences in argumentation frameworks. *Artificial Intelligence*, 173(9–10):901–934, 2009.

[11] S. H. Nielsen and S. Parsons. A generalization of Dung's abstract framework for argumentation: Arguing with sets of attacking arguments. In *Proceedings of the Third International Workshop on Argumentation in Multi-Agent Systems*, pages 7–19, Hakodate, Japan, 2006.

[12] N. Oren and T. J. Norman. Semantics for evidence-based argumentation. In *Computational Models of Argument: Proceedings of COMMA 2008*, pages 276–284, Toulouse, France, 2008.

[13] I. Rahwan, F. Zablith, and C. Reed. Laying the foundations for a world wide argument web. *Artif. Intell.*, 171(10-15):897–921, 2007.

[14] C. A. Reed and G. W. A. Rowe. Araucaria: Software for argument analysis, diagramming and representation. *Int. Journal of AI Tools*, 14(3-4), 2004.

Computational Models of Argument
P. Baroni et al. (Eds.)
IOS Press, 2010
© 2010 The authors and IOS Press. All rights reserved.
doi:10.3233/978-1-60750-619-5-391

CF2-extensions as Answer-set Models

Mauricio Osorio [a,1]

[a] *CENTIA*

Juan Carlos Nieves and Ignasi Gómez-Sebastià [b,2]
[b] *Knowledge Engineering and Machine Learning Group*

Abstract. Extension-based argumentation semantics have shown to be a suitable approach for performing practical reasoning. Since extension-based argumentation semantics were formalized in terms of relationships between atomic arguments, it has been shown that extension-based argumentation semantics based on admissible sets such as stable semantics can be characterized in terms of answer sets. In this paper, we present an approach for characterizing SCC-recursive semantics in terms of answer set models. In particular, we will show a characterization of CF2 in terms of answer set models. This result suggests that not only extension-based argumentation semantics based on admissible sets can be characterized in terms of answer sets; but also extension-based argumentation semantics based on Strongly Connected Components can be characterized in terms of answer sets.

Keywords. Argumentation Theory, Answer-set Semantics, Extension-based Argumentation Semantics.

1. Introduction

Although several approaches have been proposed for capturing representative patterns of inference in argumentation theory, Dung's approach, presented in [8], is a unifying framework which has played an influential role on argumentation research and Artificial Intelligence (AI). The kernel of Dung's framework is supported by the following extension-based argumentation semantics (also called *abstract argumentation semantics*): *grounded*, *stable*, *preferred* and *complete* semantics. Even though each of these argumentation semantics represents different patterns of selection of arguments all of them are based on the concept of an *admissible set*. An admissible set can be regarded as a coherent point of view from a conflicting set of arguments. When Dung introduced his argumentation approach, he proved that some extension-based argumentation semantics can be regarded as a special form of logic programming with *negation as failure*. This result defines a general method for generating metainterpreters for argumentation systems as well as a general method for studying the *abstract argumentation semantics'* properties in terms of logic programming semantics' properties. It is worth mentioning that following Dung's approach, other authors have defined additional argumentation seman-

[1] Universidad de las Américas, Sta. Catarina Mártir, Cholula, Puebla, 72820 México. E-Mail:**{osoriomauri@googlemail.com**
[2] Departament de Llenguatges i Sistemes Informàtics. Universitat Politècnica de Catalunya (UPC) C/Jordi Girona 1-3, E-08034 , Barcelona, Spain. E-Mail:**{jcnieves,igomez}@lsi.upc.edu**

tics, such as the semi-stable semantics [4], ideal-semantics [9] and the SCC-recursive semantics [2].

Extension-based argumentation semantics based on admissible sets have shown unexpected behaviors when computing some argumentation frameworks (for instance, frameworks presenting odd-length cycles) [2, 17]. In these cases approaches such as the SCC-recursive semantics [2] come in handy. This approach is based on splitting an argumentation framework in strongly connected components (obtaining sets of arguments whose status does not depend on the status of arguments outside the set) and processing them separately. An order (known as *directionality principle*) is defined between the resulting strongly connected components. Given two strongly connected components SCC_A and SCC_B it is said that SCC_A precedes SCC_B if there is a directed path in $\langle AR, attacks \rangle$ from any argument in SCC_A to an argument in SCC_B. Therefore, the value of (at least) one argument in SCC_B depends on the status of (at least) one argument in SCC_A. The processing of the strong connected components is performed in a recursive way, where the results of one strong connected component affect the following ones. This approach is remarkable for two reasons: a) it is powerful, as it is able to properly process semantics on argumentation frameworks where other approaches do not show proper behaviors b) it is versatile, on the definition of the approach, the base functions used to process the strongly connected components is left open, allowing the definition of a wide range of functions to capture different semantics.

According to some analysis of basic properties which can be expected from any extension-based argumentation semantics [1], CF2 argumentation semantics is considered as the most accepted from the ones defined in terms of SCC-recursive semantics [2].

In this paper, following the recent results with respect to extension-based argumentation semantics in terms of logic programming semantics with negation as failure [5, 10, 15, 16, 18], we will show that not only extension-based argumentation semantics based on admissible sets can be characterised in terms of answer set models; but also SCC-recursive semantics such as the CF2 can be characterized in terms of answer set models. In particular, we will present a characterization of CF2 in terms of answer set models. This characterization suggests an approach for characterizing other extension-based argumentation semantics based on the SCC-recursive approach and an easy-to-use form for inferring the CF2 extensions of an argumentation framework.

The rest of the paper is structured as follows: In §2, a short presentation of basic concepts of answer set programming is presented. Also a short overview of extension-based argumentation semantics is presented. In §3, an approach for characterizing SCC-recursive semantics in terms of answer set models is presented. In particular, a characterization of CF2 is formalized. This section includes a subsection for illustrating the use of our results. In the last section, our conclusions are presented.

2. Background

In this section, we present a short presentation of basic concepts. Two main topics are covered: a) the syntax of logic programs, along with the definition of *Answer set semantics*; b) extension-based argumentation semantics, including an overview of Dung's and Baroni et al.'s approaches [2, 8].

2.1. Logic Programs

This subsection introduces the syntax of logic programs, along with a brief introduction to *Answer set semantics*.

2.1.1. Syntax

A signature $\mathcal{L}$ is a finite set of elements that we call atoms. A literal is an atom, a (positive literal), or the negation of an atom *not a* (negative literal). A disjunctive clause is a clause of the form: $a_1 \vee \ldots \vee a_m \leftarrow a_{m+1}, \ldots, a_j, not\ a_{j+1}, \ldots, not\ a_n$ where a_i is an atom, $1 \leq i \leq n$. When $n = m$ and $m > 0$, the disjunctive clause is an abbreviation of the fact $a_1 \vee \ldots \vee a_m \leftarrow \top$ where $\top$ is an atom that always evaluate to true. When $m = 0$ and $n > 0$ the clause is an abbreviation of $\bot \leftarrow a_1, \ldots, a_j, not\ a_{j+1}, \ldots, not\ a_n$ where $\bot$ is an atom that always evaluate to false. Clauses of this form are called constraints. A disjunctive logic program is a finite set of disjunctive clauses. A given set of disjunctive clauses $\{\gamma_1, \ldots, \gamma_n\}$ is also represented as $\{\gamma_1; \ldots; \gamma_n\}$ to avoid ambiguities with the use of comma in the body of the clauses.

We denote by $\mathcal{L}_P$ the signature of P, i.e., the set of atoms that occur in P. Given a signature $\mathcal{L}$, we write $Prog_{\mathcal{L}}$ to denote the set of all the programs defined over $\mathcal{L}$.

2.1.2. Answer Set Semantics

The following definition of an answer set for disjunctive logic programs was presented in [12]: Let P be any disjunctive logic program. For any set $S \subseteq \mathcal{L}_P$, let P^S be the logic program obtained from P by deleting: i) each clause that has a formula *not a* in its body with $a \in S$ ii) all formulæ of the form *not a* in the bodies of the remaining clauses. Clearly P^S does not contain *not*, hence S is called an answer set of P if and only if S is a minimal model of P^S.

2.2. Extension-based argumentation semantics

This subsection introduces extension-based argumentation semantics starting from Dung's approach.

2.2.1. Dung's approach

In his work, Dung introduces the concept of argumentation framework which is defined as follows (All the definitions used in this subsection where taken from [8]):

Definition 1 *An argumentation framework is a pair* $AF = \langle AR, attacks \rangle$, *where* AR *is a set of arguments, and* attacks *is a binary relation on* AR, *i.e.* attacks $\subseteq AR \times AR$. *A attacks B (or B is attacked by A) if attacks*(A, B) *holds.*

Following Dung's reading, A attacks B (or B is attacked by A) if *attacks*(A, B) holds. A set S of arguments attacks B (or B is attacked by S) if B is attacked by an argument in S.

Definition 2

- *A set S of arguments is conflict-free if there are no arguments A, B in S such that A attacks B.*

- *An argument A ∈ AR is acceptable with respect to a set S of arguments if and only if for each argument B ∈ AR: If B attacks A then B is attacked by S.*
- *A conflict-free set of arguments S is admissible if and only if each argument in S is acceptable w.r.t. S.*

From the extension-based argumentation semantics introduced in [8], we can identify two reasoning approaches: 1.- The extension-based argumentation semantics which follows a credulous reasoning approach; and 2.- The extension-based argumentation semantics which follows a sceptical reasoning approach. From the credulous semantics, one can mention, the stable, preferred and complete semantics and from the sceptical semantics, the grounded semantics. For presenting the results of this paper only the grounded extension is relevant. The grounded semantics is defined in terms of a *characteristic function*.

Definition 3 *Let the characteristic function, denoted by F_{AF}, of an argumentation framework $AF = \langle AR, attacks \rangle$ be defined as follows:*

$$F_{AF} : 2^{AR} \rightarrow 2^{AR}$$
$$F_{AF}(S) = \{A|\ A\ is\ acceptable\ w.r.t.\ S\ \}$$

The grounded extension of an argumentation framework AF, denoted by GE_{AF}, is the least fixed point of F_{AF}

In his work [8], Dung suggests a general method for generating metainterpreters in terms of logic programming for argumentation systems. This approach is based in the following program:

Definition 4 *Given an argumentation framework $AF = \langle AR, attacks \rangle$, P_{AF} denotes the logic program defined by $P_{AF} = APU + AGU$ where*

$$APU = \{acc(x) \leftarrow not\ d(x)|x \in AR\} \cup \{d(x) \leftarrow attack(y,x), acc(y)|attack(y,x) \in attacks\}$$

and

$$AGU = \{attack(a,b) \leftarrow \top|(a,b) \in attacks\ , a \in AR, b \in AR\}$$

For each extension *E* of *AF*, *m(E)* is defined as follows:

$$m(E) = AGU \cup \{acc(a)|a \in E\} \cup \{d(b)|b\ is\ attacked\ by\ some\ a \in E\}$$

Based on P_{AF}, Dung was able to characterize the stable semantics and the grounded semantics in terms of logic programming semantics with negation as failure.

Theorem 1 *Let AF be an argumentation framework and E be an extension of AF. Then*

1. *E is a stable extension of AF if and only if m(E) is an answer set of P_{AF}*

2. *E is a grounded extension of AF if and only if $m(E) \cup \{not\ d(a)|a \in E\}$ is the well-founded model [11] of P_{AF}*

This theorem is of relevance as it: a) defines a general method for generating metainterpreters for argumentation systems, b) defines a general method for studying abstract argumentation semantics' properties in terms of logic programming semantics' properties.

2.2.2. SCC-recursiveness approach

The SCC-recursiveness approach is based on the notions of *path-equivalence* between nodes and *strongly connected components* (Please notice that, due to length restrictions, definitions in this subsection are presented informally. Formal definitions can be found in [2]).

Definition 5 *Given an argumentation framework $AF = \langle AR, \text{attacks} \rangle$, the binary relation of* path-equivalence *between nodes, denoted as $PE_{AF} \subseteq (AR \times AR)$, is defined as follows:*
— $\forall a \in AR, (a, a) \in PE_{AF}$,
— given two distinct nodes $a, b \in AR, (a, b) \in PE_{AF}$ if and only if there is a path[3] from a to b and a path from b to a.

Given an argumentation framework $AF = \langle AR, \text{attacks} \rangle$, the *strongly connected components* of *AF* are the equivalent classes of nodes which are defined according to the path-equivalence relation. The set of the strongly connected components of *AF* is denoted as $SCCS_{AF}$.

Definition 6 *Let $AF = \langle AR, \text{attacks} \rangle$ be an argumentation framework, and let $S \subseteq AR$ be a set of arguments. The* restriction *of AF to S is the argumentation framework $AF \downarrow_S = \langle S, \text{attacks} \cap (S \times S) \rangle$.*

Considering an argumentation framework, $AF = \langle AR, \text{attacks} \rangle$, a set $E \subseteq AR$ and a strongly connected component $S \in SCCS_{AF}$ the following sets can be defined: a) $D_{AF}(S, E)$ consists of the nodes of S attacked by E from outside S, b) $U_{AF}(S, E)$ consists of the nodes of S that are not attacked by E from outside S and are defended by E (i.e., their defeaters from outside S are all attacked by E), c) $P_{AF}(S, E)$ consists of the nodes of S that are not attacked by E from outside S and are not defended by E (i.e., at least one of their defeaters from outside S is not attacked by E), d) $UP_{AF}(S, E) = (S \setminus D_{AF}(S, E)) = (U_{AF}(S, E) \cup P_{AF}(S, E))$.

Here, we define $GF(AF, C)$ for an argumentation framework $AF = \langle AR, \text{attacks} \rangle$ and a set $C \subseteq AR$, representing the defended nodes of *AF*: two cases have to be considered in this respect.

If *AF* consists of exactly one strongly connected component, it does not admit a decomposition. On the other hand, if *AF* can be decomposed into several strongly connected components, then, $GF(AF, C)$ is obtained by applying recursively GF to each strongly connected component of *AF*, deprived of the nodes in $D_{AF}(S, E)$. Formally, this

---

[3]Given an argumentation framework $AF = \langle AR, \text{attacks} \rangle$ and $a, b \in AR$ there is a path between a and b if there is a sequence $\langle x_0, x_1, \ldots, x_n \rangle$ such that $\langle x_i, x_{i+1} \rangle \in \text{attacks}$ for $0 \leq i \leq n$ and $x_0 = a$ and $x_n = b$

means that for any $S \in SCCS_{AF}$, $(E \cap S) \in GF(AF \downarrow_{UP_{AF}(S,E)}, C')$, where C' represents the set of defended nodes of the restricted argumentation framework $AF \downarrow_{UP_{AF}(S,E)}$. The set C' can be determined by taking into account both the attacks coming from outside AF and those coming from other strongly connected components of AF.

Definition 7 *A given argumentation semantics S is* SCC-recursive *if and only if for any argumentation framework $AF = \langle AR, \text{attacks} \rangle$, $E_S(AF) = GF(AF, AR)$, where for any $AF = \langle AR, \text{attacks} \rangle$ and for any set $C \subseteq AR$, the function $GF(AF, C) \subseteq 2^{AR}$ is defined as follows: for any $E \subseteq AR$, $E \in GF(AF, C)$ if and only if*

- *in case $|SCCS_{AF}| = 1$, $E \in BF_S(AF, C)$,*
- *otherwise,$\forall S \in SCCS_{AF}(E \cap S) \in GF(AF \downarrow_{UP_{AF}(S,E)}, U_{AF}(S, E) \cap C)$.*

where $BF_S(AF, C)$ is a function, called base function, that, given an argumentation framework $AF = \langle AR, \text{attacks} \rangle$ such that $|SCCS_{AF}| = 1$ and a set $C \subseteq AR$, gives a subset of 2^{AR}.

Remark 1 *In the particular case where $BF_S(AF, C)$ is the function that returns the set of all maximal conflict-free sets of arguments CF2 is obtained.*

3. SCC-recursive semantics via Answer Sets

In this section, we are going to present our approach for characterizing SCC-recursive semantics in terms of answer set semantics. In particular, our approach is suitable for the class of SCC-recursive semantics defined by a conflict-free base function. This class of SCC-recursive semantics is of special interest since in [2] it was proved that any extension of these SCC-recursive semantics includes *the grounded extension*.

Like SCC-recursive semantics definition, our *declarative approach* for inferring SCC-recursive semantics is constructive and is based in three general steps: 1.-Inferring the grounded extension. 2.- Reducing the given argumentation framework by considering the inferred grounded extension. In this case, reduction is performed based on a labeling approach, labeling each argument as: *accepted*, *defeated* or *undefined*. 3.- If the reduced argumentation framework has undefined arguments, the base function is applied and the process follows in Step 1.

Observe that this approach infers the grounded semantics more than once. In order to manage the suggested approach, we define two general counters: one for inferring the grounded extension and another for controlling the general iterations suggested by Step 3.

We start by presenting a specification which characterizes the grounded semantics in terms of answer sets. In order to regard an argumentation framework as a logic program, we define the following programs: Given an argumentation framework $AF = \langle AR, \text{attacks} \rangle$,

$$\Pi_{arg} = \{ arg(a, 0) \leftarrow \top | a \in AR \}.$$
$$\Pi_{at} = \{ at(a, b) \leftarrow \top | (a, b) \in \text{attacks} \}.$$
$$\Pi_{int} = \{ time(0) \leftarrow \top; \ldots; time(n+1) \leftarrow \top;$$
$$int(0) \leftarrow \top; \ldots; int(n) \leftarrow \top; size(n) \leftarrow \top | n \text{ is the cardinality of } AR \}$$

Observe that essentially Π_{arg} and Π_{at} are mapping AF into predicates and Π_{int} is defining two counters and the number of arguments. The union of these three programs is denoted by Π_{ini}. We want to clarify to the reader that in the following programs any instantiation of a variable N in $int(N)$ will manage an iteration for inferring the grounded extension and any instantiation of a variable T in $time(T)$ will manage an iteration in the general process of inferring the SCC-recursive semantics.

Now let us introduce the following program:

$$\Pi_{GE} = \quad a\_gr(X, 0, T1) \leftarrow arg(X, T), T1 = T + 1, \; not \; not\_a\_gr(X, T) \cdot$$
$$not\_a\_gr(X, T) \leftarrow arg(X, T), at(Y, X), \; not \; d(Y, T), time(T) \cdot$$
$$a\_gr(X, N, T) \leftarrow int(N), N > 0, arg(X, T), \; not \; not\_a\_gr\_d(X, N, T), time(T) \cdot$$
$$not\_a\_gr\_d(X, N, T) \leftarrow at(Y, X), N = M + 1, \; not \; attacked(Y, M, T), arg(X, T),$$
$$arg(Y, T), time(T) \cdot$$
$$attacked(Y, M, T) \leftarrow arg(Y, T), arg(Z, T), at(Z, Y), a\_gr(Z, M, T), time(T) \cdot$$

This program is defining a characterization of the grounded semantics in terms of answer set models, as formalized in the following proposition:

Proposition 1 *Let $AF = \langle AR, attacks \rangle$ be an argumentation framework and $E \subseteq AR$. E is the grounded extension of AF if and only if M is an answer set of $\Pi_{ini} \cup \Pi_{GE}$ such that $E = \{x | a\_gr(x, N, T) \in M\}$.*

Proof: (sketch) Let M be an answer set of $\Pi_{ini} \cup \Pi_{GE}$, $n = |AR|$, $S_0 = \{x | a\_gr(x, 0, \_) \in M\}$ and $S_i = \{x | a\_gr(x, i, \_) \in M, 1 \leq i \leq n\}$. Hence, the proof follows by induction and the following observations:

1. $S_{i-1} \subseteq S_i (1 \leq i \leq n)$ and S_i is an admissible set.
2. $S_i(1 \leq i \leq n)$ characterizes the characteristic function F_{AF}.
3. Since $S_i(1 \leq i \leq n)$ is monotonic, it reaches a fix-point.

■

Given a grounded extension, one can define different states of an argument: 1.- an argument which belongs to the grounded extension can be considered as accepted (ac_gr), 2.- an argument which is attacked by an accepted argument can be considered as defeated (d_gr), and 3.- an argument which is neither accepted nor defeated can be considered undefined (i_gr). These states of the argument are captured by the following program:

$$\Pi_{gr\_states} = \quad ac\_gr(X, T) \leftarrow a\_gr(X, fixp, T), time(T), size(fixp) \cdot$$
$$d\_gr(X, T) \leftarrow at(Y, X), ac\_gr(Y, T), arg(Y, T), arg(X, T), time(T) \cdot$$
$$i\_gr(X, T) \leftarrow arg(X, T), \; not \; ac\_gr(X, T), \; not \; d\_gr(X, T), time(T) \cdot$$
$$at\_d(X, Y, T) \leftarrow arg(X, T), arg(Y, T), at(X, Y),$$
$$not \; not\_at\_d(X, Y, T), time(T) \cdot$$
$$not\_at\_d(X, Y, T) \leftarrow arg(X, T), arg(Y, T), at(X, Y), d\_gr(X, T), time(T) \cdot$$

Observe that the predicate $at\_d(X, Y, T)$ captures the arguments which are attacked by defeated arguments. Also observe that the predicate $ac\_gr(X, T)$ defines a subset of an extension of SCC-recursive semantics.

Proposition 2 *Let $AF = \langle AR, attacks \rangle$ be an argumentation framework and S be a SCC-recursive semantics such that each extension in S contains the grounded extension. If $E \in S(AF)$, then an answer set M of $\Pi_{ini} \cup \Pi_{GE} \cup \Pi_{gr\_states}$ exists, such that $\{x | ac\_gr(x, T) \in M\} \subseteq E$ and $\{x | d\_gr(x, T) \in M\} \nsubseteq E$*

Proof: (sketch) Let M be an answer set of $\Pi_{ini} \cup \Pi_{GE} \cup \Pi_{gr\_states}$, $S_{ac\_gr}(M) = \{x | ac\_gr(x, \_) \in M\}$ and $S_{d\_gr}(M) = \{x | d\_gr(x, \_) \in M\}$. Let us denote by $ASP(P)$, the answer set models of a given logic program P.

Observations:

1. By Proposition 1, if $M \in ASP(\Pi_{ini} \cup \Pi_{GE} \cup \Pi_{gr\_states})$, then $S_{ac\_gr}(M)$ is the grounded extension of AF.
2. $S_{ac\_gr}(M) \cap S_{d\_gr}(M) = \emptyset$.

If S is a SCC-recursive semantics such that each extension in S contains the grounded extension, then $GE_{AF} \in \bigcap_{E \in S(AF)} E$. By Observation 1, $GE_{AF} = S_{ac\_gr}(M)$. Then $\forall E \in S(AF), S_{ac\_gr}(M) \in E$. Therefore, by Observation 2, $\forall E \in S(AF), S_{d\_gr}(M) \notin E$.
∎

This proposition suggests that in the construction of an extension of a SCC-recursive semantics one can consider an argumentation framework restricted to undefined arguments, *i.e.*, $\{a | i\_gr(a,T) \in M\}$. This idea of recursion follows Definition 7 where the recursive step is restricted to $AF \downarrow_{UP_{AF(S,E)}}$. Observe that in order to define this restricted (*w.r.t.* undefined arguments) argumentation framework, one has to identify *the strongly connected components* that exist in the argumentation framework and follow the *directionality principle*[4].

$$
\begin{aligned}
\Pi_{AF\downarrow_{i\_gr}} = \quad & base(X,T) \vee other\_base(X,T) \leftarrow i\_gr(X,T), time(T)\cdot \\
& \leftarrow base(X,T), base(Y,T), X! = Y, not\ cycle(X,Y,T), time(T)\cdot \\
& \leftarrow base(X,T), ar(Y), X! = Y, other\_base(Y,T), cycle(X,Y,T)\cdot \\
& \leftarrow not\_base(T), time(T)\cdot \\
& \leftarrow incomplete(T), time(T)\cdot \\
& incomplete(T) \leftarrow i\_gr(X,T), not\ not\_empty(T), time(T)\cdot \\
& not\_empty(T) \leftarrow base(X,T), time(T)\cdot \\
& not\_base(T) \leftarrow base(X,T), arg(Y,T), other\_base(Y,T), at(Y,X), time(T)\cdot \\
& cycle(X,Y,T) \leftarrow path(X,Y,T), path(Y,X,T), time(T)\cdot \\
& path(X,Y,T) \leftarrow at(X,Y), arg(X,T), arg(Y,T), time(T)\cdot \\
& path(X,Y,T) \leftarrow arg(X,T), arg(Y,T), arg(Z,T), at(X,Z), \\
& \qquad\qquad path(Z,Y,T), time(T)\cdot
\end{aligned}
$$

Observe that in this program we are using predefined predicates such as $! =$ which are common in answer set solvers such as the DLV solver [7]. Once we have identified our restricted argumentation framework, the status of the arguments (identified as accepted or defeated) have to be preserved.

$$
\begin{aligned}
\Pi_{inertial} = \quad & ac(X,T1) \leftarrow T1 = T+1, ac(X,T), time(T1)\cdot \\
& d(X,T1) \leftarrow T1 = T+1, d(X,T), time(T1)\cdot \\
& ac(X,T) \leftarrow ac\_gr(X,T), time(T)\cdot \\
& d(X,T) \leftarrow d\_gr(X,T), time(T)\cdot \\
& arg(X,T1) \leftarrow arg(X), T1 = T+1, not\ ac(X,T), notd(X,T), time(T), time(T1)\cdot
\end{aligned}
$$

Observe that the last clause of this program is defining the set of arguments that have to be considered in the next iteration of the process.

In order to characterize the CF2 argumentation semantics which is a SCC-recursive semantics, we define a base function which infers maximal conflict free sets of arguments by taking into account the directionality principle.

---

[4]*Directionality principle*: Nodes defeated by an extension E play no role in the selection of nodes to be includes in E.

$$\Pi_{base\_function} = \quad d(X,T) \leftarrow ac(Y,T), at(Y,X), time(T)\cdot$$
$$ac(X,T) \leftarrow base(X,T), not\ d(X,T), time(T)\cdot$$
$$d(X,T) \leftarrow at(Y,X), base(X,T), base(Y,T), ac(Y,T), time(T)\cdot$$
$$d(X,T) \vee d(Y,T) \leftarrow at(Y,X), path\_d(X,Y,T), base(X,T),$$
$$base(Y,T), time(T)\cdot$$
$$path\_d(X,Y,T) \leftarrow at(X,Y), base(X,T), base(Y,T), time(T)\cdot$$
$$path\_d(X,Y,T) \leftarrow at(X,Z), base(X,T), base(Y,T), base(Z,T),$$
$$path\_d(Z,Y,T), time(T)\cdot$$
$$accepted(X) \leftarrow ac(X, fixp), size(fixp)\cdot$$

For connecting Π_{GE} with $\Pi_{base\_function}$, we define the program $\Pi_{GE'}$ as the program Π_{GE} plus the following rule:

$$a\_gr(X, 0, T1) \leftarrow T1 = T + 1, ac(X,T)$$

Consider the program P_{CF2} which is defined as follows: Given an argumentation framework AF

$$P_{CF2}(AF) = \Pi_{ini} \cup \Pi_{GE'} \cup \Pi_{gr\_states} \cup \Pi_{AF\downarrow_{i\_gr}} \cup \Pi_{inertial} \cup \Pi_{base\_function}$$

The following theorem shows a characterization of the CF2 argumentation semantics in terms of answer set models of the P_{CF2} program[5].

Theorem 2 *Let $AF = \langle AR, attacks \rangle$ be an argumentation framework. $E \in CF2(AF)$ if and only if there exists an answer set M of $P_{CF2}(AF)$ such that $E = \{a | accepted(a) \in M\}$.*

Proof: **(sketch)** The proof follows by Propositions 1, 2 and the following observations:

1. The programs Π_{ini} and $\Pi_{base\_function}$ characterize the maximal conflict-free sets of a given argumentation framework.
2. The program $\Pi_{inertial}$ characterizes the strongly connected components of a given argumentation framework.
3. The programs $\Pi_{inertial}$ and $\Pi_{AF\downarrow_{i\_gr}}$ induce the directionality principle.

∎

We want to point out at least two implications of this characterization of CF2:

1. By changing the behavior of $\Pi_{base\_function}$ one can characterize different SCC-recursive semantics.
2. This characterization of CF2 suggests an easy-to-use form for inferring extensions of SCC-recursive semantics such as CF2 extensions.

3.1. Applications of Theorem 2

We can find different strategies for computing extension-based argumentation semantics [3, 6, 9, 14]; however, a common point among these approaches is to address some of the following questions[6] *w.r.t.* a given extension-based argumentation semantics S, an argumentation framework $AF = \langle AR, attacks \rangle$ and $A \in AR$: 1.- Which are the extensions

---

[5]P_{CF2} - http://www.lsi.upc.edu/~jcnieves/software/CF2-ASP.dlv
[6]Notice, questions 2,3 and 6 answer 'credulous acceptance problem *w.r.t.* S', 'skeptical acceptance problem *w.r.t.* S' and 'skeptical refusal problem *w.r.t.* S' respectively

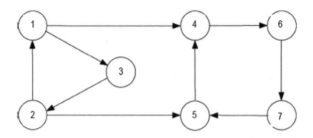

Figure   1. Graph   representation   of   the   argumentation   framework
$AF = \langle\{1, 2, 3, 4, 5, 6, 7\}, \{(1, 4), (1, 3), (2, 1), (2, 5), (3, 2), (4, 6), (6, 7), (7, 5), (5, 4)\}\rangle$

in $S(AF)$? 2.- Is A contained in an extension of $S(AF)$? 3.- Is A contained in all the extension of $S(AF)$? 4.- Which are all the extensions containing A? 5.- Which are the extensions that attacks A? 6.- Is A attacked by all the extensions of $S(AF)$?

One of the main applications of Theorem 2 is that one can take advantage of efficient answer set solvers, *e.g.*, [7], for answering the given questions *w.r.t.* SCC-recursive semantics such as CF2. For instance, the DLV system allows the use of different front-ends for performing different kinds of queries *w.r.t.* the answer set models of a given logic programs; this means that by using these front-ends one can answer the given questions *w.r.t. S, AF* and *A*. In order to illustrate these applications of Theorem 2, let *AF* be the argumentation framework of Figure 1 and `pcf2.dlv` be the program which contains $P_{CF2}(AF)$. Now we are going to answer each of the given questions.

Which are the extensions in $CF2(AF)$**?** For answering this question, let us call DLV with the filter *accepted*:

```
$ dlv pcf2.dlv -filter=accepted
{accepted(2), accepted(4), accepted(7)} {accepted(1), accepted(5),
accepted(6)} {accepted(3), accepted(4), accepted(7)} {accepted(3),
accepted(5), accepted(6)}
```

This means that the provided set of sets of arguments are all the possible CF2 extensions of the framework.

Is 5 **contained in an extension of** $CF2(AF)$**?** For answering this question, let `query1` be the file: `accepted(5)?` Now let us call DLV with the filter *accepted*, the *brave/credulous reasoning* front-end and `query1`:

```
$ dlv pcf2.dlv -brave -filter=accepted query1
accepted(5) is bravely true, evidenced by {accepted(3), accepted(5),
accepted(6)}
```

This means that it is true that the argument 5 belongs to a CF2 extension and even more we have a CF2 extension which contains the argument 5.

Is 5 **contained in all the extension of** $CF2(AF)$**?** For answering this question, let `query2` be the file: `accepted(5)?` Now let us call DLV with the filter *accepted*, the *cautious/skeptical reasoning* front-end and `query2`:

```
$ dlv pcf2.dlv -cautious -filter=accepted query2
accepted(5) is cautiously false, evidenced by {accepted(2), accepted(4),
```

```
accepted(7)}
```
This means that it is false that the argument 5 belongs to all CF2 extensions and even more, DLV provides a CF2 extension that serves as counterexample

Which are all the extensions containing 3? For answering this question, let `query3` be the file: `accepted(3)`? Now let us call DLV with the filter *accepted* and `query3`:
```
$ dlv pcf2.dlv -filter=accepted query3s
{accepted(3), accepted(5), accepted(6)} {accepted(3), accepted(4),
accepted(7)}
```
This means that the provided set of sets of arguments are all the possible CF2 extensions on the framework containing 3.

In order to manage the questions *w.r.t.* attacks, let `pcf2-at.dlv` be the program which contains $P_{CF2}(AF) \cup \{attacked(X) \leftarrow at(Y,X), accepted(Y)\}$.
Which are the extensions that attack 3? For answering this question, let `query4` be the file: `attacked(3)`? Now let us call DLV with the filter *accepted* and `query4`:
```
$ dlv pcf2-at.dlv -filter=accepted query4
{accepted(1), accepted(5), accepted(6)}
```
This means that the provided set of arguments is all the possible CF2 extensions on the framework containing arguments attacking 3.

Is 5 **attacked by all the extensions of** *CF2(AF)*? For answering this question, let `query5` be the file: `attacked(5)`? Now let us call DLV with the filter *accepted*,the *cautious/skeptical reasoning* front-end and `query5`:
```
$ dlv pcf2-at.dlv -cautious -filter=accepted query5
attacked(3) is cautiously false, evidenced by {accepted(3), accepted(5),
accepted(6)}
```
This means that it is false that the argument 5 is attacked by all CF2 extensions and even more, DLV provides a CF2 extension that serves as counterexample

4. Conclusions

The study and understanding of extension-based argumentation semantics have shown to be a crucial point in argumentation theory [1,2,8,17]. This is mainly because they capture several approaches for performing argumentation reasoning. To find relationships between them and well-acceptable approaches such as answer set semantics helps in the exploration and implementation of prominent non-monotonic reasoning approaches.

So far we have already shown that extension-based argumentation semantics based on admissible sets are able to be characterized in terms of answer set models [5,8,10,15, 16,18]; however, it is well-known that they have unexpected behaviors [2,17]. Hence, the consideration of emerging approaches seems to be crucial. The emerging approaches for defining new extension-based argumentation semantics is really diverse; however, approaches such as the ones based on SCC-recursive semantics looks sound. One can find SCC-recursive semantics such as CF2 which converges with extension-based argumentation semantics based on logic programming semantics with negation as failure [16].

Now in this paper, we have shown that not only extension-based argumentation semantics based on admissible sets can be characterized in terms of answer set models; but also extension-based argumentations semantics based on strongly connected components can be characterized in terms of answer set models. This result opens the possibility of exploring new SCC-recursive semantics which can be interpreted in a straightforward form in terms of answer set models. And of course, the possibility of implementing fast prototypes of them using answer set programming platforms [13].

Acknowledgements

We are grateful to anonymous referees for their useful comments. This research has been partially supported by the EC founded project ALIVE (FP7-IST-215890). The views expressed in this paper are not necessarily those of the ALIVE consortium.

References

[1] P. Baroni and M. Giacomin. On principle-based evaluation of extension-based argumentation semantics. *Artificial Intelligence.*, 171(10-15):675–700, 2007.

[2] P. Baroni, M. Giacomin, and G. Guida. SCC-recursiveness: a general schema for argumentation semantics. *Artificial Intelligence*, 168:162–210, October 2005.

[3] P. Besnard and S. Doutre. Checking the acceptability of a set of arguments. In *Tenth International Workshop on Non-Monotonic Reasoning (NMR 2004)*, pages 59–64, June 2004.

[4] M. Caminada. Semi-Stable semantics. In P. E. Dunne and T. J. Bench-Capon, editors, *Proceedings of COMMA*, volume 144, pages 121–130. IOS Press, 2006.

[5] J. L. Carballido, J. C. Nieves, and M. Osorio. Inferring Preferred Extensions by Pstable Semantics. *Iberoamerican Journal of Artificial Intelligence ISSN: 1137-3601*, 13(41):38–53, 2009.

[6] C. Cayrol, S. Doutre, and J. Mengin. On Decision Problems related to the preferred semantics for argumentation frameworks. *Journal of Logic and Computation*, 13(3):377–403, 2003.

[7] S. DLV. Vienna University of Technology. http://www.dbai.tuwien.ac.at/proj/dlv/, 1996.

[8] P. M. Dung. On the acceptability of arguments and its fundamental role in nonmonotonic reasoning, logic programming and n-person games. *Artificial Intelligence*, 77(2):321–358, 1995.

[9] P. M. Dung, P. Mancarella, and F. Toni. Computing ideal sceptical argumentation. *Artificial Intelligence*, 171(issues 10-15):642–674, 2007.

[10] U. Egly, S. A. Gaggl, and S. Woltran. Aspartix: Implementing argumentation frameworks using answer-set programmin. In M. G. de la Banda and E. Pontelli, editors, *International Conference of Logic Programming (ICLP)*, volume 5366 of *LNCS*, pages 734–738. Springer, 2008.

[11] A. V. Gelder, K. A. Ross, and J. S. Schlipf. The well-founded semantics for general logic programs. *Journal of the ACM*, 38(3):620–650, 1991.

[12] M. Gelfond and V. Lifschitz. Classical Negation in Logic Programs and Disjunctive Databases. *New Generation Computing*, 9:365–385, 1991.

[13] I. Gómez-Sebastià and J. C. Nieves. WizArg: Visual Argumentation Framework Solving Wizard. In *In Proceedings of CCIA'2010*. Frontiers in Artificial Intelligence and Applications, IOS Press, accepted.

[14] S. Modgil and M. Caminada. *Argumentation in Artificial Intelligence*, chapter Proof Theories and Algorithms for Abstract Argumentation Frameworks, pages 105–129. Springer, 2009.

[15] J. C. Nieves, M. Osorio, and U. Cortés. Preferred Extensions as Stable Models. *Theory and Practice of Logic Programming*, 8(4):527–543, July 2008.

[16] J. C. Nieves, M. Osorio, and C. Zepeda. A Schema for Generating Relevant Logic Programming Semantics and its Applications in Argumentation Theory. *Fundamenta Informaticae*, accepted.

[17] H. Prakken and G. A. W. Vreeswijk. Logics for defeasible argumentation. In D. Gabbay and F. Günthner, editors, *Handbook of Philosophical Logic*, volume 4, pages 219–318. Kluwer Academic Publishers,2002.

[18] K. N. Toshiko Wakaki. *Computing Argumentation Semantics in Answer Set Programming*, volume 5447/2009 of *Lecture Notes in Computer Science*, pages 254–269. 2009.

Computational Models of Argument
P. Baroni et al. (Eds.)
IOS Press, 2010
doi:10.3233/978-1-60750-619-5-403

Argumentation Mechanism Design for Preferred Semantics

Shengying Pan [a] Kate Larson [a] Iyad Rahwan [b,c,d]

[a] *Cheriton School of Computer Science, University of Waterloo, Waterloo, ON, Canada*
[b] *Masdar Institute of Science & Technology, UAE*
[c] *Massachusetts Institute of Technology, USA*
[d] *University of Edinburgh, UK*

Abstract. Recently Argumentation Mechanism Design (ArgMD) was introduced as a paradigm for studying argumentation using game-theoretic techniques. To date, this framework has been used to study under what conditions a direct mechanism based on Dung's grounded semantics is strategy-proof (i.e. truth-enforcing) when knowledge of arguments is private to self-interested agents. In this paper, we study Dung's preferred semantics in order to understand under what conditions it is possible to design strategy-proof mechanisms. This is challenging since, unlike with the grounded semantics, there may be multiple preferred extensions, forcing a mechanism to select one. We show that this gives rise to interesting strategic behaviour, and we show that in general it is not possible to have a strategy-proof mechanism that selects amongst the preferred extensions in a non-biased manner. We also investigaet refinements of preferred semantics which induce unique outcomes, namely the skeptical-preferred and ideal semantics.

1. Introduction

Argumentation has become a key model for automated reasoning and rational interaction in artificial intelligence. Key to its success has been Dung's work on abstract argumentation frameworks [6]. In this model arguments are viewed as abstract entities, with a binary defeat relation among them. This abstract framework has been beneficial for such things like the study of criteria (i.e. semantics) for evaluating outcomes of complex argument structures [1]. However, this body of work assumes that all arguments are given, a priori, for evaluation by an omniscient reasoner.

Recently there has been interest in studying strategic issues which arise in a *multi-agent* view of argumentation. In this setting, each agent has knowledge of some sub-set of the arguments, which reflects the (possibly conflicting) information available to that agent. Arguments known to different agents may overlap. However, each agent is self-interested,[1] in the sense that the agent has some preference over which arguments end up being accepted. As a result, an agent may benefit from acting strategically, by misreporting its private information (i.e. the arguments it is aware of), either passively (by hiding arguments) or actively (by stating arguments it does not believe to hold).

---

[1]Note that self-interest does not necessarily imply selfishness. One's own interests may well happen to align with those of others.

The strategic view of argumentation raises a question akin to (game-theoretic) mechanism design. Just as an auction (or a voting rule) is a rule that maps the revealed bids (or preferences) of different agents into a social outcome by allocating resources, an argumentation semantics maps the arguments revealed by different agents into a set of accepted arguments (See Figure 1). The question then becomes: *what strategic incentives are imposed by different argument evaluation criteria, when arguments are distributed among self-interested agents?*

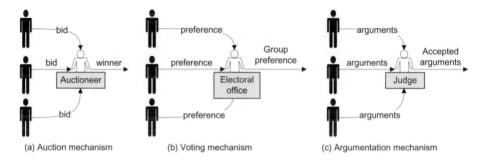

(a) Auction mechanism   (b) Voting mechanism   (c) Argumentation mechanism

Figure 1. Argumentation mechanism (semantics) analogous to auction or voting mechanism

Rahwan and Larson proposed a new approach which they called *Argumentation Mechanism Design* (ArgMD) in which argument-evaluation procedures (or semantic criteria) are analysed to understand which strategic behaviour arises [10]. Rahwan *et al* undertook a detailed case study of the *grounded semantics* and, using the ArgMD framework, provided a full characterisation of strategy-proofness (i.e. truth-telling being a dominant strategy equilibrium) under the grounded semantics when agents can both hide and lie about their arguments [11].

In this paper we extend the analysis of strategic behaviour in argumentation frameworks to incorporate the *preferred semantics*, a more credulous semantics. While the grounded semantics induces a single outcome, the preferred semantics can result in multiple outcomes. We study whether this gives rise to new strategic-behaviour on the part of the agents and provide a graph-theoretical partial characterisation of strategy-proofness under these semantics. We also provide an analysis of two refinements of the preferred semantics: the ideal and skeptical-preferred semantics.

2. Background on Abstract Argumentation

In this section we outline key elements of abstract argumentation frameworks. We begin with Dung's abstract characterisation of an argumentation system [6].

Definition 1 (Argumentation framework). *An argumentation framework is a pair $AF = \langle \mathcal{A}, \to \rangle$ where $\mathcal{A}$ is a set of arguments and $\to \subseteq \mathcal{A} \times \mathcal{A}$ is a defeat relation. We say that argument α defeats an argument β iff $(\alpha, \beta) \in \to$ and write this as $\alpha \to \beta$. For simplicity we restrict ourselves to finite argument sets.*

An argumentation framework can be represented as a directed graph in which the vertices are arguments and the directed edges characterise the defeat relationship among

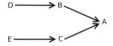

Figure 2. A simple argument graph.

Figure 3. An argumentation framework with a cycle.

arguments. An example argument graph is shown in Figure 2. Argument A has two defeaters, B and C, which are themselves defeated by arguments D and E respectively. Cycles are also allowed in the definition of an argumentation framework, as illustrated in Figure 3. In this example there are two arguments, A and B, which defeat each other.

Let $S^+ = \{\beta \in \mathcal{A}|\alpha \rightharpoonup \beta$ for some $\alpha \in S\}$. Also let $\alpha^- = \{\beta \in \mathcal{A}|\beta \rightharpoonup \alpha\}$. We first characterise the fundamental notions of conflict-free and defence.

Definition 2 (Conflict-free, Defence). *Let $\langle \mathcal{A}, \rightharpoonup \rangle$ be an argumentation framework and let $S \subseteq \mathcal{A}$ and let $\alpha \in \mathcal{A}$.*

1. *S is conflict-free iff $S \cap S^+ = \emptyset$.*
2. *S defends argument α iff $\alpha^- \subseteq S^+$. We also say that argument α is acceptable with respect to S.*

Intuitively, a set of arguments is *conflict-free* if no argument in that set defeats another. A set of arguments *defends* a given argument if it defeats all its defeaters. We now look at the *collective acceptability* of a set of arguments.

Definition 3 (Characteristic function). *Let $AF = \langle \mathcal{A}, \rightharpoonup \rangle$ be an argumentation framework. The characteristic function of AF is $\mathcal{F}_{AF} : 2^{\mathcal{A}} \to 2^{\mathcal{A}}$ such that, given $S \subseteq \mathcal{A}$, we have $\mathcal{F}_{AF}(S) = \{\alpha \in \mathcal{A}|S$ defends $\alpha\}$.*

When there is no ambiguity about the argumentation framework in question, we will use $\mathcal{F}$ instead of $\mathcal{F}_{AF}$.

Definition 4 (Acceptability semantics). *Let S be a conflict-free set of arguments in framework $\langle \mathcal{A}, \rightharpoonup \rangle$.*

1. *S is admissible iff it is conflict-free and defends every element in S (i.e. if $S \subseteq \mathcal{F}(S)$).*
2. *S is a complete extension iff $S = \mathcal{F}(S)$.*
3. *S is a preferred extension iff it is a maximal (w.r.t. set-inclusion) complete extension.*
4. *S is a grounded extension iff it is a minimal (w.r.t. set-inclusion) complete extension.*

Intuitively, a set of arguments is *admissible* if it is a conflict-free set that defends itself against any defeater. An admissible set S is a *complete extension* if and only if *all* arguments defended by S are also in S. There may be more than one complete extension, each corresponding to a particular consistent and self-defending viewpoint. A *preferred extension* is the position that cannot be extended without causing inconsistency. The *grounded extension* only accepts arguments that are not defeated as well as arguments which are defended directly or indirectly by non-defeated arguments. We note that there always exists a unique grounded extension, but there may be multiple preferred extensions. We let $\mathcal{GE}(AF)$ represent the grounded extension of argumentation framework AF and $\mathcal{PE}(AF)$ denote the set of preferred extensions. For the argumentation framework in Figure 2 we have that $\mathcal{GE}(AF) = \{D, E, A\}$ which is also the single preferred extension, while in Figure 3 $\mathcal{GE}(AF) = \{\}$ and $\mathcal{PE}(AF) = \{\{A\}, \{B\}\}$. Finally, we formally define the notions of indirect defeat and defence.

Definition 5 (Indirect defeat and defence [6]). *Let* $\alpha, \beta \in \mathcal{A}$. *We say that* α *indirectly defeats* β, *written* $\alpha \hookrightarrow \beta$, *if and only if there is an odd-length path from* α *to* β *in the argument graph. We say that* α *indirectly defends* β, *written* $\alpha \looparrowright \beta$, *if and only if there is an even-length path (with non-zero length) from* α *to* β *in the argument graph.*

3. Argumentation Mechanism Design

In this section we define the mechanism design problem for abstract argumentation as was introduced by Rahwan and Larson [10]. We define a mechanism with respect to an argumentation framework $\langle \mathcal{A}, \rightharpoonup \rangle$ with semantics $\mathcal{S}$, and we assume that there is a set $\{1, 2, \ldots, I\}$ of self-interested agents. A key notion in mechanism design is the *type* of an agent. An agent's type is all the information which is relevant to the agent when formulating its preferences over outcomes. In our framework, we define an agent's type to be its set of arguments.

Definition 6 (Agent Type). *Given an argumentation framework* $\langle \mathcal{A}, \rightharpoonup \rangle$, *the type of agent* i, $\mathcal{A}_i \subseteq \mathcal{A}$, *is the set of arguments that the agent is capable of putting forward.*

Note that $\alpha \in \mathcal{A}_i$ is not necessarily true, or even believed by i to be acceptable. It simply reflects a piece of information the agent has. Indeed, if α involved a contradiction, it would be self-defeating and hence never accepted by anyone.

A social choice function maps a type profile (vector of agent types) to a subset of arguments. In particular, we will interpret the set of arguments to be the arguments which are deemed to be acceptable if the actual types of the agents were known. We will determine the acceptability of arguments with respect to some specified semantics.

Definition 7 (Argument Acceptability Social Choice Functions). *Given an argumentation framework* $\langle \mathcal{A}, \rightharpoonup \rangle$ *with semantics* $\mathcal{S}$, *and given a type profile* $(\mathcal{A}_1, ..., \mathcal{A}_I)$ *such that* $\mathcal{A}_1 \cup \ldots \cup \mathcal{A}_I \subseteq \mathcal{A}$, *the argument acceptability social choice function* f *is defined as the set of acceptable arguments given the semantics* $\mathcal{S}$. *That is,* $f(\mathcal{A}_1, ..., \mathcal{A}_I) = Acc(\langle \mathcal{A}_1 \cup ... \cup \mathcal{A}_I, \rightharpoonup \rangle, \mathcal{S})$

As is common in the mechanism design literature, we assume that agents have preferences over the outcomes $o \in 2^{\mathcal{A}}$, and we represent these preferences using utility functions where $u_i(o, \mathcal{A}_i)$ denotes agent i's utility for outcome o when its type is argument set $\mathcal{A}_i$. Agent i prefers outcome o_1 to o_2 when $u_i(o_1, \mathcal{A}_i) > u_i(o_2, \mathcal{A}_i)$. In this paper, we assume that agents have *focal argument preferences*.

Definition 8 (Focal-Argument Preferences). *An agent* i *has focal-argument preferences if there exists some argument* $\alpha_i^* \in \mathcal{A}_i$ *such that for any outcomes* o_1, $o_2 \in \mathcal{O}$ *such that* $\alpha_i^* \in o_1$ *and* $\alpha_i^* \notin o_2$ *then* $u_i(o_1, \mathcal{A}_i) > u_i(o_2, \mathcal{A}_i)$. *Otherwise,* $u_i(o_1, \mathcal{A}_i) = u_i(o_2, \mathcal{A}_i)$.

Informally, this class of preferences can be interpreted as each agent i having a single argument, α_i^*, in which they are interested, while the other arguments are of interest only with respect to how they support α_i^*.

Agents may not have incentive to reveal their true type because they may be able to influence the final argument status assignment by lying, and thus obtain higher utility. We explicitly assume that the defeat relationship, $\rightharpoonup$, is known and understood by all agents. Then there are two ways in which an agent may lie. First, it might claim to *have* arguments which are not in its argument set (but are still part of $\mathcal{A}$). In such a case, we say that the agent *makes up* arguments. Second, it might *hide* arguments. By refusing to reveal certain arguments, an agent might be able to break defeat chains in the argument framework, thus changing the final set of acceptable arguments.

A strategy for agent i, $s_i(\mathcal{A}_i) \in \Sigma_i$, is a plan that describes what actions the agent will take for every decision that the agent might be called upon to make, for each possible piece of information that the agent may have at each time it is called to act. In our model strategies specify which arguments an agent should reveal when. The notation Σ_i denotes the *strategy space* of agent i and contains all possible legal strategies that an agent may follow.

Definition 9 (Argumentation Mechanism). *Given an argumentation framework $AF = \langle \mathcal{A}, \rightharpoonup \rangle$ and semantics $\mathcal{S}$, an argumentation mechanism is defined as*

$$\mathcal{M}_{AF}^{\mathcal{S}} = (\Sigma_1, ..., \Sigma_I, g(\cdot))$$

where Σ_i is an argumentation strategy space of agent i and $g : \Sigma_1 \times ... \times \Sigma_I \rightarrow 2^{\mathcal{A}}$.

We are particularly interested in situations where the agents' strategies are restricted so that they can only reveal sets of arguments once. Mechanisms with this particular restriction are called *direct mechanisms*.

Definition 10 (Direct Argumentation Mechanism). *Given an argumentation framework $AF = \langle \mathcal{A}, \rightharpoonup \rangle$ and semantics $\mathcal{S}$, a direct argumentation mechanism is defined as*

$$\mathcal{M}_{AF}^{\mathcal{S}} = (\Sigma_1, ..., \Sigma_I, g(\cdot))$$

where $\Sigma_i = 2^{\mathcal{A}_i}$ and $g : \Sigma_1 \times ... \times \Sigma_I \rightarrow 2^{\mathcal{A}}$.

If, given, $\mathcal{M}_{AF}^{\mathcal{S}}$ all agents are best off selecting a strategy such that $s_i(\mathcal{A}_i) = \mathcal{A}_i$ (no matter what any other agent is doing) then we say that the mechanism is *strategy-proof*. That is, agents have incentive to truthfully report their actual arguments.[2] The goal of ArgMD is to understand when and why it is possible or impossible to ensure that a mechanism is strategy-proof. The restriction to direct mechanisms is without loss of generality since the *Revelation Principle* states that if there exists a mechanism such that agents reveal their types truthfully, then there is a direct mechanism with this property [8]. Finally, we define a direct mechanism for argumentation based on the preferred semantics. We refer to a specific action of agent i as $\mathcal{A}_i^o \in \Sigma_i$.

---

[2]The term strategy-proof is used when ever all agents have incentive to truthfully report their types, even if truth-telling is only a weakly dominant strategy [8].

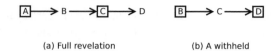

(a) Full revelation   (b) A withheld

Figure 4. Hiding an argument is beneficial

Definition 11 (Preferred Direct Argumentation Mechanism). *A preferred direct argumentation mechanism for argumentation framework $AF = \langle \mathcal{A}, \rightarrowtail \rangle$ is $\mathcal{M}_{AF}^{\mathcal{PE}} = (\Sigma_1, \ldots, \Sigma_I, g(\cdot))$ where $\Sigma_i \in 2^{\mathcal{A}}$ is the set of strategies available to each agent, and $g(\mathcal{A}_1^o, \ldots, \mathcal{A}_I^o) = Acc(\langle \mathcal{A}_1^o \cup \ldots \cup \mathcal{A}_I^o, \rightarrowtail \rangle, S^{\mathcal{PE}})$ where $S^{\mathcal{PE}}$ denotes the preferred acceptability semantics.*

4. Implementing the Preferred Extension

We start this section with an illustrative example showing why agents may have incentive to be strategic when asked to reveal their arguments.

Example 1. *Assume that there are three agents where $\mathcal{A}_1 = \{A, D\}, \mathcal{A}_2 = \{B\}$ and $\mathcal{A}_3 = \{C\}$, and with focal arguments $\alpha^*{}_1 = D, \alpha^*{}_2 = B$ and $\alpha^*{}_3 = C$. Assume also that the defeat relationship $\rightarrowtail = \{(A, B), (B, C), (C, D)\}$. If all agents reveal their arguments then the resulting argument graph is shown in Figure 4(a). There is a single preferred extension where the arguments marked by boxes in Figure 4(a) are accepted. However, if agent 1 does not reveal argument A then the unique preferred extension is shown in Figure 4(b). Note that in this outcome, agent 1's focal argument is accepted, while in the original outcome, agent 1's focal argument was not accepted. Thus, agent 1 has incentive to hide its argument A.*

This example is also illustrative of another property of argumentation frameworks. If the underlying argumentation graph is *acyclic* then the unique preferred extension is equal to the grounded extension. Thus, it immediately follows that all ArgMD results for the grounded extension also apply to preferred extensions when the underlying argumentation graph is acyclic [11].

Theorem 1. *Suppose each agent $i \in \{1, \ldots, I\}$ has a focal argument $\alpha_i^* \in \mathcal{A}_i$, and suppose that the underlying argumentation graph is acyclic. If the following conditions hold:*

- *no agent type contains an (in)direct defeat against its focal argument*
- *no argument outside any agent's type (in)directly defends its focal argument*

then $\mathcal{M}_{AF}^{\mathcal{PE}}$ is strategy-proof.

In the rest of this paper we focus our attention to argumentation frameworks where the associated argumentation graph contains at least one cycle. One challenge is that for these argumentation frameworks, $\mathcal{PE}$ may contain more than one set of acceptable arguments, and thus the social choice function must have some principled way to select from amongst the elements of $\mathcal{PE}$. We propose two minimal standard properties the social choice function must exhibit when making such a selection.

Definition 12 (Agent-Anonymous). *[8] A social choice function f is* agent-anonymous *if for any onto function* $\pi : \{1, \ldots, I\} \mapsto \{1, \ldots, I\}$, *and for any type profile* $(\mathcal{A}_1, \ldots, \mathcal{A}_I)$ *we have* $f(\mathcal{A}_1, \ldots, \mathcal{A}_I) = f(\mathcal{A}_{\pi(1)}, \ldots, \mathcal{A}_{\pi(I)})$.

Definition 13 (Argument-Anonymous). *Let* $AF = \langle \mathcal{A}, \rightharpoonup \rangle$ *be any argumentation frame-work and let* $\pi : \{1, \ldots, I\} \mapsto \{1, \ldots, I\}$ *be an onto function. Define* $AF^\pi = \langle \mathcal{A}^\pi, \rightharpoonup_\pi \rangle$ *such that for any* $\alpha_i \in \mathcal{A}$ *then* $\alpha_{\pi(i)} \in \mathcal{A}^\pi$ *and if* $\alpha_i \rightharpoonup \alpha_j$ *then* $\alpha_{\pi(i)} \rightharpoonup_\pi \alpha_{\pi(j)}$. *A social choice function is* argument anonymous *if for any type profile* $(\mathcal{A}_1, \ldots, \mathcal{A}_I)$ *we have* $f(\mathcal{A}_1, \ldots, \mathcal{A}_I) = f(\mathcal{A}_1^\pi, \ldots, \mathcal{A}_I^\pi)$.

The first property affirms that the names of the agents should not matter, while the second property states the names of the arguments should not matter. Unfortunately, there is an immediate problem when trying to enforce these properties when applying them in the preferred semantics framework.

Theorem 2. *No deterministic social choice function which selects an outcome amongst the preferred extensions is both agent- and argument-anonymous.*

Proof. (Sketch) Consider the argumentation framework shown in Figure 3, and assume that there are two agents such that $\mathcal{A}_1 = \{A\}$ and $\mathcal{A}_2 = \{B\}$ (and each agent's focal argument is its single argument). $\mathcal{PE} = \{\{A\}, \{B\}\}$ and there is no justification which would respect the agent- and argument-anonymity properties to select one extension over the other.

$\square$

Theorem 2, as stated, only applies to deterministic social choice functions. It has been suggested that allowing for *randomization* with respect to selecting outcomes may circumvent certain impossibilities [5,9]. We investigate this observation as it applies to ArgMD by defining a *preferred randomized mechanism*.

Definition 14 (Preferred Randomized Mechanism). *A preferred randomized mechanism for argumentation framework* $AF = \langle \mathcal{A}, \rightharpoonup \rangle$ *is* $\mathcal{RM}_{AF}^{\mathcal{PE}} = (\Sigma_1, \ldots, \Sigma_I, g(\cdot))$ *where:*

- $\Sigma_i \in 2^{\mathcal{A}}$ *is the set of strategies available to each agent;*
- $g : \Sigma_1 \times \ldots \times \Sigma_I \to \Delta \mathcal{PE}$ *where* $\Delta \mathcal{PE}$ *is a distribution with full support over* $\mathcal{PE}$.

Given the revealed arguments of the agents, the mechanism selects a preferred extension at random according to some pre-specified distribution. The full-support requirement implies that any preferred extension can potentially be selected. Using $\mathcal{RM}_{AF}^{\mathcal{PE}}$ we study settings where agents' types do not contain (in)direct defeats against their own focal argument since this case was strategy-proof for acyclic argumentation frameworks.

Example 2. *Assume there are 7 agents with argument sets* $\mathcal{A}_1 = \{B, F\}, \mathcal{A}_2 = \{A\}, \mathcal{A}_3 = \{C\}, \mathcal{A}_4 = \{D\}, \mathcal{A}_5 = \{E\}, \mathcal{A}_6 = \{G\}$ *and* $\mathcal{A}_7 = \{H\}$. *For agents with only one argument their sole argument is their focal argument,* α_i^*. *For agent 1,* $\alpha_1^* = F$. *Assume the full defeat relationship (when all arguments are revealed) is shown in Fig-ure 5. Note that there is no* odd-length directed path *between arguments B and F, which is equivalent to stating that there is no (in)direct defeat between them. In fact, there is no odd-length undirected path between the two arguments.*

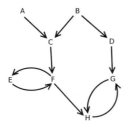

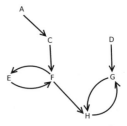

Figure 5. Argumentation graph if all agents reveal their arguments.

Figure 6. Argumentation graph if agent 1 hides argument B.

Assume the mechanism selects a preferred extension uniformly at random. All agents with only one argument (i.e. their focal argument) are best off revealing it. If all agents, including agent 1, reveal their arguments then $\mathcal{PE} = \{\{A, B, F, G\}, \{A, B, E, G\}, \{A, B, E, H\}\}$. If agent 1 hides argument B then the resulting argumentation graph is shown in Figure 6 and $\mathcal{PE} = \{\{A, D, E, H\}, \{A, D, F\}\}$. If agent 1 revealed both its arguments, then the probability that its focal argument was in the chosen outcome is $\frac{1}{3}$. However, if agent 1 hid argument B, then the probability that its focal argument was in the chosen outcome increases to $\frac{1}{2}$. Therefore, agent 1 is best off hiding argument B.

The restriction that the distribution must have full support, and our requirements of agent and argument anonymity mean that no matter what distribution is used agent 1 can always increase the probability of having its focal argument in the selected outcome by hiding its other argument. Thus, the properties which induced truth-telling for acyclic argumentation frameworks are not sufficient for non-acyclic frameworks. We now investigate a sufficient condition for truth-telling. It relies on two structural results for preferred extensions. Due to space limitation we are unable to include all proofs.

Lemma 1 characterizes the relationship between the preferred extensions of an argumentation framework, $AF = \langle \mathcal{A}, \rightarrow \rangle$, and the preferred extensions of argumentation frameworks induced by particular partitions of $\mathcal{A}$.

Lemma 1. *Let $AF = \langle \mathcal{A}, \rightarrow \rangle$ be an arbitrary argumentation framework. Let $S \subseteq \mathcal{A}, R = \mathcal{A} \setminus S$ be two non-empty subsets of $\mathcal{A}$ such that for any $\alpha \in S$ and $\beta \in R$ $(\alpha, \beta) \notin \rightarrow$ and $(\beta, \alpha) \notin \rightarrow$. Define $AF_S = \langle S, \rightarrow_S \rangle$ where $\rightarrow_S = \{(\alpha, \beta)|\alpha, \beta \in S \wedge (\alpha, \beta) \in \rightarrow\}$. Define $AF_R = \langle R, \rightarrow_R \rangle$ similarly. Then*

1. *For any preferred extension P in AF, $P \cap S$ is a preferred extension in AF_S and $P \cap R$ is a preferred extension in AF_R.*
2. *For any preferred extensions P_S in AF_S and P_R in AF_R, $P_S \cup P_R$ is a preferred extension in AF.*

Lemma 2. *Let $AF = \langle \mathcal{A}, \rightarrow \rangle$ where $\alpha, \alpha' \in \mathcal{A}$ and $AF' = \langle \mathcal{A} \setminus \{\alpha'\}, \rightarrow' \rangle$ such that $\rightarrow'$ is the restriction of $\rightarrow$ to $\mathcal{A} \setminus \{\alpha'\}$. Let $Pr_D(\alpha|\mathcal{PE}(AF))$ denote the probability that an extension containing α is selected at random under a distribution, D, with full support over $\mathcal{PE}(AF)$ and which satisfies the anonymity criteria. Assume that there is no undirected path between α and α'. Then $Pr_D(\alpha|\mathcal{PE}(AF)) = Pr_{D'}(\alpha|\mathcal{PE}(AF'))$ where D' is the restriction of D to $\mathcal{PE}(AF')$.*

Lemma 2 states that as long as there is no path between two arguments, then whether or not one argument is revealed can not influence the probability that a preferred extension containing the other argument will be chosen. We are now able to provide a partial characterization of strategy-proofness for the preferred semantics, if we assume agents will only *hide* arguments.

Theorem 3. *Suppose every agent $i \in \{1, \ldots, I\}$ has a focal argument $\alpha_i^* \in \mathcal{A}_i$. If for each agent i, $\mathcal{A}_i$ contains no argument with an undirected path to α_i^*, then $\mathcal{RM}_{AF}^{\mathcal{PE}}$ is strategy-proof.*

Proof. Let $p_i(\langle \mathcal{A}, \rightarrow \rangle)$ be the probability of a preferred extension containing agent i's focal argument to be chosen randomly from preferred extensions in argumentation framework $\langle \mathcal{A}, \rightarrow \rangle$.

Suppose the randomized mechanism is not strategy-proof, then there exists an argumentation framework $AF = \langle \mathcal{A}, \rightarrow \rangle$ such that $\exists i$, for $\mathcal{A}_i' \subset \mathcal{A}_i$ a revelation of agent i and $\mathcal{A}_{-i}' = (\mathcal{A}_1', \ldots, \mathcal{A}_{i-1}', \mathcal{A}_{i+1}', \ldots, \mathcal{A}_I')$ a revelation of all agents not including i, $p_i(\langle \mathcal{A}_i' \cup \mathcal{A}_{-i}', \rightarrow \rangle) > p_i(\langle \mathcal{A}_i \cup \mathcal{A}_{-i}', \rightarrow \rangle)$.

Let $n = |\mathcal{A}_i| - |\mathcal{A}_i'|$, $\{\beta_1, \beta_2, \ldots, \beta_n\} = \mathcal{A}_i \setminus \mathcal{A}_i'$, $\forall 1 \leq j \leq n$, there is no path (disregard direction) from β_j to i's focal argument $\hat{\alpha}^i$. By **Lemma 2**, $p_i(\langle \mathcal{A}_i \cup \mathcal{A}_{-i}', \rightarrow \rangle) = p_i(\langle (\mathcal{A}_i \setminus \{\beta_1\}) \cup \mathcal{A}_{-i}', \rightarrow \rangle) = p_i(\langle (\mathcal{A}_i \setminus \{\beta_1, \beta_2\}) \cup \mathcal{A}_{-i}', \rightarrow \rangle) = \cdots = p_i(\langle (\mathcal{A}_i \setminus \{\beta_1, \beta_2, \ldots, \beta_n\}) \cup \mathcal{A}_{-i}', \rightarrow \rangle) = p_i(\langle (\mathcal{A}_i' \cup \mathcal{A}_{-i}', \rightarrow \rangle)$, which contradicts $p_i(\langle \mathcal{A}_i' \cup \mathcal{A}_{-i}', \rightarrow \rangle) > p_i(\langle \mathcal{A}_i \cup \mathcal{A}_{-i}', \rightarrow \rangle)$. Therefore, $\mathcal{RM}_{AF}^{\mathcal{PE}}$ is strategy-proof. $\qquad \square$

Theorem 3 states that agents have no incentive to hide arguments when their focal arguments are in subgraphs disconnected from their other arguments. This is a very strong condition and is significantly stronger than the required condition for strategy-proofness for acyclic frameworks. We also note that this is only a sufficient condition. There may be other topological restrictions which would allow for strategy-proofness.

5. Refinements of the Preferred Semantics

One way of handling the multiplicity of preferred extensions is to provide additional refinements to the semantics. In this section we look at two such refinements, the *skeptical-preferred semantics* and the *ideal semantics*, both of which provide a unique extension, thus avoiding the problem faced in the last section.

Definition 15 (Skeptical-Preferred Semantics). *[2] Let $AF = \langle \mathcal{A}, \rightarrow \rangle$ be an argumentation framework and let $\mathcal{PE}(AF)$ be the set of preferred extensions. The skeptical-preferred extension is $\mathcal{SP}(AF) = \cap_{S \in \mathcal{PE}(AF)} S$.*

Clearly the skeptical-preferred extension is unique, but it may not be admissible, and thus not a complete extension.

Definition 16 (Ideal Semantics). *[7] Let $AF = \langle \mathcal{A}, \rightarrow \rangle$ be an argumentation framework. The ideal extension, $\mathcal{I}(AF)$, is the maximal (w.r.t. set-inclusion) admissible set that is a subset of each preferred extension.*

As shown by Caminada, the ideal extension always exists and is unique [3].

Proposition 1. *[3] Let $AF = \langle \mathcal{A}, \rightarrow \rangle$ be an argumentation framework. There exists exactly one maximal (w.r.t. set-inclusion) admissible set that is a subset of each preferred extension.*

The above proposition implies that $\mathcal{I}(AF) \subseteq \mathcal{SP}(AF)$.

Given these two new semantics, we define argumentation mechanisms in a similar way as we did for the preferred semantics. In particular $\mathcal{M}_{AF}^{\mathcal{SP}}$ is an argumentation mechanism where the outcome is selected using the skeptical-preferred semantics, while $\mathcal{M}_{AF}^{\mathcal{I}}$ is an argumentation mechanism where the outcome is selected using the ideal semantics. Since both the skeptical-preferred and ideal semantics result in a unique extension, we do not require randomization.

We first look at the case where agents' strategies are restricted so that they can only *hide* their arguments. While, due to space limitations, we focus on $\mathcal{M}_{AF}^{\mathcal{I}}$, we first present Lemma 3 which states what happens to the skeptical-preferred extension when a new argument is added to an argumentation framework. Any argument that had been initially acceptable w.r.t. the skeptical-preferred extension, remains acceptable in the new argumentation framework as long as the new argument did not (in)directly defeat it.

Lemma 3. *For $AF_1 = \langle \mathcal{A}, \rightarrow_1 \rangle$ and $AF_2 = \langle \mathcal{A} \cup \{\alpha'\}, \rightarrow_2 \rangle$ such that $\rightarrow_1 \subseteq \rightarrow_2$ and $(\rightarrow_2 \setminus \rightarrow_1) \subseteq (\{\alpha'\} \times \mathcal{A}) \cup (\mathcal{A} \times \{\alpha'\})$. If α is in the skeptical preferred extension of AF_1, and α' doesn't indirectly defeat α, then α is still in the skeptical preferred extension in AF_2.*

A similar result can be extended for the ideal extensions.

Lemma 4. *For $AF_1 = \langle \mathcal{A}, \rightarrow_1 \rangle$ and $AF_2 = \langle \mathcal{A} \cup \{\alpha'\}, \rightarrow_2 \rangle$ such that $\rightarrow_1 \subseteq \rightarrow_2$ and $(\rightarrow_2 \setminus \rightarrow_1) \subseteq (\{\alpha'\} \times \mathcal{A}) \cup (\mathcal{A} \times \{\alpha'\})$. If α is in the ideal extension of AF_1, and α' doesn't indirectly defeat α, then α is still in the ideal extension in AF_2.*

Proof. In an argumentation framework, the ideal extension is always a subset of the skeptical preferred extension.

Let S be the set of arguments in the ideal extension of AF_1 which are either α or (in)direct defenders of α. Then S must be admissible. Moreover, S is a subset of the ideal extension of AF_1 thus a subset of the skeptical preferred extension. $\forall \beta \in S, \beta$ is in the skeptical preferred extension of AF_1 and α' doesn't indirectly defeat β since in such case α' will indirectly defeat α. Therefore, β is in the skeptical preferred extension of AF_2 by Lemma 3. Thus S is a subset of the skeptical preferred extension of AF_2. Clearly S is still conflict-free in AF_2. Since $\alpha \in S$, if S is admissible in AF_2, by Proposition 1 and Definition 16, the ideal extension in AF_2 is a superset of S thus contains α, a contradiction. If S is not admissible in AF_2, the only possible way to break the admissibility is to have α' defeat one argument $\beta \in S$ in AF_2. But since β is an indirect defender of α, α' therefore indirectly defeats α, a contradiction. Hence, α is still in the ideal extension of AF_2. $\qquad\square$

Theorem 4. *Suppose every agent $i \in \{1, \ldots, I\}$ has a focal argument $\alpha_i^* \in \mathcal{A}_i$. If each agent's type contains no (in)direct defeat against α_i^*, then $\mathcal{M}_{AF}^{\mathcal{I}}$ is strategy-proof.*

Proof. (Sketch) Due to space limitations we only provide a sketch of the induction proof by describing the base case and induction step. The goal is to show formally that $\forall i \in$

$\{1, \ldots, I\}, u_i(Acc(\langle \mathcal{A}'_1 \cup \ldots \cup \mathcal{A}_i \cup \ldots \cup \mathcal{A}'_I, \rightarrow \rangle, \mathcal{S}^{\mathcal{I}}), \mathcal{A}_i) \geq u_i(Acc(\langle \mathcal{A}'_1 \cup \ldots \cup \mathcal{A}^{\circ}_i \cup \ldots \cup \mathcal{A}'_I, \rightarrow \rangle, \mathcal{S}^{\mathcal{I}}), \mathcal{A}_i)$ for any $\mathcal{A}^{\circ}_i \subset \mathcal{A}_i$ and $\mathcal{A}'_j \subseteq \mathcal{A}_j$.

We use induction over the sets of arguments agent i may reveal, starting from the focal argument α^*_i. We show that, considering any strategy $\mathcal{A}''_i \subseteq \mathcal{A}_i$, revealing one more argument can only increase i's chance of getting α^*_i accepted, *i.e.* it (weakly) improve i's utility. **Base Step:** If $\mathcal{A}_i = \{\hat{\alpha}^i\}$, then trivially, revealing $\mathcal{A}_i$ weakly dominates revealing $\emptyset$.

Induction Step: Suppose that revealing argument set $\mathcal{A}''_i \subseteq \mathcal{A}_i$ weakly dominates revealing any subset of $\mathcal{A}''_i$. We need to prove that revealing any set $\mathcal{A}'_i$, where $\mathcal{A}''_i \subset \mathcal{A}'_i \subseteq \mathcal{A}_i$ and $|\mathcal{A}'_i| = |\mathcal{A}''_i| + 1$, weakly dominates revealing $\mathcal{A}''_i$. This follows from Lemma 4. $\qquad \square$

We note that a similar characterisation is possible under the skeptical-preferred semantics. Interestingly, Theorem 4 provides the same characterization for when argument hiding is not beneficial for agents as for the grounded semantics [11]. This is true even though the underlying *structure* of the extensions is quite different, and the properties required for the grounded semantics characterisation do not immediately translate to the skeptical-preferred and ideal semantics due to the difference in their definitions. It is also interesting to note that if we study the situation where agents may also *make up* arguments, then we again obtain a similar characterisation as for the grounded semantics. We state the theorem for the ideal semantics, but an identical theorem also holds for the skeptical-preferred semantics.

Theorem 5. *Suppose every agent $i \in \{!, \ldots, I\}$ has a focal argument $\alpha^*_i \in \mathcal{A}_i$, and that agents can both hide or lie about arguments. If the following conditions hold:*

1. *each agent's type contains no (in)direct defeat against α^*_i (formally $\forall i \in I, \nexists \beta \in \mathcal{A}_i$ such that $\beta \hookrightarrow \alpha^*_i$);*
2. *for any agent i, no argument outside i's type (in)directly defends α^*_i (formally $\forall i \in I, \nexists \beta \in \mathcal{A} \setminus \mathcal{A}_i$ such that $\beta \looparrowright \alpha^*_i$);*

then $\mathcal{M}^{\mathcal{I}}_{AF}$ is strategy-proof.

Proof. (Sketch)

What we want to prove is that for an arbitrary $S \neq \mathcal{A}_i$: $\alpha^*_i \notin \mathcal{I}(\langle \mathcal{A}_i \cup \mathcal{A}_{-i}, \rightarrow \rangle)$ implies $\alpha^*_i \notin \mathcal{I}(\langle S \cup \mathcal{A}_{-i}, \rightarrow \rangle)$. where $\mathcal{I}(AF)$ is the ideal extension of argumentation framework AF. The rest of the proof follows a similar logic as that for the grounded extension. Due to space restrictions we refer the reader to [11]. $\qquad \square$

6. Conclusion

ArgMD is a useful paradigm for reasoning about argumentation among self-interested agents using game-theoretic techniques. To date it has been applied only to the grounded semantics, which is often criticized as taking an overly skeptical stance with respect to argument acceptability. In this paper we applied the ArgMD framework to the preferred semantics.

Unlike grounded semantics which yield a unique extension, multiple preferred extensions may exist for arbitrary argumentation frameworks. We proposed some minimal properties which ensured non-bias with respect to agents and arguments when selecting from amongst the preferred extensions. We illustrated that it was impossible to satisfy our minimal anonymity properties with a deterministic social choice function. By incorporating randomization into our mechanism, we determined conditions under which agents had incentive to reveal all their arguments. We intend to investigate less restrictive requirements on agents types, or other possible restrictions or extensions of the mechanism, so as to ensure strategy-proofness.

We also studied refinements of the preferred semantics which result in unique extensions. In particular, we were able to provide a similar characterization of strategy-proofness for the skeptical-preferred and ideal semantics, as had previously been provided for the grounded semantics. We found this interesting since the underlying structure of the extensions is quite different. We conjecture that the *uniqueness* of the extensions is important in the characterization, and intend to investigate other unique extensions (for example, the eager extension [3]).

We assumed, throughout this paper, that agents' preferences had a particular structure, that is agents had *focal-argument preferences*. One obvious question is whether the results in this paper are also applicable if agents have different preference structures, which opens up another line of future research.

It is worth noting how work reported in this paper differs from recent work on judgement aggregation in argumentation [12,4]. In judgement aggregation, all arguments are given, and each agent has preferences over how these arguments should be evaluated. In our work, on the other hand, the arguments themselves are distributed among the agents, and different argument graphs emerge based on what they choose to reveal.

References

[1]   P. Baroni and M. Giacomin. On principle-based evaluation of extension-based argumentation semantics. *Artificial Intelligence*, 171:675–700, 2007.
[2]   A. Bondarenko, P. M. Dung, R. A. Kowalski, and F. Toni. An abstract argumentation-theoretic framework for default reasoning. *Artificial Intelligence*, 93(1-2):63–101, 1997.
[3]   M. Caminada. Comparing two unique extension semantics for formal argumentation: Ideal and eager. In *Proceedings of 19th Belgian-Dutch Conference on Artificial Intelligence (BNAIC)*, pages 81–87, 2007.
[4]   M. Caminada and G. Pigozzi. On judgment aggregation in abstract argumentation. *Autonomous Agents and Multi-Agent Systems*, (to appear).
[5]   V. Conitzer and T. Sandholm. Nonexistence of voting rules that are usually hard to manipulate. In *Proceedings of the 21st AAAI*, pages 627–634, 2006.
[6]   P. M. Dung. On the acceptability of arguments and its fundamental role in nonmonotonic reasoning, logic programming and n-person games. *Artificial Intelligence*, 77:321–357, 1995.
[7]   P. M. Dung, P. Mancarella, and F. Toni. A dialectic procedure for sceptical, assumption-based argumentation. In *Proceedings of Computational Models of Argument (COMMA)*, pages 145–156, 2006.
[8]   A. Mas-Colell, M. Whinston, and J. Green. *Microeconomic Theory*. Oxford University Press, 1995.
[9]   A. Procaccia. Can approximation circumvent Gibbard-Satterthwaite? In *Proceedings of the 24th AAAI Conference on Artificial Intelligence (AAAI 2010)*, 2010.
[10] I. Rahwan and K. Larson. Mechanism design for abstract argumentation. In *Proceedings of AAMAS 2008*, pages 1031–1038, 2008.
[11] I. Rahwan, K. Larson, and F. Tohmé. A characterisation of strategy-proofness for grounded argumentation semantics. In *Proceedings of the 21st International Joint Conference on Artifical Intelligence (IJCAI 2009)*, pages 251–256, Pasadena, CA, July 2009.
[12] I. Rahwan and F. Tohmé. Collective Argument Evaluation as Judgement Aggregation. In *9th International Joint Conference on Autonomous Agents & Multi Agent Systems, AAMAS'2010, Toronto, Canada*, 2010.

Computational Models of Argument
P. Baroni et al. (Eds.)
IOS Press, 2010
doi:10.3233/978-1-60750-619-5-415

Building arguments with argumentation: the role of illocutionary force in computational models of argument

Chris REED [a] [1], Simon WELLS [a], Katarzyna BUDZYŃSKA [b,a] and
Joseph DEVEREUX [a]

[a] *School of Computing, University of Dundee, Dundee, UK*
[b] *Institute of Philosophy, Cardinal Stefan Wyszynski University in Warsaw, Poland*

Abstract. This paper builds upon the proposed dialogical extensions to the AIF, termed AIF$^+$, by making explicit the representation of the role of illocutionary force in the connection between argument structures and dialogical structures. Illocutionary force is realised in the form of Illocutionary Application (YA-) nodes that provide an explicit linkage between the locutions uttered during a dialogue and the underlying arguments expressed by the content of those locutions. This linkage is explored in the context of two contrasting dialogue games from the literature, demonstrating how the approach can support the development of computational models in which the speech-act function of communicative moves can be accounted for.

Keywords. argumentation, dialogue, AIF, speech acts, illocutionary force

1. Introduction & Background

The Argument Interchange Format [2] is an attempt to bring together a wide variety of argumentation technologies so that they can work together. [8] reviews some of the more recent applications of the AIF. An important shortcoming, however, is that the AIF does not explicitly handle dialogue, and, crucially, cannot connect the execution of dialogue protocols to the creation and manipulation of argument structures. This limitation has been explored in [5] and [11], which introduce the AIF+, but these accounts leave important questions unanswered. Here, we build on those works, but sketch a solution to one of the most important questions: how dialogic actions – locutions – generate, or warrant, or substantiate, or update parts of the argument structure. These actions, and their effects on argument structure, are defined by the dialogue games of which they form a part. Our approach builds on existing conceptions of illocutionary force developed in speech act theory, and we show how the approach can be applied to existing dialogue games from the literature. The result is that for the first time we can start to build computational models that take account of the illocutionary connection between moves in argumentative dialogues and the argument structures that underpin them – a connection that has long been taken for granted in linguistically oriented models of discourse.

2. The Argument Interchange Format (AIF)

Descriptions of the AIF are given in a number of places, as are reifications in languages such as RDF and OWL [2], [9], [7], [8]. We provide here just a very brief summary of the main concepts. The AIF uses a graph-theoretic basis for defining an "upper" ontology of the main components (or nodes) of arguments. Nodes are distinguished into those that capture information (loosely, these correspond to propositions), and those that capture relations between items of information, including relations of inference (which correspond to the application of inference rules to particular sets of propositions), relations of conflict (which represent forms of incompatibility between propositions) and relations of preference (which represent value orderings applied to particular sets of propositions). The instantiated nature of these relations is emphasised in the nomenclature, so whilst information is captured in Information (I-) nodes, relations between them are captured as Rule Application (RA-) nodes, Conflict Application (CA-) nodes and Preference Application (PA-) nodes. The general forms or patterns that these applications instantiate are given in a second part of the AIF ontology, the Forms ontology. The approach follows in the philosophical tradition of Walton [18], [19] of schematizing stereotypical patterns of reasoning – and then extending the tradition into conflict and preference. It is this schematic underpinning which gives the collective name for RA-, CA- and PA-nodes: Scheme (S-) nodes. The AIF upper ontology is designed to allow specialization and extension to particular domains and projects, in an attempt to balance the needs of interchange against the needs of idiosyncratic development.

3. Architecture: Introducing the AIF$^+$

As has been argued elsewhere [8], the job of the AIF is solely to represent argument, not to perform computation on it. Of course, the representation should have various characteristics that make the sorts of computation we are expecting to want to perform as straightforward as possible. So, for example, both analysis and mark-up of naturally occuring argument and automatic computation of acceptability status using argumentation semantics defined in the style of [3], are computations we are likely to want to perform, and therefore, to a certain extent, drive representational considerations. From a dialogical point of view, we can describe, at an abstract level, an entire class of transformations and computations that we want to perform on structures defined using the AIF$^+$. Following in a long tradition in both the multi-agent community, and before that, the discourse and pragmatics community, dialogical action can be seen as update to a shared information state. In such a model, one needs a representation of the shared state, a representation of how specific dialogical action modifies the state, and, typically, a representation of dialogue *per se*. Then one needs some sort of execution engine that allows dialogues to be conducted (or analysed) to produce both a specific dialogue history and a shared dialogue state. It is usual for the dialogue history to change only monotonically as a dialogue proceeds (that is, once something has been said it cannot be unsaid). In representation of the shared state, monotonicity is less common: perhaps for some specific dialogue protocols, modifications to the information state will happen to be monotonic, but in general, the shared state may lose information as well as gain it – after all, one would not wish to prohibit retraction or withdrawal. The AIF$^+$ takes on all three representational roles described above (*viz.* the shared state, the dialogue history and the ways in which dialogue updates the shared state), and, to be precise, treats both the general and instantiated forms of the last role. That is, both the general rules about how dialogue moves could update the shared state, and the specific application of those rules actually updating the shared state in given dialogic situations, are handled by the AIF$^+$. The shared state is represented simply by AIF structures. The dialogue history is represented by Locution

(L-) nodes, which are a special type of I-node, and the connections between L-nodes, by Transition Application (TA-) nodes, which are a special type of inference [11]. The general part of describing how dialogue moves update the state is what constitutes (a part of) the dialogue protocol. This is represented in the Forms ontology. In the AIF simpliciter, the Forms ontology describes templates that define how schemes connect premises, conclusions and other schemes of particular types. In the AIF$^+$, the role is exactly the same: the Forms ontology again describes templates that define how schemes connect premises, conclusions and other schemes. In the AIF, the schemes concern inference, conflict and preference. In the AIF$^+$, the schemes concern dialogic transitions (which were the focus of [11]) and illocutionary relations; the former connect components of dialogue, the latter connect components of a dialogue history with specific parts of an AIF structure. The AIF$^+$ thus represents all (but no more) of the information required for a general purpose dialogue execution algorithm to run a particular dialogue protocol, and create both dialogue history and underlying AIF structures. One interesting issue concerns monotonicity of the AIF structures. On the one hand, most dialogues permit some form of retraction or other nonmonotonic change to the shared information space. On the other hand, the AIF and AIF$^+$ must record all that has happened in a dialogue, including the assertions that led up to a retraction (for example). The current solution to this dilemma is to assign commitment (loosely speaking) to particular propositions nonmonotonically, but to leave the accretion of AIF structures as monotonic.

4. AIF$^+$: Ontological Extensions

In this section we introduce the ontological extensions in a little more detail, first quickly reviewing the extensions from [11] and then exploring the new, illocutionary relations in more detail. Analyzing argumentation in the context of dialogue provides insight into its important properties which are not expressible in a model of monologic argumentation. In real-life practice, an argument is commonly related to and is therefore dependent on a dialogue: "to understand an argument, it is very often highly important to know something about the context of dialogue in which the argument has occurred" [17, pp411-2] The context of a dialogue becomes especially important when we aim to evaluate the argumentation. In philosophy, the term "argument" has long been known to have two interpretations: argument$_1$ and argument$_2$ [6]. Argument$_1$ refers to an argument as a static object and is described by sentences such as "He prepared an argument". On the other hand, argument$_2$ refers to a dialogue or discussion and is described by sentences such as "they had an argument". As mentioned above, in real-life scenarios both kinds of argument coexist and interact with each other. Consider the following dialogue:

Bob: You know what? We should increase funding for science.
Alice: Really! Why do you think that?
Bob: Well, because science is necessary for successful industry.

In this argument$_2$ (dialogue), Bob and Alice jointly build an argument$_1$ (argumentation): "Funding for science should be increased since it is necessary for successful industry". The context of the argument$_2$ enables to keep track of the agents' interaction which creates the argument$_1$: the argumentation is invoked by Alice's speech act "Why do you think that?", and provided by Bob's speech acts "science is neccessary for successful industry".[2] Locutions are the fundamental building blocks of dialogue and are represented within AIF^+ in the form of L-Nodes, a subclass of I-Nodes. L-Nodes are employed to identify the individual utterances made during a dialogue. However, a dialogue is more than a mere sequence of unconnected locutions. A distinguishing feature of dialogue is the interplay between the locutors, as each locutor responds in turn to the utterances made by other participants of the dialogue. This aspect of dialogue is characterised as a form of inference called *transitional inference* and is represented by TA-Nodes, Transition Application nodes, which capture the flow of a dialogue, for example, recording that a given assertion has been made in response to an earlier question. One interesting question is how exactly L-nodes are connected to I-nodes. So for example, what is the relationship between a proposition p (e.g. "We should increase funding for science") and the proposition "X asserted p" (e.g. "Bob asserted that We should increase funding for science")? According to the original specification of the AIF, direct I-node to I-node links are prohibited (and with good reason: to do so would introduce the necessity for edge typing - obviating this requirement is one of the advantages of the AIF approach). The answer to this question is already available in the work of Searle [14] and later with Vanderveken [13]. The link between a locution (or, more precisely, a proposition that reports a locution) and its propositional content (i.e. the proposition or propositions to which the locution refers) is determined and authorized by *constitutive rules* for performing speech acts (see [1] for the role of the constitutive rules in argumentation). These rules describe in what (successfully) performing a speech act consists.

The constitutive rules can be of a number of types depending on the type of *illocutionary force* which the performer of the speech act assumes.[3] In this way, they bear more than a passing resemblance to scheme structure. These schemes are not capturing the passage of a specific inferential relation, but rather than passage of a specific linguistic relation dependent on the type of illocutionary force used in a speech act. As a result, we refer to these schemes as *illocutionary schemes* or Y schemes. Specific applications of these schemes are then, following the now familiar pattern, YA schemes. YA-nodes describe passage between L-nodes ("elements" of argument$_2$) and I-nodes ("elements" of argument$_1$ or, more rarely, argument$_2$). In the dialogue between Bob and Alice (see Fig. 1), the argument$_2$ consists of three speech acts represented by L-nodes (we use abbreviation L_i to denote subsequent locution nodes). The argument$_1$ consists of two propositions represented by I-nodes (I_i means subsequent information nodes). The interaction between the argument$_2$ and the argument$_1$ is described by means of the YA-nodes. The speech acts L_1 and L_3 have *assertive* illocutionary force connecting them with propositional contents I_1 and I_2, respectively. The passage between L_1 (resp. L_3) and I_1 (resp. I_2) is represented by YA$_1$ (resp. YA$_4$). The illocutionary node YA$_2$ links the *directive* L_2 and its propositional content I_1: not all YA-nodes are assertive schemes.

As noted above, the link between a speech act and its propositional content is *warranted (authorized)* by the constitutive rules. For instance, the assertion "Bob asserted

---

[2]A speech act $F(p)$, such as $claim(p)$, $why(p)$, consists of an illocutionary force F and a propositional content p [13]. An illocutionary force is an intention of uttering a propositional content. That is, the performer of a speech act may utter p with an intention of asserting, asking, promising and so on.

[3]Searle distinguishes five classes of speech acts: *assertives* express the speaker's belief, *directives* express his attitude about a possible future act performed by a hearer, *commissives* express the speaker's intention to do something, *expressives* express feelings toward the hearer, *declaratives* express that the speaker performs a given action. Depending on the further characteristics of an illocutionary force, each class divides into various subclasses. For example, assertives split into $claim(p)$, $deny(p)$, $guess(p)$, $argue(p)$, $rebut(p)$, etc.

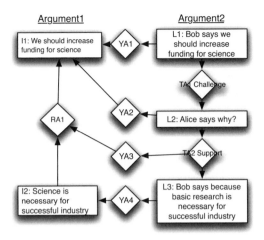

Figure 1. Illustrating the link between arguments (argument₁) and dialogue (argument₂) at the object layer.

that We should increase funding for science" is related to the proposition "We should increase funding for science", if the constitutive rules for assertives are satisfied. In natural contexts, the most important types of rules are the preparatory and sincerity rules, for which unfulfillment results in defectiveness of a speech act [13]. That is, an assertion may be successful but still defective, if its performer did not have enough evidence for the statement or he declared what in fact he disbelieves. In other words, in the case of the preparatory and sincerity rules, it is easy for a locutor not to satisfy them and still have a chance to perform a successful speech act, since a receiver may not notice their unfulfillment. Therefore, in the real-life practice they are the most often used for an attack on the YA-nodes. For example, the passage between "Bob asserted that We should increase funding for science" and "We should increase funding for science" could be blocked, if Bob was insincere. Of course, we have already met such blockers, or undercutters, before: most schemes, particularly inferential argumentation schemes, have similar components, which are represented in the AIF as presumptions or implicit premises. If we view the successful adherence to constitutive rules as presumptions on the applications of Y schemes, all of the existing AIF machinery handles the representation on attacks on the successful application of illocutionary force.

Finally, YA₃ captures the most complex relation of all. Intuitively, one might imagine Alice's question in isolation (but still connected through a YA to its propositional content), and at the same time Bob's assertion (also connected to its propositional content). They might perhaps be occurring in different dialogues. And if they were then, ceteris paribus, there would be no link between I₁ and I₂. It is only in virtue of the fact that Bob's assertion of I₂ is *responding* to Alice's question of I₁ that there is an inferential link being stated between I₂ and I₁. The link between the transitional inference that captures the notion of *responding* and the rule application that captures the inferential relationship seems to be sufficiently similar to other illocutionary schemes for it to be classed with them. It may turn out that this is hasty ontological assignment, but without any pressing need to do otherwise, the parsimonious course is preferable. What is clear, however, is that the forms that govern these YA schemes are quite complex. The

Y and T scheme forms that govern the YA and TA nodes are the AIF^+'s machinery for representing dialogue protocols, to which the next section is addressed.

In addition to delineating the relationship between locutions uttered and the underlying structure of arguments expressed during a dialogue, AIF^+ also supports representation of dialogue protocol. Protocols are described using Locution Description (LDesc-Nodes) nodes. For each locution, represented by an L-Node, there is a corresponding LDesc-Node which can in turn be linked to corresponding PreCondDesc and PostCond-Desc nodes that describe, respectively, the pre-conditions and post-conditions for legally uttering a locution. Pres and post-conditions can be represented in a number of ways and rather than create a new protocol specification language to account for this, AIF^+ supports specification of pre- and post-conditions using fragments of appropriate dialogue protocol description languages such as the Dialogue Game Description Language (DGDL) [20]. For example, the post-condition associated with the challenge move of ASD, that the content "p" of the move should be added to the listener's commitment store, can be expressed using a fragment of DGDL as follows: *store(add, {p}, CS, listener)*. The development of a dialogue, as an ordered sequence of locutions, is handled by transitional inference schemes that describe, for a given locution, the available responding locutions.

5. Examples

To show how the AIF^+ supports both argument$_1$ and argument$_2$ in such a way that the links between them can be captured, we need examples of dialogue protocols. This section describes two examples of differing complexity: the *Two Party Immediate Response* (TPI) [15,4] and *Argument Scheme Dialogue* (ASD) [12] protocols. It is important to emphasise that these protocols are simply examples of protocols that can be represented in AIF^+. We are not arguing either for their utility, or for any special role for them in the general theory of AIF^+.

5.1. Two-Party Immediate Response Protocol

The *TPI* protocol is played on a Dung argumentation framework by two players who take turns to attack each other's arguments, and to both of whom all previous moves and the whole framework are visible. For the formulation of rules we adopt the more formal and detailed specification of [4] rather than the looser specification of [15]. It has two main differences. First, it is not enough for the *defender* (the first player) simply to attack the arguments cited by the *challenger* (the second player). It cannot win without a set of arguments which both attacks all of the challenger's arguments *and* is conflict-free. That is, it must find an *admissible* set [3] which contains its thesis. Second, *TPI* permits either player to backtrack, if it is unable to attack the other's previous argument. The challenger may simply return to the most recent of the defender's previous arguments for which it has an additional attacking argument, while the defender may return to its initial thesis, and begin the game all over again, with the new stipulation that it cannot cite the set of arguments which was shown to be inadmissible in its previous attempt.

The rules of the game are as follows.

1. The initial state of the game is defined by the players's identities, the argumentation system, and the defender's initial thesis, which is an argument in the argumentation system.

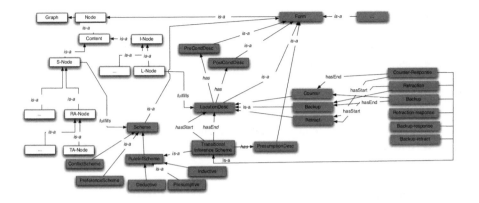

Figure 2. AIF⁺ description of the TPI dialogue protocol

2. The first move is made by the challenger.
3. Players move alternately.
4. A move must be a *counter*, a *backup*, or a *retract*.
5. A *counter* move is of the form *counter(a)*, where *a* is an argument attacking the other player's most recent argument (including the initial thesis). If the player is the defender and S is the set of arguments it has cited since its last utterance of a *retract* locution, *a* must neither (i) attack any $s \in S$; nor (ii) be attacked by any $s \in S$; nor (iii) be such that $\{a\} \cup S$ has already been shown to be an inadmissible set. If the player is the challenger, *a* must be such that the defender has not cited any argument attacking it since its most recent *retract* locution.
6. If a player can make a *counter* move, it must do so.
7. A *backup* move is of the form *backup(a,b)* where *a* and *b* are arguments. Only the challenger can make a *backup* move. *b* must attack *a* and must not have been attacked by the defender since its previous *retract* move. *a* must be the defender's most recent argument *before* its immediately previous argument for which such an attacking argument exists.
8. If the challenger cannot make a *counter* move but can make a *backup* move, it must do so.
9. A *retract* move is of the form *retract*. Only the defender can make a *retract* move, and only when (i) it cannot attack the challenger's most recent argument and (ii) its own most recent argument is not its initial thesis.
10. If the defender can make a *retract* move, it must do so.
11. When a player cannot make a move, the game ends, and the other player wins.

In the AIF⁺ representation of *TPI*, there are three LocutionDesc nodes, six TransitionInfScheme Nodes, and six PresumptionDesc nodes. The LocutionDesc nodes correspond to the three types of locution and the TransitionInfScheme nodes correspond to the *counter—counter, counter—backup, counter—retract, backup—counter, backup—retrac* and *retract—counter* transitions. The PresumptionDesc nodes correspond to the TransitionInfScheme nodes, and in each case the node expresses the presumption that the proper relation exists between the nodes which are party to the transition.

5.2. Argument Scheme Dialogue Protocol

ASD extends a simple dialectical game based upon the formal game CB [16] to incorporate argumentation schemes and critical questions. The rules of ASD are as follows:

Locution Rules

i. Statements Statement letters, S, T, U, ..., are permissible locutions, and truth functional compounds of statement letters.

ii. Withdrawals 'No commitment S' is the locution or withdrawal (retraction) of a statement.

iii. Questions The question 'S?' asks 'Is it the case that S is true?'

iv. Challenges The challenge 'Why S?' requests some statement that can serve as a basis in (a possibly defeasible) proof for S.

v. Critical Attacks The attack 'Pose C' poses the critical question C associated with an argumentation scheme.

Commitment Rules

i. After a player makes a statement, S, it is included in his commitment store.

ii. After the withdrawal of S, the statement S is deleted from the speaker's commitment store.

iii. 'Why S?' places S in the hearer's commitment store unless it is already there or unless the hearer immediately retracts his commitment to S.

iv. Every statement that is shown by the speaker to be an immediate consequence of statements that are commitments of the hearer via some rule of inference or argumentation scheme A, then becomes a commitment of the hearer's and is included in the commitment store along with all the assumptions of A.

v. No commitment may be withdrawn by the hearer that is shown by the speaker to be an immediate consequence of statements that are previous commitments of the hearer.

Dialogue Rules

R1. Each speaker takes his turn to move by advancing one locution at each turn. A No Commitment locution, however, may accompany a Why-locution as one turn.

R2. A question 'S?' must be followed by (i) a statement 'S', (ii) a statement 'Not-S', or (iii) 'No Commitment S'.

R3. 'Why S?' must be followed by (i) 'No commitment S', or (ii) some statement 'T' where S is a consequence of T.

R4. After a statement T has been offered in response to a challenge locution, Why S?, then if (S, T) is a substitution instance A of some argumentation scheme of the game, the locution pose(C) is a legal move, where C is a critical question of scheme A appropriately instantiated.

R5. After a 'Pose C' move, then either (a) if C is an assumption of its argumentation scheme, the move is followed by (i) a statement 'C', (ii) a statement 'not-C', or (iii) 'No commitment C', or (b) if C is an exception to its argumentation scheme, the move is followed by (i) a statement 'C' (ii) a statement 'not-C' (iii) 'No commitment C' , or (iv) 'Why not-C?'

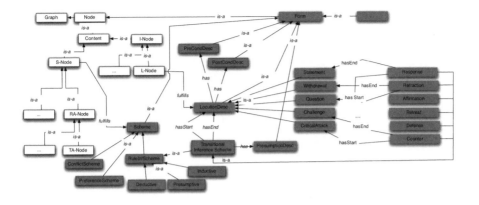

Figure 3. AIF$^+$ description of the ASD dialogue protocol

In the AIF$^+$ representation of ASD, there are five LocutionDesc nodes which correspond to the five available locutions specified in the ASD locution rules. There are also six explicit transitions, composed from these locutions, which involve particular constraints or presumptions (transitions which are simply inferable from the locutions themselves are captured by a generic, unconstrained transition scheme in much the same way that unspecified inference is captured by a generic rule of inference scheme). For example in ASD a Question locution may be followed by either a Statement or a Withdrawal. In the case of a Question → Statement sequence, the Statement is linked to the preceding Question locution by virtue of the Response transitional inference scheme. When such a *response transition* occurs there is a presumption associated with the transition, that the statement which is uttered in answer to the question actually fulfills the question → answer relationship. The locutions of ASD and the explicit transitions associated with them are illustrated in figure 3 which shows the AIF$^+$ upper ontology applied to the ASD formal game.

6. AIF$^+$: Dialogue Representation

Using the described protocols we can now provide examples to show how dialogue as well as protocols may be represented in AIF$^+$.

6.1. TPI Example

Fig. 4 represents a simple example provided by [4]. The dialogue includes a *backup* locution and a *retract* locution. The challenger first *counters* x with y, which the defender *counters* with v. The challenger then backs up to x and *counters* it with z. Since the defender has used v and v attacks w, it cannot *counter* z with w, and must *retract* to its initial position. The challenger once again *counters* x with y, and this time the defender *counters* y with u. As nothing attacks u, the challenger must *backup* to x and *counter* it with z. The defender lost its commitment to v through its *retract* locution, so this time it can *counter* z with w, and it does so. There are no further moves available to the challenger, so the defender wins the game. This dialogue may be represented in AIF$^+$ as shown in Fig. 4.

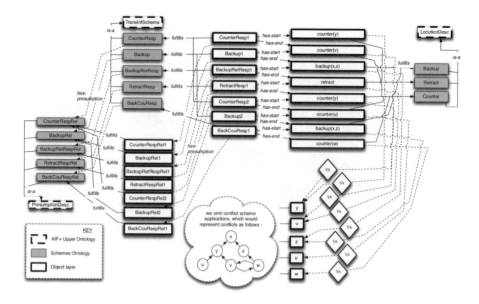

Figure 4. AIF$^+$ description of a TPI dialogue

6.2. Argument Scheme Dialogue Example

In the example ASD dialogue provided in [10], there appears the following exchange:

(L4) Alice: Well, do you remember that "expert" piece that Alf wrote in *South West-ern Ontario Philosophy Monthly* that said that most Canadian philosophers go to OSSA?

(L5) Bob: Yes, I remember.

(L6) Alice: Well, Alf should know, so we can take it that most Canadian philoso-phers do indeed go.

(L7) Bob: Yes, but he'd have a biased opinion.

(L8) Alice: Why do you think he's biased?

(L9) Bob: Er, not sure- OK so what if he wasn't biased? So what?

As shown in [10], this may be represented in formal ASD terms as follows-

(L4) Alice: (Alf said most Canadian philosophers go to OSSA)? [Question]

(L5) Bob: (Alf said most Canadian philosophers go to OSSA). [Statement]

(L6) Alice: (Most Canadian philosophers go to OSSA). [Statement]

(L7) Bob: pose(Alf is unbiased). [Critical Attack]

(L8) Alice: why(not(Alf is unbiased))? [Challenge]

(L9) Bob: no-commitment(not(Alf is unbiased)). [Withdrawal][4]

In this representation, the locutions and their propositional content are easily distinguish-able – at (L4), for instance, the locution is "(Alf said most Canadian philosophers go to OSSA)?", while its propositional content is simply "Alf said most Canadian philosophers go to OSSA". The AIF$^+$ characterisation of this dialogue history is illustrated in Figure

---

[4]In [10] L9 is erroneously listed as the *statement* "(Alf is unbiased).".

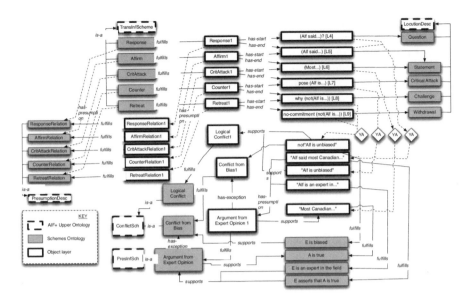

Figure 5. AIF$^+$ description of ASD dialogue

3, which falls into two main sections connected by the 'has-content' links on the right of the figure. The lower section represents the arguments appealed to during the dialogue – they are conventional AIF material. The upper section represents the actual dialogue itself. The solid-bold-bordered elements represent object-layer entities (capturing the actual data), the grey elements represent intermediate-layer entities (capturing protocols and schemes) and the dashed-bordered elements represent upper-ontology entities (capturing AIF$^+$ concepts). Some detail is omitted from Figure 3 for clarity - a fuller account of the monologic aspects of the scheme, for example, are given in [9, pp. 18-19]. The YA nodes in Figure 3 capture the relationship between the locutions and their targets or contents (or 'illocutionary points' in the language of [14]). Locution L5, for example is Bob's statement: "Yes, I remember" which might justifiably be analysed as an assertive claim in which the illocutionary point is the proposition that, "Alf said most Canadian philosophers go to OSSA." YA-schemes work just like other scheme applications in that they have multiple premises (as in the case of the L8-L9 instance), but only ever a single conclusion. They can also be attacked with conflict nodes, resulting in (claims of) defective speech acts. So for example if there were a third locutor, say John, who responded to the L5 "How can you remember? You don't read *South Western Ontario Philosophy Monthly!*", then this would be an attack on the YA-node connecting the L5 "Yes, I remember" to the I-node "Alf said most Canadian philosophers go to OSSA". This attack assumes that Bob's speech act L5 is defective (insincere).

7. Conclusions

Given that both argument$_1$ and argument$_2$ are common in computational systems, we need principled mechanisms underpinning their representation. Most challenging, we need a way of describing how the two sorts of argument interact. This paper has demonstrated how we can apply a model founded upon speech act theory to deliver exactly the required representational language. Neither the AIF nor the AIF$^+$ should tackle the myriad problems of generalised natural language mark-up. But the relationship between locutions uttered as a part of a dialogic argument and the argument structures to which they relate, plays a pivotal role in computational systems that handle natural arguments. As such, we hope that these extensions to the AIF will facilitate the development of a raft of new tools and techniques that blend arguments$_1$ and arguments$_2$.

Acknowledgements

We gratefully acknowledge the support of EPSRC under grant EP/G060347/1, and for a Doctoral Training Award to the University of Dundee that supports Joseph Devereux, and the support of the Polish Ministry of Science and Higher Education for Katarzyna Budzyńska under grant N N101 009338.

References

[1]   K. Budzynska. Argument analysis: Components of interpersonal argumentation. In *Proceedings of the COMMA 2010*, 2010.
[2]   C. Chesñevar, J. McGinnis, S. Modgil, I. Rahwan, C. Reed, G. Simari, M. South, G. Vreeswijk, and S. Willmott. Towards an argument interchange format. *Knowledge Engineering Review*, 21(4):293–316, 2006.
[3]   P. M. Dung. On the acceptability of arguments and its fundamental role in nonmonotonic reasoning, logic programming and n-person games. *Artificial Intelligence*, 77(2):321–358, 1995.
[4]   P.E. Dunne and T.J.M Bench-Capon. Two party immediate response disputes: Properties and efficiency. *Artificial Intelligence*, 149(2):221–250, 2003.
[5]   S. Modgil and J. McGinnis. Towards characterising argumentation based dialogue in the argument interchange format. In *Proceedings of the 4th International Workshop on Argumentation in Multi-Agent Systems (ArgMAS2007)*. Springer Verlag, 2008. to appear.
[6]   D. O'Keefe. Two concepts of argument. *Journal of the American Forensic Association*, 13:121–128, 1977.
[7]   I. Rahwan, I. Banihashemi, C. Reed, D. N. Walton, and S. Abdallah. Representing and classifying arguments on the semantic web. *Knowledge Engineering Review*, to appear, 2010.
[8]   I. Rahwan and C. Reed. The argument interchange format. In I Rahwan and G. Simari, editors, *Argumentation in Artificial Intelligence*. Springer, 2009.
[9]   I. Rahwan, F. Zablith, and C. Reed. Laying the foundations for a world wide argument web. *Artificial Intelligence*, 171:897–921, 2007.
[10] C. Reed and D. N. Walton. Argumentation schemes in dialogue. In H.V Hansen, C.W. Tindale, R.H. Johnson, and J.A. Blair, editors, *Dissensus and the Search for Common Ground (Proceedings of OSSA 2007)*, 2007.
[11] C. Reed, S. Wells, J. Devereux, and G. Rowe. AIF+: Dialogue in the argument interchange format. In Ph. Besnard, S. Doutre, and A. Hunter, editors, *Computational Models of Argument: Proceedings of COMMA-2008*, pages 311–323. IOS Press, 2008.
[12] C.A. Reed and D.N. Walton. Argumentation schemes in dialogue. In *Dissensus and the Search for Common Ground (Proceedings of OSSA 2007)*, 2007.
[13] J. Searle and D. Vanderveken. *Foundations of Illocutionary Logic*. Cambridge University Press, 1985.
[14] J.R. Searle. *Speech Acts: An Essay in the Philosophy of Language*. Cambridge University Press, 1969.
[15] G. Vreeswijk and H. Prakken. Credulous and sceptical argument games for preferred semantics. In *Proceedings of JELIA'2000, The 7th European Workshop on Logic for Artificial Intelligence*, number 1919 in Springer Lecture Notes in AI, pages 239–253. Berlin, Germany: Springer Verlag, 2000.
[16] D. N. Walton. *Logical Dialogue Games and Fallacies*. Uni Press of America, 1984.
[17] D. N. Walton. What is reasoning? what is an argument? *Journal of Philosophy*, 87(8):399–419, 1990.
[18] D. N. Walton. *Argumentation Schemes for Presumptive Reasoning*. Lawrence Erlbaum Associates, NJ, 1996.
[19] D. N. Walton, C. Reed, and F. Macagno. *Argumentation Schemes*. Cambridge University Press, 2009.
[20] S. Wells and C. Reed. A domain specific language for describing diverse systems of dialogue. *Journal of Applied Logic*, to appear, 2010.

Computational Models of Argument
P. Baroni et al. (Eds.)
IOS Press, 2010
doi:10.3233/978-1-60750-619-5-427

A Dynamic Argumentation Framework

Nicolás D. ROTSTEIN[1], Martín O. MOGUILLANSKY,
Alejandro J. GARCÍA, Guillermo R. SIMARI

National Research Council (CONICET), AI R&D Lab (LIDIA)
Department of Computer Science and Engineering (DCIC)
Universidad Nacional del Sur (UNS), Argentina
e-mail: nico.rotstein@abdn.ac.uk, {mom, ajg, grs}@cs.uns.edu.ar

Abstract. This article introduces the notion of dynamics for abstract argumentation frameworks. We consider evidence as the basis from which arguments may be considered valid. The proposed Dynamic Argumentation Framework (DAF) is a refinement of Dung's abstract framework (AF), enriched with additional features. Since an instance of a DAF is equivalent to an AF, the former could be viewed as a template to build different AFs, applying the same knowledge to different situations. This equivalence is important, as we can take advantage of the vast amount of study on argumentation semantics for AFs to apply it to our approach. The DAF's aim is to provide a well-structured knowledge representation tool that allows for the definition of dynamics-aware argumentation-based systems.

1. Introduction and Background

In this article we present a new abstract argumentation framework, the Dynamic Argumentation Framework (DAF), capable of dealing with dynamics through the consideration of a varying set of evidence. Depending on the contents of the set of evidence, an instance of the framework will be determined, in which some arguments hold and others do not. The extended formalisation, which is coherent with classical abstractions, will provide the opportunity to tackle new problems and applications involving dynamics, in a natural manner. Lately, frameworks for abstract argumentation have gained wide acceptance, and are the basis for the implementation of concrete formalisms. The original proposal by Dung [7] defines an abstract framework along with several notions of acceptability of arguments. Since then, many extensions were introduced to enrich this approach, not only by defining new semantics (*i.e.*, ways of accepting arguments) [2], but also by adding properties to the framework [8,14], thus broadening the field of application of the original contribution. The objective of this paper is thus two-fold: to extend the existing theory, but also to enrich current abstract models.

The DAF's purpose is to extend the usual representational capabilities of argumentation in order to model knowledge dynamics in a proper way. So far the DAF has proved to be appropriate as the basis for "argument theory change", an argumentation-based model of change that incorporates concepts from belief revision into the field of argu-

---

[1]Employed by the University of Aberdeen (Scotland, UK) for dot.rural Digital Economy Research, under the RCUK Digital Economy Programme, http://www.dotrural.ac.uk

mentation [9,11]. Similarly, ongoing work constitutes the DAF being used as the foundation to formalise dialogue, which can be implemented as an argumentation framework common to all participants. As will be clear throughout the article, the DAF allows to cope with the progression of the dialogue, providing simple operations to incorporate new arguments and conflicts, as well as to change preferences. These modifications could be triggered by the dialogue itself.

The framework defined here is a refinement of Dung's, and takes a step forward into a not-so-abstract form of argumentation. In the literature, an argument is treated as an indivisible entity that suffices to support a claim; here arguments are also indivisible, but they play a smaller role: they are aggregated into structures. These *argumental structures* can be thought as if they were arguments (in the usual sense), but we will see that they do not always guarantee the actual achievement of a claim. We will explicitly distinguish a set of premises and a claim in each argumental structure. The consideration of these features (*i.e.*, premises, inference and claim) has been part of the literature on logic and argumentation from the early stages of the area (see [12,13] and more recently in [5]). Finally, an equivalence to Dung's classical framework is provided through what we call the *active instance* of the DAF. In this way, instead of presenting a particular formalisation for argumentation semantics, we reutilise the results achieved in the literature.

2. Arguments, Argumental Structures

In this section we give the preliminary definitions from which the dynamic framework can be built, namely evidence, argument, and argumental structures.

2.1. Evidence and Arguments

Arguments are pieces of reasoning that provide backing for a *claim* from a set of *premises*. In argumentation theory, it is usually assumed that these premises (thus, the arguments they belong to) always hold, since frameworks show a snapshot of what is happening. However, as we are defining a dynamic system, it is natural to consider that evidence is in continuous change, therefore some premises could be eventually unsatisfied. We must distinguish between what we call *active* and *inactive* arguments. An argument is deemed as active if it is capable of achieving its claim. This depends on whether the argument's premises are satisfied, *i.e.*, available either as *evidence* or claims of other active arguments. The difference is that evidence is beyond discussion, whereas an argument's claim could be dismissed if that argument is defeated. On this matter, a piece of evidence could be considered as a claim supported by an "empty" argument, or it could be treated separately, as a unique entity. In this article, we choose the latter option; although we accept that the notion of evidence could be related to that of a claim, we also believe it represents a different concept. If, for instance, an argument is devised to represent that a reason for a sentence α holds with no support for it, an "empty" argument for α may be used. Such an argument could be thought as a *presumption*.

Evidence, premises and claims are assumed to belong to a common domain, an abstract language "$\mathfrak{L}$". A similar argumentation framework (without capabilities for handling dynamics) considering $\mathfrak{L}$ as first-order logic was introduced in [10]. Throughout this article, we will assume sentences in $\mathfrak{L}$ as literals, and use the complement notation to express contradictory literals such as α and $\overline{\alpha}$. As said before, an argument's premises provide backing for the claim, however, this does not mean that the claim is inferred (or entailed) from its premises. In turn, an argument is considered an indivisible reasoning step, abstracting away from the concrete connection behind premises and claim.

When speaking of a *set of evidence*, we will assume that it is a consistent set of sentences in $\mathfrak{L}$ representing the current state of the world. Evidence is considered an indivisible and self-conclusive piece of knowledge that could come, for instance, from perception or communication, or might be just an agent's own knowledge (*e.g.*, its role). As stated before, evidence "triggers" some arguments, rendering them active.

Definition 1 (Argument) *Given a language $\mathfrak{L}$, an **argument** $\mathcal{A}$ is a reasoning step for a claim $\alpha \in \mathfrak{L}$ from a set of premises $\{\beta_1, \ldots, \beta_n\} \in 2^{\mathfrak{L}}$ such that $\beta_i \neq \alpha, \beta_i \neq \overline{\alpha}, \beta_i \neq \overline{\beta_j}$, for every $i, j, 1 \leq i, j \leq n$.*

Given an argument $\mathcal{A}$, we will identify both its claim and set of premises through the functions $\mathsf{cl}(\mathcal{A})$ and $\mathsf{pr}(\mathcal{A})$, respectively. Given $\mathsf{pr}(\mathcal{A}) = \{\beta_1, \ldots, \beta_n\}$ and $\mathsf{cl}(\mathcal{A}) = \alpha$, the *interface* of $\mathcal{A}$ is denoted as the pair $\langle \{\beta_1, \ldots, \beta_n\}, \alpha \rangle$.

Example 1 *Assume an argument $\mathcal{A}$ for considering a route as being dangerous (noted 'dr') because there are known thieves in that area ('th') and security there is poor ('ps'); the interface of $\mathcal{A}$ is $\langle \{th, ps\}, dr \rangle$. Consider also an argument $\mathcal{B}$ saying that underpaid cops might provide poor security; the interface of $\mathcal{B}$ is $\langle \{upc\}, ps \rangle$.*

The notion of conflict is central in any argumentation system, and the DAF will be provided with a set containing every pair of conflicting arguments. Since the domain $\mathfrak{L}$ could include positive and negative sentences, some conflicts will automatically belong to such a set, as formalised in Def. 2. However, the conflict relation should allow for conflicts beyond the ones that are syntactically distinguishable. For instance, arguments for *go_right* and *go_left* could be declared as conflicting, rather than building artificial arguments to derive the negation of the other's claim.

Definition 2 (Conflict between Arguments) *Given a set $Args$ of arguments, the set $\bowtie \subseteq Args \times Args$ denotes a **conflict relation** over $Args$, verifying $\bowtie \supseteq \{(\mathcal{A}, \mathcal{B}) \mid \mathcal{A}, \mathcal{B} \in Args$, and either $\mathsf{cl}(\mathcal{A}) = \overline{\mathsf{cl}(\mathcal{B})}$ or $\overline{\mathsf{cl}(\mathcal{A})} \in \mathsf{pr}(\mathcal{B})\}$.*

Pairs representing conflicts between arguments model a symmetrical relation, *i.e.*, $(\mathcal{A}, \mathcal{B}) = (\mathcal{B}, \mathcal{A})$; in the examples only one of these pairs will be indicated. Following Def. 2, we will consider not only arguments whose claims/premises are syntactically in conflict, but also those specified by the knowledge engineer.

The following definition imposes conditions for an argument to be considered *coherent*. This will prevent fallacious arguments from becoming active. This will be clear next, with the definition for an active argument.

Definition 3 (Coherent Argument) *An argument $\mathcal{A}$ is **coherent** wrt. a set $\mathbf{E}$ of evidence iff $\mathcal{A}$ verifies: **(consistency wrt. E)** $\overline{\mathsf{cl}(\mathcal{A})} \notin \mathbf{E}$; **(non-redundancy wrt. E)** $\mathsf{cl}(\mathcal{A}) \notin \mathbf{E}$.*

Redundant arguments wrt. evidence are not harmful, they just introduce unnecessary information –evidence is beyond discussion and needs no reasons supporting it. In opposition, inconsistent arguments wrt. evidence may be harmful, since they could be activating other arguments, turning that reasoning chain into a fallacy, requiring further restrictions for the construction of valid reasoning chains.

As stated before, the active/inactive status of an argument might involve other arguments: sometimes it is not evidence what will be directly *activating* arguments, but *supporting arguments*, *i.e.*, arguments achieving a premise of others.

Definition 4 (Supporting Argument) *An argument $\mathcal{B}$ is a **supporting argument** of an argument $\mathcal{A}$ iff $\mathsf{cl}(\mathcal{B}) \in \mathsf{pr}(\mathcal{A})$. Let $\mathsf{cl}(\mathcal{B}) = \beta$, then we say that $\mathcal{B}$ supports $\mathcal{A}$ through β.*

Definition 5 (Active Argument) *Given a set $Args$ of arguments and a set $\mathbf{E}$ of evidence, an argument $\mathcal{A} \in Args$ is **active** wrt. $\mathbf{E}$ iff $\mathcal{A}$ is coherent and for each $\beta \in \mathsf{pr}(\mathcal{A})$ either $\beta \in \mathbf{E}$, or there is an active argument $\mathcal{B} \in Args$ that supports $\mathcal{A}$ through β.*

Example 2 *From Ex. 1, given a set of evidence $\mathbf{E}_2 = \{th, upc\}$, then $\mathcal{A}$ is active, because it can be activated by the evidence 'th' and the active (supporting) argument $\mathcal{B}$ for 'ps'. Instead, if we consider a set of evidence $\mathbf{E}_{ps} = \{ps\} \cup \mathbf{E}_2$, then argument $\mathcal{B}$ would be incoherent due to its redundancy wrt. $\mathbf{E}_{ps}$. In contrast, if we consider the set of evidence $\mathbf{E}_{nps} = \{\overline{ps}\} \cup \mathbf{E}_2$, then argument $\mathcal{B}$ will again be incoherent, because it would be inconsistent wrt. $\mathbf{E}_{nps}$. In both cases, $\mathcal{B}$ would not be active because is incoherent. Regarding $\mathcal{A}$, from the set $\mathbf{E}_{ps}$, it becomes active directly from evidence, whereas from the set $\mathbf{E}_{nps}$, it ends up being inactive since its premise 'ps' is left unsupported.*

An argument could be inactive because: it might not have enough evidence and/or active arguments to support it, and/or it might not be coherent. In both cases an inactive argument fails in being a support for reaching its associated claim.

2.2. Argumental Structures

The aggregation of arguments via the support relation needs further formalisation, giving rise to the concept of *argumental structure*. This is a core element of the framework.

Definition 6 (Argumental Structure) *Given a set $Args$ of arguments, an **argumental structure** for a claim α from $Args$ is a tree of arguments Σ verifying:*

1. *The root argument $\mathcal{A}_{top} \in Args$, called **top argument**, is such that $\mathsf{cl}(\mathcal{A}_{top}) = \alpha$, and is noted as $\mathsf{top}(\Sigma)$;*
2. *A **node** is an argument $\mathcal{A}_i \in Args$ such that for each premise $\beta \in \mathsf{pr}(\mathcal{A}_i)$ there is at most one **child** argument in $Args$ supporting $\mathcal{A}_i$ through β.*

Regarding notation for an argumental structure Σ:

- *The set of arguments belonging to Σ is noted as $\mathsf{args}(\Sigma)$.*
- *The set of premises of Σ is: $\mathsf{pr}(\Sigma) = \bigcup_{\mathcal{A} \in \mathsf{args}(\Sigma)}(\mathsf{pr}(\mathcal{A})) \setminus \bigcup_{\mathcal{A} \in \mathsf{args}(\Sigma)}(\mathsf{cl}(\mathcal{A}))$.*
- *The claim of Σ is noted as $\mathsf{cl}(\Sigma) = \alpha$.*

Note that the $\mathsf{pr}(\cdot)$ and $\mathsf{cl}(\cdot)$ functions are overloaded: now they are applied to argumental structures. This is not going to be problematic, since either usage will be rather explicit. It is important to stress that, within an argumental structure, a premise of an argument cannot be supported by more than one argument. Leaves are arguments in which all premises are not supported by any other argument in the argumental structure. From now on, when clear enough, we will refer to argumental structures just as "structures".

The notion of argumental structure is similar to an argument in the argumentation system proposed in [3]. That system uses a propositional knowledge base, and an argument is a pair $\langle \phi, \alpha \rangle$, where ϕ is a minimal consistent set of formulae that derives the sentence α. Set ϕ resembles the set of arguments in an argumental structure of the DAF, and the derivation is analogous to the tree of arguments where premises are supported by either evidence or other arguments. The properties of consistency and minimality will be fulfilled by Def. 8 for a well-formed argumental structure, and Lemma 1 proving the minimality of active argumental structures.

Example 3 *From Ex. 2 we have the argumental structure* Σ_3, *such that* $\mathsf{args}(\Sigma_3) = \{\mathcal{A}, \mathcal{B}\}$, *where its set of premises is* $\mathsf{pr}(\Sigma_3) = \{th, upc\}$ *and its claim is* $\mathsf{cl}(\Sigma_3) = \mathsf{cl}(\mathcal{A}) = dr$.

The definition for an argumental structure is not enough to ensure a sensible knowledge representation, *e.g.*, it allows for contradictory claims in a pair of arguments in the same structure. Next we define what is considered a *well-formed argumental structure*, establishing properties ensuring a sensible knowledge representation, independently from any set of evidence. Hence, all knowledge can be validated, active or not.

Definition 7 (Transitive Support) *Given a set* $Args$ *of arguments, an argument* $\mathcal{A}_i$ ***transitively supports*** *an argument* $\mathcal{A}_k$ *within* $Args$ *iff there is a sequence* $[\mathcal{A}_i, \dots, \mathcal{A}_k]$ *of arguments in* $Args$ *where* $\mathsf{cl}(\mathcal{A}_j) \in \mathsf{pr}(\mathcal{A}_{j+1})$, *for every* j *such that* $i \leq j \leq k - 1$.

Definition 8 (Well-Formed Argum. Structure) *Given a set* $Args$ *of arguments and a conflict relation* $\bowtie$ *over* $Args$, *a structure* $\Sigma \in Args$ *is* ***well-formed*** *wrt.* $\bowtie$ *iff it verifies:*

- *(Premise Consistency) There are no* $\alpha, \beta \in \mathsf{pr}(\Sigma)$ *such that* $\overline{\alpha} = \beta$;
- *(Consistency) For each argument* $\mathcal{A} \in \mathsf{args}(\Sigma)$ *there is no argument* $\mathcal{B} \in \mathsf{args}(\Sigma)$ *such that* $\mathcal{A}\bowtie\mathcal{B}$;
- *(Non-Circularity) No argument* $\mathcal{A} \in \mathsf{args}(\Sigma)$ *transitively supports an argument* $\mathcal{B} \in \mathsf{args}(\Sigma)$ *if* $\mathsf{cl}(\mathcal{B}) \in \mathsf{pr}(\mathcal{A})$;
- *(Uniformity) If* $\mathcal{A} \in \mathsf{args}(\Sigma)$ *is a child of* $\mathcal{B} \in \mathsf{args}(\Sigma)$ *in* Σ*'s tree and* $\mathcal{A}$ *supports* $\mathcal{B}$ *through* β, *then* $\mathcal{A}$ *is a child of every* $\mathcal{B}_i \in \mathsf{args}(\Sigma)$ *in* Σ*'s tree such that* $\beta \in \mathsf{pr}(\mathcal{B}_i)$, *supporting* $\mathcal{B}_i$ *through* β.

The domain of all well-formed argumental structures wrt. $Args$ *and* $\bowtie$ *is denoted as* $\mathfrak{str}_{(Args, \bowtie)}$.

Since a set of evidence is always consistent, a structure with *inconsistent premises* would never become active (see Def. 14). However, as stated above, it is useful to validate also inactive argumental structures, for instance, when performing hypothetical or abductive reasoning. The property of *consistency* invalidates inherently contradictory argumental structures. The requirement of *non-circularity* avoids taking into consideration structures yielding infinite reasoning chains. Finally, the restriction of *uniformity* does not allow heterogeneous support for a premise throughout a structure. These constraints are defined so that we can trust a well-formed structure as a sensible reasoning chain, independently from the set of evidence. The role of the set of evidence is considered by the concept of *active argument*, which is addressed by Def. 14.

Definition 9 (Argumental Substructure) *Given two argumental structures* Σ, Σ_i *from a set of arguments* $Args$, Σ_i *is an **argumental substructure** of* Σ *iff* $\mathsf{args}(\Sigma_i) \subseteq \mathsf{args}(\Sigma)$. *If* $\mathsf{args}(\Sigma_i) \subsetneq \mathsf{args}(\Sigma)$ *then* Σ_i *is a **proper argumental substructure** of* Σ.

Note that not any subset of the set of arguments of a given structure is a substructure of it. When convenient, argumental substructures will be referred just as "substructures". In the literature, a defeat relation is usually assumed, establishing ordered pairs in which the first component defeats the second one. In the DAF, the defeat relation between argumental structures is obtained through the application of a preference function over conflicting pairs. Conflict is propagated from arguments up to structures, and a preference function determines which argument (supported by the corresponding structure) prevails.

Definition 10 (Conflict between Argumental Structures) *Given a set* $Args$ *of arguments, a conflict relation* $\bowtie$ *over* $Args$, *and two argumental structures* $\Sigma_1, \Sigma_2 \in \mathsf{str}_{(Args,\bowtie)}$, *structure* Σ_1 *is in **conflict** with* Σ_2 *iff* $\mathsf{top}(\Sigma_1)\bowtie\mathsf{top}(\Sigma_2)$. *Conflict between structures is denoted as* "$\asymp$".

It could be natural to assume that a conflict $\Sigma_1 \asymp \Sigma_2$ should be inherited up to every structure containing Σ_2. However, we are interested in the recognition of the precise argumental structures that are the source of conflict.

Definition 11 (Preference Function) *Given a set* $Args$ *of arguments, a conflict relation* $\bowtie$ *over* $Args$, *and two argumental structures* $\Sigma_1, \Sigma_2 \in \mathsf{str}_{(Args,\bowtie)}$, *the **preference function** is* $\mathfrak{pref} : \mathsf{str}_{(Args,\bowtie)} \times \mathsf{str}_{(Args,\bowtie)} \to \mathsf{str}_{(Args,\bowtie)} \cup \{\epsilon\}$ *such that* $\mathfrak{pref}(\Sigma_1, \Sigma_2) = [\Sigma_1 \mid \Sigma_2 \mid \epsilon]$ *determines the preferred argumental structure; if none is preferred, the function returns* ϵ.

The preference function is defined over argumental structures and not over arguments, since, in order to decide which argument prevails, all the knowledge giving support to them should be considered. Moreover, when facing different scenarios, the same argument might be active from different active argumental structures and, consequently, the preference could change along with evidence. In this article no particular preference function will be analysed, in the examples, preferences will be given explicitly.

Example 4

Consider the argumental structures on the right, and assume the conflict relation includes only the pair $(\mathcal{A}_1, \mathcal{A}_3)$ *and that the preference function determines:* $\mathfrak{pref}(\Sigma_1, \Sigma_3) = \Sigma_1$ *and* $\mathfrak{pref}(\Sigma_2, \Sigma_3) = \Sigma_3$. *For the set of evidence* $\{a, b, e\}$, Σ_1 *and* Σ_3 *are active, in conflict, and* Σ_1 *prevails. If the set of evidence changes to* $\{c, e\}$, Σ_1 *would be inactive because* $\mathcal{A}_2$ *be-*

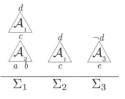

comes redundant wrt. evidence, Σ_2 *would turn to active, and* Σ_3 *remains active. In this case,* Σ_3 *is preferred to* Σ_2. *If the preference function had been defined over arguments, this would had been impossible to represent, since there would be no means to model that* $\mathcal{A}_1$ *is preferred to* $\mathcal{A}_3$ *at one moment, and that this relation is later on inverted.*

Definition 12 (Defeat between Argumental Structures) *Given a set* $Args$ *of arguments and a conflict relation* $\bowtie$ *over* $Args$, *an argumental structure* $\Sigma_1 \in \mathsf{str}_{(Args,\bowtie)}$ ***defeats*** $\Sigma_2 \in \mathsf{str}_{(Args,\bowtie)}$ *iff there is an argumental substructure* Σ_i *of* Σ_2 *such that* $\Sigma_1 \asymp \Sigma_i$ *and* $\mathfrak{pref}(\Sigma_1, \Sigma_i) = \Sigma_1$. *The structures defeat relation is denoted as* "$\Rightarrow$".

When a structure defeats another, the attack comes from the claim of the former to any claim of a substructure of the latter. The attack is not directed to an argument, but to a substructure, which is the actual portion of the structure under attack.

3. The Dynamic Argumentation Framework

We have built our approach as a refinement of Dung's argumentation framework [7] (from now on, simply "AF"). This framework is defined as a pair containing a set of arguments and a defeat relation ranging over pairs of them. The objective of our approach is to extend this theory to handle dynamics. To cope with this, we consider a set of available evidence, which determines which arguments can be used to make inferences. In Dung's approach, the consideration of a changing set of arguments would involve passing from a framework to another, but how do these frameworks relate to one another? As explained later, they could be considered as instances of a more general framework.

Definition 13 (Dynamic Argumentation Framework (DAF)) *A **DAF** is a tuple* $\langle \mathbf{E}, \mathbf{W}, \bowtie, \mathfrak{pref} \rangle$, *composed by a set* $\mathbf{E}$ *of evidence, a working set* $\mathbf{W}$ *of arguments, a conflict relation* $\bowtie \subseteq \mathbf{W} \times \mathbf{W}$, *and a preference function* $\mathfrak{pref}$ *defined over* $\mathfrak{str}_{(\mathbf{W}, \bowtie)}$.

The *working set of arguments* contains every argument that is available for use by the reasoning process. At a given moment, only the subset of active arguments will represent the current situation. The acquisition or removal of knowledge can be reflected into the working set, which would automatically affect the set of active arguments. Different instances of the set of evidence determine different instances of the DAF. Thus, when "restricting" a DAF to its associated set of evidence, we can obtain an AF in the classical sense, *i.e.*, a pair in which every argument is active, and the attack relation contains pairs of them. This "restriction" is called *active instance*, addressed in Sec. 3.1.

Example 5

Consider the structure of Ex. 3, in which knowing that there are thieves in a place and that cops in that area are underpaid leads us to think that that route is going to be dangerous (noted as 'dr'). Assuming that there are many cops ('mc') in the location, we have a reason to think that security there is good ('gs'). Another argument for this claim is that cops are volunteer ('vc'), thus more motivated to do a good job. Nonetheless, if cops are foreigners ('fc'), thus unacquainted with the place (un), they might give the idea of poor security there ('ps'). From this knowledge we can build the structures depicted on the right.

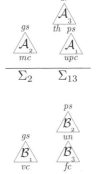

Thus, we have a DAF $\langle \mathbf{E}_5, \mathbf{W}_5, \bowtie_5, \mathfrak{pref}_5 \rangle$, *where the working set of arguments is* $\mathbf{W}_5 = \{ \mathcal{A}_1, \mathcal{A}_2, \mathcal{A}_3, \mathcal{B}_1, \mathcal{B}_2, \mathcal{B}_3 \}$. *Let consider a set of evidence* $\mathbf{E}_5 = \{ mc, upc, th \}$ *along with an empty conflict relation* $\bowtie_5 = \emptyset$. *Then, from set* $\mathbf{W}_5$, *arguments* $\mathcal{A}_1$, $\mathcal{A}_2$ *and* $\mathcal{A}_3$ *are active wrt.* $\mathbf{E}_5$, *thus reaching their claims gs, ps and dr. The latter claim is achieved via the argumental structure* Σ_{13}, *whose top argument is* $\mathcal{A}_3$. *The remaining arguments* $\mathcal{B}_1$, $\mathcal{B}_2$ *and* $\mathcal{B}_3$ *are inactive, as well as structures* Σ_1 *and* Σ_{32}, *since they have unfulfilled supports wrt.* $\mathbf{E}_5$ *and thus cannot reach their claims.*

3.1. Active Instance of a DAF

A subset of the working set is considered as the *set of active arguments* wrt. the set of evidence. This set will contain those arguments that are to be taken into account to reason in concordance with the current situation: given a DAF $\langle \mathbf{E}, \mathbf{W}, \bowtie, \mathfrak{pref} \rangle$, $\mathbb{A} = \{ \mathcal{A} \in \mathbf{W} \mid \mathcal{A}$ is active wrt. $\mathbf{E} \}$. Next we define the notion of *active argumental structure*. This will allow us to recognise those structures that are capable of achieving their claims when considering the current situation.

Definition 14 (Active Argumental Structure) *Given a set* $\mathbf{E}$ *of evidence, a well-formed argumental structure* Σ *is **active** wrt.* $\mathbf{E}$ *iff* $\mathrm{pr}(\Sigma) \subseteq \mathbf{E}$ *and every* $\mathcal{A} \in \mathrm{args}(\Sigma)$ *is a coherent argument wrt.* $\mathbf{E}$.

This definition states an important property: the support of an active argumental structure is composed just by evidence. This puts this concept nearer to the notion of active argument, showing that argumental structures can be seen as arguments in the usual way if their inner composition is abstracted away. The definition also requires every argument to be coherent wrt. the set of evidence, therefore some well-formed structures having their support satisfied by evidence will not be active due to some argument being redundant and/or inconsistent wrt. the evidence.

Proposition 1 *If* Σ *is an active argumental structure wrt. a set* $\mathbf{E}$ *of evidence, then every argument in* $\mathrm{args}(\Sigma)$ *is an active argument wrt.* $\mathbf{E}$.

Proofs were left out of this presentation due to the lack of space. Note that the reverse of this proposition is not true, as shown in the following example.

Example 6 *Consider the set of evidence* $\mathbf{E}_6 = \{a, b\}$, *and three structures* Σ_1, Σ_2 *and* Σ_3 *such that* $\mathrm{args}(\Sigma_1) = \{\mathcal{A}_1, \mathcal{A}_2\}$, $\mathrm{args}(\Sigma_2) = \{\mathcal{A}_1\}$, $\mathrm{args}(\Sigma_3) = \{\mathcal{A}_1, \mathcal{A}_3\}$, *where* $\mathcal{A}_1 = \langle \{c\}, d \rangle$, $\mathcal{A}_2 = \langle \{a, b\}, c \rangle$ *and* $\mathcal{A}_3 = \langle \{x\}, c \rangle$, *as shown on the right. From* $\mathbf{E}_6$, Σ_1 *is active, but* Σ_2 *and* Σ_3 *are not. Note that both* Σ_1 *and* Σ_2 *contain active arguments, but this condition does not ensure them to be active.*

$$
\begin{array}{ccc}
\Sigma_1 & \Sigma_2 & \Sigma_3
\end{array}
$$

Ex. 6 shows that, in a way, argumental structures have to be "complete" in order to be active. That is, they must include all the necessary arguments for their top argument to be active. Only then the premises of these structures will be satisfied by evidence.

Proposition 2 *Given a set* $\mathbf{E}$ *of evidence, an argument* $\mathcal{A}$ *is active wrt.* $\mathbf{E}$ *iff there exists an active argumental structure* Σ *wrt.* $\mathbf{E}$ *such that* $\mathrm{top}(\Sigma) = \mathcal{A}$.

Note that Prop. 2 allows for an active argument to be top argument of more than one active argumental structure, which is correct, as described in the following example.

Example 7 *Consider Ex. 6, and a set of evidence* $\mathbf{E}_7 = \{a, b, x\}$. *Now both* Σ_1 *and* Σ_3 *are active argumental structures wrt.* $\mathbf{E}_7$ *and have the same top argument.*

Definition 15 (Set of Active Argum. Structures) *Given a DAF* $F = \langle \mathbf{E}, \mathbf{W}, \bowtie, \mathfrak{pref} \rangle$, *the **set of active argumental structures** in* F *wrt.* $\mathbf{E}$ *is the maximal set* $\mathbb{S}$ *of active argumental structures from* F.

Proposition 3 *Given a DAF* $F = \langle \mathbf{E}, \mathbf{W}, \bowtie, \mathfrak{pref} \rangle$, *the set* $\mathbb{A}$ *of active arguments in* F *wrt.* $\mathbf{E}$, *and the set* $\mathbb{S}$ *of active structures in* F *wrt.* $\mathbf{E}$, *then* $\bigcup_{\Sigma \in \mathbb{S}} (\mathsf{args}(\Sigma)) = \mathbb{A}$.

Argumental structures are minimal in the sense that they include not more than the necessary arguments to determine their top argument is active. This is an important property in an argumentation setting: to prevent superfluous knowledge/information from being able to build a reason for a claim. Additionally, the incorporation of irrelevant arguments to an active structure would weaken it, providing extra points of attack.

Lemma 1 *Given an argumental structure* Σ *active wrt. a set* $\mathbf{E}$ *of evidence, there is no argumental structure* Σ_i *active wrt.* $\mathbf{E}$ *such that* $\mathsf{cl}(\Sigma) = \mathsf{cl}(\Sigma_i)$ *and* $\mathsf{args}(\Sigma_i) \subsetneq \mathsf{args}(\Sigma)$.

This lemma states that minimality is a consequence of the definition for an active argumental structure, which requires it to be well-formed.

Definition 16 (Active Defeat Relation) *Given a DAF* F, *the defeat relation* "$\Rightarrow$" *over argumental structures, and the set* $\mathbb{S}$ *of active argumental structures, the **active defeat relation** in* F *is* $\mathbb{R} = \{(\Sigma_1, \Sigma_2) \in \Rightarrow \mid \Sigma_1, \Sigma_2 \in \mathbb{S}\}$.

Next, we define the *active instance* of a given DAF, which we will show that is equivalent to an AF in the classical sense.

Definition 17 (Active Instance) *Given a DAF* $F = \langle \mathbf{E}, \mathbf{W}, \bowtie, \mathfrak{pref} \rangle$, *the **active instance** of* F *is the AF* $(\mathbb{S}, \mathbb{R})$, *where* $\mathbb{S}$ *is the set of active argumental structures from* $\mathbf{W}$ *wrt.* $\mathbf{E}$, *and* $\mathbb{R}$ *is the active attack relation between structures in* $\mathbb{S}$.

Every DAF, at any moment, has an associated active instance –an AF. Therefore, all the work done on acceptability of arguments and argumentation semantics can be applied to the DAF here defined, just by finding its active instance the set of accepted argumental structures can be obtained. Moreover, since structures hold a claim, we can go a step further and consider justification of claims, either sceptically or cautiously.

DAFs can be seen as a template for generating multiple AFs representing the same knowledge, applied to different situations. The number of active instances that can be obtained from a single DAF is quite large. Considering that each possible subset of evidence composes a different active instance of the DAF, we have that the amount of active instances is in the order of $2^{|p|}$, where $p = \bigcup_{\mathcal{A} \in \mathbf{W}} (\mathsf{pr}(\mathcal{A}))$ is the set of all premises present in the DAF.

Lemma 2 *The active instance of a DAF is **equivalent** to Dung's definition for an abstract argumentation framework.*

3.2. Updating Evidence, Working Set and Conflicts

Since the set of evidence is dynamic, it defines the particular instance of the DAF that corresponds with the current situation. In order to cope with this, the basic operations performed over a DAF are the *evidence update* and *erasure*. This mechanism should ensure the DAF reflects the new (consistent) state of the world.

Definition 18 (Evidence Update/Erasure) *Given a DAF* $\langle \mathbf{E}, \mathbf{W}, \bowtie, \mathfrak{pref} \rangle$, *and* $\mathbf{E}_1$, *a set of evidence such that for every* $\beta \in \mathbf{E}_1$, $\overline{\beta} \notin \mathbf{E}$ *(resp.,* $\beta \in \mathbf{E}$*). A (multiple) evidence update (resp., erasure) operation is* $\langle \mathbf{E} \cup \mathbf{E}_1, \mathbf{W}, \bowtie, \mathfrak{pref} \rangle$ *(resp.,* $\langle \mathbf{E} \backslash \mathbf{E}_1, \mathbf{W}, \bowtie, \mathfrak{pref} \rangle$*).*

The evidence update/erasure changes the *instance* of the DAF: it makes the set of active arguments vary. Hence, it could be seen as a form of revision [1]. However, the impact of evidence change in these sets neither performs nor is intended to be a formal revision of the theory whatsoever. Furthermore, evidence change does not modify the representation (or specification) of the knowledge about the world, but what is perceived.

Sometimes it will be mandatory to modify the working set of arguments and/or the current attack relation in order to represent changes in the knowledge specification about the world. Such a re-instantiation could be triggered by an external preference-handling mechanism, or a change operation, such as those described in [9,11]. Next, we define the expansion and contraction of a DAF by an argument, and then the analogous definitions are given for the attack relation.

Definition 19 (Argument Expansion/Contraction) *Given a DAF* $F = \langle \mathbf{E}, \mathbf{W}, \bowtie, \mathfrak{pref} \rangle$, *the result of the **expansion** (resp., **contraction**) of F by an **argument** $\mathcal{A} \notin \mathbf{W}$ (resp., $\mathcal{A} \in \mathbf{W}$) is the DAF* $\langle \mathbf{E}, \mathbf{W} \cup \{\mathcal{A}\}, \bowtie', \mathfrak{pref} \rangle$ *(resp.,* $\langle \mathbf{E}, \mathbf{W} \setminus \{\mathcal{A}\}, \bowtie', \mathfrak{pref} \rangle$*), where $\bowtie'$ is defined over* $\mathbf{W} \cup \{\mathcal{A}\}$ *(resp.,* $\mathbf{W} \setminus \{\mathcal{A}\}$*).*

Both the argument expansion and contraction have an impact on the set of conflicts. For instance, the incorporation of a new argument for α could bring about new conflicts with every argument for $\bar{\alpha}$. The opposite occurs when removing an argument: all of its associated conflicts disappear for the DAF to remain well-defined over the new working set. Those conflicts that are not syntactically detectable can be manually added or removed via the following operations.

Definition 20 (Conflict Expansion/Contraction) *Given a DAF* $F = \langle \mathbf{E}, \mathbf{W}, \bowtie, \mathfrak{pref} \rangle$, *the result of the **expansion** (resp., **contraction**) of F by a **conflict** $(\mathcal{A}, \mathcal{B})$ is the DAF* $\langle \mathbf{E}, \mathbf{W}, \bowtie \cup \{(\mathcal{A}, \mathcal{B})\}, \mathfrak{pref} \rangle$ *(resp.,* $\langle \mathbf{E}, \mathbf{W}, \bowtie \setminus \{(\mathcal{A}, \mathcal{B})\}, \mathfrak{pref} \rangle$*), with* $\{\mathcal{A}, \mathcal{B}\} \subseteq \mathbf{W}$.

The argument/conflict expansion/contraction operations allow to change the knowledge represented by the DAF. The argument expansion allows for the addition of a new reason for a certain claim. Analogously, the deletion of a reason is allowed when it is no longer considered as valid. It is important to note that both expansion and contraction of arguments are independent from the availability of evidence, but instead refers to the rationale behind the argument. In the same way, conflicts between arguments can be added/suppressed, since new conflicts can arise, and old conflicts can be no longer justified. (This also is independent from in/active attacks.) Change over the preference function is left out of this article, as it requires just a replacement of the original function.

These operations can be thought as the building blocks for a large number of more complex operations. For instance, the expansion/contraction of a DAF by a framework $(\mathbf{W}, \mathbf{R})$, where defeat pairs in $\mathbf{R}$ are obtained from "$\bowtie$" and $\mathfrak{pref}$. A merge operation between frameworks can be defined, either in a prioritised or non-prioritised fashion. One of the tasks when merging frameworks involves the determination of the new, crossed conflicts that had arisen. The kind of prioritisation would tell how to deal with inconsistency over the union of (1) the sets of evidence, (2) the working sets of arguments. A solution for (1) is to convert the conflicting pieces of evidence (*e.g.*, α) into arguments (*e.g.*, $\langle \{\}, \alpha \rangle$), while for (2) the preference function could be tweaked so that structures containing arguments in the prioritised operand are preferred to the other's. The complete formalisation of this operation is left out due to space reasons. A similar operation is defined in [6], but performed over Dung AFs (where knowledge representation is less complex than in the DAF). There, each AF is associated to an agent and the defeat relation depends on the type of merge: it might contain only those defeats accepted by all agents, or simply the ones they do not reject.

Example 8 *Consider Ex. 5 and the defeat relation* $\{(\mathcal{A}_2, \mathcal{A}_1), (\mathcal{B}_1, \mathcal{A}_1), (\mathcal{B}_2, \mathcal{B}_1)\}$:

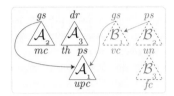

The active instance is the AF shown on the right, in (a). If we update the set of evidence by adding knowledge stating that cops are volunteer, we have that Σ_1 *becomes active, as well as its attack against* Σ_{13}, *leaving* Σ_{32} *as the only inactive structure, and* (Σ_{32}, Σ_1) *is the only inactive attack. The active instance of the updated DAF is depicted in (b). Now consider we find out that cops are foreigners and that there are few of them. We make an update of the piece of evidence 'fc' and an erasure of*

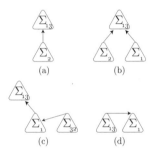

'mc'. This activates Σ_{32} *and the attack* (Σ_{32}, Σ_1), *and inactivates* Σ_2 *along with its attack against* Σ_{13}. *This active instance is shown in (c).*

Each active instance yields a particular set of accepted arguments. If we pick the grounded semantics: the active instance (a) accepts just the structure Σ_2; *the active instance (b) accepts* Σ_2 *and* Σ_1; *and the active instance (c) accepts* Σ_{32} *and* Σ_{13}. *Therefore, with this semantics, only in the latter scenario we would believe the path we are analyzing to pass through is dangerous.*

Now consider a new scenario, in which argument $\mathcal{B}_3$ *is dismissed due to the risk of being taken as xenophobic (though this was certainly not the intention), and suppose the preference between* $\mathcal{A}_1$ *and* $\mathcal{B}_1$ *is inverted. This means that* $\mathcal{B}_3$ *has to be contracted from the working set of arguments, and that the preference over* $(\mathcal{B}_1, \mathcal{A}_1)$ *has to be inverted. This new active instance is shown in (d).*

4. Conclusions and Future Work

In this article we have presented a new approach to abstract argumentation frameworks. Our model, as many others, is based on Dung's AF and represents an extension that is the basis of several research lines. From the Dynamic Argumentation Framework here defined an active instance can be obtained. This instance was shown to be equivalent to an AF; however, examples have shown that the DAF allows for a more powerful knowledge representation than the AF, by accepting the representation of change at different levels: evidence, arguments, conflicts, and preference. We contend that the DAF also yields a more realistic model, by setting apart evidence from arguments, which represent different kinds of knowledge. Agent architectures using this framework therefore could give an explicitly separate treatment to perception and reasoning. Finally, the equivalence between the active instance of the DAF and the AF is important to make the DAF compatible with the usual argumentation semantics.

Recently, some work has been done on dynamics in argumentation; in [4], the authors propose a series of principles to determine under what conditions an extension does not change when faced to a change in the framework. This article studies another aspect of the dynamics, centred on the impact of change over extensions. In our work, instead, we focus on the knowledge representation, providing constraints to avoid fallacious reasoning chains, and leaving evidence as a separate entity. As future work, results like in [4] will be helpful to provide an improved control of dynamics within the DAF.

Regarding future work, we are also interested in exploring the capability of reasoning about possible situations, and establishing a relation with the area of modal logics. The research line involving the intersection between belief change theory and argumentation will continue benefiting from the results accomplished in this dynamic framework, specially from the formalisation of distinct sources of change. Finally, the next step is to establish the theoretical foundations that relate the DAF with the classical argumentation semantics notions. The main difficulty relies on the acceptance/rejection of substructures wrt. their superstructures; for instance, it is interesting to define under what conditions the acceptance of an argumental structure implies the acceptance of all its substructures, and *vice versa*.

References

[1] Carlos Alchourrón, Peter Gärdenfors, and David Makinson. On the logic of theory change: Partial meet contraction and revision functions. *The Journal of Symbolic Logic*, 50:510–530, 1985.

[2] Pietro Baroni and Massimiliano Giacomin. On principle-based evaluation of extension-based argumentation semantics. *Artificial Intelligence*, 171(10-15):675–700, 2007.

[3] Philippe Besnard and Anthony Hunter. *Elements of Argumentation*. The MIT Press, 2008.

[4] Guido Boella, Souhila Kaci, and Leendert van der Torre. Dynamics in argumentation with single extensions: Abstraction principles and the grounded extension. In *ECSQARU*, pages 107–118, 2009.

[5] C. Chesñevar, J. McGinnis, S. Modgil, I. Rahwan, C. Reed, G. Simari, M. South, G. Vreeswijk, and S. Willmott. Towards an argument interchange format. *Knowl. Eng. Rev.*, 21(4):293–316, 2006.

[6] S. Coste-Marquis, C. Devred, S. Konieczny, M. Lagasquie-Schiex, and P. Marquis. On the merging of Dung's argumentation systems. *Artificial Intelligence*, 171(10-15):730–753, 2007.

[7] Phan Minh Dung. On the Acceptability of Arguments and its Fundamental Role in Nonmonotonic Reasoning, Logic Programming and n-person Games. *AIJ*, 77:321–357, 1995.

[8] Diego Martínez, Alejandro García, and Guillermo Simari. Modelling well-structured argumentation lines. In *IJCAI*, pages 465–470, 2007.

[9] Martín Moguillansky, Nicolás Rotstein, Marcelo Falappa, Alejandro García, and Guillermo Simari. Argument Theory Change Applied to Defeasible Logic Programming. In *AAAI*, pages 132–137, 2008.

[10] Martín Moguillansky, Nicolás Rotstein, Marcelo Falappa, and Guillermo Simari. Generalized abstract argumentation: Handling arguments in FOL fragments. *Symbolic and Quantitative Approaches to Reasoning with Uncertainty*, pages 144–155, 2009.

[11] Nicolás Rotstein, Martín Moguillansky, Marcelo Falappa, Alejandro García, and Guillermo Simari. Argument theory change: Revision upon warrant. In *COMMA*, pages 336–347, 2008.

[12] Stephen Toulmin. *The Uses of Argument*. Cambridge University Press, 1959.

[13] Douglas Walton. *Argument Structure: A Pragmatic Theory (Toronto Studies in Philosophy)*. Univ. of Toronto Press, 1996.

[14] Adam Wyner and Trevor Bench-Capon. Towards an extensible argumentation system. In *ECSQARU*, pages 283–294, 2007.

Computational Models of Argument
P. Baroni et al. (Eds.)
IOS Press, 2010
doi:10.3233/978-1-60750-619-5-439

Argumentation 3.0: how Semantic Web technologies can improve argumentation modeling in Web 2.0 environments [1]

Jodi SCHNEIDER [a] Alexandre PASSANT [a] Tudor GROZA [a] and
John G. BRESLIN [a,b]

[a] *Digital Enterprise Research Institute, National University of Ireland, Galway*
[b] *School of Engineering and Informatics, National University of Ireland, Galway*

Abstract. Argumentative discussions are common in Web 2.0 applications, but the social Web still offers limited or no explicit support for argumentation. As Web 2.0 applications become more popular, modeling argumentation happening in these systems becomes important, to enable reuse and further understanding of on-line discussions. After reviewing four genres of online conversations–Web bulletin boards, Wiki talk pages, blog comments, and microblogs–and four current Web 2.0 argumentation systems, the paper suggests how Semantic Web technologies can be used to provide an interoperability layer for argumentation modeling across applications.

Keywords. informal argumentation, social networking, argumentation tools, Semantic Web, distributed conversations

1. Motivation

Social networking systems have increased in popularity, and substantive conversations occur in 'Web 2.0' media (such as forums, wikis, blogs, microblogs, etc). People argue implicitly (i.e. in comments on blogs), but these arguments must be inferred; the argumentative structure is rarely explicit. Meanwhile, structured argumentation tools, including web-based tools (such as Debategraph[2] and Compendium[3] [4]), have slower adoption outside specialized domains such as enterprise and egovernment applications.

Many social media discussions could benefit from improved visualization and better presentation, for instance the ability to distinguish questions, disagreements, and elaborations or the ability to navigate by argument, rather than chronological order. We are inspired by earlier systems such as WIT, Hypernews, and Zest, which integrated social and argumentation features, and by recent surveys such as [9], which reviewed models for expressing the argumentation and rhetoric of scientific publications. The WIT discussion system[4] aimed to make the current state of a discussion clear, by having the user indicate

---

[1]This work was supported by Science Foundation Ireland under Grant No. SFI/09/CE/I1380 (Líon2).
[2]http://debategraph.org/ and as used, e.g. in [7]
[3]http://compendium.open.ac.uk/
[4]http://www.w3.org/WIT/User/Overview.html

"whether he was agreeing, disagreeing or asking for clarification of a point" [1]. Hyper-news[5] asks users to indicate what kind of message they are posting[6], then displays the message type as an icon in the forum's thread view. Zest [24], a prototype email browser, supported lightweight integration of IBIS-based [12] argument maps, using "criticons" such as ([?], [#], [+], [-]) to mark paragraphs as questions, statement, supporting argument, or opposing argument; a fifth criticon, [!], indicated resolution of a discussion.

Lightweight annotation schemes based on similar techniques might find adoption on the Social Web, and in addition to improved visualizations on each individual site, we would also like to enable cross-website navigation driven by arguments. That is, we would like to identify, across various wikis, weblogs and other applications, who is arguing (positively or negatively) about a particular product, topic, or position. Public policy and shared events may discussed across various different platforms but need to be viewed globally: Consider conversations provoked by the U.S. Health Care policy debates or the infamous 'hand ball' in the World Cup qualification of 2009. While many people talk about the same topic, there is little support for gathering conversations, in part because we lack shared identifiers for these topics (e.g. URIs). Cross-website navigation would make it possible to display all the arguments related to a URI (that URI could represent a blog post or a topic); we call this *"object-centred argumentation"*, since social media is centered on objects of interest, around which conversations develop [11].

We believe that Semantic Web technologies, that focus on interoperability between applications by relying on common data formats (RDF) and models or *ontologies* (RDFS/OWL), could play an important role in this. On the one hand, various characteristics of social media systems have been modeled using Semantic Web technologies [6], for instance via models such as FOAF[7] and SIOC [2]. On the other hand, separate models based on Semantic Web technologies have been proposed for argumentation, such as IBIS-OWL[8], SALT [10], and Scholarly Ontologies [19], and further the Argument Interchange Format (AIF) has been expressed in RDF [3]. Despite a similar metadata modeling layer via RDF(S)/OWL, there are still many gaps between these models.

To fill these gaps, our goal is to identify the needs of the Social Web community in terms of argumentation, and determine how social media argumentation patterns can be represented. Bridges–formal models and/or mappings–will be needed between the two sorts of ontologies: those for representing social media and those for representing argumentation, in order to bring the Social Web ('Web 2.0') and the Semantic Web together into a Social Semantic Web ('Web 3.0') for argumentation–'Argumentation 3.0'.

This paper is organized as follows: First, we discuss use cases in social media, based on well-known applications. Second, we review existing Web-based tools for argumentation. Third, we work towards requirements for social media argumentation, based on a survey of users. Fourth, we review Semantic Web models for argumentation, considering their relation to social media. Finally we conclude, highlighting the need for an ecosystem approach.

---

[5]http://www.hypernews.org/HyperNews/get/hypernews/reading.html
[6]None, Question, Note, Warning, Feedback, Idea, More, News, Ok, Sad, Angry, Agree, Disagree
[7]http://www.foaf-project.org/
[8]http://purl.org/ibis

2. Argumentation in the Social Web

The Social Web includes many Web sites, each with its own affordances and interaction patterns, which affect which types of conversations are well-supported, and thus what kind and how much argumentation occurs[9]. In this section, we consider typical discussion environments from four types of social media: forums, wikis, blogs, and microblogs.

The message board has been a popular feature of Internet-based communication since mailing lists and Usenet newsgroups. Most forums employ some threaded display methods, where users post and reply to threads on a particular topic. Forums share some rhetorical characteristics of mailing lists, such as the tendency to quote previous comments, as well as some social conventions, such as the use of +1 to indicate agreement. On some boards, thumbs-up and thumbs-down signs are used, providing visual cues.

Wiki software saves a complete history of each page, and allows pages to be edited directly in a Web browser, facilitating collaboration. Wikipedia Talk pages often host argumentative discussions about editing articles, such as whether and how a topic should be covered, or whether particular sources are reliable. However, they lack some typical affordances: signatures, posting dates, and indentation are added manually, by social convention, whereas other systems store and display this information along with the message content. Only social convention prevents editing others' comments, and in some cases (e.g. responses to peer reviews), long comments are split by responses. While Talk pages are intended to support editing, discussions often remain after they have had their intended effect on page editing. When message volume is manageable, the topical, rather than chronological, order of wiki discussions has some advantages for coherence.

Blogs often include a comments section where readers can leave a response, and this format has been adopted by major newspapers, juxtaposing readers' reactions with the newspaper article cum blog post. This fragments the conversation about news items, since reactions to a newspaper story reside only on the platform for that paper, even though many news articles cover the same event, each from its own perspective. Blog comments can include long threads with substantive comments, or substantial back-and-forth replies between an author and one or more commenters. Replies may be threaded, and comments usually list the date and author (perhaps also with a visual cue such as an avatar). Even though a comment responds to a blog post at a given time, posts can be updated, and usually only the most recent version is publicly viewable.

Microblogging is a newer trend; Twitter[10], is characteristic, and its brief posts (limited to 140 characters) are each globally available at a URI, and typically publicly viewable. In microblogging, each message stands by its own and forms part of a stream; some messages may also have secondary status as a reply to another user or as a retweet/repost broadcasting a prior message (similar to forwarding an email). The popularity of retweets [5] points to an inherent need to quote, even in very brief messages. While stream-based services make it difficult to maintain the coherence of a dialogue, short personal opinions, reactions, and interpretations are easy to post, and can be gathered through collation methods such as hashtags[11]; preceding a word with a # symbol creates a link to other messages using the tag, but reduces the space available for message content.

---

[9]Argumentation may be explicit and commonplace (in task-based collaboration on wikis) or harder to spot (in microblogging where dialogue is comparatively rare).

[10]http://twitter.com

[11]For instance, [17] used hashtags to gather tweets about the U.S. Presidential debates.

3. Web-based Argumentation Tools and Social Web Systems for Argumentation

This section provides an overview of four Social Web systems for argumentation: Cohere, Debategraph, Debatepedia, and LivingVote. These systems were chosen based on exploration of argumentation literature, Web searches, and Web browsing. At a minimum, the systems needed to be currently available and publicly viewable. They were chosen due to their influence, wide use, or novelty; after the selection period, another relevant system, the Climate Collaboratorium[12] came to light.

Cohere[13] is a knowledge-mapping website, which allows user to view and create maps, or import them from Compendium. Maps consist of ideas, which can be taken from the site's public, global pool of ideas, or added to a user's private collection. Cohere offers sorting options and several views, including map, timeline, argument, and argument listing views. Although all the data resides on Cohere's server, plugins provide some integration with external sites: users can clip ideas and save websites from Firefox (similar to social bookmarking), or tweet from Cohere (using a Jetpack extension). Ideas can be private or shared, allowing the possibility of finding arguments and ideas which interact with your own, and suggesting that truly distributed systems could be useful.

Debategraph[14] is a wiki debate visualization tool which has been adopted for use at the Kyoto climate change summit and is being tested by EU projects such as WAVE[15]. Visualizations can be embedded in other websites, and Debategraph encourages users to add hyperlinks within graphs. Debategraph's user interface is elaborate, and its navigation methods may take some time to get used to: As the focus changes, so does the graph, and for a novice user it can be confusing to figure out how to get back to a previous view. The learning curve to effective use is its main disadvantage.

Debatepedia[16] bills itself as the "the Wikipedia of pros and cons". Sponsored by the International Debate Education Association, Debatepedia is a collaborative community effort to summarize arguments. Each argument page provides an overview, then a list of issues, with pros and cons supported by news articles and similar sources. It provides an intuitive editing environment, where users can edit just the relevant section, such as the pro or con for a topic. Debatepedia's biggest weakness is the lack of alternate visualizations; this could be overcome by using the existing separation of pros and cons.

At Living Vote[17], users discuss pro and con arguments of issues, creating argument maps. A tree view provides a coherent view of the argument, which can be drilled down, where arguments and their counterarguments are presented side-by-side. To vote, users must answer questions designed to test whether they've read the arguments. Living Vote also prunes unhelpful arguments and aims to provide a "complete, persistent, constantly changing and up-to-date record of everyone's opinion on an issue as well as the arguments that led them to that opinion, weighted by each voter's understanding and participation". Complex arguments, where a position supports one issue but argues against another, are not supported by Living Vote's current interface. Living Vote succeeds at summarizing large-scale policy debates and deserves further examination by those interested in vote-based approaches.

---

[12]http://www.climatecollaboratorium.org/
[13]http://cohere.open.ac.uk/
[14]http://debategraph.org/
[15]http://www.wave-project.eu/
[16]http://debatepedia.idebate.org/
[17]http://www.LivingVote.org/

4. What Users Say They Want in Argumentation

To begin to understand users' perceptions of which features they value in online discussions, we conducted two prototype surveys of users[18]. Survey responses were solicited first on Twitter (8 replies) and then for a second, slightly modified survey[19], by email in our Semantic Web lab (23 replies). Respondents rated the following ten items as "Important", "Not Important", or "Maybe Important", based on the question "When you're commenting in an online discussion or argument, which of these are most important to you?" 1. It's easy to use [usability] 2. I can see the whole conversation (even if it's on multiple social networks) [integration] 3. I can quote or reference earlier parts of the discussion [referential context] 4. I can indicate the topic I'm discussing [topical context] 5. There's enough space to write my own message [appropriate length] 6. I can add or view comments on the document, at the part or section where they apply [view context] 7. I can tell who wrote earlier messages [author context] 8. I know whether a comment is up-to-date (not superseded) [currency/temporal context] 9. There are extra features useful in my domain/area of interest [modularity/topical integration] 10. It's easy to see the messages I care about [visualization/sorting].

Usability and appropriate length were the most important features to users; next were author, temporal, or referential context and visualization/sorting; then topical context or integration; and the least important features were view context and modularity/topical integration. The lack of emphasis on integration is interesting; from one perspective the Social Web is fundamentally distributed, yet, from the researcher perspective, integration seems fundamental to facilitating dialogue and argumentation in these distributed conversations. The question about appropriate length was proposed with microblogs in mind, but even those reaching the survey from an email link emphasized this aspect.

One respondant suggested five additional aspects for reading and scanning online discussions, which should be considered in further studies: 1. a view of the reputation or role of the contributor (reputation) 2. an overview of a participant's interests/past contributions by topic (summarization) 3. indicator of sentiment in an argument discussion thread (sentiment) 4. indicator of possible repetitiveness/circularity (redundancy) 5. indication of a consensus emerging in an argument (consensus).

A disadvantage of studies of this kind is that it is hard to distinguish regular interaction with the medium from specific argumentation support. Similarly, case studies of how people are using social media for argumentation could be helpful, however those require a clear understanding of what argumentation can and should mean in the context of social media, a question which deserves further consideration.

One fundamental question is what amount of complexity users are willing to adopt in order to reap the benefits of argumentation; previous research has emphasized incremental formalization [18] because users do not generally understand the larger structure of an argument from the outset (see e.g. [19], page 29), and even experienced users can have difficulty holding a complex argumentation model in their heads (page 27, ibid). This leads us to believe that only a simple argumentation model will gain use in social media, unless the complexity can be mitigated by good interfaces and familiar metaphors.

---

[18]Further information at http://jodischneider.com/pubs/suppinfo/2010COMMA/

[19]Items were randomized for the first survey but not for the second survey, and one item, [view context] was at first described as "I can annotate documents or messages". The second survey also gave slightly more context, including the keywords in brackets and the indication that "We're trying to establish requirements for arguments (discussions where there's disagreement or differences in viewpoints)."

5. Semantic Web Models for Argumentation

The Semantic Web's strengths include modularity–easing integration of domain knowledge and topical models–and integration–allowing distributed systems to interoperate–along with the ability to reference anything (providing author, topic, or referential context), at any granuarlity addressable with a URI. Push-based Semantic Web protocols such as sparqlPuSH[20] can facilitate currency. Yet users' most important criteria–usability and appropriate length–depend on particular models and the implementations of those models, whose simplicity, for instance, varies considerably. To understand these factors, we next focus on five Semantic Web models for argumentation: AIF, AIF-RDF, DILIGENT, OWL IBIS, and SWAN/SIOC, and comment on their applicability to social media.

AIF [3], an RDF-based format for argument interchange, has been combined with the Dialogue Game Description Language (DGDL), to create Argument Blogging [22]. With a JavaScript plugin, bloggers add argumentative relations to their own posts, selecting whether they want to support or refute a highlighted statement, or attack an inference between statements. Even though blogs are still published at their usual location, this code allows the distributed conversation to be centralized and stored in a single database, facilitating collation and visualization. Argument Blogging's effectiveness is in its ability to hide the complication of the AIF ontology, simplifying to just three choices. Similar approaches could be used on forums and wikis, but for microblogging, this approach would need some modification, perhaps using a registry and a brief command language such as Zest's. Wide adoption would require cooperation of major blog hosts, since many bloggers use hosted systems rather than administering their own blog.

Rahwan's work on the AIF-RDF ontology and ArgDF system looks promising [16], [15]. AIF-RDF's strengths lie in its use of standards (AIF and RDF) and its ability to represent full argument schemes. To make a new argument, in the latest public demo of ArgDF[21], a user must first choose an argumentation scheme by name, then add statements in the appropriate structure. However, most users do not have formal training in logic or argumentation, and while they may recognize (and even use) complex arguments, their ability to formalize these arguments lags behind. Incremental formalization suggests that users might first present their arguments, and then edit them to match an appropriate scheme; if this scheme were suggested (perhaps with NLP detection of the argument type [13]), AIF-RDF could back a powerful and user-friendly environment. However, developing a generic interface for AIF-RDF, which could accompany existing social media, seems challenging due to the inherent abstraction of argumentation schemes.

DILIGENT [20] is primarily a methodology for engineering an ontology; the acronym comes from certain letters in the phrase "DIstributed, Loosely-controlled and evolvInG". Argumentation is used to track the process, in part because externalizing the information exchanged during ontology creation could help avoid rehashing discussions as new people join the process or later review the ontology. DILIGENT's strength is its previous use in collaborative ontology engineering, using IM and wikis [21], in which Talk pages are used to store "elaborations, arguments, positions and decisions ordered chronologically". However DILIGENT has over 30 terms, including terms such

---

[20]http://code.google.com/p/sparqlpush/
[21]http://dundee.argdf.org/

as `Issue`, `position-on`, `Justification`, and `Decision`; the intricacies which make it an ideal model for design support detract from its use by the layman.

The IBIS OWL Model[22] is an RDF representation of IBIS, providing URIs and PSIs for these ten terms: `Idea`, `Question`, `Argument`, `Decision`, `Reference`, `Note`, `Map`, `refersTo`, `pro`, and `con`. The brevity, simplicity and clarity of the terms are promising for casual use across social media, but that use has not yet been tested.

SWAN/SIOC [14] harmonizes the argumentation aspects of models for neuromedicine and online communities. SWAN/SIOC's argumentation is based around specifying 11 types of relationships between items such as `inconsistentWith`, `motivatedBy`, and `discusses`. The system mediates and moderates this complexity, leading to the success of the model in scientific online communities such as a Parkinson's disease discussion site[23], where the intricacy of SWAN/SIOC is suited to representing the relationships between scientific arguments. These distinctions would not match some more general discussions, where they might be overly complex.

6. Conclusions & Future Work

With the rise of Web 2.0 systems, discussions happen everywhere on the Web, and argumentation is often present in those discussions. Semantic Web models have been developed and used to structure social media as well as in argumentation.

For forums and blogs, the approach taken by Argument Blogging needs mainly evangelism and integration with hosted systems to help the World Wide Argument Web [16] emerge, and a federated network in order to make it scalable and resistant to disruption.

For wikis, argumentation should use the inherent structure–the change over time. For instance, comments could be connected to particular text chunks, as in Commentpress[24] [8]. On some heavily-trafficked wiki Talk pages, FAQs are used to represent the current consensus, guarding against repetition and redundancy, but discouraging the involvement of new users; with a dialogue game system, perhaps based on MAgtALO [23], newcomers could interactively persuade or be persuaded, and the existing community would need to get involved only when new arguments warrant reexamining the consensus.

For microblogging, brevity is an overwhelming limitation; even indicating what is being argued about can be challenging, if a URI must fit in the message. Twitter Annotations[25] and client-based semantic annotations such as SMOB[26] provide a way forward, without depending on special fields for URIs or argumentative structure within a message.

Despite the proliferation of Semantic Web models for argumentation, a unified standard for argumentation on the Social Web is still lacking. We cannot yet collate arguments *across* social media, to find, for instance where microbloggers express approval of or provide brief counterpoints to blog posts, or where forums and listservs point to and extend wiki Talk page disputes. In short, we lack an ecosystem approach. In future research, we will work towards an argumentation ecosystem for social media, aligning Semantic Web models for argumentation with those for social media.

---

[22]http://purl.org/ibis
[23]http://www.pdonlineresearch.org/
[24]http://www.futureofthebook.org/commentpress/
[25]http://apiwiki.twitter.com/Annotations-Overview
[26]http://smob.me/

References

[1]   Tim Berners-Lee. *Weaving the Web*. Harper Paperbacks, 1st edition, 2000.

[2]   John G. Breslin, Andreas Harth, Uldis Bojars, and Stefan Decker. Towards Semantically-Interlinked
      Online Communities. In *The Semantic Web: Research and Applications*, pages 500–514. Springer, 2005.

[3]   Carlos Chesnevar, Jarred McGinnis, Sanjay Modgil, Iyad Rahwan, Chris Reed, Guillermo Simari,
      Matthew South, Gerard Vreeswijk, and Steven Willmott. Towards an Argument Interchange Format.
      The Knowledge Engineering Review, 21(04):293–316, 2006.

[4]   Jeff Conklin, Albert Selvin, Simon Buckingham Shum, and Maarten Sierhuis. Facilitated hypertext
      for collective sensemaking: 15 years on from gIBIS. In *Proceedings of the 12th ACM conference on
      Hypertext and Hypermedia*, pages 123–124. ACM, 2001.

[5]   danah boyd, Scott Golder, and Gilad Lotan. Tweet, tweet, retweet: Conversational aspects of retweeting
      on Twitter. In *HICSS-43*. IEEE, 2010.

[6]   Ben Kei Daniel, Alexandre Passant, Sheila Kinsella, Uldis Bojars, John G. Breslin, and Stefan Decker.
      Understanding online communities by using Semantic Web technologies. In *Handbook of Research on
      Methods and Techniques for Studying Virtual Communities: Paradigms and Phenomena*. Information
      Science Publishing, 2010.

[7]   Aldo de Moor, Jack Park, and Madalina Croitoru. Argumentation map generation with conceptual
      graphs: the case for ESSENCE. In *CS-TIW 2009*, 2009.

[8]   Kathleen Fitzpatrick. CommentPress: new (Social) structures for new (Networked) texts. *Journal of
      Electronic Publishing*, 10(3), 2007.

[9]   Tudor Groza, Siegfried Handschuh, Tim Clark, Simon Buckingham Shum, and Anita de Waard. A
      short survey of discourse representation models. In *Proceedings of the Workshop on Semantic Web
      Applications in Scientific Discourse (SWASD 2009) at SWC-2009*, volume 523. CEUR-WS.org, 2009.

[10] Tudor Groza, Siegfried Handschuh, Knud Möller, and Stefan Decker. SALT - semantically annotated
      LaTeX for scientific publications. In *The Semantic Web: Research and Applications*. Springer, 2007.

[11] K.D. Knorr-Cetina. Sociality with objects: Social relations in postsocial knowledge societies. *Theory,
      Culture and Society*, 14(4):1–30, 1997.

[12] Werner Kunz and Horst W.J. Rittel. Issues as elements of information systems. Working Paper 131,
      Center for Planning and Development Research, University of California at Berkeley, 1970.

[13] Raquel Mochales Palau and Marie-Francine Moens. Automatic argumentation detection and its role
      in law and the Semantic Web. In *Law, Ontologies and the Semantic Web - Channelling the Legal
      Information Flood*, pages 115–129. IOS Press, 2009.

[14] Alexandre Passant, Paolo Ciccarese, John G. Breslin, and Tim Clark. SWAN/SIOC: aligning scien-
      tific discourse representation and social semantics. In *Proceedings of the Workshop on Semantic Web
      Applications in Scientific Discourse (SWASD 2009) at (ISWC-2009)*, volume 523. CEUR-WS.org, 2009.

[15] Iyad Rahwan. Mass argumentation and the Semantic Web. *Web Semantics: Science, Services and Agents
      on the World Wide Web*, 6(1):29–37, 2008.

[16] Iyad Rahwan, Fouad Zablith, and Chris Reed. Laying the foundations for a World Wide Argument Web.
      Artificial Intelligence, 171(10-15):897–921, 2007.

[17] David A. Shamma, Lyndon Kennedy, and Elizabeth F. Churchill. Tweet the debates. In *Proceedings of
      the first SIGMM workshop on Social Media*, pages 3–10. ACM, 2009.

[18] Frank M. Shipman and Catherine C. Marshall. Formality considered harmful: Experiences, emerging
      themes, and directions on the use of formal representations in interactive systems. *Computer Supported
      Cooperative Work*, 8(4):333–352, 1999.

[19] Simon J. Buckingham Shum, Victoria Uren, Gangmin Li, Bertrand Sereno, and Clara Mancini. Mod-
      eling naturalistic argumentation in research literatures: Representation and interaction design issues.
      International Journal of Intelligent Systems, 22(1):17–47, 2007.

[20] Christoph Tempich, H. Sofia Pinto, York Sure, and Steffen Staab. An argumentation ontology for DIs-
      tributed, loosely-controlled and evolvInG engineering processes of oNTologies (DILIGENT). In *The
      Semantic Web: Research and Applications*, pages 241–256. Springer, 2005.

[21] Christoph Tempich, Elena Simperl, Markus Luczak, Rudi Studer, and H. Sofia Pinto. Argumentation-
      Based ontology engineering. *IEEE Intelligent Systems*, 22(6):52–59, 2007.

[22] Simon Wells, Colin Gourlay, and Chris Reed. Argument blogging. In *CMNA 2009*, Pasadena, CA, 2009.

[23] Simon Wells and Chris Reed. MAgtALO: an Agent-Based system for persuasive online interaction. In
      AISB 2008, 2008.

[24] Ka-Ping Yee. Zest: Discussion mapping for mailing lists. In *CSCW 2002*. ACM, 2002.

Computational Models of Argument
P. Baroni et al. (Eds.)
IOS Press, 2010
doi:10.3233/978-1-60750-619-5-447

Pipelining Argumentation Technologies

Mark SNAITH, Joseph DEVEREUX, John LAWRENCE and Chris REED

School of Computing, University of Dundee, Dundee, DD1 4HN, UK

Abstract. Software tools for working with argument generally exist as large systems that wrap their entire feature set in the application as a whole. This approach, while perfectly valid, can result in users having to use small parts of multiple systems to carry out a specific task. In this paper, we present a series of web services, that each encapsulate small pieces of functionality for working with argument. We then demonstrate two example systems built by connecting these services in the form of a UNIX-style pipeline.

Keywords. Argumentation Engine, Dung, Dungine, Dung-O-Matic, Web Services

1. Introduction

Argumentation tools such as Araucaria [9], Rationale [12], AVERS [1] and Cohere [10] all provide distinct features for working with argument. However, each system wraps its entire feature set in the application as a whole, meaning individual components cannot be used independently. As a result, users may find themselves having to use multiple systems to carry out a specific task.

We present here a solution to this problem, that involves breaking down argumentation tools into small components, deploying these components as web services, then constructing UNIX-style pipelines to link them together as one large system, with specific functionality.

The advantages of this approach are that components can be used in multiple systems that require overlapping functionality, but only one instance of each component is required (on a remote web server). Additionally, adopting a web services approach allows existing, legacy systems to interact with new technologies, and vice versa (see section 4.2).

2. Web services

In creating our web services, we decided to use the REST (REpresentational State Transfer) architecture [7], because this is simpler to interact with than protocol-based approaches such as SOAP (Simple Object Access Protocol).

In addition, REST allows for simpler construction of services, which can be written in any language that allows parameters to be posted to it. We illustrate this point in the deployment of our services; most were written in Java using the RESTlet framework[1], however one was written in PHP.

---

[1] `http://www.restlet.org/`

2.1. Dungine

Dungine is a Dung reasoner, for the computation of arguments in the grounded extension and every preferred extension of a given framework [11]. It exists as a Java library, which we have wrapped in a RESTful interface.

The interface both accepts and returns an adapted RDF reification of the Argument Interchange Format (AIF) [4] (see section 2.5). Additionally, the type of semantics required (i.e. grounded or preferred) is indicated by a boolean parameter. The returned AIF contains labellings to indicate argument acceptability under the chosen semantics.

2.2. Dung-O-Matic

Dung-O-Matic is a Dung reasoner that identifies several extensions of an argumentation framework:

- the admissible sets [13]
- the preferred extensions
- the grounded extension [5]
- the stable extensions
- the semi-stable extensions [2,3]
- the ideal extension [6]
- the eager extension [3]

It can also answer any corresponding question about any argument in the framework, such as whether or not it is in the grounded extension.

This service accepts and returns the same adapted RDF reification of the AIF as the Dungine service, with the returned AIF containing labellings to indicate argument acceptability for all semantics.

2.3. ArgDB

ArgDB is an AIF reification which allows for the storage and retrieval of argument data in multiple forms. It consists of two main components:

- A web service interface which allows for the addition and retrieval of elements corresponding to the top level concepts of the AIF ontology. For example nodes, edges and schemes can all be posted individually to ArgDB. Received elements are checked for validity and that they do not currently exist in the database before adding them. The web service also offers the ability to query an ArgDB installation for the arguments it contains.
- An underlying database for the storage of each of these elements.

ArgDB currently uses a MySQL database, though it is designed to support a wide range of databases with the web service abstracting the database interaction

Additional components allow for addition and retrieval of AIF-DF directly from ArgDB through a RESTful interface, though these are not a core part of the database solution and could easily be replaced by components to handle input and output of other AIF reifications.

2.4. AML to AIF

Our AML to AIF translation module accepts Argument Markup Language (AML), as used by Araucaria [9], and translates it into AIF-DF, for insertion into ArgDB. AML "propositions" are translated into AIF I-Nodes, while AIF S-Nodes are created based on the edges between propositions (expressed in AML as "Convergent Argument" (CA) and "Linked Argument" (LA)).

This was developed to allow users to save arguments analysed in Araucaria (which does not currently support AIF) into ArgDB.

2.5. Dot to AIF/AIF to Dot

A further two translation services allow for translation between Dot language ("Dot") and AIF-DF, and vice versa.

Dot is a simple language that allows graphs to be expressed in plain text[2]. We see this as an ideal way of constructing Dung-style argument frameworks [5], which can be represented as directed graphs.

While there is presently no support for argument frameworks in the AIF, we have adapted it slightly to provide this. This was done to illustrate a distinct advantage of our pipelining approach: if and when official support for argument frameworks is added to the AIF, modifying this small component will be considerably easier than modifying a full system.

2.6. AVERS to AIF

Our final web service is still under development, but we include it here to illustrate a further advantage to our approach.

This service will translate the data used by AVERS [1] into AIF-DF. AVERS uses a version of Dot language for representation of argument, which is slightly different to the version accepted by the Dot to AIF translation service. Specifically, AVERS encodes various visual conventions in the Dot representation (ellipses correspond to inferences, etc.). Those conventions all correspond to ontological categories in the AIF specification, so constructing the mapping from AVERS Dot output to AIF-DF is straightforward because there is a common ontological backdrop provided by the AIF. Implementation is similarly straightforward, because the Dot-AIF parser is trivially extended to be sensitive to the AIF conventions implicit in AVERS Dot.

This shows that modularity enhances incremental development – by having small components with limited functionality, it is much easier to adapt those components to fulfil a slightly different goal.

3. Pipelining

It is our goal to create pipelines out of our web services, where the output from one is sent as the input to another, and so on. The concept of pipelining is not new; UNIX

---

[2]http://www.graphviz.org/doc/info/lang.html

systems have offered support for this approach for many years. However, applying this to argument technology is new.

An example of pipelines emerging on the web is through *Yahoo! Pipes*[3]. A drag-and-drop interface is provided, allowing various components for manipulating data to be linked together [Figure 1].

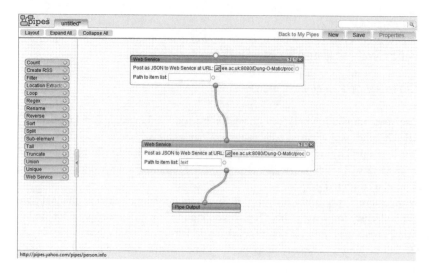

Figure 1. Yahoo! Pipes screenshot

4. Systems

We now present two systems built using different pipelines through our web services.

4.1. OVA-gen

OVA-gen is a tool for the construction and analysis of Dung-style argument frameworks [5].

It consists of a graphical "point-and-click" interface, which sits in front of two pipelines, consisting of Dung-O-Matic and Dungine for acceptability computation, and the Dot to AIF/AIF to Dot translators. The pipeline construction can bee seen in figure 2.

The user interface was developed as part of the Online Visualisation of Argument (OVA) project, which aims to deploy easy-to-use tools for online argument visualisation[4].

A menu bar is provided at the top of the interface, allowing the user to select which semantics they wish to compute, along with which computation engine to use (for example, "Grounded (Dungine)" or "Preferred (Dung-O-Matic)").

---

[3]http://pipes.yahoo.com
[4]http://www.arg.dundee.ac.uk/?page_id=143

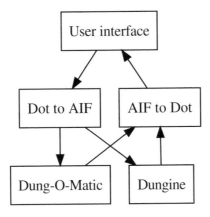

Figure 2. OVA-gen pipeline

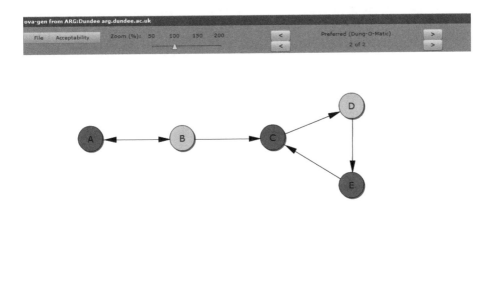

Figure 3. OVA-gen user interface

When the semantics are returned, the arguments in the framework are rendered green if they are acceptable under those semantics, or red if they are not. Under semantics that can yield more than one extension, buttons are provided for scrolling through the different extensions.

Finally, when semantics have been computed, any subsequent arguments added to the framework will immediately be rendered as acceptable. When new attacks are added, all renderings are updated to reflect the presence of that attack.

The user interface can be seen in figure 3.

4.2. ArauAIF

ArauAIF is a pipeline that takes arguments saved in the AraucariaDB in AML, translates them into AIF and inserts them into ArgDB. Its structure can be seen in figure 4.

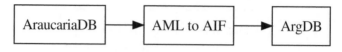

Figure 4. ArauAIF pipeline

The purpose of this pipeline is to allow users to continue using Araucaria and its connection to AraucariaDB, while also having the ability to save their analyses in AIF, into ArgDB. This benefits ArgDB and the World Wide Argument Web (WWAW)[8], because it allows Araucaria's existing userbase to seamlessly contribute to this emerging platform.

Addtionally, we have another pipeline that carries out the reverse process, translating AIF to AML, allowing AIF analyses to be loaded into Araucaria for examination and manipulation. However, this pipeline has its limitations, which are detailed in section 5.

5. Limitations & Problems

It is not our intention here to present an idealistic view of using web service pipelines for argumentation technologies. During the course of this work, we encountered several challenges, some of which remain unresolved.

Connecting our components to existing systems (such as in section 4.2) presented a problem as to how we obtain the data from the application. Our solution was to use data that was saved in the original format and convert that — so in the case of Araucaria, analyses are first saved as AML in the AraucariaDB, then translated to AIF for insertion into ArgDB.

Another issue related to the ArauAIF pipeline is that while AML is tree-based, AIF is graph-based. This is fine for translation from the former to the latter, but when we reverse the process, we find that certain analyses in AIF cannot be converted, limiting the level of interaction between Araucaria and the WWAW.

There is also the more general issue of web services only being available so long as the servers hosting them remain "live". If a server hosting a particular component (or pipeline) goes down, the functionality that it offers would no longer be available to the application employing it. The emergence of new technolgies for redundancy, such as cloud computing, could address this, but it remains an issue nonetheless[5].

6. Conclusions and future work

In this paper we have presented several web services that each encapsulate small pieces of functionality for working with argumentation. We have then demonstrated how these web services can be connected in the form of a pipeline to create larger systems.

---

[5]And of course, redundancy does not address the even wider issue of the client requiring an Internet connection to make use of web services.

The work presented here shows only the first steps towards a pipelining approach. Further work will be required to simplify pipeline construction; it is our intention to create a "construction toolkit" for building argumentation systems, similar in principle to that of Yahoo! pipes (section 3), but with specific components for argumentation, instead of more general tools for working with data. It would then potentially be possible to provide an open platform for developers to submit their web services for inclusion in the toolkit.

At the moment, though, we have shown how existing, reusable argumentation services can be composed into nontrivial applications in several different domains.

References

[1] S. W. Van Den Braak. Avers: An argument visualization tool for representing stories about evidence. In *In Proceedings of the 11th International Conference on Artificial Intelligence and Law*, pages 11–15. ACM Press, 2007.

[2] M. Caminada. Semi-stable semantics. In *Proceedings of the 1st International Conference on Computational Models of Argument (COMMA 2006)*, 2006.

[3] M. Caminada. Comparing two unique extension semantics for formal argumentation: Ideal and eager. In *Proceedings of BNAIC 2007*, 2007.

[4] C. Chesnevar, J. McGinnis, S. Modgil, I. Rahwan, C. Reed, G. Simari, M. South, G. Vreeswijk, and S. Willmott. Towards an argument interchange format. *The Knowledge Engineering Review*, 21(4):293–316, 2006.

[5] P. M. Dung. On the acceptability of arguments and its fundamental role in nonmonotonic reasoning, logic programming and n-person games. *Artificial Intelligence*, 77:321–357, 1995.

[6] P.M. Dung, P. Mancarella, and F. Toni. Computing ideal sceptical argumentation. *Artificial Intelligence*, 171:642–674, 2007.

[7] R.T. Fielding and R.N. Taylor. Principled design of the modern web architecture. *ACM Trans. Internet Technol.*, 2(2):115–150, 2002.

[8] I. Rahwan, F. Zablith, and C. Reed. Laying the foundations for a world wide argument web. *Artificial Intelligence*, 171:897–921, 2007.

[9] C. Reed and G. Rowe. Araucaria: software for argument analysis, diagramming and representation. *International Journal on Artificial Intelligence Tools*, 13:961–980, 2004.

[10] S. Buckingham Shum. Cohere: Towards web 2.0 argumentation. In *Proceedings of the 2nd International Conference on Computational Models of Argument (COMMA 2008)*, 2008.

[11] M. South, G. Vreeswijk, and J. Fox. Dungine: a java dung reasoner. In *Proceedings of the 2nd International Conference on Computational Models of Argument (COMMA 2008)*, 2008.

[12] T. van Gelder. The rationale for rationale. *Law, Probability and Risk*, 6(1–4):23–42, 2007.

[13] G. A. W. Vreeswijk. An algorithm to compute minimally grounded and admissible defence sets in argument systems. In *Proceedings of the 1st International Conference on Computational Models of Argument (COMMA 2006)*, 2006.

Computational Models of Argument
P. Baroni et al. (Eds.)
IOS Press, 2010
doi:10.3233/978-1-60750-619-5-455

455

Argumentation and rules with exceptions

Bart VERHEIJ

Artificial Intelligence, University of Groningen

Abstract. Models of argumentation often take a given set of rules or conditionals as a starting point. Arguments to support or attack a position are then built from these rules. In this paper, an attempt is made to develop constraints on rules and their exceptions in such a way that they correspond exactly to arguments that successfully support their conclusions. The constraints take the form of properties of nonmonotonic consequence relations, similar to the ones that have been studied for cumulative inference.

1. Introduction

Consider the following information: p, p is a prima facie reason for q, q is a prima facie reason for r, r is an exception that undercuts the support of q by p. Formally: $p, p \Rightarrow q, q \Rightarrow r, r \Rightarrow \neg(p \Rightarrow q)$ (see the argument depicted on the left in Figure 1). The example is essentially the important and well-known example used by Pollock (1995, p. 119 [6]) in his groundbreaking work on defeasible argumentation. The issue with this theory can be summarized as follows:

> Either p successfully supports q, or it does not. Assume that it does. Then r is also successfully supported, as q supports r and that link is not disputed. But if r is successfully supported, the assumption that p successfully supports q is contradicted since r attacks the link between p and q. So assume the second possibility that p does not successfully support q. But only an attack by r can break the link between p and q, so r should be successfully supported. But it isn't, as the successful support of r requires the successful support of q based on p, which contradicts the assumption. Paradox!

There are two possible kinds of responses. A first kind is to reconsider the way in which we construct and evaluate arguments. This is the route taken by Pollock: he adapts his approach to the determination of defeat status. But there is a second kind of response, namely that the input information is in some sense flawed. For instance, the input theory could be 'inconsistent' or 'incomplete' in a sense that is relevant in the context of argumentation with pros and cons. It is this second kind of response that is pursued in the present paper. We will establish constraints for rules and their exceptions in such a way that they correspond closely to argumentation. The constraints will take the form of logical properties of a consequence relation associated with argumentative input information. With respect to non-monotonic logic more generally, a similar type of response has been followed in the important work that led to the theory of cumulative inference (Kraus et al. 1990 [4]; see also the overview by Makinson 1994 [5]). Until now, the connection of nonmonotonic consequence relations with argumentation seems to only have been touched upon (but see Bochman 2005 [2]).

In this paper, the relation between the nonmonotonic consequence relations and arguments that successfully support their conclusion is studied. The following equivalence will be formally elaborated:

ϕ defeasibly implies ψ ($\phi \mid\!\sim \psi$) if and only if there is an argument from ϕ that successfully supports the conclusion ψ.

For instance, when there is a witness testimony (t), of a witness claiming that the suspect was at the crime scene (p), an argument for the conclusion that the suspect committed the crime (c) can be expressed as $[t, t \Rightarrow p, p \Rightarrow c]$. If the conclusion c is successfully supported by the argument, c is a defeasible consequence of t, denoted $t \mid\!\sim c$. When the witness is lying (l), there is an attacking argument $[l]$, since lying makes a witness testimony unreliable ($l \Rightarrow \neg(t \Rightarrow p)$). As a result, the extended argument $[t, t \Rightarrow p, p \Rightarrow c, e]$ does not successfully support the conclusion c. If there are no other arguments, c is not a defeasible consequence of t and l together ($t \wedge l \not\mid\!\sim c$).

A useful role in the analysis is played by what is here called the *case made* by an argument, that will be defined as the conjunction of all claims made by the argument. For instance, the case made by the argument $[t, t \Rightarrow p, p \Rightarrow c]$ is $t \wedge p \wedge c$.

In our proposal, the normal situation is that, given certain premises, exactly one set of conclusions follows. However, in the context of argumentation it can also occur that more than one position is defensible; a choice still can be made, but the current premises do not decide the choice. Consider for example two witness testimonies (t_1 and t_2), the first witness claiming that the suspect was at the crime scene (p), the second that he was not ($\neg p$). If now both testimonies are of equal strength, no choice between $t_1 \wedge t_2 \wedge p$ and $t_1 \wedge t_2 \wedge \neg p$ can be made. In the formalism proposed here, it is a matter of the input information (not of logic) how this is addressed. It is possible, firstly, to make no choice (neither $t_1 \wedge t_2 \wedge p$ nor $t_1 \wedge t_2 \wedge \neg p$ is defensible), secondly, to not decide about p (making $t_1 \wedge t_2$ defensible, and leaving the status of p and $\neg p$ open) and, thirdly, to consider both options $t_1 \wedge t_2 \wedge p$ and $t_1 \wedge t_2 \wedge \neg p$ defensible. Each of these styles are reasonable under different circumstances (perhaps reflecting different proof standards), so each can be modeled. Of course there is also the possibility that one option is chosen, but that represents a different situation: then one of the testimonies is stronger. When for instance t_1 is stronger, $t_1 \wedge t_2 \wedge p$ is defensible, and $t_1 \wedge t_2 \wedge \neg p$ is not.

Our strategy is as follows. The start is a formalization of rules and the exceptions to them (section 2). Then the notions of argument, argument attack and defensibility are defined (section 3). The core of the paper is section 4 in which argumentation on the basis of rules with exceptions is studied in terms of the properties of nonmonotonic consequence relations. Then follows a discussion of the results (section 5), and the conclusion (section 6).

2. Rules with exceptions

As logical object language, we use a language L for standard truth-functional propositional calculus with connectives $\neg$, $\wedge$, $\vee$, $\leftrightarrow$ and $\top$, and its associated monotonic consequence relation, denoted $\vdash$. The language L is the language in which the premises, conclusions and exceptions that occur in an argument are expressed. Statements are connected in an argument on the basis of the inference and exception rules from which argu-

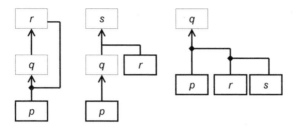

Figure 1. Some arguments

ments are built. Such input information from which arguments are built and subsequently evaluated is formalized in the concept of a *(defeasible) rule system*.

Definition 2.1. A *(defeasible) rule system* is a triple $\mathcal{R} = (L, R, X)$, where R is a set of expressions of the form $\phi \Rightarrow \psi$, where ϕ and ψ are elements of L, and X is a set of expressions of the form $\neg(\phi \Rightarrow \psi)$, where ϕ and ψ are elements of L. The elements of R are the *inference rules* of the system $\mathcal{R}$, the elements of X the *exception rules*.

Inference rules are the *warrants* or *licenses* that allow one to draw (possibly defeasible) conclusions, while exception rules express the *prohibition* to draw a conclusion. Exception rules are here treated on a par with inference rules: both are part of the input information. The conditional connective $\Rightarrow$ is not used in L, so an inference rule $\phi \Rightarrow \psi$ is not an element of L, nor is an exception rule $\neg(\phi \Rightarrow \psi)$. An example of an inference rule is — following the famous example by Pollock — that when an object looks red, it can be inferred that it is red. Formally: $l \Rightarrow r$. An example of an exception rule excluding this inference rule is that when an object looks red and is illuminated by a red light, it cannot be inferred that it is red. Formally: $\neg(l \wedge i \Rightarrow r)$.

In the following, rule systems will be *logical*, in the sense that sentences can be replaced by logically equivalent sentences (from the perspective of the language L and its consequence relation $\vdash$): When $\vdash \phi \leftrightarrow \phi'$ and $\vdash \psi \leftrightarrow \psi'$ it holds that $\phi \Rightarrow \psi \in R$ if and only if $\phi' \Rightarrow \psi' \in R$, and that $\neg(\phi \Rightarrow \psi) \in X$ if and only if $\neg(\phi' \Rightarrow \psi') \in X$.

Exception rules can express exceptions to inference rules. We use the following terminology.

Definition 2.2. Let $\mathcal{R} = (L, R, X)$ be a rule system. A sentence ϵ expresses an *exception to a rule* $\phi \Rightarrow \psi$ in R if $\neg(\phi \wedge \epsilon \Rightarrow \psi) \in X$. A sentence δ *reinstates* the inference from ϕ to ψ excluded by the exception ϵ if $\phi \wedge \epsilon \wedge \delta \Rightarrow \psi \in R$.

Notation: An exception rule $\neg(\phi \wedge \epsilon \Rightarrow \psi)$ is also written $\epsilon \Rightarrow \neg(\phi \Rightarrow \psi)$. An inference rule $\phi \wedge \epsilon \wedge \delta \Rightarrow \psi$ reinstating an inference rule $\phi \Rightarrow \psi$ excluded by the exception rule $\neg(\phi \wedge \epsilon \Rightarrow \psi)$ is also written $\delta \Rightarrow \neg(\epsilon \Rightarrow \neg(\phi \Rightarrow \psi))$. By this notation (which reflects the intended meaning), the inference and exception rules used in the argument on the left in Figure 1 can be represented as $p \Rightarrow q, q \Rightarrow r, r \Rightarrow \neg(p \Rightarrow q)$, as we did in the introduction. The argument on the right uses the rules $p \Rightarrow q, r \Rightarrow \neg(p \Rightarrow q)$ and $s \Rightarrow \neg(r \Rightarrow \neg(p \Rightarrow q))$. By this notation, the arrows in the figure correspond exactly to (nested) conditional sentences (cf. the relation between argument diagrams and the logical language of DefLog developed by Verheij 2003 [10]).

3. Arguments, argument attack and defensible cases

Given a rule system, arguments are the result of chaining inference rules, and counterarguments are the result of exception rules. Our arguments are *dialectical* in the sense that they can contain both pros and cons.

Definition 3.1. Let $\mathcal{R} = (L, R, X)$ be a rule system. Then the set of *arguments* is inductively defined as follows:

1. The empty list $[]$ is an argument from $\top$ making the case $\top$.
2. If $[\alpha_0, \ldots, \alpha_n]$ (with each $\alpha_i \in L \cup R \cup X$) is an argument from ϕ making the case ψ (with $\phi \in L$ and $\psi \in L$), then

   (a) $[\alpha_0, \ldots, \alpha_n, \phi']$ with $\phi' \in L$ is an argument from $\phi \wedge \phi'$ making the case $\psi \wedge \phi'$.
   (b) $[\alpha_0, \ldots, \alpha_n, \phi' \Rightarrow \psi']$ with $\phi' \Rightarrow \psi' \in R$ and $\psi \vdash \phi'$ is an argument from ϕ making the case $\psi \wedge \psi'$.
   (c) $[\alpha_0, \ldots, \alpha_n, \neg(\phi' \Rightarrow \psi')]$ with $\neg(\phi' \Rightarrow \psi') \in X$ and $\psi \vdash \phi'$ is an argument from ϕ making the case ψ.

An argument $[\alpha_0, \ldots, \alpha_n]$ from ϕ making the case ψ has each $\chi \in L$ with $\phi \vdash \chi$ as a *premise*, and each $\chi \in L$ with $\psi \vdash \chi$ as a *conclusion*.

The case made by an argument can be thought of as the 'overall position' supported by the argument; it is the conjunction of all claims made in the argument. Adding a premise or applying an inference rule can extend the case made by an argument, but adding an exception rule does not. For instance, the argument $[p, p \Rightarrow q, q \Rightarrow r]$ is an argument from p making the case $p \wedge q \wedge r$. The argument $[p, p \Rightarrow q, q \Rightarrow r, r \Rightarrow \neg(p \Rightarrow q)]$ (the one on the left in Figure 1), which is equivalent to $[p, p \Rightarrow q, q \Rightarrow r, \neg(p \wedge r \Rightarrow q)]$, is an argument from p making the case $p \wedge q \wedge r$. The argument in the middle of the figure, $[p, p \Rightarrow q, r, q \wedge r \Rightarrow s]$, is an argument from $p \wedge r$ with s as one of its conclusions. It is an argument making the case $p \wedge q \wedge r \wedge s$. The argument on the right is $[p, p \Rightarrow q, r, r \Rightarrow \neg(p \Rightarrow q), s, s \Rightarrow \neg(r \Rightarrow \neg(p \Rightarrow q))]$, or equivalently, $[p, p \Rightarrow q, r, \neg(p \wedge r \Rightarrow q), s, p \wedge r \wedge s \Rightarrow q]$, which is an argument from $p \wedge r \wedge s$ with q as a conclusion. The argument makes the case $p \wedge q \wedge r \wedge s$.

Argument attack is defined in terms of exception rules: argument attack occurs when an argument supports an exception to a conclusion of another argument. Coherent arguments do not attack themselves, and defensible arguments attack their attackers.

Definition 3.2. Let $\mathcal{R} = (L, R, X)$ be a rule system and A an argument from ϕ with a conclusion ψ. Then an argument A' *attacks* A if A' has a conclusion ψ' such that $\neg(\phi \wedge \psi' \Rightarrow \psi) \in X$. An argument is *coherent* if it does not attack itself; otherwise *incoherent*. An argument A from ϕ *defends its case* if A is coherent and attacks all arguments from ϕ that attack A.

An attacking argument can contain the exception rule needed for the attack, but does not have to. So when $\neg(p_1 \wedge e \Rightarrow q)$ (which is the same as $e \Rightarrow \neg(p \Rightarrow q)$) is an exception rule, both $[p_2, p_2 \Rightarrow e]$ and $[p_2, p_2 \Rightarrow e, \neg(p_1 \wedge e \Rightarrow q)]$ attack $[p_1, p_1 \Rightarrow q]$. When $e \Rightarrow \neg(p \Rightarrow q) \in X$, the argument $[e]$ attacks the argument $[p, p \Rightarrow q]$. When $\neg(p \wedge r \Rightarrow q) \in X$, the argument $[p, p \Rightarrow q, q \Rightarrow r]$ is incoherent. To be defensible, an argument needs to attack only those attacking arguments that start from the same premises. For instance, if e is an exception to $p \Rightarrow q$ (and there are no other exceptions in the system), then $[p, p \Rightarrow q]$ is defensible, while $[p, p \Rightarrow q, e]$ is not, as the latter does not defend itself against the attack by the argument $[p, e]$.

It can occur that different cases are defensible, while they do not go together. For instance, one can perhaps both defend a weekend trip to Paris or one to London, but not both (cf. the so-called Nixon diamond in non-monotonic logic). A formal example in the present setting is the following. Consider the rule system with $p \Rightarrow q$, $p \Rightarrow r$, $r \Rightarrow \neg(p \Rightarrow q)$ and $q \Rightarrow \neg(p \Rightarrow r)$ as only (inference and exception) rules. Then the argument $[p, p \Rightarrow q]$ is coherent. The only argument from the same premises attacking $[p, p \Rightarrow q]$ is $[p, p \Rightarrow r]$, and this attack is attacked. So $[p, p \Rightarrow q]$ defends its case. In this system a second argument is defensible, namely by the argument $[p, p \Rightarrow r]$. However, the two cases cannot be defended simultaneously, as they exclude each other. This is reflected by the fact that the argument $[p, p \Rightarrow q, p \Rightarrow r]$ attacks itself.

4. Argumentation on the basis of rules with exceptions as nonmonotonic inference

Now we can start our study of connections between argumentation and rules with exceptions from the perspective of non-monotonic consequence relations. Consider the following properties of consequence relations:

1. (Logical equivalence)
   If $\phi \mathrel{\vert\!\sim} \psi$, $\vdash \phi \leftrightarrow \phi'$ and $\vdash \psi \leftrightarrow \psi'$, then $\phi' \mathrel{\vert\!\sim} \psi'$.
2. (Restricted reflexivity)
   If $\phi \mathrel{\vert\!\sim} \psi$, then $\phi \mathrel{\vert\!\sim} \phi$.
3. (Antecedence)
   If $\phi \mathrel{\vert\!\sim} \psi$, then $\phi \mathrel{\vert\!\sim} \phi \wedge \psi$.
4. (Right weakening)
   If $\phi \mathrel{\vert\!\sim} \psi$ and $\psi \vdash \chi$, then $\phi \mathrel{\vert\!\sim} \chi$.
5. (Conjunctive cautious monotony)
   If $\phi \mathrel{\vert\!\sim} \psi \wedge \chi$, then $\phi \wedge \psi \mathrel{\vert\!\sim} \chi$.

These properties characterize the arguments that do not attack themselves, in the sense of the following two theorems.

Theorem 4.1. *Let $\mathcal{R} = (L, R, X)$ be a rule system and let $\phi \mathrel{\vert\!\sim_c} \psi$ denote that there is a coherent argument from ϕ with a conclusion ψ. Then $\mathrel{\vert\!\sim_c}$ obeys the properties (1) to (5) above.*

Theorem 4.2. *Let $\mathrel{\vert\!\sim}$ be a consequence relation obeying the properties (1) to (5) above, and $\mathcal{R}_{\vert\!\sim}$ the associated rule system defined by $R_{\vert\!\sim} := \{\phi \Rightarrow \psi \mid \phi \mathrel{\vert\!\sim} \psi\}$, and $X_{\vert\!\sim} := \{\neg(\phi \Rightarrow \psi) \mid \phi \mathrel{\not\vert\!\sim} \psi\}$. Then the following are equivalent:*

1. $\phi \mathrel{\vert\!\sim} \psi$
2. $[\phi, \phi \Rightarrow \psi]$ *is coherent.*
3. *There is an $\mathcal{R}_{\vert\!\sim}$-argument from ϕ with a conclusion ψ that is coherent.*

When properties (1) to (5) hold, we speak of *coherent argumentation*.

A coherent argument does not always defend itself. Consider for instance the rule system consisting of the inference rules $a \Rightarrow b$ and $a \Rightarrow c$ and the exception rule $\neg(a \wedge c \Rightarrow b)$. Then the argument $[a, a \Rightarrow b]$ from a making the case $a \wedge b$ is coherent, but does not defend itself against the attack by $[a, a \Rightarrow c]$.

The following additional property is needed to ensure defensibility:

6. (Mutual attack)
   If $\phi \mathrel{\vert\!\sim} \psi$, $\phi \mathrel{\vert\!\sim} \chi$ and $\phi \wedge \psi \mathrel{\not\vert\!\sim} \chi$, then $\phi \wedge \chi \mathrel{\not\vert\!\sim} \psi$.

Theorem 4.3. *Let $\mathcal{R} = (L, R, X)$ be a rule system and let $\phi \mathrel{\vert\!\sim}_c \psi$ denote that there is a defensible argument from ϕ with a conclusion ψ. Then $\mathrel{\vert\!\sim}_c$ obeys the properties (1) to (6) above.*

Theorem 4.4. *Let $\mathrel{\vert\!\sim}$ be a consequence relation obeying the properties (1) to (6) above, and $\mathcal{R}_{\vert\!\sim}$ the associated rule system defined by $R_{\vert\!\sim} := \{\phi \Rightarrow \psi \mid \phi \mathrel{\vert\!\sim} \psi\}$, and $X_{\vert\!\sim} := \{\neg(\phi \Rightarrow \psi) \mid \phi \mathrel{\not\vert\!\sim} \psi\}$. Then the following are equivalent:*

1. $\phi \mathrel{\vert\!\sim} \psi$
2. $[\phi, \phi \Rightarrow \psi]$ *is defensible.*
3. *There is an $\mathcal{R}_{\vert\!\sim}$-argument from ϕ with a conclusion ψ that is defensible.*

When properties (1) to (6) hold, we speak of *defensible argumentation*.

Can an argument always be extended by an inference rule to which there is no exception? The answer is no. Consider for instance the rule system consisting of the inference rules $a \Rightarrow b$ and $a \wedge b \Rightarrow c$ and the exception rule $\neg(a \Rightarrow b \wedge c)$. Then the argument $[a, a \Rightarrow b]$ making the case $a \wedge b$ is coherent and the inference rule $a \wedge b \Rightarrow c$ has a satisfied antecedent and no exception given $a \wedge b$. Still $A = [a, a \Rightarrow b, a \wedge b \Rightarrow c]$ is not coherent as it attacks itself. One can say that the argument is defeated by 'sequential weakening' (cf. Verheij 1996 [9]). The following property forbids such defeat by sequential weakening.

7. (Conjunctive cumulative transitivity, Conjunctive cut)
   If $\phi \mathrel{\vert\!\sim} \psi$ and $\phi \wedge \psi \mathrel{\vert\!\sim} \chi$, then $\phi \mathrel{\vert\!\sim} \psi \wedge \chi$.

Given the other properties, this property is equivalent to (Conclusions are compatible or mutually exclusive) 'If $\phi \mathrel{\vert\!\sim} \psi$ and $\phi \mathrel{\vert\!\sim} \chi$, then either $\phi \mathrel{\vert\!\sim} \psi \wedge \chi$ or ($\phi \wedge \psi \mathrel{\not\vert\!\sim} \chi$ and $\phi \wedge \chi \mathrel{\not\vert\!\sim} \psi$)'.

When there is no defeat by sequential weakening, coherent argumentation implies defensible argumentation, as can be seen using the following proposition.

Proposition 4.5. *If a consequence relation obeys (Logical equivalence), (Conjunctive cautious monotony) and (Conjunctive cumulative transitivity, Conjunctive cut), then it obeys (Mutual attack).*

When properties (1) to (7) hold, we speak of *reason-based argumentation*.

5. Discussion

We have looked at argumentation and rules with exceptions from the perspective of nonmonotonic consequence relations.

The first kind of inference that we distinguished was *coherent argumentation*, obeying the properties (1) to (5). It is related to the system that Bochman (2001, p. 140 [1]) refers to as basic inference and that goes back to van Benthem (1984 [7]). Coherent argumentation is somewhat more minimal than basic inference. For basic inference, (Restricted reflexivity) also obtains, but in the unrestricted form (Reflexivity) $\phi \mathrel{|\!\sim} \phi$. We keep the restriction to allow the possibility of incoherent premises, i.e., premises from which no conclusions can be drawn (the 'no extensions' possibility in non-monotonic logic). Basic inference also has the property (Deduction) 'If $\phi \wedge \psi \mathrel{|\!\sim} \chi$, then $\phi \mathrel{|\!\sim} \psi \rightarrow \chi$', which does not in general obtain for our systems. The property (Conjunctive cautious monotony) of basic inference holds for coherent argumentation. In our approach, this property reflects that an argument does not attack itself.

The second kind of inference was *defensible argumentation*, obeying the properties (1) to (6). Dung's notion of admissibility (1995 [3]) for abstract argumentation frameworks is close in spirit to our notion of a defensible argument: an admissible set of arguments in the sense of Dung is one that does not attack itself and that attacks its attackers. However, whereas Dung abstracts from arguments structure and argument attack is given, here arguments are constructed using (defeasible) inference rules, and argument attack is the result of exception rules. Also, for the most constrained kind of inference that we have considered, reason-based argumentation, the argument attack relation is particularly well-behaved: arguments are either compatible or mutually attacking.

The third kind of inference that we distinguished is *reason-based argumentation*. Of the three systems proposed, it is closest to cumulative inference as studied by Kraus et al. (1990 [4]). Like basic inference mentioned above, cumulative inference has full (Reflexivity), but a more important difference is that it has (And) 'If $\phi \mathrel{|\!\sim} \psi$ and $\phi \mathrel{|\!\sim} \chi$, then $\phi \mathrel{|\!\sim} \psi \wedge \chi$'. By (And), in cumulative inference, conclusions can always be drawn simultaneously, while in our systems one conclusion can exclude another. An example is the rule system consisting of the inference rules $a \Rightarrow b$ and $a \Rightarrow c$ and the exception rules $\neg(a \wedge b \Rightarrow c)$ and $\neg(a \wedge c \Rightarrow b)$. Then $a \mathrel{|\!\sim} b$ and $a \mathrel{|\!\sim} c$ (using defensible arguments), but $a \mathrel{|\!\!\not\sim} b \wedge c$ (there is even no coherent argument). Cumulative inference also has a stronger version of our (Cumulative cautious monotony), namely (Cautious monotony) 'If $\phi \mathrel{|\!\sim} \psi$ and $\phi \mathrel{|\!\sim} \chi$, then $\phi \wedge \psi \mathrel{|\!\sim} \chi$'. When (And) holds, the difference disappears. The property (Cut) 'If $\phi \mathrel{|\!\sim} \psi$ and $\phi \wedge \psi \mathrel{|\!\sim} \chi$, then $\phi \mathrel{|\!\sim} \chi$' of cumulative inference holds for reason-based argumentation, but in the stronger form of (Conjunctive cumulative transitivity, Conjunctive cut). Since (And) does not obtain for reason-based argumentation, (Cut) is a bit too weak for what is needed; our (Conjunctive cumulative transitivity, Conjunctive cut) does the job. It seems to be a new proposal. As a consequence of the fact that our constraints are not the same as those for cumulative inference, the preferential model semantics of cumulative inference does not apply to reason-based argumentation. However, since the constraints of reason-based argumentation inference do obtain for cumulative inference, our results connecting rules with exceptions and argumentation work also for cumulative inference. In other words, one could say that our approach provides an 'argumentation interpretation' of cumulative inference.

Veltman (1996 [8]) has studied rules with exceptions semantically. He does so in the context of update semantics. In his system, rules can have what he calls 'nonaccidental exceptions', i.e., exceptions that obtain conditionally. He focuses on contradicting exceptions and does not treat Pollock's undercutting defeaters.

B. Verheij / Argumentation and Rules with Exceptions

6. Conclusion

In this paper, argumentation has been formalized in such a way that the arguments that are constructed using rules with exceptions can be studied from the perspective of non-monotonic consequence relations. Properties have been given that characterize when arguments are coherent (i.e., not self-attacking) and when they are defensible. Three kinds of inference have been distinguished in terms of the properties of consequence relations: coherent argumentation, in which arguments do not attack themselves, defensible argumentation, in which arguments attack all their attackers, and reason-based argumentation, in which arguments can always be extended when there is a non-excluded rule with satisfied antecedent. In reason-based argumentation, there is no 'defeat by sequential weakening' (cf. Verheij 1996 [9]).

References

[1] A. Bochman. *A logical theory of nonmonotonic inference and belief change*. Springer, Berlin, 2001.
[2] A. Bochman. Propositional argumentation and causal reasoning. In *International Joint Conference on Artificial Intelligence*, volume 19, pages 388–393, 2005.
[3] P.M. Dung. On the acceptability of arguments and its fundamental role in nonmonotonic reasoning, logic programming and n-person games. *Artificial Intelligence*, 77:321–357, 1995.
[4] S. Kraus, D. Lehmann, and M. Magidor. Nonmonotonic reasoning, preferential models and cumulative logics. *Artificial Intelligence*, 44:167–207, 1990.
[5] D. Makinson. General patterns in nonmonotonic reasoning. In D.M. Gabbay, C.J. Hogger, and J.A. Robinson, editors, *Handbook of Logic in Artificial Intelligence and Logic Programming. Volume 3. Nonmonotonic Reasoning and Uncertain Reasoning*, pages 35–110. Clarendon Press, Oxford, 1994.
[6] J.L. Pollock. *Cognitive Carpentry: A Blueprint for How to Build a Person*. The MIT Press, Cambridge (Massachusetts), 1995.
[7] J. van Benthem. Foundations of conditional logic. *Journal of Philosophical Logic*, pages 303–349, 1984.
[8] F. Veltman. Defaults in update semantics. *Journal of Philosophical Logic*, 25(3):221–261, 1996.
[9] B. Verheij. *Rules, Reasons, Arguments. Formal studies of argumentation and defeat*. Dissertation Universiteit Maastricht, Maastricht, 1996.
[10] B. Verheij. Artificial argument assistants for defeasible argumentation. *Artificial Intelligence*, 150(1–2):291–324, 2003.

Computational Models of Argument
P. Baroni et al. (Eds.)
IOS Press, 2010
doi:10.3233/978-1-60750-619-5-463

Lower Bounds on Argument Verification in Computational Dialectic

Gerard Vreeswijk[a]

[a] *Utrecht University, The Netherlands*

Abstract. An argument may be considered sound ("admissible" or "RSA-compliable" in informal logic) if it is well-formed and fulfills a number of reasonable semantic criteria. When agents exchange arguments, not all incoming arguments are sound.

This paper formulates two results. First, it gives lower bounds for the verification rate of incoming arguments, given an estimate of the percentage of incoming sound arguments and a predefined tolerance of error. Second, it prescribes what percentage of incoming arguments must be verified if there is no prescribed error tolerance, but there is a tradeoff between cost of verification and cost of error.

Keywords. Computational dialectic, defeasible reasoning, argumentation and machine learning, probability and statistics, numeric status assignment.

1. Introduction

Computational dialectic studies argumentation performed by computers. The motivation is that computers are sometimes better debaters than human beings, because they have the resources, patience and precision to argue about complex issues.

A problem with computational dialectic is that argumentation software (or any software for that matter) is by nature unable to understand the arguments it processes. At its very best a computer program knows how to manipulate formal structures but actually does not have a clue what these structures are about. This is a problem, especially in a dialectic context. When an agent receives arguments from another agent, these arguments typically contain new material of which the validity can only be verified by actually looking at the content of the argument offered. Such a verification can only be performed by a human being. If Agent A is engaged in a dispute it can of course throw an argument back at B but then B has to make sure that this response makes sense, has meaning and is relevant. Suppose, for example, that A is a conscientious agent that is pretty sure that every argument it puts forward is double checked and makes sense. Agent B, on the other hand, is a formalist, and is programmed to play the argument game in a way that is formally correct. Otherwise, B does not care much about the contents of its arguments. If we further stick to the rule that the one which has the last argument wins, then it is not hard to imagine that Agent B will win most of its disputes, simply by countering all arguments of A with formal nonsense. Thus, a problem with computational dialectic is that disputes cannot be entirely conducted on formal grounds and must in some way at some moments be checked back to reality.

This paper addresses the following problem:

"What percentage of incoming arguments must be verified to keep the status assignment of arguments in line with the actual status assignment?"

A small example may clarify the problem. Suppose A puts forward argument a. It may then happen that there is an agent B that puts forward b to attack a. (For example because A asked for opposition to test a.) Normally, then, b would defeat a so that in most argument semantics s, we would have $s(a) = 0$ and $s(b) = 1$. If, however, A knows that only 80% of B's arguments are sound it may derive that a is out with probability 0.2. To eliminate this uncertainty, A can select b for verification. Verification involves costs but may be beneficial if A has serious interests to be relatively sure about the status of a proper, for example, if assigning a wrong status to a would incur a heavy penalty. This is the problem defined in a nutshell.

Given that errors are costly, a related problem is the following:

"What percentage of incoming arguments must be verified if there no prescribed error tolerance, but there is a tradeoff between cost of verification and cost of error?"

This problem is more of an economic problem, and has connections to optimisation in operations research and microeconomy [5,11].

The research reported here falls in the category of numeric status assignment to arguments. Existing research in this area [2,4,9,10,12,15,16,17] typically involves weights, probabilities or variable degrees of justification. However, most theories are concerned with uncertainty on attack relations, rather than with uncertainty on the arguments themselves. Moreover, the domain of application of the above mentioned research is not so much verification, and deducing lower bounds for verification, as well as different ways to represent uncertainty in argument graphs. An exception is [4]. However, this work is concerned is with the computational complexity of deriving *greatest* (i.e., precise, or optimal) lower bounds for tolerance. On a technical note the theory of Bayesian belief networks [6,14] is more than capable to compute exact complementary probabilities in defeat graphs. Again, the point is that error estimation does not need exact rates of verification. Rather, it needs simple (preferably polynomial) lower bounds. These are the points addressed in this paper.

The research reported here also falls in the category of cost-benefit analysis of (formal) argumentation. Work of [8,13] is relevant in this respect. However, the cost-benefit analysis in, for instance, [13] is contemplative and the graphs therein are merely suggestive, in the sense that they are based on neither a mathematical analysis nor on data from experiments.

This paper is organised as follows.

- Section 2 describes a model for argument verification. It also attempts to describe the underlying assumptions and the context.
- Section 3 is concerned with the first problem. It determines two lower bounds for argument verification, one based on an estimate of the percentage of sound arguments where attack is independent, and one based on an estimate of the percentage of sound arguments where attack is dependent (in the sense that additional attackers that are "in" do not further influence the status of the argument attacked).
- Section 4 is concerned with the second problem. It determines a verification rate in cases where both verification and errors involve costs.
- Section 5 discusses related work in more detail.

2. Model

To model argument verification, a number of concepts must be introduced, such as "player," "agent," "soundness," "justly accepted," "verification rate," and "probability of receiving a sound argument". These concepts are now introduced.

Players and agents

The present model presupposes *players* and *agents*. Players are human beings that use agents to represent their interests. Agents argue on behalf of players by constructing arguments that are then exchanged with other agents (owned by other players) Agents argue autonomously. Thus, argumentation takes place without immediate supervision of (or interference by) players. Because agents cannot have knowledge of the semantics of arguments, the model assumes that players provide agents with the material to construct arguments. (Think of a knowledge base of facts and inference rules.) Such a supply process would typically happen off line and is beyond the cope of this paper.

Soundness

The present model assumes that arguments must satisfy certain standards of construction and sensibility in order to be entitled to play a role in the argumentation process at all.

In mathematical logic, a proof is considered to be sound if all its steps are semantically valid. Similarly, an argument might considered to be sound if a reasonable player after inspection is forced to accept this argument in and of itself, provided it is not attacked (let alone defeated) by other arguments. The following are examples of conditions that may be demanded.

- The argument conforms to elementary syntactic standards. [For example, it is delivered in the agreed upon argument interchange format (AIF).]
- Inferences are instances of accepted rules of inference. [Further standards of acceptance may then be that rules of inference must be common knowledge, or must be traceable to established argument inference scheme repositories, or must simply be known to the receiver.]
- Rules of inference must have been applied correctly.
- Inferences connect logically from one sub-argument to the next.
- Variable-substitutions have been applied correctly.
- The argument makes sense. [This is vague, but the idea is that players have the right to filter out dialectic spam.]
- Premise check. Some theories of formal argumentation demand that, for an argument to be sound, the premises must also accepted by the receiver. [Some other theories leave this to the dialectic process itself, and then such a check does not need to be performed.]
- The argument put forward in the capacity of an attacker must indeed attack the argument it claims to attack. [This may include checks on negation of conclusions of (sub-) arguments, and checks on the strength of the attacking argument that is minimally required.]

There may well be more conditions.[1]

An essential aspect of the model is that most but not all arguments emitted by agents are sound. Agents receive arguments in response to the arguments they produce and emit. The idea is that players sample a small fraction of these arguments to verify their soundness. The model assumes that the verification of arguments is a process with certain costs. Hence, not all arguments can be verified. On the other hand, players cannot totally refrain from checking arguments, because they have to to avoid that their agents are fooled by (formally correct but) unsound arguments.

Verification rate

The model distinguishes two important events. First, there is the event that a player decides not to accept an incoming argument at face value, and selects it to examine its structure and content. It is assumed that verification is performed randomly at a certain rate θ, which is called the *verification rate*. Further, it is assumed that a verification always and unambiguously reveals the status of an argument, i.e., a verification reveals whether the verified argument is indeed sound. The parameter θ is within control of the player, and can be used to enforce a certain quality standard in processing arguments. This idea is further elaborated in Sec. 3. Second, there is the event that a player receives a sound argument. We assume this is a random event that is beyond the control of the player and is Bernoulli distributed with parameter η. (Cf. [18].) It is assumed that the soundness is independent of verification. I.e., it is assumed that $\Pr(\eta) = \Pr(\eta|\theta)$. Since the soundness of arguments may depend on the agents that send them, it is possible to differentiate η per agent i, thus working with different probabilities η_i. The idea to estimate these probabilities through sampling is further elaborated in Sec. 4.

If a player accepts an argument that happens to be sound (a player may not know this due to lack of verification), then that argument is said to be *justly accepted*. For the purpose of the analysis, the probability that incoming arguments are justly accepted can be reduced to the probability

$$\alpha = 1 - (1 - \theta)(1 - \eta).$$

The idea is to bring α close to one, either by knowing that most incoming arguments are sound, or else by setting a high verification rate.

Independence

Let a be an argument, and let $Att(a)$ denote the set of all possible attackers of a. The justified acceptance of attackers is not necessarily independent. Thus, it is not immediately clear that a justified acceptance of elements in $Att(a)$, for any argument a, are independent events. More specifically, an assumption of independence rests on two assumptions. The first assumption is that players select arguments for inspection at random. This is a

---

[1]The informal notion of soundness as it is introduced here can be compared to the notion of admissibility as it is known in informal logic. There, an argument or chain of reasoning is said to be *admissible* if it meets the requirements of the "RSA triangle," viz. relevance, sufficiency and acceptability [7]. (The last bullet point of the list thus seem to refer to relevance.) The term soundness is adhered to here nevertheless because the term admissibility already possesses a specific meaning in computational theories of argument, mainly due to [3].

reasonable assumption, and if it does not hold we may simply enforce it by stipulating that players do select arguments randomly. The second assumption is that the soundness of attackers is not correlated. This latter assumption is somewhat more controversial, because one may expect that some arguments are more prone to rebuttal by unsound arguments than others. (Think of an irrefutable argument that is otherwise highly undesirable from a certain agent's point of view.) For now, this second assumption is adopted for reasons of simplicity. (Later, in a section on the so-called min norm, a solution in cases where attackers do in fact mutually reinforce their soundness is discussed.)

If the above assumptions hold, then the probability that a is justly accepted is given by

$$j(a) = \alpha \cdot \Pi_{b \in Att(a)}(1 - j(b)) \tag{1}$$

(If $Att(a) = \emptyset$ we assume this product is 1 and $j(a) = \alpha$.) It is important to emphasise that Eq. (1) is not a definition, but follows from the laws of probability.

Definition 2.1 (Probabilistic status assignment). The process of incorporating probabilities of acceptance due to not verifying unsound arguments is called *probabilistic status assignment*.

The *error* of a probabilistic status assignment j on a particular argument a is defined as $|s(a) - j(a)|$, where $s :$ Arguments $\rightarrow \{0, 1\}$ is a conventional status assignment on arguments. (If there is more than one status assignment s, for example in the case of preferred or stable semantics, then one such status assignment must be chosen.) For a set of arguments, the error is defined as the supremum of the errors of the individual arguments. (For finite sets this is just the maximum.)

Example 2.1. Suppose

$$a \leftarrow b \leftarrow c \leftarrow d.$$

In a Dung type argumentation system [3], $j(a) = j(c) = 0$ and $j(b) = j(d) = 1$. With a probability α that an argument is justly accepted, we have $j(d) = \alpha$, $j(c) = \alpha(1 - \alpha) = \alpha - \alpha^2$, $j(b) = \alpha(1 - \alpha + \alpha^2) = \alpha - \alpha^2 + \alpha^3$, and so forth. Generally, $j(a) = \Sigma_{i=1}^{n}(-1)^{n+1}\alpha^n$ if a is at the end of a linear defeat chain of length n, which goes to $\alpha/(\alpha + 1)$ for large n.

Remarks:

1. This example already hints at lower bounds for probabilistic status assignment of root arguments, since $j^2(a) \rightsquigarrow 1$ (reinstatement) whenever $\alpha \rightsquigarrow 1$, for every n, and for every argument in the chain of length n.
2. In this example, defeat is discontinuous for large n and $\alpha = 1$. Later results that assume continuity must therefore stipulate finite attack chains.

3. Results

This section determines two lower bounds for argument verification, one based on an estimate of the percentage of sound arguments where attack is independent, and one based on an estimate of the percentage of sound arguments where attack is dependent.

Claim 3.1. *Probabilistic status assignment is continuous. In particular, the following two properties hold.*

1. *If, for at least one $b \in Att(a)$: $j(b) \leadsto 1$, then $j(a) \leadsto 0$.*
2. *If, for all $b \in Att(a)$, $j(b) \leadsto 0$, then $j(a) \leadsto 1$.*

Proof. This claim follows from the continuity of functions of the form

$$f : [0,1]^n \to [0,1] : (x_1, \ldots, x_n) \mapsto \alpha \cdot \Pi_{i=1}^n (1 - x_i)$$

for every integer $n \geq 0$ and every real constant $0 \leq \alpha \leq 1$.   □

(In the borderline case $n = 0$, f reduces to a constant function of the form $\{0\} \to [0,1] : 0 \mapsto \alpha$ which is also continuous.)

The two above properties inductively apply through attack chains of finite length, hence to finite (or finite parts of) Dung graphs. This observation leads to the following claim.

Claim 3.2. *Suppose the length of attack chains is bounded. Then for every $\varepsilon, \eta > 0$ there exists a verification rate $\theta > 0$ such that the error on probabilistic status assignments does not exceed ε.*

Proof. Let $\varepsilon, \eta > 0$ be given. Due to Claim (3.1) and the boundedness of attack chains there exists an $0 < \alpha \leq 1$ such that the error of status assignments j on individual arguments does not exceed ε. Solving $\alpha = 1 - (1 - \theta)(1 - \eta)$ for θ yields the desired verification rate θ.   □

Remarks:

1. Because $\theta = (\eta - \alpha)/(\eta - 1)$, a verification rate only exists if $\eta < 1$.
2. A player can enforce 100% soundness on accepted arguments by letting $\alpha = 1$. However, then also $\theta = 1$, which means that every incoming argument must be verified. Since it is assumed that the verification of arguments is a costly operation, θ, hence α, should be kept as low as possible.

Claim 3.2 is qualitative. Given $\varepsilon, \eta > 0$, it does not specify a concrete value for θ. It only specifies that such a value exists.

We now try to derive a concrete lower bound for θ. To this end, Claim 3.1 is sharpened.

Claim 3.3. *Probabilistic status assignment satisfies the following two properties.*

1. *If $j(b) \geq 1 - \iota$ for at least one $b \in Att(a)$, then $j(a) \leq \alpha\varepsilon$.*
2. *If $j(b) \leq \varepsilon$ for all $b \in Att(a)$, then $j(a) \geq \alpha(1 - \varepsilon)^n$.*

Proof. Elementary.   □

Item (1), is not problematic, since the probability of acceptance remains smaller than ε. This probability may then be propagated further into the defeat chain. Item (2), however, is more problematic because the error (the difference between pure defeat status and probabilistic defeat status) increases every step of the defeat chain, and there is nothing we can do about it, i.e., $\alpha(1-\varepsilon)^n$ is the greatest lower bound on acceptance in case all attackers remain undefeated with probability ε.

To derive a concrete upper bound for θ nonetheless, the attention will be focused on

$$\phi(x) = \alpha(1-\varepsilon)^n.$$

For the moment, it will be assumed that the number of attackers an argument may have is bounded by $n = 2$. Later it will be argued that this upper bound can easily be generalised to arbitrary $n > 2$.

The function ϕ^2 can be used to estimate the error in an elementary defence chain of length two. A problem with ϕ^2 and iterations of it, is that it is difficult to seize its amplitude for repeated applications of ϕ:

$$\phi^0(\alpha) = \alpha$$

$$\phi^1(\alpha) = \alpha(1-\alpha)^2$$

$$\phi^2(\alpha) = \alpha(1-\alpha(1-\alpha)^2)^2 = \alpha - 2\alpha^2 + 5\alpha^3 - 6\alpha^4 + 6\alpha^5 - 4\alpha^6 + \alpha^7$$

$$\vdots$$

One way to predict the development of these expressions is to use generating functions. (These are formal power series in one indeterminate, whose coefficients encode information about a sequence of numbers and that is indexed by the natural numbers.) However, a problem is that different levels of attack produce different polynomials.

Another solution is to find a simple (preferably polynomial) function on $[0,1]$ that acts as a lower bound on iterations of ϕ^2. This method actually works, at least for $n = 2$. To this end, there is the following result.

Lemma 3.4. *Let* $\phi(x) = \alpha(1-x)^2$. *Then for every function* $f : [0,1] \to R$,

$$x^\kappa \leq f(x) \quad \Rightarrow \quad x^\kappa \leq \phi^2 f(x). \tag{2}$$

where $\kappa = 3.81884154$.

Proof. The proof amounts to verifying that

$$\alpha(1-\alpha(1-\alpha^\kappa)^2)^2 \geq \alpha^\kappa,$$

for $0 \leq \alpha \leq 1$, which is indeed the case. $\qquad\qquad\square$

Remarks:

1. The inequality is tight. That is, there is a value for α for which the inequality becomes an equality. (This is for $\alpha = 3/4$.)

2. The inequality does not hold for other values of κ. (For other values of κ, the function $\alpha(1 - \alpha(1 - \alpha^\kappa)^2)^2 - \alpha^\kappa$ possess two zero points near $\alpha = 3/4$.)

Thus, there do not exist better lower estimations of the form x^κ, and κ is unique.

Theorem 3.5. *Suppose the length of attack chains is bounded, and all arguments have at most two attackers. Let $\varepsilon, \eta > 0$ be given, and let θ be the verification rate. If*

$$\theta \geq \frac{\eta - (1 - \varepsilon)^{1/3.8188415}}{\eta - 1} \tag{3}$$

the error of status assignments j on individual arguments does not exceed ε.

Proof. Two different types of attack structures are considered: attack structures that are "saturated," and those that are not. An attack structure is called *saturated*[2] if all attack chains have length $2n$, for some $n \geq 0$. A saturated attack structure is the worst case with respect to errors in probabilistic status assignment. (As a verification: if the *depth* of a saturated attack structure is defined as the length of the attack chains in it, then the number of arguments in a saturated structure of depth n is $2^n - 1$.)

Case I. Saturated. If the error in leaves (arguments without attackers) is smaller than $1 - \alpha$, then Lemma 3.4 ensures that the error of the root argument in a saturated attack structure is smaller than $1 - \alpha^\kappa$. Solving $\varepsilon \leq 1 - \alpha^\kappa$ for ε yields $\alpha \geq (1 - \varepsilon)^{1/\kappa}$. As in the qualitative continuity claim above (Claim 3.2), the required verification rate θ is obtained by solving $\alpha = 1 - (1 - \theta)(1 - \eta)$ for θ, which yields Eq. (3).

Case II. Other. These are obtained by deleting paths of length one, *or* paths of length two, from saturated structures, starting at the leaves. Every structure embedded in a saturated structure may thus be obtained. For paths of length one Claim 3.3.1 applies; for paths of length two Lemma 3.4 applies (but then to less iterations of ϕ^2). □

Although the length of attack chains must be bounded, it is not limited. This is due to the fact that inequality (2) may be applied an arbitrary number of times.

The min norm

The product in Eq. (1) is an iterated composition of binary products. A binary product is a special case of a so-called *triangular norm* (t-norm). A t-norm $\wedge : [0,1]^2 \to [0,1]$ is the continuous counterpart (and a conservative extension) of the discrete conjunction $\wedge : \{0,1\}^2 \to \{0,1\}$ and is by definition commutative, associative, monotone, and has 1 as a unity element.[3] It is a well-known fact that the ordinary min-function on $[0,1]^2$ is, despite its name, the largest t-norm. I.e., if $\wedge$ is a t-norm, then $\wedge(x,y) \leq min\{x,y\}$ for all x, y. In particular, the min norm is larger than the product norm. To represent the fact that the number of undefeated attackers is irrelevant in determining the defeat status of an argument, the use of the min-norm rather than the product-norm in Eq. (1) might be considered. In this way

$$j(a) = \alpha \cdot min\{1 - j(b) \mid b \in Att(a)\}.$$

---

[2]This is a bit of a pretentious term. On the other hand, it seems to cover the load.
[3]Monotonicity: if $b \leq c$ then $a \wedge b \leq a \wedge c$. One as unity: $a \wedge 1 = a$.

Unlike the product norm, the min norm does not "fade out" during propagation. Therefore, the minimum verification rate θ in this case is much easier to deduce.

Theorem 3.6. *Let $\varepsilon, \eta > 0$ be given. If the verification rate θ is such that*

$$\theta \geq 1 + \frac{\varepsilon}{\eta - 1} \tag{4}$$

then the error of status assignments j on individual arguments does not exceed ε.

Proof. Set $\alpha = 1 - \varepsilon$ and solve $\alpha = 1 - (1 - \theta)(1 - \eta)$ for θ. $\square$

Contrary to the conditions in Theorem 3.5, there are no restrictions on the number of attackers. Also Eq. (4) is much simpler. The downside is that status assignment based on the min norm lacks a probabilistic basis.

4. Learning

This section is concerned with estimating the probability of receiving sound arguments, and with tradeoffs that are involved between costs of verification and costs of errors.

If η_i is the probability that an argument received from player i is sound, then this probability may be estimated through exploration (i.e., by sampling arguments manually for verification). However, sampling is a human activity and might therefore be costly. On the other hand, it is reasonable to assume that errors involve costs as well. Thus, there is a tradeoff.

Since verification is a human activity, it is unreasonable to assume that verification costs linearly depend on the verification rate. (For computers this would be a reasonable assumption.) Instead, the law of diminishing marginal returns for human labour prescribes that verification has increasing relative costs, say $C_1 \theta^\beta$, for some constant $C_1 > 0$ and $\beta > 1$. (Cf. [5,11].) Further, it is assumed that the costs for errors is C_2 per error per argument, $C_2 > 0$. The expected cost is then

$$C(\theta) = C_1 \theta^\beta + C_2 \varepsilon$$

Because the error ε can be controlled by θ, the expected cost effectively depends on θ and η. For example, if θ is determined by Eq. (3), then the expected cost per argument would be

$$C(\theta) = C_1 \theta^\beta + C_2 (1 - (\theta + \eta - \theta\eta)^\kappa) \tag{5}$$

where the right term is obtained by solving Eq. (3) for ε, and $\kappa = 3.81884154$. In this way, the verification rate θ is directly controlled by the estimated probability η.

As an example let $C_1 = 8$, $C_2 = 9$, $\beta = 2$ and $\eta = 0.65$. This yields Fig. 1, where the plots faithfully depict the real functions. The dashed decreasing curve represents the expected cost of error as a function of θ, the dashed increasing curve represents the expected cost of verification, and the solid hanging curve represents the cost function. The dotted lines accentuate the concavity and convexity of the cost functions. The vertical dotted line represents the unique stationary point with minimal costs.

The cost function is not always convex. If it is, however, then there is a proper tradeoff, and cost is minimised for the unique stationary point for which $dC(\theta)/d\theta = 0$ ($\theta = 0.38$ in the example). If the law of increasing costs of human argument verification does not hold, then the cost function is never convex, and interesting tradeoffs would never occur. Hence, the assumption that human argument verification suffers from diminishing returns, is crucial to the above analysis.

5. Related work

Conventional argument semantics (with names as grounded, stable, and preferred) are two-valued. They map arguments to either one of two statuses, viz. "in" and "out". Lately much work is done to make this picture more colourful and realistic. Various avenues are explored such as variable degrees of justification, graduality in acceptance, probability of acceptance, and inconsistency tolerance in weighted argument systems.

The philosopher and epistemologist Pollock probably was one of the first who proposed to incorporate uncertainty in formal theories of argumentation. He did this by means of so-called *variable degrees of justification.*[4] In [15] Pollock

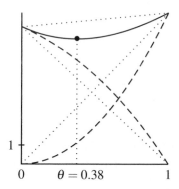

Fig. 1: Tradeoff between cost of verification and cost of errors.

addresses the question how the degree of justification of a belief is determined. It is argued that argument strength cannot be modelled by probability. Instead the so-called weakest link principle applies, which says that the degree of justification an argument is the minimum of the degrees of justification of its premises and the strengths of the reasons employed in the argument. The objective of [15] is to epistemically justify a certain numerical status assignment, rather than to calculate probabilities on two-values assignments.

Another important contribution to numeric status assignment is made by Cayrol *et al.* [2]. They propose to differentiate among acceptance of arguments by means of what is called *graduality in acceptance*. This notion partitions arguments in more than the two usual subsets of "in" and "out". Cayrol *et al.* [2] as well as Besnard *et al.* [1, p. 97] also introduce the important concepts intrinsic vs. interaction-based values of arguments. The intrinsic value of an argument represents its degree of acceptance independent of its interactions with other arguments. The interaction-based value, then, represents the degree of acceptance after it has been tested dialectically.

---

[4]Pollock might be considered as the founding father of computational dialectic. He was an established philosopher with a remarkable affinity for computer programming.

A different but related approach is taken by Riveret *et al.*[16,17]. There, probabilistic status assignments are used to let parties pro and con develop strategies on the basis of their appreciation of the probability that an adjudicator will accept their arguments or the arguments of their adversary. Like the work presented here, this approach also incorporates costs and gains that must be balanced to obtain a maximal expected utility from engaging in a legal dispute. Paper [17]

Dunne *et al.* [4] study inconsistency tolerance in *weighted argument systems* (WASs), which are Dung systems in which attacks are associated with a weight, indicating the relative strength of the attack. An inconsistency budget is used that characterises how much inconsistency one is prepared to tolerate: given an inconsistency budget β, attacks are disregarded up to a total cost of β. The authors suggest that weights may represent a subjective belief (in the form of a ranking or a probability), or a number of votes. For example, a weight p on the attack of argument b on argument a might be understood as the belief that (a decision-maker considers) a is false when b is true. This interpretation comes very close to the model presented in this paper. Dunne *et al.* are also involved also with lower bounds for tolerance, as they formulate a problem to find the smallest amount of inconsistency that is needed to tolerate in order to make s (where s is a discrete status assignment) a solution.

From a more general perspective, the research presented here fits in a recent line of research that investigates the costs and benefits of engaging in (formal) argument. Karunatillake *et al.* [8] and Paglieri *et al.* [13], for example, are concerned with the costs and benefits of engaging in a process of argument at all, and with the question whether it is more beneficial not to argue and be silent or switch to negotiation [8]. The titles of both publications ("Why argue?" and "Is it worth arguing?") betrays these questions are not answered yet (or at least not yet answered satisfactorily) and that further research is needed.

6. Discussion and conclusions

The research in this paper, namely to obtain lower bounds for argument verification, fits in a larger context of cost-benefit analysis in formal argumentation. It thus is a further contribution to the realisation of practical forms of computational dialectic.

Research may be continued in the following directions. From a theoretical point of view, it is desirable to deduce lower bounds in case there are more than two attackers. For individual cases, this is easy, since the same line of reasoning may be applied (although other values for κ will be obtained). However, the challenge is to generalise the deduction of lower bounds for a variable upper bound on attackers.

From a more practical point of view, the model presented here must be refined so that it can be applied. It is reasonable, for example, to demand that challenges ("please explain", or "why do you think this is true?") must also open to inspection. This is quite some other issue, however, because the meaning and relevance of challenges cannot be derived by inspecting the challenges themselves, but can only be derived from the dialogical context. Also the assumption that players may reject arguments as unsound without having to explain why, is unrealistic in te present model or at least undesirable. Rather, the act to reject arguments as unsound should be incorporated in the dialectic process, so that such acts can be challenged just as any other (dialectic) move.

References

[1]   Philippe Besnard and Anthony Hunter. *Elements of Argumentation*. The MIT Press, 2008.

[2]   Claudette Cayrol and Marie-Christine Lagasquie-Schiex. Graduality in argumentation. *Journal of Artificial Intelligence Research*, 23(1):245–297, 2005.

[3]   Phan Minh Dung. On the acceptability of arguments and its fundamental role in nonmonotonic reasoning, logic programming, and n-person games. *Artificial Intelligence*, 77(2):321–357, 1995.

[4]   Paul E. Dunne, Anthony Hunter, Peter McBurney, Simon Parsons, and Michael Wooldridge. Inconsistency tolerance in weighted argument systems. In *Proc. of The 8th Int. Conf. on Autonomous Agents and Multiagent Systems (AAMAS'09)*, pages 851–858, 2009.

[5]   James M. Henderson and Richard E. Quandt. *Microeconomic theory: a mathematical approach*. McGraw-Hill, New York, 3rd edition, 1980.

[6]   F. V. Jensen. *An Introduction to Bayesian Networks*. UCL Press, London, 1996.

[7]   Ralph H. Johnson and J. Anthony Blair. *Logical Self-Defense*. IDEBATE Press, 2006.

[8]   Nishan Karunatillake and Nicholas R. Jennings. *Is it worth arguing?*, volume 3366 of *Springer Lecture Notes in AI*, pages 234–250. Springer-Verlag, 2004.

[9]   Paul Krause, Simon Ambler, Morten Elvang-Gøransson, and John Fox. A logic of argumentation for reasoning under uncertainty. *Computational Intelligence*, 11:113–131, 1995.

[10] Diego C. Martínez, Alejandro Javier García, and Guillermo Ricardo Simari. An abstract argumentation framework with varied-strength attacks. In *Principles of Knowledge Representation and Reasoning: Proc. of the 11th Int. Conf., KR 2008, Sydney, Australia, September 16-19, 2008*, pages 135–144. AAAI Press, 2008.

[11] Andreu Mas-Colell, Michael D. Whinston, and Jerry R. Green. *Microeconomic Theory*. Oxford University Press, New York, 1995.

[12] Paul-Amaury Matt and Francesca Toni. A game-theoretic measure of argument strength for abstract argumentation. In *Proc. of the Journées Européennes sur la Logique en Intelligence Artificielle (JELIA)*, pages 285–297. Springer, 2008.

[13] Fabio Paglieri and Cristiano Castelfranchi. Why argue? Towards a cost-benefit analysis of argumentation. *Argument and Computation*, 1(1):71–91, 2010.

[14] Judea Pearl. *Probabilistic Reasoning in Intelligent Systems: Networks of Plausible Inference*. Morgan Kaufmann, Inc., Palo Alto CA, 2 edition, 1994.

[15] John L. Pollock. Defeasible reasoning with variable degrees of justification. *Artificial Intelligence*, 133(1-2):233–282, 2001.

[16] Régis Riveret, Antonino Rotolo, Giovanni Sartor, Henry Prakken, and Bram Roth. Success chances in argument games: a probabilistic approach to legal disputes. In *Proc. of the 2007 Conf. on Legal Knowledge and Information Systems*, pages 99–108, Amsterdam, The Netherlands, 2007. IOS Press.

[17] Giovanni Sartor, Michel Rudnianski, Antonino Rotolo, Régis Riveret, and Eunate Mayor. Why lawyers are nice (or nasty): a game-theoretical argumentation exercise. In *ICAIL '09: Proc. of the 12th Int. Conf. on Artificial Intelligence and Law*, pages 108–117, New York, NY, USA, 2009. ACM.

[18] Albert N. Shiryaev. *Probability*, volume 95 of *Springer GTM*. Springer, New York, Berlin, 2nd edition, 1995.

Computational Models of Argument
P. Baroni et al. (Eds.)
IOS Press, 2010
doi:10.3233/978-1-60750-619-5-475

Arguing in Groups

Maya Wardeh, Frans Coenen and Trevor Bench-Capon
Department of Computer Science, University of Liverpool, UK.

Abstract. We have previously introduced the notion of *arguing from experience*, whereby agents debate a classification problem using arguments based on association rules mined *"on the fly"* from their individual datasets. In this paper we extend PISA, which allows for n agents to argue about cases which have n possible classifications. By allowing any number of agents to participate all the agents supporting a given classification can form a collaborative group for the purposes of the dialogue. We describe how the system is organised, give an example, and report results which suggest that allowing groups in this way has a beneficial effect on the quality of the result.

1. Introduction

Arguing from Experience was introduced in [11] to provide a computational model of argument based on inductive reasoning from past experience. Instead of drawing rules from a knowledge base, arguments were constructed on the fly using Association Rule Mining (ARM) techniques [5, 10]. The setting is a debate about how to classify an example, and the associations provide reasons for and against particular classifications. This form of argument differs from the typical belief based arguments (e.g. [8]) where persuasion occurs through one participant telling the other(s) something previously unknown, either a fact or a rule. Such argument from experience has several advantages: it is a common form of natural argument; it avoids the knowledge acquisition bottleneck; the arguments are not constrained by a predetermined theory; and it can allow the different experiences of different agents to be considered.

The PADUA framework [11] allowed two agents to dispute a binary classification. This was extended in [9] to the *PISA Framework* to allow more than two players, and to support argue about problems with a range of classifications, with each participant championing a different possibility. In this paper we discuss an extension to PISA to allow groups of agents to argue for a classification. Agents advocating the same or a similar thesis can confer and jointly select which arguments to put forward. This extension raises a number of issues: (i) the process by which such agents can collaborate: we suggest that such agents should form what we term a *Group of Participants*, (ii) how to form such group and what roles to assign to its members, and finally, (iii) how to facilitate the discussion within these groups in order to produce a single argument to present to opponents. Finally we give a short discussion of whether groups improve the quality of the classifications.

2. PISA Framework for Arguing from Experience

2.1. Arguing from Experience Dialogue Model

Association Rules (ARs) [1] are probabilistic relationships expressed as rules of the form $A \rightarrow W$ which should be read as follows: *"if A is true then W is likely to be true"*, or *"A is a reason to think W is true"* where A and W are disjoint subsets of some global set of attributes. In the context of *Arguing from Experience*, ARs represent a means to draw arguments from individual experiences. Such arguments (as represented by the rules) can be read as follows: *"In my experience, typically things with features A are Ws: this case has those features, so it is likely to be a W"*. Likelihood is usually represented in terms of a confidence value expressed as a percentage, calculated as *support(A $\cup$ W)×100/support(A)* where the support of an attribute set is the number of records in the dataset in which the attribute set occurs. To limit the number of rules generated only attribute sets with support and confidence above user specified support thresholds are considered.

Six speech acts have been identified for the basic moves the dialogue allowing a position to be stated, attacked and refined:

- **Stating a position** (SA1)**:** Presentation of an AR expressing a generalisation of experience.
- **Attacking a position**: There are three ways in which an opponent's AR can be attacked: (SA2) distinguishing the AR by adding an additional premise (attribute to the antecedent) so that the AR's confidence is reduced; (SA3) observing an additional consequent on which AR does not match the case under consideration; (SA4) present a counter Rule.
- **Refining a position**: There are two ways to modify a previously played AR so as to address attacks: (SA5) add an additional premise (attribute to the antecedent) to increase the confidence, (SA6) withdraw a consequent from the AR.

For each move a finite set of legal next moves is available (Table 1). These speech acts have strong resemblance to those used in arguing on the basis of legal precedents (e.g. [3]). However, here, unlike legal decisions, authority for the rules comes from the frequency of occurrence in the set of examples rather than endorsement of a particular decision by an appropriate court

2.2. The PISA Framework

PISA is directed at dialogues where there exists a range of conclusions, and each of the participants is the advocate of one of these conclusions. The framework comprises three key components: (i) a number of Participant Agents (players), (ii) a mediator agent, the *chairperson*, who does not advocate any position, but rather manages and facilitates communication between the clashing Participant Agents, (iii) A central argument structure, termed the *Argumentation Tree*, which stores the arguments exchanged in the course of PISA dialogues. In the following each of these three components will be briefly discussed.

Move (speech act)	Label	Next Move
SA1	Propose Rule	SA3, SA 2, SA 4
SA 2	Distinguish	SA3, SA5, SA1
SA 3	Unwanted Cons	SA 6, SA 1
SA 4	Counter Rule	SA3, SA2, SA1
SA 5	Increase Conf	SA3, SA2, SA4
SA 6	Withdraw Unwanted Cons	SA3, SA2, SA4

Table 1. Legal moves in Arguing from Experience dialogues.

Each Participant Agent has its own repository of experience, in the form of a tabular dataset. Using their distinct databases, PISA Participant Agents produce reasons for and against conclusions by mining Association Rules (ARs) from their datasets. Additionally, the agents are equipped with a strategy model (Section 2) to help them in generating their arguments.

The Chairperson is a neutral agent which administers a variety of tasks aimed at facilitating multiparty *Arguing from Experience* dialogues. It has the following responsibilities:

– Starting the dialogue.
– Making decisions regarding agents requesting to join or to withdraw.
– Monitoring the dialogue, i.e. registering which agents have taken part.
– Maintaining the Argumentation Tree
– Terminating the dialogue, once a termination condition is satisfied.
– Announcing the game's winner through consultation of the Argumentation Tree.
– Excluding (removing) participants from the game if they fail to contribute in the game for a predetermined number of rounds.

The *Argumentation Tree* is the central data structure representing the arguments exchanged in a dialogue, and the attack relations between these arguments. The tree acts as a mediating artifact for the dialogue as described in [7]. The nodes of the argumentation tree represent the arguments exchanged and the links the attack relations between the arguments. There are two types of links: *explicit* links representing direct attacks, and *implicit* links representing indirect attacks. Each node can have one of four colours: green, blue, red or purple. Green nodes are introduced when a new AR is proposed (SA1,SA4,SA5,SA6). Blue nodes only attempt to undermine an existing node (SA2, SA3). Red nodes are those directly under attack and purple nodes are those indirectly attacked. Further detail regarding the PISA Argumentation Tree can be found in [9]. The Argumentation Tree indicates the *"winner"* on completion of the game as follows:

– **Rule1:** If all the green nodes belong to the same participant, that participant is the winner. This condition is realised only when no other participant has played an undefeated move with higher or similar confidence. Note that rules with higher confidence defeat (indirectly) any other rules with lower confidence (via *implicit* links).
– **Rule2:** If there are no green nodes, and all the blue nodes were played by the same participant, that participant wins.

2.3. PISA dialogue protocol

Assuming that we have a case to classify, and a number of PISA Participant agents, each promoting one of the possible classifications in the domain from which this case was drawn; then PISA *dialogue protocol* works as follows:

1. Before the start of the dialogue the chairperson selects one participant (P1) to start the dialogue.
2. At the first round P1 proposes a new argument: ARG1 (with confidence above the user-defined threshold). The chairperson instantiates a new argumentation tree, rooted on ARG1. If P1 fails to play an opening move, the chairperson selects another participant to commence the dialogue. If all the participants fail to propose an opening argument, the dialogue terminates with failure.
3. In the second round the other participants attempt to attack ARG1 using any of the available attacking speech acts. If all the participants fail to attack ARG1, the dialogue terminates, and the case is classified according to ARG1.
4. Before the beginning of each of the subsequent round, the chairperson removes the Participant Agents that have not taken part in the last m rounds from the dialogue. If only one agent remains after all the other participants have withdrawn or have been removed the dialogue is terminated, and the case classified according to the class promoted by this last participant. Otherwise, any participant who can play a legal move (as defined in Table 1) can do so.
5. If a round passes without any participant making a legal move, the dialogue will terminate in the following round if no moves are made (payers are aware of this).
6. If two subsequent rounds pass without any new moves, or if n rounds have passed without reaching an agreement, the dialogue terminates and the winner(s) identified. If no winner can be identified, a tie-break dialogue can be instantiated between the tied parties (commencing from step 1). Otherwise, the case under discussion is classified according to the winner's promoted class.

Note that in each round all players who wish to play moves do so simultaneously. This, we argue in [9], leads to a fairer result than sequential turn taking.

3. Strategy Model for PISA

In PISA players' strategies can be a key factor in determining the winner of the dialogues, as the more sophisticated the strategy used the greater the agent's chances of winning against their opponents. PISA strategies are categorized according to the understanding of the status of the argumentation tree. This is the state of the tree at the start of each round. Players can either take this status into consideration or not. Strategies that take this status into account are to be considered "smarter" than those who do not. PISA strategies fall into three main strategy types (types 1, 2 and 3) defining when, and how frequently, opponents are to be attacked, as follows:

Type1 - Attack whenever possible: Players attack whenever they can. Players may adopt this strategy to enhance their chances of winning the game by being as aggressive as possible.
Type2 - Attack only when needed: Players attack their opponent only when needed, typically when all their proposed rules so far have been successfully attacked by other

players, or when their attempts to undermine all the other players have failed (because the other players successfully defended their positions). In other words the strategy is for the player to wait as long as its current proposal is secure (not under attacked). Note that due to the nature of PISA dialogues, some nodes may be left un-attacked for a number of rounds.

Both these types of strategy are divided into three sub-types:

Sub-type1.   Attack whenever possible by proposing new rules.

Sub-type2.   Attack whenever possible by undermining the opponent.

Sub-type3.   Tree dependent attack whenever possible according to the nature of the argumentation tree. This strategy combines the previous two giving the players the freedom to use either of them. For example if proposing a counter rule would not yield the best undefeated rule, the player will first attempt to reduce the confidence of the current best rule.

Type3 - Attack to prevent forecasted threat: Using this type of strategy a player attempts to anticipate likely attacks and therefore either change its proposal or attacks the other players before they have the chance to attack. Where an attack takes the form of proposing new rules we say that the player is in *build mode*, whereas if the attack uses undermining we say the player is in *destroy mode*.

4. Arguing in Groups in PISA

Having introduced the PISA framework for multiparty Arguing from Experience the process whereby PISA agents can collaborate together to jointly produce their arguments can be considered. In PISA, where there are more agents than opinions, individual *Participant Agents* advocating the same thesis (e.g. the same possible classification) are required to "join forces" and act as a single *Group of Participants*. Each groups acts as a single player. The proposed notion of groups prevents individual players sharing the same objective from arguing without consulting each other and consequently causing contradictions amongst themselves or attacking each other. Group formation in PISA is a straightforward process: before the start of a new dialogue all participants advocating the same thesis (classification) are required to form a *Group of Participants*. This also applies to new agents joining an ongoing dialogue.

In each group, one member is selected to be the leader of the group who is usually the *smartest* and *most experienced* member of the group. A player's *smartness* relates to its strategy. Hence, the smartest member is the one with the most sophisticated strategy amongst the group's members, where strategies are ranked according to their level of understanding of the history and the progress of the dialogue. Type 3 strategies are smarter than Type 2 strategies which are smarter than those of Type 1. Experience is measured in terms of the size of the data set available to the agent. The leader guides the inter-group dialogue, and selects which of the moves suggested by the group's members to play in the next round. This inter-group dialogue is a variation of *targeted broadcasting* where only group members can "*listen*" to what is being discussed. The leader can also redirect other members' moves against different opponents, or advise them to follow its (the leader's) own strategy. This allows the group to benefit from the different strategies suggested by members as well as from their different experiences.

4.1. Groups Types

The Group Leader (GL) has authority over the other members of the group. This allows the leader to perform the following tasks:

1. **Homogenous groups:** Groups of players which apply the same strategy. In such groups the most experienced player (the one with the largest background dataset) is the group's leader. If two or more of the group members share the same level of experience then one of them is selected at random to represent the group.
2. **Heterogeneous groups:** Groups of players with different strategies. Therefore a strategy ranking is applied to determine who is the *smartest* player amongst the group and thus best suited to be its leader. If two or more players have the smartest strategy then the most experienced one is selected. If they also have the same amount of experience then one of them is selected at random.

4.2. The Role of the Group Leader (GL)

The Group Leader (GL) has authority over the other members of the group that allows the leader to perform the following tasks:

- *Selecting the best move at every round of the dialogue, from the candidate moves suggested by the group's members.* Here, the differences in the members' experiences will greatly influence the leader's decision: members with different experience will often promote different content for their chosen moves, even where all the members apply similar strategies.
- *The leader can compel the more experienced members (if any) to act according to the leader's strategy.* If a more experienced member suggests one move, in a given round, and if the leader assumes that a better type of move could be produced by this member, then the leader can ask this player to attempt to generate the leader's choice. Additional conditions are applied to ensure that the leader exercises the above authority only when needed if the experienced members of the group apply weak strategies, and where other members have failed to produce adequate moves.
- The leader can redirect moves suggested by the other members against opponents other than the ones they have chosen. For instance, if one member suggests an "increase confidence" move against one opponent, then the leader may change this move to a "propose new rule" directed at another opponent (possibly because this opponent threatens the group more). The leader is allowed to redirect the members' moves only when redirection is more rewarding than the original move.

The role of the leader is not fixed, and it may change during the course of the dialogue when a new member joins the group, or when the current leader leaves the dialogue. Therefore PISA uses a token-based technique to identify the group's leader, similar to that of [2] where the token is used as a sign of decision power amongst a team of software agents.

4.3. Intergroup dialogue model

At the start of a new round, if the leader applies a *wait and see* strategy (Type 2), then the leader assesses the argumentation tree and makes a decision if the group should participate or not. If there is no need to take part in the round, the leader passes the round. Otherwise, or if it is using a Type 1 strategy, it requests the other members to suggest moves, and the following dialogue sequence occurs:

1. Once all the group members have suggested moves according to their strategies and experience, the leader compares the member's moves against its own strategy and selects the best move (e.g. if applying a build strategy, then the move with the highest confidence), and submits it.
2. Otherwise if the leader cannot find a move that follows its own strategy and cannot generate this move itself then it can use the submitted moves (if possible) according to its own strategy (e.g. transform an increase confidence move to counter attack).
3. Otherwise if there exists at least one group member such that the member's experience exceeds a predefined limit, then the leader can ask this member to generate a move using the leader's strategy. If a successful move is generated, the leader submits it to the chairperson. Otherwise the leader re-submits the request to the other group members.
4. Otherwise if no successful moves were generated, then the leader can select a move from the initially submitted moves to play. If all the group members fail to suggest any move, the leader passes the round and submits no moves.

5. Example

This section illustrates the notion of groups as described in the previous sections by means of an example using an artificial dataset representing a fictional housing benefit scenario. This scenario concerns a fictional benefit, Retired Persons Housing Allowance (RPHA) (e.g. [4, 6]), which is payable to a person who is of an age appropriate to retirement, whose housing costs exceed one fifth of their available income, and whose capital is inadequate to meet their housing costs. Such persons should also be resident in the country, or be absent only by virtue of "*service to the nation*", and should have an established connection with the UK labour force. The scenario was interpreted in such a way that four classes could be identified:

− *(Fully) Entitled*: The candidate satisfies all of the above conditions (e.g. [4]).
− *Entitled with Priority*: The candidate satisfies all of the above and one of the following: (i) has paid contributions in four out of the last five years and either has no more than £2000 capital, or the housing costs are substantially more than is needed for entitlement. Or (ii) is a member of the armed forces and has paid contributions in each of the last five years.
− *Partially Entitled*: The candidate satisfies the age condition, and also satisfies one of the following: (i) has paid contributions in four out of the last five years and either has no more than £1000 above the original capital limit (£3000), or the

housing costs are only slightly below what is required for entitlement, or (ii) is employed in the Merchant Navy and has paid contributions in all the last five years.
— *Not Entitled*: The candidate fails to satisfy any of the above.

The example assumes four different benefit offices providing RPHA in four different regions, each has a dataset of 1500 benefit records. Each dataset is assigned to a PISA Participant Agent. Thus a total of four Participant Agents would engage in dialogues regarding the classification of RPHA claims, each agent defending one of the above four classifications. The support and confidence thresholds were set to 1% and 50% respectively (the default thresholds in the data mining community). Given the case of a female applicant, aged 78 years, who is a UK resident whose capital and income fall in the right range (≤2000£ and ≤15%, respectively), and who has paid contributions in four out of the last five years, according to the above listed conditions listed, the case should be classified as *Entitled with Priority*.

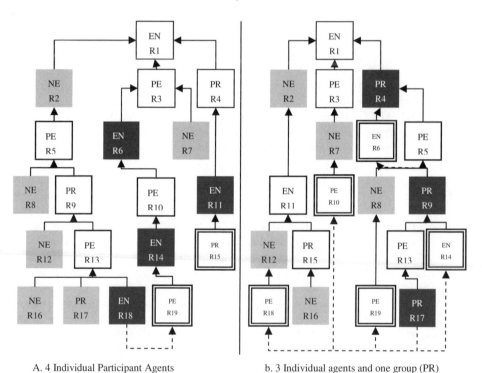

A. 4 Individual Participant Agents   b. 3 Individual agents and one group (PR)

Figure 1. Example argumentation Trees.

The dialogue might proceed as illustrated by the argument tree presented in Figure 1(a). The diagram features four agents labelled PR (Priority Entitled), EN (Entitled), PE (Partially Entitled) and NE (Not Entitled) who all apply the same "build attack when possible" strategy. The diagram should be viewed in conjunction with Table 2 which presents the dialogue. The dialogue commences when the chairperson invites EN to propose the opening argument, EN proposes R1. R1 is then attacked by the other three agents in the second round (R2, R3 and R4). At the end of round 2 PE is ahead as it has the best un-attacked rule. In round three PE proposes a counter rule against NE's previous rule (R5), EN proposes a new rule (R6) to attack the current best rule (R3) and NE distinguishes PE's argument (R7). Thus PE maintains its lead. Note that PR has not contributed to round three.

1	**R1:** EN - Proposes a New Rule: Residency = UK and Contrib Y1= paid → **entitled.** c = 50.61%.
2	**R2:** NE - Distinguishes a previous move. The case has the additional feature: Contrib Y5 = not paid→ **entitled** with c 20.0% only. **R3:** PE- Proposes a Counter Rule against a move previously played by EN: Contrib Y1= paid and Contrib Y2= paid → **priority entitled.** c = 54.79%. **R2:** PR - Distinguishes a previous move. The case has the additional feature: Capital<2000£ → **entitled** with c= 35.66% only.
3	**R5:** PE- Proposes a Counter Rule against a move previously played by NE: Contrib Y1 = paid, Contrib Y2=paid and Contrib Y3=paid→**partially entitled.** c = 62.29%. **R6:** EN- Proposes a New Rule against a move previously played by PE: Income<15% and Contrib Y2= paid→ **entitled.** c = 54.83%. **R7:** NE distinguishes PE's argument by pointing out that capital<2000£ and residence=UK only gives partial benefits with c = 19.24%.
4	**R8:** NE - Distinguishes PE's previous move (round 3). The case has the additional feature: Residence = UK→ **partially entitled** with c 27.60% only. **R9:** PR- Proposes a New Rule against a move previously played by PE: Gender=female. 75<Age<80, Income<15%, Capital<2000£ and Contrib Y2= paid→ **priority entitled.** c = 74.83%. **R10:** PE - Increases the confidence of a previous rule by stating that the case has additional feature: Gender=female→**partially entitled.** c = 70.05%. **R11:** EN - Proposes a New Rule against a move previously played by PE: Residency= UK, Contrib Y3= paid and Contrib Y4= paid→**entitled.** c = 69.12%.
5	**R8:** NE - Distinguishes PE's previous move (round 4). The case has the additional features: Residence=UK and Contrib Y5=not paid → **partially entitled** with c 23.71% only **R13:** PE- Proposes a New Rule against a move previously played by PR. The case has the following features: Gender=female, Contrib Y1= paid, Contrib Y2=paid and Contrib Y3=paid. Therefore the case should classify as (partially entitled). c = 76.83%. **R14:** EN- Proposes a New Rule against a move previously played by PR. The case has the following features: Gender=female, 75<Age<80, Residency=UK and Contrib Y2= paid. Therefore the case should classify as (entitled). c = 74.24%. **R15:** PR - Increases the confidence of a previous rule by stating that the case has additional features: Contrib Y3=paid, Contrib Y4= paid →**entitled.** c = 75.58%.
6	**R16:** NE - distinguishes PE's argument (R13) by pointing out that the additional features: Residency=UK and Capital<2000£ only gives partial benefits with 25.36% confidence. **R17:** PR - distinguishes PE's argument (R13) by pointing out that the additional features: Income<15% and Capital<2000£ only gives partial benefits with 14.22% confidence. **R18:** EN- Proposes a New Rule against a move previously played by PE: 75<Age<80, Residency=UK and Contrib Y5= Not paid→ entitled. c = 83.54%. **R19:** PE- Proposes a New Rule against a move previously played by EN: Gender=female, 75<Age<80, Contrib Y1 = paid, Contrib Y2= paid, Contrib Y3=paid, Contrib Y4=paid → **partially entitled.** c = 82.69%.

Table 2. The result-dialogue of the first example (c = confidence).

In round four: NE distinguishes PE's rule from round three (R8), PR proposes a counter rule against PE's rule of round three (R9), PE increases the confidence of its previous move (R3) by playing R10 and EN proposes a new rule R11. Now PR is winning, but in the fifth round its winning rule (R10) can be distinguished by NE (R12).

Additionally, both EN and PE have moves in this round (R13 and R14, respectively). PR however increases the confidence in its previous move (R4) by playing R15, the resulting rule however does not have enough confidence to maintain PR's win. In the sixth round NE distinguishes PE's argument (R13) using R16, PR distinguishes R13 using R17, and EN and PE plays new rules (R18 and R19 respectively). No more arguments are now possible, and so the final classification is that the candidate should be entitled to normal rather than priority benefit, which is the wrong classification.

Let us now assume that the data available to the office arguing that the case should classify as "*priority entitled*", is divided between four PISA Participant Agents as follows: P1 (25%), P2 (15%), P3 (35%) and P4 (25%), such that these agents are joined in one group with P2 being the most experienced agent. Let us also assume that P1 and P2 apply a build strategy and that P1 is selected as the Group Leader (GL). And that P3 and P4 applies a destroy strategy. The new dialogue commences in the same manner as the previous one, and EN proposes the same rule R1 as before. In round two, the other three agents attack R1, EN and PE play the same moves they have used in the previous example (R2 and R3). PR however, attacks using a different rule (Figure 1 (b)). Both Leader and P2 propose a counter rule against EN's move from round one, while P3 and P4 suggest distinguishing this move. GL chooses its own move, as it has the highest confidence and consequently plays R4`[1]:

PR - Proposes a Counter Rule against a move previously played by EN. Gender= female and Capital<2000£ →**priority entitled**. c=53.89%.

In round three, PE, EN and NE play the same moves as before (R5`, R6 and R7 respectively). However, here PE directs its move against PR's previous move (R4`). In round 4, NE and PE play the same moves (R8 and R10) as before, EN also has the same move (R11`), but here it is directed against NE's move from round two (R2). In the PR group, players P2 and P4 have no moves, the leader suggests a counter move against PE but it cannot be played (has confidence of 61.83% only), and P3 suggest distinguishing PE's move from the last round (R6). The leader however requests the following from P3: Request_Move("propose counter rule", confidence>62.29%). P3 succeeds in mining the requested move, and GL puts forward the resulting move (R9`).

R9` : PR- Proposes a New Rule against a move previously played by PE. 75<Age<80, Income<15%, Capital<2000£ and Contrib Y2= Paid→ **priority entitled**. c = 72.13%.

In round five, NE PE and EN play the same moves as before (R12, R13 and R14, respectively). In The group PR, a similar decision to the previous round is taken, and the leader plays forward the move requested from P3:

R15`: PR- Proposes a Counter Rule against a move previously played by PE: 75<Age<80, Income<15%, Contrib Y1 =Paid, Contrib Y2= Paid and Contrib Y3=Paid→ **priority entitled**. c = 77.34%.

Finally, in round six, all participants make moves: PE and EN play the same moves as the first example (R18 and R19, respectively). EN PR's argument (R15`) by pointing out that Residency=UK and Contribution Y5=not paid, only gives partial benefits with 33.69% confidence. Similarly to the previous rounds, the leader of group PR directs its members to play the following move:

R17`: PR- Proposes a Counter Rule against a move previously played by PE: 75<Age<80, Income<15%, Contrib Y1=Paid, Contrib Y2= Paid, Contrib Y3=Paid and Contrib Y4=Paid→**priority entitled**. c = 84.55%.

---

[1] Primed rules (e.g. R4`) represent rules (or moves) that are different in the second dialogue, for instance: R4` is different from R4. Whereas, R1,R2 and R3 are identical in both dialogues.

No more arguments are possible at this stage, and so the final classification is that the candidate should classify as priority entitled. Note that the right class emerged as a result of PR being a group of four agents; even though each agent had less data than the first example, they were able to generate better arguments.

6. Experiments

This section provides an analysis of how the performance of PISA relates to the number of players in each group (assuming homogenous groups only and that all members have the same amount of experience, therefore the process of selecting a GL is random). Two experiments were conducted to investigate the operation of groups.

The first experiment provided evidence on the operation of groups within PISA. This experiment assumed that the amount of data available to each group was fixed and equally divided amongst its members. Thus, if too many players were assigned to a single group, each will be assigned a very small dataset and the members will not be able to mine adequate rules. Five cross validation tests were carried out using the same Housing Benefits dataset (6000 records in total) used to generate the above example. PISA was run using four groups comprising (respectively) 2, 4, 6, 8 and 10 players each, each group corresponding to one of the possible four classes in the dataset. In each test the original dataset was divided equally amongst the players. Figure2(a) presents the results of these tests, which indicate that, in general, PISA operates better when using groups of players. More than one agent advocating the same classification, using the notion of groups, seems to have positive effects on the accuracy of the resulting dialogues, due to the fact that a range of arguments can be mined from different datasets, each presenting different experience. Thus more options will be available to the group as a whole, from which the group's leader can select the best course of action. However, the increase in accuracy is proportional to the amount of data given to each agent in the dialogues. If the data is not sufficient to mine adequate ARs, the operation of PISA will not benefit from dividing the data any further.

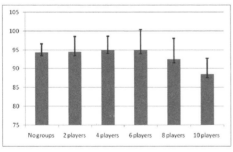
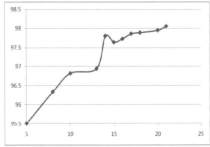

a. A of the TCV tests using same number of players per group. Error bars represent the standard deviation. Y axis represents the accuracy obtained from each test.

b. Relation between number of players and PISA accuracy when players are given fixed amount of data

Figure 2.Empirical Results.

The second experiment was conducted to investigate the relationship between the amount of data available to the group as a whole and the performance of the group. For this purpose, a number of Housing Benefits datasets, each comprising 1000 records, were generated. PISA was run with four groups, each comprising the same number of players. But here, each player was given one of the generated datasets. Thus, the more players that join a group, the more experience available to the group as a whole. A number of cross validation tests were conducted. For each test, the number of players in each group was randomly generated. Figure2(b) shows the result of these tests. Note that the overall accuracy benefits from the increase in the size of the groups. For instance, the average accuracy when each group comprised five players was 95.50%. However as more members were added, the accuracy increased to reach 98.06%.

7. Conclusion and Future Work

We have provided a mechanism by which any number of agents can participate in a dialogue to decide how a case should be classified using arguments mined *"on the fly"*, from their individual datasets. The agents form groups supporting each possible classification and these groups collaborate to decide on the best next move. Using groups can improve the quality of the classification, even when the data is simply divided amongst different agents so that no more data is available than if each classification was supported by a single agent. Our experiments suggest that for any given problem there is an optimal size for the agent's datasets, and allowing the available data to be divided amongst agents in this way ensures that any amount of data can be deployed to the best effect. Further experiments show that more data improves the classification quality, provided that data can be used in optimally sized chunks. In future work it would be interesting to explore dynamic groups, whereby agents that become convinced by a different classification can join the appropriate group rather than leaving the game. Also, we would like to explore the effect of coalitions whereby two groups can temporarily join forces against a currently stronger adversary.

References

[1] R. Agrawal, T. Imielinski and A. Swami. Mining association rules between sets of items in large databases. In Proc. ACM SIGMOD Conf. on Management of Data (SIGMOD'93). ACM Press, (1993), 207 -- 216.
[2] S. Ambroszkiewicz, O. Matyja and W. Penczek. Team Formation by Self-Interested Mobile Agents. In *Multi-Agent Systems, Lecutre notes in computer science*, Springer, (1998), 1 -- 15.
[3] K. D. Ashley. Modelling Legal Argument. MIT Press, Cambridge, MA, USA, (1990).
[4] T.J.M. Bench-Capon. Neural Nets and Open Texture. In *Proc. 4th Int. Conf. on AI and Law* (ICAIL'94). ACM Press: Amsterdam (1994), 292 -- 297.
[5] F. Coenen, P. H. Leng, and S. Ahmed. Data structure for association rule mining: T-trees and p-trees. In *IEEE Trans. Knowl. Data Eng.*, **16(6)**, (2004), 774 -- 778.
[6] M. Mozina, J. Zabkar, T. Bench-Capon and I. Bratko. Argument based machine learning applied to law. In Artif. Intell., **13 (1)**, Springer (2005), 53 -- 73.
[7] E. Oliva, M. Viroli, A. Omicini and P. McBurney. Argumentation and artifact for dialogue support. In *Proc. 5th Intl. Workshop on Argumentation in MAS* (ArgMAS'08). Portugal,(2008), 24 -- 39.
[8] H. Prakken. Formal systems for persuasion dialogue. In *The Knowledge Eng. Review*, **21**. Cambridge University Press (2006),163 -- 188.
[9] M. Wardeh, T. Bench-Capon and F.P. Coenen . Multi-Party Argument from Experience. In *Proc. 6th Intl. Workshop on Argumentation in MAS* (ArgMAS'09). Hungary (2009), 216 -- 235.
[10] M. Wardeh, T. Bench-Capon and F.P. Coenen. Dynamic Rule Mining for Argumentation Based Systems. In *Proc. AI 07,* Cambridge, UK. Springer, London, (2007), 65 -- 78.
[11] M. Wardeh, T. Bench-Capon and F.P. Coenen. *Arguments from Experience: The PADUA Protocol*. In *Proc. COMMA'08.* Toulouse, France. IOS press, (2008), 405 -- 416.

Computational Models of Argument
P. Baroni et al. (Eds.)
IOS Press, 2010

Author Index